Eighth Edition

SALTWATER FISHING IN CALIFORNIA

Secrets of the Pacific Experts

by Ronnie Kovach

featuring these expert Pacific Ocean anglers . . .

- Bill Beebe, Jr.
- Captain Fred Benko
- Captain Buzz Brizendine
- Mike Callan
- Steve Carson
- Riley Compton, Jr.
- Abe Cuanang
- Angelo Cuanang
- Ron De La Mare
- Curt Dills
- Jim Emmett
- Jerry Esten
- Dick Gaumer
- Captain Steve Giffin
- Captain Ron Hart
- Leonard Hashimoto
- Pete Haynes
- Captain Russ Izor

- Al Kalin
- Ray Lawry
- Bill Lescher
- Don McAdams
- Captain Kit McNear
- Joe Mendosa
- Bill Miyagawa
- Captain Mark Pisano
- Bryan Porter
- Carl Riccardi
- John Rowe
- Captain Tom Schlauch
- Captain Paul Strasser
- Bob Suekawa
- Glenn Ueda
- Dick Uranga
- Captain Allyn Watson

MARKETSCOPE
BOOKS

119 Richard Ct.
Aptos, CA 95003
(831) 688-7535

ISBN 0-934061-45-9

"The leading publisher of fishing books for California Anglers"

About This Expanded and Updated Edition

The first editions of this book were a big surprise. We had no idea that so many thousands of Californians would buy a book about saltwater angling. Outdoor writers praised it and anglers obviously found it useful. It's still selling at a fast pace, but now we've decided to make it even bigger and better. More strategies, More tactics. More tips and tricks. Quite simply, this new edition has more of everything for the California angler. We hope you like it.

The Editor

ISBN 0-934061-45-9

Cover Design: Electric Art Studios
                Mountain View, CA

Technical
Illustrations by: Linda Kovach

Dedication

This final book of the California fishing trilogy is dedicated to the preservation of our last great frontier here on Earth —the sea. Take only what you can use from these waters and future bounties will be shared by our sons and daughters.

Acknowledgments

I wish to thank the following saltwater experts for their kind asssistance and for the insights with which they provided me in writing this book:

Bill Beebe, Jr., Captain Fred Benko, Captain Buzz Brizendine, Mike Callan, Steve Carson, Riley Compton, Dr., Abe Cuanang, Angelo Cuanang, Ron De La Mare, Curt Dills, Jim Emmett, Jerry Esten, Dick Gaumer, Capt. Steve Giffin, Captain Ron Hart, Leonard Hashimoto, Pete Haynes, Capt. Russ Izor, Al Kalin, Ray Lawry, Bill Lescher, Don McAdams, Capt. Kit McNear, Joe Mendosa, Bill Miyagawa, Captain Mark Pisano, Bryan Porter, Carl Riccardi, John Rowe, Capt. Tom Schlauch, Captain Paul Strasser, and Bob Suekawa, Glenn Ueda, Dick Uranga, Captain Allyn Watson.

Thank you long-time fishing friend, Mark Grinyer, for the following poem:

> Salt spray and deep sea mist
> tonight, break rainbows out of light,
> but the upturned wakes of ships that start
> together into night, and then run far apart,
> lead fishermen to different grounds, to cast
> their different fates.

> from "A Fishing Poem to Ron"

> by Mark Grinyer

Finally, above all, thank you once again, Linda, my dear wife, editor, illustrator, and personal consultant for all the hard work to make the California fishing trilogy a reality.

Great Books

Fishing in Northern California

Marketscope Books publishes the bestselling **Fishing in Northern California** (8 1/2 x 11 inches, 240 pages). It includes "How To Catch" sections on all freshwater fish as well as salmon, steelhead, sturgeon, shad, kokanee, lingcod, clams, sharks, rock crab, crawdads, stripers, etc. Plus, there are sections on all major NorCal fishing waters (over 50 lakes, the Delta, Coastal Rivers, Valley Rivers, Mountain Trout and the Pacific Ocean). All these waters are mapped in detail!

Fishing in Southern California

Marketscope Books also publishes the bestselling **Fishing in Southern California** (8 1/2 x 11 inches, 256 pages). It includes "How To Catch" sections on all freshwater fish as well as barracuda, bonito, calico bass, grunion, halibut, marlin, sea bass and yellowtail. Plus, there are sections on major SoCal fishing waters (45 lakes, the Salton Sea, Colorado River, Mountain Trout and the Pacific Ocean). All these waters are mapped in detail!

Bass Fishing in California

At last, a bass fishing book just for Californians -- both beginners and veterans. This book explains in detail how to catch more and larger bass in California's unique waters. But, most valuable, it includes a comprehensive guide, with maps, to 40 of California's best bass lakes, up and down the state. This classic has now been expanded to include scores of advanced bass-producing techniques. 8 1/2 x 11, 240 pages.

Trout Fishing in California

Trout fishing is special in California and now there is a special book for the California trout anglers. It covers, in detail, how to catch trout in lakes or streams, with line, bait or flies, by trolling, casting or still fishing, from boat or shore. And even better for California anglers, this is a guide to the best trout waters all over the state. Detailed info and precise maps are featured. 8 1/2 x 11, 224 pages.

Saltwater Fishing in California

California is blessed with over 800 miles of Pacific Ocean coastline. This is a marvelous resource for all Golden State anglers. And now there is a book that covers it all. Surf fishing. Kelp fishing. Harbor and Bay fishing. Poke poling. And more. Don't go saltwater fishing without it. Both veteran anglers and beginners are finding this book a necessity. It explains, in detail, how to catch albacore, barracuda, bass, bonito, halibut, rockfish, sharks, salmon, stripers, yellowtail and striped marlin. And there is a large "How-To and Where-To" Guide for hot spots all along the coast. And don't be without the Saltwater Sportfish I.D. Section. This book has become a standard because it explains in simple, straightforward language how to catch fish in the Pacific, off California. 8 1/2 x 11, 256 pages.

Contents

Order Form 4

Fishing Map 9

BOOK I—Catching Fish in California's Saltwater 11

The California Coast: An Immense and Varied Fishery 12
Up and Down the Coast 12
San Diego to Santa Barbara 13
Santa Barbara to Monterey Bay 13
San Francisco to Oregon 14
What's Ahead in this Book 14

The Basics: Tackle Selection for Coastal Angling 15
Premium Lines 15
The Conventional Outfit 16
Saltwater Spinning Combos 18
The Popping Rod 18
Surf Fishing Options 18
Trolling and Bottom Fishing Rigs 19
Which Outfit to Use 20
Simple Tackle Storage Systems 20
Other Accessories 21
Terminal Tackle 21
Southern California Live Bait Tackle 21
North Coast Tackle 22
Rock Cod Gear 22
Surf, Jetty, and Bay Paraphernalia 22

Bait Fishin': 'Chovies, Squid, Crabs, and More 23
Live Anchovies 23
Live Sardines 24
Live Squid 24
Live Smelt 25
Live Pacific Mackerel 25
Brown and Junk Baits 26
Mudsuckers 26
Bullheads 26
Shiner Perch 27
Frozen Cut and Strip Baits 27
More Baits for Surf and Bays 28
Summary 30

Lure Fishin': Candy Bars, Lunker Thumpers, Salty Magics and More 31
Candy Bar Style Jigs 31
Diamond Jigs 33
Soft Plastic Baits 33
Saltwater Plugs 38
Saltwater Spoons 35
"Feathers" 37
Bucktails and Other Jigs 38
Surface Plugs 38
Other Exotics 38

Trolling Tactics: Ridin' the Wake 40
Trolling Rods and Reels 40
Trolling Options 41
More Trolling Tips and Downriggers 43
Trolling the Ropes 45
Trolling Bait 45
Summary 45

Party Boating: Learning the Strategy 46
Choosing a Party Boat 46
Party Boat Practices 47
Time to Rotate! 47
Jackpot Fishing 48
Other Party Boat Equipment 49
Summary 49

Boat Fishin': Doing It Your Way 51
Key Equipment 51
Fishing Electronics 52
Fish Storage 53
Advantages of Private Boats 53
Disadvantages of Private Boats 54
The Art of Chumming 54
Summary 54

Pier Fishin': Plaudits for Piers 56
Southern vs. Northern Piers 56
Pier Tackle 57
Specialized Pier Rigs 57
The Bonito Trolley 58
The Halibut Trolley 59
Bonito Splashers 59
Secret Shiny Sinkers 59
Pier Plastics 60
Spoonin' the Pier 60
Plugs for the Pier? 61
Big Bait Tricks 61
Sidewinder Magic 61
More Float Tips 61
The Slider Rig 62
More Pier Fishing Tips 62
Summary 63

Surfin' Safari: Fishin' California's Beaches 64
Surf Casting Rods, Reels, and Lines 64
More Surf Fishing Gear 65
Surf Baits 66
Basic Terminal Rigs 67
Surf Sinkers 68
Reading the Water 69
Perch 70
Corbina 70
Croakers 71
Halibut 71
Calicos and Sandies 71
Starry Flounder 71
Cabezon 72
White Sea Bass 72
Striped Bass 72
Sharks and Rays 72
Summary 73

Rock and Breakwater Fishin': Jetty Jockeys and Wall Bangers 74
Rods and Reels 74
Terminal Gear 75
Typical Baits 76
Artificial Lures 76
A Year 'Round Fishery 77
Fishing "Walls" at Night 77

Contents (cont.)

Kelp Fishin': Offshore Underwater Forests 82
    "Pot-Holing" Through the Kelp 83
    Troll Outside the Kelp 84
    Floating Kelp Paddies 85
    Summary 85

Harbor and Bay Fishin': Sheltered Action 87
    Look for Moving Water 87
    Fish Structure 88
    Bay Tackle and Rigs 88
    Baits and Rigs for Harbors and Bays 89
    Lures for Bay Fishing 90
    Plastics, Cranks, and Spoons for the Bay 91
    Summary 92

Poke Poling: Just Pokin' Around the Coast 94
    The Poke Pole 94
    Watch the Water 95
    Poke Poling Equipment and Gear 95
    A South Coast Variation 95
    Pokin' Lures 95
    Summary 96

Albacore: Jig Strike! 97
    Locating Albacore 97
    Four Basic Outfits 98
    Trolling Tactics 98
    More Trolling Secrets 100
    Albies on Live Bait 101
    A Multiple Hooking Trick 101
    Fishing the Slide 101
    Other Tunas 102
    Summary 102

Barracuda: Pacific Torpedoes! 103
    Scooters on Bait 103
    Barries on Lures 104
    Summary 105

Saltwater Bass: Grumpers, Bulls and Whites 106
    Sandies 106
    Grumpers on Bait 106
    Sandies on Lures 107
    Calicos 109
    Bull Bass on Bait 109
    Calicos on Lures 110
    Fishing the Pots 110
    White Sea Bass 111
    Summary 111

Bonito: Tricks for a Bongo Bonanza 113
    Bongos on Bait 113
    Bonies on Lures 114
    Summary 114

Halibut: Bottom Bouncin' for Barndoors 115
    Finding Halibut 116
    Barndoors on Bait 116
    Flatties on Artificials 117
    Summary 118

Catchin' Rockfish: Cowcod, Chilipeppers, Lings
and More 119
    The Shallow Bite 119
    The Deep-Water Action 120
    Lingcod 122
    Summary 123

Sharks: Leopards, Threshers and Company 125
    Bay Area Sharkin' 125
    Trolling and Drifting for Sharks 126
    Handling Sharks 128
    Bat Rays 128
    Summary 128

Salmon: Kings of the Coast 129
    Trolling for Kings 129
    Mooch for Chinooks 131
    Spoon Drifting for Salmon 133
    Salmon Near the Shore 133
    Summary 133

Stripers: Linesides from Surf and Bay 134
    Working the Surfline 134
    Linesides in the Bay 136
    Lures in the Bay 137
    Stripers from the Bank 138
    Summary 139

Yellowtail: Pacific Yellow Fever 140
    Tails on Bait 140
    Yellows on the Iron 141
    Trolling for Yellowtail 142
    Summary 142

Striped Marlin: Big Game Fishin'—
California Style 143
    Stripers on the Troll 143
    Stripes on Bait 145
    Use Your Eyeballs! 146
    Summary 146

BOOK II—California Saltwater: A "Where-to" and "How-to" Guide 147
    Coronado Islands 148
    San Diego Coast and Offshore 149
    San Diego Bay and Mission Bay 150
    San Clemente Island 150
    Oceanside Area 151
    Dana Harbor Area 152
    Newport Harbor 153
    Santa Catalina Island 153
    Huntington Beach to Seal Beach 154
    Long Beach Harbor Area 155
    Kings Harbor and Redondo Beach Pier 156
    Marina Del Rey 156
    Santa Monica Bay and Malibu 157
    Ventura and Oxnard 158
    Channel Islands 159
    Santa Barbara Area 159
    San Luis Obispo and Morro Bay Northward 160
    Monterey and Carmel Bays 161
    Moss Landing and Santa Cruz 161
    Pillar Point and Half Moon Bay 162
    Pacifica Surfline 162
    San Francisco Bay Halibut 163
    San Francisco Bay Striper 163
    San Francisco Bay Sharks 164
    San Francisco Bay Potluck 164
    Farallon Islands Area 164
    Bodega and Tomales Bays 165
    Ft. Ross and Timber Cove Area 165
    Ft. Bragg and Shelter Cover Area 165
    Eureka and Humboldt Bay 166
    Crescent City Area 166

Pacific Ocean Fishing Maps 167
  San Diego Area 168
  Solana Beach to Dana Point 169
  Los Angeles Area 170
  Santa Monica Area 171
  Ventura Area 172
  Santa Barbara Area 173
  SoCal Islands (Map I) 174
  SoCal Islands (Map II) 175
  Central Coast 176
  Monterey Bay Area 177
  San Francisco Area 178
  San Francisco Bay 179
  Pt. Reyes to Ft. Ross 180
  Ft. Ross to Cape Mendocino 181
  El River to Oregon Border 182

BOOK III—More Good Stuff 183

Party Boat Lessons 184
  Pick the Right Boat 184
  Learn to Ask More Questions! 184
  Skippers on the Cutting Edge 185
    Boat Handling 185
    Controlling the Crew 185
    Innovation 186
    A Demand for Precision 186
    The Gambler Aspect 186
    Patience and Perseverance 187
    Lessons to be Learned 187
  More Party Boat Strategy 187
    Come Prepared! 188
    Develop Rapport 188
    Hooking Live Baits 188
    Fish the Bow 188
    Understand Kelp Paddies 188
    Another Tip—Throw Plastics! 189
    Longer Rods for Live Baits 189
    Remain Flexible! 189
  The Pros' Hot Tips! 189
    The Night Bite 190
    Select Primo Baits 190
    Fish Big Baits! 190
    Feather Your Bait! 190
    Fish Deep! 191
    Vary Retrieves 191
    Checking Line and Knots 191
    Use Your Drag 191
    Follow Your Line! 192
    Light-Lining 192
    Multiple Outfits 192
    Pros Love Lures! 193
    Dump the Chutes! 193
    Again—Learn to Be Adaptable 193
  How to Win Jackpots 193
  The Hidden Essentials 194
    Polarized Eyewear 194

Small Craft Lessons 196
  Basic Tactics 196
    Limited Range 196
    Limited Bait 197
    Small Craft Trolling 198
    Lots of Pluses! 198
  Drift Fishing Basics 199
    Drift Baits 199
    Setting a Drift Pattern 201
    Be Experimental 202

Tackle Lessons 203
  Use the Right Hook 203
    Live Bait Hooks 203
    Baitholder Hooks 204
    Lead Head Hooks 204
    Jig Hooks 205
    Spoon Hooks 205
    Plug Hooks 205
    Worth the Effort! 206
    Circle Hooks 206
  Hooking Strategies 206
    Anchovies 206
    Sardines 207
    Mackerel 207
    Brown Baits 207
    Squid 208
    Strip Baits 208
    'Dads 208
    Match the Hook! 208
    Use Good Line! 209
    Light-Line Fever 209
  No Dinkers with Sinkers 210
  When Equipment Fails 211
    Spooling 211
    Extraneous Hardware 211
    Wrong Lure—Wrong Time 211

Advanced Lure Lessons 212
  Soft Plastics on Parade 212
  The History of Soft Plastics 212
  Fork-Tails 212
  Tube Baits 213
  Tube Driftin' 214
  The S-L-O-W Yo-Yo 214
  Knob-Tail Shads 215
  Whip-Tail Grubs 215
  Sickle-Tails 215
  Split-Tail Grubs 215
  Versatile Lures! 216
  More on Lead Heads 216
  Pumpin' the Eel 217
  Saltwater Scents 217
    Home Remedies 218
    Liquid Blends 218
    Pastes and Slime 219
    Built-In Scents 219
    Be Creative! 220
  South Coast Trolling 220
    Bass on the Troll 220
    Trolll for Bonito 221
    Barracuda on the Troll 222
    Drag Lures for Yellowtail 222
    Tuna and Dorado on the Troll 223
  More Trolling Tips 224
  Spoonin' the Pacific Coast 224
    Types of Saltwater Spoons 224
    Bass on Spoons 225
    Spoon 'Cuda! 225
    Bonito Spoonin' 226
    Yellowtail Spoons 226
    Tuna Spoons 226
    Spoon Bottom Grabbers 226
    Salmon Spoons 226
    Spoon Stripers! 227
    All-Season Lures! 227
  Packing Iron 227

Contents (cont.)

The Inner Game of Fishing 229
   Creative Fishing 229
   Catching vs. Fishing 229
      Water Temperature 230
      Water Color 230
      Current 230
      Bait 230
      Everyone Welcome 230
   "Positive Fish Attitude" 231
   Practice Catch and Release 231

Saltwater Sportfish Identification Guide 232
   Spiny Dogfish 233
   Shark, Common Thresher 233
   Shark, Bonito 233
   Shark, Gray Smoothhound 233
   Shark, Brown Smoothhound 234
   Shark, Leopard 234
   Shark, Blue 234
   Shovelnose Guitarfish 234
   Bat Ray 235
   Round Stingray 235
   Sturgeon, Green 235
   Sturgeon, White 235
   Salmon, Chinook (King) 236
   Salmon, Coho (Silver) 236
   California Lizardfish 236
   Pacific Hake (Whiting) 236
   Pacific Tomcod 237
   California Grunion 237
   Jacksmelt 237
   Sculpin 238
   Rockfish, Black 238
   Rockfish, Blue 238
   Bocaccio 238
   Chilipepper 239
   Cowcod 239
   Rockfish, Olive 239
   Rockfish, Yellowtail 240
   Rockfish, Canary 240
   Rockfish, Vermillion 240
   Rockfish, Copper 240
   Rockfish, Widow 241
   Rockfish, Greenspotted 241
   Rockfish, Starry 241

   Sablefish 241
   Lingcod 242
   Kelp Greenling 242
   Pacific Staghorn Sculpin 242
   Cabezon 242
   Bass, Striped 243
   Bass, Giant Sea 243
   Bass, Kelp 243
   Bass, Barred Sand 244
   Bass, Spotted Sand 244
   Mackerel, Jack 244
   Yellowtail 245
   Sargo 245
   Queenfish 245
   White Sea Bass 245
   Yellowfin Croaker 246
   California Corbina 246
   Croaker, White 246
   Croaker, Spotfin 246
   Opaleye 247
   Halfmoon 247
   Surfperch, Silver 247
   Surfperch, Walleye 248
   Surfperch, Shiner 248
   Surfperch, Redtail 248
   Surfperch, Rubberlip 249
   Surfperch, Barred 249
   Sheephead, California 249
   Barracuda, California 249
   Giant Kelpfish 250
   Mackerel, Pacific 250
   Skipjack 250
   Bonito, Pacific 250
   Albacore 251
   Tuna, Bigeye 251
   Tuna, Bluefin 252
   Tuna, Yellowfin 252
   Swordfish 252
   Marlin, Striped 253
   Halibut, California 253
   Sanddab, Pacific 253
   Sanddab, Longfin 253
   Halibut, Pacific 254
   Flounder, Starry 254
   Sole, Petrale 254

Extra: The "Non-Mono" Controversy 255

California Saltwater Fishing Map

See detailed maps on pages 168-182

Crescent City

Humboldt Bay
Eureka

Cape Mendocino

Pt. Bragg

Pt. Arena

Bodega Bay
Pt. Reyes

San Francisco Bay

Farallon Is.

San Jose

Monterey Bay
Monterey

Morro Bay

Pt. Conception

Santa Barbara
Ventura

Santa Monica Bay
Los Angeles

San Miguel

Long Beach/San Pedro Harbor

Santa Rosa

Anacapa

Santa Cruz

San Nicholas

Catalina

San Clemente

San Diego

Coronado Is.

BOOK I

Catching Fish
in
California's
Saltwater

The California Coast: An Immense and Varied Fishery

Saltwater fishermen have a tendency to underestimate the wealth of angling possibilities that lie off the California coast. More often than not, exotic locales such as Baja California, Hawaii, the Florida Keys, Australia, and New Zealand receive all the accolades as saltwater havens.

The fact of the matter is that this great state offers some of the finest saltwater angling to be found anywhere in the world—and on a year around basis. When you stop to examine the desirable marine species that abound off our shores, you will realize that California is indeed a saltwater bonanza.

Up and Down the Coast

Unlike, for example, bass and trout fishing where the same techniques apply up and down the state, saltwater angling in California is more regionally diverse. By this I mean that marine anglers in the Southern region of the state have their particular brand of fishing as do those living along the Central Coast and those in the North. Why is this the case?

Well, for one thing, in contrast to freshwater species, many marine game fish are pelagic or migratory by nature. They are much less sedentary than inland fish like trout or bass. They must follow the water currents which play host to the baitfish that comprise their major dietary needs. For instance, whether or not large numbers of yellowtail are caught off San Diego depends to a large extent on water temperature and coloration. Ideal conditions result in good numbers of bait species such as anchovies, smelt, sardines, and squid moving offshore. If the water is too cold or too dirty—no bait, no yellowtail. Similar ecological relationships govern the albacore tuna and salmon fisheries in the Central and Northern sectors. However, not all saltwater fish are pelagic. The surf fishes, such as corbina and spotfin croaker, pretty much stay in their shallow water zones all through the year along the Southern beaches.

Similarly, the myriad of rockfish varieties popularly sought around the Monterey peninsula also assume a sort of "home-guard" residency for this portion of the coast. Water temperature is the critical ingredient.

This is especially true once the angler turns the corner at Point Conception above Santa Barbara and heads north. The coastline here is very rugged and exposed to prevailing northwest winds. These winds have a tendency to work with the current to bring up colder water from the depths which displaces the otherwise warmer surface layer. This process of wind and current "upwelling" typically occurs in the spring so the shore here remains fairly cold all year long in contrast to offshore waters that warm in summer along the Southern Coast.

So what this means in terms of the angling opportunities is that the Central and Northern regions can sustain large populations of cold water dwellers that are not migratory species. In some sense the fishery in this part of the state has greater stability—the rockfishes, lingcod, eels, etc. are always there. On the other hand, Southern Californians are somewhat more dependent on optimal movements of warm, bait-laden currents for banner catches of such game fish as bonito, barracuda, or yellowtail.

Thus, if we take into account such variables as water temperature, wind exposure, the offshore topography, and the proliferation of forage bait, a very complex portrait of the California marine fishery emerges. A thumbnail sketch of this environment follows.

San Diego to Santa Barbara

Starting in the Southland, migratory species move up from Baja California when water temperatures approach the 65 to 70 degree mark. Extensive summertime action on bonito, barracuda, and yellowtail occurs under the right warm water conditions. If water temperatures soar higher, as they have recently in so-called El Niño years, then even more exotic species may head towards San Diego. These include yellowfin and bigeye tuna as well as spectacular dolphinfish or "dorado." The Coronado Islands just below San Diego are a perennial prime fishing ground.

Other offshore species can be caught on an all-year basis from San Diego to Santa Barbara. These include calico and sand bass, occasional flurries of white sea bass, halibut, assorted sharks and rays, and the ever present tomcod as well as green and Spanish mackerel. Sometimes these game fish are taken just a few hundred yards offshore. Other times, private and party boats will venture to the outer banks and test the waters around Catalina and San Clemente Islands to the west and south or the Channel Islands above Los Angeles to the north.

In the winter, deep-water rockfish are prime quarry with surface fishing grinding down. Lingcod, chilipeppers, salmon groupers, barberpoles, strawberries, bank perch, reds, and the large cowcod round out this mixed bag. These members of the rockfish family are catchable even in the warm months along deep canyons down to 900 feet. But, with intensified surface action in the warmer months, Southern Californians turn to the various bass, barracuda, bonito, yellowtail, and tuna species.

For the most part, Southern beaches tend to have fairly smooth sandy bottoms with sporadic rocky outcroppings and some adjacent kelp beds. The surf fisherman or jetty jockey can try for numerous surf perches—barred, rubberlip, shiner, forktail -- halibut, sand and calico bass, shallow water rockfish, cabezon, yellowfin and spotfin croaker as well as corbina.

Southern California's piers, harbors, and bays hold similar smorgasbords of marine game fish. These piers provide sanctuary for perch, halibut, mackerel, tomcod, occasional runs of bonito, sharks and rays. Major boat harbors such as San Diego, Mission, Dana, Newport, and Huntington have thriving populations of spotted bay bass, halibut and turbot, croakers, sharks, rays, sargo, and modest invasions of small bonito and barracuda.

Santa Barbara to Monterey Bay

Heading above Santa Barbara the complexion of the fishing changes dramatically. As I mentioned, Point Conception seems to be an ecological dividing line for saltwater fish, especially for the dominant pelagic species. Occasionally there will be catches of some wayward bonito or barracuda that find their way up above the point. Similarly, there are intermittent accounts of species indigenous to the Central and Northern sector that end up in the fish sacks of Southern Californians. Recent runs of salmon taken within a mile of Newport Beach exemplify this reversed, minor migration into southern territory.

Kelp beds can be very thick from Santa Barbara up to Monterey. Calico bass—an otherwise warmer water species—can be found in considerable numbers at times in the Santa Barbara area. To a lesser extent, there will also be sporadic yellowtail or white sea bass catches here. But, for the most part, lingcod, rockfish, some halibut, and mackerel comprise the bulk of offshore tallies as we move up the Central Coast.

Pier and surf fishing from Santa Barbara to Morro Bay can be a viable option to offshore angling especially with the scarcity of sport fishing landings. Assorted surfperch, cabezon, olive, kelp, and grass rockfish, along with a few halibut comprise the catch.

As we motor further north into the Pismo Beach and Avila Bay areas, the coastline varies from smooth sandy beaches to hard-to-fish, rocky outcroppings. Surf casters often face stiff winds on these unprotected beaches. But, numerous surf species such as barred, calico, and silver perch along with jack smelt are available for the accomplished long-rodder.

Central coasters have devised their own unique technique termed "poke poling" for yanking such species as monkeyface eels, greenling, cabezon, and lingcod from the deeper pockets formed by rocks and boulders along the surfline. (In a later chapter I'll examine this method in detail.)

Similar cold water action awaits surf casters and offshore boaters out of Morro Bay. Starry flounder, walleye and shiner surfperch, jacksmelt, lings, eels and various rockfish are resident options. Both Morro Bay and Avila Beach also experience stellar runs of albacore during the fall in some years when outside currents bring the schools of tuna into party boat range.

Continuing above Morro Bay, more poke poling and surf casting are available on relatively unpressured beaches. Pier fishermen can find much solitude on the limited number of piers that are found from here to Monterey. Jacksmelt, cabezon, mackerel, and shallow rockfish are staple catches.

Shore fishermen who can challenge the tough access from Morro Bay to Monterey can be treated to some excellent surf fishing for perch, along with rock hopping for lings, greenling, cabezon, kelp, blue, grass and olive rockfish. Check for local restrictions. Some of this coastline is a protected ecological preserve.

The assorted piers, landings, and sloughs that encompass Monterey Bay provide a variety of cold water, marine angling treasures. Salmon, striped bass, perch, sanddabs, halibut, petrale sole, flounder, lingcod, cabezon, greenling, kelp and grass rockfish, sculpin, jacksmelt, sablefish and sharks are on this area's menu of diverse sport fish. Party boaters, skiff fishermen, surf casters, poke polers, and rock hoppers alike can share in the bounty!

San Francisco to Oregon

Once into San Francisco Bay, striped bass, salmon, and shark are the mainstays for enthusiasts interested in larger gamefish. Boaters and shore-liners can take advantage of stripers from inside the bay, from the piers, or along the surfline at Pacifica. Salmon, shark, lingcod, and larger rockfish species inhabit the area's deeper waters. The offshore Farallon Islands similarly offer some phenomenal opportunities for the "rock cod" fanatic. Late summer runs of albacore also frequently occur in these deeper offshore waters.

Pier anglers in the San Francisco area similarly harvest a number of smaller species. Jacksmelt, perch, tomcod (a.k.a. white croaker), sharks, rays, starry flounder, and often striped bass and shallow rockfish are taken off these Northern piers.

Pushing further up the coast to the Oregon border, there are numerous sandy beaches, docks, bays, piers, and rocky shorelines that host cold water species. Tomales Bay, for example, is renowned for its shark population. Skiff fishermen also have some limited action on stripers, salmon, perch, and starry flounder. Surfperch are overwhelmingly the number one catch from the beach. But, there are also some monkeyface eels for the pokers along with rockfish, greenling, cabezon, and lingcod to be caught both off the rocks and in outside waters—all the way to the Oregon state line.

What's Ahead in this Book

You've just read an overview of the California saltwater fishing scene. It is truly a diversified complex of different fisheries. In the following chapters, each of these locals and their various fisheries will be considered in great detail.

I will give the reader an extensive overview of the angling possibilities that exist along the California Coast. I will focus on the tackle, as well as how to use the baits, terminal rigs, and artificial lures to catch each species. Much of this information has been gleaned from veteran saltwater fishermen. These include party boat and charter boat captains, professional guides, tackle experts, landing operators, and assorted local authorities.

If your appetite for more information increases as you read the various chapters, there are a few other texts worth considering for your library. These include: A Field Guide to the Pacific Coast Fishes of North America by Eschmeyer and Hammann; Inshore Fishes of California by John L. Baxter and the California Department of Fish and Game; and Marine Sportfish Identification by the California Department of Fish and Game.

The Basics: Tackle Selection for Coastal Angling

Over the years, I have written many articles, delivered numerous lectures, and taught a variety of courses on the California fishing scene. Whether I was referring to trout, bass, or saltwater techniques, the one thing I have always stressed is to keep your tackle simple!

Also, it is critical to buy the best equipment you can afford. With today's technology, the higher quality rods and reels are made to last. It is a far better investment to purchase one or two top-of-the-line saltwater outfits—at least to start with—than a boat load of cheaper gear.

Another tip: rather than building up a war chest of different lures, rigs, terminal gear, etc., try to stockpile only the tackle you need for the species you're after. Work to develop a level of expertise with a relatively narrow selection of baits and lures. Master these techniques first, acquire a modicum of confidence, and then slowly add to your repertoire.

As was noted earlier, there are clear regional differences between Southern and Northern approaches to coastal fishing as a result of dramatic climate, species, and topographical variations. Thus, a certain amount of forethought is required in selecting outfits for fishing the different regions. For instance, the live bait rods utilized for throwing an anchovy on boiling albacore in the South might have limited application for chasing these tuna along the North Coast. Here, live bait is less accessible and trolling is often more appropriate. Similarly, the surf rods used for shallow water corbina in Carlsbad will differ from those used for chucking a lure for stripers off Pacifica.

So, let's look at some of the basic tips for proper tackle selection which apply regardless of where in California you fish. Then we will focus on some of the more specific variations that are intrinsic to the different fisheries.

Premium Lines

Professional anglers realize that the line and the corresponding knot are the most important links between themselves and the fish. Far too often, saltwater fishermen spend considerable dollars on the latest technological advances in rods and reels but then scrimp on line. They sometimes purchase not only a poor quality line, but also fail to change the line on their reels frequently enough.

A major share of saltwater fishing in the Golden State will require using monofilament line. A premium grade mono exemplifies certain characteristics that set it apart from the cheaper varieties. To begin with, better quality lines are fairly uniform in terms of diameter. This means that the premium line will be rather consistent in its measured breaking test. An inexpensive 1/4 pound spool of "bulk mono," as it is commonly termed, in 20 pound test can conceivably have spots that are higher or lower in breaking strength than the overall average test of 20 pounds. This is not the case with premium lines which have precise extrusion measurements consistent throughout the spool.

Higher quality monofilament will also have better knot strength and abrasion resistance than cheaper versions. These are equally important features, well worth the extra cost. The marine environment plays havoc with monofilament. Constant exposure to sun and salt has a tendency to deteriorate line. This process is reduced to some degree with premium mono. But, still it is imperative to change monofilament every few trips to insure maximum freshness and strength.

As for line color, this becomes a matter of personal choice as far as monofilament is concerned. Color is probably one of the more controversial debates among the fraternity of saltwater buffs. Live bait fishermen are sometimes adamant that fluorescent lines spook the fish under tough conditions. But even here, the evidence is somewhat sketchy at best, with live baiters disagreeing among themselves. Some prefer only clear lines. Others stand by light blues, greens, pearl, or even pink colorations. Trollers who like to use monofilament cloud the picture further. Many of these fishermen recommend going back to fluorescent shades to increase visability when following a lure dragged behind the boat. Be a little experimental—but above all buy premium grade monofilament. Berkley's new Vanish fluorocarbon line is yet another option. Fluorocarbon, in contrast to mono, is almost totally invisible. It sinks three times faster and has great knot strength. But fluorocarbon is somewhat "stiff" and hard to cast for novices.

The same applies to braided lines used for some big game trolling and deep-water rockfishing. Manufacturers have really improved the quality of these fabric-based lines. Even the more modestly priced spools of brand-name dacron perform adequately for the deep bite.

The reason for buying this type of fishing line is to minimize stretching at great depths. This allows the angler to feel the strike in a more pronounced manner as it is transmitted up to the rod tip. One option to consider is either Berkley's Fireline or Whiplash, which are somewhat more expensive than traditional dacron line, but well worth the investment. These thin diameter alternatives to monofilament permit you to put more cloth line onto a particular casting reel without sacrificing breaking test or resistance to stretching, which can be a real plus. Some big game fishermen actually prefer a braided line to a monofilament. One group feels that the mono stretches too much for use on larger fish and thus prefers the braided material. On the flip side of the argument, another group of trollers believes that a braided line is too "unforgiving" and will not allow for making any mistakes in playing the fish.

Most baitcasting and spinning reels will hold roughly 200 to 300 yards of a particular pound test in monofilament. Manufacturers sell their premium monos in 200 to 1000 yard spools. For most coastal fishing, 250 to 300 yards is ample. If you need more line to fill the spool, use some cheaper backing line or build the spool up with masking tape. Hardcore saltwater aficionados might want to consider purchasing even larger 2000 to 3000 yard spools of their favorite monofilament for greater savings.

Rock cod reels will usually house 300 to 500 yards of braided line. This type of line is typically sold in these two quantities. But here again, larger bulk spools are available. These may prove more economical in the long run for the frequent deep-water specialist.

The Conventional Outfit

Saltwater anglers fishing the California Coast should have at least one good "conventional" or baitcasting outfit. Saltwater baitcasting reels feature a revolving spool in contrast to fixed spool spinners. Significant strides in the quality of these reels have been made in the last decade. The two major bugaboos with this style of reel were (1) too much backlash, and (2) spools that were too heavy to cast light lures and baits. Both of these problems have been worked out to a great extent.

Borrowing a page from the freshwater bassin' marketplace, baitcasting reel makers such as Zebco-Quantum, Daiwa, and Penn now have models with magnetic braking systems. Although this engineering feature means that these reels cost more, they are virtually free of excessive spool overruns or "backlash." For the anglers who simply cannot "educate" their thumbs to apply the necessary braking force, a magnetic baitcaster is worth the extra money.

Similarly, with the advent of modern graphite and aluminum tooling, both the saltwater reel and the revolving spool have been made lighter. This doesn't mean that the reels or spools are any less durable than those with the older heavier metal components. The aluminum spools, in particular, have opened up an entirely new dimension for using light lines and small baits with casting outfits. Prior to this, most light-lining was practiced with spinning gear or small baitcasters with highly temperamental plastic spools.

I suggest that anglers at either end of the state invest in one good medium-sized conventional reel. Models like the Penn #140 Squidder and the basic #500 Jigmaster are solid choices. The high speed, ball bearing Penn 955, 965, and 975 miniature International reels have also garnered a strong following in recent years. These styles will store ample amounts of 12 to 30 pound monofilament. This will suffice for most surface, bottom, surfcasting, and even many light trolling situations.

Baitcasting reels are essential to fighting and playing out large saltwater fish. The key feature is their superior drag systems. The standard "star drag" (named because of the star-shaped wheel used for adjustment, etc.) is clearly smoother and more powerful than drag systems found on spinning reels. Penn, Shimano and Daiwa took the star drag design one step further when they incorporated a lever drag system into their line of medium-sized baitcasters. These are miniature drag mechanisms similar to those found on expensive, big game fishing reels.

Better quality conventional reels have ball bearings that facilitate greater distance and smoothness in casting. When possible, think about upgrading your purchase and buy the ball-bearing models. Likewise, most baitcasting reels are now made in faster 4, 5 or even 7:1 gear ratios. For every complete turn of the handle, the spool revolves five times. This feature can be a real boon to gathering up line quickly on a "freight-training" fish.

The latest in ultralite high speed technology is the Penn GS series. The GS 525, 535, and 545 graphite frame

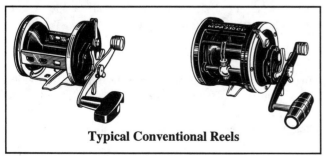

Typical Conventional Reels

casting reels have become a huge favorite among serious West Coast bait and lure casters. With their 6:1 gear ratios, these models allow the angler to make cast after cast for hours at a time, holding a very light reel and retrieving quite rapidly.

Some baitcasting reels such as many of the Penn models, come with a backup spool. This can be helpful if conditions change from what you customarily expect. If the fish are real "twitchy," as they say, switch to a lighter line test. If you are using larger-than-usual baits and/or the fish are breaking off, scale up in line strength. This is just another option to consider when buying a sturdy baitcaster.

Conventional reels, surprisingly, can cast medium to heavy weights further than spinning models. This makes sense when you think about it. The line coming off of a baitcaster pays out against a revolving spool with minimal resistance—but, with a modest amount of weight being casted. As the spool turns, it facilitates the smooth even flow of the line off the reel. By comparison, as line leaves a spinning reel, it must go up and around the lip of the fixed spool. This creates more resistance and friction as the line uncoils further down into the spool. Spinning reels work fine with super-light lures or bait offerings. But, for maximum distance with say, 2 to 6 ounces of weight, the conventional model excels. This is why long-distance casting records are established using baitcasting reels rather than spinning gear. This is also the reason why seasoned surf casters throwing up to 100 yards from the bank opt for a conventional setup.

If you had to select just one length rod and action for a baitcasting outfit, stay in the 7 to 7 1/2 foot medium to light action range. This basic live-bait taper has enough sensitivity and power for most offshore fishing along the California Coast. The Penn Sabre model 270 is perhaps the most popular rod ever sold for all-purpose California saltwater fishing. It is rated for 12-30 pound test line and is equally suitable for calico bass to albacore.

For some time, the regional differences that separated Northern anglers from their Southern California cousins was most apparent in the style of rods preferred in each area. Back in the late fifties and early sixties, the average length casting rod for Southern California saltwater fishing was somewhere around eight feet. Northern California anglers seemed to prefer a shorter, stouter rod with minimal action often referred to as a "boat rod." Many of these early distinctions in regional preferences were dictated by bait presentation.

In Southern California, much offshore angling is done with live offerings. Anchovies, sardines, smelt, greenback and Spanish mackerel, squid, tomcod, and small 7/11 perch comprise the major types of live bait tossed. A majority of these baits are fished right on or just under the surface. Hence, it is necessary to throw these baits some distance without the addition of much weight. Southern California anglers practice the art of "fly-lining" whereby live baits are cast out and allowed to swim unencumbered, stripping off more line, while the reel remains out of gear.

Rod designers along the South Coast eventually modified these lengthy slow-tapered rods into shorter models with powerful butt sections and fast-action tips. Southern Californians have readily endorsed this new design. Party boaters in particular found that the fast-taper rods allowed them to throw a weightless anchovy great distances. But equally important, the prominent butt sections provided adequate strength to play out large fish.

The live bait situation in Northern California is a hit or miss proposition. However, interest in this technique has increased in recent years. A lot of North Coast fishermen prefer to "mooch" dead baits along the bottom ,or in a trolling capacity, as is done with stripers or salmon at times. Thus, there hasn't been an overwhelming need for the shorter hyperbolic rods used by the Southern California sportfishing fleet. Still, North Coast anglers are finding greater utility with these fast-taper models over the stiffer, slow-tapered boat rods used in the past.

Saltwater Spinning Combos

Spinning reels definitely belong on the California saltwater scene. Models vary widely in terms of quality and cost. The finer products have components made with graphite, anodized aluminum, or stainless steel. I believe that ball bearings are critical for saltwater spinners. Models with bushings just don't seem to reel as smoothly after repeated outings compared to those with ball bearings.

For some time saltwater veterans have complained that the primary drawback to the spinning reel was that it is too risky and cumbersome to flip over the bait, allowing the fish to peel off line as it makes its run. Now there are numerous spinners that make it possible to actually throw the spinning reel in and out of free spool without manipu-

lating the bail. This can have tremendous application when the angler has to rely on super-light mono in order to get game fish to strike a fly-lined bait.

A good all-purpose saltwater spinner will hold about 200 to 250 yards of 20 pound test line. A reel with this capacity is usually strong enough to hold everything from yellowtail to stripers. Another possibility is to purchase a slightly smaller model that holds about 200 yards of 15 pound string. A light to medium rig like this can be a lot of fun on smaller pelagic species such as bonito. This is also a good combo for rock hopping and chucking lures on school stripers in San Francisco Bay.

A matching spinning rod can vary from 7 to 8 foot lengths. A single piece model will be stronger but more inconvenient to travel with. The shorter rod provides a lot of sport with small lures and live bait. The lengthier eight footers will allow you to throw further. These are trade-offs worth weighing before you select a spinning rod. Attach the reel to the rod and feel how it balances in your hand. If you are casting from the shore, remember that you may need distance but you also want to be comfortable.

The Popping Rod

This type of rod is typically a one piece, 6 to 7 1/2 foot blank with small baitcasting guides. The popping rod is relatively short but powerful. It is not as strong as fast-taper, off-shore rods whose blanks have thicker walls. A popping rod fills the void between heavy freshwater and light saltwater tackle. As a matter of fact, these blanks are made to balance best with freshwater baitcasting reels.

Fished with 10 to 15 pound mono, the popping outfit has tremendous utility for light-line, live-bait fishing, tossing hardware from the bank, walking a gentle surfline, or working back bays, lagoons, and harbors. If your budget permits, definitely think about adding a popping outfit to your collection of saltwater rods and reels.

I personally helped design the new Penn Sabre GLS series of graphite rods. Models such as the GLS 700, 760, and 800 were tested pulling on lingcod at 300 foot depths, as well as fighting yellow tuna on the surface. Don't underestimate the power of these graphite blanks. They are an excellent addition to your overall tackle arsenal when you must fish 10 to 20 pound mono.

Surf Fishing Options

Surf fishermen in the Golden State are fairly well divided as to what type of rod and reel is most suitable for our waters. In the Southland, numerous anglers are reverting back to super-light combos for combing the shallow

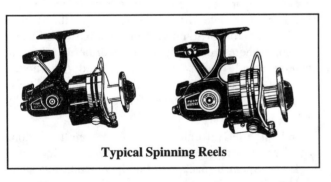

Typical Spinning Reels

surfline. Smaller inshore species such as barred perch, spotfin croaker, and corbina are more readily caught on 6 to 12 pound mono. Hence, if conditions are right, you will see a lot of medium freshwater or light saltwater spinning outfits, or popping rods and conventional reels along the Southern beaches.

However, if the surf is rough, or if distance is critical, the fish are large, or the bottom rocky—then shift to the magnum gear. There are spots along the South Coast—for example South Laguna or Malibu Beach—where proficient surf casters have to reach offshore kelp beds as they hunt for big calicos or "bull bass." This requires up to an 80 to 90 yard cast. Powerful rods capable of handling 4 to 6 ounces of lead and 25 to 30 pound mono are essential. Conversely, there are times in the North when a 10 to 12 pound rod comes in handy in hunting stripers. Surf fishermen often toss artificial lures with spinning reels fitted with 10 to 12 pound test teamed with the long surf sticks.

There are other stretches of beach along the central and northern coastline where the angler can get by with a lighter outfit—if the conditions permit. When the tidal surge is strong and the wind is blowing right into your cast, it's time to bring out the "heavy artillery" and throw a conventional reel matched with a 10 to 13 foot rod.

Granted, many of the surf species caught along our coast are smaller perch and rockfish. However, I must reiterate that the longer rod can be a valuable asset. A 2 to 3 pound perch is a real prize. So, in some sense these smaller surf fishes are dramatically out-scaled by the big rods, heavy sinkers, and 20 to 30 pound line. The point is, that in order to make the cast under very inclement conditions, a longer rod teamed with strong lines and larger sinker is your only chance to stay in the hunt and maintain contact with the bottom. Also note that almost every surf rod sold in the West today comes with large spinning guides. This allows the surf caster to use either a spinning or a conventional reel as conditions and skill dictate.

Trolling and Bottom Fishing Rigs

If your pocketbook allows for another outfit, then invest in a heavy duty rig that can double for either trolling or serious bottom fishing. Most sport fishing landings from San Diego to San Francisco have these combos available on a daily rental basis. Whether or not to invest in a complete outfit depends upon how much you plan to use the big gear over the years. There is no substitute for personally owning all your rods and reels. With your own equipment, you always know the condition of the drag,

the line, and the overall performance ability of the rod and reel. This can be essential in landing a trophy fish.

So if you can afford a heavy-duty reel, decide if you want it strictly for bottom fishing or for trolling as well. Some manufacturers such as Penn and Daiwa market large reels with super-slow high-leverage gear ratios for pulling up many pounds of lead sinkers and rockfish from the bottom. Reels in this genre do not require sophisticated drags or ball-bearing drives. They are used primarily for deep-water drops. They will store anywhere from 300 to 500 yards or more of 50 to 80 pound monofilament or braided line.

Reels with similar capacities are required for trolling. But in this situation more precision is needed with regard to drag smoothness, spool tolerance, and ease and speed in retrieving line on a fast-charging game fish. These reels are somewhat "overpowered" for bottom fishing, but they can be modified for the deep-water game. You can purchase an oversized extension handle that gives you more leverage and comfort when hauling large loads of rockfish from the depths. Then when seasons shift, remove the spool with the dacron line, replace it with one filled with monofilament, change back to the shorter handle, and you are back in the trolling business!

In regard to trolling or bottom fishing rods, many skippers recommend a single piece model, preferably with the glass blank running all the way through the handle. The older, East Coast style rod with detachable butt section is passable for bottom bouncing smaller species. But if you are dragging in a 20 pound albacore or hoisting up 30 pounds of rock cod with a two-piece model, too much strain is placed on where the sections are connected. Don't risk a broken rod—invest in a one-piece blank.

A good bottom or trolling rod should minimally have a roller tip guide. This tip top looks like a miniature pulley and functions in the same manner. With the internal roller, much potential line friction and hence, wear is dissipated on the retrieve. If you can step up in quality, look for a bottom trolling rod with not only a roller tip top, but also a lead stripper roller guide. This feature reduces additional line friction. The ultimate, of course, is to own a trolling rod with a full set of rollers. These models are usually expensive and may not be that critical for the weekend angler.

Better grade trolling rods feature AFCO rollers which are considered to be some of the finest components available.

Which Outfit to Use

As a very rough rule of thumb, I switch to casting outfits when I need to fish 20 pound test or greater—or, if I am looking for larger species. I do this whether I am surface fishing for yellowtail or stripers, or bottom bouncing for halibut or shark. There is simply no substitute for the leverage and smooth drag that you receive from a conventional reel, along with larger line capacities and greater casting potential.

With regard to rod components, saltwater fishermen do not have to make a significant investment in graphite or boron composite blanks as is occurring in some freshwater circles. The quality-grade fiberglass rod is fine. Graphite and boron are more sensitive, but in contrast to fiberglass blanks, they are more susceptible to chipping and cracking. For marine conditions, fiberglass rods have withstood the test of time. They can take a beating against boat rails, rocks, pier decks, and sandy beaches. If you want to experiment with some of the new, light composite materials, purchase a graphite popping rod. This blank can also be used for freshwater bassin' and serious trout trolling.

Simple Tackle Storage Systems

An angler can easily become confused at times when he is trying to decide what type of tackle box to purchase. Over the years, as a shore angler, charter and private boater, and adventure traveler, I have had to make many decisions as to what kind of tackle box would be most suitable for a particular situation.

The Flambeau Products company has designed a series of tackle storage systems that help the fisherman narrow down his choices when it comes to choosing the correct box. Here are some of my personal favorites.

Tackle Station 2000. This is the ultimate "big box" for the true "collector" of fishing toys. It combines the best of soft, airline type carry-on luggage with rugged "hard box" technology. For small boaters, the nice thing about this type of soft box with hard internal plastic trays is that it won't scratch or mar those expensive interiors. This is also an excellent magnum class box to take on a fishing expedition when you need to travel by plane.

ST Soft-Sided Tackle System. These handy nylon boxes are one of my all-time favorites. They can be carried along the bank, on an airplane, or on any boat. Each nylon case has a series of 4 to 6 individual plastic boxes with an infinite number of ways to compartmentalize each box. Extra boxes are inexpensive. I purchase extra boxes and have each labeled and loaded with the tackle and lures I

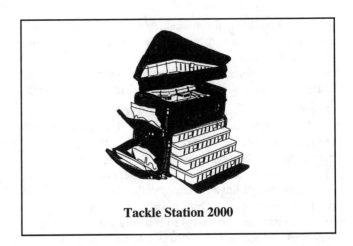

Tackle Station 2000

use for a particular locale. Then, depending on my destination, I simply pack one of these soft-sided cases with the 4 to 6 boxes that will specifically work for that outing. This saves the hassle of carrying lots of items I don't need. The various types of tackle I need are readily available in their own separate box.

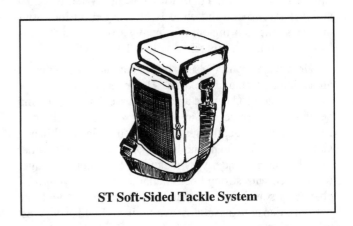

ST Soft-Sided Tackle System

Infinity Boxes. When it comes to traditional hard boxes, it is difficult to beat these units. A series of plastic trays are aligned vertically in a nest "chest of drawers" fashion. These too are excellent quick-access boxes for the private boater and have lots of extra storage space.

This box can be added to "infinitely." Flambeau markets extra expansion trays so that you can create even taller Infinity boxes to house more tackle. These models are excellent for big plugs, larger spoons, plastics, and oversized lures used to challenge big fish.

Top Force. This is a two-level box that looks like a mini suitcase. It can hold lots of tackle and is easy to tote around. It is perfect for the rental boat angler, smaller skiff owner, or shore angler. It also stores conveniently in cars, trucks, or planes.

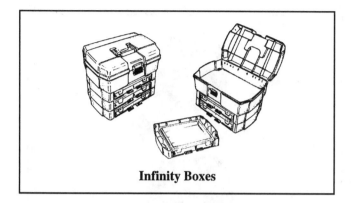

Infinity Boxes

The Top Force is also a good option if you want to bring along an extra reel and some accessory spools of monofilament. Space is dedicated for these items with this hard, compact tackle box.

Top Force

Other Accessories

A saltwater angler shouldn't leave home without some kind of cutting device. It really puts a strain on the dental work to bite through 30 to 50 pound monofilament. A pair of dikes make an excellent tool for marine purposes. Equally important is some form of hook remover. Needlenose pliers will suffice. Better yet are the surgical hemostats marketed by Izorline as "Dr. Fisherman." Using this long-nosed tool allows you to remove hooks deeply entrenched without tearing up the fish. This is important where size limits apply and immature sub-legal specimens must be returned—alive.

Polaroid sunglasses are also a valuable asset. Whether you are fishing from a boat or jetty jockeying off the rocks, polaroids definitely help you to monitor the water for bait or fish activity. Many fresh and saltwater pros, as well as

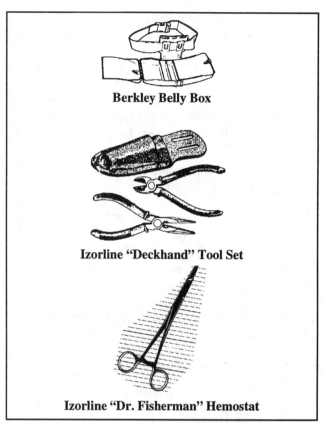

Berkley Belly Box

Izorline "Deckhand" Tool Set

Izorline "Dr. Fisherman" Hemostat

skippers, are now using more expensive models designed by such manufacturers as Mako and Fitovers.

These polarized lenses are made from high quality optical glass, and as you would expert, they do cost more than plastic. With the peripheral leather sun shields that come with some of these models, you will encounter minimal glare and optimal clarity. Polarized sunglasses in this class are designed to be worn for long periods when the angler is paying constant attention to the water.

Terminal Tackle

Unlike freshwater fishing, the terminal tackle used from one end of the state to the other for saltwater tactics is highly varied. I'll try to give the reader a brief synopsis—almost like a "quickie grocery list"—of the basic terminal gear used for certain coastal areas. As you read further into the following chapters, greater details will be given on how to rig for specific techniques with both bait and lures.

Southern California Live Bait Tackle

Short-shanked ringed live baithooks are the staples for serious fly-liners. Most novices buy the Eagle Claw #318-

N model in nickel finish. Local veterans strongly suggest using the more subdued bronze color. The trade-off? The bronze live bait hooks seem to rust more easily but they won't spook touchy fish. A growing number of pros have switched to the more expensive Eagle Claw "Black Pearl" lazer sharp hooks. The #113 model in particular is so strong with its welded ring, it's practically impossible to break on even the largest of Pacific gamefish. These may very well be the sharpest hooks available in this style.

Eagle Claw hook sizes range from #2 to #4 for normal anchovy baits. Scale up to #1 or #1/0 for larger offerings. Keep a pack of #4/0 for mackerel or squid. Throw in a few #1/0 to #3/0 treble hooks (3x-strong, cadmium plated) for specialized yellowtail baits.

Twist-on rubber core sinkers are still widely used for fishing baits below the surface. An assortment of 1/8 to 3/8 ounce rubber cores is adequate. Keep a few larger 3/4 to 1 1/2 ouncers handy for fishing deeper along with some 1 to 2 ounce chrome-ringed sinkers for halibut tactics. In addition, some large lead split-shot sinkers sometimes work better than rubber core models. Likewise, stock a few 1/2 to 2 ounce sliding-egg sinkers for other bottom bouncing options.

North Coast Tackle

Nickel-plated Sealy hooks in sizes 3/0 to 7/0 are popular for stripers. Double and single snelled hook slider rigs are sold throughout the North with special striper spreaders. These pre-tied leaders are the easiest for the novice to fish. Hooks, swivels, and related hardware can be purchased separately for the more advanced striper fishermen.

A lot of salmon will be caught by trolling. Sinkers utilized in a trolling release setup will be necessary in 1 to 3 pound weights. Hooks similar to those utilized for stripers are used for salmon trolling, but check local tackle stores for preferred double-hook harnesses. If live anchovies are available, standard Eagle Claw #318-N #2 to #4 short-shank baitholder hooks are required. Have a supply of sliding sinkers in your North Coast box. Weights should range form 1/4 to 1 ounce for salmon and striper offerings. In addition, you will need to buy metallic chrome flashers or dodgers as attractors for salmon action. Here again, rely upon landing operators to recommend the current "hot ticket" for trolling.

Rock Cod Gear

The first thing to purchase is a rail board to help balance heavy rock cod outfits against the boat's wooden railing. Keep a stock of assorted, pre-tied commercial gangions,

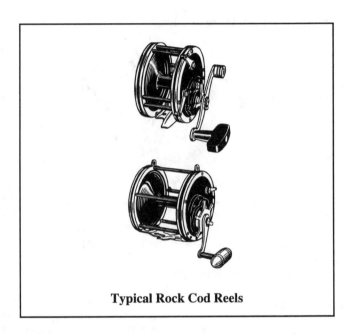

Typical Rock Cod Reels

ranging in hook sizes from #1/0 to #7/0. (Check with local landings to determine the size of rockfish that are showing.) Gangions with colored shrimp flies or plastic lures should also be included. Keep a small knife handy for filleting frozen or fresh strip bait. Sinkers, like the gangions, depend in part on the species and depth fished. An assortment could range from 10 to 12 ounces up to 5 pounds.

Surf, Jetty, and Bay Paraphernalia

Depending upon tidal variables, be prepared with an array of surf sinkers in 1 to 4 ounces on up to 6 ounces if your rod and reel will handle it. Long-shank Eagle Claw #181 bronze baitholders in sizes #6 to #1/0 can cover a wide variety of surf, bay, and jetty conditions. Sinker designs should be mixed with spoon, bulldozer, claw pyramid, and torpedo shapes thrown in the tackle pack. A bait knife and bait bucket along with a cutting board are important additions. A sand spike is helpful if you don't want to hold your rod all the time. A gunny sack serves to keep your catch fresh. Most of the gear can be consolidated into the bait bucket to make movement easier. Chest waders are another option depending on water temperature and casting access.

Remember, these are simplified "shopping lists." As we get into more extensive discussions of specific saltwater methods, invariably you will want to add some "trick" lure or different terminal gear to your tackle arsenals, but the equipment mentioned in this chapter will be enough to get you started with a well-rounded, basic assortment of gear.

Bait Fishin': 'Chovies, Squid, Crabs, and More

Estimates would have to range in the upper 90 percent bracket for the number of saltwater species caught on bait compared to artificial lures. The tasty morsels used to catch our marine fish off the California Coast can be separated into three principle categories: live, cut, and surf baits. In this chapter, I'll itemize these diverse baits, tell how they can be obtained, and describe proper hooking technique. Additional information will follow in subsequent chapters on the specific species and the baits they feed upon.

Live Anchovies

Without a doubt, live anchovies are the integral component of the sport fishing fleets in Southern California. Without ample numbers of this small bait fish, entire seasons can be lost by the party boat fleets.

'Chovies, as they are commonly termed, are gathered by commercial net boats off the coast. The fish are held in special receiving tanks built into these bait boats. Often, when anchovies are in abundance, the commercial operators transfer their catch into floating bait re-

ceivers. These platforms are usually situated inside a harbor that hosts a sport fishing landing.

Both party boats and private yachts pull up to the receivers and fill their bait tanks with anchovies. These are a delicate bait fish requiring constant aeration. Occasionally, tackle shops on the ends of some piers also sell live anchovies. Pier anglers equipped with bait buckets and miniature battery-operated aerators take advantage of this primo bait fish.

Handle anchovies very carefully. Try to keep the scales intact. It is best to almost "cradle" them in the palm of your hand as you corner one in the bait tank.

Size can be a misleading factor in picking a good 'chovy from a loaded tank. It is better to isolate a highly active small to medium-sized bait instead of another, lethargic "race horse." Equally important is coloration. A select number of anchovies in the bait tank have a greenish hue to their skin. "Greenies" are claimed to be the heartiest, most active specimens. Personal experience seems to support this thesis.

Most saltwater anglers prefer to use short-shank live bait hooks for 'chovy fishing. Gear the hook to the size of the bait and the diameter of the line. Small Eagle Claw #318-N #8 or #6 hooks are used with "pinheads" and 10 to 15 pound test mono. #2 to #4's are staples for medium-sized 'chovies and 15 to 30 pound line. Scale all the way up to 1/0 to 2/0 for larger baits.

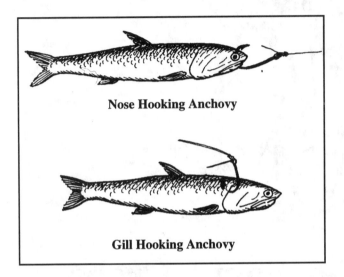

Nose Hooking Anchovy

Gill Hooking Anchovy

The most popular hooking technique is to gently insert and pull the point through the outer edge of the gill collar. This is a favored tactic for fly-lining the bait near the surface. If you are going to fish the 'chovy closer to the bottom with a heavier sinker, then hook it through both the upper and lower lips. This serves to keep the bait fish from inadvertently drowning.

Often, pesky seagulls dive and pick at anchovies fished on the surface. Similarly, hordes of mackerel or Catalina blue perch devour the 'chovies at sub-surface levels while larger game fish lie underneath the activity. By hooking an anchovy through the body near the anal fin, the bait will head downward.

Live Sardines

For many years, sardines practically disappeared from the South Coast. Commercial fishermen put a considerable dent into this bait fish population. However, in recent seasons, sardines have returned. At certain times, sport fishers will have tanks full of these baits instead of anchovies.

Live sardines are hooked basically in the same fashion as 'chovies. Some veterans prefer to use a #1/0 to #3/0 bronze or nickel treble hook with jumbo-class sardines. The theory is that often a large single hook gets fouled and inadvertently re-embeds itself into the sardine. This makes hook penetration nearly impossible. A treble hook, in contrast, always has at least 1 to 2 barbs exposed for greater penetration. The big sardine can be hooked in the dorsal or anal fin area with a treble hook.

In the Southland, there are actually days when game fish like yellowtail want a puny anchovy instead of a frisky, larger sardine. So, there are no guarantees that even this premium bait fish will always work.

Live Squid

Almost any pelagic game fish will attack a live squid. Southern Californians call a tankful of these cephalopods "candy" because they are so deadly. Sand bass, calico bass, white sea bass, halibut, yellowtail, bonito, lingcod, rock cod, albacore, and stripers all eat squid.

Like anchovies and sardines, much of the live squid used by sport fishing boats is pre-captured by commercial bait operations. But, where the conditions are right, party boat skippers hang a large light over the side of the boat in the middle of the night and wait for the squid to float to the surface. Using brail nets, deck hands will herd the squid and transfer them into the bait tanks.

If the squid fail to float and ball up in quantity, then another approach will be tried. Deck hands will ask the passengers to rig up two or three "squid jigs" in tandem, about 15 inches apart on their regular outfits. Add another similar length of leader to the bottom jig and attach a 2 to 6 ounce chrome torpedo sinker. The squid jig is a rather unusual lure made from plastic or cloth. Some have built-in battery-operated lights for added attraction. The key feature of the jig is the rows of metal prongs that stick out from the thickest section. When the jig is lowered down and then slowly lifted vertically, the squid grasps onto the prongs. You can feel the dull resistance of the squid as it hooks itself on the jig. Reel up in a nice, slow steady fashion and unhook the squid in the bait tank. The best depth for using the jigging strategy is about 100 feet.

Live squid fish best if hooked once through the tail, and maybe back in and through the body for security. Don't be timid as far as hook size is concerned with these creatures. Escalate to Eagle Claw #113H Black Pearl Lazer Sharp #3/0 to #5/0 live bait models—and sharpen the points on these bigger hooks for best penetration. In handling the bait, grasp the squid behind the head with the tentacles well in front of your hand. Keep the squid aimed away from other anglers should it inadvertently decide to squirt its ink.

There are a few piers along our coast —for example, at King's Harbor in Redondo Beach—that occasionally

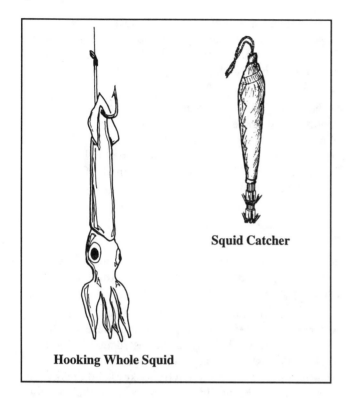

Squid Catcher

Hooking Whole Squid

sell live squid for immediate usage. This can be an unexpected treat for pier fishermen who are usually relegated to frozen baits.

Squid begin the spawning ritual in early December in Southern California and in January in the North. The spawn proceeds in the Southland sometimes through April and up until May on the North Coast. Using electronics, skippers look for squid along deep sub-marine canyons with sandy or muddy bottoms. Keep in mind that in some years the squid remain submerged at depths well over 600 feet. When this occurs, an entire season may pass, with limited, if any, of this prized "candy" bait.

Live Smelt

Sometimes these shimmering bait fish end up with anchovies or sardines in bait receivers. Other times, boat fishermen may come across a school of these little firecrackers and will start catching them with tiny jig fly gangions. In past years, anglers used the popular "Lucky Joe" rig. This was comprised of nothing more than alternating little hooks draped with red or yellow yarn. The problem was that the smelt became too "educated" and were no longer fooled by the yarn all the time. Some enterprising anglers found that a new series of miniature gangion-fly setups from Japan would produce when the Lucky Joe rigs

wouldn't. These tiny little jig flies are made with a combination of a bead, wax paper, and feathers. They are terrific when jigged up and down for small bait fish.

Smelt can also be netted at times with larger throw nets. They can be taken near the surfline and inside sheltered bays. These bait fish can be hooked and presented in a manner similar to anchovies or sardines. The size of the hook should match the length of the bait. For the larger 8 to 10 inch smelt, use an Eagle Claw #318-N #2/0 to #3/0 short-shank bait hook. In some cases, the smelt are so "hot" that they almost swim too fast for a surface bait. Deck hands sometimes clip the fins to slow the smelt down when crossing paths with a big bull bass or yellowtail.

Live Pacific Mackerel

Pacific mackerel are characterized by vertical green stripes. They are also called "greenback" mackerel. These larger bait fish are highly prolific and can often be a nuisance when other game fish are being sought. They can have voracious appetites.

Pac macks can be caught on small pieces of anchovy on a #6 to #2 hook. It doesn't make too much difference if the 'chovy is fresh or frozen. Sometimes, the only way they can be caught in harbors and bays is tediously like this, one-at-a-time. However, in open water, especially under a floating kelp patty, look for greenbacks to strike a jig fly gangion. As I mentioned with smelt, try one of the micro-jig rigs for an improved catch. Also, use a chrome 1 to 2 ounce torpedo sinker to get the jig flies to sink. But use the shiny sinker without a hook. Too many times, 4 or 5 macks will climb on to the jig fly leader. The fish snagged on the treble hook can nearly foul up the rest of the gangion.

Mackerel can be fly-lined with larger Eagle Claw #318-N #4/0 to #7/0 short-shank hooks when the game fish are on the surface. Some anglers prefer to hook the mack through the nose slits, while others pin it under the anal fin. Another ploy is to use larger #1/0 to #3/0 treble hooks through the nose or lower fin. South Coasters have found that fewer yellowtail are lost by using the treble hook-mackerel combo.

Pacific jack mackerel are often termed "Spanish" mackerel. They are brownish-gold in color and are commonly smaller than the more hearty greenbacks. They are also excellent bait for yellowtail, big bass, sharks, halibut, and lingcods. "Spanish" are most easily taken with the jig fly methods. An Eagle Claw #118 or #113 #1/0 to #4/0 short-shank hook through the two nasal pores is the preferred hooking method.

Brown and Junk Baits

Invariably, commercial bait boats net a collection of smaller fishes that get mixed in with anchovies or sardines in the receivers. This potpourri of species include small tomcod, queenfish, 7-11 and shiner perch, and baby sargo. Many anglers consider this grouping to be "junk bait." Accomplished saltwater pros rate brown bait as a "delicious addition" to the diets of such game fish as calico bass, yellowtail, and white sea bass.

Kit McNear is a long-time charter boat skipper in the Santa Barbara area. He passes along the following tip to small boaters from Ventura south who want to garner some of this junk bait. McNear recommends using your own brown bait net to sift through the bait receivers. A long-handled model with 1 1/2 inch mesh allows the anchovies to pass through while capturing the brown bait.

Some of this bait can also be caught using jig fly leaders around piers, docks, jetties, and pilings. The tomcod (or white croaker) in particular, congregate in these areas. The tommy croakers also strike chunks of anchovy, thin strips of squid, or frozen shrimp fished on a single hook or used as tippets on jig fly gangions.

Brown baits can be hooked behind the dorsal fin, through the nasal pores, or next to the anal fin. Hook sizes range from #1/0 to #5/0, depending upon the size of the bait fish. Private boat owners who prefer to fish brown baits should try to segregate them from the scoops of live anchovies by using two separate bait tanks.

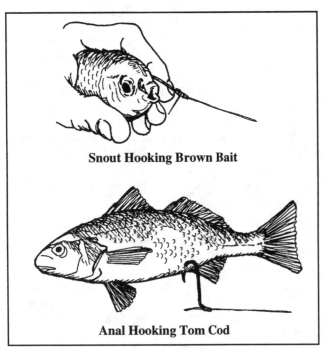

Snout Hooking Brown Bait

Anal Hooking Tom Cod

Southland pier anglers probably recognize some of these brown baits in their catches. Next time you bring in that unwanted tomcod, think twice before throwing him back out as bait. A big halibut or bull bass might be waiting for this larger feast!

Northern Californians can take advantage of a similar condition with other "junk baits." Try using live, small blue rockfish, little sanddabs, or whole herring for good size lingcods. This is parallel to brown bait fishing in the Southland. These big lings will hit the smaller fish off the shallow water reefs with a vengeance!

Mudsuckers

This member of the goby family can be caught in baited fish traps in some Northern tidal flats. Mudsuckers are usually purchased through bait stores.

Interestingly, they can be kept in just an inch or two of water and blanketed with damp seaweed. These little baits are remarkably tough. They can be casted repeatedly with minimal damage. They are a key target for striped bass. But, in Southern California, jetty jockeys and breakwall fishermen have found mudsuckers to be lethal on big calicos that live among the rocks.

Mudsuckers can be fly-lined without a sinker or fished closer to the bottom. A wire Sealy or bronze long-shank baitholder hook works fine. Depending upon the size of the 'suckers anywhere from a Eagle Claw #181 bronze, long-shank baitholder #2 to #4/0 hook should suffice. Local anglers note that it is often important to "pump" your rod once in a while when bait fishing with mudsuckers. The sudden movement of the rod, they relate, makes the mudsucker swim in a more frantic manner.

Bullheads

This is another small, durable bait fish essential to the Northern California striper fishery. Bullheads are saltwater sculpins and are indigenous to our bays and brackish waters. They can be worked along the same lines as mudsuckers. However, some pros feel that it is better to kill the bullhead first before you cast it. They point out that the live bullhead will burrow into the muddy bottom, disappearing out of sight. Long-time striper snipers feel that as long as the dead bullhead is fresh, with an ample coasting of slime still intact, it will outperform a live model.

On this note, locals emphasize that if you purchase frozen bullheads, check to make certain that there is plenty of slime left on them. This slime apparently has some essential qualities which can enhance the bite when striper fishing.

Shiner Perch

North Coasters also appreciate the value of these tiny perch as a striper appetizer. Shiners can be caught in baited traps or by rod and reel. An Eagle Claw #181 #12 baitholder hook tipped with a small piece of shrimp take a share of these bait fish. Work around the docks, piers, and pilings. Shiners can be fly-lined or weighted with a small shot. The best hooking is behind the dorsal fin so that the bait swims fairly unencumbered.

Frozen Cut and Strip Baits

West Coast anglers—both Northerners and Southerners alike—for some reason don't fish as much cut bait as do East Coast fishermen. A variety of the live offerings just listed can be frozen down for future trips. Many baits, including squid, anchovies, and mackerel, are commercially sold in the frozen state. Here is a brief rundown on some of the popular entrees that can be cut or stripped.

Frozen Anchovies: Bait stores from San Diego to Eureka usually stock a supply of frozen 'chovies. Don't confuse these with salted anchovies. Both work, but the relatively fresh frozen ones will be more effective.

Frozen 'chovies can be fished whole and hooked similarly to the way they would be in the live state. However, you might try a long-shank baitholder hook instead of the short-shank live bait model. The baitholder style holds the frozen bait fish better with the additional barbs on the shank. Anchovies like this can be drifted, mooched, still fished, surf casted, or trolled.

Another tip is to cut the 'chovy to create a more attractive natural scent in the water. This can be done in a number of ways. One technique is to cut the bait in half. Then slice through the anchovy's midsection about 2/3 into the half section. Place your hook through the "meatier" uncut portion of the fish. This creates a "scissor-like" effect with the two strips of skin flapping together. The frozen sections have a very life-like appearance when they are slowly pulled through the water or are struck by current.

You can also make an incision with your bait knife into the abdomen of the frozen 'chovy, or cut out a small chunk from the lower head section. Either cut allows more odor to flow from the bait while leaving the anchovy pretty

Frozen 'chovy Hooking (Scissors Effect)

much intact. The same techniques apply to frozen sardines when they are available. Smart saltwater bait fishermen now also use a few drops of Berkley Strike in the saltwater flavor for extra insurance when using frozen 'chovies or sardines.

Frozen Dead Squid: You can usually purchase a pound tray of frozen squid at most bait stores for a very nominal fee. But also check your local fish markets for fresh stocks. Buy the "calamari" from the seafood section and freeze for usage in the next few days.

Frozen squid will catch just about any major game fish in the whole, uncut version. Surf casters, party boaters, rock codders, shark hunters, and trollers will hunt their prey with fresh dead squid when the live critters are not available.

One trick that enhances the effectiveness of dead squid is to move it, if possible. I discovered this many years ago on a spotty yellowtail bite off San Diego (what sport skippers term a "pick"). The fish were fussy and not too interested in our live 'chovies. I pinned on a whole, thawed squid, casted it, and slowly "pumped" it back to the stern. This pumping action made the tentacles flair, giving the bait the illusion of being very much alive. I got my 'tail that day on this tactic and have seen the scenario repeated many times by long-time party boaters.

Another variation on this theme is a little trick deck hands sometimes pull to impress their customers—and it often works! Take a frozen squid and carefully insert a live anchovy into its stomach cavity. Gently cast, drift, or slow-troll this combo. The wriggling 'chovy makes the squid dance from side to side. These erratic movements sometimes result in blind strikes from otherwise touchy game fish.

Frozen squid can also be cut into diagonal or longitudinal strips. The smaller sections serve as excellent trailers behind lures or as tippets on rockfish gangions. They can be diced into further chunks for smaller quarry. The longer strips can also be fly-lined and "pumped and twitched" back to the boat or shore.

Every few years, and frequently in El Nino conditions, schools or jumbo squid invade our coastal waters. These magnum cephalopods are too large to use for bait whole (except maybe for shark or swordfish). But, filleted into long, 12 inch strips, the jumbos can be sensational on certain game fish like yellowtail and large bonito.

The tentacles themselves from a frozen squid should be tried as another form of trailer. The tentacles are tough, leather-like in texture, and won't tear off easily from the hook. They yield a very snake-like, undulating action on a retrieve or a drift when laced behind a plastic or feather jig.

Mackerel and Bonito Slabs: Both greenback and Spanish mackerel can be good strip baits along with frozen bonito. With the mackerel, sometimes an entire side fillet works best. This pennant-shaped strip can be still fished from the bank, trolled, mooched, drifted, or fly-lined near the surface. Smaller strips work as tippets or trailers on jigs or gangions.

For the bonito, remove one side of the fillet from a one to two pound fish and then re-section the slab into 4 to 6 long skinny fillets. Fish the longer fillet sections on the surface for bigger game fish, or near the bottom for sharks and rays. Cut these fillets into smaller chunks for trailers or gangion tippets. Some of the bigger calico, sand bass, lingcod, yellowtail, and tuna are caught on "slab" bait each season.

Mackerel and bonito strips fish especially well when pinned onto a circle hook. It is almost impossible for yellowtail or tuna to "strip" the chunk of soft "meat" when using the circle hook. Try the Eagle Claw #2004 or #200S models in sizes 4/0 to 8/0 for fishing the "strip bait."

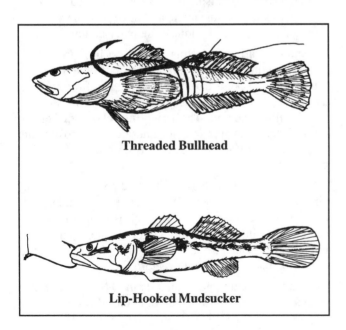

Threaded Bullhead

Lip-Hooked Mudsucker

More Baits for Surf and Bays

There is a wealth of other fresh, natural baits that are suitable for certain types of surf or bay fishing. Here is a brief listing.

Sandcrabs: This ubiquitous little creature is a key forage bait for many of the inshore surf fishes. Sandcrabs are found all along the coast. You can dig them up by hand or use a wire mesh sand crab trap to sift for them through the waves' backwash.

Sandcrabs molt at certain times of the year. Many surf anglers feel that you will get more bites from a soft-shelled sandcrab in this molting stage. This is probably true. Yet, the flip side to this equation is that the hard-shell varieties produce the larger surf fish.

Here is a little trick that I stumbled across some years ago that sort of compromises the soft-shell/hard-shell dilemma. Take a hard-shell crab and peel away part of the shell to expose some of the viscera. The hard-shell stays on the hook better. When slightly cut open in this manner, it has the appearance of a more vulnerable soft-shell crab.

Sandcrabs should be hooked with either wire Octopus, Sealy, or bronze baitholders. Match the hook to correspond to the size of the crab. Hooks range from #6 to #1 for most conditions. Sandcrabs will nail almost all the surfperches, corbina, spotfin croaker, and sand sharks. They should always be fished fresh. Many tackle stores stock both hard-shell and the primo soft-shell crabs during different times of the year.

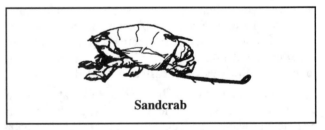

Sandcrab

Clams: Pismo clams are viable baits for many resident fish found in the surf line and in lagoons, back bays, and sheltered harbors. Pismos can be dug using shovels, but a pitchfork or clam rake is better. You must always check for up-to-date posting with regard to seasons and size limits. If you prefer to gather your own clams for bait, the ones you keep must meet the legal size requirements.

Almost all of the clams can be converted to good fish bait. Some anglers prefer to use the siphon part, others swear by the foot. Another group likes to fish the gut. Long-shank baitholders are the best hooks to use with pismos. Depending upon the size of fish sought, the hooks will range from #6 to #1. Both the Eagle Claw bronze #181 long-shank baitholder and #197 nickel light wire circle hooks excel when fishing sand crabs in the surf.

Razor clams do not have the culinary value of Pismos. You can find them in the muddy sloughs and back bays. The Elkhorn Slough, Alamitos, Mission and San Diego Bays sustain a major population of razor clams. Dedicated clammers often use a specialized suction pump made from PVC pipe to extract razors from the mud. These pumps are sometimes sold at local bait shops. Use the same size range of hooks for razors as with Pismos. Most bait dealers stock at least one or the other clams throughout the year.

Rock and Bay Mussels: These are probably some of the easiest baits to gather yourself. Both varieties are indigenous throughout the coastline. Rock mussels are the larger and tougher of the two. They can be found along tide pools, shoreline rocks, and pier pilings.

Bay mussels are typically found inside the quiet harbors. The meat from the bay mussel is much softer than the rock species. There are times when surf and bay fishes prefer one over the other. Most coastal bait shops have ample stocks of each mussel all year long.

If you decide to eat your leftover mussels after your outing—be careful! Watch for posted warnings. At certain times of the year, mussels assume a dangerous level of toxicity, harmful for human consumption. Mussels in this condition, although unfit for us to eat, are still acceptable as bait, with no after effects for the fish or fisherman.

Mussels can be hooked similarly to clams. If the meat is exceptionally soft, secure the bait to the hook with some orange thread. Fresh mussels are far superior to the canisters of frozen mussel meat that some bait vendors sell.

Shrimp: (Ghost, Mud, and Grass) There are a variety of shrimp that can be dug or pumped from the back bays, mudflats, and estuaries. Ghost shrimp are perhaps the easiest to pump or shovel at low tide. This species is sold in both the North and the South. Grass and mud shrimp are more popular in the San Francisco Bay Area.

Most anglers prefer to thread shrimp onto either a long-shank, Sealy wire, or Gamakatsu hook. Enter in from the tail portion and work the hook back out into the head section, leaving the point buried. Hook sizes vary depending again on how large the different shrimp are that you are using. The better bait shops in the coastal regions will stock live shrimp that are obtained from commercial pumpers.

Sidewinder Crabs: These little one to two inch rock crabs can be gathered by hand around inshore rocks, tidal pools, and near the mud and eel grass. Sidewinders can be rigged with Eagle Claw #197 fine wire circle hooks or #181 long-shank #1 to #4 baitholders. Try to embed the hook and hide it into the body portion of the tiny crab. Sidewinders are superb baits for large perch— more on this later!

Marine Worms: There are a number of marine worms that can be utilized as baits for inshore species. Bloodworms are a staple in many Southern bait shops. They live in muddy sloughs and the more energetic angler may try to dig his own. This worm has four sets of jaws, and it will bite! Be careful in handling them. Bloodworms can be cut into pieces or used whole.

Pile worms are more centipede-like in appearance. They root in the sand, mud, barnacles, mussel mass, and pier pilings. These worms are a staple bait for Northern California anglers.

The tubeworm is the most bizarre of all. It will build itself a parchment-like tubular home and lives securely inside. They can be found in mud banks, quiet bays, and even under rocks and along pier pilings. A trained eye can spot the tubal openings in the mudflats, signaling a place to start digging. Tube worms look like frankfurters upon first glance. A popular way to fish them is to cut the tube into smaller strips and thread them onto a long-shank bait hook.

Grunion: The California grunion is akin to other members of the jacksmelt clan. Grunion are primarily a South Coast bait fish, not often found above Point Conception. These little silver fish spawn from March until August. Newspapers will report when a run is scheduled. Some runs are protected to insure propogation of the species and no grunion hunting is allowed at that particular time.

Grunion beach themselves at high tide as the waves wash them into the sand. They may only be gathered by hand—and a fishing license is required. Fry up and eat all you want of these tasty little fish. Then freeze down the remainder.

Frozen grunion make fantastic cut baits for larger surf fish such as calico bass, halibut, and shark. Some anglers fish the grunion whole. I have found it works better to cut the grunion in half then slice it up the center about two-thirds of the way through. (This is the same procedure outlined for anchovies and sardines.) Use a fairly large #1/0 to #4/0 Eagle Claw circle or baitholder hook for maximum effectiveness. A chunk of frozen grunion can be cast a long way from the beach.

Moss and Peas: The opaleye is a member of the half-moon family of fishes. It ranges from Baja to San Francisco and prefers rocky areas near adjacent kelp beds. Opaleye are tough fighters on parity with freshwater bluegill. The best method for catching them is using natural moss or frozen peas. The moss can be gathered off the rocks and "balled up" onto a bait hook, #8 to #4. Or try frozen green peas threaded onto a long-shank hook.

Abalone: A final bait to consider is abalone. Like grunion, "abs" are a gastronomical delight in their own right. I've included them in this section because divers and fishermen often discard the "trimmings" once the major meaty portion is removed from the shell. Save these slivers of meat and freeze them down. They make absolutely stellar bait for offshore rockfish! Sheephead, sculpin, cabezon, and the multitude of kelp and deep-water rockfishes will really pounce on a chunk of abalone meat. Both short-shank and long-shank bait hooks in #1 to #4 sizes will work fine with this gourmet bait. Note: As with clams that you collect yourself, if you dive for abalone be certain to observe size, season, and bag limits for this mollusk.

Summary

As you can see, there is a mind-boggling smorgasbord of baits that can be used for our coastal fish. Keep in mind a few helpful pointers: (1) Try to always use fresh bait when possible—either "fresh live" or "fresh dead." Examine packages closely for freezer burn and deterioration when purchasing frozen bait; (2) Change bait regularly. Always try to make the best presentation possible. Hide the hooks and replace tattered or "picked at" baits with fresh offerings; and (3) be experimental! Try different baits. Fish combination offerings. Try different strip and cut configurations. Move the bait more often when still fishing.

Lure Fishin': Candy Bars, Lunker Thumpers, Salty Magics and More

One of the most challenging aspects of saltwater fishing is to get certain marine species to bite on an artificial lure. In contrast to freshwater lakes and streams, the saltwater environment abounds with a variety of natural baits. To fool ocean fish into striking a lure requires some cunning and expertise.

In this chapter, I'll talk about the basic types of saltwater lures that are used along the California Coast. Some of these models are designed especially for a particular species, while others are multi-purpose offerings. In later chapters, I'll discuss more specialized techniques used to catch distinct varieties, including the possibilities of using artificial lures.

Candy Bar Style Jigs

One of the oldest forms of saltwater lures used for Pacific species is the candy bar style jig. The term "jig" in itself is somewhat of a misnomer when used to describe this type of lure. When most anglers think of a jig, they conjure up an image of a feathered or skirted lead head with a single hook for either fresh or saltwater conditions.

By comparison, the candy bar design is far removed from its skirted namesakes. Candy bar jigs are basically semi-rectangular shaped bars of cast-metal with large treble hooks. The original candy bar models were made by the Starman Company and popularized through the 60's and mid-70's, especially in Southern California. The company changed hands and for a while the original candy bars were difficult to obtain with limited production. They are, however, now available in five different patterns and are sold primarily in select coastal tackle shops catering to the serious saltwater enthusiast.

Over the years, a variety of local manufacturers have brought out their own versions of candy bar-shaped jigs. The term "candy bar" has become a generic word describing this specific style of metal lures. Some of the most popular models on the market today are made by Jerry Jigs, Ironman, Salas, and Tady.

This style of lure is made to swim from side to side. It is designed to replicate a fleeing bait fish such as an anchovy, sardine, mackerel, or smelt. Interestingly, this swimming action also simulates the movements of squid —another prime morsel for larger game fish.

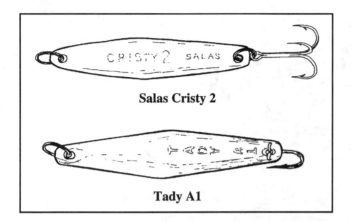

Salas Cristy 2

Tady A1

Many candy bar style jigs are made in either "light" or "heavy" weights. For example, Salas' ever-popular 6x model is available in either light or heavy styles. Put side by side, in the same color pattern, they appear to be identical. However, when you pick one up, the difference is apparent. The "light" model is usually made from an aluminum alloy, while the "heavy" is made from cast iron.

The "light" jigs are made to swim just under the surface of the water. This is termed a "surface grind." The lure is cast out and then retrieved back to the boat as it darts from side to side a few feet below the surface. The "heavy" version can usually be casted further. It will swim considerably deeper than the "light" model and often without as much erratic action.

Heavy jigs in this configuration also have other unique applications. Both Southern and Northern California party boaters will simply drop the heavy lures straight to the bottom. They are made to sink quickly and larger models can be worked all the way to 600 feet. (More on this tactic later.)

Sometimes strikes will occur "on the sink" as the heavy jig falls to the bottom. Other times fishermen will use an exaggerated "lift'n drop" technique to yo-yo the heavy jig up and down off the bottom. Invariably, many species will respond to this yo-yoing action by striking the jig on the "drop" portion of the lift'n drop motion.

Sometimes saltwater fish hold deep, but not necessarily on the bottom, so that the only way to get consistent action is to use a heavy jig through the strike zone. Heavy candy bar styles can be lowered to levels somewhat below where the fish are presumably stratified and then reeled through those deep strike zones.

Jigs in the candy bar design are made in a wide array of sizes and colors. Sizes vary somewhat according to the bait the jig is supposed to represent. There are tiny candy bars designed to replicate 3 inch pinhead anchovies.

Others in lengths of over 8 inches mimic larger Spanish mackerel. It is important to carry an assortment of sizes to accommodate a range of conditions, a variety of bait fish, and the depth necessary to work the jig. Party boat skippers, deck hands, landing operators, and local bait and tackle dealers can be extremely helpful in recommending the right jigs to buy for your area.

I might add, on this note, that these same people are excellent sources for recommending all types of lures for your outing—not just jigs. Remember, they make a living on your repeated success. It is in their best interest to provide you with up-to-date, accurate information!

As for jig colors, you can keep your selection fairly narrow with a solid lineup of proven patterns. These include: blue and white, green and yellow, solid white, green mackerel, and chrome. Another color scheme proven to be effective for both surface-feeding species and rockfish is a "scrambled egg" effect with highlights of brown, yellow, white, or even orange.

Here's a little coloration trick that a few saltwater anglers practice to keep their lure expenses down. Consider painting your old, outdated candy bar style jigs in solid white primer. Then with proper masking and some inexpensive spray paint, you can come up with your own unique variations on a particular pattern. If that jig color runs "cold"—as often happens with saltwater fishing—just sand the current finish down, re-shoot it with white primer, and start all over again.

Here are some other pointers: first, most candy bar jigs feature larger saltwater grade treble hooks. This type of hook is nearly impossible to bend out, and is impervious to rapid rusting. However, unlike bronze wire or forged treble hooks, these models need to be sharpened recurrently to maximize hook penetration. Saltwater anglers can be remiss in this facet of tackle preparation. Invest in a good file and keep a sharp point on these large treble hooks. The extra effort may mean a jackpot fish!

Second, don't make the mistake of using a snap-swivel with this type of lure. Tie directly to the soldered ring. A snap-swivel added to the ring will dampen the erratic swimming action of the jig.

Third, Luhr Jensen markets an adhesive Prismlite scale-like paper. Cut a piece of this material and add it to your old, favorite "iron." The new effect can be dramatic! All of a sudden your old jig will show traces of the brillant prism finish from this nifty Primslite paper.

One final point: There are many times when a good jig fisherman can thoroughly trounce others who are using baits. Why is this the case? To begin with, jigs are made for casting and retrieving. You can cover a lot of territory with a jig whether you are bottom bouncing outside the Farallons or surface grinding off the Coronados. Second, jigs seem to have a propensity for catching bigger fish. Many times I have seen the largest yellowtail or the heaviest cowcod on a boat come in on a jig. It may be that saltwater fish—even with the abundance of bait—can become wary of a live or cut offering with a hook in it. Larger, more aggressive or territorial fish see the jig as an imposing intruder of sorts which may trigger the strike behavior from the bigger species.

Diamond Jigs

The original Diamond Jigs are made by the Bridgeport Brass foundry. Other manufacturers such as Ironman and Luhr Jensen also market this lure. They are chrome plated, highly polished, elongated diamond-sided bars of brass. Diamond Jigs are sold primarily for bottom fishing along the California Coast. They are a staple among veteran rock codders. This lure works best when fished deep with a yo-yo technique.

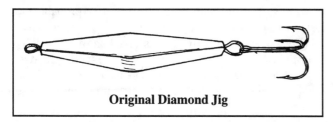

Original Diamond Jig

Other manufacturers have similar shaped jigs now on the market. They are cheaper than the original Diamond model because they are brass plated rather than solid brass. As with most types of fishing, it pays to buy the best. The bright surface on the patented Diamond models will last for many years with its smoothly polished, high luster finish.

Soft Plastic Baits

Most of the saltwater lures made from soft plastic evolved from freshwater lure technology, specifically in the bass fishing realm. Some of the first soft plastic lures to hit the California marketplace were nothing more than larger, thick-bodied versions of freshwater grubs. Boone's Tout, Haddock's Split Tail, and Bagley's Salty Dog are all examples of these rather unspectacular-looking lures. These baits produce on an extensive range of coastal species when jigged or drifted along the bottom.

One subtle way to dress up these saltwater grubs is to add a contrasting vinyl skirt, similar to that used for freshwater spinnerbaits. The skirt should be reversed (see diagram) so that it flares out. In the water, the pulsating skirt resembles the tentacles of small squid resting on the bottom. Next, cut a small 2 to 3 inch strip of frozen squid or mackerel. Use this as a trailer with the grubs. Squirt on a few drops of Berkley Saltwater Attractant or use Berkley's other concoction in a paste-like form and you have a remarkably productive bait! The lure will retain the Strike especially well if you add the vinyl skirt which absorbs the scent compound.

In the next step in the evolution of soft plastic lures for saltwater fishing, manufacturers recognized how volatile

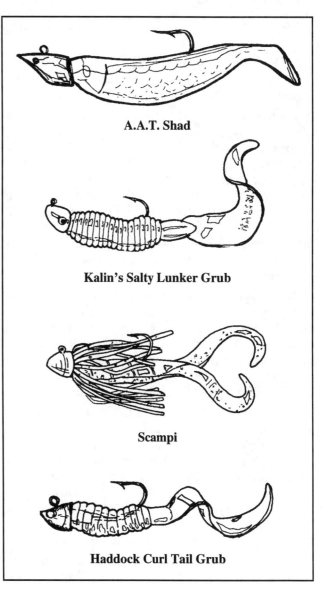

A.A.T. Shad

Kalin's Salty Lunker Grub

Scampi

Haddock Curl Tail Grub

a plastic grub could be if it had a pair of swimming "legs" or tails. Scampi Lures in San Diego took the basic flat single-tail saltwater grub and redesigned it, giving it a pair of sensational swimming legs. The now famous Scampi Lure heralded in an entire new era of marine fishing along the coast for lure chuckers!

The double-tail grubs like the original Scampi produce under all sorts of conditions. Some manufacturers make their styles in softer plastic to increase the swimming tail effect. Haddock's Lunker Thumper, the Mojo, and Bobo are classic examples of using the softer plastic rather than the Scampi models. Keep in mind that the softer baits will get bit off more frequently than those made from harder plastic.

Rock hoppers and jetty jockeys use them, and party boaters, trollers, pier fishermen, and even rock codders have found tremendous application for these swimming baits. In later chapters, I will go into greater detail with regard to the more species-specific ways to fish these lures. For now, let's focus on the basic rigging with a single-hook lead head.

The most popular way to rig the double-tail grub is to lace it onto a single-hook lead head. Sizes vary depending upon the length of the grub tail itself, the depth and casting distance required, and the type of bait the lure is simulating. For example, small 3 inch grubs are suitable for harbors and bays, longer 5 to 6 inch models for open water, and larger 8 to 10 inch versions for deep-water rock codding or even big game like albacore. The weight of the jig head gets correspondingly heavier with the larger size trailers and the greater depth desired. The best overall size is a 3/4 to 1 1/4 ounce lead head.

Surprisingly, you don't have to be too creative in fishing this type of saltwater lure. Some of the best results come on a straight cast and retrieve. Other times, for example with calico and bass, the fish seem to prefer a slow-sinking action. Thus, many strikes occur on the fall with these species. It does help however, to sometimes "countdown" the grub until you find the proper strike zone.

Here's a good illustration of this. Let's say, for example, you are fishing sand bass in 80 feet of water. These fish are notorious for layering through different depths, instead of being stratified only along the bottom or near the surface. Begin by, say, counting to five after the lure hits the water then retrieving. Keep adding a few seconds to the count until you start getting bit. Once you determine the right count, you can continue to swim the plastic grubs through this primary strike zone cast after cast.

Returning full-circle and borrowing a page from freshwater bass fishermen, a recent rage among marine anglers has been to use large, single curl-tail grubs. The late Leonard Hashimoto was a Southern California lure de-signer famous for his inlaid abalone-head trolling feather designs. Hashimoto also found that frequently a more subtle, single curl-tail bait outproduces the conventional twin-tail models. Hashimoto's Salty Magic lure has been a well-kept secret among many saltwater bassers. The trick, he notes, is to use an even lighter lead head than is typically used with Scampi's and similar double-tail models. A 1/2 ounce lead head produces an extremely seductive falling action when matched with the Salty Magic. Both the Salty Magic and Caba Caba Tube are now practically "extinct." If you find these lures on a dusty tackle shop wall, buy them—they really work!

Hashimoto's other unusual baits are the hollow-bodied, soft plastic Caba Caba Tube and the Pacific Eel. The Caba Caba replicates a small live squid, while the Pacific Eel mimics the real thing.

Al Kalin is a veteran bass angler who has designed a large 5 inch sickle-tail grub to cover both saltwater and inland species. Kalin's Salty Lunker Grub is rigged similarly to a Tout or a Scampi using a single-hook lead head. These are super soft baits, but they produce under so many different variables—trolling, casting, or bottom bouncing. Of all the soft plastic baits, the Lunker Grub has probably the greatest action with its super flagellating tail. Aggressive pelagic fish such as striped bass and bonito will really clobber fast-moving grubs like these. An exciting alternative to Kalin's model is Berkley's saltwater Power Grub, heavily scented with "high octane" fish attractant.

Another form of soft plastic lure with an extensive saltwater track record has been the knob-tail design. These are also popularly known as "swimbaits." These baits, perhaps more so than the candy bar jigs or plastic grubs, come most closely to actually looking like a bait fish. Kalin's Lunker Shad, Worm King, Berkley Power Swimbait, A.A. Worms, and Fish Trap are favorite models in West Coast swimbaits.

The trick to using one of these knob-tail lures is to monitor your speed. At times, the fish want the bait to swim slowly, other situations dictate a fast-swimming action. Southern Californians, in particular, have found these lures to their liking when fishing calico and sand bass. The knob-tail baits closely resemble natural "brown baits" such as tomcod and queenfish when tossed in front of a hungry bull bass.

A final entrant in this saltwater plastic bait sweepstakes is one of this writer's all-time favorites—the Stingaroo. This lure was designed by Dr. Phillip Gallo, interestingly, a psychology professor in San Diego. His idea was to dramatically imitate the swimming style of squid down to the pulsation of the tentacles. Gallo's Stingaroo does precisely that with its unique design and four squid-like tentacles. The problem is that the Stingaroo is out of circulation, though some can still be found collecting dust on some tackle shop walls. Here again, if you can find one—buy it! It is a phenomenal bait for everything from salmon and stripers to yellowtail and albacore. The Stingaroo is particularly potent as a big fish catcher on large calico "bull" bass or lunker size "grumper" sand bass.

As for colors in selecting soft plastic lures, you can really go crazy with the awesome array the different manufacturers market in these baits. The following is kind of a shopping list for the different styles and the color schemes that seem to work best with those designs.

Basic Grubs	Single-Curl Tails
smoke	smoke/black flake
watermelon	amber/black flake
motor oil	chartreuse/black flake
smoke/sparkle	motor oil flake
black	solid silver
Double-Tails	Knob-Tail Minnows
root beer flake	gold/chartreuse
lime flake	silver flake
silver flake	motor oil flake
fluorescent pink	green/blue 'chovy
chartreuse	root beer

In addition to stocking the above colors, follow local reports in your area for new patterns that the fish are starting to key in on.

Saltwater Plugs

East Coast fishermen have been successfully using saltwater plugs for years. Perhaps due to the availability of live bait, Californians have not often found it necessary to use these bait fish replicas. As a general rule, the various wood and plastic minnows sold for saltwater purposes are considerably more expensive than either candy bar style or soft plastic jigs. This may also limit their wide-spread usage. Finally, party boat skippers are not too fond of this type of lure which features at least two prominent treble hooks and sometimes three. In the hand of an inexperienced caster on a crowded passenger boat, this could spell real danger. Nevertheless, for the private boat owner, it would be a wise decision to keep a small stock of some saltwater plugs handy, especially if live bait supplies dry up at your landing.

Overwhelmingly, the best overall models are the Magnum series of saltwater Rapala baits. These are larger versions of the popular freshwater minnows used for trout and bass. The saltwater Rapalas feature stronger, cadmium treble hooks, stainless split rings, and a brilliant marine finish. The most popular models are in the "CD" series. These countdown baits are made to sink and are significantly heavier than minnow baits designed to float. They can be either trolled or free-casted from the boat. The CD-18 is a popular favorite with its elongated diving bill. More compact, scaled-down patterns in the CD-14 size are preferred for smaller pelagic species. The CD-14 is also a bonafide killer on albacore tuna of all sizes. During my Eagle Claw Fishing Schools, we have recurrently found marauding schools of yellowtail and yellowfin tuna by trolling the big CD-18 Magnum Rapalas. For private yacht owners who do not have extensive supplies of the chum bait, the CD-18 Magnum Rapalas can be a "day-saver," perhaps replicating live mackerel or sardines better than any other artificial lure.

The light tackle enthusiast armed with a freshwater baitcasting outfit or spinning rod and reel can also get into the act using the larger bass or trout size Rapalas. One of my favorites is the CD-11, which is perfect for taking bonito on light gear. Be sure to thoroughly rinse these smaller plugs in freshwater before putting them away for the day. These baits usually come with stock bronze treble hooks and they will corrode quickly in the saltwater environment. Veteran lightliners often keep a stock of extra replacement trebles on hand so as to maintain sharp new hooks on these smaller Rapalas for every outing. The primary colors for Rapalas used in saltwater include the silver/black back, silver/blue back, green/gold mackerel, blue/silver mackerel, and fire tiger.

Also note that Rapala recently introduced a new "stainless steel" finish in their Rapala CD series plugs. The metallic finish seems to be more "bite proof," and draws more strikes, especially on bright, sunny days. Try my favorite: the new "clown" color, featuring a mix of chartreuse, orange, and silver. It's a killer on tuna and yellowtail!

Other manufacturers have baits similar to the Rapala that will also perform well in saltwater. The Luhr Jensen Fingerling line of plastic minnows is an excellent lure that comes in a wide range of colors. Popular finishes for saltwater Fingerlings are greens, blues, browns, and mackerel.

Rebel also markets a well-made series of plastic lures in both floating and sinking models. These also have a fairly hard plastic finish which makes them perfect for larger, toothy game fish. There are times when stripers and barracuda for example, prefer a plug twitched on the surface rather then jerked below it. Also floating minnows made from plastic tend to be heavier than similar-sized plugs constructed from balsa wood. Thus, the plastic baits will be easier to cast to surface-feeding fish. The floating Rebels fit these requirements perfectly. The basic silver/black back coloration is a staple along with silver/blue back.

Again, I want to emphasize how important it is to keep the hooks sharp on these minnow-style lures. Saltwater plays havoc on these big trebles and they will dull after a few trips. An alternative tip to consider is to replace the trebles with either single Siwash hooks or stainless steel double hooks. These strong single or double hooks were made for tough marine game fish and they can be sharpened to needlepoint perfection. Also in a wide-open bite on fish like barracuda, it's a lot easier to remove single hooks than trebles when the action is hot and furious. Many saltwater skippers note that you actually get a stronger hook-set and maintain better leverage by using a single hook on your lures instead of doubles or trebles. Manufacturers persist in loading up these baits with the large treble hooks because this is what the average fisherman presumably wants. The theory that three hook points are better than one is simply not always the case!

More conventional diving plugs or so-called "crankbaits" sometimes find their way to the ocean. For example, Bagley's giant diving Bang-O lure is simply a magnum-sized version of their popular freshwater bass bait. Southern Californians have used the diving Bang-O primarily as a trolling lure for members of the tuna family. It will also perform well at times when cranked through a school of hungry yellowtail. To emphasize again, the problem with a big bulky plug like the Bang-O is that it is difficult to cast in the hands of a novice. This creates a safety problem on a loaded party boat. So, baits in this class are probably more suitable for the private yacht owner or on smaller charter boats.

Saltwater Spoons

Far and away, one of the most versatile lures in the saltwater war chest is the basic spoon. Salmon, yellowtail, albacore, stripers, sand and calico bass, rockfish, and even some of the surf fishes will readily strike a shiny spoon.

These lures are designed for surface-feeding game fish. However, heavier, thicker-bodied models can also have application on a deep-water yo-yo bite. For saltwater conditions it is best to tie directly to the split ring on the spoon. Often, fishermen think that a snap-swivel is imperative in using larger lures like these. The snap-swivel will eliminate line twist to a certain degree, but it has a tendency to dramatically dampen the action of the spoon or jig. So tie a strong knot, and tie it directly to the split ring.

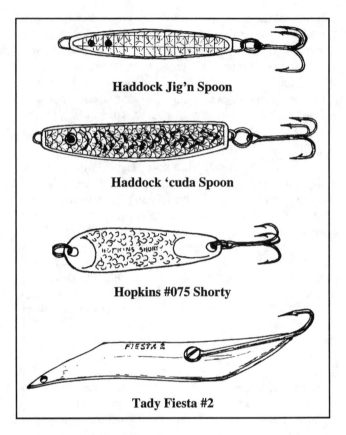

Haddock Jig'n Spoon

Haddock 'cuda Spoon

Hopkins #075 Shorty

Tady Fiesta #2

The basic size range for most saltwater spoons used along the California Cast is roughly 1/2 to 2 ounces. The size of the spoon corresponds to both the quarry sought and the natural bait fish the spoon is supposed to imitate.

Some models such as the Pixie and Kastmaster are shaped along traditional lines with a wide surface area. This type of spoon is made to slowly wobble from side to side giving off a prominent "flash." Other models such as the ever popular Krocadile are much narrower and generate a tighter side-to-side wobble with a more subtle "flash." There are times when game fish prefer one action over the other.

Another type of spoon gaining a rapid following with the saltwater angling crowd is a thin slab style design with minimal lateral action. These spoons originated in Scandinavia and are imported under such popular names as the Swedish Pimple and Sildeglimp. Domestic manufacturers in the West have brought out their own regional replicas of these European spoons and they produce phenomenally well!

Haddock's Jig'n Spoon, the Luhr Jensen Crippled Herring and Deep Stinger, the Rader, and the Hopkin's Spoon, and the Scampi Coaster exemplify this Swedish design. You can throw these lures a long way with great wind resistance. Quite frequently, surface feeders such as bonito, stripers, and barracuda will hit one of these slim spoons on a medium-to-fast retrieve below the surface. It also helps to give the rod a few twitches to create a more erratic swimming effect with these simple baits.

But overall, spoons in this super narrow genre produce the greatest results simply jigged off the bottom. A yo-yoing technique with long exaggerated lifts and drops will generate many strikes. With most spoon-jigging, the fish will hit the lure as it is fluttering down on the fall after the lifting motion. Watch for slight "ticks" in the line, unusual slackness, or the line suddenly moving to the side—all telltale signs of a fish inhaling the spoon on the drop!

Unlike the plastic Stingaroo, one lure that has been brought back from near extinction is the Tady wobbling spoon. Generations of Southern Californians and more recently, North Coasters, have found this remarkable spoon to produce under the most adverse conditions. You can still find some around in limited quantities in certain tackle shops. What is most appealing about the Tady Wobbler is that it is made in finishes that are appropriate for the Western saltwater fishery. Such basic stock saltwater colors as blue and white, green and yellow, sardine, and scrambled egg were also found in this relic spoon.

With regard to spoon coloration, nickel and gold finishes in the more conventional models seem to be the best options season after season. Haddock uses a brilliant prismlite finish on the popular 1 1/4 ounce Jig'n Spoon for coastal angling. Such color schemes as "blue anchovy," "greenback mackerel," and "brown bait gold" typify the range and regional flavor of these locally made spoons.

Quite frequently, spooning action can become hot and furious on schooling game fish. It might be wise to carry a few models with single hooks instead of large trebles. As I mentioned with saltwater plugs, it sometimes becomes very hectic to remove treble hooks, re-bend them, or re-sharpen them during a wide-open bite. A strong, needle-sharp single hook is a viable alternative.

"Feathers"

In my estimation, of all the saltwater lures sold along the West Coast today, the feathered jig receives the least amount of angler interest. Perhaps it is because "feathers" as they are sometimes termed, appear to be too simple. They clearly do not have the eye appeal of, say, a computer-designed plug or a hand-painted candy bar jig. But, with the exception of a handful of "old timers" few saltwater fishermen really know how to fish the "feather."

The most rudimentary feathered casting jigs are nothing more than a chrome-plated lead head with some colored feathers wrapped onto the hook shank. Most forms of this jig are manufactured in Asia. The design has been around for a long time and was pioneered by commercial fishermen. Feathers are sold primarily in 1/2 to 1 1/4 ounce weights. They can be trolled or casted. If the latter method is preferred, the angler has to bring some of his own creative energies to bear to become a competent feather fisherman. Simply casted out and retrieved back in, the feather is unlikely to produce much in the way of strikes. Rather, some kind of darting, swimming effect has to be imparted to the lure. This is done on the retrieve.

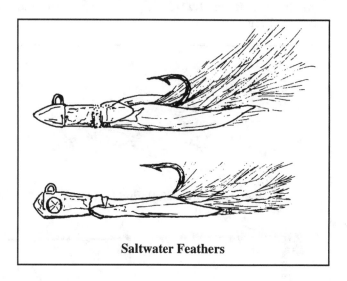

Saltwater Feathers

Tom Schlauch is a veteran charter boat skipper who is also a virtuoso with a feather. Schlauch notes that a long rod in the 7 1/2 to 8 1/2 foot range performs best for feather fishing. He points out that the trick to using the feather is in the retrieve. You have to gently "lift and pump" the rod to make the feather dart and glide through the water. This mimics a streaking anchovy.

Feathered jigs designed for casting are tied on single-hook lead heads. The hooks on these imported lures have historically been notoriously dull right out of the package. It is thus critical to pre-sharpen these jigs before your outing. You will find many game fish will "mouth" the feather rather than viciously strike it. Hence, a sharp hook will result in better penetration and far more catches.

There are only a few color patterns necessary for most serious feather fishing. These include blue and white, green and yellow, and red and white. A real sleeper used sometimes by commercial fishermen is a solid white feather jig.

Bucktails and Other Jigs

Northern Californians have recognized the importance of the simple bucktail hair jigs for years with regard to the striper fishery. Long-time favorites, the Hair Raiser and the Banjo Eye styles have become legendary striper catchers in the San Francisco area.

Like their feathered counterparts used along the Southern Coast, the Bucktail models perform well either casted or trolled. Interestingly, a "do-nothing" type of retrieve sometimes works best with these jigs for stripers. Cast the jig out, let it settle into the strike zone, and just reel it back in. But also, try a bottom bouncing approach. Hop the jig along the structure and watch for that soft "tick" in the line, signalling a strike.

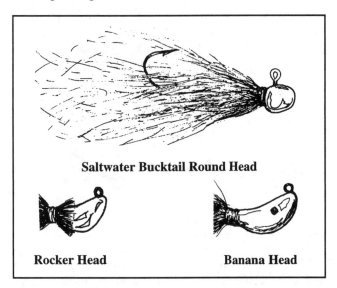

Saltwater Bucktail Round Head

Rocker Head   **Banana Head**

Numerous other single-hook jigs work on stripers and should definitely be tried for more southern-based species. Brawley's live rubber Bass Bug, the Scrounger with its hallmark oscillating plastic diving lip, and the Worm Tail jig are regionally proven winners.

The most commonly used colors in this collection of North Coast jigs include solid white, black, white and red, and chartreuse. Some locals feel that the jig head itself has to be red in order for it to work. I might add, in the Holy Mother of All El Niños (1997), I experienced phenomenal results on both dorado and yellowfin tuna when experimenting with traditional bucktail jigs, deep into Mexican waters. The simple, single-hook design works especially well on acrobatic dorado. Best colors? Chartreuse or yellow.

Surface Plugs

When saltwater anglers think of surface plugs, striper fishing immediately comes to mind. Northern Califor-

Cordell Pencil Popper

nians throw such magnum-sized surface lures as the Cordell Pencil Popper, Rapala Husky Jerk, Yozuri Hydro Tiger, Rebel Pop-R, Scudders, and Windcheaters from the shore, the surf, or from small craft.

But, surprisingly, surface plugs also produce some spectacular action on more pelagic game fish such as bonito, bass, barracuda, tuna and dorado. Few recreational anglers think of these South Coast species as having the inclination to strike a floating plug—but, at times they will! Because of the treble hook situation, large surf plugs are not readily welcomed by party boat captains and their deck hands. But if you take the time to learn how to cast and work these bulk top-water baits carefully, the results can be sensational. During one Eagle Claw School, for example, we tallied over three dozen yellowfin tuna in the 25- to 35-pound class on these big surface plugs. Try the new Rapala Skitter Pop in both saltwater sizes and finishes. This is an excellent surface lure for yellowfin tuna.

Other Exotics

There are a few other unusual artificial lures that produce quite well in the marine environment. For example, a modification of the freshwater tail spinner jig is the Straggler Chopper made expressly for saltwater usage. The Chopper is nothing more than a wedge-shaped chunk of painted lead, a lone treble hook on the bottom, with a fast whirling nickle spinner blade comprising the tail action. This lure can also be thrown considerable distances with ease. It works best on a straight retrieve, especially for calico bass.

There aren't many Choppers left on tackle shop walls anymore. But if you see one, buy it! It really is a secret calico killer!

As I briefly mentioned, hollow tubular baits are also now appearing on the saltwater scene in a variety of capacities: as drift baits, trolling lures, rock cod trailers, etc. For years these lures were the rage of tournament freshwater bass fishermen. Some enterprising manufacturers found that huge 7-inch versions of these freshwater tube baits would also produce remarkably well in salt water.

The most common technique to rig these baits is to lace them onto a 1 to 4 ounce jig head with a barb on the shank

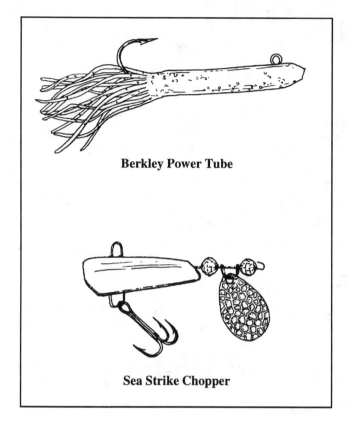

Berkley Power Tube

Sea Strike Chopper

to keep the tube from sliding down. Do not expect great action from this soft plastic lure. Baits like the Canyon Lures Tora Tube, Berkley Power Tube, or Crappie John's Saltwater Finger Jig were meant to sashay back and forth through the water seductively with the multitude of tiny tentacles pulsating from the tail portion.

Halibut will ambush these tube baits on a drift as will salmon. Various rockfish will strike the tubes used as trailers on rock cod gangions. Similarly, try dropping one of these lures through "pot holes" in offshore kelp beds. Big lingcod especially will eagerly hit these giant slow-falling tube baits on lighter 10 to 20 pound lines.

Here's a hot tip to use when fishing tubular lures in saltwater. The hollow cavity design makes these baits highly palatable to fish when they are touchy feeders. Because this lure body actually compresses upon impact, many anglers theorize that the fish sense it is a live, wounded bait fish when they chomp on it. But, the hollow body construction has further benefits. Take some saltwater Berkley saltwater liquid or gel Fish Attractant and squirt it into the tube. The slow, time-release feature of this compound produces a virtual "chum slick" behind the tube bait. Since this form of artificial lure is meant to be worked slowly, the graduallly dissipating Strike works in perfect conjunction with the plastic bait!

Trolling Tactics: Ridin' the Wake

Quite frequently both private craft operators and party boat skippers must make a strong effort to locate marauding pelagic game fish. Marine species in this category will follow the optimum currents that play host to migrating schools of bait fish. Put simply: if you can find the bait fish, you have a good shot at finding the game fish.

Trolling an artificial lure behind the boat is one of the best strategies for locating concentrations of game fish. In this chapter I'll outline some of the rudimentary features of this approach, highlighting when necessary the distinction between Northern and Southern techniques. More specialized trolling secrets for specific species such as salmon and albacore will follow in subsequent chapters.

Trolling Rods and Reels

Almost any conventional reel can function in a trolling capacity. The key variable is whether or not a particular model stores enough line for a specific size and species of game fish.

For larger, extremely fast-moving albacore tuna, for example, a reel in the 4/0 size class is appropriate. This model will hold close to 300+ yards of 50 pound monofilament. Remember, for ocean species, especially for larger pelagic game fish such as albacore or yellowtail, line can be stripped off of a reel quickly when trolling. Once the fish strikes, both the fish's ability to pull line as well as the boat's speed, force line to drag off the reel, which necessitates having reels with considerable line capacities.

Smaller, less speedy species, such as stripers, salmon, bonito, barracuda, or bass can be handled with baitcasting models up to about the 2/0 classification. Many of these offshore game fish can be tackled with, say, a Penn Jigmaster or the newer Penn GS 525, 535, or 545 spooled with 300 yards of 20 pound string.

Light-liners can also try their luck at trolling on special charter boats or private skiffs. Larger freshwater baitcasters designed for bass, steelhead, or salmon will work for offshore trolling up to a point. If the skipper is fairly adept at boat handling, he can follow the fish hooked on lighter 10 to 15 pound mono. However, on big albacore or yellowtail, both the drag mechanisms and the overall spool capacity of such smaller reels may impede the ability to play out larger game fish.

As for saltwater spinning reels and their application to offshore trolling—it's probably best to leave them at home if you are party boating. Their usage for the trolling game is restricted for a number of reasons: modest line capacity with heavier monofilament; limited drag and gearing for subduing bruiser-class fish; and above all, line twist often generated from a trolled lure coming off a fixed spinning reel spool.

Private boaters can definitely give their spinning gear a workout trolling for smaller quarry such as bonito, barracuda, calico bass, and stripers. It might pay, in this case, to pull your lure on a 5 to 6 foot length of leader line joined to your main monofilament with a ball-bearing swivel. The swivel will minimize line twist to a considerable degree.

With regard to trolling rods, it is usually best to scale down in length. Shorter, 5 1/2 to 6/12 foot rods are both stouter and more maneuverable, particularly when used on the stern of a crowded party boat. Consider the Penn Sabre #655, 660, or Penn International II light trolling models. If albacore, yellowfin tuna, or yellowtail are your primary candidates for an offshore trolling trip, then invest in a quality trolling rod with at least a roller tip guide and a front lead roller stripper. The optimal purchase would be a rod with a full set of roller guides. These rollers act like a miniature pulley system. They dissipate line friction and wear, especially on a fish that hits the lure and turns away like a runaway freight train.

North coasters can find numerous models of so-called "boat rods" in the seven foot class that are quite suitable for salmon and striper trolling. These rods have heavier actions and thicker butts than conventional live bait models. They are often used to slowly drag a two pound sinker along the deep bottoms in the San Francisco Bay region. Boat rods in this genre should not be confused with standard deep-water rock cod models. The latter usually have at least a roller tiptop and are super strong, often accommodating 5+ pounds of lead at the end of the line. Boat rods do not require that more pronounced roller guide. Northern California anglers usually use 20 to 40 pound test monofilament for this slow-trolling method with stout 7 foot boat rods.

More popular 6 to 7 foot live bait rods used for slinging anchovies or sardines can also be used for trolling. You will receive a lot of action and sport when you troll with a live bait model. As was noted, these rods typically have powerful butt sections, with softer hyperbolic tip actions necessary to delicately fly-line a pinhead 'chovy. Models in this design are perfect for trolling small-to-medium-sized lures just below the surface on 15 to 20 pound monofilament.

Some party boat captains permit the use of live bait rods for trolling if they are hunting down smaller game fish. But, for 15 to 20 pound class albacore tuna or yellowtail, invariably the skipper wants the fishermen to bring out the heavy artillery. There are two important reasons for this. First, these larger pelagic species are schooling fish. If the angler can quickly—I emphasize quickly—bring in the trolled fish, the rest of the school will often follow up to the stern of the boat. If that lead fish is lost in the ensuing fight, it will often "spook" the rest of the school and shut off the bite.

Second, party boat skippers depend upon high fish counts published daily for their boats to promote their business and to maintain full passenger loads. They cannot afford to have fish lost because an angler preferred to use a light outfit for sporting purposes during a trolling run. Also, it is not uncommon for the fish caught by trolling to be significantly larger than those taken with bait. Thus, it is in both the angler's and the skipper's best interest not to let these larger trophies get away.

Trolling Options

Usually, when we think of trolling, the use of artificial lures comes to mind. Fish will often strike a trolled lure more readily than one that is casted. Trolled behind the boat, the lure blends in more easily with the prop wash, the wake, and any natural wave or current action present at the time. Because trolling speed is also more or less constant, the opportunity for the game fish to scrutinize the offering carefully is diminished. Here then, is a brief listing of some of the more popular trolling lures used along the California Coast.

Minnow-shaped Baits: These plastic replicas of natural bait fish catch practically anything that may be near the surface when trolled behind the boat. The Rapalas are the most detailed and are more readily available than the Rebels, Bagleys, Bill Norman, and Storm counterparts. But take care to closely examine which minnow plug you select.

To start with, it is important to try to match the bait fish indigenous to the area. For instance, if schools of pinhead anchovies are congregating off the coast, it would probably be best to troll silver with black or blue back minnows. On the other hand, if Pacific mackerel are loaded under the offshore floating kelp paddies, then yellowtail trollers would be wise to drag along a mackerel-patterned plug.

The length of the lure can also be critical at times. Here again, think about the size of the bait fish where you are trolling. A 6 to 8 inch lure most closely replicates the size of Spanish or Pacific mackerel, a 3 to 5 inch plug approximates the length of an anchovy, smelt, or sardine.

The construction of the minnow-shaped lure in itself can also effect its potency as a trolled bait. Most manufacturers market their lures in either floating or sinking models. The floating versions perhaps have a little better action than a sinking minnow. But, the problem is that in rough seas, it is often difficult to get the floater to plane deep enough below the waves and swells. For this reason alone, the sinking models are probably a wiser investment.

Some manufacturers also use metal diving lips to drive the lures below the surface. The metal lips found on many of the saltwater Rapalas, Ciscos, and L&S Mirro Lures are made to withstand the attack of large marine species. The more traditional plastic diving lips simply will not hold up to the constant hammering these plugs get when dragged through schools of hungry game fish.

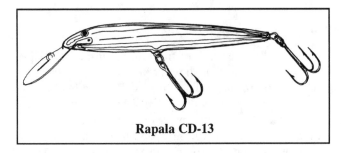

Rapala CD-13

Some minnow-shaped baits can be trolled faster than others. You will have to experiment on this note. It is important to generate a solid, throbbing vibration from the plug as it dives to the proper depths. As a general rule, the more line you let out and the faster you troll, the deeper these lures will dive. There is however, a point of diminishing returns. If you pull the plug too fast, the water pressure will "load up" on the diving lip and the lure will plane to the surface. (When you see your lure "water ski" like this, slow down!)

For trolling purposes, you must keep the treble hooks on these plugs filed to needle-sharp consistency. A large saltwater fish can create a lot of leverage and torque against one of these minnow-style plugs as it shakes its head from side to side. Hence, it is imperative to get a good hook set and as deep a penetration as possible.

Feathered Jigs: Assorted feathered jigs trolled through the wake have been catching saltwater fish for centuries. The simplest construction, a chrome lead head with a few brightly colored feathers and a single hook, performs

under a wide range of conditions. They can be pulled fast and literally skipped through the waves or slowly skimmed under the surface. Here again, that hook has to be honed to perfection.

Variations along this line using bucktail material instead of feathers perform equally well. Although lures such as the Hair Raiser and Banjo Eye Dude have received notoriety in the North as deadly striper baits, they perform equally well on barracuda, bonito, and occasionally calico and sand bass.

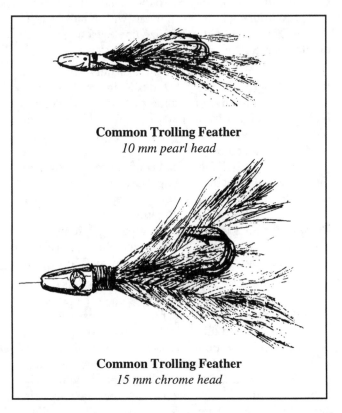

Common Trolling Feather
10 mm pearl head

Common Trolling Feather
15 mm chrome head

More elaborate feathered jigs with lustrous abalone or plastic heads are used primarily for members of the tuna family and sometimes yellowtail. These trolling feathers are sold both un-rigged and rigged. The un-rigged models require a larger cadmium double hook for proper presentation. There is a hole running through the nose portion of the jig. Thread your line (usually 30 to 50 pound mono or heavier) through this hole and tie in the double hook. When the albacore or yellowtail strikes the lure, the feathers slide freely up the main line out of the way of the double hook. This permits the angler to obtain much more leverage on the fish without the cumbersome feathered jig in the way of the hook.

Pre-tied trolling feathers like these are also sold commercially over-the-counter at tackle stores and landings. The manufacturers include the feathered jig, double hook, and 6 to 8 feet of leader line tied to a snap-swivel. All you have to do is tie your primary line to the snap-swivel. Although there is some obvious convenience in purchasing these larger feathers pre-rigged, they are considerably more costly than rigging you own. Also, the variety of colors available in the pre-rigged setups is narrow, with about four basic color schemes usually available. By rigging your own feathers, you can select the colors the fish are currently eating just prior to your trip. The Severstrand Tuna Feather, Tuna Clone, and Area Rule Engineering Tu-Nob are classic West Coast trolling feathers—although the "feather" portion is often replaced by brilliant, long-lasting vinyl skirting material.

Plastic Lures: In recent years, both party boat and private skiff owners have found tremendous application for trolling soft plastic baits or "plastics" as they are termed. Single-tail lures such as the Salty Magic or Kalin's Salty Lunker Grub, The Berkley Power Pogey and Power Minnow, or A.A. Worms' classic Monarch grub, along with double-tail models including Haddock's Lunker Thumper, the Mojo, or Scampi, perform reasonably well as a trolling option. Almost all game fish will make a pass at these sensuous tail-shakin' baits.

Here are a couple of tips worth noting when using plastics on a trolling run. First, consider using heavier lead heads than normal to keep these lures down beneath the swells and wakes. Normally, many skippers and deck hands will recommend using a light 1/2 to 3/4 ounce head when free-casting plastics. (The lighter lead heads allow the lure to fall more slowly.) But, in a trolling capacity, upscale the jig head to from 3/4 to 1 1/2 ounces to keep the bait down.

Second, think about using dramatically larger plastics than you normally would for free-casting from an anchored boat. A.A.Worms' Monarch, for example, fishes with a 2 ounce jig head. Larger game fish such as yellowtail, stripers, and albacore will jump on this lure on a medium-to-slow troll. Similarly, Kalin's Giant Salty Grub and Berkley's new 8 inch Magnum Power Grub can be pulled with a 4 to 10 ounce head. It has actually recorded catches of marlin in warmer Southern waters!

Third, be experimental with trolling plastics. The array of color variations available in these swimming tails is virtually endless. Marine game fish can be as finicky as their freshwater cousins. Sometimes it helps to show them something different while trolling. Plastics offer the angler a full gamut of unique colorations to drag by the fish.

Spoons: Larger saltwater spoons can be very effective when a slowly trolled lure is required. The key here is S-L-O-W-L-Y. Too often the recreational angler makes the mistake of trying to troll a spoon in the same manner as a minnow bait or a feather. It simply won't work. Spoons such as the popular Krocadile or Blue Fox Pixie have a narrow rotational plane in which to move from side to side. At higher speeds, the spoons begin to spin rather than wobble, which defeats their intended presentation. Here too (as I mentioned in reference to trying spinning gear for trolling) consider using a 5 to 6 foot leader and a ball-bearing swivel to minimize potential line twist from the spoon.

More Trolling Tips and Downriggers

A heavy torpedo-shaped sinker can often be employed as a means to troll a lure through deeper strike zones. Take two quality ball-bearing snap-swivels and attach one to each end of the ringed sinker. Tie your primary line to one end and a 5 to 6 foot length of leader with your lure to the other. I have used anywhere from an 8 ounce up to a one

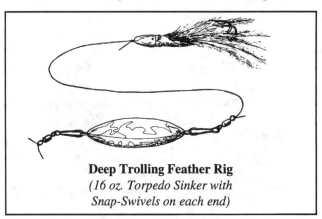

Deep Trolling Feather Rig
(16 oz. Torpedo Sinker with Snap-Swivels on each end)

pound torpedo sinker like this to troll feathers deeper. This combination has proven effective on both yellowtail and albacore.

However, perhaps a better alternative is to invest in a downrigger. This device has been a productive tool and a boon to the North Coast salmon fishermen. Southland anglers have been truly remiss in not applying down riggers to warm water marine conditions.

Many fishermen shy away from purchasing a downrigger because the unit appears too complicated and imposing. In reality, they are simple to both comprehend and to operate.

The unit itself is comprised of a metal or graphite boom (similar to a crane) with a pulley at one end. A large wheel with wire line passes off the main wheel and through the tiptop pulley at the end of the boom. Attached to the end of the wire is a heavy (2 to 5 pound) trolling ball weight. This weight appears to be almost like a shot-put, but it has a small built-in keel on the bottom. More importantly, the prominent sinker also features a line release clip affixed to the weight.

Now then, here's how a downrigger works. Clip your main line with the lure tied onto the sinker release. You should allow for anywhere from 5 to 10 feet of line between your lure and the release clip. Next, lower the ball sinker to the depth that you desire the lure to travel. As the wire line is unreeled from the major wheel, the ball sinker takes the lure—attached to your main monofilament line—down to the proper strike zone.

When the lure gets bit, the mono releases from the line clip and you are able to play the fish as you normally would. That is, the ball sinker remains free below the boat, totally removed from your monofilament. Have your partner reel in the wire line and trolling ball as you play out the fish.

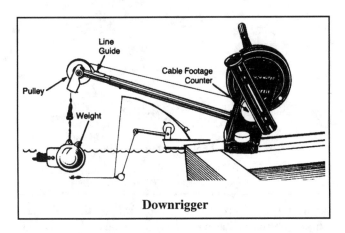

Downrigger

The downrigger concept may open new, untapped horizons for the Southern California fishery. Party boat skippers can definitely use them more frequently to prospect the depths for albacore, tuna, and yellowtail. Big game fishermen may also find some application on bill fish species.

But, private boaters should also weigh the investment. School fish such as calico, sand, and striped bass will often stratify some distance below the surface. Without massive quantities of chumming baits to bring these fish up (assuming they will surface to the chum) the downrigger tactic lets the angler put the lure in the most viable strike zone.

The issue of light versus heavy line for offshore trolling also arises. As with most types of fishing, there are always tradeoffs to ponder. Light line may get bit better than a heavier mono. But, light line also stretches more, sometimes making hook sets more difficult with a lot of line out behind the boat. On the other hand, light line is sometimes necessary because the lures "swim" better with less restriction. Light line is also more sporty. But if the fish can't be hooked properly, or the line continues to break off, what good is it? These are good arguments pro and con, for going "light" or "heavy" when trolling. The final decision must be one of personal preference.

Here's another tip: keep the hardware attached to the line minimal and of top-notch quality. Don't overload your trolled lure with excessive swivels. Buy only the better cross-lock or ball-bearing varieties to maximize strength in playing the fish and to minimize line twist.

Vary your presentations! Sometimes a change in trolling speed—faster or slower—can suddenly trigger a strike. Mix up the style of baits trolled. If you troll two or more rods, think about initially beginning your day by dragging both patented winners and more experimental baits. The lures that are historical winners will "cover your bets," the more innovative selections will handle the "long shots." So often, tried and true lures suddenly no longer produce. By having something different—yet plausibly effective—you may discover a new hot bait or an emergent trolling pattern perhaps untapped before.

With regard to coloration for trolled lures, it is essential to be flexible and investigate diverse patterns and shades. As with lure shape and action, marine species can become overly pressured by seeing the same repertoire of colors day after day. A new dimension of this offshore tactic opened up with the advent of the Color-C-Lector. This electronic device is a specialized hand-held light meter that keys in on the colors game fish are most easily able to see under prevailing light and water conditions.

The Color-C-Lector is powered by a 9 volt transistor battery. It consists of three bands on the meter which identify water clarity (muddy, stained and clear). Most offshore conditions are clear, however, around bays and estuaries a more stained condition can be found. The angler lowers a light-sensitive probe, attached by a cord to the meter, to the depth that the lure is travelling and obtains a color reading. This indicates which scheme of a 26 color range is most visible to the fish at that precise depth and under that specific water clarity.

The key is to lower the probe to the depth at which the lure is being trolled. If you are using feathers tied directly to the line, the probe should be lowered 2 to 5 feet below the surface. If you are pulling, say, a Rapala CD-14 Magnum plug on a fast troll, then a 12 to 15 foot reading is necessary.

Shrewd offshore trollers should take color readings throughout the day. Wave action, light intensity, cloud cover, photoplankton, barometric pressure, and pollution levels can all affect the readings as you troll through different territory. For years, veteran albacore fishermen have noted that the tuna will home in on a variety of colors during a full day of trolling. They may start with a dark purple or black feather in the morning, switch to a "psychedelic" orange and yellow by midday, then back to a darker green and blue combo by twilight. The Color-C-Lector may serve to take some of the guesswork out of the selection of marine trolling colors. Freshwater bass, panfish, and trout anglers have many documented successes with this novel instrument. It may definitely be an even greater value to the complex saltwater fisheries! To my knowledge, few Color-C-Lector units are sold these days. However, if you can find a used one, buy it. These units have really produced for me!

Trolling the Ropes

One special trolling ploy is worth mentioning. Most party boats and private craft have stainless steel or hard plastic rod holders designed especially for trolling. The angler simply places the butt section of the rod into the holder, lets out a prescribed length of line, flips the reel in gear, and sits and waits.

Sometimes, however, excessive chop, swell, or wave action makes it difficult to keep the lure beneath the surface without heavy sinkers or downriggers. Veteran skipper, Tom Schlauch, formerly of the charter boat, Dreamer, has found that using a short piece of parachute cord and a brass marine clip is a handy remedy to this problem.

Schlauch uses a length of cord about two feet long and ties it to the back stern railing. He attaches a heavy duty brass clip to the other end. Larger reels have built-in rings used for big game harnesses into which you can clip the rope. On smaller live-bait reels, clip the cord to the metal cross-support bars.

Next, literally lower the rod and reel over the stern! The trolling lines will ride low to the water, keeping the lures down through the wake. This is a strange sight indeed! The trolling outfits appear to be barely tied to the stern railing with the rod tips flipping barely above the water line. But, it is even stranger to see that rod get bit! At the instant of the strike, the rod elevates and extends, stretched out perpendicular to the water, hanging out on the ropes tied to the stern. Quickly run over, grab the reel,

set the hook, detach the clip, and fight the fish.

You can troll the ropes with practically any class of tackle. This trick also works quite well for boats that do not have permanent rod holders. Commercially made, trolling straps are now sold by Izorline for those who like to troll "the ropes."

Trolling Bait

Don't falsely assume that trolling has to be conducted using only artificial lures. Larger smelt, sardines, herring, or tomcod can be slowly trolled.

Cut or frozen baits similarly can also be productive at times. As a matter of fact, frozen anchovies are the most commonly trolled bait used for salmon, on both private, party, and commercial fishing boats. Trolled frozen anchovies are probably more popular than all other lures combined. Frozen squid trolled slowly along the kelp beds can also nail bass or even yellowtail. Lace the baits —either alive or frozen—on long-shank baitholder hooks. (Short-shank live bait hooks will work in a pinch. Check local landings for the best recommendations.) Sometimes the bait will troll best unencumbered without any sinker. Other times, a weight facilitates in keeping the trolled offering down below the waves.

A simple rig is to use a 1/2 to 2 ounce sliding-egg sinker. Run your main line through the weight and tie it off to a ball-bearing swivel. Next, tie to the swivel a 3 to 4 foot length of leader line with live or dead bait hooked at the other end.

Bead Chain Company also makes a variety of keel leads up to 2 ounces that have a swivel molded at both ends of the sinker. This Bead Chain keel weight provides optimal stability when trolled ahead of either lures or baits.

Summary

Offshore trolling plays an integral role in the saltwater enthusiast's ability to locate fish. Be precise in your tackle care and selection of lures for trolling. This method routinely catches larger specimens that can really test your gear. Be innovative in your trolling attack. Vary lures, colors, and boat speeds. Mix up your offerings to cover all the bases. Don't get locked into the more conservative approaches.

Hooks must be pre-sharpened. Manufacturers simply don't put the extra effort and expense into honing hooks on most lures. Trollers must do this for themselves. Take these extra steps and the trophy might be waiting at the other end of the line!

Party Boating: Learning the Strategy

There are numerous sport fishing landings that operate along the coastline from San Diego to the Oregon border. Most of these companies have some type of open party fleet. "Party boats," as they are known, are available on a first come, first serve basis. Most landings also accept reservations in advance. This is a good idea, particularly during the busy summer season, weekends, or at the peak of a run of game fish.

Many landings also have a more modest number of charter boats for hire. The skippers make these boats available for exclusive groups such as civic or fishing clubs, private businesses, or even small groups of fishermen who desire a day of fishing on the ocean without the crowds on a party boat.

Party boats generally average anywhere from 60 to 100 feet in length. Besides the skipper, there are usually two or more deck hands and possibly a person to run the galley if food is prepared on board. These boats are designed to carry optimal passenger loads, sometimes reaching up to 70 persons. Charter boats are generally smaller 35 to 60 foot vessels. Some are "six-pack" operations, set up for a skipper, deck hand, and six passengers. Others can accommodate over 20 anglers in a charter package.

Choosing a Party Boat

In selecting a party boat, the uninformed angler is often at a disadvantage. The chances of maximizing your luck in fishing among a group of strangers can be improved with a little research. Consult with your local tackle store salespersons. Ask for their recommendations—not all boats, and especially not all crews, are alike. Review the outdoor tabloids. These publications routinely print stories about the skippers and boats that are highly successful.

Finally, most major newspapers publish the "fish counts" for each landing in their area on a daily basis. Although you may not be able to find any information on a particular boat, the fish counts will at least give you some idea of which landings are running "hot" or "cold."

Party boat fees vary primarily with regard to the length of the trip. Some landings operate a 1/2 day party boat that leaves the dock around 6:00 am and returns at noon. There are also some 1/2 day afternoon shifts that leave at 1:00 pm and are back in port by 6:00 pm.

It is also possible to pay for a 3/4 day outing. This spans about 8 or 9 hours, leaving the dock at 3:00 or 4:00 am and returning around noon. Full-day trips often leave the harbor at midnight or in the early morning and return around 2:00 to 3:00 pm.

During the warm summer months, some landings also offer special twilight trips. This allows many anglers the opportunity to fish midweek, right after work. The boats usually leave around 5:00 or 6:00 pm and return at 11:00 or 12:00 pm. The "night bite" can often be fantastic on these runs with lighter crowds and therefore less angling pressure.

The longer the time spent on the water, the more opportunities for tapping the prime fish-holding areas. The half-day boats must remain near areas not too far off the beach. Full-day outings may take the fishermen to the farther banks and islands, sometimes over 50 miles from the landing.

On these extended trips, most vessels offer a sleeping bunk as an option for more comfortable travel. I strongly recommend paying the extra few dollars for a bunk. You will sleep better and be more rested for the action at hand in the morning. Most boats will not allow you to bring sleeping bags or similar gear. If you have some distance to travel before reaching the fishing grounds, you can "crash" in the galley or on the open-air deck if you didn't sign up for a bunk.

Along a similar line, many skippers will not permit the angler to bring an ice chest on board—no matter how small and compact it is. This is done for two reasons: (1) There is only so much room on the deck to move about and ice chests get in the way. The captain doesn't want his customers stumbling around on misplaced and unsecured ice chests nor does he want the boxes moving about on the decks in rough seas. (2) There are a limited number of ways the crew can insure profit on a sport fishing boat. One is through the galley. The skipper wants his customers to purchase breakfast and lunch in his galley to maximize a modest amount of profit from this part of his business. This is no different from movie theatres, concert halls, stadiums, and amusement parks "forcing" customers to buy refreshments on the premises. So, if you want to bring along an ice chest, check with the landing first to make sure they are allowed.

Party Boat Practices

Once you are on the boat, the deck hand will usually sign you up for the ship's Coast Guard log. He will also ask if you would like to participate in the "jackpot." This is the big fish derby—winner take all. For a modest investment, the fisherman can take a chance on the jackpot which might add to the excitement of the day's fishing.

Depending upon the boat or the species sought, gunny sacks may also be sold for storing your catch on the deck. Or numbers and tickets will be given for identifying fish in a cold fish hold. Many boats also hand out "rotation numbers" at the time of the sign-in (more on this later).

If you are only a casual angler without any equipment, you can rent tackle from the landing. "Rent rods" are usually maintained in good working order. Some landings offer both conventional and spinning tackle. I am not a big proponent of using rental tackle on these excursions. If you want to experience, say, rock codding for the first time, then a rent rod might be the best way to go until you decide if you like the sport. But, if you envision yourself as a fairly regular rider on these boats, definitely take the plunge and purchase your own equipment.

Similarly, many party boats offer hooks, sinkers, and lures for sale in the galley. Think twice about relying upon the boat's stock of available items. For one thing, you will pay a premium price for these goods once out to sea. For another, too often stock levels are not maintained and the boat will run out of a certain hook or sinker. Then you may find yourself in the embarrassing position of having to "mooch" off other passengers. So, take that extra effort to purchase your terminal gear ahead of time rather than relying on the boat's stockpile, except in emergency situations.

Almost always, the party boat captain provides bait for his passengers. Whether it is live, freshly dead, frozen, or cut, there is usually an ample supply for the number of passengers on a given day. But, occasionally someone slips up and the bait supplies run thin. Or, the fish "turn off" of the bait that the skipper has on board and seem to prefer another offering. More than once this writer has salvaged his fishing trip by bringing his own "private stash" of bait along. My favorite? A small 1 to 2 pound tray of frozen squid. Fish it whole, stripped, or as tippets for lures.

Time to Rotate!

To insure that everyone has a reasonably fair shot at the stern, the passengers are given rotation numbers. The skipper announces which group of fishermen are to occupy the stern section first. The remaining anglers are assigned positions above the stern, working all the way back to the bow.

Why is the stern such a premium spot? At anchor, the party boat crew begins to toss out scoopfuls of live chum off the stern, when it is available. Game fish come up near the surface behind the boat to feed on the chum. Therefore, anglers positioned in the rear portion of the boat have a tremendous advantage over other passengers at catching these feeding fish in the chum line.

Even if live chum is not available, the stern still affords the angler the best positioning on the party boat. The captain must anchor his vessel bow-first into the wind and current. Otherwise he could swamp the craft by taking waves and swells over the stern. Thus, anglers in the rear section of the boat typically have it easiest, being able to cast their baited hooks back into the flowing current or closest to the structure the skipper is anchoring near (for example: a kelp bed, reef, or sunken wreck).

Theoretically, all passengers are supposed to be given roughly the same opportunity to fish the stern. In reality, this doesn't always happen. Invariably there will be certain fishermen—affectionately referred to as "stern hogs" —that will try to position themselves in the rear of the boat regardless of their rotation assignment. It is up to other paying customers to inform the "intruder" that it is time for him to "rotate." If he doesn't budge, report it to the deck hand or skipper if necessary. All paying customers deserve a fair shot at fishing the stern, irrespective of their level of fishing expertise.

Once in the stern, there is a subtle observation you can make that may enhance your catch potential in this prime spot. As the deckhands stand atop the bait tank, they will usually toss the live bait with one hand or the other. Right-handed chunkers seem to throw the bait toward the stern's left corner; left-handers, towards the right. Try to position yourself on the "hot corner" where the chum seems to be most highly concentrated.

On speedy pelagic species, or even on some of the larger "bulldog" type fighters like sharks and lingcod, anglers may have to move along the party boat railing to follow their fish. Veteran party boaters can be heard to emphatically yell, "Hot rail—coming through!" This gets the other anglers to move out of the way—quickly.

Fishermen who prefer to throw jigs or other lures are usually not permitted to work the crowded stern. Many jig fishermen who need to make an overhead cast are safer throwing their lures from the bow area. Large saltwater treble hooks can be nearly lethal if they are whipped around a crowded stern.

If the skipper decides to set up a drift pattern, then it is best, when possible, for all anglers to fish the windward side of the boat. In this situation, the party boater must bring heavy enough sinkers to maintain contact with the bottom. Check with the landings before your departure and find out how much weight is needed if the skipper decides to drift. Here again, don't rely upon the boat's limited tackle shop to keep you supplied once at sea.

Being well-prepared and ready to meet the challenge of shifting conditions is especially important for the Northern California fleet. So-called "pot luck" trips are run on a regular basis out of North Coast ports. There can be a lot of drifting or slow trolling involved here as the skipper lets the anglers fish for a potpourri of pelagic and bottom-dwelling species. If live bait is available, the boat may drift for halibut, stripers, or salmon, sometimes right off the beach.

But, in rougher water, anglers will have to switch to a 2 pound sinker release program and drift dead bait along the deeper bottom. In either situation, it is up to the passengers to have the proper terminal gear handy to accommodate the different conditions. Some Northern landings now have reasonably priced "pot luck kits" for sale along with the rental rods for the occasional passenger.

Jackpot Fishing

If you intend to fish for money through the jackpot cash pool established on the party boat, here are a few helpful pointers the pros pass along:

1. Think "Big Bait = Big Fish." A larger sardine from the bait tank may often produce the whopper of the trip. Likewise, if the tank is full of anchovies, the angler who selects one of the few "brown baits" (tomcod, perch, queenfish, or pompano) swimming with the 'chovies and fly-lines it, may end up with the "J.P." fish.

Frozen baits such as whole squid can be equally potent on larger class game fish and members of the rockfish family. A strip of freshly caught mackerel or a strip from the belly of a smaller rockfish can be dynamite! Hook these on a deepwater rock cod gangion. This often results in the biggest lingcod caught on the boat that day.

Strips and frozen chunks of bait should also be utilized as trailers for plastic lures. Larger "bull bass" (calicos) and "grumpers" (sand bass) often seek out these more elaborate offerings when everyone else is fishing an anchovy.

2. Use Artificial Lures More Frequently. Trophy-class fish are prone to hit artificial baits. The candy bar jig, spoon, feathers, or assorted plastics regularly take some of the larger fish caught on the trip. This holds true for both surface-feeding and bottom-dwelling species.

3. Use Light Line with Live Bait. Accomplished party boaters often scale down in line test to maximize their chances at catching not only more fish, but larger specimens. This is especially effective on a touchy surface bite. Lighter lines allow the live baits to swim more freely. The smaller diameter evident with premium-grade mono is also less obvious to really "spooky" feeders. But greater skill and dexterity will be needed to play fish out on a light rig on a crowded party boat. This will only come with the experience accumulated from repeated outings.

4. Sharpen Those Hooks! Throughout the previous chapters, I have harped on the need for sharp hooks. This is never more important than when big fish and jackpot monies are on the line. Most party boat anglers won't put in the extra work to pre-sharpen both their bait hooks and those on their lures. Those who take this extra precaution often walk away with a few extra dollars in their pocket at the end of a trip!

5. What Counts for the "J.P."? This is a good question and it varies from landing to landing. Its a good idea to find out what qualifies for "J.P." contention from the start. For instance, on albacore runs trolling is disqualified for jackpot fishing. Only a few anglers get a chance to troll during the day. On other trips, so-called "trash fish" such as sharks or rays are not included in the "J.P." contest. Know what species and techniques qualify before you enter the pool.

Other Party Boat Equipment

Ironically, one of the primary pieces of equipment necessary for successful party boating has nothing to do with tackle itself. A good pair of rubber deck boots can be a valuable investment for the frequent passenger. The decks on these boats can get quite bloody and slippery on a "wide-open" bite. Deck hands recurrently wash the surface down to prevent excessive slipping. Still, when you have some fast and furious "hot rail" action at hand, sure, dry footing is absolutely a must. A wet party boat is no place for that pair of potentially slippery old sneakers you use in the garden.

Next, wear a hat and polarized glasses when possible. The hat will obviously keep the glare off the ocean to a minimum. But, it will also keep flying fish scales from the chumming out of your hair. Polarized lenses help to actually see fish that are near the surface. The polarization effect cuts through the glare dramatically, and allows the angler to see cruising fish in the chum line.

A "crying towel" can also be another useful piece of equipment often overlooked by party boat anglers. It helps sometimes to have clean, slime-free hands when tying and removing hooks.

With regard to removing hooks, deck hands will help you when you need assistance. It might be better, however, to carry your own set of needle-nose pliers or surgical hemostats. Sometimes during a wide-open bite, it may be a matter of time before the crew gets to your hooked fish. Do the work yourself and get that line back in the water!

Finally, such personal incidentals such as seasick medication, sun screen, or aspirin must be carried on board by the angler. Don't expect the boat to have a stock of these often important medicinal aides.

Summary

For many Californians, the party boat is the primary means for them to spend a day ocean fishing. Landing operators specialize in all types of open party trips—rock cod, striper, salmon, lingcod, sand bass, yellowtail, albacore, or even shark. The angler has a wide range of skippers, boats, and trips to select from.

Do your homework and come prepared for the day's fishing. Monitor your local sources from tackle shops and landings to outdoor columns and fellow fishermen for the most reliable tips regarding proper tackle and equipment.

Above all, remember that you, as a paying customer, deserve a fair shake and an equal opportunity to catch fish on these boats. Any evidence of differential treatment should be brought to the attention of the boat's captain or the sport fishing landing itself. A skipper and his crew build their business on repeat clientele. It is in their best interest to insure that all passengers are treated fairly.

Finally, if you enjoyed your trip regardless of the total catch, leave a tip with the deck hands. They will be grateful for this courtesy. Similarly, if you win the jackpot, consider giving a chunk to the crew. The deck hands, like waitresses, depend on customer tips to augment their daily wages.

Boat Fishin': Doing It Your Way

Some saltwater enthusiasts prefer to fish from their own boats. The California Coast offers year 'round opportunities for the private boat owner. Before I delineate the distinct pluses and minuses in fishing from these craft, let's review a basic checklist of equipment necessary for successful and safe private saltwater boating.

Key Equipment

In my estimation, the most important piece of equipment I look for before boarding a private vessel—of any size —is a radio. I prefer VHF, but I'll settle for a CB if we are planning to fish local waters close to shore. You might also consider investing in a satellite cell phone, which will let you call from virtually anywhere in the world.

I am often amazed how some private yacht owners with luxurious, fast offshore boats, fail to have a ship-to-shore radio on boat. The "big pond" can become ruthlessly dangerous at times with little warning. A long-range radio transmission may be your only hope and salvation if you experience engine failure many miles out to sea.

Many marine radios also have a built-in radio directional finder (RDF). This is a valuable feature especially in the fog should you become lost. The radio homes in on a signal from the shore which then serves as a beacon of sorts to follow until visual bearings can be taken.

A compass goes hand in hand with a radio. Along with a compass, it is helpful to have navigational charts or a Dial-A-Course wheel that helps you set your course for the trip. Don't rely upon following other boats out or completely on visual landmarks. Boats have a way of separating from each other on the ocean and landmarks can often become obscured with fluctuating marine weather.

Review current written Coast Guard regulations for small craft. In addition to proper flotation devices, count on having an anchor, ample anchor rope (check current requirements), signal flares, a horn, a buoy ring or similar float that can be thrown, and a well-stocked first aid kit.

Some skippers planning on multi-day trips or traveling long distances carry on extra supplies of water and emergency provisions. In addition, minor mechanical problems can sometimes be remedied by keeping tools, spare oil, and fresh spark plugs on board.

With regard to fuel, I am flabbergasted that some novice boaters: (a) have no idea how much fuel their craft consumes; (b) don't know the capacity of their fuel tank(s); and (c) fail to leave the dock with full tanks. There are no floating fuel docks or gas stations once you're out to sea. The Coast Guard no longer responds except in life-threatening situations. Private towing vessels will be happy to come out and refuel your boat or tow you in—for some rather healthy fees!

Other additional equipment worth considering include a gaff and a landing net. Scale both of these items to the quarry sought. If you are out after albacore, you will need a fairly long handled gaff. One of those small 3 to 4 foot "pea shooters" may not be long enough to reach down to stick fish showing "deep color." Similarly, salmon fishermen must have a net on board as required by law. A small trout net suitable for freshwater lakes will not suffice for a 10 to 20 pound king salmon.

Nets are also a good idea for evaluating catches of potentially sub-legal white sea bass, barracuda, or halibut. It also helps to have a measuring device as a permanent fixture on your boat whenever length restrictions apply to a certain species.

Rod holders and/or trolling ropes add to the comfort for the trip. Very few anglers want to actually hold the rod and reel for great lengths of time when trolling. Rod holders also permit you to fish more than one outfit at a time when either drifting or still fishing on the bottom. Because of the crowded conditions on a party boat, anglers are strongly advised to fish only one rod at a time. Private craft offer the fishermen the luxury of setting out as many rigs as they want, assuming that they are reasonably able to attend to them. (There can be a fine line between "sport fishing" and a full-blown commercial operation!)

Fishing Electronics

When it comes to additional electronics, the sky's the limit. A sea temp gauge can be a valuable instrument to monitor the different areas for optimal water temperatures. Fish-finding devices are also important and highly recommended if you can afford one.

These units can be divided into three basic categories: fish locators, graphs, and liquid crystal recorders. Locators, or "flashers" as they are sometimes termed, are the most rudimentary. They send out a sonar signal which is deflected off the bottom. Novice boaters will be able to read the depth of the water easily with these simple units. More sophisticated readings of the bottom terrain, schools of bait fish, and potentially larger prey are possible with a fish locator—but it will take some practice to master the device.

A paper graph recorder is a far superior option. These units may cost a few hundred dollars more than a flasher, but they will provide you with an accurate graphic picture of the bottom. The paper scroll actually gives an inked image of the bottom topography. Schools of game fish, rockfish, underwater canyons, ledges, reefs, kelp forests, and wrecks vividly appear on the paper.

Another option that is gaining in popularity is the liquid crystal recorder. The LCR is a compromise between a flasher and a graph. It is a very thin compact unit. The picture received on the narrow screen is a computerized impression of the bottom and everything from there to the surface. The markings are not as articulated as those on the paper graph recorder. But they are clearly superior to having to discern the flashes from a fish locator.

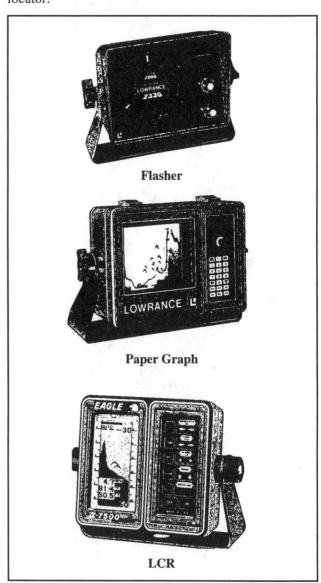

Flasher

Paper Graph

LCR

Liquid crystal recorders are becoming more and more advanced each season. Many anglers prefer the LCRs because they do not require replacing the paper scrolls as do graph recorders. The resolution of the underwater terrain is usually more than adequate for the occasional angler and the units cost much less than paper graphs. The most sophisticated LCRs measure in feet or fathoms, have variations in the size of the digital readings, and allow the viewer to actually enlarge or bracket a particular strike zone where the fish are holding (e.g., 20-40 feet). The most expensive models also have built-in sea temp and boat speed gauges. Other electronics to add to your vessel would be either a basic GPS (Global Positioning Satellite) unit or a GPS/plotter combo that allows you to retrace your course from one way point to another. Slowly, but surely, GPS technology is replacing Loran as the major electronic means for finding out where you're going— and where you have been.

It pays to have a qualified boat rigger install your electronics, especially on more elaborate private craft. They will make certain that the transducer—the signal sending device—is mounted properly for maximum performance. They will also be sure to wire the units properly so as to avoid serious electrical shorts or similar faults in the boat's electrical system.

Fish Storage

A final equipment concern is what to do with the catch? Most private boats do not have the space for a separate refrigeration hold. Wet gunny sacks are useful on small outboards, but won't always preserve the catch until you get home.

The new wave of heavy-duty plastic foam ice chests made by Igloo, Coleman, Thermos, and Gott are perfect for this situation. They range in size from small 30 quart models on up to jumbo 200 quarts. These larger models can actually be tied on the swim step of private yachts to form a refrigerated storage hold for larger sizes or greater quantities of game fish. Some of the bigger chests also have built-in cushions on their top lids which can provide extra seating on a small boat.

These chests, compared to the clunkier metal models of yesteryear, are impervious to saltwater, won't rust, and will really take a beating in rough seas. They also won't mar expensive decks, woodwork, or metal fixtures as will the heavy metal-cased models.

That should give you a fairly extensive menu of the items needed for a properly rigged, privately owned saltwater boat. Now let's focus on some of the advantages and disadvantages that are inherent in owning your own rig.

Advantages of Private Boats

Some fishermen simply have to be in total control of their outing. This is possible when you fish from a private boat. These boats are typically faster than party boats. You can leave for the fishing grounds later, and stay out longer than you could on most party boats. You come and go when you want to.

Anglers can also select who they want to fish with when they own their own craft. You can never really tell who will end up with you in a crowded stern on an open party trip. There are times when tempers may flare on a party boat. Some anglers do not have the expertise to play fish properly, to keep from crossing other people's lines, or to know how to move down the rail quickly. More accomplished saltwater fishing buffs may find this situation frustrating, in addition to the overall congestion when the fishing is "hot." On a private vessel, crowding is not a problem nor do you usually have to deal with the angling whims of complete strangers.

Private boats also afford the angler more opportunities for creative fishing. There can be a lot of space and room, for instance, to use lighter gear, maybe even freshwater tackle, to generate the maximum sport from the various marine species. Trolling is also less problematic. On a packed party boat, the skipper has to divide the trolling time between as many passengers as possible. (This can be a real problem, especially if it is the only way the fish are being caught that day.) Private skippers can troll to their heart's content.

There are also some places that are rich "honey holes," holding quantities of fish that party boats won't venture near. For example, quite often party boat skippers will not take a chance on fishing close to the beach. Some feel it is too dangerous to put these larger vessels in jeopardy should there be a mechanical failure near the surfline. In contrast, smaller private craft routinely fish this type of water.

Party boats also won't usually explore the shallow water found within the many harbors and bays along the coast. Sometimes it is hard to maneuver a long, 60 to 100 foot boat in these areas. But also, the passengers didn't pay top dollar for a "harbor cruise." Most party boaters expect to travel some distance to fish open ocean.

Similarly, the offshore kelp beds, particularly from around Malibu to up past Santa Barbara, are a sanctuary for a diverse smorgasbord of both game fish and kelp dwellers. Larger party boats have a difficult time positioning themselves near the floating kelp. Anchoring is sometimes impossible. Smaller boats—particularly aluminum outboards—can actually glide over the kelp and fish the numerous "pot holes" of open water. It is possible to nail everything from big calicos to 30 pound class white sea bass in these little openings (more on "pot holing" in the kelp fishing chapter).

There are numerous small rock piles that protrude above the water up and down the coast. When the surge breaks over these rocks, fishermen describe them as "boilers." There can be a lot of trophy-sized bass and rockfish that feed inside these boilers where the turbulence creates a frothy whirlpool effect. Not too many party boat captains will fish this structure. For one thing, it is dangerous to put a large boat near the rocks. But also, spots such as these and pot holes in the kelp are not large enough for a full boat load of paying passengers to share. These are not concerns for the private boat owner.

Disadvantages of Private Boats

There are also distinct disadvantages that must be weighed before deciding whether or not to fish from your own boat or to go as a party boater. For one thing, the size of your craft always has to come into consideration. If you own a 16 foot aluminum boat with 60 horsepower outboard, you might want to think twice about making an albacore run 45 miles out to sea. The seaworthiness of one's boat must be weighed, anticipating distance to be travelled and a "worse case scenario" of how the craft would handle in rough water.

Other pragmatic concerns include fuel and live bait capacities. Obviously, it would be ridiculous to take your own boat if it didn't have the range in terms of fuel capacity to get you there and back. Don't play Russian roulette with marginal decisions in this regard. If, for example, your boat had a 50 mile total range, this might be fine for travelling 20 miles and back. But always remember to anticipate additional fuel consumption such as trolling once you get there.

The bait situation poses a similar problem. Most private boats, even the most luxurious yachts, usually can't compete with the party boats when it comes to chumming power. If the fish you are seeking need continual chum to keep them "up" and feeding, you may be at a clear disadvantage with your own boat. There have been a few occasions while fishing from a private boat that I have watched party boat anglers shoulder to shoulder in the stern catching fish, while my boat simply ran out of chum. I would gladly have switched places, taking my licks in the crowded stern.

Another often overlooked problem intrinsic to fishing in smaller private boats involves anchoring. There are certain spots along the coast that require anchoring to maximize the chances of taking fish. The offshore oil derricks along Huntington Beach present such a problem. There are times when the big yellowtail decide to feed around these rigs. First, a boat needs to have considerable chum to bring these battlers to the surface. But second, to maintain proper position so the chum can work, the boat has to be anchored. The problem: the depth here may be over 250 feet with a lot of current. That means large anchors and a lot of rope to let out scope. Most private boats are not equipped for deep water anchoring nor do they have the power winches to bring the "hook" up when they are ready to move.

The Art of Chumming

If you do have a bait tank, there are a few simple guidelines to follow when chumming. Try to maintain a fairly constant flow with the bait. Don't become too erratic; for example, a scoopful here, a handful next, then two scoops. Be careful not to overfeed the fish. The chum is meant to get them interested in feeding and to eventually take your baited hook or artificial lure. There is a very fine line between keeping the fish on the "edge" of feeding interest and spoiling them with too much chum.

It is also essential to position your boat properly. In simple terms, you want to have the chum flowing back behind the stern with the current. The optimal effect is to have fish that are facing into the current come up and eat the chum, heading towards the fishermen in the stern.

But what if you do not have an aerated bait tank or run out of live chum? There may still be ways to salvage the bite. Ron De La Mare is a veteran saltwater tackle expert who fishes from a lot of small private boats. Frequently these craft leave the harbor without any live bait to speak of. De La Mare has devised his own form of chum using a mixture of Berkley Saltwater Attractant, cut squid, and sand.

Take the squid and slice it up into small mouth-sized pieces. Put the squid and a garden spadeful of sand in a bucket. Add ample quantities of Berkley Saltwater Attractant to coat the squid and mix the sand in. The sand adheres to the squid, the attractant sticks to the sand. As you drip some of this chum overboard, the Berkley Saltwater Attractant slowly releases its scent as it sinks to the bottom. This tactic works remarkably well for sand bass, sometimes calicos, and various shallow water rockfish species.

Summary

Owning your own saltwater boat can definitely open up a wealth of new opportunities for the serious angler. Light-lining, trolling, using jigs more often—you name it—it's your boat, so the techniques are unlimited. There are no crowds, rotation sequences, or "hot railers" to contend with.

But, in owning your own craft, there are certain responsibilities you assume that you didn't have as a party boat passenger. It is now up to you— as the skipper—to insure the vessel is in top mechanical shape. All electronics, navigation, life-saving, and first aid equipment is now your legal responsibility for both your own and your passenger's welfare.

It is also up to you—as the skipper—to make rational decisions as to what are your craft's safe, reasonable limits.

Finally, once at the helm, you have joined the ranks of sport fishing captains. Certain "rules of the road" and proper etiquette among skippers themselves must be observed at all times. Do not, for example, crowd the charter fleet or the party boats. Do not "sponge" off their chum lines. Do not cut across their sterns. Remember—these skippers are doing this for their daily living. They depend upon their fish counts for continued patronage. Learn to share the water and find your own fish.

Pier Fishin': Plaudits for Piers

Public piers and wharfs offer some of the most inexpensive fishing available in the Golden State. Outside of privately owned lakes or ponds, piers are practically the only places Californians can fish for free. No license is required for fishing these structures.

Upon first glance, pier fishing may appear to be pretty simple: you find a spot to sit, cast out, and wait for a bite. In reality, there are a number of sophisticated tactics you can use when working your baits or lures from a pier which will enhance your potential to catch fish.

There are also distinct differences in the complexion of the inshore fisheries of Southern and Northern California piers. Much of this can be attributed to water temperature variations. There is a wider array of both inshore species and pelagic game fish that are found off the Southland piers. Perch, corbina, croaker, along with calico and bass, bonito, barracuda, and even yellowtail are possible prey off Southern California's piers. Piers along the Central and Northern Coast, such as those at Pismo Beach or Avila and Monterey Bays, have a less diverse selection of species to fish for due to the colder currents. Major game fish taken at Northern California piers include salmon, stripers, halibut, flounder, sturgeon, and kingfish.

In this chapter, I will focus on some of the more innovative ways to catch fish from our diverse piers. I'll outline the appropriate equipment to use, the different terminal rigs, and the special methods for catching species indigenous to these areas.

Southern vs. Northern Piers

The piers in Southern California characteristically are long and lead to open water and sandy bottoms. There are only a handful of piers or wharfs inside sheltered bays in this part of the state. The Shelter Island pier in San Diego Bay and Stearn's Wharf in Santa Barbara are examples of piers within harbors in the Southland.

In contrast, there are a wider variety of piers in the northern sector of the state. Because of the expansive nature of the San Francisco Bay complex, there are numerous piers from Berkeley to San Mateo that are situated in the calmer waters of the Bay. Other piers like the one at Pacifica lead to cold waters as they face the ocean adjacent to the sandy beach. Northern piers also differ sharply from those in the South Coast in terms of the availability of live bait. Southern piers sell ample quantities of live anchovies or sometimes even sardines or squid for the anglers at certain times of the year. Live bait for pier operations in the North is a real bonus and a rare commodity. The prevalence or absence of the bait definitely affects the options available to the dedicated pier angler.

Pier Tackle

Pier fishing in general is really a matter of choice, much depending on the size of the fish you are seeking. Small freshwater spin-cast outfits on up to Penn 4/0 Senators can be used off these structures. The light rigs will handle everything from perch, tomcod, and queenfish, to mackerel and bonito. Use magnum gear for sharks and bat rays.

Many regular pier fishermen will carry two or three outfits to cover a range of options. A lightweight freshwater combo spooled with 6 to 10 pound test mono is great for smaller fish. It doesn't particularly matter whether you select closed-face spin-cast or open-face spinning gear. A 6 to 7 foot fiberglass or graphite rod is perfect for perch, tom cod, small "boneheads" (bonito), and the like. Casting is minimal with this tackle. Most presentations will be right below the pier next to the pilings.

A medium 8 foot spin or casting rod is better for the larger species. Here again, either a conventional reel or a spinner is fine, spooled with about 200 yards of 15 to 20 pound monofilament. You will need this stouter outfit for bringing up halibut, bigger bonito, lingcod, barracuda, stripers, salmon, sand or calico bass. A stray "peanut" size (5 to 8 pound) yellowtail could also be subdued with this kind of tackle. The longer rods and large spool capacities are also necessary for making further casts off the pier.

Shark hunters prefer a heavy action fiberglass rod in 8 foot lengths. A Penn 113H-4/0 or Daiwa 4/0 reel, filled with 400+ yards of 30 pound mono complements the "bazooka-like" rod. This rig is able to handle 200 pound or better sharks and bat rays. (I'll talk about these later.)

Specialized Pier Rigs

Typical Smelt Catchers: Jack smelt are one of the most common fish sought by pier anglers up and down the state. Jack smelt look very similar to grunion. They can be found in water 5 to 50 feet deep and are commonly under 12 inches in length—though larger specimens do show up in catches.

Smelt can be caught from piers quite readily with small pieces of bait (e.g. pile worms, mussels, squid, anchovies) laced onto a series of snag hooks. This kind of multiple hook and leader rig is sold throughout tackle stores along the coast and often at the pier concession stands that sell bait and tackle. A variation on this theme is a pre-tied "surf leader" you can purchase. This style of leader has only 2 to 3 baitholder hooks tied off of the main leader line, with a sinker on the end of the setup.

In Northern California pier anglers have devised another method to fish the snag rigs for smelt. Some use a standard plastic bobber snapped up above the leader to keep the bait suspended just below the surface. A sinker remains on the bottom of the leader to slow the drift.

Another variation of this smelt rig has been popularized off the Berkeley Pier. Fishermen will take a chunk

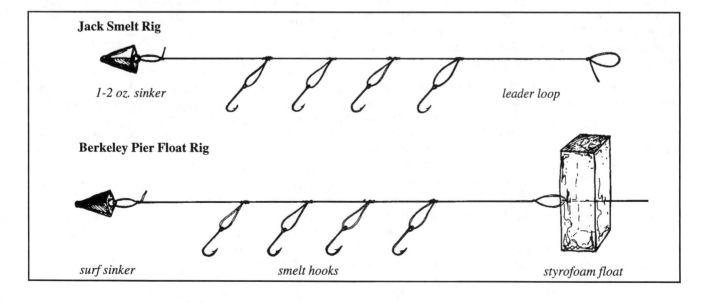

Jack Smelt Rig

1-2 oz. sinker   *leader loop*

Berkeley Pier Float Rig

surf sinker   *smelt hooks*   *styrofoam float*

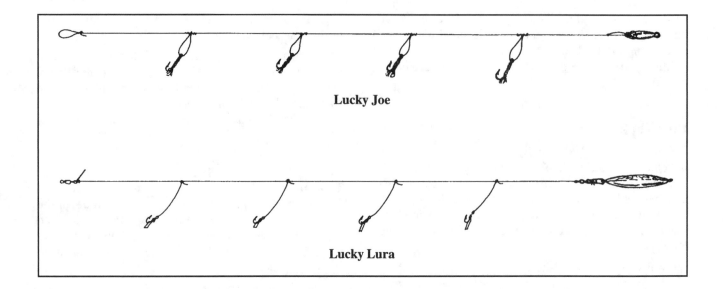

Lucky Joe

Lucky Lura

of styrofoam used for packing insulation and run their line through it to form a highly visible, inexpensive float. Then, attach the snag hooks to the main line along with a 1 to 2 ounce pyramid sinker on the bottom to stabilize it. Both pile worms and chunks of grass shrimp are favored baits.

Jig fly rigs will also take a number of smelt when the bite is "on." The old standby, generically termed, a "Lucky Joe," is a series of snag hooks with alternating red and yellow yarn. These can be fished with or without a tippet of cut bait.

But in recent years, it seems that even the smelt have become more choosy about artificial lures. Izorline imports a unique snag fly rig, the Lucky Lura, from Asia. This is comprised of a series of luminous beads and tiny, wax paper like "flies." The smelt often go crazy for this rig! Use size #4 or #7 in the Lucky Lura. For added attraction snap a 1 1/8 ounce Haddock Structure Spoon to the bottom of the rig instead of a sinker.

I might add that putting either a shiny chrome torpedo sinker with a treble hook or a conventional spoon on the end of a snag fly rig often produces some unexpected results. Smaller fish such as smelt will strike the little snag hooks. But larger game fish such as bonito will be drawn to the snagged smaller fish and the flash of the spoon. So don't be surprised if you feel another "thump" on the end of your line as a larger predator goes for the spoon!

Another tactic for smelt is a favorite of the North Coast pier veterans. Normally, these small mouth "silversides" won't strike an artificial lure. But when the smelt are spawning, try a tiny, 1/4 ounce, silver Kastmaster spoon with a feather trailer worked near the bottom. This tactic often produces some of the larger smelt of the season.

The Bonito Trolley

These smaller pelagic tuna can put up an awesome tussle when caught off the piers. Usually you won't find any great numbers of these warm water species too much further north than Morro Bay.

Bonito love a live anchovy. But there is a problem. Even if you can obtain the bait alive, how do you get it out, away from the pier? The 'chovy must be fly-lined with minimal weight. The bonito feed near the surface, and want the bait to appear as lively as possible. Enterprising anglers in the Southland have devised a unique "trolley" rig for using live bait fish such as anchovies or sardines from a pier.

The trolling rig is easy to put together. Tie a 2 to 4 ounce pyramid sinker to the end of your main line. Make a long cast. The pyramid sinker will descend and embed itself in the soft sand. Next, take about a 3 to 4 foot length of 15 to 20 pound test mono. Tie an Eagle Claw #318-N #2 to #4 live bait hook to one end. Thread the other end through a large clear Casta-Bubble float. Once through the bubble, tie this end of the leader to the swivel portion of a snap-swivel. Push the float up against the swivel, then butt the other end with a small B.B. shot. This keeps the bubble from sliding down onto the hook. Next, bait the hook with a live 'chovy, open up the snap (on the snap-swivel), and hook it over the main line. Close the snap shut and let the float and 'chovy slide down the trolley line.

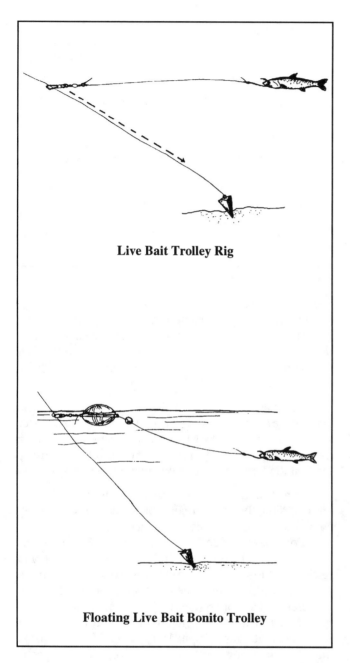

Live Bait Trolley Rig

Floating Live Bait Bonito Trolley

The Halibut Trolley

Halibut and smaller members of the flatfish family are equally fond of live bait. Halibut and flounders can also be very touchy feeders. A variation of the bonito trolley will work as a means to get a live bait to these bottom fish. Instead of using the float to keep the 'chovy near the surface, let the leader slide all the way to the bottom. The snap-swivel will rest up against the pyramid sinker. Quite frequently other game fish—including halibut—may strike the 'chovy as it trollies down the line before it hits the bottom.

Bonito Splashers

As schooling creatures, bonito are often attracted to the noise created by a cluster of bait fish thrashing near the surface. Anglers working high above the water off of piers can simulate this effect with a bonito splasher. There are different ways to construct the splasher setup. One of the easiest is to once again rely upon the versatile clear Casta-Bubble.

Using a medium-sized saltwater spinning reel and an 8+ foot long rod, run your line through a fluorescent bead, then a Casta-Bubble, then through another bead, and tie it off to a swivel. Pinch a small B.B. shot just above the float and the first bead to keep them from sliding up the line. Next, tie a 7+ foot length of leader to the rear swivel and a bonito feather to the other end. This fly is nothing more than a very crude, single-hook streamer made with yellow, white, or blue feathers. Some South Coast bait shops sell the flies with a piece of shiny mylar for added flash.

The object of the splasher rig is to create a commotion for the bonito to follow, eventually striking the fly as it trails behind. Make a long cast. (Fill the Casta-Bubble halfway with water for extra weight and distance.) Work the float back in towards the pier with rhythmic strokes from the long rod. The bubble will "pop" and splash, with the subtle streamer fly darting behind it. The bonito will home in on the noise and then viciously strike the feathers. The bonito splasher is an incredibly creative approach for taking these feisty game fish from the pier!

Secret Shiny Sinkers

A few pier fishermen have found another unique way to take halibut from these structures. Instead of using live bait from the ends of the pier, try working the surflines on piers that jut out from the beach. Take a 2 to 4 ounce shiny chrome torpedo sinker with a treble hook or a Luhr Jensen "Hot

When the float/leader combo hits the water, the anchovy will swim unencumbered near the surface. But now the fun begins! When a bonito eats the 'chovy it will pull the Casta-Bubble down. You have to quickly reel in your main line. When the pyramid sinker butts up against the float and swivel, set the hook!

This trolley rig is a lot less complicated than it sounds. It is an absolutely invaluable strategy for surface feeders such as bonito.

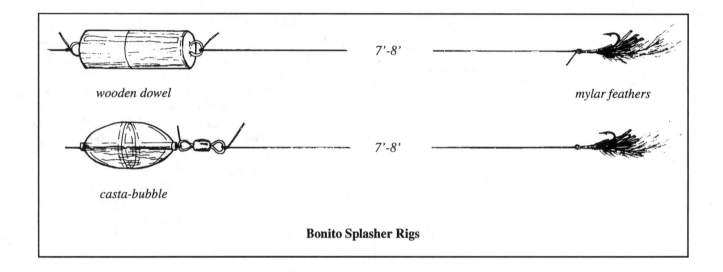

wooden dowel

7'-8'

mylar feathers

casta-bubble

7'-8'

Bonito Splasher Rigs

Diamond" or Diamond Jig and cast it towards the surfline. Let the heavy sinker-lure plow through the sandy bottom just the other side of the breakers.

Halibut will lie outside the surf, picking off grunion, anchovies, or smelt near the bottom. The shiny sinker resembles one of these small silver bait fish as it tumbles in the sand. Normally there aren't too many obstructions for the sinker to get hung up on. So, on anything that feels like a strike, swing hard, and set the hook!

Pier Plastics

Soft plastic lures can also be effective at times fished off the pier. In the Goleta area, for example, a local favorite is to use ultralight tackle and small crappie jigs tipped with a tiny piece of squid. Little mini-jigs like these made out of soft plastic, can provide some great sport with light tackle for mackerel, smelt, and assorted perch.

Further south, fishermen working Newport, Balboa, or Aliso Piers can catch a stray calico or sand bass throwing Salty Magics, Scampis, or Lunker Thumpers out to deeper water. These baits also perform best in this situation with a 1 x 3 inch squid tippet. Make long casts and fish darker patterns towards dusk, at night, and in the pre-dawn period. Rarely will the calicos move into the waters around the pier in broad daylight.

Spoonin' the Pier

Saltwater spoons can also rack up some hefty catches at times—both in the North and the South. Along the Central Coast in the Monterey area, lingcod occasionally move into the waters near the pier on an incoming tide. Flashing spoons such as the popular Krocadile casted long distances and retrieved off the bottom can account for an occasional catch. Salmon are another spoonin' possibility in the North if the conditions are right.

In the San Francisco Bay Area, local pier specialists wait for the run of school stripers to start. Silver Kastmaster spoons in heavier 3/4 to 1 ounce sizes will often take a limit of these linesiders when they cruise around the many piers in the Berkeley and Oakland area.

Further south, bonito, barracuda, yellowfin croaker, and occasionally sand and calico bass will attack a brightly colored spoon. Krocadiles, Crippled Herring Kastmasters, Blue Fox Pixies, Haddock Jig'n Spoons, and Rader Spoons will occasionally produce, following a long cast and retrieved below the surface. Gold, silver, and prismlite patterns are all effective when the fish eat this kind of lure. The great thing about spoons in this design is that they can be chucked out a long way, many yards away from the pier into water that is rarely tapped by most pier fishermen. On piers facing open water, scale up in size, and cast spoons in the 3/4 to 1 1/2 ounce weight range.

Sometimes a smaller spoon will perform better off the piers found in quiet bays or harbors, even though the game fish may be the same size as those found off piers leading to sea. For example, a favorite technique on the small Shelter Island Pier in San Diego Bay is to take a light 5/8 ounce Krocadile spoon and yo-yo it on 6 to 8 pound test line at a 45 degree angle. Both bonito and Pacific mackerel will strike the more compact spoon retrieved in this fashion.

Plugs for the Pier?

Believe it or not, it is possible to use a narrow assortment of minnow-like plugs off of the pier. On piers such as Berkeley's that do not stand too high off the water, a simple cast-and-retrieve technique will sometimes work. Both Rapalas, Rebels, and the Cordell Spot can be super for striped bass.

Southland piers at Huntington, Ocean, and Aliso are quite high above the water. But there are still ways to try a plug off of these higher structures.

Using a medium-weight spinning outfit, tie the end of the line to a 4 to 10 ounce torpedo sinker. Onto the other end of the sinker, run a 6 to 7 foot length of leader. Tie a **floating** #9, 11, or 13 silver or blue Rapala or Rebel to the other end of the leader.

I recommend the floating versions of these lures because they have more action than the sinking models. And, you don't have to worry about getting these minnow-shaped plugs down since the heavy ringed sinker will do that for you.

I have used this setup to catch bonito when they were holding deep and wouldn't hit a live anchovy on a trolley rig. A blue-black Rebel or Rapala are my favorite picks for this innovative tactic. Consider also trying the new Rapala Husky Jerk minnows or Luhr Jensen P.J. Shiner for this innovative pier strategy.

Big Bait Tricks

Another rather creative ploy for catching braggin' size fish from the pier involves catching your own live bait—albeit sometimes inadvertently. Live smelt, for instance, are excellent baits for big halibut. This is where that two-rod versatility comes in handy when pier fishing. Catch the smelt on the lighter rig, then pin it on your heavier outfit and try for a larger fish.

The ever present tomcod, queenfish, and smaller perches can all be effective for halibut and bull bass. Smaller rockfish, either stripped or fished whole, along with Spanish or Pacific mackerel can also interest a large lingcod in the Central Coast. The adage "Big Bait = Big Fish" applies equally well to pier fishing.

Sidewinder Magic

Long-time saltwater tackle dealer and pier specialist, Steve Carson, has found another tactic worth mentioning for nailing large perch. Carson notes that some piers such as those in Venice and Santa Monica, are long and thin with rounded or T-shaped extensions at the end. He suggests getting up to where the extension begins at the running end of the pier and pitch little sidewinder crabs among the pilings.

The sidewinders can be caught along the rock piles, jetties, and breakwalls at low tide. Using a 4 to 6 inch wooden dowel with screw-eyes at each end as a wooden float, Carson connects a 5 to 7 foot leader to the dowel with a sidewinder hooked at the other end.

The trick, he observes, is to gently cast this splasher-bait combo underneath the pier between the pilings. By using the prominent wood float, you can actually "guide" the sidewinder from piling to piling.

Understand that this water underneath many of our piers rarely ever gets fished! Magnum-sized white piling, rubberlip, and buttermouth perch will inhale the small crab. The bait slowly drifts suspended underneath the dowel, putting the sidewinder right against the pilings. The heavy wood float permits you to make a more precise cast. Also, the pilings can become so concentrated in an area like this that it is virtually impossible to fish it by using a sinker. The large wooden float is the secret!

Other baits such as piling and blood worms, assorted clams or mussels, and chunks of anchovies should also be tried with this method.

More Float Tips

The ubiquitous red and white plastic bobber can be used extensively when pier fishing—North or South—when

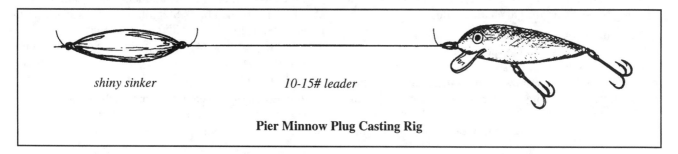

shiny sinker   10-15# leader

Pier Minnow Plug Casting Rig

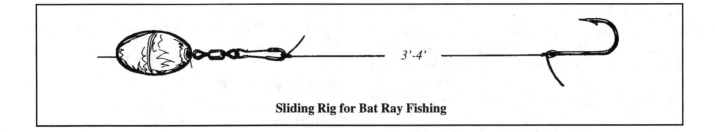

Sliding Rig for Bat Ray Fishing

drifting a dead anchovy, smelt, herring, grunion, or sardine. Steelhead, king, and silver salmon will often hit an anchovy drifted outside the surfline in this manner utilizing a simple bobber.

Mackerel, small barracuda, and sometimes even a super hungry bonito will also strike the dead 'chovy drifted like this. The bobber keeps the bait suspended below the surface while the current and wave action gives it a wounded or fluttering appearance.

The Slider Rig

Of all the assorted pre-tied leader and rigs available at the bait and tackle stores, anglers would be hard pressed to match the basic slider setup for everyday pier fishing. This is the old standby used in both fresh and saltwater.

Take a 1/2 to 5 ounce egg sinker (depending upon what you are after and the size of the bait). Slide your main line through it and butt it off with a snap-swivel. Add your own leader, a commercial leader, or a snelled hook to the snap and you are ready to go.

The slider can be used with virtually any kind of bait —dead or alive: anchovies, smelt, grunion, sardines, brown baits, squid, crabs, shrimps, worms, mudsuckers, bullheads, strips, chunks, or even larger whole fish.

A popular shark or ray strategy from the pier is to fish, for example, that Penn #113H, 4/0 Senator reel I mentioned filled with 30 to 40 pound line. Construct a slider rig using a 5 ounce egg sinker and a 60 pound test leader matched with 4/0 to 10/0 hook. Chicken or duck livers, whole squid, mackerel, or bonito fillets round out the offering for some midnight shark action.

A lot of my own pier fishing has occurred late at night off the Huntington and Newport Piers. This is the time when the crowds of tourists have returned to their hotel rooms and the pier becomes a quiet sanctuary for nocturnal feeders. My favorite tactic is to fish a whole squid on a slider rig with 15 pound test mono and a light saltwater combo. My quarry? Those bizarre-looking shovelnose

sharks. On light tackle, these critters can really give you a tussle. It seems invariably that the larger "shovels" always know exactly where the pilings are—even in the dark. Although not a prized game fish by any means, shovelnose shark offer some great sport on the light string in the middle of the night.

More Pier Fishing Tips

If live bait is available at your favorite pier or if you think you can catch your own, purchase a small battery-operated aerator. These miniature pumps run off of a D-size battery and clip onto the side of a plastic bucket. This little aerator can keep fragile anchovies alive for some time.

There are basically three ways to bring a large fish up from the pier. Probably the safest is to use a large hoop net on a rope lowered under the catch. The net is especially valuable if there is any question of a sub-legal ("short") fish on the end of the line: e.g. halibut, lingcod, white sea bass, barracuda.

Another approach would be to use a large pier gaff. This is nothing more than a mammoth-sized treble hook, weighted with lead, that is lowered down by a rope. I have personally witnessed 100 pound bat rays hoisted high up onto the pier with these menacing-looking gaffs.

A final option—which any dedicated shark hunter keeps open—is to literally walk your catch back towards the beach, get off the pier, and fight the brute from the sand. This is obviously the best way to go with 200+ pound sharks, initially hooked from the pier.

Since live chum is not available for pier anglers, how about some crushed bait? Step on some mussels, clams, barnacles, and the like and literally kick the mess over the side of the pier where you are fishing. Smaller species such as smelt, perch, and croakers will be attracted to this makeshift chum slick.

A question often asked is when to fish the piers. These structures are also governed by tidal flow. As with most inshore marine angling, the incoming tide is a premium period. If you are looking for solitude, pier fishing can definitely provide this in the chilly winter and early spring. Similarly, if you wait for the tourists and plank walkers to leave, both the later evening and pre-dawn hours in the summer will result in a fairly empty pier.

Novice pier fishermen also often miss the bet because they are not sure where to situate themselves, particularly in the longer structures leading out to sea. There are no hard and fast guidelines, but there are some rough rules of thumb which may help in fishing long coastal piers.

The end of this kind of pier typically attracts the larger game fish including calico bass, bonito, lings, barracuda, salmon, stripers, and halibut. Sharks also gravitate to this area since it has immediate access to open ocean which plays upon their roaming instincts.

Perch—rubberlip, walleye, striped, black, white piling, and redtail varieties—like the pier's midsection, where the pilings and barnacle growth is thickest. In the Northern areas, monkeyface eels and shallow water rockfish also look for sanctuary among the pilings.

Within the surfline, everyday residents such as corbina, barred perch, yellowfin and spotfin croaker, halibut, and smelt can be taken from the pier. Sand sharks, leopard sharks, guitarfish, skates, and rays will also scavenge near the breakers.

Summary

California's piers are one of the most relaxing places along the coastline to fish. Anglers on limited incomes or those with limited interest can find a diversity of activity off of these structures for a modest cost. Many longtime friendships are also cultivated as pier regulars meet and exchange stories over repeated outings.

As with any form of fishing, there will always be a small legion of anglers who excel at a particular facet of the sport. The same holds true for the pier fishing fraternity.

Consider trying some of the tips and secrets passed along in this chapter. Be experimental when working the piers. Fish that live "brown bait," try throwing artificial lures, and try new and unusual offerings. Game fish situated around this kind of structure become quite touchy after a period of angler pressure. Reach into that "bag of tricks," show them something different, and watch your pier catch improve!

Surfin' Safari: Fishin' California's Beaches

Of all the forms of saltwater angling that are available along the Golden Coast, surf fishing offers some of the best solitude, sport, and challenge. It takes some time to become an accomplished surf caster. There is a "science" to matching the right tackle to the prevailing conditions, selecting the right baits to use, and finding the right stretch of beach to fish.

Surf Casting Rods, Reels, and Lines

Traditionally speaking, most images of the lonely surf fishermen conjure up "old salts" chuckin' long 13 to 15 foot rods. To some degree, this depiction—as far as tackle is concerned—is not too far off base.

The surfline can be an extremely difficult environment to master. The crashing waves, tidal surge, ripping currents—and perhaps worst of all, drifting kelp—can really put the angler's expertise to the test. These conditions, combined with wind and spray, often necessitate using heavy-duty equipment in order to simply reach the fish and then to keep the bait fairly stationary when it gets there.

Surflines vary along the Pacific Coast. Sometimes there are only one or two major "rolls," along other stretches there could be six or more. These may vary with regard to beach topography (e.g. the presence of reefs or shelves, or with shifts in offshore swells and winds). Frequently, the surf fisherman has to make a long presentation, fighting coastal winds as they blow directly onto the beach.

With long 11 to 15 foot rods, distance casts are possible The lengthier rod, in conjunction with using the heavier sinkers for both distance and anchoring power, allows the adept surf fisherman to fire off 60 to 70 yard casts. It is not uncommon, especially the further north you go, to see anglers chuckin' 4 to 6 ounces of lead sinker with these long sticks. Keep in mind that the size of quarry may be 1 to 2 pound perch. So, the length and power generated from this kind of rod does not always correspond to the fighting ability or weight of the game fish. The big surf rod is simply needed to tame the conditions.

The longer rods also serve one other important requirement. They keep the monofilament line far above the churning waves and drifting kelp. An 11 to 15 foot surf stick keeps most of the line from slapping the water and hence from being subjected to the current and the tidal drift.

However, if you are not ready to splurge and purchase a rod with obviously very limited application, then review some of my recommendations in "The Basics" chapter. For a lot of water, particularly in the Southern sector where the surf is usually a little calmer, the 8 foot live bait rod used for party boating will do nicely. You can always purchase a long 3 to 5 foot tall "sand spike" (rod holder) to help elevate the shorter rod above the waves.

For anglers who prefer to be more mobile in working a beach (and I'll make a strong argument for this shortly) heavy freshwater or light saltwater outfits can be used in moderately calm conditions. Medium-weight spinners, smaller casting reels, and shorter spin or popping rods have gained in popularity among the surf casting fraternity in recent years. Many of the inshore species are found in less than 6 feet of water. Consequently, shorter casts with lighter gear can frequently be employed to take fish from the shallow surf zones.

Reels are somewhat less problematic for surf fishing. Many anglers prefer larger conventional models in the Penn Jigmaster, Squidder, or GS 535, 545, and 555 class. These heftier casting reels store plenty of big diameter line. But more importantly, as was noted in "The Basics" chapter, when it comes to handling large sinkers over long distances, the conventional reels will clearly outcast the spinning models.

There are times however, especially in windy weather, where a spinning reel will be more manageable. Numerous manufacturers such as Quantum, Penn, and Daiwa have models designed for rugged conditions like this. They will handle up to 25 pound test with fast gear ratios, and heavy-duty gearing. Check out the Penn 9500—perhaps the largest spinner in the world. You can fish over 300 yards of 30 pound test mono with the 9500. Its oversize drag is suitable for everything from 60 pound stripers to 150 pound striped marlin.

Some surf casters strongly believe that it is best to stay with either graphite or plastic-framed reels—spinning or conventional. They theorize that reels made from these materials, in contrast to those with metal casings, will last longer for their brand of fishing. It is certainly true that the salt spray and intermittent submerging of the reel can play havoc on the equipment in terms of corrosion. Still, if the tackle—both rods and reels—are washed down with fresh water at the end of the outing and re-lubricated in key external locations (e.g. line rollers), there is no

reason not to use metal-case reels under these circumstances. Make reel selections based on budget requirements, workmanship, ease-of-handling, and balance with your rod. Take that extra time to clean up your gear and it will last for many years.

Line requirements vary depending upon the surf conditions. A good all-around monofilament for surf casting is 25 pound test. Not that many anglers use 25 pound mono for offshore fishing. They usually purchase either 20 or 30 pound test. But I find that 25 pound string is a good compromise. You can fill most saltwater-sized spin reels up with about 200 yards of 25 pound mono, and conventional models with 250 yards. This diameter line is still small enough to maximize distance, yet thick enough to minimize excessive abrasion and breaking from rocks or kelp.

Other outfits can be spooled with anything from as small as 4 pound test with freshwater ultralight gear on up to 12 to 20 pound test with poppin' rods and live bait combos. Here again though, I want to emphasize the importance of buying premium grade mono. Surf fishing is comparatively inexpensive once you make the initial investment of a rod or reel. But this kind of angling can really tear up monofilament. Don't lose that big bull calico or halibut because your cheaper line frayed too easily on the rocky bottom!

More Surf Fishing Gear

As was noted, sand spikes can be an invaluable aid when using shorter rods. And some fishermen also have no interest in holding a heavy-duty surf outfit for hours at a time. The sand spike offers a respite from working with this magnum gear.

But also, sometimes it really helps to use two outfits simultaneously. The sand spike also helps here. Throw that 11 to 15 footer working beyond the shallow water. Certain species like calicos, cabezon, white sea bass, stripers, salmon, and shark feed in the deeper holes and ledges out some distance from the shore. Then, with your lighter rig, work the shallows for perch, smelt, croakers, corbina, and the like. Stay in proximity to your long-range outfit. If the big stick gets bit, quickly put your lightweight setup in the spike as you grab for the other rig.

This tactic—fishing two rods at the same time—really maximizes your chances on certain stretches of beach that are known to hold fish. However, if you have to prospect for productive water, you will have to outfit yourself for greater mobility. One of the most well-designed pieces of equipment you can own in this situation is the Berkley Fishing Partner. This nearly indestructible tackle box straps around the angler's waist. (It comes with its own interlocking web belt.) The larger model is deep enough to carry bait, hooks, sinkers, leaders, and lures while walking the beach. Everything you need for some serious surf fishing can be consolidated within this handy belly box. With a stringer tied to the web belt, there is no need to travel back and forth up to higher sand to either re-bait your hooks or stash away your catch.

Let's talk about stringers for a moment. Don't try to use that inexpensive model with the safety pin style clips that kept your trout or bass from getting away. These clips will thoroughly rust after one trip to the ocean. There are similar stringers made which feature stainless steel components. These are great, but costly. A better alternative is to use a stringer with hard nylon clips. These will hold 3 to 5 pound class fish and won't rust.

In Southern California, it is often possible to wade in your swimsuit while surf casting during the summer months. But overall, it would probably be wise to purchase a pair of hip boots or waders for the more frequent colder conditions.

Hip boots are fine if you rarely venture into the water. Some surf fishermen prefer to wade out further both when casting and playing the fish. In this situation, chest-high waders are essential.

Many anglers opt for the more traditional, heavy-weight rubberized nylon or canvas models. These are rather "clunky" but they offer a reasonable amount of insulation and protection. Another option is to buy a pair of the lighter stocking-foot waders. With these, the fisherman wears an old pair of tennis shoes outside the lightweight nylon footing. Even though the stocking-foot versions are chest-high, the surf caster could probably actually swim in them should he or she take an unexpected fall. This would be a tough and dangerous proposition with the heavier rubberized waders.

In either case, regardless of whether you select the rubberized or stocking-foot versions, take an old belt and buckle it around you chest. This little trick will help to keep water from quickly filling up the waders if you accidentally tumble into the surf. A more recent and considerably more expensive innovation is neoprene waders. This design is an offshoot of wet suit construction. The neoprene material is super light and warm. Swimming in an emergency is definitely possible with neoprene waders. An investment in these will escalate your start-up costs for some serious surf fishing, but the comfort may be worth it.

If you decide to fish from a stationary position off the beach, then take along a cutting board and inexpensive bait knife. Rock and bay mussels as well as Pismo clams can be pried open with the cheap blade. Chunks of anchovy along with fillets or strips of mackerel, bonito, grunion, sardine, herring, or innkeeper worms may also need to be cut.

If you decide to collect your own bait, then there are a few more accessories you will need to acquire. Sandcrabs can be scooped by hand, but a sandcrab trap is a lot more efficient. In the shallow water the angler can drag one of these traps through the sand looking for the crabs. The water and sand sift through the mesh wire leaving the crabs on the screen. These are sold at local bait shops.

If you want to dig your own Pismo clams, then you will need either a shovel, pitchfork, or better yet, a clam rake. This beats bending over constantly to poke through the sand with your hands.

Ghost shrimp and razor clams, as well as different varieties of worms can be dug up in the back bays and tidal sloughs. More sophisticated bait-diggers use suction pumps made from heavy PVC pipe. These pumps can cover a lot of territory quickly and really cut down on the labor of having to dig through the mud. Many bait shops stock them.

Finally, one piece of often overlooked equipment for a successful surfin' safari are polarized sunglasses. The polarized lenses reduce the glare, but also allow the angler to discover the "darker" water, signalling a hole or drop-off, or even schools of bait fish (more on this in a moment). This type of glass also makes it possible to literally see game fish in the water when they are up shallow. Corbina stalkers, in particular, will benefit from this feature.

Surf Baits

Chapter 3 gave a comprehensive breakdown of the assorted baits used for fishing the California Coast. Many of these such as anchovies, have a "crossover" element to them in that they can be used for both inshore and offshore species.

For purposes of clarity, here's a checklist of the major species of surf fish found along our beaches and the dominant baits used to catch them. A more detailed discussion of the actual techniques will follow later in this chapter.

Surf Sportfish	Sand Crabs	Bay Mussel	Rock Mussel	Pismo Clams	Razor Clams	Innkeeper Worms	Blood Worms	Pile Worms	Strip Mackerel	Strip Bonito	Squid	Anchovy	Smelt	Grunion	Ghust Shrimp
								Dominant Baits							
Perch	x	x	x	x	x	x	x	x	x	x		x			x
Corbine	x	x	x	x	x	x	x								x
Croakers	x	x	x	x	x	x	x								x
Halibut		x	x	x	x		x	x			x	x	x	x	x
Calico Bass											x	x	x	x	
Sand Bass				x	x						x	x	x	x	
Starry Flounder		x	x	x	x							x			
Cabezon											x				
White Sea Bass											x	x	x	x	
Striped Bass											x	x	x		
Sharks/Rays				x	x				x	x	x	x	x	x	x

Basic Terminal Rigs

Surf fishing along our coastline is not an overly complicated endeavor with regard to constructing the proper terminal rigs. There are basically three distinct setups that have great versatility for a variety of species when casting from the beach.

The Double Surf Leader: Far and away this commercially tied rig is the one that is most commonly used up and down the coast. This leader consists of a swivel at one end where you connect your main line coming off the reel. The other end has a snap-swivel. Open up the snap and clip it to the eye ring on the surf sinker. Between the two swivels, the leader has two pre-tied loops.

You can take separate lengths of monofilament and tie into the loops. Using two leaders like this, with two different hooks and baits, can add a lot of diversity to your presentation.

Another tip is to purchase pre-tied snelled hooks. You can simply run the snelled leaders through the surf leader loops, cinching them by creating a "hitch" without having to tie any further knots.

Double surf leaders come in a range of line tests. Lighter 10 pound mono is used for smaller species such as perch. The snap-swivels at the end of the 10 to 15 pound leaders are smaller to correspondingly match with lighter surf weights in the 1 to 2 ounce size. This is an important feature to consider. The weaker snaps will not withstand the shock that occurs in whipping out a 4 to 6 ounce sinker. You will have to scale up to the 20 pound surf leaders when using the heavier weights.

Also, don't shortchange your outing by using the "cheapie" snelled hooks. Both the hooks and the mono that these snells are tied with are typically poor quality. Stay with better grade snelled hooks in case you set-up on a real lunker from the surfline!

Three-Way Swivel Rig: This is a very simple setup to put together. Tie your line to a three-way swivel. On one of the remaining swivels, either hitch a snelled hook, or run your own custom length mono leader and tie your own hook. On the remaining swivel, run another length of leader—usually shorter than that for the hook—and tie your sinker to it. It is best to use a heavier test monofilament for the leader attached to the surf weight. In this

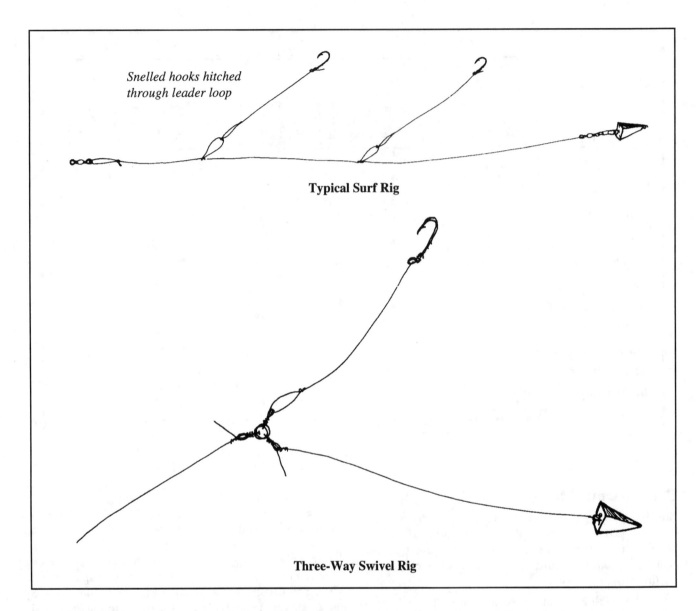

*Snelled hooks hitched
through leader loop*

Typical Surf Rig

Three-Way Swivel Rig

way, if the bait leader gets snagged on the bottom, you can still salvage the more costly sinker. The angler needs the lighter mono on the leader line with the hook to encourage strikes from spooky fish.

Sliding Sinker Rig: This is nothing more than a variation of the slider rig discussed for pier fishing. But, instead of using primarily a hollowed-out egg weight, any surf sinker with the brass eyelet will work.

Pass your line through the eyelet and tie it off to a snap-swivel. The weight will now butt up against the swivel, sliding no further down the line. Use fairly large hardware to keep the eyelet from sliding over the swivel.

Next, add your own length of leader line and hook or snap on a snelled hook. (In this situation, try to use snells with longer leaders so there is ample space between the sinker and the baited hook.) The slider rig works particularly well with touchy feeders.

Surf Sinkers

Selecting the proper surf sinker is an integral facet of the sport that is often overlooked by the novice fisherman. Sinker choice depends in part upon the angler's assessment of the prevailing conditions. The sinkers are molded into different shapes for specific reasons. Here is a breakdown of styles commonly used along the coast.

1. Spoon: The flat-sided spoon sinker is designed for smooth sandy bottoms. It allows the bait to drift along with the tidal surge.

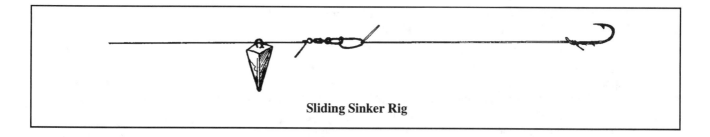

Sliding Sinker Rig

2. Pyramid: This sinker provides excellent anchoring along sandy bottoms. When it lands, the pointed end of the weight impacts itself into the sand. The pyramid design is suitable for fishing a more stationary bait.

3. Bulldozer: Along more broken up or hardened bottoms, the bulldozer sinker plows into the terrain. It provides a degree of anchoring or slow-drifting.

4. Claw: The claw, a distinctively shaped weight used to drag the bait slowly along a sandy bottom, can be used in place of a spoon sinker when the current is rough or fast moving.

5. Dollar: A popular variation on the flat spoon sinker, the dollar weight is more rounded and thicker. It too, is used for slow movement in faster water.

6. Torpedo: Use this slender-shaped sinker for sliding through broken rocks and kelp-laden bottoms.

Two other surf sinkers have become legendary over the years, but seem to appear less frequently on the beach as the sport becomes more sophisticated. Old automobile spark plugs can still be used for weights. They approximate pyramid sinkers in terms of anchoring ability and are somewhere in the 2 to 4 ounce range.

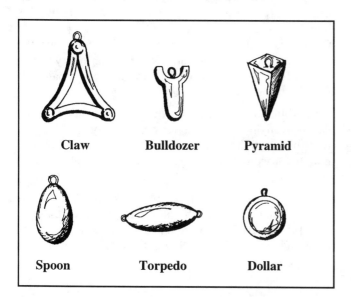

| Claw | Bulldozer | Pyramid |

| Spoon | Torpedo | Dollar |

The other "legend" is constructed by taking an empty cloth bag that Bull Durham smoking tobacco comes in. (This is the stuff for those who prefer to "roll their own.") Fill this tiny bag with sand, tie it off, and you have an excellent sinker for fishing among the rocks.

Reading the Water

It is critical to learn to "read" the water when surf fishing. To the beginning angler looking both directions down the beach, the water "all looks the same." There are, however, some subtle variables to consider that can be assessed by using your polarized glasses.

Look for the darker water. This indicates a ledge or shelf, or deep hole. Pockets of deeper water will also be evident along the surfline as characteristic "flat" spots with active wave action adjacent to this calmer water. These are good locations for all sorts of game fish to congregate because bait gets trapped inside these troughs.

Next, look for stretches of beach which slope dramatically more than the other portions of shoreline. These areas can serve as prime feeding inclines for marauding surf fish.

If you monitor the way in which waves break, you can often decipher where the reefs are—if any—along a particular beach. Bigger game fish and rockfish species will feed along these rocky reefs. The waves seem to be shallower, yet more extended as they break over a reef in contrast to flat sandy stretches.

When feasible, try to make casts to any rocky outcroppings near the surfline. These "boilers" provide additional sanctuary for numerous surf fish.

Finally, if time permits study the beach at low tide. This little ploy can help you to discover where some of the key rocks, pockets, reefs, or ledges lie. Many of these structures are submerged at high tide.

Once you have a good feel for the area you think should be holding fish, consider whether to work it from a stationary or more mobile attack. As I noted, some of the larger game fish like bull calicos, cabezon, lings, or white sea bass hold up in small pockets or along a certain reef. It is probably best to work this narrow band of water thoroughly when looking for these larger trophies.

Other species such as perch, corbina, croaker, surf smelt, and even halibut and stripers seem more transitory in their movement along the surfline. In this situation, it might pay to move along the beach trying to intercept any of these shallow feeders. I term this "controlled bait soakin'." In contrast to more conventional "still fishing," you will be able to cover a lot more territory hunting for aggressive feeding fish.

Now that you are properly outfitted and have learned to read the water, let's focus more precisely on the different techniques used to catch the primary surf fishes of California.

Perch

There are 21 different species of perch off the California Coast. Most can be caught from the surf. The dominance of one variety over the others is clearly apparent as we travel from South to North. For instance, in the Southland, the barred surfperch is numero uno. In Northern California all the way to Eureka, it's the redtail.

Surfperch are the most prolific of all the types of fish within a cast from the beach. An extensive collection of baits work for surfperch. Sand crabs—both hard and soft shell—mussels, clams, assorted worms, and chunks of anchovies produce consistently. Don't underestimate strip baits, especially for the larger spawners. Small strips of mackerel and bonito are dynamite at times for these bigger perch. In a pinch, here's another tip: strip-fillet a smaller perch and use it for bait. Sometimes the jumbo perch will strike this over all other baits.

Keep your hooks and leaders on the lighter side for surfperch. Smaller #2 to #6 baitholders on 6 to 12 pound leaders are best. Any of the major terminal rigs will work fine.

Another key point: too often anglers make the mistake of persisting in fishing surfperch deep. A certain number of these fish can be caught in the 4 to 6 foot range. Don't be surprised if your catch improves as you survey the knee-deep water on the incoming tide.

Surfperch will also strike artificial lures. This is one of my favorite forms of surf casting during the winter spawning runs of these fish. Small, brightly colored trout spinners such as the Bang Tail, Shyster, Mepps Lightning, or Rooster Tail can be fished on light 4 to 8 pound mono in the shallow water. Use spinners with yellow, red, orange, or white feathers.

Tiny curl-tail grubs such as the Scrounger and the Haddock Grub can really put a dent into the perch population when the shallow bite is "wide open." Silver and lime green are especially effective with the curl-tail grubs, teamed with a 1/8 ounce jighead.

Try fishing a motor oil colored Berkley Power Grub on a sliding egg sinker setup. Run 6 pound test monofilament through a 1/8 to 1/2 ounce egg sinker and tie off to a snap swivel. Then tie on 18 to 30 inches of 6 pound leader, with a Power Grub laced onto a long-shank #181 size 6-1/0 baitholder hook. This combo nails a lot of perch, croaker, and corbina found in the shallow surf lines. A recent "hot" tip has been to also work the surf lines with a 1/8 ounce darter head jig teamed with a motor oil, 3-4 inch grub or a miniature A.A. Worms swimbait.

Wobbling spoons such as the Kastmaster, Hot Shot, Krocadile, or Haddock Structure Spoon in 3/8 to 5/8 ounces also take surfperch. These lures can be exceptionally potent when the fish are feeding out in the deeper water. Cast the spoon out, let it flutter to the bottom, and then slowly retrieve it in through the waves.

I have caught numerous surfperch on these various lures and I am still amazed at how hard they strike the hardware. On light freshwater tackle, these fish are incredibly strong battlers and the larger fish seem to zero in on the lures!

Corbina

These are without question one of the more challenging species to master from the beach. These members of the croaker family are shallow water denizens. This is an important feature to keep in mind for understanding this bite. The corbina are highly hook shy and very skittish. Quite frequently, you can make visual contact with the fish in less than a foot of water. In this situation try to cast 5 to 15 feet to either side of the corbina. Let the bait drift into the trough where they are working.

Corbina are primarily a South Coast resident. They can be caught all season long with July and August recognized as the prime months. They average 1 to 3 pounds in weight with a 5 pounder assuming "lunker" status.

It is estimated that 50% of the corbina's diet is comprised of sand crabs. Obviously, for this reason they are your primary baits for these fish. Corbina will also strike strips of innkeeper worms, mussels, and ghost shrimp. As with perch, keep your tackle scaled down with these spooky fish.

Some Southlanders armed only with light spinning outfits and 6 pound mono have been racking up impressive catches of this otherwise tough-to-catch surf dweller. The trick is to "split-shot" the corbina.

Take a small lead shot and crimp it 18 to 30 inches above the end of 6 pound mono. Tie on a #4 to #8 bronze baitholder hook, preferably with a ghost shrimp or soft-shell crab. Make a delicate lob cast toward the feeding fish and hold on when they decide to eat the bait. Corbina can make some rather exciting runs on the light string in the shallow water!

Croakers

Yellowfin croaker and its larger cousin, the spotfin, are prized catches in the surf fisherman's bounty. They are excellent eating and tough fighters as well. These fish are also inclined to be found in warmer water. The yellowfin averages 1 to 2 pounds, the spotfins are somewhat larger. "Spots" pushing the 7 to 8 pound mark are a reality for the knowledgeable surf caster.

Behaviorally speaking, these croakers are similar to the corbina, but perhaps not as spooky. They prefer the shallower 2 to 3 foot water. Favorite baits include ghost shrimp, bloodworms, sand crabs, and mussels. General surf rigs and baitholder hooks perform quite well on either the yellowfin or spotfin croaker.

Halibut

Only a small number of California anglers actively seek halibut from the surfline. These are tough fish to find and they put up a hearty battle when dragged through the waves.

Halibut prefer sandy bottoms. They eat most bait fish offerings either whole or halved—anchovies, smelt, sardines, herring, or grunion. They can also be taken on rock or bay mussels, and bloodworms, as well as Pismo or razor clams. But day in and day out, the bait fish mentioned are your best bets.

I use a sliding rig for halibut. These fish are toothy critters, but seem to have an uncanny way of "mouthing" the bait. I like them to feel as little resistance as possible when they start picking at the bait, hence the slider setup.

But, don't underestimate using lures on these larger flatfish. Chrome spoons, in particular, often produce some stellar catches, sometimes striking right at your feet at the end of the retrieve! Halibut are a lot more aggressive and mobile than fishermen give them credit for being. They will quickly swim and pounce on a spoon

fished through the surf if you retrieve it along the sandy bottom.

Calicos and Sandies

One of the most exciting adventures surf fishermen can have is to fish these bass at night from Santa Barbara south to the Mexican border. Normally calico and sand bass are offshore feeders. However, at night it is not uncommon to find them within the surfline, primarily in water with reefs, rocks, and kelp.

Heavy gear is needed to work for these fish. Big "grumper" sandies to 8 pounds and "bull" calicos up to 10 pounds are a strong reality from a moonlit beach. A full moon is indeed one of the best times to take a shot at these nocturnal bass.

Long 11 to 15 foot rods, 25 to 30 pound monofilament, and either conventional or super strong spinning reels are in order. I recommend using anywhere from a 4 to 6 ounce torpedo sinker for sliding through this rough terrain. Both three-way swivel and slider combinations will work. Hooks must be extra sharp and top-quality baitholders. A 5 to 10 pound fish exerts awesome leverage against the angler and his equipment when fought through the surf.

Whole squid, anchovies, smelt, or sardines catch surf-bound calico or sand bass. The hot combination however, is frozen grunion. You have to catch your own grunion during one of the legally scheduled runs. They are not sold commercially. Freeze the bait fish down until your next bassin' trip. Use it either whole or halved with a #4/0 baitholder hook.

Calicos and to a greater degree, sandies, occasionally show up during the daylight hours around beaches with kelp beds nearby. The same baits used for the night-bite will produce with limited results.

Another option is to cast single-tail A.A. Worms Monarchs and Berkley Power Grubs or Berkley Power Minnows and Lunker Thumpers and retrieve them through the kelp back to the beach. Root beer, lime, black, and chartreuse flake colors seem to fish best. Dawn and twilight are good times to try the plastics on both the calicos and sandies.

Starry Flounder

This smaller flat fish will readily take petite offerings such as clams, mussels, and pieces of 'chovies. Lighter leaders and smaller #4 to #6 hooks will improve your success. Almost any terminal rig will suffice.

Cabezon

These rockfish can be taken shallow, primarily during the winter, all along the coast from Malib and north. "Cabs" are usually taken as incidental catches by anglers fishing for bass, halibut, or shark. Usually they will be lurking some distance from the bank in the kelp and rocks. They have unusual blue flesh but don't let that throw you; they make great eating and the flesh turns white when cooked.

Slider and three-way swivel rigs work best. Use large #2/0 to #4/0 baitholder hooks on 20+ pound test leaders. These fish are like bulldogs and they head right back into the rocks after they are hooked. You only need one primary bait for cabezon—frozen squid. Use tackle similar to that described for calico and sand bass. A 3 to 4 pound "cab" puts up a voracious fight when hauled in through the surf!

White Sea Bass

"Whites" are always "front page news" when an angler takes one off the beach. These giant croaker cruise the surfline along warmer stretches. There can be anywhere from 5 to 30 pounders that can be found close to the bank like this.

It's time to bring out the "artillery" if you're planning on catching white seabass from the surf: powerful rods, 25 to 30 pound test line, heavy-duty conventional reels, 4 to 6 ounces of lead, and big baits. Three-way swivel or slider rigs are fine. Only make sure that your leaders are at least 20 pound test. Whole frozen squid or grunion are preferred offerings.

Look for sandy beaches with deeper holes or shallow scattered rocks. Be prepared to follow these fish some distance down the beach. A white seabass from the surf is a true trophy for any dedicated surf fisherman!

Striped Bass

North Coasters value a striper caught through the waves in the way Southlanders revere a big calico or white taken from the beach.

Surf casters in the North use medium to heavy rods and reels looking for schools of stripers boiling in the surf. Some veteran striper snipers prefer a 10 foot surf rod for casting out to schooling fish. They feel that the shorter rod gives them greater accuracy than a longer 11 to 15 footer for pinpoint casting to schools working close to the beach. Better quality spinners or conventional reels are

necessary to withstand the rigors of constant casting for these cruising fish.

One key to locating stripers in the surf is to look for feeding birds. The birds flock to the anchovies below in the surf. The stripers are usually nearby, pushing the bait to the surface. But, you may have to start your hunt early. If there is a lot of bait around, the birds will quickly gorge themselves and then stop "picking" and return to the beach. Your hunt then becomes a more or less random affair, without the assistance of the birds to locate the school.

Here is another tip worth noting: look for black masses of shallow inshore water. This often signals a huge concentration of 'chovies balled up tight. There is an excellent chance that the stripers are underneath herding the bait into these "meatballs."

The stripers can be taken on fresh or dead 'chovies with traditional surf rigs. However, better action can often be found using lures. This is definitely true if the fish have an abundance of bait to feed upon. An artificial lure has a way of standing apart from all the routine natural baits the stripers can eat. So, as is often the case with game fish, a well-presented lure can raise the interest level, arouse curiosity, and stimulate some strikes from otherwise well-fed fish.

Some of the bona fide winning striper lures include the Kastmaster, Mikey Mouse, Krocadile, Hopkins spoon, Keel Squid, and Hair Raiser Jigs. Pencil Poppers, Mikey Minnows, Wind Cheaters, Scooters, and Dashers also produce, especially on a sustained surface bite.

Northern striper specialists state that the primo territory for stalking these brutes from the shore is from Baker's Beach south to Linda Mar Beach. Pacifica is often heralded as the striper beach for this kind of surf casting. Both sandy and rocky stretches harbor these prize game fish. July and August are considered to be the best months for surf-bound striper action. With this type of surf casting, it pays to visit local bait shops to inquire as to which lures in particular have been effective in recent days.

Sharks and Rays

Almost any bait can inadvertently nail a shark or ray in the surf. Smaller shovelnose and thornback sharks, along with dogfish sharks, will readily chomp on frozen 'chovies, ghost shrimp, and bay mussels. If you want some real excitement, fish these sharks with 6 pound mono on a freshwater spinning outfit in the shallow surf lines.

Still, if you want to concentrate on the bigger members of this class of fish—the 10 to 20 pound leopard sharks or the bat rays—then definitely bait with whole frozen squid or large mackerel or bonito strips.

Stout rods, heavier line, 20 to 40 pound leaders and bigger #4/0-#10/0 hooks are the tools of the serious shark hunter. Use either Eagle Claw #181 long-shank baitholder or #197 circle hooks for these smaller, in-shore sharks. I prefer a slider rig because I want plenty of space between the hooked fish and the remaining hardware—the swivel and sinker.

Leopards or double-digit weight bat rays caught from the surf, and more so at night, can put up quite a tussel with their twisting, head-shakin' actions. Remember, these are genuine members of the shark family and they should be handled with some care!

Summary

Surf fishing along the California Coast can be an amazing adventure, often producing some truly phenomenal catches. There is a lot to be said about the beauty and solitude of fishing from a desolate beach. But always keep in mind that the ocean can be a very fickle friend. Marine weather and tidal conditions can dramatically change in a short period of time. Always be on the lookout for danger and potential hazards, particularly when wading out into the surf.

Take your time in playing out surf fish. Maintain constant pressure and a tight line but remember you have the surge and undertow working against you. Many novice surf casters lose that prize trophy by trying to "horse" the fish in while fighting the surf. Learn to time your retrieve with the waves. As the wave breaks, let the fish glide in toward shore. Quickly wind the slack and allow the fish to fight the drag when the waves recede back out. Start the process all over again until you finally beach your fish. When appropriate, think lighter leaders and presentations to shallow water. Don't get caught up in the trap of thinking that the only way to get bit is to cast as far as you can. Sometimes distance is important in the surf fishing game—but not always.

Finally, learn to monitor the tides. Purchase an economical little tide table book at your local bait shop. Key in on the incoming and outgoing tides. This is when an exchange of water is greatest, with increased food being washed through the waves, generating increased feeding activity. Also, keep a log as to which tidal conditions produce the best result for certain species of surf fish.

Rock and Breakwater Fishin': Jetty Jockeys and Wall Bangers

The Pacific Coastline from San Diego to the Canadian border is dotted with numerous jetties and rocky outcroppings. These structures provide sanctuary for a wealth of inshore marine species, ranging from bonito, barracuda, halibut, and calico bass in the Southland to lingcod, salmon, and a myriad of rockfish in the North. In addition, sharks, rays, flatfish, and even eels can spice up the menu of fish taken from the coastal rocks.

Rock hoppers and jetty jockeys are a rare breed of saltwater fishermen. Quite frequently this type of angling requires considerable physical fortitude to withstand the elements. Steep rocks, slippery concrete, crashing waves, and offshore swells can add both to the adventure and to the danger of this type of fishing.

Although the species of game fish may vary by location, there are some fundamental guidelines to observe if you want to give this style of shallow water ocean fishing a try. In this chapter, I will explain how to get started in fishing rocks and jetties, with a particular focus on the tackle and baits used.

Rods and Reels

There is probably no single rod and reel combo that will universally suffice for fishing up and down the entire coastline, but there are a variety of options to consider. To begin with, many recreational anglers feel most comfortable using open-face spinning reels. These reels are relatively easy to operate. They are excellent for casting baits into the wind without the annoying back-lash that can occur with casting reels.

The spinner should hold about 200 to 250 yards of 20 pound test monofilament. Here again, I recommend purchasing a brand name quality reel, preferably with a ball-bearing drive. Tackle for this style of fishing can really take a beating being constantly exposed to sand, salt spray, and accidental dropping. The 20 pound test line also gives the angler some edge in "horsing out" larger, unexpected catches from the rocks and kelp.

A two-piece 8 to 9 foot fiberglass medium-action spinning rod matches well with the medium to heavy saltwater spinning reel. This combination is suitable for casting both lures and baits. It should have enough "beef" to handle a good sized lingcod or a "bull" calico bass.

However, if longer casts are needed, or if heavier monofilament is necessary to pry the fish out of those shallow haunts, then a standard saltwater baitcasting reel should be considered. Any of the medium-sized conventional reels that hold 200 to 300 yards of 20 pound test will perform quite well.

Most rock hoppers or jetty jockeys prefer to stay with a spinning rod when using the saltwater casting reel. In this way they can switch back and forth from spinning to baitcasting reels without changing rods, depending upon tidal conditions and the size of the quarry.

It is not necessary to invest in magnum-sized 11 to 14 foot surf rods for fishing these rock piles and jetties. Super long casts are usually not that critical, since many species are located in close proximity to the structure. Here too, that 8 to 9 foot fiberglass spinning rod will handle a wide range of rock and breakwall fishing.

Terminal Gear

Depending upon the terrain, it helps to be somewhat mobile in fishing these rocks. Many of the best angling opportunities are situated where the tidal conditions are most turbulent. This includes scattered boulders that lie adjacent to deeper water and the end portions of jetties or breakwalls. Game fish gravitate to these areas since tidal currents often wash natural baits into these pockets. However, wave action can become outright dangerous at times, requiring sure footing and the ability to quickly scramble for high ground when the surge is powerful. Thus, it is probably best to keep your tackle simple and compact in case you have to "evacuate" your prime spot in seconds.

Rock and jetty angling doesn't require an extensive repertoire of hooks, sinkers, baits, and lures as does offshore party boat fishing. You won't need that cumbersome five drawer wooden tackle box for rock hopping or working the jetties. Some rock fishermen prefer to carry most of their gear on their backs in sturdy nylon knapsacks. This allows them to keep both hands free in case they need to brace themselves or maneuver among the boulders. Another possibility is to use one of those lightweight "belly boxes" I mentioned earlier which strap around the waist such as Berkley's Fishing Partner. Most rock hoppers still prefer a gunny sack wetted down to store their fish. The sack can be stuffed into a backpack

or placed on the beach for even better security from the waves.

Jetty jockeys can often be seen carrying the ubiquitous 5 gallon bucket. Terminal rigs, bait, lunch, and the day's catch can be transported in one of those recycled plastic containers. Also, should a rogue wave inadvertently crash over the jetty and wash your bucket out to sea, your loss will be minimal and easily replaced.

As for hooks and sinkers, sizes and styles vary up and down the coast. Local bait stores are excellent places to inquire as to the best type of hook and weight and shape of sinker to use in your area. However, there are a couple of general points worth mentioning.

First, many novice rock fishermen are inclined to use sinkers that are much too heavy for working the shallower water. A lighter weight sinker will get hung up less in the rocks and permits the bait to move about more freely in the current or wave wash.

Second, beginners also have a tendency to select hooks that are too large for smaller species and conversely, too small for larger game fish. It is practically impossible to use one single size hook for all the species in one area. For example, a smaller #6 to #8 baitholder hook would be appropriate in fishing mussels for perch off the jetty. But, switch to a larger #4/0 heavy-duty forged hook when tossing out a whole frozen squid for bass or sharks. Try to be precise in selecting the proper hooks and weights. Gear up for the prevailing conditions and the species you are seeking.

Finally, a recent trend has been to use some type of float or bobber as part of your terminal system. Popping corks have been widely used for a long time in the Gulf States of the South. Now, Pacific Coast anglers are finding some important uses for these floats. The West Coast "Bonito Splasher" will definitely work off these jetties in warmer coastal waters.

If you decide to use a wooden dowel or Casta Bubble it will be considerably heavier than a traditional popping cork. They are used to make long casts off the jetties or breakwalls. By "jerking" or "popping" the rig, the commotion generated from the splasher attracts marauding schools of bonito to strike the feather, as I have noted, off the piers. The small tuna are terrific fighters, especially from off the rocks. Medium-sized 8 to 9 foot spinning rods are commonly used with these West Coast splashers while walking the rocky jetties.

But, floats can also be utilized for baitfishing along the rocks. Baits can be suspended above the boulders, jetties, or breakwalls by using a bobber. Similarly, a plastic float fished on the edge of a kelp bed outside the rock piles can be deadly on cruising kelp fish. Usually it is still necessary to pinch a lead shot about midway between the float and the hook. This will keep the bait in the strike zone longer so that the bobber won't drift into the rocks too quickly.

Typical Baits

There is a virtual shopping list of live and cut baits that can be used for Western rock hopping or jetty fishing. Some have a general appeal all along the coast while others are more restricted to a specific area or game fish species. Here is a brief rundown of some of the routine offerings used by West Coast anglers fishing the rocks.

Shellfish are probably the most commonly used bait. Rock and bay mussels as well as pismo and razor clams will take a major portion of the diverse rockfish and perch found near the shore. Members of the flounder family including both turbot and California halibut will also strike the meatier portion of shellfish. Always try to use fresh shellfish when possible. Fresh stock will usually outfish frozen mussels or clams. Most of these popular mollusks are sold at local bait shops or they may be gathered by hand. Mussels can be pried from the rocks or pier pilings. Pismo clams can be dug in the surf at low tide and razors are usually found in the mud in the back bays.

Live saltwater crayfish or "ghost shrimp" are another hot bait along with large grass shrimp found in the North Coastal areas. Ghost shrimp can be fished whole, threaded onto a long shank baitholder hook. Grass shrimp can be cut into smaller sections for the inshore species. Commercially packaged frozen shrimp sold at your local supermarket will also suffice, when the fresh varieties are hard to find. An interesting recent finding is that many of the fish that live around these rocky structures will also eagerly strike freshwater crawdads. These should be hooked between the nose plate with a #6-#1/0 baitholder hook.

Assorted saltwater worms are another favorite, especially for the Western jetty jockeys. Bloodworms and piling worms are great for both rockfish, flatfish, and numerous kinds of perch. It is usually best to cut these worms into compact portions, particularly when fishing for the smaller marine species. On this note, greater catches and less bait-stealing will result when working the rocks by using a modest portion of bait meticulously threaded onto the hook.

Occasional bait dealers sell live bait fish such as anchovies or mudsuckers for fishing the jetties and breakwalls. These can be kept alive in bait buckets for a limited time. Veteran rock fishermen use small battery-operated aerators that clip onto the lip of the bucket to increase the longevity of these baits.

Frozen anchovies, sardines, smelt, or squid are also integral offerings for the West Coast rock hopper or jetty jockey. Again, depending upon the size of the fish you are seeking, these baits can be presented either whole or in cut portions. Sharks, eels, calico bass, halibut, lings, cabezon, and even sheephead will pounce on one of these larger offerings fished whole. Sometimes it helps to run a knife partially through one half section of an anchovy or sardine. Carefully slice about three quarters of the way through the bait fish chunk. Put the hook through the unsliced meatier section. This little filleting trick makes the two lateral sides of the frozen chunk wave back and forth in scissor-like fashion in the water. This gives the bait the appearance of a live, fluttering bait fish.

One other rather esoteric bait is also worth carrying if you venture along the Southern California Coast. Local anglers have found that opaleye—a member of the half-moon family of fish—are vegetarian by nature. These tough saltwater panfish will strike frozen peas threaded on a baitholder hook. Jetty jockeys in the Southland will attest that a 1 to 2 pound opaleye caught off the rocks is a phenomenally tough scrapper.

Artificial Lures

Anglers fishing the rocky areas along the West Coast are somewhat remiss in not using artificial lures more often. As was mentioned, bonito can be caught throughout the year casting out splashers and feathers to deeper water. But barracuda, calico and sand bass, lingcod and larger members of the rockfish group as well as exotic needle-fish will also strike a well-presented lure.

Shiny spoons such as the Krocadile, Hopkins, and Haddock Jig'n Spoon will catch these species off the rocks. Try throwing candy bar style jigs in smaller sizes made by Tady, Jerry Jigs, Salas, and Ironman to nail many of these inshore species casted from the rock walls. Chrome, blue and white, or green and yellow combinations are the standard colors to try.

One of my favorite lures for this type of fishing is a #11 Countdown Rapala Minnow in blue and silver patterns. Using medium freshwater spinning tackle, I have caught numerous game fish off the rocks cranking this balsa wood plug a few feet below the surface. However, be prepared to replace the bronze treble hooks on a regular basis since they corrode quickly.

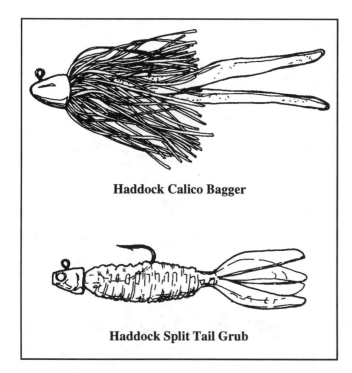

Haddock Calico Bagger

Haddock Split Tail Grub

Soft plastic baits with swimming tail actions are perhaps the most versatile lures you can use. They can be casted a modest distance with the medium saltwater gear, and further with heavy freshwater outfits. Haddock's Kreepy Krawler and Lunker Thumper, the Mojo, or Scampi have seductive, fluttering plastic tails. Laced onto a 1/4 to 1 ounce jig head, these plastic baits can be deadly fished from the rocks or jetties. Historically, root beer flake, chartreuse, pink, lime, and silver flake color schemes have been the most productive patterns with these lures fished in this type of terrain. A variety of species will hit these slow-swimming baits. And, again, at night consider tossing Berkley Power Grubs or Power swimbaits with the built-in fish attractant.

A Year 'Round Fishery

The rocky outcroppings that are found along this Pacific shoreline hold fish all year long. This includes the more pelagic species such as bonito, barracuda, and calico bass. Try to be versatile in working the rocks. Experiment with different baits and terminal rigs. Don't overlook the potential of artificial lures.

When possible, monitor the tide. Some species bite best on either an incoming or outgoing tide. Similarly, some fish are more commonly found on the calm harbor side of a jetty while others seem to prefer the more turbulent rocks facing the open ocean.

Above all be careful! This type of fishing can be exciting with the potpourri of fish available for the accomplished angler. But, never take the sea for granted. Calm waters can quickly turn treacherous with changing weather. When possible, try to fish the rocks with a fellow enthusiast. The buddy system is extra insurance that help is near if the wave and weather conditions unexpectedly take a change for the worse.

Fishing "Walls" at Night

Did you ever consider fishing for calico and sand bass at night? This is, without a doubt, one of the more interesting and challenging varieties of marine angling found in the Golden State. Bob Suekawa is a long time local manufacturer of the popular line of Haddock lures. He has been fishing these expansive rocky structures in Southern California for over 20 years. He is considered to be an authority on challenging these offshore jetties in the middle of the night.

The Long Beach Federal Breakwater, Marina del Rey Wall, and the Santa Monica rocks are examples of distinct rocky jetties, each separated by a channel leading to the open sea. Local anglers collectively refer to structures like these as "Walls." They are located within 1 1/2 miles from the shore and are accessible by private boat from a variety of small craft harbors.

Most anglers visiting the various Walls are recreational fishermen who work them primarily in daylight hours. There can be a modest bite on perch, halibut, rockfish, and a few scattered sand bass, as well as the occasional bonito or barracuda. However, the real secret is to fish the Walls after dark.

By sunset, pleasure boat traffic has dwindled down completely. Winds have usually subsided and the water surrounding the jetties can assume an eerie calm. This time of day calico bass are the prime targets of veteran Wall fishermen. These are very tough fighters, sometimes reaching weights over 10 pounds. A 5 pounder caught off the breakwater is a true trophy.

Many Wall regulars feel that both calicos and sand bass put on a stronger fight in the darkness and along the breakwaters than when caught in the offshore ocean waters. Locals theorize that some of the calicos, in particular, become "home-guard" fish, living only in the sanctuary of the rocky crevices. The growth of calico bass is very slow compared to other pelagic species of saltwater game fish, so calicos over 7 to 8 pounds have

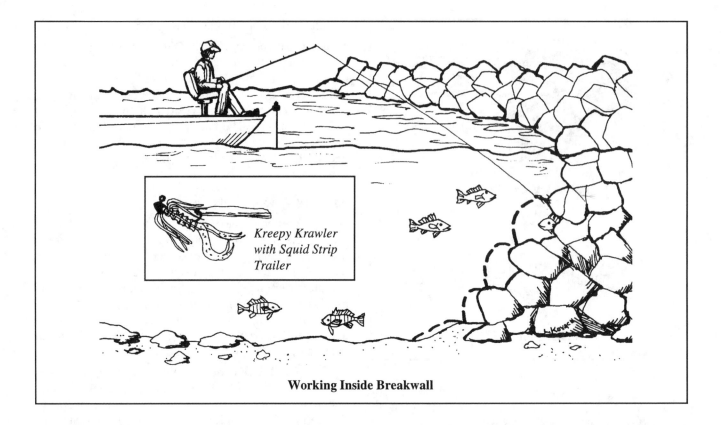

*Kreepy Krawler
with Squid Strip
Trailer*

Working Inside Breakwall

saltwater game fish, so calicos over 7 to 8 pounds have probably lived along the Walls for over 10 years. They are wary and very smart, but they are also nocturnal feeders, giving the "hawg hunters" a better shot at the bigger specimens.

Wall fishermen have the choice of sampling either the "inside" or the "outside" of a Wall. The inside waters are calmer, with the wave and surge action broken by the shelter of the rocky Walls. Many anglers fishing out of small aluminum or fiberglass boats feel safest working the "inside." On the other hand, the "outside" may hold the bigger fish. There is less fishing pressure on the outside, plus there is more food washed off the rocks into the foam by the pounding of the waves. But, it is clearly more dangerous.

Most Wall fishermen rely upon electric trolling motors to keep moving along the jetty, casting to the rocks, and retrieving the bait back to the boat. Suekawa points out one very interesting feature about fishing a Wall. He notes that often you can motor and cast down one side without any strikes. Then, all of a sudden, you can reverse and work your way back along the same stretch and the action becomes "wide open." He speculates that even the slightest change in tidal flow can activate the bite like an "On-Off" switch. The best activity seems to occur with a full moon, prominent current, and at the height of the solunar tables.

The large rock slabs and boulders that comprise the breakwalls actually extend out some distance under the water in a staircase-like fashion. The calicos are typically found up tight in the broken rocks and will often attack the lure the instant it hits the water. In contrast, the sand bass seem to congregate just at the edge where the rocks meet the hard-packed, sandy bottom. It is important to work your lures all the way down the incline of the Wall, checking for calicos against the rocks, and sandies out in deeper water all the way out to the boat.

Interestingly, on some super calm evenings, you can actually employ a saltwater version of the flippin' method used by freshwater bass fishermen to fish shallow areas. Using longer 7 1/2 to 8 foot rods, motor carefully on the inside of the Wall just to the edge of the submerged boulders. Believe it or not, you can gently pitch or flip lures in an almost vertical presentation directly into the rocks. Without substantial tidal surge, the calicos in particular will root right into the boulders. The vertical flippin' technique puts the jig straight down into the cracks and holes where the bigger fish live. Be prepared for a jolting strike and swing hard!

As for the proper tackle for this type of moonlight safari, stout rods and baitcasting reels are a must. Heavy duty freshwater bassin' gear is usually adequate. Strong graphite or fiberglass rods in 6 to 7 1/2 foot lengths are ample for making the 50 to 60 foot long casts to the rocks. Baitcasting reels spooled with 15 to 20 pound monofilament are matched with these stronger rods. Casting reels with some type of magnetic breaking system can be a real boon for this type of night fishing. Turn the anti-inertia setting up a little higher than normal to minimize the chance of bothersome backlash in the dark.

Drags are usually locked down fairly tight. You don't want to have these fish, calicos in particular, to run back into the sharp rocks. Be prepared to lose a lot of lures over the course of an evening's fishing. Invariably even the heavier monofilament will become frayed and nicked from contact with the rocks. You should recurrently check the last 18 inches of line and re-tie as necessary.

Also, many anglers have some initial problem with night vision and depth perception when fishing Walls. It may take some practice to consistently make a cast that will land tight up against the rocks without overshooting and embedding the lure into the boulders.

In addition, you can't let the bait sink too far. As with freshwater bassin', the Wall fisherman will have to develop a sensitive feel that allows him to either "hop" the lure over or to "swim" it just above the rocks. Try to maintain a moderately tight line to get a good strong hook-set on these tough saltwater bass.

Both species—calicos and sand bass alike—are very tenacious fish. The strike can be very vicious. However, once hooked near the Walls, count on these bass to make a beeline right back to the boulders. Hence, it's important to keep steady pressure on the fish, heading them away from the rocks.

Most seasoned breakwater fishermen use artificial lures in stalking nighttime sandies and calicos. Plastic baits are overwhelmingly the choice of locals who fish these rocks. Popular swimming lures such as the Scampi, Salty Magic, Berkley Power Grubs and Power swimbaits, Mojo, Lunker Thumper, Fish Traps, and A.A. Worms Shad Tail produce quite well. Preferred colors include the basic root beer flake, lime, hot pink, and smoke. Perhaps the single hottest color to hit the scene since rootbeer/flake is tomato/pepper. This is a killer shade on the breakwalls. Twin T's made a lure years ago called the Lunker Legs that also excels as a swimming bait if you can find any on some dusty shelf.

More conventional freshwater bass lures also take their share of these nocturnal feeders. The Haddock

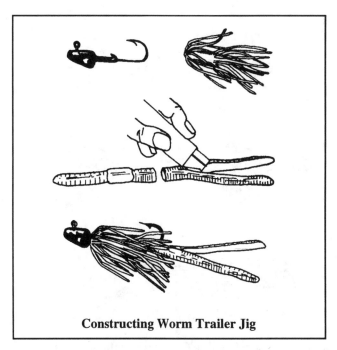

Constructing Worm Trailer Jig

Kreepy Krawler and Garland Spider jigs work if the fish are keying on a swimming bait. Large curl-tail plastic worms such as the Gator Tail and Boogie Tail models also produce when fished on an open-hook jig head. Similarly, Kalin's new 5 inch Salty Grub that is widely used in freshwater bassin' circles has produced some sensational nighttime catches on the Walls. Pink, green, orange, salt'n pepper, silver, black, motor oil, root beer, and red seem to all work at one time or another.

Suekawa prefers his own unique Haddock Split Tail Grub as perhaps the "sleeper" bait of the lot. The Split Tail Grub is a thick, fat-bodied bait with a tail divided into four separate sections. This effect creates a very slow, subtle swimming action in contrast to more active curl-tail or fork-tail lures.

But here's the key secret that Suekawa passes along: no matter what plastic lure you select for using on the Walls, tip it with a strip of frozen squid. What he does is to take about a pound of whole frozen squid, thaw it, and strip it into small 3 x 1/2 inch tippets. These are all pre-cut and placed in a small bait bucket before he reaches the Wall. It is tough enough fishing in the dark, let alone having to filet out frozen squid. The "jig'n squid" combo is reminiscent of the way in which freshwater bassers use pork rind trailers with their assorted jigs. (As a matter of fact, some "old timers" still use pork rind tipped jigs out on the Walls with consistently good results.) For an added attraction squirt some saltwater Berkley Saltwater Fish Attractant on to the jig'n squid. There are times when this extra scent seems to stimulate the bass into a more active feeding mode.

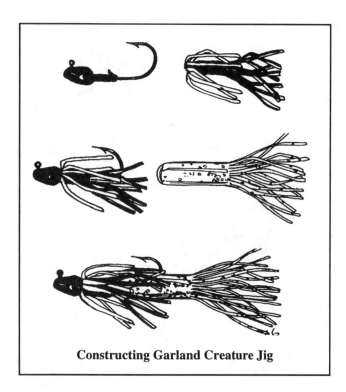

Constructing Garland Creature Jig

The cadmium-plated hooks, although much duller than the wire versions are very strong. Suekawa notes that the bass along the Walls are remarkably aggressive fish. As is often the case, they actually impale themselves on the lure as they ambush the jig and head back to the rocks. Thus, the cadmium hooks seem to work just fine even without any pre-sharpening. Also jig heads with the wire hooks become severely rusted after just one night's fishing in the salty air. This won't happen with the cadmium-plated models. One other somewhat obsure yet highly potent lure for catching calico bass at night is the magnum-size spinnerbait. These safety pin designed lures were made primarily for freshwater bass. But they are practically snagproof, and the larger whirling blades draw strikes from calicos along the rocky breakwalls. Try the Haddock or the Blue Fox versions in 3/4 to 1 ounce models, with white pulsating vinyl skirts and large tandem nickel-plated blades.

Fishing the diverse breakwalls that line our coasts can be an exciting alternative to more traditional offshore party boat fishing. The Walls produce all year long. Suekawa feels that for Southern California they are best in late spring and early summer during the spawning season when droves of sand bass move into the shallow waters. But, even the dead of winter can be productive with the right combination of moon and tidal action, especially in Northern California for various rockfish species.

You must remain constantly alert when fishing an area like these in the dark. Running lights are essential. Private boaters can be expected to be visited by Coast Guard patrols if navigational lights are not turned on. There is also a lot of flotsam and floating debris at times in the harbors. Keep your speed down and motor out to the Walls with caution.

Once there, keep an eye out for shifts in tidal conditions. If you prefer to work the outside, be especially on guard for unexpected swells created by the taxi boats that run all night long shuttling back and forth to the offshore oil rigs, along with freighters, tankers, and other craft. If the winds kick up and the sea becomes too rough on the outside Walls—don't fight it! You can still salvage much of the outing by seeking protection on the calmer inside rocks.

One further note: It might be wise to keep a compass in your boat. The coastal fog can become really thick all of a sudden, turning a clear night into a navigational nightmare. Also many veteran Wallbangers dress in foul weather gear, since the nighttime air can become very misty and wet.

For anglers who prefer to use natural baits, Suekawa recommends two options. Large, whole frozen or fresh squid can be sensational at times pinned onto a 3/8 or 5/8 ounce plain jig head. Live mudsuckers fly-lined into the rocks would be the other choice. With either, don't be surprised if you tie into a real "hawg" some night, as a wayward white sea bass bushwacks the bait.

With regard to the jig heads themselves, Suekawa recommends anywhere from 3/8 to 3/4 ounces of lead depending on tidal conditions. The lighter heads will fall slower which sometimes triggers more strikes than a heavier, faster-falling jig. The larger lead heads however are somewhat easier to cast and control when there is a lot of surge. A compromise is to take a vinyl spinnerbait skirt and slide it onto the heavier jig head. This adds bulk to the lure making it displace more water. It also gives the bait a more prominent silhouette in the darkness which can be very beneficial for this kind of night fishing. The vinyl skirt also permits the jig'n squid to fall somewhat more slowly, tantalizingly drifting just above the rocks.

Most pros who fish the Walls also prefer to use jigs with the heavier gauge cadmium hooks instead of the more traditional wire hooks found on freshwater baits. The thinner wire hooks will certainly provide better penetration on the hook set. However, they will become either blunt or bend too easily after repeatedly bumping into the rocks.

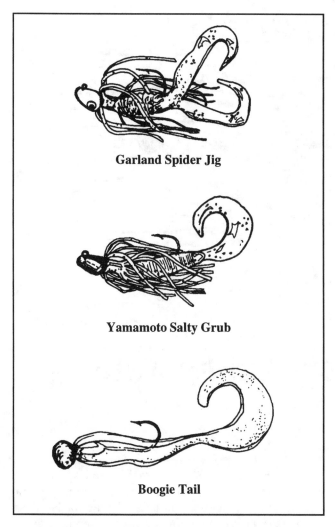

Garland Spider Jig

Yamamoto Salty Grub

Boogie Tail

The Walls usually hold plenty of calicos and sandies in the Southland but they are not always lunkers. Some evenings the pesky little ones will mount an all-out attack on your jigs, while the "toads" seem to be hiding in the rocks. Consider keeping a lighter spinning outfit spooled with 6 to 8 pound mono. Even the "shorts" offer one of the best fights pound for pound of any fish I've caught on light tackle. You will experience that the ratio of fish caught per angling hour spent on one of the Walls is one of the highest found anywhere in the West!

Kelp Fishin': Offshore Underwater Forests

From San Diego to above the Monterey Peninsula, intermittent yet expansive blankets of kelp can be found a short distance from the beach. Depending upon the locale, there are numerous species of saltwater fish that assume a year 'round resident status in these underwater forests.

In Northern California, a myriad of shallow water rockfish species abound in the kelp. Party boat anglers and small craft skippers can sample blue, olive, black, copper, starry, and rosy rockfishes. Sable fish, petrale sole, Pacific sanddab and kelp greenling are also found in mixed amounts with the basic rockfish fare. The prize game fish found on a season long basis along the edge of the kelp for North Coasters is the voracious and aggressive lingcod.

Concentrated kelp bed angling pretty much ranges as far north as Point Reyes above San Francisco. Continuing up the coast, offshore anglers focus more on rocky reefs and opportunities to fish pelagic game fish such as salmon, striper, or albacore.

It is important to note that particularly in warmer water years—especially during the so-called El Nino condition—certain more Southern-based species will migrate into these North Coast kelp beds. Bonito, barracuda, and mackerel are an added bonus for Northern anglers if the warmer currents move offshore.

The kelp beds along the Central Coast from San Simeon to Santa Barbara are loaded with fish. Lingcod, rockfish, and cabezon are ever-present in the kelp-strewn areas. But, also tackle-busting white sea bass are a strong possibility. Bonito, mackerel, and barracuda can be frequently taken in these waters, primarily in the warmer summer months.

Boaters working in the Ventura and Santa Barbara stretch have a wide gamut of species to choose from when it comes to prospecting the offshore kelp beds. There are still plenty of cold water rockfish to be found along with cabezon, sculpin, and lingcod. Bonito, barracuda, mackerel, and white sea bass will stage intermittent flurries. But the major game fish of the kelp forests in this region are calico, and to a lesser degree, sand bass and bruiser-class yellowtail.

The kelp beds that form rings around the Channel Islands off Santa Barbara generate one of the richest, yet relatively untapped, harvests along the coast. San Miguel, Santa Rosa, Santa Cruz, San Nicholas, Santa Barbara, and Anacapa Islands can offer tremendous opportunities for calico bass, yellowtail, white sea bass, and lingcod. Sheepshead, whitefish, barracuda, bonito, mackerel, cabezon, johnny bass, and blue rockfish round out the scorecard for this angling mecca.

Southern California has perhaps the best overall blend of kelp fishing opportunities found along the coastline for day in and day out action. Bass, barracuda, and bonito—the "three B's" as local skippers term them—along with the prolific Spanish and greenback mackerels are regular dwellers in the Horseshoe Kelp out of San Pedro, the Barn Kelp near Oceanside, and the La Jolla Kelp beds just north of San Diego. The calico bass, in particular, is the principle game fish sought by Southland skippers exploring these popular kelp blankets.

White sea bass, sand bass, sheepshead, whitefish, cabezon, olive and vermillion rockfish, and even a stray halibut or shallow water lingcod are all viable possibilities. Under the right conditions, prize yellowtail and the less frequent visitors—bluefin and yellowfin tuna—can be taken along the kelp line.

Southern Cal's offshore treasures are Catalina and San Clemente Islands. All of the above mentioned species are challenged at these isles by both private boaters and the sport fishing fleet. Further south, the Coronado Islands—North, South, and Middle ground rocks provide a similar haven for kelp-dwelling species, with a special emphasis on the yellowtail and white sea bass catches.

In subsequent chapters, more precise information and details will be given as to how to catch a particular species from each of these waters. For purposes of this chapter, I will focus on some of the more generalized features of kelp bed fishing.

"Pot-Holing" Through the Kelp

To begin with, some anglers falsely assume that there are no kelp beds in the areas they are fishing because there are no obvious signs of the vegetation. Depending upon the current, tidal surge, and swells, there are times when the kelp is considerably below the surface and not readily visible. Other days the kelp will be "up." In some locales, for instance the highly frequented Horseshoe Kelp off of San Pedro, most of the kelp stringers are always submerged well below the surface.

Most fishermen are more accustomed to fishing the beds where the kelp forms a "mat" on top of the water.

There are a couple of strategies that work particularly well when you can see the kelp beds in this manner.

As I mentioned previously, smaller boats, including aluminum skiffs and rubberized inflatables can really take advantage of thick kelp. The trick is to glide over the prominent mat and fish the "potholes" or openings in the beds. Once inside the potholes, anchoring won't be necessary. Often the kelp around the perimeter of the hole is enough to keep a smaller craft fairly stationary. If this doesn't work, try tying a rope to some of the kelp stringers. This should hold the boat while you fish the openings.

Vertical drops are all that are needed to fish the potholes. Live anchovies, sardines, or smelt are effective as are shellfish and especially abalone trimmings. Whole, fresh, or frozen squid pinned onto a #4/0 live bait hook is my favorite option. This bait catches everything from rockfish to white sea bass.

The easiest bait rig to use in these openings is a split-shot rig. Tie on your hook and crimp a medium to large-sized lead shot about 12 to 24 inches above it, and you're ready to pothole.

Vertical jigging should also be tried in the open pockets. Captain Russ Izor, original builder of the party boat, First String, out of San Pedro pioneered the saltwater counterpart to the freshwater jig and pig combo (a lead head with a pork rind trailer). Izor took a green scale Bomber Gumpy Jig with a nylon bristle tail and simply hooked a whole squid behind the lure. The "jig'n squid" combination has taken a lot of bull calicos over the years among the party boat fleet. However, this strange offering also produces some astonishing catches in the kelp lowered through the sporadic openings.

I'm still not sure if the green-colored Bomber jig really does anything to enhance this lure-bait package. Some saltwater fishermen are emphatically sold on the green-scale finish of the jig, claiming that it triggers the strikes, and not the squid. Other veterans believe that this is nonsense. They cite equally strong results using a simple unpainted lead head with a whole squid trailer.

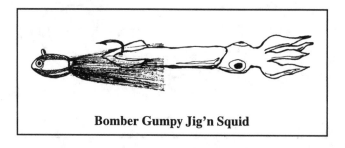

Bomber Gumpy Jig'n Squid

I have personally caught some big bull bass using both the Bomber and the simplified lead head through the potholes with squid trailers. I prefer to stay with the Bomber jig. I feel that if the squid gets stripped, at least I still have a reasonably appealing lure down there as a secondary alternative for the fish. It is unlikely that calicos or other species will bite a bare, unpainted lead head.

With either setup it is not necessary to "yo-yo" the bait using an exaggerated lift-and-drop motion with the rod. As a matter of fact, many strikes will occur as you slowly let out line, allowing the lure to spiral down in a slow-swimming action through the kelp.

"Potholers" also rely heavily upon the full range of plastics for this kind of kelp fishing. The A.A. Worms' Monarch grub, Haddock's Lunker Thumper, the Scampi, Mojo, and Berkley's Power Grub and Power Eel have all proven effective with this unique vertical approach. But, consider scaling up in line test—dramatically! When the bull calicos or white sea bass inhale baits or lures in the middle of these kelp beds, hold on! The bigger fish invariably try to back into the thick of the kelp and wrap you up. It is not out of the ordinary to fish 30 pound "string" with soft plastic lures or jig'n squid combos, with conventional reels, and the drag hammered tight.

Spoons and jigs are also effective when fished through the kelp openings. Haddock's 1 1/8 ounce Jig'n Spoon in either 'chovy, chartreuse prism, or "brown bait" patterns is hard to top. If you find that the jig is getting snagged too much on the kelp stringers while you are yo-yoing through the potholes, replace the treble with a single hook.

Another tip comes from charter boat skipper and calico expert, Kit McNear. After backing down into the kelp, McNear will sometimes borrow a page out of the freshwater bassin' book. He rigs up a large curl-tail plastic worm and fishes it Texas-style through the narrowest passages. The Texas rig is nothing more than using a sliding bullet weight and a large plastic worm hook embedded into the body of the lure. This makes the worm

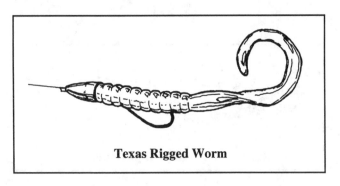

Texas Rigged Worm

practically weedless. Push a toothpick into the nose of the sinker and break off the wooden point, leaving it in the bullet weight. This keeps the sinker from sliding and fouling in the kelp.

Diamond jigs in the smaller 1 to 2 ounce sizes; chrome, green and yellow, or blue and white candy bar style jigs also work with the yo-yo stroke through the kelp. The Salas Christy #2 or #3 is a favorite in the heavier metal composition, along with the Ironman #2 and small Jerry Jig.

Bear in mind that there is no telling what "treasures" these lures will jig up from deep within the kelp forests. I have caught some magnum-sized rockfish on the jig'n squid mono, for example, while probing the potholes primarily for calicos. I have also hooked fish on 30 and 40 pound mono that I simply couldn't tear away from the adjacent kelp strings—presumably big white sea bass.

No matter what artificial lure you decide to fish in these subtle openings, always try to tip it with frozen squid if possible. Do this even with the spoons and candy bar jigs as well as the assorted plastic lures. Sometimes a whole squid will produce fewer strikes but larger specimens. But also, a big chunk of squid behind some of the baits has a tendency to restrict the action. So in this case, use a small 1 x 3" tippet, which is often just enough to add a little flavor to the lure.

As a final note, a small number of adventuresome anglers have also been working these potholes on a more "intimate basis" so to speak. Don't be surprised to see fishermen dressed in wet suits paddling out in float tubes to fish artificial lures vertically in the narrowest openings, hunting primarily big bull calicos. This is the ultimate sport—"mano-a-mano" (hand to hand)—that an angler could experience in fishing for trophy size calico bass.

Troll Outside the Kelp

With proper boat maneuvering, anglers can also encounter a bonanza of pelagic species by trolling along the kelp beds.

Feathers are a popular lure choice since most come with single hooks which ride upward. The smaller chrome head feathers will barely troll beneath the surface and yet they remain fairly snag-free from the kelp. Barracuda, calico bass, mackerel, and bonito are kelp bed residents who will strike feathers dragged near the edge.

A number CD-13 Magnum or the smaller CD-11 Magnum Rapala minnow can be dynamite trolled outside the kelp lines. A blue or black version of this sinking plug works best. The "three B's" —bass, bonito, and barracuda—eat them as do mackerel, and occasionally yellowtail and rockfish.

Assorted plastics can also be surprise winners when pulled near the kelp. It is important to throttle down and use a fairly slow speed for trolling these lures. The Salty Magic, Mojo, Scampi, and Lunker Thumper can generate strikes from both calicos and sand bass on a slow troll outside the kelp line. Also consider larger A.A. Worms and Berkley Power swimbaits, along with 4 inch Possum Lures for calicos on the slow-troll.

To a lesser degree, small to medium-sized candy bar-shaped jigs are also viable for trolling the beds. Stay with proven patterns such as blue and white, green and yellow, solid white, or chrome. Most surface-feeding species can be enticed to occasionally hit the jigs.

Floating Kelp Paddies

Saltwater fishermen in the Southern region sometimes find the smaller floating kelp paddies to be loaded with all kinds of marine game fish. Most paddy fishing is done in the late spring through fall.

There is no telling which paddies are "loaded" with fish and which ones are barren or "dry" as the skippers say. Numerous pelagic species such as bonito, mackerel, yellowtail, yellowfin, and bluefin tuna, skipjack, and even albacore or dorado further out, can be found resting under these masses of broken kelp.

With the larger species, anywhere from a solitary "loner" fish to entire schools can be drifting with the kelp paddy. Veteran party boat and charter captains feel that the isolated paddies they stumble across twenty miles or more off the shore are the most fertile. It makes sense why this would be the case. Kelp paddies adrift far out to sea can establish themselves as a floating oasis and the only isolated shelter for miles around. Cruising schools of game fish can often find ample amounts of smaller bait fish under the paddies and will thus drift many miles while lazily feeding on this forage.

Kelp paddies vary in size from about the size of a large cardboard box to a square acre. Most are worth exploring, especially in a warm water year.

The best technique is to quietly position your boat above the paddy and drift down along side it. Definitely shut down the engine and keep all noise on the deck and elsewhere to an absolute minimum. Paddy fish can be quite skittish.

If possible, a tankful of fresh 'chovies would be a real bonus. This permits chumming the outer perimeter of the paddy. This will often draw game fish out from underneath the kelp and into the chum line. It is important not to drift too close to the paddy. Fish can be lying both underneath and on the outside edges some distance from the actual kelp.

Polarized sunglasses can be a real boon for "paddy jumping." It is not uncommon for both party boat and private skippers to actually see everything from mackerel to sulking yellowtail underneath the floating kelp.

Lighter 10 to 20 pound mono gets bit better under the paddies. Standard live bait outfits—either spinning or conventional—will work. Use short-shank live-bait hooks to correspond to the size of the offering ('chovies, sardines, smelt, brown baits, or mackerel).

Frozen squid can also be fly-lined or slowly drifted alongside the floating kelp. If you need to get either the baitfish or the squid down further beneath the surface, pinch on a single prominent lead split shot 12 to 24 inches above the hook.

Free-casting or yo-yoing jigs around the patties also produce at times. Solid chrome, blue or green mackerel, blue and white, and green and yellow are staples for jig selection and paddy jumping. Popular models include Tady A1and AA, heavy Jerry Jig, Ironman #3 and #5, Salas CP-105 and 6XJR.

The array of standard trolling lures sometimes work equally well if the boat does not have any chum power. Countdown Magnum Rapalas, Rebels, Bagley Bang-O's, and similar minnow-shaped plugs are definitely worth a try. Silver and mackerel patterns are best. Assorted plastics and either jigs or spoons can be similarly pulled on the outside perimeter of the paddies, slowly.

Bonito or larger tuna feathers are also highly effective at times for trolling the floating kelp. Yellowtail, albacore, tuna, and dorado will jet out from around the paddy to attack these brightly colored feathers during the warmer months.

It is a big ocean and floating kelp paddies are not always easy to locate. Many private boaters monitor weekly fishing reports from the sport fishing landings to garner a general idea of how far out to go when looking for this kind of kelp oasis. Coastal tackle stores will similarly also provide the small craft owner with information, when available, as to where the highest concentration and most productive kelp paddies are being seen.

Summary

Kelp provides the various marine fishes along the California Coast with precious shelter and food sources. The species that are found in and around these underwater forests can be exceptionally tough to land, the closer to the kelp you fish. It is thus important to keep your tackle in top condition with quality rods and reels matched with tough premium grade mono if you want to put kelp species on the deck.

Harbor and Bay Fishin':
Sheltered Action

For many Californians, harbors and bays are the primary places where they fish for saltwater species. The complexion of these inlets varies along Northern and Southern lines as does the offshore fishing. In the latter portion of this book I will go into greater detail on how and when to fish the specific harbors and bays. In this chapter I want to give the angler some more general idea of how to approach these quiet waters.

Look for Moving Water

Whether you fish off the bank or from a boat, you usually can't go wrong working moving water in harbors and bays. By "moving" I am referring to tidal flow, backwashes, whirlpools, and eddies. I have fished numerous times, for instance, in Newport Harbor with local expert, Jim Emmett. Even when using strictly artificial lures, Emmett is always on the lookout for flowing water. All types of game fish found in this particular harbor—ranging from halibut and croaker to sand sharks and bay bass—gravitate to areas like this. The trick is to watch for junctures where the currents cut into otherwise still water.

The mouths of harbors and bays leading to open ocean similarly form a place where the currents collide with calmer waters. Pelagic species such as bonito in the South or stripers in the North can frequently be taken in these areas. Colder ocean currents often push the bait fish into the warmer waters of the harbors and bays. Game fish will typically follow, sometimes travelling some distance into the backwaters of these inlets.

The main channels cut deep into some bays—for example, San Diego and San Francisco Bays—and are used for navigational purposes for large commercial and naval vessels. These channels also can have considerable current ripping through them. Numerous varieties of game fish will traverse these underwater passages, looking for morsels of food swept up in the current.

Here's where modern electronics are a tremendous help. In some locations, the deep channels are marked with navigational buoys, but not always. By monitoring graphs and LCR's for dramatic changes in depth, private boaters can find the channels. More importantly, it is essential to pinpoint the edges of these canyons. This topographical "break" or drop-off is where different game fish species lurk to ambush schools of bait.

Some harbors, such as Kings Harbor in Redondo Beach have thermal outlets from steam power plants. When warm water is released into this harbor an incredible "blow hole" effect occurs. The swirling warmer water can attract hordes of bait fish and pelagic travellers like bonito, barracuda, and even yellowtail into this quiet sanctuary. In the dead of winter when water outside the harbor can be considerably colder, the thermal outlet provides a haven for prominent schools of game fish. Anglers can actually work their lures or baits into this blow hole from boats or by shore casting. Or they can key in on the water on the perimeter of the whirlpool if the fish seem to prefer less turbulence.

Finally, pay attention to tide tables. For most harbors and bays, your chances are maximized fishing on a fast-moving incoming tide. In San Francisco Bay, for example, this is so critical that much of the striper party boat fleet coordinates the day's outing with major tidal flow. But the importance of water movement can vary between the diverse harbors and bays. San Francisco and Newport Bays seem to perform best with a lot of water being exchanged with the tides. San Diego Bay, in contrast, is at its peak usually with a limited exchange of water. Local landings and tackle stores can help you zero in on what is optimal for your area.

Fish Structure

Depending upon the locale, there can be an extensive structure that will attract fish in these quiet waters. Both functional and deteriorated wooden or concrete pilings used for supporting wharfs, docks, or bridges are excellent spots to try. Rocky outcroppings and scattered chunks of broken concrete block are equally good fish-holding areas.

North Coasters pounding the waters near Berkeley, Emeryville, Angel Island, the San Mateo Bridge, and Coyote Point will quickly recognize that perch are drawn to these structures. Similarly, the scattered pilings in the backwaters of Newport Bay provide hiding places for spotted bay bass, sargo, and yellowfin croaker.

Small piers and boat or fuel docks within many harbors also host large populations of sport fish. The boat docks and pilings sustain considerable barnacle and mussel growth. Smaller bait fish and crabs are attracted to these structures and game fish follow.

The boat moorings themselves provide shade and cover for game fish. They can hide in the darker water created underneath moored boats lying in wait to ambush an errant bait fish or crustacean.

Boat docks and moorings are often situated in deeper water so that sailboat skegs and power boat motors won't scrape the bottom. Sometimes this difference in depth, especially when it is near the bank or dock, can form feeding pockets for larger harbor residents.

Similarly, fuel docks can be phenomenally good places to try. Too often anglers falsely assume that because of all the boat traffic, fish won't move into the waters under these structures. Game fish that have resided in these harbors and bays for long periods of time become acclimated to the commotion created by passing boats. The wood, concrete, or similar material used to build these floating gas stations can play host, once again, to barnacles, mussels, crabs, and schools of bait.

A bait receiver can also be an "oasis in the desert" for an otherwise sterile harbor. Invariably, bait fish minnows escape from the holding tanks or transfer nets. These baits will typically remain in close proximity to the floating receivers. Depending upon harbor regulations, it is always a good gamble to investigate the water where these bait tanks are located.

You can fish alongside the receivers in most harbors. Some will let you tie up to them. Don't overlook actually fishing through the slats and boards that comprise the decking of these floating structures. I had one memorable trip in San Diego Bay on a party boat on the way to the sand bass grounds. We stopped to take on bait at the receiver. With nothing else to do, I lowered a rather unassuming plastic grub down through the cracks on the wooden deck. By the time we had filled our live bait tanks, I had a limit of ten sandies in my gunny sack! This scenario is repeated often by anglers shrewd enough to try the receivers.

Bay Tackle and Rigs

Fishermen working off the bank or from boats can get by with a sparse amount of tackle when it comes to bay and harbor angling. Almost any of the assorted outfits previously mentioned will suffice for at least one form of fishing or another within these waters.

For example, ultralight freshwater gear with 4 to 6 pound test mono is superb for fishing piling perch in Northern California or for swimming artificial lures in San Diego's Mission Bay. Without question, there is a place for light-lining in these harbors. Natural baits are presented more delicately and the fish readily chomp at them. Artificial lures—especially small plastic models like the Scrounger, Canyon Lure's Cap'n Gown, Haddock's Kreepy Krawler, or Kalin's Salty Lunker Grub—swim better with lighter line.

Heavier freshwater tackle such as baitcasting reels and stouter popping rods have excellent utility in these areas. They are strong enough to tame a striper, halibut, bonito, or even a yellowtail. But, they are lightweight enough to provide a lot of sporting fight.

Heavy freshwater or lighter saltwater outfits like these are also perfect for trolling in the harbors. School stripers to the North, and bonito or bay bass in the South can put up quite a tussle when caught while trolling the bays. Saltwater species of this genre strike a trolled lure hard—even the 1 to 2 pounders—and broken lines will result with ultralight tackle.

Bank anglers fishing these inlets can get away with lighter outfits. There are places like the rocks along Berkeley or the Quivara Basin in San Diego's Mission Bay, where shoreliners can experience a lot of sport chuckin' artificial lures from the shore. Freshwater bassin' gear will suffice in this situation.

But frequently, the bank fishermen may be at a disadvantage when fishing in some bays and harbors unless they can get their baits out into more productive water. Here's where a longer 8 to 9 foot spinning rod or even an 11 to 15 foot surf stick helps to neutralize this disadvantage. Sometimes even fishing for smaller species such as smelt from within these harbors requires a long distance cast.

If larger game fish are the main quarry on your expedition to the bay, then traditional live bait outfits are in order. Conventional reels will be best teamed with 6 1/2 to 8 foot live bait rods. Potluck fishermen using live 'chovies or shiner perch drift for stripers and halibut in San Francisco Bay with this type of tackle. Blow hole experts use similar live bait combos for fooling bruiser yellowtail in Kings Harbor.

Sharks and rays pose another problem altogether. Shark hunters in San Diego are looking for 100 pound class bat rays. San Francisco Bay has its counterparts with behemoth 6 and 7 gill sharks (more on both fisheries in later chapters). In either case, heavy-duty reels in the 3/0 to 4/0 range and 50 to 80 pound mono with thick-barreled rods round out the magnum gear for this type of bay fishing.

Baits and Rigs for Harbors and Bays

Most of the regionally popular bait selections itemized in previous chapters will work for those same game fish when they are found in harbors and bays. But, don't get lazy in fishing these baits here. There is a great temptation to simply "still fish" your offering in the quiet solitude of some of these waters.

A better option is to practice some "controlled bait soakin'." Whether it is stripers, perch, bass, croaker, or whatever, make an effort to keep your bait moving at a modest pace. If you are anchored in a boat or bait fishing from the shore, reel in your offering a few feet every so often.

Here's where some potent fish attractant like Berkley's Saltwater Fish Attractant really comes in handy. Soak your bait heavily in this concoction. After you cast it out, start to inch it back in, pausing intermittently for 30 seconds or more. The attractant leaves a tantalizing chum slick in the water, drawing in fish from some distance to attack the bait.

This tactic is very important if you are still fishing bait in some of the calmer, more stagnant waters found in these harbors and bays. The combination of the moving bait and the chemical attractant consistently triggers strikes when simple bait dunkin' fails.

Something else worth noting in fishing these waters is to consider catching your own live bait fish. Anglers adept at using either dip or throw nets can gather up both anchovies and smelt inside the bays and harbors. There is no question that a lively critter will usually outfish a frozen bait fish—hands down!

That bait bucket outfitted with a portable aerator used for pier fishing also works perfectly for boat or shore anglers stalking inside the harbors and bays. Likewise, consider carrying at least two rod and reel combos for these trips. If you catch a small shiner perch, smelt, queenfish, mackerel, or tomcod, pin it onto a heavier rig and fish for the lunkers!

With regard to basic terminal rigs for "quiet water" fishing, keep it simple. The sliding-egg sinker combo works if you are fishing a hard bottom. Some bay fishermen like to use the slider with a three-way swivel so they can lay two different baits out. The double combo surf leaders are also very suitable for smaller species such as perch and smelt. Consider using a lighter dipsey sinker (bell-shaped with a swivel eyelet) for fishing near the docks and pilings with the surf leaders. They will hang up less. Light-liners can fish a basic split-shot setup for perch, smelt, corbina, croakers, and smaller flatfish.

If the bottom is rocky, many of the above-mentioned rigs may get hung up either still fishing or drifting. An alternative is to use a three-way setup with a lighter leader connecting the sinker. This way, if the weight gets snagged, you can break it off while salvaging both the three-way

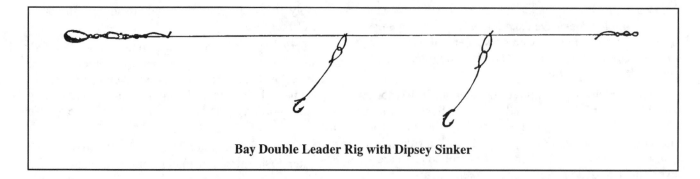

Bay Double Leader Rig with Dipsey Sinker

swivel and the hook and leader. You might also use a pencil lead in place of a more traditional pyramid or spoon sinker. The pencil weight is soft and malleable and bends easily as it bangs into the rocks. It has limited anchoring ability but it is relatively snag-free.

Also, remember that some of the fish found in these sheltered inlets are touchy feeders. Hence, it is important to not only have the best baits on the hook, preferably fresh over frozen, but also to make sure that the hook gets carefully covered. Even rather unspectacular perch and smelt will turn their noses up at an improperly baited hook.

Chumming is sometimes difficult while prospecting harbors and bays. Party boats often have some "fire power" in San Francisco Bay, whereas sport fishing boats rarely ever explore the backwaters of Southern California. Shore fishermen and private boaters can chop up assorted frozen baits or cracked shellfish and throw them over the side or out from shore as a makeshift chum line.

Floats and bobbers also have a place in the bay angler's tackle box. These can be fished as they are, off piers and jetties. Inside the harbor, you can use a float to suspend your bait and let it drift lazily while fishing from docks, small piers, or from the inside rocks. Both baited hooks and/or small artificials (jig flies, marabou feathers, tiny grubs, and tube lures) can be fished under the drifting float.

Lures for Bay Fishing

Diverse species require specific artificial lures inside the harbors and bays. In Northern California, anglers prefer one set of lures. Fishermen trolling Newport Harbor for spotted bay bass rely upon another. However, before examining these lures and patented tactics, let's review some more general points to be made when using artificials inside these waters.

First, as you may have gathered, it is equally important to fish the moving water with lures as it is with natural baits. As a matter of fact, in the flowing water, game fish —and the bigger specimens at that—are often more likely to strike the artificial over the live offering. This is probably due to both the unique appearance and swimming action of the lure. Game fish feeding in current don't have time to study the bait. If they wait too long, the morsel will be swept away. (This is analogous to stream fishing for trout.) So, if the fish sees the lure moving erratically in the current, it will often strike out with a vengeance, fearful that its food will quickly move out of range.

Lures should definitely be trolled or bounced along the edge of a channel. Positioning the boat on the outside lip of the break and casting to deep water, bringing the lure up the side, works for many game fish found inside the bays.

Striper fishermen similarly learn to "walk" their baits and lures just above the rocky bottoms to take advantage of this structure. South Coast bay busters quietly parachute their tiny plastic baits down the sides of pilings and docks looking for scrappy sand and spotted bay bass. Locating and using structure is the foundation for a lot of free-casting with lures while sampling harbors and bays.

As with freshwater stream fishing, bay species will face the current as it washes food down in their direction. So, with natural bait, and more so with lures, make your presentation up above the fish and retrieve it directly in front of them. Time is wasted if the angler can clearly discern the direction of the current but ends up casting his lure to the fish's back.

Because of the effect of current, it is sometimes beneficial to drop the rod tip when you feel a fish hit the lure. The theory is that the slight slack in the line creates a more natural feel to the fish and they may hold onto the lure longer. Once that small amount of slack is straightened out—swing and set!

Plastics, Cranks, and Spoons for the Bay

Many of the soft plastic lures previously discussed will work quite well in the quiet waters of harbors and bays. Ultralight tube baits like tiny Berkley Power Tubes or Garland's Fat Gitzits are excellent. Scroungers, Berkley Power Grubs, and plastic worms can also be sensational on all kinds of bay residents. Perch, croaker, corbina, halibut, stripers, as well as sand and spotted bay bass will eat these soft plastics.

Medium-sized plastic swimming baits including the Salty Magic, Lunker Thumper, and Scampi also produce at times for larger fish such as halibut found in these harbors and bays. All of these lures mentioned here perform either free-casting from docks, piers, the bank, or from boats working the current, drop-offs, channels, and structure within the bay.

Soft plastic lures are also highly effective slow-drifted in these areas. The easiest technique is to use two or three different rods per angler with assorted lures. Lean the rods on the side of the boat and let the drift and current work the lures in a slow, bottom-bouncing action.

Slow-swimming knob-tail lures have also put a major dent into the population of bay game fish, especially the smaller species such as turbot, perch, croaker, sargo, and spotted bay and sand bass. Most of these fish-like replicas are made from hand-poured soft plastic, including those sold by A.A. Worms, Fish Trap, Berkley, Worm King, and Kalins. They are meant to be casted or drifted on a 1/8 ounce lead head. The tantalizing tail action imitates a small perch or anchovy. The results can be fantastic using a knob-tail bait and lighter 6 to 8 pound monofilament. Don't hesitate to fish these miniature lures through shallow areas with a lot of current.

Assorted crankbaits normally associated with freshwater bassin' also produce in this water. Some anglers cast and retrieve these lures towards shoreline targets. Others prefer to set up trolling patterns, dragging the crankplugs along the edges of channels and drop-offs. Deep-diving plugs such as Bombers, Hellbenders, Waterdogs, Luhr Jensen Deep Secrets, Rapala Deep Magnums, Poe's Super Cedars, and Mann's Deep Hawgs can really stir up some commotion as they plow the 10 to 20 foot depths of the harbor. Likewise, don't overlook the wide range of possibilities for casting or trolling medium-to-deep diving Rebels and Rapala minnows in the harbors. Larger game fish will definitely zero in on these 'chovy replicas from North to South. Another option is to slow-troll the new 3 and 4 inch Possum Lures. The Possum is neither a soft swimbait, nor a hard plastic plug. Instead, it has a plastic diving lip with a soft plastic, segmented tail section. The Possum Lure combines the best of "soft" and "hard" lure technology. It is terrific for light tackle bay action!

Another important option is to toss spoons around the docks, piers, pilings, boat moorings, rocks, riprap, and similar structures found in many of our harbors. Dick Gaumer is a long-time Southern California writer, lecturer, and spoonin' specialist. He has essentially made a

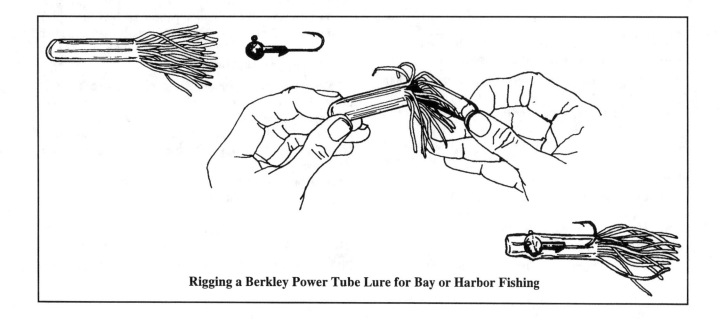

Rigging a Berkley Power Tube Lure for Bay or Harbor Fishing

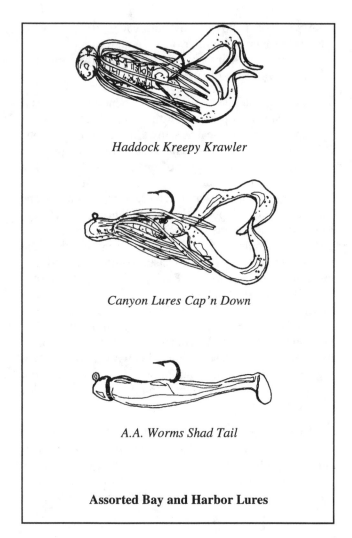

Haddock Kreepy Krawler

Canyon Lures Cap'n Down

A.A. Worms Shad Tail

Assorted Bay and Harbor Lures

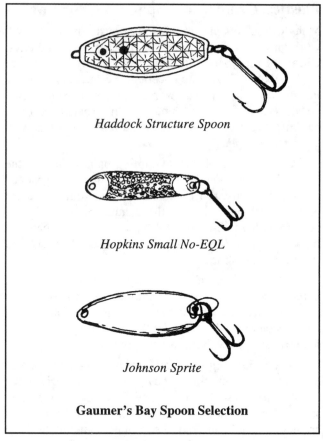

Haddock Structure Spoon

Hopkins Small No-EQL

Johnson Sprite

Gaumer's Bay Spoon Selection

study over the years of how these simple shiny spoons can be used in a vertical presentation in salt water.

Gaumer's strategy is relatively basic: simply pitch the spoon alongside pilings, underneath moored boats, around rocks, or comparable structure. Be prepared for strikes on the fall as the lure flutters towards the bottom. Once the spoon hits the bottom, jig it in a short lift-'n-drop action. Here too, look for the fish to hit the spoon as it drops slowly.

A number of smaller spoons in the 1/4 to 5/8 ounce class are perfect for this type of bay action. The Johnson Sprite, Hopkins NO-EQL, and Haddock Structure Spoon are some of Gaumer's favorite models.

This spoon expert also recommends adding a dull watermelon green grub as a trailer with the spoon. Re-move the stock treble hook, replace it with a single hook, and lace on the grub trailer. Gaumer theorizes that the more subdued icy green coloration in the grub matches perfectly with the vibrant flash of a lightly polished spoon. Grubs in a more opulent pattern such as "hot" pink or lime, according to Gaumer, may actually spook the fish with too much "flash." The spoons should be preferably in a chrome or nickel finish.

More traditional spoonin' tactics also work inside these sheltered zones. Basic cast-and-retrieve or slow-trolling with spoons account for numerous tallies of bonito and stripers. These pelagic monsters are more accustomed to attacking a more active lure as they do in open ocean. Krocadiles, Rader Spoons, Jig'n Spoons, or larger Hopkins models can be used to lure these more aggressive species when they migrate into the bays.

Summary

Fishing in bays and harbors requires some forethought with regard to proper tackle selection, rigging, baits and lures. These areas host various marine species on a year 'round basis. Both shore anglers, private craft, and party boaters can take advantage of this type of fishery. There are four simple "rules of thumb" that will enhance your catch ratio when fishing bays and harbors: (1) look for current, (2) work around structure, (3) keep your bait fresh and moving, and (4) be more experimental tossing artificials for larger fish when conditions permit.

Poke Poling: Just Pokin' Around the Coast

One of the more exotic forms of coastal angling is practiced only by a handful of aficionados. Poke poling is not only an inexpensive sport, it can also be a highly productive one in terms of numbers of fish caught. A variety of species can be taken with this unique presentation. Small lingcod, a multitude of perch, olive and china rockfish, opaleye, cabezon, greenling, reef cod, small flatfish, sculpin, and monkeyface eels are some of the inshore species accessible to the accomplished poke poler.

Poke polers usually use super long rods in the 10 to 18 foot range. The object is to carefully place a baited offering into the most minuscule cracks and openings between inshore tidal rocks. When the fish jump on these baits—hold on! The strike can be hard, but move importantly, that fish wants to head right back into its rocky shelter. The angler has to be alert and quick in order to pry fish out of these spots.

The Poke Pole

The elongated rod is the most integral piece of equipment in the poke poler's array of gear. Technically speaking, any bamboo, fiberglass, graphite, or similar composite rod blank can be used as a poke pole. The reason for the extra long 10 to 18 foot lengths is to be able to reach out and lower baits directly over the fish in those hard-to-get-to holes. It would be practically impossible to make a cast with a more conventional rod and reel combo to hit these cracks and tidal pockets.

To get into some of these nooks and crannies, the angler will actually have to "poke" the tip of the rod into the tight areas. Most commercially made bamboo or fiberglass "cane poles" have tip sections that are small in diameter. They are therefore fragile and susceptible to breaking or cracking with repeated "pokes" into the rocky structure.

For this reason, some poke polers actually cut down the tip portions of the store-bought cane poles, often up to a foot. Then they wrap on an extension piece of wire —about 18 to 24 inches—roughly the thickness of a coat hanger. You can use thread or electrical tape to lash this wire tip extension to the end of the bamboo or fiberglass rod blank. Form a tip "eye" by bending the wire in a circle. Then attach a 12 to 24 inch length of leader in 20 to 40 pound test monofilament.

You will note that there are no true guides on the poke pole aside from the handmade tiptop constructed by bending the heavy gauge wire. Nor are there any reels involved. When the fish strikes, the angler rears back and yanks his prey from out of the cracks.

Poke poling in this manner has been primarily a Central and North Coast phenomenon. This precise methodology will also work in the Southland, although the rocky outcroppings are not as prominent below Santa Barbara.

Watch the Water

Veteran poke polers learn to observe tide tables for this inshore approach. Some recommend "poking" primarily at minus tides and making sure you are at the water three hours before the low point. The lower the tide, the better the fishing.

The months of April and May typically have some extraordinarily low tides. These are definitely periods to think about some serious poke poling. Wintertime is also favorable for this tactic since many rockfish species spawn during this season. It also helps to wear polaroid sunglasses. As with other forms of marine angling, these lenses allow you to see the darker water which means a deeper pocket. Even fishing practically on the shore like this, the various species will gravitate to those cracks and openings formed by channels leading to deep water. It stands to reason why this is so. These narrow passages serve as "feeding funnels" where all sorts of morsels become trapped along the sides and in the back of the pocket.

Also look for fish in adjacent tidal pools around the rocks right underneath you. They can be hugging tight to the boulders and in whirlpools, eddies, and gentle tidal washes.

It is important to present each bait carefully in the most precise way. Take that extra effort to lower your leader and hook in those difficult-to-reach spots. Let the bait sit there for a minute or two. Give the fish a chance to locate the offering in all the churned-up water.

Poke Poling Equipment and Gear

As for baits, it is hard to beat shellfish and squid for this inshore attack. Anywhere from an Eagle Claw #181 #1 to #4 baitholder hook will suffice tied to the 20 to 40 pound mono. Chunks of squid, clam, mussel, or abalone trim-

mings will produce. Sometimes it might help to pinch a medium-sized lead shot on the lower six inches of the leader to keep the bait as vertical as possible.

Poke polers should invest in a good pair of hip waders. There are endless slippery rocks and crashing waves to keep you on your toes. Sure, dry footing is essential. (See "The Basics" chapter for information on selecting hip waders.)

A South Coast Variation

Poke poling with the short leader and long rod is indeed applicable anywhere tight, accessible shoreline rocks are found. Along the Southern California Coast, however, in the areas near Corona del Mar and Palos Verdes, anglers practice a variation of North Coast poke poling fishing from taller, steeper rocks.

Using similar long, 10 to 18 foot rods, Southlanders leave the fiberglass or bamboo tip sections intact. The "rods"—actually blanks—are still stripped of all hardware. No reel seats, no guides, only a tiptop.

A length of line ranging from 8 to 14 feet is simply tied to the tip eyelet. Anywhere from 10 to 20 pound monofilament is fine, depending upon the conditions and the size of the fish being sought. Again, pinch on a medium lead shot 18 to 24 inches above the baited hook and lower this split-shot rig into the crevices.

Another ploy is to add an old-fashioned red and white bobber or one of the more artistic oriental quill floats about 3 to 5 feet above the baited hook. This allows the offering to drift slowly while keeping the hook suspended off the bottom. Bobbers also have the obvious added advantage of letting the angler see the strike more easily.

Pokin' Lures

Strange as it may sound, you can also lower some of the more popular plastic saltwater lures into these dark inshore pockets. Berkley Power Eel, Haddock's Lunker Thumper, Kalin's Salty Grub, the Scampi, Mojo, Scrounger, and even plastic worms will frequently get bit when poked around these rocks.

Similarly, small shiny spoons such as Kastmasters, Krocodiles, Blue Fox Pixies, or Crippled Herring may also be attacked when dropped into the quieter cracks and crevices. Marabou feathered jigs and even freshwater spinners like the Shyster and Roostertail may also work at times.

Summary

Poke poling is a rather unusual form of saltwater angling with few practitioners. Since the low tide period is overwhelmingly the best time for this technique, poke poling is something that can be done as a casual half-day outing. This is not to say that the fish won't bushwack a bait or a lure in these spots all day long—they definitely will! Besides low tide, also consider working these tidal rocks in the early morning or at dusk. Fish are much less wary with the dimly lit sky, especially when it comes to striking a bait!

Finally, keep in mind that not all rocks are alike. Some recurrently teem with fish. Make notes after your poke poling adventure to isolate the better fish-holding rocks for your next trip. Where possible, try to be somewhat mobile, and explore a range of different outcroppings along a given stretch of shoreline.

Albacore: Jig Strike!

In saltwater angling circles throughout California, there is probably nothing more exciting than the first reports of albacore being caught off the coast. This white meat tuna is the legendary "chicken of the sea." With their extraordinarily long pectoral fins, these migratory fish can actually traverse the Pacific in one year.

Albacore follow the cooler, greenish offshore currents, moving along the Pacific Coastline toward the Oregon border before they swing further out to sea. One important aspect of this sport involves finding the schools of albacore. Usually, the commercial fleet will radio in reports of their catches in semi-local waters around mid-July for the Southern bite. Northern sport fishing operators can expect albies to move in their direction by late August or September. For example, in recent years huge schools of big—40 to 60 pound albies—have been found off of Santa Cruz to San Francisco Bay as early as mid-July.

These time frames are highly tentative at best. There are certain conditions that must be met before the albacore travel within range of the sport fishing boats and private yachts. Many Southern California landings depend upon these game fish and the full boatloads of anglers their arrival generates. But, these pelagic warriors are extremely temperamental and often bypass our coastal waters for two or three seasons in a row. Conditions simply have to be nearly perfect.

Albacore trips are the most expensive single-day outings staged by the sport fishing landings. Many one-day trips last over 20 hours, since much time is spent running to the fishing grounds. Some landings now package 2 to 4 day trips to maximize fishing time once the tuna are located. Many albacore fanatics feel that this kind of mini long-range trip is the best value. These prized fish only "show" off our coast sporadically, they figure, so for the extra money, they maximize their chances of catching some albies with these longer outings. Also, these multi-day packages typically have reduced passenger loads compared to one-day junkets.

Locating Albacore

Many veteran sport fishing captains feel that water temperature and color are the pivotal variables to be considered in locating these fish. As soon as the skippers feel that the albacore are within sport fishing range—usually about 100 miles from the landing —all-day party and charter boats are launched to look for the longfins. Private vessels soon follow.

Once in the vicinity of the fish (based on reports from commercial boats or "scouting missions" sent by the landings) the skippers focus on water temperatures in the 63 to 65 degree range.

Private boaters who do not have temperature gauges in their craft can still receive accurate information from a pool thermometer. It is possible to gather recurrent samples of water using a bucket and immerse the thermometer to take temperature readings.

Next look for good, clean greenish-colored water. The albies gravitate to this band of offshore current. Sophisticated electronics are concurrently used to monitor sea temperature and water color. Fish finders will show you the sub-marine canyons and ledges where schools of bait are typically found. The tuna are frequently located on those same breaks foraging on the bait. Some skippers now actually use their sonar devices to pinpoint the schools of albacore and then fish them deep, well below the surface (more on this later).

Even without highly technical sonar equipment, you can use your eyes for spotting other potential telltale signs of albacore activity. Watch for birds dipping and feeding on the water. This may mean a school of tuna is pushing bait fish to the surface. Be on the lookout for floating kelp paddies. As I mentioned earlier, this migrating vegetation can form a major refuge for pelagic game fish—especially albacore. Veteran party and charter boat skippers now also monitor their sonar devices, looking for deep "meter marks" of albies suspended at 90-300 foot depths. It is not uncommon for the captain to leave his fish finder on, and all of a sudden stop the boat in the "middle of nowhere" over a school of tuna holding deep.

Finally, always keep your eyes peeled for major surface boils. There is nothing more exciting than to be cruising for hours without a sign of life and then to suddenly stumble upon a square acre of albacore boiling on the surface!

Now that we are in the area where the albies should be, let's gear up and examine the ways to catch them!

Four Basic Outfits

The general consensus is that it is best to carry at least four outfits on an albacore excursion. A medium-class trolling rig is essential. Party boaters will typically have a random drawing to see which anglers will get a chance to troll from the stern. Not all fishermen want to stand a "trolling watch" at the rail; they may pass up the opportunity, preferring to stay in the galley or their bunks. But it is often the case that the trolled fish may be the only albacore caught that day as the schools refuse to come to the boat.

A Penn 113-H to Penn 114-H (4/0 to 6/0 size) big-game reel, loaded with 50 to 80 pound mono is the basic albacore trolling outfit teamed with a roller guide rod in the 50 to 80 pound I.G.F.A. class. The new Penn 10 and 15 KG series of two-speed reels are also terrific for making albacore trolling even more easy when you have to haul in a 30-40 pound longfin quickly.

Most anglers want to take a shot at tossing live bait to the longfins. Here, two setups with medium-sized conventional reels are needed. The baitcasters should hold about 300 yards of 15 to 20 pound test monofilament. The rods are typical 6 1/2 to 7 foot hyperbolic (fast taper) live bait rods—preferably single piece blanks. The action can be hot and furious on a wide-open albacore bite, so expect some tangles and broken lines. Having that extra back-up outfit ready saves a lot of time, particularly if the "jig stop" is short, with only a sparse number of fish taken on live bait.

The fourth outfit should be a larger size casting reel capable of spooling 300 yards of 30 pound string matched with a heavy-duty 6 1/2 to 7 foot bait rod. This rig can be used for throwing jigs or other lures on the albies. Also, you never know when a school of 30 to 40 pounders will attack the chum line, so the heavy gear is more properly matched for these "big guys."

Albacore trips are no place for spinning outfits—not even the best of the models. These fish can make sizzling runs and really put a strain on the equipment. The star drag system, heavy gearing, and larger spool capacities intrinsic to baitcasting equipment are more suitable for fish in this class. Statistics kept over the years indicate that the average size albacore caught off California is right around 22 pounds. These are too large to have to rely upon spinning gear to tame.

Trolling Tactics

Most skippers recommend trolling for albacore at a modest 6 to 10 knots. There are times however, due to major offshore swells, that the boat will have to throttle down to keep the lures in the water.

As for lures, feathered jigs are the overwhelmingly best option for these game fish. The standard rig is a 15 mm Severstrand Trolling Feather or Tuna Clone, or an Area Rule Engineering unique Tu-Nob with a double hook. I recommend using a 50 to 80 pound leader about 5 to 6 feet in length with a ball-bearing swivel attached to the main line. It is not necessary to use a wire leader.

The 15 mm feather is most popular. However, there are times when a smaller 10 mm model works better. Use the Severstrand TC100 model when a tiny feather is

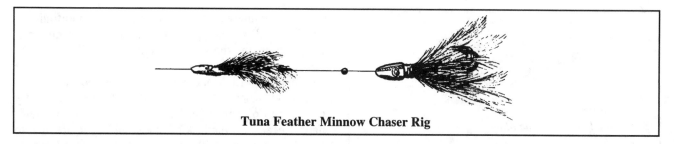

Tuna Feather Minnow Chaser Rig

needed. Party boat captains usually let the trollers know what the albies have been hitting on so they can key in on the proper feather size. Private boaters might consider dragging a variety of jigs in different sizes if they are not privy to information garnered in recent days.

There are a few other little tricks worth noting that you can experiment with in using feathers. Run your leader line through a smaller 10 mm feather and secure it about 3 to 4 feet above the end of the mono. To secure it and keep it from sliding any further, pinch a small lead shot behind it. Note that this feather thus does not have a hook in it. Next, thread on a larger 15 mm model to the end of the line tied to a double hook. When this setup is trolled through the water, it gives the illusion of a larger bait fish (the 15 mm jig) chasing a smaller prey (the 10 mm jig).

A variation of this chaser rig is to run a series of 10 mm —or even 15 mm—feathers spaced about 12 to 18 inches apart in tandem. This "daisy chain" effect was borrowed from East Coast tuna fishermen who have used it for years with great success. The daisy chain of 3 to 6 feathers spaced apart simulates an entire school of bait fish when trolled at modest speeds. Or, you can replace the smaller tuna feathers with soft plastic, squid-like "hoochies." These lures, originally designed for Salmon mooching, excel when strung together to form an albacore daisy chain setup.

With regard to selecting the proper trolling feather color, this can become a frustrating hit-or-miss proposition. There are, however, a couple of broad, general guidelines that the reader may find helpful.

First, stay with dark-colored feathers in the morning or under overcast skies. Colors like solid black, black and purple, green and blue, or black and green, present a better silhouette for the fish to see under dim light conditions.

As the morning haze clears, switch to more opulent patterns. Popular combinations include the "basic three":

green and yellow, blue and white, and red and white. Other combinations that produce are "zucchini"—a white, yellow, orange, and chartreuse blend of feathers; "the Mexican Flag"—red, white, and green; and the "Fourth of July"—red, white, and blue.

Sometimes it helps to devise your own unique color scheme in the field. For example, take a 15 mm jig in black and purple and thread it on top of another 15 mm model in, say, green and blue. Now you have a lure comprised of the two jigs riding tandem against each other that is larger both in terms of length and bulk, with twice as many feathers. I have personally found that this combination produces when traditional, single 15 mm jigs aren't getting bit. There are larger feathered jigs available with bigger heads and more feathers used for trophy tuna. However, by rigging two 15 mm models in tandem, you still maintain a slimmer profile to the lure which is less imposing to smaller 10 to 20 pound albacore than a large tuna feather.

Another tip I discovered some years ago came from Leonard Hashimoto, one of the principle designers of the popular tuna feathers. Hashimoto found that in banner albacore years, a number of the commercial operators trolling for the longfins were requesting a 15 mm feather in solid white. This jig is fairly unspectacular looking, especially on the retailer's shelf. But, I was given some to try and they can be deadly! Severstrand markets their solid white model, along with Area Rule Engineering's variation, a color they call "ghost."

I have used solid white feathers in both dim and bright light conditions. A pearl pink or even chartreuse head works fine. If your local tackle stores don't have this trolling color in stock, inquire if they can special order it for you. Most of the albacore feathers sold along the coast are made by local manufacturers such as Severstrand and Area Rule Engineering. If you can get a few of your fishing friends to

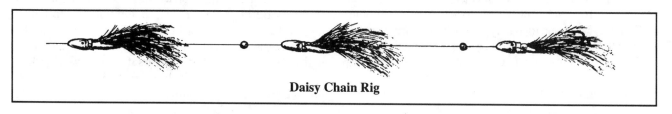

Daisy Chain Rig

*(Two 15mm feathers,
one pushed up inside the other)*

Tandem Hooked Feathers

go in for a half a dozen apiece, the dealer may consider putting in an order for solid white feathers.

Instead of a traditional feathered jig, there are also models that utilize brightly colored, "psychedelic" plastic skirts. The Seven Strand Hex Head with its radical six-sided, chrome head is an effective alternative to try in lieu of 10 to 15 mm feathers. These can also be rigged in a "chaser" setup or tandem for greater body and length.

For private boaters, when you troll lures in this genre, it is important at times to vary direction. In one situation, the albies may want the lure trolled up swell, another time down swell. Sometimes it helps to zigzag the lure as the boat moves along to create a more erratic effect with the feathers.

Some skippers also like to "box in" a particular area where they believe the fish are holding. They simply set up a trolling pattern in the shape of a box, running approximately equidistant in four directions to concentrate on a confined location.

Novice trollers often make the mistake of letting out too much line. On party boats and private charters, the crew will carefully set the jigs back behind the boat at the proper distance. A good rule of thumb is to let out no more than 40 to 80 feet of line—max. You want to troll the feathers in the wake or just outside it. Don't worry if the jig occasionally skips along the surface. This makes it look even more like a fleeing bait fish.

On private yachts, try to run at least two different lengths of line, at least initially, to decipher the pattern for the day. It is not uncommon for the albacore to bite "short" while the jig is just barely beyond the prop wash.

I have found times when the albies would not strike a feather trolled directly on the surface. Here's where that heavier 8 to 16 ounce ringed torpedo weight I talked about in Chapter 5 comes in handy. Clip ball-bearing snap-swivels to both ends of the sinker. Tie your main line and the leader to the feathers to each end of the weight. This will keep the feathers considerably below the surface at normal trolling speeds.

Another interesting tactic I've had the opportunity to try firsthand was demonstrated to me by a commercial tuna fisherman who worked from a small 22 foot boat. Instead of using monofilament line on his trolling reels, he would spool with Monel wire. The wire does not stretch like mono. When an albacore strikes a feather tied directly to a strand of wire line, he practically hooks himself—hard. Because of the lack of line stretch, you are able to reel the longfins in with considerable ease. Another benefit is that the wire will help to keep the feathers below the surface and riding more evenly since it is much heavier than mono.

Wire line like this does, however, break easily if it is inadvertently bent in any one spot. Careful winding and handling are essential in using this material instead of monofilament. It is better and safer to spool the wire onto a narrow-bodied reel such as a Penn 49 or 349 series. The wire is easier to wind in and to lay onto the reel with the narrow spool design.

It is absolutely imperative to reel that jig fish in quickly. Hopefully the school will follow. If there are multiple rods trolling on the stern, immediately take your reel out of gear and let your feather drop back a few feet if your jig is not the first bit. This little ploy sometimes results in a few additional jig fish being caught. By dropping back your feather, you may get a more wary albie to bite that didn't follow the first jig-caught fish to the boat.

More Trolling Secrets

Large saltwater plugs can be trolled for albacore. Usually party boat skippers prefer to use feathers because they are more manageable with a double hook, in contrast to sharp trebles, and they foul up less.

But there are times when the longfins will readily attack a plug trolled at about 7 to 8 knots. The Rapala CD-14 and CD-18 Magnums are probably the best overall plugs for trolling for albacore. Try gold/green mackerel, blue/silver mackerel, silver/black back fire tiger in these plugs. Likewise, throttle down and drag a saltwater-sized Rapala behind the stern. These also can be highly productive at times.

Larger plastic baits such as A.A. Worms swimbaits or the new Berkley Power swimbaits can be trolled at moderate speeds for albacore. Here it pays to be experimental, with such a wide array of colors available with these lures. Again, it's fairly safe to stay with darker, opaque colors under dimly lit skies, switching to bright schemes with sunny conditions.

Albies on Live Bait

Most albacore are caught on live bait, usually anchovies. At times they will strike both live squid and smaller sardines, but over the years, they prefer the anchovies. After the jig fish is reeled in, wait for the boat to come to a fairly complete stop. I like to begin bait fishing by fly-lining a 'chovy weightless, without a sinker. Hook sizes will range from small Eagle Claw #318-N #6 live bait hooks for pinhead anchovies, on up to #1/0 hooks for "race horse" size baits.

I will state it once again: it is critical to be highly selective in picking a 'chovy from the bait tank. Try to find a greenback if possible. Avoid selecting a red-nose bait, no matter how large it is. Their noses are red from banging against the tank. Expect red-nose 'chovies to be more lethargic and possibly injured.

As for hooking methods, start with hooking the anchovy gently under the gill cover. If the bait is particularly small, then consider a nose hooking. To get the 'chovy to swim deeper without adding any weight, try hooking it under the anal fin.

Even with bait fishing, there are a lot of insiders' secrets that separate the experts from the novices. For example, the albacore veterans will invariably plant themselves in the downwind corner of the stern. This is where the bait will concentrate the best from the chumming process. It is also important to keep changing baits—frequently. Allow 3 to 5 minutes of soakin' the 'chovy, then get another bait from the tank.

Keep your line perpendicular to the boat at all times. By "squaring off" with your bait, you will have a better feel for the strike and ultimate control of the fish when it makes its first run.

There are varying opinions as to what is the best method to employ once you get bit. Some anglers will actually fish the reel in gear, holding the rod trip high. When the fish strikes and pulls the rod down to the horizon, they swing and set. Others prefer to free-spool the bait, let the albie run for 5 to 6 seconds, throw the reel into gear and set. Once the fish is hooked, be prepared to move—QUICKLY! With the yell of "Hot Rail—Comin' Through," follow your fish around the boat. Keep your rod fairly high, with your line out away from the other anglers as much as possible. When you see the fish in the clear water toward the end of the fight, call out "color," which informs either deck hands or friends you are ready for the gaff.

If the albacore are holding deeper, much below the surface, fly-line the 'chovy by adding a sinker. A large split-shot pinched 12 to 18 inches above the bait will work as will the more traditional rubber core, twist-on sinkers. It is not uncommon, on deep fish (known as a "plunker bite") to use as much as 1 to 1 1/2 ounces of weight to get to the longfins.

A Multiple Hooking Trick

If you stalk albacore from a private boat let me pass along an interesting strategy for live bait fishing. To begin with, realize that due to the size of the vessel, you may have limited chum power. Because of this, you may get only one or two chances during the day to hold fish near the boat. On a small craft with two or three anglers, have at least two or three live bait outfits rigged and ready to go.

As the jig fish is being reeled in, the other passengers can fly-line a 'chovy. Once a live bait hookup occurs, leave the reel in gear, but place the rod in a rod holder. Then quickly bait up and cast a second—or even a third rig if the second gets bit! Place the second or third rods in holders also.

Then, as strange as this scenario may seem, go back and play the first albacore out. It will have been "soaking" there while you were sticking a second or third fish. In my firsthand experience with this multiple hookup tactic, I found that the longfins simply sulk at the end of the line as long as they feel no pressure from the angler starting to pump the rod. And it is truly an amazing sight to see three or four albies on the ends of rods sitting in rod holders waiting to be reeled in!

In this way, even with limited chum capabilities, small boaters can have the maximum opportunity to nail albacore on live bait following a jig stop.

Fishing the Slide

While the jig fish is being reeled in, the captain will shut the boat down and it will kind of glide to a halt before the drift pattern is set. At this time, albacore may come rapidly charging toward the boat, following the jig fish. Some of the pros will quickly head for the corner and simply lower a bait or lure down into the water and let the momentum of the boat pay out the line. This is termed "fishing the slide." There are two basic methods for nailing albies in this situation.

The first involves using live bait. Take a 1 to 1 1/2 ounce chrome-plated double ring sinker and tie it to your live bait outfit. To the other end of the ring tie a 18 to 24 inch length of leader with your live bait hook. As you "shoot" this rig over the side, the heavier sinker keeps the bait down, but also serves as an attractant to the following fish.

The second technique involves using artificial baits. Candy bar style jigs, spoons, and even plastic tail-swimming lures can be "shot" out over the stern and then retrieved as the boat comes to a stop. For some reason, red-colored lures—for example, a Salas Yo-Yo 4 heavy jig in red and white—have always caught their share of albies on the slide. But other colors such as blue and white, sardine, mackerel, and solid chrome are also viable patterns. Metallic flake finishes in the plastics including blue, silver, smoke/sparkle, green, and root beer should be tried. Popular "iron" in this genre are the Salas CP-105 and 6XJR, Tady A1 and AA, and the Ironman #3 or #5. Also, try to drop a great swimming Jerry Jig surface iron back on the slide where the albies are hot.

All of the above-mentioned lures can also be used in a more conventional cast-and-surface-retrieve, or in a deeper yo-yoing presentation. On party boats, however, this has to be done on the bow—if the situation permits it —due to greater numbers of anglers bunched at the stern. Albacore caught on lures retrieved in this fashion can be terrific sport and an alternative to fighting the crowds on the stern.

In recent years, a lot of albacore have been caught on the "slide" using the soft plastic A.A. Worms, Berkley Power, and Fish Trap swimbaits. These lures replicate larger anchovies or small sardines—a favorite forage of the longfin tuna. I actually add a drop or two of super glue to insure that the soft plastic body of the swimbait stays securely attached to the 1/2 to 2 ounce lead head. Otherwise, the tuna will frequently pull the plastic body down along the shank of the hook following an albacore "short" strike.

Other Tunas

Bigeye and yellowfin tuna migrate up the coast especially during warmer El Nino seasons. Many of the same tactics described for albacore will work for these pelagic battlers. However, consider scaling up in tackle.

Schools of yellowfin in the 12 to 20 pound range have come in just a few miles off the Southern California Coast in recent years. The standard 4/0 trolling outfit and companion live bait setups used for albacore will work on yellowfin in this size bracket. But, further offshore, marauding schools of 50 to 150 pound yellowfin and their bigeye cousins will really tear up light to medium-sized tackle. Fish in this range are termed "gorillas" by the local anglers. Trolling tackle should be in the 60 pound class, live bait outfits in the 30 to 50 pound range. Larger reels, greater spool capacities, and stouter rods are in order.

The same cast iron jigs outlined for fishing the slide or yo-yoing for albacore will work for yellowfin. But also consider "dropping back" with a big CD-18 Magnum Rapala or a Jerry Jig surface-swimming jig. Dorado

mixed in with the yellowfin tuna will also attack any of these lures fished on the slide.

These bigger tuna will eat everything from a 15 mm feather on up to a medium-sized marlin jig. Live bait fishing is best with mackerel or sardines, using the smaller 'chovies primarily as chum.

Bluefin tuna are another story all together. Although these fish many frequently top the 30 to 40 pound mark, many anglers are adamant that these are the spookiest of the tunas. So, some experts scale down dramatically in hook size and line test. It is not uncommon to see veteran party boaters using smaller reels, loaded with 300 yards of 12 pound string, softer-tipped rods, and tiny #6 to #8 bronze live bait hooks. Some feel that the bronze hooks create a less unnatural flash than chrome-plated models.

Bluefin are primarily caught locally off the Southern Coast using these light-line tactics. This is a very precise form of finesse, saltwater angling. Bluefin, which often school with albacore, will more readily hit the feathered jigs, heavier mono, and larger hooks. But, don't be surprised to see schools of 12 to 30 pound bluefin cruising off the nearby kelp beds, and around our offshore islands. These will usually be taken by accomplished light-liners. When bluefin tuna are really skittish, switch to Berkley's Vanish fluorocarbon line. Unlike monofilament, the Vanish is almost totally invisible and can be deadly on bluefin.

I might add that bluefin will also definitely strike candy bar style jigs and occasionally spoons like the Crippled Herring, Deep Stinger, or Krocadile. Solid chrome, blue and chrome, and blue and white patterns are historically the best colors.

Summary

Albacore fishing can be tantamount to seeing the World Series in person for many of California's saltwater buffs. For Central and Northern anglers opportunities to make a run at these fish are rarer than for Southland fishermen. So it is important to scan your outdoor press for up-to-the-minute reports of possible longfin activity.

Count on a 16 to 22 hour trip in order to reach the offshore schools of albacore. Shorter trips are possible in the Central and Northern parts if the schools swing close to the shore. The albacore as well as the yellowfin, bluefin, and bigeye tuna will really put a test to even the best tackle. Top quality rods, reels, and monofilament line is a must. Some fishermen will only have one or two days at most to take a shot at these pelagic bruisers. With considerable time and money invested in one of these offshore adventures, don't scrimp on tackle—go "first class" with the best gear you can afford. The difference will be worth it!

Barracuda: Pacific Torpedoes!

Barracuda are kind of like the comedian, Rodney Dangerfield—they simply don't get the respect they deserve. On one hand, our Pacific variety are occasionally confused with the more stereotyped and menacing Atlantic barracuda. On the other hand, "scooters," "barries," "'cuda" or just plain "slime" as they are sometimes known, are often fished as an afterthought. The assorted larger stripers, salmon, tuna, bonito, bass, and of course, albacore and yellowtail, are all more highly sought after than barracuda.

But, the fact of the matter is, 'cuda are sensational sport on medium-to-light gear. They frequent Southern California waters on practically an all-year basis, and they readily devour both live bait and artificial lures. In warm water years, barries have made it all the way up to San Francisco, providing Northerners with an unusual treat from this Southern visitor.

'Cuda are primarily a coastal school fish. They are found inside harbors and bays, around bait receivers, along outside kelp beds, and around offshore southern islands. Like tuna, scooters will push bait to the surface. So look for signs of schooling activity such as dipping birds, surface boils, or sometimes fish humping clear out of the water. The Coronado Islands, the Barn Kelp off

Oceanside, the Horseshoe Kelp near Long Beach, and Santa Monica Bay are all popular barracuda hot spots.

Scooters on Bait

Years ago, saltwater fishermen strongly believed that you had to use a wire leader to catch barries. Hundreds of thousands of Blue Ribbon Shorty's were sold in the Southland. This was a wire leader about eight inches long, tied to a short-shank live bait hook. The theory was that the compact wire leader would maximize the strike-to-catch ratio of these exceptionally toothy game fish. Back in the late fifties and sixties, there were large populations of 'cuda and 7 to 10 pound "logs" were often weighed in at the docks.

This fishery, like many in the West, has been impacted. A 28 inch minimum size limit has helped to restore it to some degree. But these fish are still somewhat pressured, so it will take more expertise to fool them. To begin with, discard the notion of fishing 'cuda with wire leaders. Tie directly to your line.

Charter Boat skipper, Tom Schlauch of the Dreamer out of Long Beach, specializes in fishing scooters. He has found that his barracuda counts have risen dramatically in past seasons by not only tying hooks directly to the monofilament, but also scaling all the way down to 10 to 12 pound string. Without question, some fish will be lost, sawing through the fine diameter line. But, live anchovies will swim better, and the barries have a harder time seeing the light mono.

Stay with standard Eagle Claw live bait hooks—either nickel or bronze—in sizes #6 to #1/0 depending on the size of the 'chovies. You might also try the Eagle Claw #254 long-shank or the #197 circle models to minimize getting bit off by the 'cuda. As with most live bait fishing, it is probably best to start out with a weightless, fly-lined bait on the surface. If the scooters are down deeper, use a light rubber core sinker or a pinch of shot.

Whether you are fishing on the surface or working your baits deeper, it's important to let barracuda run with the anchovy. These fish will pick up the bait, run with it a little, mouth it, turn with it, then make a longer sustained run as they finally eat it. Have a little patience, wait a few moments before you set up on the 'cuda.

Another little trick is to rig up a ringed chrome torpedo sinker as was discussed for fishing the slide with albacore. The chrome sinker attached above the leader and the bait will definitely attract the barries with its flash as it settles beneath the surface.

Another tip: learn to "pump" your bait when fishing for barracuda. If the 'chovy is being worked below the surface, once you reach a reasonable depth where you think the fish are holding, slowly lift the rod tip and "pump" the bait back to the boat. This "pumping" retrieve is basically a slow lift-wind-drop-pause-slow lift motion.

The three principle hooking techniques for the anchovies work with barracuda: gill hook for surface fly-lining; anal fin hook for deeper swimming bait; and nose hook with pinhead 'chovies.

Also, in playing out 'cuda on light 10 to 20 pound test lines, it pays to keep constant pressure on the fish. Try not to "stroke" the barrie with jerky, pumping actions once the fish is hooked. This has the effect of causing the fine diameter mono to chafe against the scooter's numerous teeth and eventually break from the fraying. This simple practice of slowly reeling in the barracuda with constant pressure applied is a hot secret the party boat pros use to raise their personal fish counts on barries.

After each 'cuda you catch on live bait is landed, take time to check the last 18 inches of your line for nicks and frays. I encourage you to do this after every fish. Re-tie hooks as necessary.

Barries on Lures

On a wide-open barracuda bite, accomplished lure fishermen can put a major dent in the scooter population. First, use jigs, plastics, spoons, or plugs with single hooks. Replace the trebles when possible. Barries are a lot easier to handle when caught on single-hook lures. The solitary hook will give you better leverage on the fish, but will also be easier to remove from that toothy mouth.

Saltwater spoons such as the Krocadile, Crippled Herring, Deep Stinger, and Haddock's Jig'n spoon series are terrific lures for these fish. Nickel, gold, blue prism 'chovy, mackerel, and nickel/fluorescent stripe are winning combinations in spoons for 'cuda. The Tady metal wobbler—when you can find it—has also been a time-proven killer for barracuda.

Spoons can be retrieved on a straight surface grind or yo-yoed off the bottom. With the surface retrieve, here's a little trick to try. As you are winding the spoon barely under the surface, stop every once in a while to let the lure flutter down. Many times the 'cuda will strike the spoon on the sink like this. A "stop'n go" retrieve is also applicable to fishing cast-metal jigs.

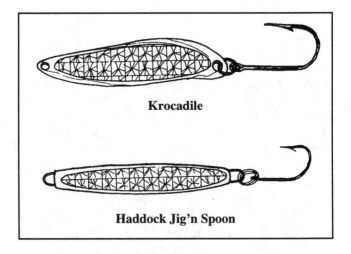

Krocadile

Haddock Jig'n Spoon

On this note, the traditional candy bar style jigs are excellent for barries, but drop down in length to a 3 to 5 inch model. Use the "light" alloy jigs for the surface crank and the "heavy" versions for yo-yoing. Barracuda prefer candy bar designs in solid chrome, chrome and blue, sardine, mackerel, blue and white, and green and yellow. The real "sleeper" in barrie jigs used primarily by long-time scooter fishermen is solid white. Definitely add a smaller Ironman, Jerry Jig, Salas, or Tady in simple solid white to your repertoire of 'cuda lures.

Barries will frequently climb all over plastic tail-swimming lures. Scampis, Lunker Thumpers, Berkley Power Pogeys, Mojos, A.A. Worms swimbaits, or Optimum swimbaits—they'll all work—can really get torn apart by these toothy torpedoes. The new Possum Lures are actually pretty rugged compared to traditional soft plastic swimbaits, and will withstand most 'cuda attacks. Popular metal flake patterns ranging from green, blue, and silver to root beer, purple, and black will all produce. Make certain to sharpen the cadmium hooks used with most of these soft plastic baits to insure maximum penetration with the barracuda.

Rapalas and Rebel plugs likewise catch a lot of 'cuda throughout the season. These plugs are too dangerous to use in most party boat and charter situations. But private boaters can have a field day with them both trolling and free-casting to the 'cuda. Be prepared, however, to change treble hooks frequently. The head-shaking, twisting action from a 6 to 7 pound "log" barrie will annihilate the bronze trebles on the smaller plugs.

A single, long-shank, Siwash hook should be considered as a replacement for the weaker bronze trebles.

With Rapalas and Rebels, stay with the basics. Silver with black back, chrome with blue back, and mackerel finishes will work fine with the scooters. Once again, tie directly to the plug—do not use a snap-swivel.

Feather fishermen are a dying breed. But those who can rhythmically stroke-pump a single-hook chrome Japanese head can rack up awesome scores of scooters. Barracuda love a feather twitched under the surface. Veteran feather fishermen prefer longer 8 foot, soft-tip parabolic rods to give them an exaggerated, yet gentle jerk on the feather. Be prepared for many strikes to occur after the pull, as the feather is lying nearly motionless in the water. Red and white, blue and white, and solid white feathers are the top picks for anglers wanting to add a new dimension to their barrie fishing.

Summary

Barracuda comprise a major portion of the sport fish counts in the Southland. In certain years, they will migrate all the way up into the Monterey area. They are fantastic sport, especially on light line.

Don't hesitate to toss lures on these game fish when you are into a school of barries. Greater numbers of fish, and some of the larger "log" barracuda can be caught by the accomplished lure fisherman.

Saltwater Bass: Grumpers, Bulls and Whites

When it comes to finding saltwater game fish that will bite all year long, it's hard to beat calico and sand bass. Both of these fish are primarily warmer water species, but they will migrate well above Point Conception at times. In Southern California, they play an integral role in the fish counts for numerous landings.

Sandies

Barred sand bass are clearly the easier of the two species to fool. These fish move into close coastal waters between May and July. This is the prime spawning period for sandies as they school up on hard packed sand and muddy bottoms.

Sand bass can be found in anywhere from 40 to 100 foot depths. Occasionally catches are made in shallower water, with sandies sometimes being taken from piers or even in the surf. But, the greatest volume of fish are found in that 40 to 100 foot water.

There is no telling where sand bass will show in numbers. Historically, the Imperial Beach area to the far south, Oceanside, and the Huntington Beach Flats have been havens for major sand bass activity.

Schools of sandies will light up a graph recorder or an LCR. Many private boaters wait for the first reports of the fish moving up onto the flats. Then they can easily follow the fleet out to the general area where the fish are holding.

Don't be surprised to find these fish layered from the bottom to the surface. Numerous times I have watched party boat anglers bouncing jigs on the bottom nailing fish in 60 feet of water, while fly-liners in the stern were also racking up the sandies.

Grumpers on Bait

Sand bass are one of the easier game fish to catch with live bait. They can be chummed to the surface with fresh 'chovies. Assorted cut baits like squid or mackerel can be chunked and also used as chum in a pinch. These fish seem to have a "frenzy mentality." Once you start catching a few, more and more sandies will often follow, balling up under the boat.

Sliding Egg Sinker Sand Bass Live Bait Rig

Standard live bait outfits are more than adequate for a sand bass safari. Popping rods with heavy-duty freshwater baitcasters spooled with 10 to 12 pound test line are perfect. Most spinning gear will also subdue these bass.

Anchovies hooked in practically any place and lowered to the bottom are the common practice for bait fishing sandies. Most anglers twist on a 1/2 to 2 ounce rubber core sinker to maintain contact with the bottom. Others prefer to use a sliding egg sinker (1/2 to 1 ounce) rig with an 18 to 24 inch leader.

A simple variation is to run your line through a sliding-egg sinker and tie your hook directly to the end. The weight then actually butts up against the hook. This setup gets the bait right to the bottom. The sand bass are not particularly selective feeders and they will jump on the live bait. As they tug on the 'chovy, it will slide freely away from the egg sinker. This is a simple rig but it really works quite well when you want that bait presented as deep as possible.

Some long-time sand bassers also use a double live bait setup. You can construct this by using a sliding sinker and a three-way swivel. Use two different lengths of leader line and two live bait hooks. When the sandies are schooled tight, this double rig can put a 10 fish limit on the deck with five drops!

Another one of my favorite setups is to use a 2 to 4 ounce chrome torpedo sinker for a slider. Thread your line through one of the rings and butt it with a swivel. Attach an 18 to 24 inch length of leader with the live bait hook. The chrome weight acts as a flashy attractant in contrast to a bland, sliding-egg sinker.

If you want to get tricky, add a split ring and either a single or a small treble hook to the torpedo weight. Sometimes the sand bass will hit the shiny sinker as it is falling to the bottom. Or, as you stick a bass on the live bait leader, don't be startled to feel another "thunk" on your way up as a second sandy hits the chrome weight with the stinger hook!

Other baits besides live anchovies will take sand bass. Some of the biggest "grumpers" (6 to 8 pounders) I have seen were caught on whole frozen squid or healthy strips of fresh mackerel fillet. Sand bass are voracious feeders without the most discriminating palate. Don't hesitate to try different and larger baits if you want to put one of those grumpers in the gunny sack.

Sandies on Lures

Novice anglers can have an absolute field day using artificials for sand bass. There are also occasions where

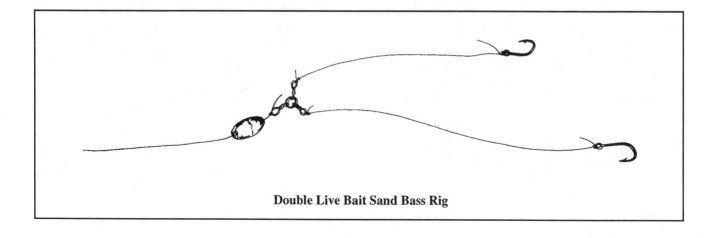

Double Live Bait Sand Bass Rig

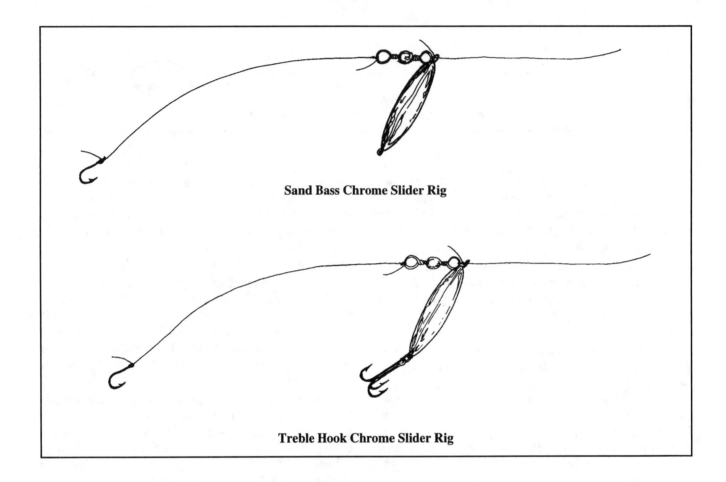

Sand Bass Chrome Slider Rig

Treble Hook Chrome Slider Rig

the lure fishermen will thoroughly trounce the bait soakers when the sandies want a slow-swimming presentation.

Soft plastics excel on these fish. You name it—Salty Magics, Mojos, Possum Lures, Optimum lures, A.A. Worms swimbaits, Scampis, Lunker Thumpers, Scroungers, and Kalin's Salty Grubs all work. Use heavier 1 to 1 1/2 ounce jig heads for bouncing the plastics off the bottom. Switch to lighter 1/2 to 3/4 ounce heads if the fish are suspended and seem to want a slow-falling bait.

At one time or another, almost all the various colors produce. Root beer flake, lime flake, and two fluorescent colors—chartreuse and hot pink—always lead the sand bass parade. The fish will definitely hit the plastics without any trimmings. However, you will generate more strikes by adding a small 1 x 3 inch frozen squid tippet to the plastic jig. As a bonus, squirt some Berkley Saltwater Attractant all over the jig'n squid combo.

Sand bass—and particularly the larger grumpers—will eat the "iron." Don't think twice about lowering a 3 to 5 inch candy bar jig in a heavy pattern over the side. The

sandies will eat the cast-metal jig on the yo-yo—both on the lift and the drop. Solid chrome, solid white, scrambled egg, and blue and white are popular candy bar colors for sand bassin'.

Smaller Diamond Jigs with highly polished finishes are similarly effective on a yo-yo for sandies. The Hopkins spoon in either gold or nickel patterns along with the Haddock Jig'n Spoon are equally productive.

As a final note, sand bass can also be taken on the troll. Small boaters can often drag a medium-to-large size Rapala minnow through the potential sand bass grounds. On one outing with my father, we were trying to meter the bass off of San Onofre. Hordes of mackerel confused our electronics, so we decided to troll CD-18 Rapalas. We quickly struck sandies at 15 feet below the surface. Little did we know that the fish were layered like a ten-story building from top to bottom. After landing a nice four pounder, we stopped the boat and began to toss plastic lures. We racked up a three-person, thirty-fish limit in less than an hour! Trolling the plugs in the basic area helped us locate the huge school of bass.

Calicos

In contrast to sand bass, calicos prefer the shelter of offshore rocks, kelp, and sunken reefs. To be sure, there are situations in which the sandies will be mixed in with the calico bass near offshore kelp or, as I noted, inside some of the major breakwaters. But generally, anglers seem to key in on either one or the other species.

Kit McNear is a veteran charter boat skipper who works the Santa Barbara area. He specializes in finding calico bass. McNear stresses the need for private boaters to invest in a high quality graph recorder or LCR unit. Using his electronics, he concentrates on locating hard bottom adjacent to the offshore kelp beds. As was noted in earlier chapters, calicos will definitely hole up in thick kelp; but, sometimes larger boats can't position themselves into the kelp beds so all passengers can fish equally. This is where the outside area comprised of the hard bottom becomes a major alternative spot.

McNear continues his search by looking for other places where few people fish for calicos. The boiler rocks outside the kelp line can sometimes hold enough bass for private boats and smaller charter craft.

Similarly, he recommends seeking out water movement on the windward side of our offshore islands. Fish an incoming rising high tide, and work your baits or lures in tight to the kelp. Novice party boat anglers are too hesitant at times to throw near the kelp. But, this is where the larger "bull" calicos live. Cast your offerings as close to the kelp stringers as possible, or anywhere around the islands where a churning white water condition exists from tidal surge.

Bull Bass on Bait

Medium-weight live bait outfits are compatible for fishing calicos, spooled with 15 to 20 pound test mono. High quality spinning tackle is also a viable option but is best suited for open water instead of kelp bed areas. As with barracuda, if you can get by using a lighter line, say 10 to 12 pound string, you will get bit more. This is particularly true when using anchovies.

Standard live bait procedures work when fishing calicos with 'chovies. Gill, nose, and anal fin hooking is applicable depending upon the size of the bait and whether or not the bass are feeding deep or on the surface. Hook sizes range from #1 to #6 for most 'chovy-caught calicos.

But, as Kit McNear notes, bull bass are rarely caught on anchovies. He recommends that private boaters use their 'chovies primarily for chumming purposes. If you want big bass—use big baits!

Smelt, grunion, and sardines can often tally up some larger specimens. These are fished best either gill-hooked or through the anal fin, and fly-lined without any sinker.

Long-time tackle representative and big game specialist, Mike Callan, has put on some awesome demonstrations fishing big bull bass using whole live Spanish or greenback mackerel. Callan uses longer 8 foot heavy-duty jig Sticks and 20 to 40 pound test line, and larger #4/0 to #6/0 Eagle Claw #318-N live bait hooks. Pinning the hook through the mackerel's nostrils, he will make long lob casts into the fringes of the kelp.

There are a couple of tricks involved here with fishing macks for bull calicos. First, the cast has to be a gentle lob, with the help from the longer rod. If you exert too much force on the cast, the hook will pull out of the mackerel. Secondly, once the mack hits the kelp, let it free-swim through the stringers. You have to give calicos this size some time to eat the big bait. When you set up on the fish, swing hard. Keep a fairly tight drag and pull the bass away from the kelp stringers out into open water.

Live mackerel are not always available in great quantities to sustain a group of party boat anglers. Instead, look through the bait tanks for various "brown baits" (tomcod, queenfish, herring, 7-11 perch, and baby pompano). Brown baits should be hooked either through the back below the dorsal fin, through the anal fin, or slightly below the pectoral fin. Brown baits usually fish best on a weightless fly-line, but sometimes it helps to use a small weight to get them down deeper.

Don't give up if you run out of fresh brown baits with only dead tomcod, herring, or queenfish remaining in the tank. The dead baits will still catch big bass, but there's a secret to making them work. If the brown bait is somewhat "stiff," bend it back and forth a little to make it more pliable and life-like.

After you cast the dead brown bait out, slowly "walk" it back in. This involves twitching the rod and slowly "pumping" the bait. This action will give the dead bait the illusion of a fluttering wounded morsel. It is up to the angler to then impart some of this life-like action to the dead brown bait.

One of this writer's favorite techniques is to fish big calicos with either whole live or frozen squid. Calicos are nocturnal feeders. Party boats will frequently arrive at the prime bass fishing areas in the wee hours of the morning while it is still pitch dark. They will set out an anchor and wait for daylight before starting a chum line.

If you can't sleep, or if you're interested in doing some serious "hawg huntin'" take out a medium to heavy outfit (20-40 pound mono) and rig up a chrome ring torpedo sinker (1 to 2 ounce) with an 18 inch leader and a #4/0 live bait hook. Fish a whole squid right on the bottom. I have caught some big bull bass by doing this at night, while the remaining passengers were deep in slumber in their bunks. Sharks, rays, and even a maverick white seabass are also possible takers of this midnight squid rig.

In the winter months, party boats will often have tankfuls of live squid. Passenger loads are traditionally light this time of year, and the calico bassin' can be fantastic! Big wintertime fish will readily strike the squid. You can fly-line these cephalopods, with or without a sinker, using a sliding-egg sinker rig or the chrome torpedo weight setup first mentioned. Veteran party boat pros await eagerly for the arrival of the squid in the Southland during the winter. This is the time to nail some lunker calicos with minimal passenger loads.

Calicos on Lures

Unlike sand bass, calicos seem much more temperamental when it comes to striking artificial lures. There are times when they literally inhale plastic baits, then the next day, they won't touch anything but a live 'chovy.

It is always worth the effort to intermittently make a few casts with plastics or a jig or spoon, even if the calicos are wide-open on live bait. Sometimes a larger fish will home in on the strange-looking intruder and crunch the artificial bait.

Plastic tail-swimming lures are far and away the most potent artificials for calicos. McNear relates that his logs indicate a plastic tail in root beer flake pattern is clearly the #1 color combination for calico bass. His second favorite is lime green with gold flake.

Other color schemes such as metallic silver, metallic blue, solid black, red, or purple should also be stocked in the calico arsenal. Personally, I have found that the dark opaque patterns such as red, purple, or black are productive at night or under dim light conditions.

If the fish are holding near the bottom, McNear recommends using a 1 to 2 ounce lead head with a double-tail plastic lure. However, if the bass are suspended some distance off the bottom—as calicos often are—then he shifts to a single-tail lure. His preference is a smoke with red flake tail, teamed with a bright red head.

McNear will then fish the calicos on the fall, or lure drop. He will use a lighter 1/2 to 3/4 ounce head, often adding a plastic skirt to the lure to make it sink more slowly. Calicos suspended like this can be very "twitchy" feeders. To insure both a slow-falling bait and super hook penetration, McNear suggests using jig heads with fine wire hooks instead of the heavier, duller cadmium hooks typically matched with saltwater plastics. Always be prepared for strikes as the lure is sinking.

McNear provides us with some further expert insights into this important fishery. He speculates that bigger calicos prefer to eat the plastics on the fall because they will expend less energy than they would if they had to chase a retrieved bait. Anglers become too impatient and fail to let the plastic offering glide down through the suspended fish. Instead, they cast out and quickly start retrieving the lure. This usually results in catching the smaller, more aggressive bass on the retrieve. Be patient —fish the fall for larger calicos!

Saltwater enthusiasts who like to throw "iron" can also nail an occasional bull bass. Here I recommend using larger jigs such as the Tady 45, Jerry Jig Surface Iron, or the Salas 7x, preferably a light model with a single hook. Cast-metal jigs in this construction can practically be thrown right on top of the kelp stringers and retrieved back to the boat.

Smaller 3 to 5 inch models work in both light versions for surface action and heavy weights for suspended calicos. One thing to keep in mind when fishing calicos on the iron—slow down a little with the retrieve. These fish are not as prone to eat a jig on a fast grind as is, for example, a yellowtail. A more moderate speed is needed. Try Ironman #2 or #4, Tady #AA, Salas Christy #1 or #2, or a small Jerry Jig.

Calicos will eat jigs in green and yellow, blue and white, chrome and blue, sardine, and mackerel finishes. One of my all-time favorites is a blue and white jig with a solid black underside. Throw the iron on about 30 pound string. This will allow you to pull both the jig and the bass out of the kelp stringers without excessive line stretch.

Smaller spoons such as Haddock's 1 1/8 ounce Jig'n Spoon in blue 'chovy finish, or the 3/4 to 1 ounce chrome Hopkins models will also catch calicos. These lures work particularly well on a yo-yo, but usually account for the smaller 1 to 2 pound "legals" (12 inch bass).

Fishing the Pots

Here is a very important piece of information for private boaters seeking calicos from October through March. Commercial lobster fishermen set out their lobster traps or "pots" on small rocky pinnacles up and down the Central through Southern Coast. These submerged rockpiles are sometimes difficult to discern, especially for small boaters with limited experience with electronics.

Look for the buoys that are set out to mark the location of these lobster traps. I have found that the best way to fish the pots is to set up drift patterns using plastic baits. Motor up above the buoy and then try to drift alongside it.

With a private boat, don't hesitate to set out multiple lines. Tail-swimming plastic lures with a tippet of squid are the best combinations to use. But here is one of my well-kept secrets: try a non-swimming grub. I have found that there are times when the calicos during these months are lethargic. They don't readily pounce on a swimming lure, but they will gently mouth a slow-moving grub. Try Haddock's large split-tail grub with a vinyl skirt and a squid trailer on the drift like this. My personal preference in colors include: white grub/red skirt, yellow grub/green and yellow skirt, motor oil grub/black skirt, and silver grub/black and silver skirt.

Over the years, when the calicos are gorged on small pelagic crabs, definitely switch to light line and the Haddock Kreepy Krawler. Use the Kreepy Krawler in the tomato/pepper color. You'll be amazed at how big "bull" bass will inhale this little bait!

Drifting the pots in this manner can result in some stellar calico catches in these colder months—and big bull bass to boot! Sand bass, white sea bass, halibut, and assorted rockfish can also be taken on these drifts using the plastic baits.

White Sea Bass

These fish are not true saltwater bass. They are actually members of the croaker family, akin to such fish as tomcod and corbina. "Whites" are a rather mysterious species. In past years, the number of sea bass was significantly depleted with commercial operations and sport fishers keeping immature fish. The imposition of minimum size limit of 28 inches combined with a two-fish maximum daily bag limit has helped to some degree to restore this delicate fishery. Still, you never really know where a straggler white or for that matter, an entire school will show up.

The Ribbon Kelp along the Coronado Islands out of San Diego, the Palos Verdes Peninsula, and Deep Hole near Malibu are areas that sometimes sustain a flurry of white sea bass activity. Whites can be taken, however, at times as far north as Morro Bay and San Simeon.

Whites are not overly picky feeders. Most are caught on bottom-bouncing baits, though don't eliminate the possibility of sticking a fly-line sea bass on the surface. Some are caught incidentally using anchovies.

But, if the bite is "on" in a certain locale for whites, think BIG! Whole fresh or frozen squid on live mackerel are strong candidates for a major meal for these giant croakers. The slider rig is a good way to fish whites, using heavier 1 to 5 ounce egg sinkers depending upon depth and current.

Buzz Brizendine is the owner-operator of the San Diego based sport fisher, the Prowler. Brizendine concurs that white sea bass are a highly unpredictable game fish. But, if he can gather a tankful of live squid for his customers in the winter, Brizendine has a sure-fire technique for white sea bass—if they are in the area.

The trick is to use a heavy ring sinker, somewhere between 6 and 12 ounces. Tie it to the end of your 20 to 30 pound test line. Then about 12 to 15 inches above the weight, tie a dropper loop. Next, add an 8 to 12 inch length of leader with a magnum size #6/0 live bait hook. Assuming that there are ample amounts of bait available, Brizendine will pin two live squid onto the #6/0 hook.

This dropper rig is potent at considerable depths. Brizendine has recorded catches of white sea bass using this setup all the way down to 270 feet.

Smaller white sea bass are sporadically taken on plastics, drifted and bounced along the bottom. The Optimum Swimbait, large Scampi, Berkley Power swimbait, and A.A. Worms' big swimbaits will nail "whites" quite often slowly retrieved on a 3/4 to 3 ounce lead head, usually on or near the bottom. However, for serious lure chuckin', use a larger size jig in solid white or chrome for these fish. Most whites caught on the "iron" will be taken on a yo-yo bite, with the exaggerated lift'n drop technique. The Salas 6X and 7X, Jerry Jig Surface Iron, and Tady #45 will work for this technique on white sea bass. Don't think twice about adding a whole live or dead squid pinned onto one or two of the jig's treble hook points for extra effect. This "jig-n-squid" combo is a jackpot winner! Veteran saltwater pros prefer a solid white jig for the sea bass. A recent innovation is the new "glow-white" pattern, a milky white color that actually glows in the dark under water.

Whites can be caught all through the season and they will eat at night. They are tenacious battlers and should be fished with conventional tackle and 20 to 40 pound test line. Stout rods are necessary as 40 pound class whites or larger are a real possibility along our coast!

Summary

Saltwater bassin' is an important aspect of the Central to Southern California marine fishery. These fish—calicos, sandies, and white sea bass—are available on a year 'round basis.

If you want the bigger "toads" in these species—the "grumper" sandies and the "bull" calicos, as well as the whites themselves—think Big Bait. Do not fall into the rut of simply fishing anchovies for these species because that is what everyone else on the boat is doing. The trophy specimens will routinely be taken on larger offerings by the saltwater pros "in the know." I emphasize again, fish these big baits or lures on or near the bottom where the trophy bass live.

Bonito: Tricks for a Bongo Bonanza

Bonito are, without a doubt, one of the real treasures of the California Coast. For some reason however—perhaps over-commercial catching—their numbers have dwindled over the past years. These diminutive members of the tuna family are legendary fighters. Pound for pound, it would be hard to find many species—salt or freshwater —that compare with the bonito's spectacular power.

"Bongos" or "boneheads"—as they are called by deck hands—are reasonably easy to catch. They have an affinity to both live bait and artificial lures. Most bonito are caught in Southern California, but they will travel all the way above Monterey in some warm current years. Huge, double-digit class bonito are also sporadically encountered off of San Nicholas Island and the remote Cortez Bank.

Bongos on Bait

A fly-lined anchovy is without question numero uno as far as bonito baits are concerned. The fish will, on occasion, strike sardines, smelt, or even whole squid, but 'chovies are the preferred choice.

Light to medium-weight spinning or casting gear will handle most school bonies in the 1 to 4 pound range. Lighter 10 to 12 pound test mono will get bit better and naturally provides greater sport with these small tuna. These are times, however, when you may run into a school of 8 to 12 pound bonito. Bongos in this class will be sheer terror on the light gear. A conventional outfit spooled with 20 pound string would be more appropriate on bruisers this size.

Live bait hooks range in size from #1 to #6 depending upon the quality of the anchovies. Use a split-shot or a small rubber core sinker if you need to get the bait down below the surface.

If you are careful, there is another trick you can try on both party and private boats when you are confronted with a tank of small pinhead anchovies. Using spinning tackle, and preferably an 8 to 8 1/2 foot rod, run your line through a large, clear Casta-Bubble float and fill it about half way with water. (To fill the bubble, submerge it in the bait tank.) Butt the sliding float with a snap-swivel and add a 5 to 7 foot length of leader with a #6 bait hook. Nose or gill hook the tiny 'chovy, and make your cast

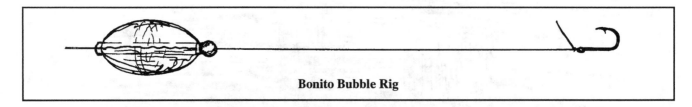

Bonito Bubble Rig

with this bait'n bubble combo. You have to watch behind you when using the super long leader so you don't hook other anglers.

The weighted bobber provides you with considerable extra distance when other fly-liners are fighting the size of the fly-weight pinheads. The bubble will ride on the surface, but so will your bait. When the bonies hit the small 'chovy, they will feel no resistance on the initial run, pulling the bait and leader through the sliding float.

Bonies on Lures

Bonito will usually strike a shiny artificial without much hesitation. Small boaters working inshore harbors and bays will find that the 1/2 ounce Kastmaster spoon used for trout fishing is a dynamite bonito lure. Fish it on 8 to 12 pound test line. Other spoons such as smaller Krocadiles, Haddock's 3/8 ounce Jig'n spoon, and the Hopkin's NO-EQL are also excellent for school bonito in the quiet water, along with the smaller Luhr Jensen Deep Stinger and Mr. Champ models.

Outside along the kelp lines, on the flats, or at the islands, I prefer to throw cast-metal jigs. The Salas Christy 2 in blue/white/green has been a hot bonie color; a strong back-up model has been a blue and white Tady AA. Solid chrome, chrome and blue, sardine, mackerel, and green and yellow are also effective bonito colors in candy bar models. Use the heavier styles for a yo-yo grind, the light alloy versions for surface-feeding bonies. Alternate hot styles are the Ironman #1 and #2.

Haddock's 1 1/8 ounce Jig'n Spoon in blue 'chovy finish would be my next choice in open water fishing for bonito. This slim spoon casts a mile on light to medium tackle. The bongos hit it with a vengeance on both the surface wind or a yo-yo retrieve. Although they are dwindling in numbers, veteran feather fishermen will also hammer the bonito, stroking and pumping single-hook chrome heads. Blue and white, solid white, green and yellow, and red and white will all produce.

Bonito are easy prey for trolling. Nothing fancy is required. A single-hook chrome head, a small 10 mm tuna feather, CD-9, 11 or 13 Magnum Rapalas, saltwater 4 inch Possum Lures with heavier gauge wire hooks, or even silver, blue, or green-colored plastics will catch bongos on the troll. The speedy little tuna will hit the lures at 6 to 10 knots.

Summary

Bonito are incredible fighters and comprise a major portion of the sport catch for the Southern fleet. They are excellent game fish for the novice saltwater buff to hone their skills on. Many anglers discard bonito as "trash fish" as far as their culinary value is concerned. I too was of that opinion until Captain Russ Izor shared some of his secrets for preparing bongos. The trick is to cut off the head, let the fish bleed, and ice it as soon as possible. This can be tough to do on a party boat, so the next best thing is to keep the bonies wet in the gunny sack.

When you get home, fillet the fish and trim around the black dorsal vein. Remove the meat and place it in a frying pan filled with about 1/2 inch of beer. Poach the fillet on both sides in the warm beer. Let the fish cool. Mash it up with a fork, add mayonnaise, a dash of mustard or relish, and you have an incredibly tasty tuna salad!

Halibut: Bottom Bouncin' for Barndoors

California halibut are one of the toughest species to fool along our coastline. These toothy flatfish reach weights of over 40 pounds and put up a respectable fight on medium-weight gear. The challenge to halibut fishing however, is less in the actual playing of the fish, but more in finding them and getting them to eat a lure or bait.

In this chapter, I'll highlight some of the different techniques used both in the South and in the North to take halibut. Southern Californians prospecting the bottom in Santa Monica, Newport, Mission, and San Diego Bays, the backside of Catalina Island, the Huntington Flats, and South Island at the Coronados have their favorite tactics. Trophy flatties are also routinely nailed at Santa Rosa and San Miguel islands. Halibut anglers in the San Francisco Bay Area drag the bottoms around Angel, Alcatraz, and Treasure Islands, Deep Hole, Raccoon Straits, the International Airport, and off of Candlestick Park. They too have their patented methods for nailing flatties.

As I delineate these regional differences, keep in mind that it pays to be experimental in this sport. South Coasters can learn from Northern fishermen and vice versa. Evaluate all these methods and try them in your particular locale. The halibut may be surprised to see something new!

Finding Halibut

Halibut are most active between the months of March and October, with summer being the best overall season. These fish can be taken from the surfline, beyond it, around the kelp beds, on the flats, around offshore islands, and in secluded harbors and bays.

Halibut fishing is best with a major interchange of tidal flow. A high tide is usually better than low tide for working outside waters. Experts agree that two hours before the turning tide is the best time to try for halibut.

In the bays and estuaries, the incoming tide with its exchange of clearer water is the optimum condition. High tide, slightly beyond the surfline, is similarly the prime time to look for halibut along this 6 to 10 foot depth. (As a matter of fact, it is not uncommon to see anglers on surfboards, drifting bait or lures, off the Southern beaches a few yards off the breakers!)

Halibut can be found on sandy beaches of offshore islands. Inside harbors, look for flatties around the floating bait receivers. In the winter months, head to the back beaches of quiet bays—halibut will gravitate to the warmer shallow water.

Barndoors on Bait

California halibut typically lie semi-submerged into the sand, lazily waiting for an errant bait fish or other marine creature to pass nearby. There are occasions when these fish will suspend or even take a bait fly-lined on the surface. But for the most part, count on finding 'buts near the bottom.

Anchovies are probably the principle bait used to fool halibut from both ends of the state. Sometimes live squid are also used in Southern California, along with smelt, grunion, or sardines. Northerners prefer live mudsuckers along with the 'chovy offerings. (Keep in mind that some bait shops in Southern California also sporadically keep stocks of mudsuckers on hand.)

In both regions, "brown baits" are often used by the pros to score on the bigger "barndoor" class fish topping the 20 pound mark. Tomcod, herring, queenfish, and shiner perch—fished whole and alive—are excellent baits for trophy flatties.

The slider rig is used in both areas. South Coasters usually prefer a 1/2 to 2 ounce sliding-egg sinker. Northerners, because of the rushing currents, opt for sliding weights up to 12 ounces. The leader can be anywhere from 10 to 20 pound mono with a short-shank, live bait hook.

If you are using anchovies or sardines, an Eagle Claw #318-N or #113 #1 to #4 hook should be adequate. With squid or larger brown baits, a #3/0 to #4/0 short-shank, live bait hook is necessary. Eagle Claw fine wire #197 circle hooks are also an excellent alternative for halibut when drifting small anchovies. Just remember—don't set the hook with circle models. Leave the reel in gear, and the cam-action of the Eagle Claw circle hooks makes the set for you!

Southern Californians also like to fish halibut with a dropper rig basically like the one described for white sea bass fishing. A 1 to 4 ounce sinker is attached to the bottom of the rig. The sinker can be either a chrome or plain ringed model, or a spoon shape designed for easy drifting.

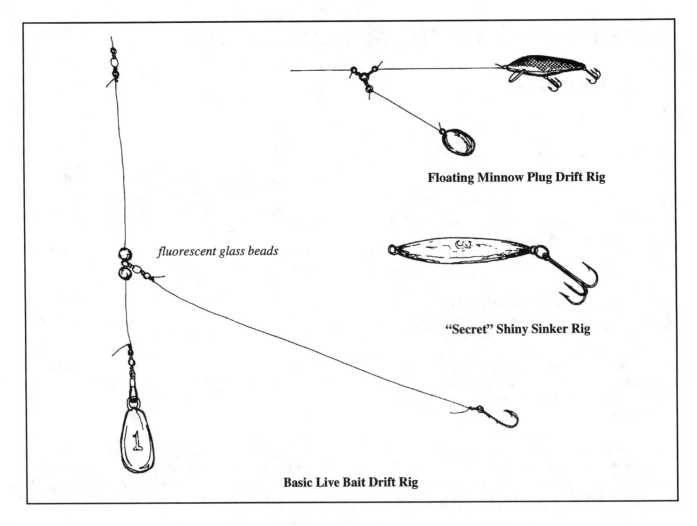

Floating Minnow Plug Drift Rig

fluorescent glass beads

"Secret" Shiny Sinker Rig

Basic Live Bait Drift Rig

On this note, most of the time the halibut want a slow-moving bait. If you use these rigs from the beach or a pier, then slowly reel the bait in, pausing intermittently to enhance the amount of territory covered. If you fish from a boat, then set up slow drift patterns for the 'buts. Remember, these fish characteristically will not move too far to attack a bait. You have to bring it to them.

In Northern California, another preferred rig for halibut is the standard three-way swivel setup. But, instead of using lighter 10 to 20 pound test mono leaders, Northern anglers attach a 50 pound test piece of line, with a #3/0 hook. This is the patented configuration for drifting a live shiner perch for barndoor halibut. Due to ripping currents in San Francisco Bay, be prepared to use a heavier 10 to 12 ounce torpedo or spoon sinker on a short leader to complete the three-way swivel rig.

Now then, there are a few modifications that you can make to these basic halibut rigs. First, instead of using a short-shank bait hook, substitute it with a #8 or #10 treble hook for anchovies, a #4 to #6 treble for bigger baits. Hook the bait fish through the nose or under the anal fin. The nose-hooking, I might mention, is probably best for slow-drifting, since it keeps the bait swimming fairly naturally through the water.

The treble hook may get snagged a little more frequently. But, it will also provide an extra amount of insurance when setting the hook on these touchy feeders. The treble hooks should be bronze. Their color blends in better with the bait and are sharper than nickel or cadmium-plated trebles.

Another secret tip is to hook two modest-sized 'chovies onto a treble hook, each on a separate barb. The commotion and flash created by two live bait fish being drifted along the bottom may be too much for even the laziest halibut to resist.

The actual "bite" itself can be perplexing and nerve-racking when a halibut decides to eat the bait. I prefer fishing the 'buts with conventional tackle, since it often helps to keep the reel in free spool following that initial "tick" or "tug" on the line.

The trick is to be patient. You almost have to coax the halibut into swallowing the bait. One way to do this is to fish them with the reel out of gear. As the halibut hits the bait, start to use your fingertips and gently "roll" the spool of your reel, taking in a small portion of line. As you nudge the bait slowly away from the 'but expect the fish to pull back. Again, "roll" the spool to tease the bait away from the fish. Eventually, the halibut will mouth the bait with

more aggressiveness and hopefully you will feel dull resistance on the end of the line. Now is the moment of glory! Go ahead and set, but do it in a rather cautious, "mushy" manner. Don't try to swing hard on the halibut —you may pull the bait away.

This give-and-take ritual may last well over 30 seconds from the initial "tap tap" you feel. It's a real art to entice these fish by free-spooling and "rolling" the line, but the results may well be worth the patience. This technique is very much akin to "mooching" for salmon, popularized in the Pacific Northwest.

A final tip to consider is adding a trap hook to the live bait offering. Simply tie a dropper loop above the bait with a short 6 to 8 inch length of leader. Tie a small treble hook to the leader. Embed the treble into the other end of the bait away from the main hook. Although the trap setup may impede the overall lively action of the bait, better catch-to-strike ratios might result.

Flatties on Artificials

Halibut will definitely strike an artificial lure. Here, as with bait drifting, there are Northern and Southern approaches to this dimension of the sport.

To begin with, slow-trolling at 4 to 5 knots is the name of the game. Don't expect these bottom-dwelling flatfish to swim after a lure trolled much faster than this.

Next, the object is to get the lure down so it plods along the bottom. South Coast fishermen look for smooth sandy bottoms to troll their lures. Anglers working the Central Coast from Cayucos to San Simeon look for similar sandy stretches. Northern aficionados exploring San Francisco Bay prefer broken bottoms with clay and sand as prime halibut territory.

Long minnow-shaped plugs can be trolled for halibut. The Bagley Bang-O in 'chovy and mackerel finishes has been a favorite in the Bay Area, slow-trolled and bounced along the bottom. South Coast fishermen have had similar success with deeper-diving, spoon-billed models made by Rebel and Rapala.

The slow-troll speed will be adequate to get these plugs down into the shallow flats of harbors and bays or in the 6 to 10 foot depths along the surfline.

Another interesting method is to use a three-way swivel rig to get a lightweight floating minnow plug to suspend just above the bottom on a slow-troll. Take a 2 to 4 ounce flat spoon sinker and tie it to one eye of the three-way swivel with 6 to 8 inches of leader line. On a longer length ,(24 to 30 inches) of 10 to 12 pound test leader, tie a floating Rebel or a #9, 11 or 13-S Rapala in silver finish. The floating plug will wiggle slightly above the bottom as the sinker drags along in the sand. This setup is terrific for working outside the surflines or in sheltered bays and harbors.

Plastic tail-swimming lures can be similarly bottom bounced for halibut. Here, a drift is usually more effective than a slow-troll. Lunker Thumpers, Mojos, Scampis, Berkley Power Pogeys and Grubs, Salty Lunker Grubs, and the Scrounger will work. The squid tippet should also be used to spice up these plastic baits in a bottom-bouncing capacity. The A.A.T. Tora Tubes, A.A. Worms, Pacific Eels, and Sea Reapers are also bonafide halibut killers, along with Optimum swimbaits in a variety of sizes.

Northern anglers have also had some excellent results working the popular bucktail Hair Raiser Jigs along the bottom for halibut. South Coasters have been reluctant to use hair jigs for marine species. This is really an oversight. The slow sashaying of the deer hair in the water can be exceptionally tantalizing to finicky feeders. Hair Raisers in yellow, white, or red are proven winners for halibut.

I might add that I like to have jigs in this design for another reason. I am a strong proponent of using fish scents in the marine environment to attract saltwater species. A deer hair jig like the Hair Raiser saturated in Berkley Saltwater Attractant, for instance, can be a "hot" enticement for hook-shy halibut.

Shiny spoons can also be slowly trolled along the bottom or fan-casted from an anchored or drifting boat for halibut. The Kastmaster, Krocadile, Diamond Jig, and smaller Hexbar designs account for many legal-sized flatties during the season. The important thing is to keep the lure plodding slowly along the bottom where the halibut are lurking.

Summary

Halibut are one of the truly fine-eating fish that you can seek along the California Coast. They are very touchy feeders and require much finessing especially if you are using bait.

Don't force these fish to bite. They have a tendency to "mouth" the bait and must often be teased or coaxed to eat the offering more aggressively.

Once hooked, take your time playing in the fish. Don't try to initiate some quick, spectacular short pumps in an effort to "stroke" the halibut right in. Instead, maintain constant, even pressure, allowing the fish to fight the drag. Always gaff halibut broadside against the flat surface.

Catchin' Rockfish: Cowcod, Chilipeppers, Lings and More

There are over 52 varieties of rockfish found along the California Coast. These include such regional favorites as vermillion, goldeneye, gopher, china, bolina, grass, copper, blue, barber pole, strawberry, rougheye, chilipepper, and cowcod. The popular culinary fare known as "Pacific red snapper" is actually a collection of red, blue, yellow, brown, and black rockfishes.

There are basically two approaches for fishing these bottom dwellers: shallow or deep. The shallow bite focuses on somewhere in the 20 to 150 foot range. The deep-water action can take place all the way down to 600 foot depths. Please keep in mind that in recent years there has been much state and federal legislation limiting where, when, and even how deep you can fish for rockfish. Be sure to check current regulations to make sure you are "legal" when going after these bottom species.

The Shallow Bite

Assorted species of rockfish including black, china, blue, copper, tree, gopher, canary, bolina, black, and johnny bass can be caught in the shallow canyons and ledges along the coast. Anglers using medium-weight, conventional baitcasting outfits with 6 ounces to one pound sinkers can take advantage of this shallow water bite.

A variety of terminal combinations will suffice. The three-way swivel setup, the dropper rig, a slider combo —they'll all work. It really depends upon how much bait you want to present at one time.

For sheer sporting purposes, some rock fishermen prefer to drop only one or two baited hooks. This works particularly well if you like to use light 10 to 15 pound test line, and a 2 to 6 ounce sinker. Rockfish caught at shallower depths will put up a fairly decent scrap on the lighter string.

If you have heavier 20 to 50 pound test line on your reel, you can go all out and tie on a rock cod gangion with a one pound weight. The rock cod gangion is a commercially tied leader, comprised of usually five sequentially spaced hooks. It has a snap-swivel on the bottom of the leader to add a heavy sinker. The front portion of the gangion has a lone swivel to which you attach your main line.

The gangion allows the angler to bait all five hooks and present them at one time on a single "drop." You can load the hooks with the same offering or a combination of rockfish treats. The object of the gangion is to allow you to catch more than one fish on a single drop instead of having to reel up after each hook set. When you feel that first strike, set the hook, but then let the gangion rest. Repeat this procedure with a few more strikes until you are satisfied that a number of fish are on the hooks. Go ahead and reel up. You may have anywhere from one to five rockfish on a single drop! For the smaller rockfish species caught on the shallower banks, a gangion with #4/0 or #5/0 hooks is usually sufficient.

There are numerous kinds of bait that will work at these depths. Live anchovies, when available, are hard to beat. Simply nose-hook them and lower them down to the bottom. With freshly dead or frozen 'chovies, I like to run the hook once through the body behind the gill area and then re-embed the hook in the midsection. It often helps to double up the anchovies and pin two onto the hook. This makes it more difficult for the fish to steal the bait. Smelt, sardines, or grunion can be fished in this same manner.

Frozen squid is an equally potent bait for rockfish—at any depth. You can either fish it in chunks or strip it. A gangion loaded with fresh, dead squid can be an awesome combination.

Pieces of shellfish such as abalone, clams, or mussels as well as shrimp, also work at times, primarily on the shallow water denizens. Consider squirting ample amounts of Berkley Saltwater Attractant on whatever offerings you decide upon before making the drop.

Shallow water rockfish will definitely pounce on a lure yo-yoed over the rocky bottom. A lot of anglers like to use a softer tipped, hyperbolic rod to drop medium-sized candy bar jigs and spoons on these fish. When bounced down to 150 feet, the Salas, Tady, Ironman, Jerry Jigs, and Tony's Jackpot models in 4 to 6 inch lengths will often rack up good numbers of rockfish. Popular colors include chrome, blue and white, scrambled egg, solid white, and blue and chrome.

Sometimes, however, the shallow water species will also strike smaller artificial lures all the way down to that 150 foot level. There is a growing fraternity of anglers—this writer included—who prefer to probe the bottom with super light tackle.

If conditions permit, take out some of that freshwater bassin' gear and work artificial lures over these reefs and rocky structures. You will find that 1 to 3 pound rockfish on 6 to 10 pound mono are terrific fighters when you try to pry them from the depths.

The possibilities are endless as far as choice of artificials is concerned. A multitude of conventional soft plastic saltwater lures will work—Salty Magics, Mojos, and Scampis. Also, use plastics more commonly associated with freshwater bassin'. The Kalin Salty Lunker Grub, A.A. Worms' Giant Sea Reaper and Pacific Eel, Canyon Lure's Magnum Fatzee tube baits, and assorted 4 to 6 inch plastic worms are some dynamite possibilities. And especially don't overlook Berkley's Power Pogey, Grub, Tube, and Eel at these greater depths.

Light bucktail or feathered jigs bounced along the bottom will also nail shallow water rockfish. Likewise, the smaller plastic tail-swimming jigs such as Haddock's Kreepy Krawler or the Garland Spider will prove effective along the deep banks.

All sorts of smaller spoons and candy bar style jigs should be yo-yoed in this situation. Haddock's 1 1/8 ounce Jig'n Spoon, the 5/8 to 2 ounce Krocadile, the Deep Stinger in 1-3 ounce, along with a 2-4 ounce Crippled Herring, or the tiny Salas Pee Wee jigs are strong possibilities for shallow water rockfish. Chrome, blue and white, or practically any prism-like finish will work.

I have personally had some outstanding days on party boats using my freshwater baitcasting outfits and artificials like these to clobber the shallow rockfish. I have found that there are times when I will not only take more fish, but also larger specimens using artificials, compared to other anglers soaking gangions full of bait.

Rockfish will respond very well to light line. But, it is important to get a strong hook set on the fish and keep the pressure on. This will help to move the fish out, away from the rocks. Maintain a tight line and use a steady retrieve back to the surface. This light mono will have a lot of stretch worked at these depths and it is also easy for the rockfish to spit the hook. So, take your time playing the fish, avoid "short pumping" with quick jerks. Instead, maintain that steady pressure and enjoy the fight back to the surface.

The Deep-Water Action

Usually "rock codding" is identified with bazooka-like rods, wench-like reels, heavy line, and back-breaking work. Well, to some degree this depiction isn't too far off base. But, with proper tackle selection, there are ways to minimize the physical strain that can be generated from dragging up 600 to 800 feet of line from the bottom.

First, as was noted in the section on tackle selection, it is important to purchase a high quality reel in the 4/0 to 6/0 range. The reel has to hold at least 300 yards of 50 pound class dacron. Don't try to cut corners and opt for a smaller baitcasting model for this style of fishing.

Next, add a power handle to enhance your leverage when reeling. These are sold as accessory items at most tackle stores. The oversized handle will make reeling a lot easier, providing considerable leverage for grinding in a full gangion of fish.

The deep-water rock cod rod should definitely have at least a roller tiptop. Better models have roller guides the full length of the blank. The more rollers—the less line friction and the easier it is to wind up the heavy sinkers and full gangions.

A rock cod plate or "rail board" is another necessary piece of equipment for the deep-water bite. The plate bolts onto the lower portion of the rod blank. It allows the angler to brace the heavy rod and reel against the boat railing. This serves to reduce a lot of the twisting and turning that would otherwise be inherent in trying to handle such heavy-duty gear.

The reels can be filled with either Berkley Whiplash or Fireline. These braided lines have finer diameters for comparable breaking tests, allowing the angler to fill the reel with more line. Most veteran rock codders recommend against using monofilament at these depths. There is too much stretch with the mono and the fabric lines usually have greater abrasion resistance.

An alternative to consider is wire line. The wire line has hardly any stretch. I have fished it down to 600 feet for rock cod and it is amazing stuff. The "strike" is so pronounced, even at these great depths, that it is as if the fish is only a few feet below the surface. The angler is thus able to set the hook quickly and to get strong penetration into the rockfish due to minimal line stretch. Wire is expensive to use and highly temperamental. It can often literally break in half if there is a bend formed in the strand. It takes some skill and expertise to fish this material, but the results can be worth the extra investment and effort.

Now that we're set up for the deep-water action, we'll be looking for chilipeppers, salmon grouper, starries, reds, goldeneyes, yellowtail rockfish, canaries, and larger cowcod. We need to use anywhere from 1 to 6 pounds of lead.

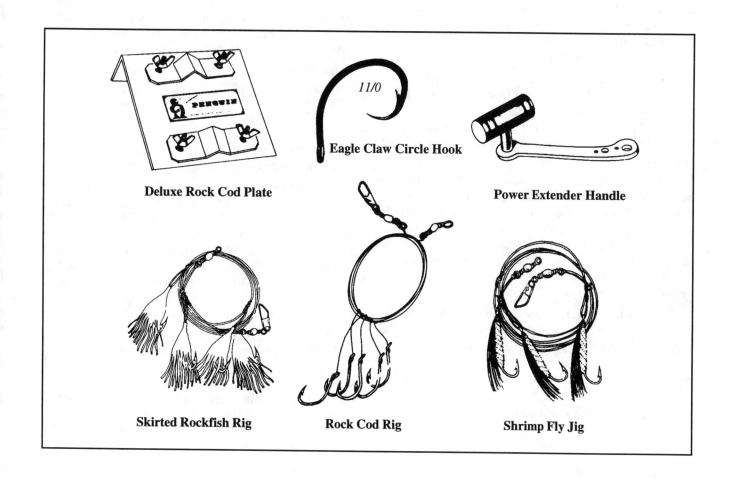

Deluxe Rock Cod Plate

11/0

Eagle Claw Circle Hook

Power Extender Handle

Skirted Rockfish Rig

Rock Cod Rig

Shrimp Fly Jig

The configuration of the gangion hooks themselves is worth commenting upon. Most fishermen purchase their gangions with thin wire Sealy-type hooks tied to 50 to 80 pound mono. This style hook can be sharpened fairly easily. But, as you drop deeper and deeper, it is easier for the rockfish to steal the bait.

An alternative is to use heavier gangions with the rather strange-looking tuna-circle hooks. These thick, cadmium-plated models, actually have the points turned inward toward the center of the hook. Upon first glance, it seems impossible for a fish to impale itself on the barb with this unique design. But the tuna-circle hooks really do work—especially for deep-water rock codding. The rockfish can't steal the bait easily with this circular hook design. They will continue to eat the bait eventually swallowing it deep.

I learned a trick from some of the shrewd party boat deck hands who moonlight at fishing rock cod commercially. What they do is to put the tuna-circle hook in a vice and carefully open up the gap between the point and the rest of the hook. Use pliers to grasp the point portion and gently bend it outward. By doing this, the point is slightly more exposed. Although this increases the potential for bait-stealing a little, it also enhances hook penetration. It is critical with this trick then, to take a file to the tuna-circle hooks and hone the points to needle sharpness.

Another deep-water strategy is to join gangions together, increasing your offerings from 5 to 10 or 15 baits. Simply clip the gangions together with the snap-swivels. However, I recommend using pliers to crimp the swivels shut tight so that they won't inadvertently open up with the weight of additional fish.

There are commercially made gangions sometimes sold at tackle stores and at landings that feature a greater number of hooks on a wire leader. These are worth the extra money for fishing beyond that 300 foot range. The wire leaders won't fray or stretch. The hooks on the gangions in this class tend to be spaced perfectly, allowing the bait to stand apart from the main leader in a natural fashion.

The Eagle Claw fish hook company also markets brilliantly colored rock cod rigs featuring their patented circle hooks. The circle hook design requires no hook setting. The cam-action of the circle basically sets itself which becomes a real advantage—fishing your reel-in gear at 200 to 600 foot depths.

The same baits itemized for the shallow approach will work with the deep-water attack. Also consider using strips of other game fish as an added bonus. Mackerel fillets or strips of smaller rockfish can be sensational at times. These offerings will catch larger rockfish. If you have ample supplies of whole squid, pin these onto a gangion. The "cods" will eat the big bait.

Large, brightly colored shrimp fly rigs also take their share of rockfish. Sometimes it is better to add a whole anchovy, a chunk of squid, or a strip of mackerel as a trailer to the shrimp fly gangion.

In lieu of using a shrimp fly setup, there are other little tricks you can employ to dress up the basic gangion. Fasten on strips of brightly colored cloth, colorful (deflated) balloons, or strands of fluorescent yarn. These can be fished either by themselves or with a natural bait as a trailer.

Another option is to add soft plastic trailers to the gangion hooks. Single or double-tail grubs, tube lures, chunks of plastic worms—they'll all work at times laced onto gangions. The brighter, more opulent fluorescent colors seem to give the best results at these depths.

Another recent innovation has been to add a chemical luminescent light tube to the bottom of the gangion, usually tied above the rock cod weight. The light emitted from this chemical tube illuminates the gangion and the multiple offerings tied above it. Many anglers firmly believe the light draws rockfish into the area.

It is important to maintain contact with the bottom during a rock cod drift. Although you may be working at 300 foot depths, you may have to let out 450 feet of line to stay on the bottom. This is because of the drift of the boat. It is usually difficult due to wind and current to fish straight up and down while rock codding beyond 150 feet. So pay out line as needed to stay near the bottom with your bait.

Rock codders have also found that heavy 15 to 32 ounce jigs will often produce spectacular results, especially on bigger fish. The larger Salas PL-68, Tady 45 Heavy, Jerry Jig Heavy, Ironman #6, and Tony Jackpot models, along with DiClad, Hexbar, and Diamond Jigs are popular favorites up and down the coast. Chrome and white are preferred colors once you hit that 300 foot mark. Another tip is to add a piece of strip bait or a whole squid to the "iron" and yo-yo it off the bottom. This method also accounts for trophy bottom fish.

Be prepared to work either the gangions or the heavy jig slightly above the bottom at times. On party boats, the skipper may tell the passengers to take a few "turns" on the reel to take the bait up off the bottom. This is because the fish are being metered above the ocean floor. Private boaters should also rely upon their electronics to pinpoint similar concentrations of rockfish suspended off the ocean floor.

Lingcod

Lings present an entirely different perspective to rockfishing, worthy of a separate discussion. Lingcod are vicious bottom dwellers. They are typically caught in 90 to 150 foot depths. They can be found at much shallower depths in Northern California as the big females come in to spawn in November and December. They can also be taken much deeper, caught incidentally on rock cod gear at 600 foot depths.

Lingcod do not have swim bladders as do other rockfish. For this reason, they do not suffer the bends as do other species whose bladders blow out on the way to the surface. Lings will thus fight the angler all the way up from the bottom. These amazing game fish have been found to live as deep as 1400 feet.

The prime areas for fishing lingcod start around the Oxnard-Ventura area and continue north toward colder waters. Lings are frequently caught below San Diego, but the greatest numbers of fish are in the North. Some of the legendary hunting grounds for lingcod include Ventura, Oxnard, Avila and Morro Bays, the Farallon Islands, Point Reyes, Fanny Shoals, Bodega Bay, Fort Ross, Timber Cove, Half Moon Bay, and Cape San Martin.

Saltwater anglers working specifically for lings usually bring out heavy-duty baitcasters filled with 30 to 50 pound mono, matched with stout rods. Lings can also be caught on conventional gangions or shrimp fly rigs. These fish are more piscivorous than other species—that is, they like to eat smaller game fish. A baby rockfish, a sanddab, or a medium herring is a perfect meal. So are whole squid, a small octopus, or a large strip of mackerel or rock cod belly. Lings like big baits!

Many lingcodders prefer to thread these larger baits through the head onto an Eagle Claw #2004 circle hook in #6/0 to #8/0 size. But then they add a #4/0 or #5/0 treble hook to the tail portion of the bait forming a trap setup. (The treble is connected by a short leader to the single hook.)

Another tactic to use with lings is to tie your main line to a three-way swivel. Use a short leader with an 8 to 20 ounce sinker to keep the rig down. On a longer 60 to 80 pound test piece of mono, tie on a #6/0 to #10/0 single hook. Then tie this leader to the other eyelet on the three-way swivel. The heavy 60 to 80 pound line will resist abrasion from the rocks where the lings live. Next pin on a 1/2 to 2 pound live blue rock cod to the large single hook. This combination is a real hawg hunter.

On this note, don't be surprised if a big ling bushwacks a smaller rockfish as you haul it up from the bottom. Many magnum-sized lingcod are caught in this manner. The ling will inhale the small rockfish. The spines on the fins will lodge into the lingcod's throat. You can actually play the ling all the way to the surface like this without actually having it hooked. Be prepared for a quick gaff job once you see color on the fish.

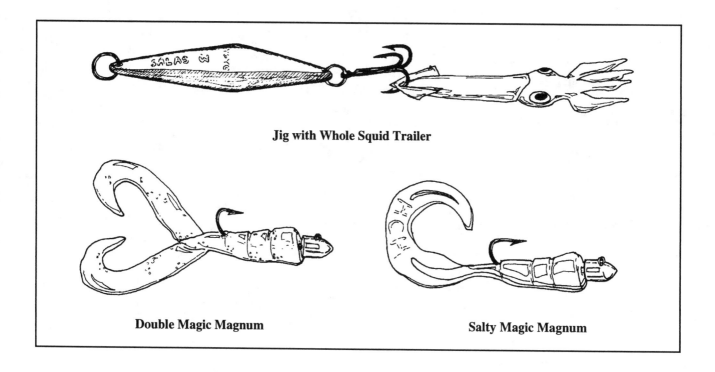

Jig with Whole Squid Trailer

Double Magic Magnum

Salty Magic Magnum

Lingcod are phenomenal sport on lures. The spawners are particularly aggressive fish when they move up into 10 to 20 feet of water. They readily annihilate soft plastics. All of the various models aforementioned are viable options—as long as you try a root beer flake pattern. This is overwhelmingly the preferred shade in soft plastic jigs.

However, on our famous "Lingcod Universities"—a winter version of my Eagle Claw Fishing Schools—we have found lingcod to also readily strike soft plastic A.A. Worms large swimbaits, Berkley Power Pogeys and Power Eels, Optimum swimbaits, and A.A.T. Pacific Eels and Giant Sea Reapers in black, pink, hot orange, or blue/white patterns.

Don't think twice about yo-yoing the iron for lings. Hex Bars, Diamond Jigs, heavy Jerry Jigs, Tony's Jackpot jigs and other candy bar shapes will produce. The three best colors are chrome, solid white, and copper. Red/yellow, red/orange have also come on strong amoung rock codders who like to yo-yo the deep "iron." Be prepared for a lot of strikes to occur on the fall. Once on the bottom, use a short yo-yo action, letting the jig lift-and-fall about three feet with each stroking action.

Here too, as with bigger rock cod, try adding a whole squid to the jig as a bonus for the lings. Also, a large jig fished below a gangion or a shrimp fly rig has been a proven winner with lingcod. The flash of the bigger lure below the gangion of bait or shrimp flies, gives the illusion of a medium-sized fish thrashing through a school of bait. This will often excite the lings into devouring the jig.

Summary

Fishing deep for rockfish and lings can be an exciting adventure from the Southern to the Northern portions of the State. There is no telling what species lurk in these deeper environments. It can be a true potpourri for the taking. It also doesn't have to be strictly a "meat trip." These bottom dwellers are prone to eat an artificial lure. They can be fooled on light tackle—and they will put up a pretty good fight in the shallower water. With this kind of fishing, perhaps more so than any other type outlined in this book, it pays to be experimental.

Use quality lines and take extra care to pre-sharpen all your hooks on both the lures and the gangions. It is a long way up to the surface on some of the drops you will make. Don't give that fish a chance to throw the hook or break the line. Make no doubt about it, this will indeed be some of the best table fare you will find in the Pacific!

Sharks: Leopards, Threshers and Company

For a long time sharks and rays were generally relegated to the category of "trash fish" as far as marine anglers were concerned. In recent years, an increasing number of saltwater enthusiasts have experienced the thrill and excitement of fishing these toothy game fish. More and more anglers are looking to sharks and rays as an alternative to other types of big game fishing.

Not all sharks are sought by the weekend fisherman. Some, like the shovelnose, are basically nuisances. Others, such as the leopard and the thresher are not only fished for their fighting qualities, but for culinary reasons as well. Broiled, barbecued, and smoked shark meat, from some of the prime species, is often compared to such fine table fare as broadbill swordfish. As more anglers come into contact with these predators and try shark meat, fishing for these game fish will continue to grow in popularity.

Some of the sharks I'll discuss in this chapter such as the thresher and the leopard range from the Mexican to the Canadian borders. Others, like the mako, are primarily found in the South, while the six and seven gill variety are found in colder Northern waters.

There are basically three dominant ways to fish shark: (a) still-fishing at anchor; (b) trolling; or (c) chum-slick drifting. The first strategy is most commonly practiced in San Francisco Bay. The latter two tactics work on a variety of species when you hunt sharks in open sea.

Bay Area Sharkin'

Anglers in the San Francisco Bay Area set their sights primarily on six and seven gills, soupfin, and leopard sharks. The "big boys" are the seven gills, also known as "cow sharks." These sharks can reach weights of over 200 pounds in the cold waters of the Bay. The "soupys" push close to 100 pounds while a big leopard tops out at about 40 pounds.

In contrast to shark fishing in the Southland, most Bay Area anglers prefer to fish them at anchor. It's possible to fish all the way down to 90 foot depths probing the deep channels around Marin, Angel Island, The Bay Bridge, Hunter's Point, and the Dumbarton Bridge. So, it is important for the private boaters to have a decent depth finder and carry plenty of anchor line.

Most of the action, however, will occur in the 20 to 60 foot level in the channels. Occasionally, it is also possible to catch sharks from the bank in the Bay, primarily leopards and small, less desirable dogfish.

Angelo Cuanang is considered a major authority on this Bay Area sharkin'. The six and seven gills will eat a large offering. He recommends using a chunk of tail section of a dogfish, a small shark locally called a stickle back. A strip of striper belly, or actual salmon stomach is another prime bait for these "big boys." If you want to really get elaborate, try a combination of a strip of fish topped with fresh dead squid. It will take anywhere from 1 to 3 pounds of sinker to keep the bait on the bottom if the deep currents are ripping.

Cuanang notes that it is important to match your tackle to the size of your quarry. When it comes to 100 to 300 pound seven gills, it's time to bring out the "artillery." His basic rig consists of a reel in the Daiwa 400 H or Penn 4/0 class size. He fills it with 200 yards of .025 diameter single strand stainless steel wire backed with heavy Dacron line. His typical rod for monster bay sharks like this is a 20 pound IGFA big game rod.

The best time to fish the "big boys" according to Cuanang is in that 1 to 2 hour span at the height or the bottom of the tidal flow. Occasionally the six and seven gills will hit a chunk of bait on the drift. But most Bay Area shark specialists feel that better catches result from anchoring on the edge of the deep channels. The best fishing for the larger seven gill sharks is during the spring and fall months. Soupfins are taken most frequently during the spring and on through summer.

As for the actual setup for hooking these larger offerings, Cuanang has also designed a rather specialized rig. He starts by tying a #3/0 swivel to a 4 foot length of 120 pound test monofilament. He then slips onto the large diameter mono a rubber sliding sinker sleeve. This allows the heavy sinker to easily slide up and down along the 4 foot leader. Next, Cuanang attaches a 24 to 30 inch length of 200 pound test piano or 49 strand braided wire to a lower swivel. (This swivel is also used to butt off the sliding sleeve.) Tied to the other end of this leader is a 10/0 to 13/0 Kirby-style hook.

Medium-range conventional reels that hold 300 yards of 25 to 30 pound test mono filled with aluminum spools are perfect on the smaller sharks. A medium to heavy 7 to 8 foot single-piece live bait rod is equally suitable for this kind of sharkin'.

The 10 to 40 pound sharks including the leopards, soupfins, and dogfish can be taken on more conventional, commercially made shark leaders consisting of sturdy 50 to 60 pound test wire and a single hook and swivel. A basic sliding sinker setup is perfect. Use frozen squid, smelt, anchovies, grunion, grass or ghost shrimp, and mudsuckers. At certain times of the year, Bay Area bait vendors will also sell a slimy sculpin-like fish called a "midshipman" which makes an excellent shark tantalizer.

Trolling and Drifting for Sharks

Once out in open water, sharks can also be pursued in more traditional ways by either trolling or drifting through a chum slick. The trolling technique is used primarily for 100 to 300 pound makos or thresher sharks. Big game 50 to 80 pound class gear is necessary for this slow-down approach. Usually, the shark experts prefer to slow-troll a whole bonito, mackerel or squid. Fresh bonito or mackerel is the best ticket. If you have to rely upon frozen bonito or macks, try to remove the backbone of the fish before pinning it on a hook. This will make the bait more flexible and life-like in the water.

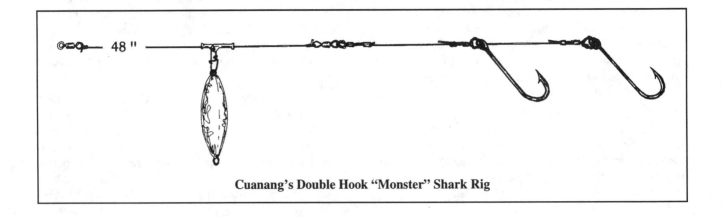

Cuanang's Double Hook "Monster" Shark Rig

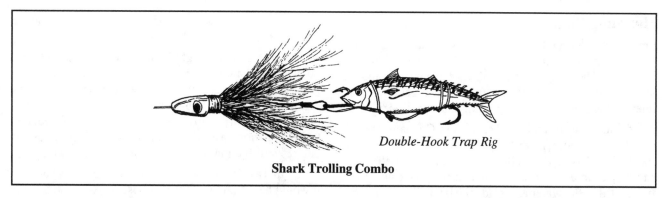

Double-Hook Trap Rig

Shark Trolling Combo

These baits are often pinned onto a unique trolling feather combination. This is made by running a heavy wire leader through standard brightly colored 15 mm or larger tuna feather. A #10/0 to #12/0 Eagle Claw #2004 black pearl circle hook is attached to the wire. A double-trap effect is constructed by attaching a stronger hook of about equal size to a short wire cable to the rear. This stinger wire is then tied into the loop formed by the cable on the lead hook. Crimped metal sleeves secure the wire cables together. The mouth of the dead bonito or mackerel is stapled shut to keep the bait from spinning on a slow-troll.

Some shark fishermen also use a downrigger to drag their baits into deeper strike zones. Sharks will lay out in the deep canyons and sub-marine ledges. The downrigger gets a slowly trolled mackerel or bonito into this strata.

Makos will sometimes strike an artificial lure trolled at modest speeds of about seven knots. It is not uncommon to nail one of these missiles while trolling a large tuna or marlin jig. The super husky, #CD-18 sinking Rapala lure has also accounted for a few prominent mako tallies. Threshers will typically smack at the lure with their tails and get foul-hooked in the jig. A tail-wrapped thresher, even on heavy string, could provide the angler with a battle lasting many hours.

A highly efficient means to both locate and catch sharks is to use a controlled chumming program. East Coast fishermen are frequently without the benefit of live bait. In its place, they grind up small bunker bait fish, place the ground meat into drums, and gradually disperse it over the side of the boat. This has the effect of leaving an aromatic chum slick on top of the water. The game fish are attracted to the film and move up the line toward the anglers in the stern.

West Coast sharkers have implemented a similar procedure to lure makos, threshers, and blue sharks to the boat. Instead of using bunker minnows, take relatively fresh mackerel, bonito, brown baits, smelt, or squid—in any combination—and mash up the blend in a meat grinder. Freeze it down in a milk carton to form a block of chum.

Next, when you motor into prime open-water shark territory (e.g. the La Jolla Trench, Oceanside, or Monterey Bay) peel away the wax milk carton and place the block of ground chum in a wire fish basket. These are widely sold for storing your panfish catch. Tie a rope to the handle of the basket and drag it with the chum block behind the boat. The block will slowly defrost, leaving an oily slick behind it. As an added enticement, empty a bottle of saltwater Berkley Saltwater Attractant onto the frozen block. Also, every so often, toss out some larger pieces of squid, mackerel, 'chovy, or bonito to spice up the chum line.

As an alternative, many landings and bait stores sell a five pound block of frozen squid. You can place this in the basket. It will not work as well as the ground fish meat, but it might suffice in a pinch, especially if you pour on some of the Strike compound for extra effect.

Once a shark shows in the chum line, don't be surprised if others follow. It may seem like all of a sudden the ocean becomes "alive" with these denizens of the deep coming from out of nowhere. This provides additional excitement for the hunt.

You can use anything from 10 to 12 pound ultralight saltwater outfits on up to 50 to 80 pound string and marlin-style gear. But, you will need about 10 to 15 feet of 60 to 100 pound monofilament or heavy stainless steel wire for a leader. That #2022 wide-gap Eagle Claw circle hook in a #8/0 to #12/0 size is perfect for fly-lining a slab of bait back into the chum slick.

Sharks can be tough fighters. The makos (also termed bonito sharks) and the threshers with their sickle-like tails, will sometimes put on some pretty spectacular surface fireworks. The makos will often skyrocket to the surface and turn a cartwheel in the air.

Handling Sharks

Let's never forget that these are potentially dangerous critters. This is true for even the smaller 20 pound leopards and blues. These fish have prominent teeth that can indeed inflict injury to the less-than-careful angler. Many anglers release sharks at boatside by cutting the wire leader.

If you want to land sharks, Angelo Cuanang recommends using a homemade bang stick to subdue these game fish before they are brought on board. The 12 or 20 gauge shotgun charge is detonated against the shark while the fish is still in the water alongside the boat. The bang stick has been utilized for years by scuba divers who encounter sharks. They are usually homemade by the divers.

In lieu of owning a bang stick, a fish billy and a gaff are your next best options. Saltwater pros recommend sticking the makos right behind the front dorsal fin. A similar swipe of the gaff works best with the threshers, but be careful of the tail. Thresher sharks can whip that awesome tail quickly with great force, slashing violently at would-be targets. It wouldn't be a bad idea to perhaps carry a flying gaff to keep the shark some distance from the boat. If possible, avoid gaffing the shark on its side. The fish can put up a lot of twisting action, making it tough to handle in this position.

Most shark hunters recommend bleeding the catch almost immediately after the fish is boated. This serves to keep the meat from becoming tainted.

Bat Rays

There is a small fraternity of saltwater anglers who like to play tug-o-war with bruiser bat rays. San Diego and Newport Harbors, Mission Bay, Santa Barbara, the Elkhorn Slough at Moss Landing, and the Monterey Peninsula are only a few spots to fish for rays.

"Bats" can range up to well over 100 pounds in weight. They generate tremendous resistance in the water once they start flopping those wings. They will hang tight to the bottom, occasionally planing to the surface. It takes some stout gear, preferable 40 pound test mono or heavier, teamed with strong live bait rods.

Bat rays can be caught both from the bank and from boats. The channels leading into sheltered harbors are good areas to try as well as the territory around floating bait receivers. These fish are nocturnal feeders with much of the best action occurring after dark. They are frequently taken as incidental catches during the daylight hours by anglers still fishing or drifting bait in these bays.

If I had to pick one setup to use for fishing big bat rays, it would be a sliding egg sinker. Use anywhere from 2 to 5 ounces of weight depending upon the current. Butt the sinker with a heavy-duty ball-bearing swivel. Clip on a 3 to 5 foot wire leader (60 to 80 pound test) with a single Eagle Claw #113 Black Pearl or #2004 circle #6/0 to #10/0 hook. Double-hook a whole frozen squid onto the leader and wait for the ensuing battle.

Other options include a slab of cut mackerel or bonito. Clams, bloodworms, shrimp, and even bloody chicken livers will produce at times. To avoid bait-stealers, consider adding a rear booby trap hook, similar to the trolling rig I mentioned in the previous section.

Summary

Sharks and rays are terrific alternatives for the weekend angler wishing to experience the thrill of big game fishing at a fraction of the cost associated with bill fishing and other exotic species. Sharks can put up a respectable fight and their potential as a fine food fish is slowly being discovered.

Treat these marine predators with respect. Even the most seemingly innocuous species can inflict a serious wound or do damage to the inside of a boat. Be careful with "jaws," and pass the word along—shark fishing is great sport!

Never—and I emphasize NEVER!—kill a shark for the mere fun of it. These ancient and magnificent creatures occupy an important part of our planet's marine ecosystem. It is up to us, the sportfishing community, to set an example of what prudent conservation is all about.

Salmon: Kings of the Coast

North Coasters react to the first reports of salmon activity in the same way Southlanders get excited about albacore. Feisty chinook, or king salmon, are one of the premium saltwater game fish caught off the Central and Northern coastlines. But before you go salmon hunting, be sure to check state regulations and possible closures for these two prime species.

For this chapter, I want to review the primary techniques Californians use to catch these fish. Salmon can be exceptionally aggressive biters at times, then all of a sudden "shut off" with a serious case of marine lockjaw. The accomplished chinook fisherman has to develop an array of specialized tactics. Let's focus first on some of the rudimentary trolling methods.

Trolling for Kings

King salmon can be taken from mid-February through the first part of November during a typical season. In the early part of the run, veteran salmon experts rely upon trolling to find the fish scattered over a large area.

Most salmon trolling is done at depths around 20 to 60 feet. Popular trolling areas are in San Francisco Bay outside of the Golden Gate Bridge between Duxbury Point and the Farallon Islands, Pillar Point, Monterey,

and Humboldt Bays, Pacifica, Muir Beach, Half Moon Bay, Rock Point, Stinson Beach, and Bolinas Point.

Salmon trolling is best at 2 to 4 miles per hour. There are a variety of trolling tactics that will work. All are worth trying.

Perhaps the simplest is to set up a sinker release system. The release mechanism itself is nothing more than a spring loaded device that is used to hold a fairly heavy 1 to 3 pound ball weight down until the chinook strikes. Your main line is attached to one end of the sinker release. The cast-iron weight is snapped into the release bar and your leader with either a natural bait or a lure is tied to the rear eye of the sinker release. (Sometimes a flasher or dodger is also used as an attractor. More on these in a moment.)

Now then, when the salmon hits the trolled lure or bait, the pressure from the strike pulls the spring on the release device, opening the clip that holds the cast-iron weight. The sinker is automatically released and falls to the bottom. The cast-iron weights are comparatively inexpensive in contrast to smooth, slick sinkers poured from quality lead. The cast-iron ball looks crude; but remember, it sinks to the bottom and becomes totally disposable.

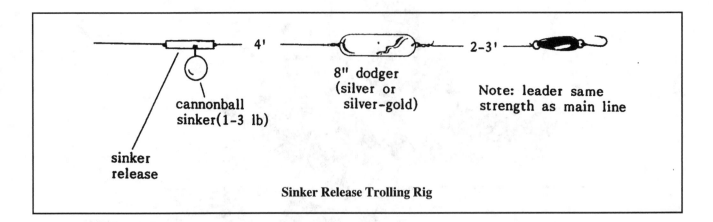

4'

8" dodger
(silver or
silver-gold)

2-3'

cannonball
sinker(1-3 lb)

Note: leader same
strength as main line

sinker
release

Sinker Release Trolling Rig

Many anglers are adamant that they will receive more strikes trolling for salmon if they use large metal attractors. Dodgers are made to rotate through the water in a side-to-side motion. This slow wobble effect can be maintained only at modest speeds. Flashers, on the other hand, actually rotate on a 360 degree plane. This spinning effect allows the fisherman to troll somewhat faster using the flasher.

The most popular colors preferred in dodgers and flashers for salmon trolling are nickel, prism, or a hammered brass and chrome 50/50 combination. Some local experts recommend a precise length of 14 inches of leader between the attractor and the lure or trolled bait. Planing devices can also be used to take either bait or lures to the proper depths where salmon are holding. Planers have been popular in certain inland trout circles for many years.

Interestingly, the unit itself is quite simple to understand. The planer is akin to the diving lip of a crankplug. But to get the "lip" to go deeper, it is weighted. You tie your main line to the front or lip portion of the planer. Then a leader with either bait or a lure (with or without a flasher or dodger in between) is tied to the rear of the unit. As you let out line, the diving plane sort of "cocks" itself into position to "dig" in, and takes the offering down. But, when the salmon strikes the lure or bait, the planer "trips" into a neutral plane. The lip no longer digs in and the device can be retrieved with minimal resistance.

Some of the popular diving planes sold for salmon fishing along the California Coast are the Deep Six, Pink Lady, Depth Glider, and Fish Seeker. Read the instructions carefully with each model. Some will clearly dive deeper than others. Try to obtain reports from local sources as to what depths the salmon are cruising and use planers with corresponding diving capabilities.

Both sinker release and diving plane systems for trolling require fairly stout tackle and heavier monofilament lines. With diving planes, 12 to 15 pound test for your main line would be the bare minimum. For sinker release outfits, dragging 1 to 3 pounds of cast-iron requires at least 20 pound string.

An alternative method which allows the angler to troll much lighter line with the optimal depth control is to use

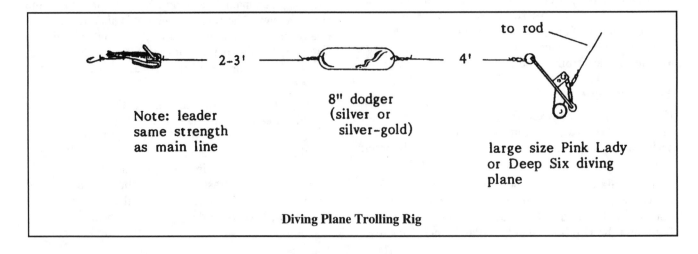

to rod

2-3'

8" dodger
(silver or
silver-gold)

4'

Note: leader
same strength
as main line

large size Pink Lady
or Deep Six diving
plane

Diving Plane Trolling Rig

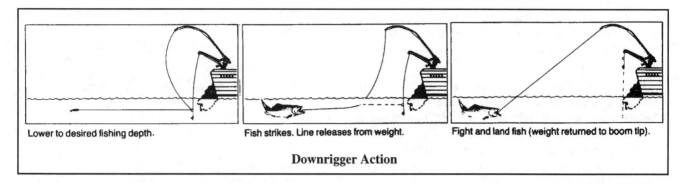

Lower to desired fishing depth.   Fish strikes. Line releases from weight.   Fight and land fish (weight returned to boom tip).

Downrigger Action

a downrigger. (This approach is outlined in the earlier chapter dedicated to trolling techniques.) The downrigger can accommodate anywhere from the lightest to the heaviest monofilament permitting the angler to play the salmon up from deep water without any major encumbrances.

Anchovies are the principle natural bait used for salmon trolling. They are typically threaded onto either a crowbar hook harness or a plastic baitholder rig. The crowbar hook is the more traditional setup. But more and more salmon slammers now prefer one of the popular plastic baitholders. These are sold as Rotary Salmon Killers or Herring Aids. They help to provide a more natural spinning and wobbling motion when the frozen 'chovy is dragged through the water.

The anchovies can be trolled behind any one of three primary setups: (1) a cannonball sinker release system, (2) a diving plane, or (3) a downrigger. The first two methods also commonly involve adding a dodger to the leader to generate greater flash and attraction.

Numerous lures can be slow-trolled for kings. The "hoochie" is a generic term used to describe the popular plastic squid-like jig dragged behind any of the basic trolling combinations. Shiny spoons such as the Krocadile and Apex will also produce on the slow troll. The key to remember is to throttle down when you pull lures in this genre. These fish are somewhat cautious in their feeding habits when it comes to trolled offerings. They won't usually annihilate a fast-moving lure as will tuna or yellowtail.

The deep trolling approach is essential when the chinooks are disbursed, or when the sea is rough with a lot of chop and swells. If you are a private boater, try to be a little imaginative when you drag the lures or bait behind the boat. You will find that your success ratio at salmon trolling will dramatically improve if you are more creative with your trolling patterns. How is this done?

Well, to begin with, vary your line of direction. Instead of trolling in a routine straight line, pull your lures or bait

in an "S" pattern. As the line swings through the different curves in this trolling sequence, the lures or bait will increase then decrease in action. This appears much more life-like to the salmon. Natural bait fish don't swim in straight lines, at the same pace, in the same manner all the time. By varying the boat's direction, this more natural erratic movement is imparted into your trolled offerings.

Here's another trick, that private boaters can try to generate a similar effect. As you are trolling along, intermittently throw your motor into neutral, then back into gear again. As you put the boat into the neutral position, your trolled bait or lures will start to flutter to the bottom. Putting the boat back into gear starts the bait or lures moving quicker along the normal plane. This subtle "go-and-stop-and-go" procedure gives the trolled offerings the illusion of dying, wounded bait fish—a natural target for finicky salmon.

Finally, there seems to be some evidence that quite frequently the largest kings are caught at greater depths. Try letting out more line to get the trolled bait or lure down deeper. This can be especially effective on a party boat if you troll slightly deeper than the other passengers. You may end up with the jackpot king!

Mooch for Chinooks

Veteran party boat and private boat captains will use both their electronics and their "eyeballs" as they say, to pinpoint concentrations of bait. Once the "meatballs" of bait are located, the marauding schools of salmon should be nearby.

Skippers will often try to make a visual sighting of "dark water." This distinctive patch of discoloration indicates a ball of bait—anchovies, smelt, or even squid or shrimp. Sometimes you can literally see a fish oil slick and smell the aroma of live bait that has been slashed by cruising schools of salmon.

Also be on the lookout for signs of boiling kings on the surface. Stretches of ocean where currents converge are similarly observable with the naked eye and are potentially good bait-holding areas.

Without visual sightings, your chart recorder or liquid crystal unit is your next best tool to use to locate the bait. Many salmon experts feel that the first two hours of daylight and twilight are the best times to find these game fish along with the schools of bait. So definitely plan on starting out early and staying out late with a potential lull in the midday action.

Once the bait fish are located, it's time to start "mooching." This tactic is a patented drifting method for nailing the kings. Mooching is excellent, especially inside the more quiet waters of the northern and central bays. It is usually a better strategy to use for salmon when you pinpoint concentrations of the fish. Mooching also seems to account for the larger chinooks weighed in annually in Central and Northern California.

Mooching doesn't require the heavier gear associated with sinker releases or planers. As a matter of fact, most salmon buffs prefer a longer, whippier, parabolic rod in 8 to 9 foot lengths for this particular line of attack. In addition to the more sensitive lengthy rods, moochers like to use lighter 10 to 15 pound mono with heavy freshwater class baitcasting reels.

The fine diameter line gets bit more, the parabolic rods telegraph the super touchy strike better, and there isn't that much worry about playing a 20 to 30 pound king on light string in open water. Mooching is really the "hot ticket" when it comes to both sport and greater action with this delicate fishery.

The object of mooching is to drift live or dead baits across schools of bait fish in pursuit of salmon. You must pay out line as the boat drifts to keep the bait near the bottom. Usually a live anchovy is mooched best with the nose-hooking technique previously discussed. An Eagle Claw #318-N #2 to #3/0 live bait hook is the standard combo, depending upon the size of the anchovy. Herring can also be mooched. With larger bait fish, consider using a double-hook trap setup.

The terminal rigs utilized with the mooching approach can vary, a lot depending upon personal preference. The basic sliding-egg sinker system works fine with the nose-hooked 'chovy or for trap-hooked bait fish drifted along the bottom. Another option is to use a 1/2 to 4 ounce crescent weight for this kind of salmon drifting. The keel-shape design, evident with this type of sinker, rides particularly well on a slow drift in more turbulent current.

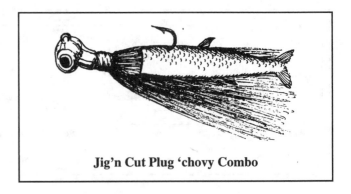

Jig'n Cut Plug 'chovy Combo

A favorite setup among local salmon anglers is the sliding sleeve with a dipsey sinker. The sliding sleeve is constructed from rubber tubing with the weight clipped to the middle of the sleeve. The nice thing about the design of this mooching rig is that you can quickly change weights depending upon conditions by easily snapping on different sinkers to the sleeve.

Once you get your bait down to the bottom, an integral trick to the mooching program is to gently "pump" the rod every so often. By lifting and dropping the rod in this manner much more tantalizing action is given to the bait. Salmon seem to really prefer a slow-fluttering offering.

As you drift along, the rod is usually placed in a rod holder, taken out for intermittent pumping action. The drift of the boat down swell also instills a lot of action as the bait bounces along. But keep in mind that even the biggest kings will often strike in the most nerve-racking, "picky" way. This is where some skillful, patient rod-handling comes into play.

The soft-tipped, parabolic rods will telegraph the telltale "tick" of the initial strike. Immediately drop the rod and give the fish some slack to further mouth the bait. When you feel the gentle resistance or pulling on the line on the second tap, swing and set.

Sometimes, you will have to feather the spool, rolling it with your finger tips or continue to lift-and-drop the rod in a gentle pumping motion and generally engage in a war of nerves as you coax the chinook to really eat the bait. This is all part of the challenge with the mooching strategy —but, it does many trophy kings in the ice chest.

It is also possible to mooch with either artificial lures or a cut plug of bait as a trailer to a salmon jig. Abe Cuanang is one of Northern California's foremost salmon experts. Using basic 8 to 9 foot steelhead rods, with freshwater-sized baitcasting reels, Cuanang will mooch many lunker kings with jigs. He likes to work 4 to 5 outfits at one time, letting out line to cover 10, 15, 20, and 25 foot depths. The rods remain on holders or along the boat railing. Cuanang's trick is to use a strip of anchovy teamed with a white, banana-head jig (for example, the popular Hair Raiser model).

This jig'n plug bait combo is deadly in the warmer summer months on the chinooks. Cuanang recommends drifting a jig in 1/4 to 1 ounce patterns. The lighter heads will generate more action, but the heavier models are needed in rough seas. He will also let out more line with his assorted outfits as the day evolves, probing deeper strike zones.

I should note that this tactic is akin to the drifting that Southland anglers do using soft plastic baits along off-shore kelp beds and reefs. With both methods, the waves and current help to make the jigs bob and dart like an errant bait fish.

Cuanang also suggests that the small craft owner invests in a sea anchor for successful mooching. This parachute-like anchor will slow the drift down significantly, letting hook-shy salmon catch up with the bouncing jigs.

These basic mooching strategies can also be tried in Southern California. Salmon are sometimes found— albeit rarely—as far south as Newport Beach. Local tackle expert, Mike Callan, has employed the standard sliding sinker setup and a live anchovy to boat some hefty double-digit kings in the Southland. Callan observes that the salmon are usually found less than a mile offshore, making them easily accessible to the small boat owners.

Spoon Drifting for Salmon

Abe Cuanang has also perfected another interesting ploy for coastal salmon fishing. Instead of using jigs or bait in a mooching program, he will yo-yo a spoon in a vertical presentation as the boat drifts along.

The key is to home in on the meatballs of bait. Once in the vicinity of the bait concentrations, Cuanang likes to yo-yo a brightly polished spoon for school salmon. The versatile Haddock Jig'n Spoon, Krocadile, Mr. Champ and Hopkins models in chrome finishes are perfect for this vertical spoonin' method. As with all spoonin', be prepared for strikes on the fall following the lifting action.

Soft plastics can also be worked vertically along a drift pattern. Lures such as the Haddock Kreepy Krawler, A.A.

Worms Swimbait, Fish Trap, and Berkley Power Pogey and Power Minnow have been racking up some impressive tallies of the kings. Both single and double-tail grubs are also worth experimenting with for salmon. Try them when a slow-swimming lure is needed. Definitely explore these different possibilities to expand your repertoire of king salmon tricks.

Salmon Near the Shore

Northern anglers will sometimes experience an additional treat when these gamesters migrate off the surfline or within a cast from the public piers. Almost all of the patented techniques outlined in this chapter can be modi-fied for tossing bait on salmon feeding near the shore.

Assorted lures ranging from shiny spoons and tube lures to hair jigs with a plug of cut bait can be worked from the piers or cast into the surf. There are however, two additional strategies worth mentioning that could prove to be deadly if the chinooks range near the public piers.

Review the live bait trolley rigs I outlined in the pier fishing chapter. A lively anchovy slid down the line from high above the water on a pier will definitely produce strikes on shallow water kings.

Similarly, use a styrofoam bobber, with about 6 to 8 feet of mono under the float to form the leader. Tie on a #2 to #3/0 live bait hook to the leader. Pin on a fresh dead, or preferably, a live 'chovy hooked through the nose or gill cover. Add a large split-shot midway to the leader to keep the bait fish fairly vertically below the float. Use a lob cast, and let the anchovy drift in the current below the styrofoam bobber. Salmon cruising in the vicinity of the pier will sometimes go crazy for this combination.

Summary

Salmon are terrific sport, especially on light tackle. These fish have excellent eyesight and they can be exceptionally spooky at times. You will get bit more if you stay with lighter lines, fresher bait—even if it's dead—and careful rigging of the lures and bait fish.

If you decide to mooch for salmon, keep your hooks extremely sharp. Be prepared to spend some time "teas-ing" this game fish into eating your bait. The effort spent will be well worth it!

Stripers: Linesides from Surf and Bay

Striped bass are one of the primary game fish sought by Northern California saltwater sportsmen. There has probably been more written about this particular fish with regard to the North Coast fishery than all other species combined.

This chapter is a primer of sorts to get you started as a "striper sniper." There is a wealth of other information available that will provide you with even more sophisticated tools to track these intriguing fish.

Begin to monitor accounts published in weekly outdoor newspaper columns. These seasonal reports are essential to follow in order to get a general idea of where the stripers are schooling. Next, visit area tackle stores. Develop a rapport with the proprietor. Try to buy your bait and at least some portion of your terminal gear from these shops. In exchange, the sales personnel may turn you on to valuable insiders' tips of "where, when, and how" to fish stripers.

Finally, if your thirst for striped bass has intensified after reading this chapter, I strongly recommend Abe Cuanang's classic text, San Francisco Bay Striper (Angler Publications, 1983).

Working the Surfline

In the surf fishing chapter, I described how to cast for striped bass while working the beach. Similar action can be experienced as both party and charter boats, as well as smaller private craft, maneuver for position barely outside the surfline.

Usually by early June, huge schools of linesides will cruise within the breakers south of the Golden Gate, herding masses of anchovies or any other available bait fish. These stripers can be smaller 8 to 10 pound school fish, on up to 20 to 30 pound class brutes.

As was noted in the surf fishing chapter, keep a keen eye open for telltale signs of nearby striper activity. This can be signalled by sea birds dipping into the water, visual sightings of "dark water" (meatballs of bait), or surface boils.

If you are lucky enough to first see an indication of surface-feeding fish, definitely take a shot at them with artificial lures. Top-water plugs in larger freshwater or saltwater sizes such as the Arbogast Dasher, Heddon Lucky 13, Bomber Model Long-A, magnum class Rapalas and Rebels, or the Cordell Pencil Popper are time-proven striper killers.

Expect to make a fairly long cast, keeping the boat some distance from the surface frenzy. A medium-action 8 to 9 foot saltwater spinning rod and a spinner filled with 20 pound mono should do the trick. Heavy-duty freshwater popping rods will also work for this type of casting. However, novice striper fishermen will probably find the spinning combos easier to cast when using these large bulky plugs, especially in the wind.

Other lure possibilities should also be explored when the stripers are near the beach. Spoons such as the ever popular Krocadile, Luhr Jensen Champ, Haddock Jig 'n Spoon, Tony Acetta Pet, and the Kastmaster are excellent choices under these conditions. The traditional solid chrome, chrome and blue, or chrome and red color schemes produce annually for fan-casting for stripers from the boat.

Slab-shaped crankplugs in beefier sizes are similarly effective. The Cordell Spot is a standout lure for plugs in this genre along with the Rapala Rattlin' Rap, Rattle Trap and Luhr Jensen Sugar Shad.

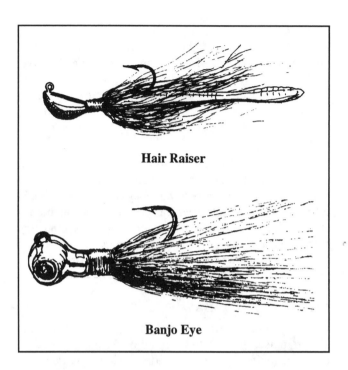

Hair Raiser

Banjo Eye

Kastmaster with Bucktail Trailer

But one of the simplest lures to use for surfline stripers is the hair jig. Models enjoying great popularity over past seasons are the Hair Raiser, the Banjo Eye, and the Worm Tail. The latter is a hair jig featuring a long, white plastic curly-tail worm as a trailer. On this note, include soft plastic jigs such as the Scrounger, Salty Magic, and Kalin Lunker Grub in your striper arsenal.

Here are a couple of fairly basic rules of thumb to observe when tossing lures on striped bass. These guidelines are appropriate whether you are spot-casting outside the surfline or inside the more sheltered bays.

First, learn to vary your retrieve to key in on the pace at which the stripers appear to be feeding. For example, if the fish are in a wild surface-feeding frenzy, then consider ripping that crank plug, surface lure, spoon, or jig back to the boat fairly rapidly. If they seem touchy, slow down your retrieve.

Second, if the stripers become skittish, or if the water clarity is high, or the bite simply appears to have ground down, then switch to smaller lures and lighter monofilament.

Third and last, mix up your presentations as conditions change throughout the day. For instance, when the linesides are "hot," a swimming jig with a curly-tail may be the ticket. When the action cools, it might be better to use a slow sashaying jig with minimal tail movement.

If fan-casting from the boat isn't your fancy this close to the beach, slow-trolling is a viable alternative. Spoons, jigs, and crankplugs are adaptable to this method. Sometimes the lure will have to be pulled through a specific fish-holding strata some distance above the bottom. Other times the stripers may be sulking near the bottom and a deep diving lure will work better.

Party boats will often chum with live bait in the surfline. If you have this kind of fire power at your disposal, then live bait drifting or fly-lining a 'chovy, smelt, herring, or sardine will produce.

A nose or gill-hooked anchovy with a small 1/4 to 3/8 ounce rubber core sinker or a larger split-shot crimped above the bait will get bit when drifted gently behind the boat. If more weight is needed to fight the current or wave action, then a sliding sinker rig or a three-way swivel setup will be necessary. The sinkers can vary from 1 to 4 ounces in weight.

Stripers will continue to chase bait fish along the beach from late June through early September. Boat positioning is critical with this approach. To be effective, the boater will frequently have to pilot his craft perilously close to the beach. The stripers will gravitate to the sandy or rocky points, along with narrow creases where the shoreline takes a turn forming a feeding funnel for trapped bait fish.

Fishing spots like this require considerable boat handling skill and full attention to the surf conditions. Many veteran private boaters recommend fishing the surfline in teamwork fashion. One person should be responsible for staying on the wheel while the others fish. Then rotate that responsibility. But someone has to maintain control of the boat at all times when working this close to the shore.

Linesides in the Bay

By late summer, stripers should start migrating into the San Francisco Bay. After gorging themselves on ocean-bred anchovies for the past months along the Pacifica, Rockaway, and Lindeman beaches, the big linesides follow the schools of bait inland. Activity now begins to heat up in such legendary striper haunts as Candlestick Park, Hunter's Point, and the San Mateo Bridge in the southwest bay, and the Alameda Rocks, the Berkeley Flats, and the Oakland Estuary in the northeast section. Schools of stripers also inhabit San Francisco Bay from mid-May through early fall. These fish come down from the Delta in late spring.

Party boat skippers will run so-called "potluck" trips on which they drift for stripers, salmon, or halibut in the expanses of the Bay. The object of most Bay drifting is to keep the bait roughly 3 feet above the bottom. Mudsuckers are considered the primo bait for stripers. But live shiner perch, bullheads, anchovies, squid, grass shrimp, herring, and smelt are also on the seasonal menu for these Northern game fish.

Let's elaborate on some of these baits for a moment. The mudsuckers are sold at area bait shops. They are usually fished live on the drift, hooked through both lips with either a long-shank baitholder or short-shank live bait hook. Shiner perch can be caught around the pilings in the Bay using pieces of pile worm or shrimp on a tiny #10 to #14 baitholder hook. They can then be placed in aerated live wells or bait buckets. Hook the shiners as you would a "brown bait" to fly-line it either behind the dorsal fin, under the anal fin, or through the nose.

Anchovies and smelt, of course, produce best when alive. Standard live bait hooking procedures previously discussed are appropriate. Frozen versions of these bait fish, along with herring also work. Whole bait fish, halves, or chunks can be tried.

Remember the little tip I passed along in earlier chapters on how to slice a halved 'chovy partially up the center to create a scissor effect with the flaps of meat? Well, this also helps to lure stripers to this bait. Locals also like to make an incision in the whole dead bait fish, again primarily to emit scent and fish oils to attract the striped bass.

Veteran striper snipers will disagree among themselves as to whether it is best to fish bullheads alive or dead. One theory recommends drifting a live bullhead available from area bait vendors. This lively sculpin-like bait fish drifted slowly along the bottom is a tantalizing morsel for a hungry striper. But the other school of thought suggests drifting only dead bullheads. The reason is that live bullheads have a tendency to burrow into the mud.

So, some experts prefer to take live bullheads, kill them first, then use them for bait. You can, however, purchase frozen bullheads at the bait shops. If you do this, always make sure there is a lot of slime coating left on the bait as you look through the packaging. This slime layer dissipates an apparent odor in the water that attracts the snipers. The slime also has luminescent properties that make the bullhead practically glow in the Bay's cloudy water.

A variety of routine drifting rigs will be suitable with the above-mentioned baits. The basic sliding egg sinker setup, a three-way swivel combo, a split-shot rig—all of these will produce when drifting for stripers in San Francisco Bay. Sinker size will vary depending upon currents, tidal conditions, and the bottom topography.

Quite a few of the area's regular anglers also recommend using a double-hook trap setup when drifting these different baits, especially with bullheads, cut 'chovies, smelt, or herring.

Also consider using a large chunk of styrofoam tied above the bait as a drift bobber. A favorite tactic is to fish a live shiner perch 5 to 8 feet underneath the float and let it drift in the current.

You will also often hear long-time striper fishermen talk about "walking" their baits off the bottom. This is an important technique, requiring some finessing with, again,

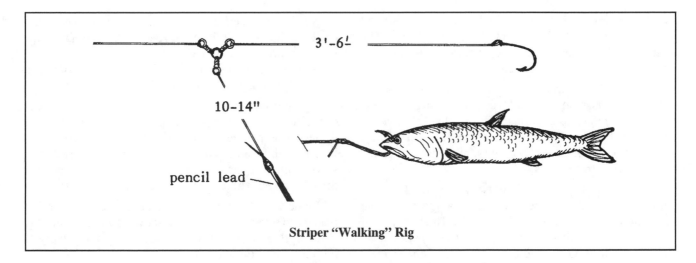

Striper "Walking" Rig

the object being to keep the bait from hanging up on the bottom terrain.

One strategy is to use a three-way swivel combination. On a lighter, 8 to 12 inch leader tie on your sinker. A very soft flexible pencil lead can be used in this situation. This kind of sinker hangs up less than conventional weights. On a heavier, 18 to 36 inch leader, tie on your bait. The trick is to kind of "pump" the rod tip as you either drift or cast-and-retrieve, easing the bait above the rocks and along the ledges. If the weight gets hung up or if the fish heads for the rocks, the lighter leader with the sinker will break off first, either saving the bait, or allowing you to play the striper without any further hang-ups. In many ways, this is quite similar to mooching for salmon.

A variation on this theme is to "chrome" the stripers. Tie a 1 to 4 ounce shiny chrome ringed torpedo sinker to your main line. Run an 18 to 36 inch leader with your bait on the other end of the weight. After you cast, be prepared for strikes on the fall, as the shiny sinker creates a lot of "flash" on the way down. The torpedo weight can then be either bounced along the bottom or "pumped" and retrieved above it through shallower strike zones.

Here are a couple of other pointers to keep in mind for fishing stripers in the Bay with live bait. First, if you feel uncomfortable working drift patterns, consider fishing the linesides at anchor. This is a particularly good tactic if you want to zero in on a lunker using bullheads for bait. Try to fish at the peak of high tide if possible.

Second, give these fish plenty of time to eat the larger offerings such as mudsuckers or bullheads. Leave the reel in free-spool, allowing the bass to mouth the big bait with minimal resistance. Don't underestimate the magnitude of the initial strike. It may take the form of nothing more than a subtle "tick" in the line. In sum, it pays to be patient when still fishing or drifting for striped bass.

Lures in the Bay

Many of the lures mentioned in the earlier discussion of stripers from the surfline, will be effective in the quieter waters of the Bay. Also consider using both the large and more compact plugs associated with freshwater bassin'. Long distance casting may not always be that critical. Both medium saltwater spinning and freshwater popping outfits are perfect for bay striper snipin'.

When you switch to artificials, there are a couple of things to look for to enhance your chances. Always keep your eyes peeled for surface activity: birds picking at bait,

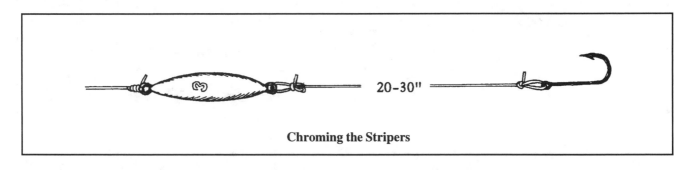

Chroming the Stripers

swirls, boiling fish. Fire casts wherever you can find moving currents. And, toss your lures up-current. The stripers will be facing into the current, waiting for wayward bait to flow down to them.

Next, seek out structure in the Bay. Striped bass will establish ambush points on all types of obstructions. Boat docks, rock piles, riprap, bridge pilings, channel markers, chunks of broken asphalt or concrete, old duck blinds, broken pipe, rock jetties, and piers, all constitute prime structure for striped bass.

Stripers "wolf pack" in schools trying to herd the bait into pockets created by the structure. As aggressive as the fish can become, they also spook easily. The best way to stalk those game fish in the shallow waters is to use an electric trolling motor and come up behind the stripers quietly. You can actually follow the schools with the trolling motor as they migrate over the shallow flats.

There are regional favorites that Bay Area locals like to toss when a lure bite materializes. Large freshwater plugs such as the Cordell Spot, Rebels, and CD-11, 13, 14 and 18 Magnum Rapalas persist at nailing Bay stripers. A black or white Hair Raiser jig is another killer. Other banana-head jigs with a red head and white skirt, or red head with orange skirt are equally productive. The Worm-Tail models are also frequently used, commonly in white, for both drifting or spot-casting towards structure. More traditional freshwater bassin' jigs such as the Haddock Kreepy Krawler, Klein Weapon, and Stanley Jigs are equally worth trying. If the water is real dirty, select a jig with a relatively bulky skirt. This lure will displace more water and the bulky body will show up better under murky conditions.

Spoons of practically any shape are possible striper catchers. It is hard to beat the Kastmaster and Krocadile series in chrome. These will cast well, with minimal wind resistance. Other spoons to try are the Luhr Jensen Champ, Crippled Herring, and Haddock Jig 'n Spoon.

Another interesting option is to present two lures at one time. You can buy a wire spreader rig at local tackle dealers. The spreader frame allows you to tie two different leaders with diverse baits for real variety when drifting or slow-trolling. A popular combination is a Tony Acetta Pet Spoon teamed with a hair jig on separate leaders.

Some anglers will also use Pink Ladys or similar planers to take spoons or plugs down deeper in the Bay while trolling for stripers. The basic setup and principles outlined for using these planing devices for salmon are pretty much applicable for striper deep-trolling.

Stripers from the Bank

The wide range of tactics I have discussed, for taking stripers from within the surfline or in San Francisco Bay, can also apply to certain shoreline locations. The assorted bait rigs are quite suitable for making long casts from the bank. Obviously, the acquisition and handling of live bait will be problematic for the shoreline striper hunter. Still, various fresh dead or frozen offerings will produce.

Here again, look for "signs of life"—current, swirls, birds, boils. It will definitely help to move the bait by reeling in every so often to give it a more life-like appearance.

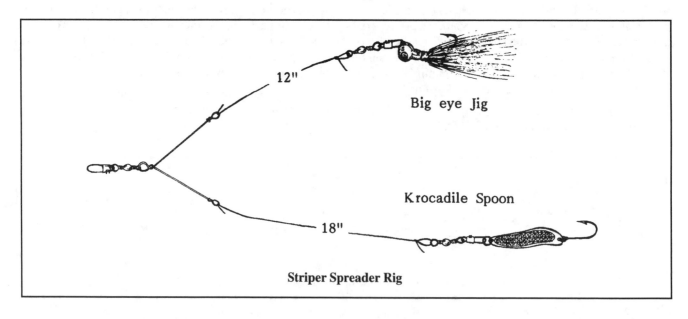

12"

Big eye Jig

Krocadile Spoon

18"

Striper Spreader Rig

Bank walkers chuckin' lures for linesides should similarly take advantage of any visual structure within casting distance from the bank. Also, look for stripers against shady bridge pilings seeking respite from summer heat.

The magnum plugs used for surf casting are perfect for making a long cast from the bank. Pencil Poppers, Creek Chub Dashers, jumbo Rebels,and CD-11, CD-13 and CD-14 Magnum Rapalas, along with Rapala saltwater Skitter Pops, can be worked on or below the surface depending on the feeding mode of the stripers. These fish are also nocturnal creatures and they will readily crash on a surface lure worked diligently in the dark. This is another added dimension for the accomplished striper sniper pounding the shoreline with big plugs.

Stripers will also slaughter soft plastics! Mojos, Salty Magics, Pacific Eels, A.A. Worms swimbaits, Optimum lures, and Lunker Thumpers will all catch stripers from the shoreline.

Throw your lures in places where currents converge—always look for that moving water! Above all, try to remain mobile. These are marauding game fish, and they will move as they follow the schools of bait. Remember, by the time striped bass move inside the Bay, they have basically become shallow water feeders. Hence you may not be at that much of a disadvantage being relegated to the bank once these fish begin their migration from the ocean to the Bay.

Summary

Striped bass are both excellent sport and fine eating. When the fish are concentrated, the bite can go "wide-open" for both bait soakers and lure fishermen. Learn to "read" the water when you fish for stripers. There are vast expanses of "dead" water found along stretches of beachfront access or the quiet water in San Francisco Bay. Learn to rely upon your "eyeballs" and instincts to home in on these Northern game fish. Be on the constant lookout for any indication of striper activity and then be prepared to move quickly to follow the fish.

Yellowtail: Pacific Yellow Fever

Next to albacore, yellowtail are the most prized game fish found along the Southern California Coast. Favorite hot spots for these jumbo members of the jack family of fishes include the Coronado Islands, Catalina and San Clemente Islands, the La Jolla and Horseshoe Kelp, and the oil rigs outside of Huntington Beach. Occasionally, schools of yellowtail will also migrate with warmer currents into the kelp beds off the Central Coast and the Channel Islands.

Tails on Bait

Yellowtail are frequently touchy feeders. One day the fish can "show" in a particular area and have absolutely no interest in biting. A return trip the next day may result in wide-open activity.

It is important to keep your live bait offering fresh and lively. Most fishermen will use somewhere around 20 pound test string when fishing 'chovies for yellowtail. Anything heavier tends to restrict the free movement of the small bait fish. This is especially true for a fly-lined anchovy. Novice anglers sometimes over-scale their tackle for yellows. They think that it is necessary to use 30 to 40 pound test line on these 10 to 25 pound fish. Especially on crowded party boats, you will usually get bit more with 15 to 20 pound mono, smaller Eagle Claw #318-N #2 to #4 live bait hooks, and a lively greenback anchovy.

Now, if you are lucky enough to have a tankful of live squid, the 'tails will usually go crazy for this "candy." I still prefer using the 15 to 20 pound mono. It allows the squid to swim more freely and the fish are less spooked with the finer line. However, use anywhere from a #2/0 to #4/0 Eagle Claw #318-N live bait hook with the squid. Hook the squid through the tail.

Either fly-line these cephalopods or use a twist-on rubber core sinker or a split-shot to get them down deeper. With squid, more so than with anchovies, let the yellows run some distance once they pick up the bait. Leave your reel in free-spool if you are using conventional tackle. If you prefer spinning gear, fly-line the bait with the bail open. You have to give the 'tails some time to eat the squid.

Yellowtail will also readily attack a Spanish or greenback mackerel fly-lined on the surface. Now you may want to consider using heavier string. A lot of veteran Southland anglers wouldn't think of fishing yellows on macks with any less than 30 pound mono. Larger #3/0 to #6/0 live bait hooks are recommended. However, as I mentioned, these gamesters can become real spooky at times. It often pays to throw a mackerel on 20 pound test line if the bite seems to have dwindled for those tossing 30 to 40 pound test. My feeling—in any type of sport fishing —is that I would rather get bit first, then worry about playing the fish later.

In the past few years, local party and charter boat skippers have been having their clients fish large treble hooks with mackerel for yellowtail. They note that a lot of 'tails are missed due to the touchy nature of these sport fish when they hit the bait—particularly large mackerel. The trick is to hook the mack gently through the nostril using only one of the three points of the treble. The remaining two points of the hook are left exposed. If you want the mackerel to swim deeper, a similar procedure can be followed, running a single point in the anal fin area.

When a yellow runs with the bait with this kind of hooking, the angler can set up more quickly on the fish. Instead of relying upon only one point to penetrate the fish as is the case with a single live bait hook, you now have two additional points that may stick.

The treble hook trick has been a central ploy used for yanking larger home-guard 'tails away from the floating oil rigs outside of Huntington Beach. At one time there were quite a few larger 18 to 25 pound resident fish that cruise around these platforms. Once these yellows make a run with the bait, they will invariably head for the wire cables that help to support the legs of the structures.

By using the larger treble hooks combined with 30 to 40 pound mono, the fisherman is able to set up quickly on the 'tail and keep the fish away from the cables. Many bruiser-class yellows have been salvaged with this combination of big treble, big line.

Yellowtail are also suckers for live smelt or sardines. These baits work particularly well along the kelp stringers fly-lined on the surface. (See the chapter on kelp fishing for more on yellowtail in the "weeds.") Occasionally, a stray yellow or two will be taken on brown bait. This, however, is usually an incidental catch as the anglers work the brown baits for bull calicos.

Yellowtail can also be fooled with one other rather unusual bait—striped bonito. This tactic doesn't produce all the time, but when it does, the action can be pretty spectacular. Simply cut long strips from an average 1 to 3 pound bonito. The strips should be cut lengthwise, somewhere around 10 to 15 inches in length and about an inch wide. Put an Eagle Claw #113 Black Pearl #4/0 short-shank baitholder hook through one end of the strip. Be sure to leave the shiny bonito skin on the strip.

Cast this extraordinarily long filet out, usually without a weight. The secret is to let the strip drift out into the current, then "walk" it back in towards the boat. As your reel is on free-spool, roll the spool with your fingers to pick up line in little spurts. Twitch the rod tip once in awhile when doing this. This slow retrieve-twitching concerto makes the strip undulate in the water, seductively moving like a snake.

It is important to keep the reel in free-spool. When the yellows hit this long strip bait, they will literally pull and tug at it, shaking it the way a dog plays with an old newspaper. You have to let the fish really run some distance with the giant strip without feeling resistance. Hence, it is imperative to give the 'tail a lot of line on the free-spool.

Usually, lighter 15 to 20 pound mono works best for the bonito strip. The lighter line allows the angler to impart more natural movement to the strip.

Yellowtail will sometimes hit other dead baits. A fresh dead mackerel will often work. Here too, the fisherman must kind of "walk" and "twitch" the mack back to life, to give it a more natural appearance.

Frozen, or better yet, fresh dead squid will also account for some limited action on yellows. The bait can be fly-lined or slightly weighted to drift out into the current. The "twitching" technique also works with frozen squid. However, don't forget that little secret trick I mentioned earlier regarding putting a live 'chovy inside a dead squid to make it look alive.

Although most yellowtail are caught near the surface with bait, it is not impossible to find that these fish respond to a deep presentation. This occurs typically in the winter months. If you have live squid, try fishing it on a sliding sinker rig all the way down to 150 feet. Numerous large yellowtail have been caught in this manner in the dead of winter. There are populations of home-guard fish that stay around out local waters and they will seek deeper, more temperate thermoclines in the colder months. Dead squid can also be worked deep on a slider for yellows.

Yellows on the Iron

One of the most exciting events is to be on a wide-open yellowtail bite when the fish are on the "iron." Yellows will occasionally really hammer the cast-iron jigs. There are two basic programs to use: (a) the surface grind; or (b) the yo-yo.

'Tails will frequently come out from the kelp stringers, boiler rocks, or submerged reefs to strike a candy bar jig retrieved across the surface with fairly long casts on conventional tackle. When these game fish hit the iron, hold on! They generate tremendous impact when they nail the jig and instantly turn and run. It takes good equipment—baitcasting recommended—to subdue these rockets on the iron.

Most anglers prefer to use 30 to 40 pound mono to throw surface jigs on the 'tails. The heavier string won't stretch much upon impact. It also allows the fisherman to apply leverage to turn the fish away from the kelp and rocks. If I could recommend one surface jig for yellowtail, day in and day out, it would be a tougher choice between a "light" Jerry Jig or the new Ironman Candyman. Every one of these lures seems to swim perfectly—no "duds"!

Depending upon what the 'tails seem to prefer, the jigs range in length from 4 to 8 inches—and, in the "light" slow-sinking alloy. Routine color schemes include blue and white, blue, green and yellow, sardine, chrome, blue and chrome, and scrambled egg. I always make it a point to phone the landing in advance to find out what specific patterns and models the yellows have been hitting.

It takes a considerably fast retrieve to get the right action out of these lures for yellowtail fishing. Slower retrieves may work for barracuda and bass, but not usually for yellows. This is another reason for using quality saltwater baitcasting reels with at least 4:1 and preferably 5:1 gear ratios. You will be doing a lot of winding on a surface jig bite. The conventional reels in contrast to spinners are made to withstand the rigors of this type of hard work.

Also, as a general rule, the 'tails prefer a constant steady wind—none of that tricky "stop'n go" stuff I talked about for 'cuda fishing. And, whatever you do, don't add a snap-swivel to the jig—tie directly to the line ring.

If the yellows are feeding deeper, then a yo-yo approach may perform best. This is the situation where you can try the "heavy" counterparts of your favorite surface iron. Many anglers like to use a stout, shorter 6 to 7 foot rod for the yo-yo bite, compared to 8 to 9 foot models for making long casts with surface jigs.

There isn't really much casting needed with the yo-yo strategy. Point the rod tip towards the water, throw the reel into free-spool and let the jig shoot straight down toward the bottom. Sometimes the yellowtail will strike the jig on the fall. Popular models to try with heavy yo-yo iron are the Ironman #3 and #5, and Jerry Jig Heavy models, Salas CP-105 and 6X JR, and Tady AA and A1.

Once the jig hits the bottom, there are two ways to yo-yo it. In some situations, a typical slow lift-and-drop motion works best (usually in the winter). In others, it is better to wind the jig back in quickly, immediately after it bumps the bottom. This is also termed a "yo-yo grind."

Again, I want to harp on the need for sharp hooks. The stock trebles found on both the surface and yo-yo iron are not sharp enough when purchased off the shelf. You must take a file to these trebles before your trip. It is relatively easy for the 'tails to twist and turn their heads, quickly dislodging a dull treble.

Trolling for Yellowtail

This strategy is not used too often and I have mentioned it in previous chapters. But to review, there are times when the 'tails will eat a lure dragged behind the stern.

Perhaps the best overall choice is the balsa and plastic saltwater minnows resembling bait fish. Bagley's Balsa Bang-O, the Rapala Magnum CD-14 and CD-18, and various plastic Rebels should be trolled at moderately fast speeds. Typical color patterns that work are silver/black back, silver/blue back, mackerel and fire tiger.

You can also drag smaller 10 to 15 mm feathers for yellowtail. Sometimes this method works super for locating schools of breezing fish. I prefer to pull the feathers on a 20 to 30 pound test leader line about 5 feet in length attached to an 8 ounce ringed torpedo sinker. (The weight should have ball-bearing swivels clipped to each ring for tying the lines to.) Some anglers like to troll the feathers near the surface. Others, myself included, find they get bit better if the feather is made to ride deeper below the commotion created by the wake. Best models include the Salas 6X or 7X, Tady #45, the new Jerry Jig Surface Iron, and the Ironman Candyman.

A final option is to drag candy bar style jigs through schools of "breezers." Both light and heavy models have been effective. It is important, however, if you decide to troll the iron for yellows, that you throttle down. These jigs will start to spin if you pull them too fast.

Summary

Yellowtail are fantastic sport. It seems though, that they have become tougher to fool each successive season. No doubt the effects of commercial fishing, depletion of bait fish, angler pressure, and pollution have all taken their toll on this important fishery.

It will take some cunning and expertise to trick these game fish. Your tackle has to be in topnotch condition. 'Tails will make scorching runs across the surface, then long sulking dives to the bottom. Many Southlanders claim that each yellowtail has its own personality—each puts up a different fight.

Striped Marlin: Big Game Fishin'— California Style

From late July through mid November, private yacht owners and charter boat operators prospect the offshore waters of Southern California for striped marlin. "Stripes," unlike their larger blue or black cousins, range somewhere between 100 and 175 pounds on the average in the Southland. A 200 pound specimen is a real wall hanger, though catches topping well over the 300 pound mark have been recorded off this coast.

Most of the striped marlin fishing occurs from San Diego to the far South, and northward around San Clemente and Catalina Islands, extending further north occasionally to the outside of the Channel Islands. There are basically two ways that Southern California anglers fish for marlin: (1) trolling and (2) live bait drifting or casting.

Stripers on the Troll

Perhaps the simplest strategy for the beginning marlin fisherman to employ is a basic trolling program. You will need a quality reel in the 4/0 class. It should hold 300 to 500 yards of 30 to 50 pound string. In recent years, most local pros have switched to premium grade mono in this line category. A smaller number of anglers still prefer the more expensive and less stretchable Micron fabric line. Either will suffice. The rod should be somewhere in an IGFA 20 to 50 pound range with roller guides and tiptop.

Many Southland marlin hunters prefer to fight the fish standing at the rail instead of from a fighting chair. The lighter 30 pound outfits are perfect for this kind of "stand-up fishing" combined with either a reel harness, or minimally, a rod butt apron. Heavier gear in the 80 pound class will usually wear the angler down from a stand-up position. This more traditional magnum-sized outfit performs best from a fighting chair.

Years ago the common way to troll for stripes off the Southern California coast was to drag a bridled fresh or frozen flying fish. This tactic is practically extinct. It has been replaced with so-called brightly colored "psychedelic" marlin jigs.

These are really jumbo versions of big tuna feathers. But instead of having feathers, they have highly opulent plastic skirts laced over multi-colored faceted beads. Marlin jigs in this genre are sold commercially rigged

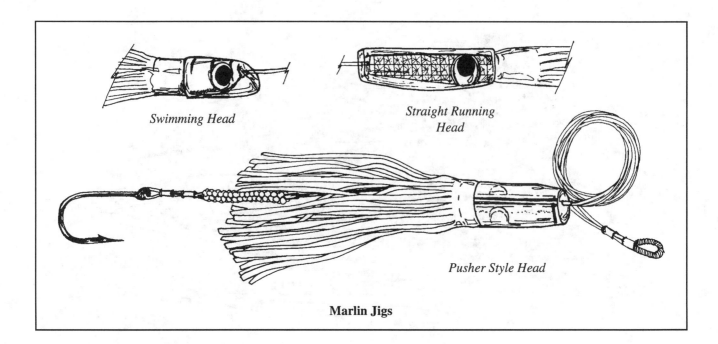

Swimming Head

Straight Running Head

Pusher Style Head

Marlin Jigs

with either a single or double-hook trap setup on 100 to 200 pound test monofilament leader.

I might add that the size of the hooks and the diameter of the leaders may vary from model to model. This is because of the diverse swimming action that you can get from the different kinds of jigs. The object for the manufacturer is to create the best swimming jig possible, combined with the right configuration of hooks and leader material.

Marlin jigs are commonly sold by such regionally favorite names as Seven Strand, California Lures, Door Knobs, Pro Soft, and Zucker. These are expensive lures for an expensive dimension of the sport. Expect to pay anywhere from $15 to $60 for a winning marlin jig. Many models have a lot of handwork involved in their construction. Also, without fail, take a file to the stock hooks and hone them to perfection.

The time-proven color schemes for jigs used by the best marlin skippers are as follows: green and yellow mackerel, green and yellow, black and green ("Mean Joe Green"), black and purple, red and yellow ("bleeding mackerel"), and red and black ("goat fish").

As you would with trolling feathers for tuna, plan on making changes in color patterns throughout the day. Consider starting with darker colors in the early morning (e.g. black and purple) and switching to more brilliant tones by midday (e.g. red and yellow). Don't get locked into one favorite pattern trip after trip. Stripes here in the Southland are quite unpredictable. What works today may

be totally "dead" tomorrow as far as jig color and models are concerned.

Most trolling is done behind the boat through the third and fifth wake. As strange as this may sound, each vessel seems to troll differently. Sometimes the prop wash is significantly unique from one style of craft to another. Hence, the same model jig can actually "swim" differently behind each different boat. But, staying within the third to fifth wake will probably be a safe distance of line to let out in dragging the marlin jig. Some boats are said to get bit "short" while others are known for getting bit "long." Experiment to find out which style is best for you and your vessel.

Many boats are equipped with outriggers. These long extension poles allow the angler to clip his line to the outrigger tip and thus troll to the outside of the boat's wake. This is helpful in setting up a diverse trolling pattern with three or more rods. The fisherman can then spread his jigs across the wake more evenly to cover wider strike territory. A common ploy is to run three lines off the stern in rod holders each at different lengths behind the boat. Then have two additional outfits clipped to the outriggers. When a marlin strikes one of the outside lines, it will snap free from the outrigger pole, permitting the angler to set up on the fish.

Marlin trolling is usually done at 7 to 9 knots. The boat pilot has to "gun" the throttle for 4 to 5 seconds following the strike to help drive the hook home into the fish's hard mouth. It will also help at times to vary trolling directions

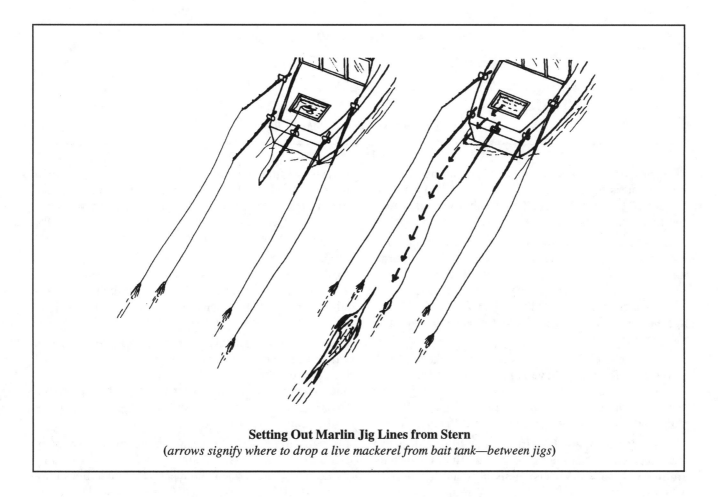

Setting Out Marlin Jig Lines from Stern
(*arrows signify where to drop a live mackerel from bait tank—between jigs*)

while keeping your speed relatively constant. As with any type of trolling program, it pays to be a little experimental. Also, don't be surprised if a good sized mako or thresher shark decides to beat a marlin to your jig!

Stripes on Bait

A more challenging approach to corralling one of these prized bill fish is to try to bait a marlin. The trick is to "make" mackerel. You have to have either a "diaper bag" style bait tank or a built-in one with proper water circulation. The mackerel—either Spanish or greenback—can be jigged from under floating kelp paddies, around oil platforms, or sometimes near the docks and bait receivers.

The typical live bait outfit consists of a conventional reel in the Penn GS 555, 10 KG, or larger class filled with 30 to 40 pound test mono. The rod is usually a thick-walled 6 to 7 foot live bait action with a special marlin tiptop. (This is basically a modified roller guide capable of handling the big diameter monofilament used with live bait leaders.)

You can purchase commercially tied marlin live bait leaders. These are comprised of about an 8 foot length of 80 to 150 pound test monofilament. Tie on a heavy-duty ball-bearing snap-swivel and clip the snap into the loop of the pre-tied leader. Or, tie your main line only to a strong ball-bearing swivel (without the snap) and hitch the entire 8 foot leader through the eyelet and the loop. (This is the same procedure I talked about in regard to hitching a simple snelled hook through a swivel eyelet without using any additional knots.)

Many experts such as big game fisherman, Ron De La Mare, recommend another alternative. De La Mare prefers 30 pound mono for his primary line. Then using a nail knot to join two strands of monofilament, he splices on a 10 to 12 foot section of 80 pound mono. Next, he ties the 80 pound test to a sturdy ball-bearing swivel (no snap). Then, to the other eye of the swivel he runs a 3 to 5 foot strand of 125 pound test monofilament.

The 80 pound test spliced to the 30 pound test main line serves as a shock leader. By using the nail knot, the

De La Mare's Live Bait Marlin Rig

80 pound test mono is easily reeled up through the rod guides and is equally easy to cast. The 125 pound test connected to the swivel handles the abrasion against the marlin and its bill.

It is practically impossible to actually cast the commercially tied live bait leaders because of the extraordinarily long 8 foot piece of monofilament. The angler will have to strip off line gently as he lowers these long leaders with a baited mackerel into the water. With De La Mare's specialized leader, you can actually make an overhand cast on feeding fish.

The mackerel themselves should be hooked through the nostrils. It is best to have a live bait outfit all set up and ready to go. Have a mackerel hooked and resting in the bait tank with the leader dangling over the side. You're now ready for action if you encounter a "feeder."

You can also slowly drift or slow-troll with a live mackerel with either the lighter bait outfit or the heavier trolling rod and reel. This is commonly done only in areas where the marlin are "showing." Throttle way down, dragging the mackerel at no more than 1 or 2 knots.

Use Your Eyeballs!

The most accomplished marlin fishermen in Southern California rely upon good binoculars more than their tackle. They are constantly on the lookout for any "signs of life." Working in 64+ degree, clear, deep blue water, they will continually scan for birds on a "pick," i.e. dipping and diving for bait fish. This is a good sign that marlin are nearby, pushing meatballs of bait to the surface.

Veteran bill fish skippers also use an interesting typology to identify the feeding mode of the striped marlin. Each classification requires a slightly different tactic.

(1) "Feeders": These are basically striped marlin thrashing through a school of bait. Birds will usually be in the vicinity picking at the bait fish. You can troll on the perimeter of the feeding activity or cast a live mackerel directly into the commotion. Some captains actually like to run over the top of the feeders and drop a live bait at the precise spot where the fish were last seen. Presumably the marlin have momentarily sounded but may still be directly under the bait.

(2) "Tailers": Skippers also call these "eyeball fish." They are usually seen down swell with their large tails sticking up. You must get down swell on a tailer and put the bait or trolled lure in front of the fish.

(3) "Sleepers": This is an interesting phenomena to witness firsthand. The marlin appear to be listless as if they are actually sleeping. You will typically spot the tail and sometimes the dorsal fin or the "hump" that the dorsal folds into. Cast live mackerel on the sleepers aiming close to the head of the fish.

(4) "Jumpers": Marlin seen putting on a display of freeform aerial fireworks are usually not in a feeding mode. These are termed "jumpers." Chasing after jumpers can often be a "sucker's bite," with the fish showing no interest in trolled lures or live bait.

Summary

You can experience big game fishing, California-style, at its finest when you start chasing striped marlin. The fish are big and tough. It requires excellent boat handling as well as angling skill to land a marlin in our Southland waters. Hooks must be perfectly honed. This is of paramount importance. The tackle and especially the reel drags must be in precise working order.

Marlin fishing is not for small boats. It is not uncommon to be out well over 50 miles from the beach for striped marlin. Full navigational and electronic equipment is strongly recommended. However, numerous charter boats run out of San Diego, Newport, Long Beach, and San Pedro for sportsmen who do not own boats, but who want to try their luck at local big game fishing.

BOOK II

California Saltwater:
A "Where-to"
and "How-to" Guide

California Saltwater:
A "Where-to" and "How-to" Guide*

The remainder of this book highlights the major saltwater fishing locales in California. It is organized in a south to north manner.

Information has been gleaned from a variety of sources in order to give the reader a thumbnail sketch of each particular area. Personal experience, field reports from local experts, interviews with skippers and landing operators, and published accounts in regional tabloids have been utilized to assemble this reference section.

It is important to note that even the strongest historical patterns that game fish demonstrate over a period of time can quickly change. The effects of angling pressure, boat traffic, water temperature fluctuations, and pollution can dramatically alter such otherwise long-standing assumptions of how, when, and where a particular species feeds. Hence, it is important to constantly monitor up-to-the-minute information wherever it is made available for a specific fishery. Also, as I mentioned in the rockfish section, there has been a landslide of both federal and state regulations put into effect in recent years, restricting when, where, and even how deep you

can fish. Be certain you review current rules and regulations—they often change from year to year.

A series of California saltwater fishing maps are included at the end of this section. They are organized from south to north. All of the areas described in this book are illustrated, in detail, on these maps. Note that these maps are not to be used for navigational purposes.

Coronado Islands

Technically speaking, the four rocky outcroppings that comprise the Islas Los Coronados are actually in Mexican waters. They are located about seven miles off of the Baja Peninsula and 10 to 12 miles south of San Diego Harbor. Sport fishing boats from Point Loma, H & M, Fisherman's, Seaforth, and Imperial Beach landings all make runs to these islands.

The Coronados are considered the yellowtail capital of the Southern California sport fishing fleet. Numerous other species abound off these desolate islands. The largest structure is South Island, with two smaller outcroppings to the north forming the Middle Ground Rocks. Above the Middle Ground and closest to San Diego is North Island.

*See the California Saltwater Information Directory on page 167.

There are no facilities at the Coronados. There are a few primitive dwellings for Mexican fishing families. Private boaters must be totally self-contained when venturing from San Diego into these waters. Adequate fuel, food, water, first aid supplies, and mechanical equipment must be carried on board. You will also need a Mexican fishing license to fish here. This can be obtained at tackle stores in the San Diego area for a modest fee. Party boat passengers are covered, as the Mexican license is incorporated into the all-day ticket. Don't be surprised to have a small Mexican gun boat actually come alongside your vessel to inspect your license documents.

Places to Fish: Four prime places to fish in the Coronado chain are: (1) the northeast portion of North Island known affectionately as "Pukey Point"; (2) the stretch around the Middle Ground Rocks; (3) the Ribbon Kelp on the eastern edge of South Island; and (4) an area roughly ten miles below South Island known as the Rock Pile.

"Pukey" is legendary for its yellowtail bite in rough water. Bonito, barracuda, and occasional bluefin tuna will also migrate off this rocky slope. The Middle Grounds can also be a hot bed of activity on breezing schools of yellows and scooters. White sea bass stage occasional flurries in the Ribbon Kelp, and yellowtail and numerous varieties of shallow water rockfish are found at the Rock Pile.

Best Times: The Coronados can be fished all year long. The yellowtail bite heats up in the spring through fall. However, in the winter large "home-guard" fish are sometimes caught working live squid or jigs deep. Bonito and barracuda are similarly a spring-to-fall proposition as far as sheer numbers are concerned. The whites can appear sporadically on the dock totals at any time, with the greatest numbers of this species are usually taken in the winter. Surprisingly, the Coronados are not recognized as a major calico bass fishery. This species can be caught intermittently around the kelp and reefs surrounding the rocky islands. Rockfish are an all year possibility here.

Tips and Tricks: If the yellows are on live 'chovies, then always try to find a frisky greenback in the bait tank. Both Spanish and Pacific mackerel will be the "hot ticket" at times at the Islands when the yellows are on big baits. Use treble hooks to maximize hooking. Live squid is perhaps the best all-around bait for both the yellowtail and whites. Fly-line this "candy" or work it off the bottom with a sliding-egg sinker.

As for artificials, the Tady 45 candy bar style jig in blue and white sardine has been a favorite of local skippers for a surface grind along with the Jerry Jig Surface Iron. A Salas Christy #2 in heavy, or a Tady AA also in heavy, in a blue/white/green pattern is a bona fide killer on the yo-yo grind, as well as the Ironman #3 and #5 in scrambled egg, blue/white or blue/chrome.

San Diego Coast and Offshore

There are numerous sandy beaches to the north and south of San Diego Harbor that offer some outstanding surf fishing. Torrey Pines, noted more for its famous golf course, is a local barred perch spot. The Silver Strand, Ocean Beach, and Imperial Beach are similarly good perch and corbina stretches with minimal angling pressure.

Sport fishing landings from San Diego, Islandia, and Seaforth in Mission Bay often sample the offshore bite along these coastal waters. The Point Loma and La Jolla kelp beds are important fisheries for pelagic species.

Places to Fish: In Ocean Beach, there is a little, short rocky groin near the O.B. Pier that can be a real secret hot spot. Few surf fishermen try it, but the perch bite there can be phenomenal at times. Most of the other stretches of beach in this southern portion are fairly nondescript sandy runs. Look for subtle pockets, reefs, and troughs to fish. However, there are occasionally some decent calico bass caught at the cliffs by Swamis and Cardiff.

The Point Loma kelp is a popular spot for the San Diego party boat fleet. Barracuda, bonito, as well as calico and sand bass are found here, sometimes all through the year. Yellowtail are another strong option in this kelp bed. Sheepshead, sculpin, shallow water rockfish, and a stray white sea bass round out the selection of game fish in the Point Loma kelp. Further to the north, the La Jolla kelp is similar to the Point Loma beds. Identical species abound in these kelp forests.

Best Times: Summer is probably the best overall time to fish these southern beaches. Corbina action is intensified along with catches of spotfin and yellowfin croaker. The barred perch spawn in the winter, so this will be the season to look for the larger specimens.

Imperial Beach also stages some incredible sand bass action when the spawning runs begin in late spring. Some flurries of spring and summer yellowtail also occur along the La Jolla kelp. Wintertime spells good shallow water rockfishing along the La Jolla trench.

As mentioned, the Pt. Loma kelp is fishable all year. Summertime action is intensified on yellowtail, the "three B's," and even some maverick bluefin tuna. The same holds true for the La Jolla kelp. The deep-water canyons formed by the La Jolla trench are a popular rock cod area during the wintertime.

Tips and Tricks: The surf perch along these stretches will eat artificial lures. Small freshwater trout spinners like the Rooster Tail, Shyster, and Mepps Lightning are worth trying on freshwater gear. The tiny Scrounger and similarly a small crappie jig can often produce limit catches of the barred perch in the shallows. Also try the Haddock curl-tail grub with a small lead head in motor oil color. On this note, fish the corbina typically in less than three feet of water. Split-shot a sandcrab, ghost shrimp, or fresh mussel on 6 pound test line.

San Diego Bay and Mission Bay

Both of these expansive waterways can provide yearlong angling opportunities. Most of the fishing done in these bays is either from the shore or from small private craft. There are, however, outboard skiffs for rent. You can call Seaforth Boat Rentals (619: 223-1681) for fishing Mission Bay or H & M Landing (619: 222-1144) for renting skiffs for San Diego Bay. Live bait is also available from bait receivers in the harbors.

Private launch facilities are accessible at Campland by the Bay in Mission Bay. Public launching is available at Shelter Island, San Diego Bay; Bayside Park, San Diego Bay, Chula Vista; 24th Street, San Diego Bay, National City; Glorietta Bay, Silver Strand Coronado; Dana Landing, Mission Bay; and Santa Clara Point, Mission Bay.

Places to Fish: Wherever the bait receivers are situated, fish are usually nearby. These include halibut, bonito, barracuda, sharks, rays, mackerel, croakers, perch, as well as sand and spotted bay bass.

The deep edges of the main ship channel in San Diego Bay are excellent places to drift both lures and live bait. Start from the bait barge below Ballast Point and work to the mouth of the harbor. The areas near Harbor Island and the Shelter Island Pier are also local hot spots in this bay. Fishing around the Coronado Bridge can be equally productive.

Inside Mission Bay head toward the Ventura Bridge for both bass and halibut action. Definitely fish the pilings slightly north of this bridge. There are seasonal weed beds which are also prime territory for sandies and spotted bay bass. Fiesta Island is without a doubt one of the premier spotfin croaker fisheries, when the run is on (usually a minus tide). The Quivara Basin has sporadic flurries of mackerel, bonito, or pencil-size 'cuda. For the secret bat ray spot, head to Mariners Point inside Mission Bay.

Best Times: This harbor complex has full twelve month fishing potential. Boat traffic, water skiing and other recreational usage is obviously impacted in the warmer months. The period of October through May is probably the best time frame to sample both San Diego and Mission Bays. The bass activity can be sensational in the winter months when most other forms of saltwater angling get tough.

Tips and Tricks: A smorgasbord of soft plastic lures will work for a variety of species in these harbors. The A.A. Worms Shad Tail (on a 1/8 ounce darter head), Salty Magics, and Scampis in both small and medium patterns are especially effective.

Use green and gold, root beer flake, hot pink, salt'n pepper, and motor oil shades in soft plastics. Also, some locals rave about using the Scrounger lure for catching bay bass inside the weed beds. They claim the oscillating lip in this bait helps to push it through the grass beds. Definitely toss the Berkley Power Grubs here in these two bays.

Bomber Gumpy Jigs in white, black, or orange/brown, tipped with a squid trailer are another possibility. Bass, halibut, and sometimes croaker will attack the jigs and plastics bounced along the channels.

Bonito, barracuda, mackerel, and even an occasional halibut or yellowfin croaker—along with spotted and sand bass—will eat a spoon jigged off the bottom. The 1 1/4 ounce Haddock Jig'n Spoons in blue, 'chovy' or mackerel finishes are dynamite. Be prepared for strikes on the flutter-fall. The bonies and scooters, plus the larger macks will jump on a chrome 5/8 ounce Krocadile retrieved below the surface.

Live 'chovies, smelt or brown bait are viable alternatives for halibut and big sand bass. Whole squid works super here for sharks, rays, and the "grumper" class sandies. Ghost shrimp and razor clams are good bets for croaker, corbina, perch, and halibut. Slider rigs are a favorite setup for bay bait dunkers.

San Clemente Island

San Clemente Island can be an incredible bonanza for the saltwater buff willing to make a good five hour run from the Southern California mainland. Both party boats and private charters make all-day excursions to this isolated island on an intermittent basis. Consult with landing operators from Redondo, Newport Beach, San Pedro, Long Beach, Dana Harbor, Oceanside, and San Diego for scheduled trips to 'Clemente.

Private boaters should proceed with the basic precepts of marine safety in mind. This island is considerable distance from shore and there are no facilities for fuel or provisions available here. A quality VHF radio is a must for this trip via private craft.

Places to Fish: Pyramid Head and China Point are favorite spots on the southeast end of the island to fish. The kelp beds here are thick, and provide sanctuary for big "bull" calicos. Bonito and barracuda also move along this kelp line. Yellowtail cruise this kelp recurrently, and it is a good place to make live squid in the winter. The White Rock sector on the mid-eastern side of the island is a potential yellowtail stretch.

At the far west end of 'Clemente known as the Isthmus similar opportunities exist for some serious bassin'. Bird Rock and Castle Rock to the outside are potential hot spots for calicos. The windward, southwest side of the Island is another area to work for bluefins. Shark hunters looking for blues, makos, and threshers can work the channel between 'Clemente and Catalina Islands. Striped marlin are also a possibility.

Best Times: With a tankful of live squid, the calico basser can find solid action on tap all year long. Brown baits and 'chovies, mackerel and smelt produce calicos in the warmer months. 'Clemente has a wealth of shallow and deep-water rockfish for the taking. Meter a likely-looking reef, pinnacle, or high spot and try for salmon grouper, whitefish, or sheepshead with squid. Again, these species are available all year long. The island is fairly unpressured, and home-guard yellows can be found at any time. The best seasons will be early spring through fall for the surface-feeding 'tails, bonito, and barries. White sea bass and halibut are occasionally caught and these too can end up in the daily fish counts any trip. The bluefin tuna are primarily a summer bite as they migrate towards San Clemente. Sporadic pockets of striped marlin appear in late summer through fall.

Tip and Tricks: Standard live bait, fly-lining tactics work for the yellowtail. If you can commandeer live squid, smelt, Spanish, or Pacific mackerel, then go for the big calicos and yellows along the kelp stringers. These fish are not as spooky as the coastal residents. Thus, 30 pound string may be quite appropriate for turning them away from 'Clemente's thick kelp.

The bluefin will require some finessin'. Start by fly-lining primo 'chovies with 10 to 12 pound test monofilament and Eagle Claw #181 #6 to #8 baitholder hooks. They will also sometimes strike a solid chrome jig, such as a Salas yo-yo #4, CP 105, Ironman #2 and #3 and Jerry Jig Heavy.

Soft plastics in all the patented colors will nail the calicos—root beer flake, chartreuse, silver flake, and mack-erel shades. The Bomber Gumpy Jig and squid combo is quite deadly here. The yellowtail will eat traditional "iron" both on a surface grind and yo-yo. Switch to 40 to 60 pound test line and bottom bounce for rockfish with heavy Salas, Tady, Jerry Jig, Ironman, and Diamond Jigs.

Oceanside Area

There are some interesting possibilities in this southern sector for a variety of saltwater angling. Helgren's Landing inside the Oceanside Harbor itself makes half-day and full-day excursions to the Barn Kelp and offshore islands as well as rockfish junkets in the winter. A cross section of pelagic species frequent this area. Yellowtail, calicos, sand bass, mackerel, occasional white sea bass, and halibut are staple fare along with lots of bonito and barracuda.

The Carlsbad Lagoon is a real "sleeper" frequented primarily by local area anglers. Spotfin croaker, big bat rays, halibut, and even a rogue white sea bass are potential catches in this waterway.

The Encino Lagoon and Oceanside Harbor are similarly worthwhile spots to try, both exhibiting comparatively limited fishing pressure.

Places to Fish: Give the locations outlined above some serious attention. The shallow water lagoons are perfect spots for the light line enthusiast to try his or her tricks. Here are some more areas to focus on.

The Barn Kelp is historically one of the most prolific kelp beds to find South Coast game fish on a year round basis. Further to the north, the waters off of the San Onofre nuclear power plant have been excellent sand bass territory when the spawning run is in full swing.

Best Times: Spring is exceptional along this southern sector. The sand bass gravitate towards the hard muddy bottoms in this area. From June through later summer, the sandy bite can be simply wide-open! The three B's along with yellowtail are similarly a summer proposition.

The lagoon fishing is also probably at its height in the warmer months, particularly for sand and spotted bay bass and spotfin croaker. But, because this shallow water remains warmer than ocean currents, the lagoons remain viable possibilities all season long. Also, take a shot at the south jetty in Oceanside Harbor for some potential bonito action.

Tips and Tricks: Spotfin and yellowfin croaker, sargo, and corbina will eat bloodworms, ghost shrimp, and bay mussels along the beaches and inside the lagoons. Barred perch will also attack Scroungers and colored spinners within the surfline.

Spotted bay bass in Carlsbad lagoon will jump on Scroungers and A.A. Worms Shad Tails fished on light string. Stay with silver or clear anchovy-like patterns. Grubs also produce in Carlsbad and Encino lagoons. A red lead head teamed with a smoke sparkle grub is a local favorite. Consider some nighttime "monster fishing" using squid for giant bat rays in these lagoons.

Dana Harbor Area

The Dana Harbor area, nestled between Long Beach to the north and San Diego to the south, is one of the most diverse angling havens of the Southland. Dana Harbor itself is a full facility complex. Rental skiffs and sailboats, party boats, bait and tackle shops, bait receiver, public launch ramps, boat hoist, and fuel dock are all available at Dana.

The harbor is also surrounded by a major jetty and a shorter finger wall of rocks bordering the inner boat basins. Numerous game fish abound in the harbor basin: halibut, sand and spotted bay bass, spotfin croaker, bonito, halibut, mackerel, and corbina. Along the outside rocks and jetties, sheepshead, opaleye, calicos, sculpin, and sharks and rays are all possibilities. To the north, the rocks and kelp of South Laguna are prime calico haunts. Some yellowtail and the seasonal flurry of bonito and barracuda are taken in the offshore kelp. The Aliso Pier in this north sector also kicks out modest catches of the three B's, sporadic halibut, and surf perch. Anglers working the sandy beach near South Laguna also nail corbina, barred perch, croaker, and sometimes, a halibut.

Motoring south of Dana, there is the San Clemente Pier which is on parity with Aliso with regard to angling opportunities. The offshore kelp similarly will play sanctuary for bass, bonito, scooters, 'tails, mackerel, and sometimes, white sea bass.

Places to Fish: Inside Dana Harbor, work around the dock pilings and under and between the boat moorings for spotted bay bass. The mouth into the West Basin is a good spot to try for spotfin croaker. The bait receiver can be sensational at times. Halibut, bonito, barracuda, sand bass, small white sea bass, and mackerel feed around the receiver.

Outside the harbor, the rock walls facing the ocean usually produce much better than the inside structure. Your best chances for bonito are on the ends of the rocks at the mouth of the harbor. Bass, sheepshead, opaleye, and sculpin are also caught in the midsection of the walls on the ocean side.

Don't overlook the whistler buoy as you venture north from Dana. Bonito, barracuda, calicos, and halibut are routinely nailed near this buoy. The ends of the Aliso and San Clemente Piers are worth trying with small craft.

The 14 Mile Bank off of Dana Harbor is a legendary rock cod alley. Marlin, tuna, and albacore are also taken in this deep offshore water.

Best Times: The dominant pelagic species, the three B's and yellowtail, are commonly caught in the greatest numbers from spring through fall along the kelp beds. The spotfin croaker, corbina, and spotted bay bass are similarly warm weather options. Halibut, mackerel, sculpin, sheepshead, sharks, rays, spotted and sand bass can be taken in the harbor itself all through the year.

Both piers—Aliso and San Clemente—demonstrate the best activity in the warmer months. Surf fishing equally excels in this period. Calicos taken from the rocky beaches in this area seem to be caught mostly in the pre-dawn period. Opaleye from the rocks offer some exceptional winter action. The 14 Mile Bank holds a full array of deep-water rockfish all through the year.

Tips and Tricks: Rock hoppers make their way down to the rocky outcroppings of South Laguna. Here they cast soft plastic lures directly into the waves and around the rocks and kelp. Scampis, Mojos, Power Pogeys and Power Minnows, Salty Magics, and Scroungers are regular favorites. Stay with root beer flake, silver flake, blue, chartreuse and gold, and black and purple patterns. Use the darker colors in the wee hours of the morning or at dusk. Most of the calico activity found off these rocks occurs in the early morning.

In the winter locate the commercial lobster traps and set up drift patterns with jig'n squid combos. Both sand bass and calicos will eat the drifted jigs.

Surface feeding fish will strike spoons—chrome Krocodiles, 'chovy-colored Haddock Jig'n Spoons, or larger Kastmasters casted or yo-yoed off the bottom. Try trolling Rebels and Rapalas barely outside the kelp line. Yellowtail, calicos, bonito, 'cuda, and even sand bass will attack these minnows on a medium-to-deep troll.

Fish the spotfin croaker on lighter 10 to 12 pound line and live ghost shrimp inside the harbor. Work the bait receiver area with live anchovies, split-shotted near the bottom.

The opaleye will eat frozen green peas fished below a float. Another trick is to try a small green feather or some green yarn glued to a baitholder hook. Moss gathered off the rocks is another opaleye favorite.

Newport Harbor

One of the most interesting "hot beds" of activity in the Southland is Newport Harbor. This shallow bay plays host to a prominent population of spotted bay bass, some sandies, halibut, croaker, corbina, mackerel, bonito, barracuda, sand sharks, rays, and a stray striper or two.

Rental skiffs are available at the Balboa Pavilion. Live anchovies are provided with the small outboard. The main launch ramp for private vessels is at Newport Dunes. There are ample fuel docks, mini-tackle marts, and places to purchase provisions along the waterway.

Places to Fish: Halibut can usually be found on the hard mud or sandy bottoms. Drift or troll the main channel for sandies and bay bass. The Coast Guard dock, the area around the Reuben E. Lee restaurant, and the front sector of the Balboa Pavilion have been historically good spots for bass, perch, croakers, and occasional halibut. Stripers, in limited numbers, usually stay in the back bay.

The spotted bay bass are highly prolific in Newport Bay. Key in on the dock pilings and under the moored boats. Look for signs of eel grass and places where currents converge. Spotties will gravitate to this type of water. Corbina are frequently taken in the surfline on razor clams and bay mussels along Balboa Pier. Newport and Balboa Piers also have occasional runs of halibut and bonito.

Best Times: Here again, this harbor is a viable proposition all season long. It gets pretty hectic in the summer though, with vacation crowds, tourists, and pleasure boaters cruising the bay. Newport Harbor can be a real windfall in the winter months when the water temperature on the outside ocean is considerably colder than that of the bay. The fall and spring are usually the best periods for a multi-species bite.

Tidal conditions play an integral role in this fishery. Plan on optimal action to occur 1 1/2 hours before low tide and one hour prior to a prominent high tide.

Shore fishing from the bank, rocks, jetties, piers, and docks, along with still fishing, drifting or trolling from small craft are typical ways to approach this bay.

Tips and Tricks: A multitude of natural baits will produce in Newport Harbor. Live anchovies are a good bet for bonito and barries. Halibut prefer a live offering, but they will also strike a fresh dead 'chovy. Frozen grunion, sardines, or smelt are also on the flatfish menu. The croaker, perch, and corbina will annihilate live ghost shrimp. Razor or pismo clams, rock or bay mussel, or bloodworms are next best choices. Shark and rays will jump on practically anything, but it's hard to beat whole squid. Big spotfin croaker will eat innkeeper worms.

Soft plastic lures are the name of the game in this harbor. Knob-tails like the A.A. Worms Shad, curl-tails such as the Salty Magic, Scampi, and Lunker Thumper are effective. Try to use the smaller versions of these baits for the spotted and sand bass.

Experiment with plastic worms and straight or sickletail grubs commonly used for freshwater bass. Popular colors for plastics used inside Newport Bay are pearl, orange, pink, motor oil, salt'n pepper, chartreuse and gold, lime, root beer flake, brown, and silver flake.

Tube lures like the Fatzee, Berkley Power Tube, or Fat Gitzit in freshwater bassin' sizes pitched gently along the pilings are another secret tactic. So is a Johnson Sprite, or Haddock Structure Spoon. The spotties will invariably hit the spoon as it glides down the pilings. You can also drift with both the soft plastic lures or jig the spoons along with the current. A recent innovation is to use a float tube inside this harbor. Fan-cast or drift with the lures outlined above.

Trollers will often have a field day on assorted game fish in Newport Harbor. Drag medium-sized Rebels, Rapalas, Bomber Long-A's, and conventional, solid chrome freshwater bassin' crankbaits. Bonito, barracuda, and the bass species will attack these lures trolled through the bay. Basic anchovy or mackerel colorations are best: silver, black/white, blue/black, green/yellow, or solid chrome.

Outside the harbor look for isolated rocky groins to host barred surf perch. A regional favorite is to cast a lime green mini Scrounger on ultralight tackle to nail the perch from these rocky outcroppings.

Santa Catalina Island

This is the most popular of the offshore islands along the California Coast. Located roughly 25 miles from the mainland, Catalina is 22 miles long and 7 miles wide. An abundance of saltwater game fish can be caught around the island all through the seasons.

Avalon is the tourist hamlet and major outpost on the island. Full facilities ranging from groceries and fuel to overnight lodging and boat moorings are available at Avalon. Sport fishing boats from San Pedro, Long Beach, Redondo Beach, Newport Beach, Seal Beach, and Dana Harbor make full-day runs to Catalina. These boats, however, do not stop over in Avalon.

Places to Fish: An overwhelming number of both private and party boat captains prefer to fish the lee side of the island facing the mainland. The windward side can somtimes become rough with high gales and swells crashing into the rocky shoreline.

The tip of the West End is a favorite hot spot for big bull calico fishing inside the floating kelp stringers. Yellowtail and bluefin tuna, along with bonito and barracuda will breeze through this outer point of Catalina.

Emerald and Cherry Coves, and the Isthmus near the center of the Island are good areas for yellowtail. Halibut drifting occurs from Goat Harbor to the beaches north of Avalon. Bonito and barracuda and some small shallow water rockfish are also possiblities along this stretch.

At the East End near The Slide, yellowtail, bonies, and scooters can be found cruising within a mile from the bank.

Rock codding for deep-water species is best at both ends of Catalina. Similarly, the marlin bite usually materializes at the outer fringes of the island.

The West End and The Slide are long-time hot spots for the marlin fraternity.

Best Times: The major pelagic species—bonito, barracuda, and yellowtail—are typically a spring-to-fall proposition. Yellows, as well as calico bass, can be taken all year long, and especially in winter if live squid is available. Halibut drifting is best in the spring.

Tips and Tricks: The big bull bass and yellowtail fisheries are the major attractions of the Catalina fishery. The calicos have a penchant for whole squid (live or frozen) pinned behind a 1 to 2 ounce lead head. The Bomber Gumpy Jig has become legendary as a Catalina calico killer. Next, gear up with numerous soft plastic swimming baits. Both double and curl-tail models are effective. Salty Magics, A.A. Worms swimbaits, Power Pogeys, Haddock Lunker Thumpers and Mojos are best. The very popular root beer flake pattern is the standard color. As an added tip, fish dark-colored plastics like purple or black at night or before dawn for the calicos. And don't forget the Tora Tubes, especially in winter when live squid are in.

The bull bass will devour a whole Spanish or greenback mackerel fly-lined in the kelp. Brown baits should equally be tossed on heavier line for kelp-grown bull bass. Big, home-guard yellows will similarly stage a "mack attack" here.

Fly-lined 'chovies will take the barries and boneheads as well as smaller calicos. When available, live squid fly-lined or split-shotted will also hammer yellowtail, halibut,

or a stray white sea bass. Most halibut are taken here, however, drifting live or frozen 'chovies along the sandy beaches. White sea bass at Catalina will also attack solid white jigs like the Ironman #5, Tady A1 and Salas 6X JR, laced with a whole squid.

Huntington Beach to Seal Beach

The Huntington Beach Pier has been a landmark for California's surfing community for many years. Unfortunately, this structure has not generated that much fishing success in past seasons. Occasionally, the H.B. Pier will be invaded by schools of mackerel or small bonito. Most of the action, however, is on small perch, a few halibut, and tomcod, herring, and queen fish.

On the other hand, the Seal Beach Pier seems to attract a more thriving population of surface feeders. At times, there can be outstanding bonito action off this pier along with keeper-sized halibut, yellowfin, croaker, and sargo.

There are plenty of restaurants and hotels that lie between these two piers. Seal Beach operates a sport fishing landing and private craft can be launched from Huntington Harbor.

Places to Fish: Apart from the piers, consider surf casting from the beach. The bluffs north of Huntington are good for barred perch. Windy Bolsa Chica State Beach between Huntington and Sunset Beaches is another barred perch stretch. The beach around Surfside can kick out a smorgasbord of surf fish ranging from sharks and halibut to corbina and yellowfin croaker.

Small flounder, halibut, and turbot can be found in Huntington Harbor. The spotted bay bass for some reason are not as prolific in this basin as in Newport Bay. But, there are some keepers for the taking. Also check out the area under and around the Pacific Coast Highway bridge connecting Surfside and Seal Beach for shallow lagoon species. The San Gabriel River Channel is another "sleeper" spot for small bonito.

The Huntington Flats and the offshore oil platforms have been a favorite run for sport fishing and private boats. Halibut, bonito, and barracuda frequent the flats. But the big news occurs when the sand bass move in to spawn. The offshore oil rigs provide sanctuary for some large, home-guard yellowtail, along with calico bass, bonito, and mackerel.

Best Times: Spring through fall seems to be the best period for this area. Surface action for bonito declines off these piers in the winter. Larger barred perch will move off Huntington and Bolsa Chica beaches during the colder months, but the corbina and yellowfin bite is best in summer.

The sand bass bite heats up in late spring and early summer in the flats. Similarly, look for the yellows on the oil rigs during this time of year.

Tips and Tricks: Trolley rigs with live bait—when available—are best for bonito off the Seal Beach Pier. Lucky Joes, bonito splashers, and Krocadile spoons are also effective. Spoons and freshwater spinners in bright colors will get bit by the bonito in the San Gabriel River Channel.

Think about pumping your own live ghost shrimp in the tidal flats around Huntington Harbor. These are sensational bait for flounder, turbot, and small halibut in the Harbor or the lagoon. Soft-shell sandcrabs, bloodworms, and bay mussels will intermittently seduce the barred perch, corbina, and yellowfin croaker.

Sand bass are absolute suckers for soft plastic lures tipped with squid once the spawning run is in full swing. The bruiser yellowtail that live among the oil rigs prefer live mackerel, squid, or anchovies. Fish the "macks" on 30 pound string and a treble hook. Hold on! These homeguard 'tails know just where to run in an attempt to break you off on the rigs.

Long Beach Harbor Area

This is one of the most underrated saltwater hot beds in Southern California. Within this harbor complex there are jetties, piers, breakwalls, and even offshore oil islands to fish.

Small boat owners can launch their craft from Cabrillo Beach in the San Pedro area, Golden Shores off Ocean Blvd. in Long Beach, or the Second Street ramp in Alamitos Bay.

A potpourri of inshore game fish are accessible within the harbor. Bonito and mackerel are frequently caught off the Belmont Pier, around the famous Queen Mary cruise ship, and on the outside of the jetty and breakwalls. Spotted bay bass, sandies, and calicos are highly sought after species in this harbor area. Halibut, croakers, perch, sharks, and rays are also possible alternatives here.

Places to Fish: The breakwalls themselves can be phenomenal spots for nighttime calico and sand bass activity. Calicos seem to prefer the water on the outside of the walls whereas sand bass gravitate to the calm inside waters. The water around the Queen Mary is deep and provides an excellent haunt for bass and halibut. The oil islands are definitely worth trying, particularly Island Chaffee to the far south.

Sporadic catches of bonito, mackerel, bass, halibut, sharks, and rays are made off the public jetty and Belmont Pier. The Pier "J" area is especially good for runs of bonito.

To the north, the adventuresome can experience some fantastic surf casting for big calicos off the rocks on the Palos Verdes peninsula. Sheepshead, surf perch, and opaleye are also found off these jagged bluffs.

Best Times: There can be a lot of activity in the spring when the bass and halibut spawn. But, the harbor can provide steady action all year long. It is not uncommon to have some banner evenings working the Federal Breakwall in the middle of winter.

Tips and Tricks: Soft plastics and light lines are the name of the game in Long Beach Harbor. Local experts fish with freshwater bassin' outfits spooled with 6 to 12 pound test mono. A variety of swimming baits are perfect when matched with the freshwater combos. Use 1/4 to 1 ounce lead heads. Spice the jigs with a squid trailer for extra attraction.

Haddock Kreepy Krawlers, Haddock Split-Tail Grubs, A.A. Worms Shad Tail, Salty Magics, Scampis, Mojos, Kalin Salty Lunker Grubs, Berkley Power Grub and Power Pogey, as well as Fatzee and Fat Gitzit tube baits will produce. Popular colors include: root beer flake, chartreuse flake, hot pink flake, hot orange, chartreuse and gold, black, red, silver, white, champagne, and smoke sparkle, and of course, tomato/pepper.

Larger 6 to 8 inch plastic worms, sinking Rapalas, and Rebels, in addition to deep-diving crankplugs will also catch bass and halibut.

Bonito and mackerel will jump on the Rebels and Rapalas trolled around the Queen Mary. Bonito splasher rigs can be effectively used off the jetties and the Belmont Pier. A longer 8 to 11 foot rod is needed.

Spoonin' with Haddock Jig'n Spoons, the Hopkins #075 and No-Equal, and the Johnson Sprite will also work for bonito, occasional flurries of pencil barracuda, and of course, the ever present mackerel. Another tip is to drop these spoons alongside the deep pier and dock pilings found within this harbor.

Natural baits such as live 'chovies, smelt, or tomcod will take fish—especially larger halibut. The perch inside the pilings favor ghost shrimp, clams, bloodworms, and cut anchovies split-shotted off the bottom on light line.

Halibut can also be taken drifting a frozen anchovy behind a three-way swivel. Onto the other end of the second swivel eye attach a leader with a chrome sinker for an attractor to be bounced along the sand. Work this combo near the oil islands.

Expert calico fishermen will take their share of big bull bass tossing soft plastic lures from the rocks and coves off Palos Verdes.

Finally, consider sampling some of the action or flat-fish species such as sanddabs, halibut, and turbot in the shallow harbors in the Long Beach area. Bahia Marina, Anaheim Bay, and Colorado Lagoon are good local "in-spots" along with the channel running into Marine stadium. Corbina and spotfin croaker are also stalked in this area by local anglers. Use Hopkins and Kastmaster spoons for the smaller halibut and innkeeper and bloodworms for the croaker and corbina.

Kings Harbor and Redondo Beach Pier

Located in Redondo Beach, this small harbor has declined somewhat in recent years in fishing popularity. There are no longer outboard skiffs for rent, which once made this a haven for light tackle enthusiasts. Still, private boats can be launched from a sling operation for a modest fee. Redondo Sportfishing is located here, with a fleet of half, three-quarter, and full-day party boats.

Places to Fish: The rock walls and jetties that enclose Kings Harbor are accessible by foot. Jetty jockeys can cast for bonito and mackerel, particularly at the ends of the breakwalls. Perch, opaleye, halibut, tomcod, smelt, and an occasional sand bass can be caught all along the length of these rocks.

The water inside the harbor itself attracts schools of bonito, barracuda, mackerel, and sometimes even yellowtail. Kings has a thermal "blow hole" resulting from a warm water outlet of the Edison Power Company. This often acts as a magnet for firecracker-sized yellows and bonito. The water is warm and oxygenated.

The Redondo Pier is minuscule, but fishing for bonito can be outstanding if you like to fish shoulder to shoulder. To the north, the Hermosa Pier sometimes can be excellent for a winter run of barred surfperch. The Manhattan Pier, similarly, has some good perch fishing. While in the area, also try 18th, 19th, and 26th Street for shallow water surf fishes.

Best Times: Like most Southern California harbors, Kings suffers from extensive recreational boat traffic in the summer. Almost any time of the year can be produc-tive inside the harbor. Early spring is prime time for bonito, still winter is also favored by many locals. The water inside Kings Harbor can be significantly warmer than outside currents in the Palos Verdes area. Pelagic game fish will migrate into Kings following schools of anchovies with the onset of cold weather.

Tips and Tricks: The standard fare of rockfishing baits catch fish off the jetties. Ghost shrimp, clams, mussels, sand crabs, frozen anchovies, and squid are staple offer-ings.

Perhaps the most intriguing prospect in Kings Harbor is to cast splasher rigs for bonito from the rocks. These small tuna can be terrors on light tackle. Use a bonito fly behind either a Casta-Bubble or wood splasher.

The bonito will also strike trolled or casted CD-9 and CD-11 Magnum Rapalas and Rebels (silver/blue back, blue/black back), Krocadile spoons and scaled down "iron" like the Salas Christy 1 or Pee Wee jigs. Old standby bonito feathers will also produce (blue/white, red/white, green/yellow, solid white).

Stray yellows usually hit fly-lined 'chovies or a live mackerel. Or, "walk" a whole frozen squid barely under the surface. It is also possible on rare occasions to nail a yellow while casting lures from the rocks with surf casting gear. Stay with smaller candy bar jigs in scrambled egg, blue and white, solid chrome, or sardine patterns. I recom-mend Ironman #2, Tady AA, Salas Christy 1, and light Jerry Jigs.

A rare bonus occurs when the bait receiver situated in the harbor has live squid for sale. Small boaters can take advantage of this and fly-line the "candy" in the inner harbor for a possible big, home-guard yellowtail!

Marina Del Rey

This is one of the largest small boat harbors in the world. Full facilities, including a private launch area, a sport fishing operation and harbor cruises are available at Marina del Rey. Restaurants and hotels abound in this water wonderland.

Places to Fish: There are actually some fish to be caught inside the harbor. Spotted bay bass, sandies, and halibut are possibilities. The other areas to fish are along the short breakwall or the long jetty leading out to the ocean.

Big calicos and sand bass are nocturnal targets for the small group of wallbangers who have discovered Marina del Rey. Jetty jockeys take mixed catches of tomcod, queenfish, small calicos and sand bass, halibut, bonito, and barracuda.

Fish the bonies and scooters on the ocean side of the jetty and towards the end. The sandy beach adjacent to the north side of the jetty occasionally has some nice corbina lurking in the sloping pockets.

Best Times: Marina del Rey can afford decent fishing all through the seasons. The resident bass and halibut population will eat especially well from spring through fall.

Breakwall fishermen can key in on the warmer months; but, don't be surprised to find a reasonably good bite in the dead of winter. Time your "moonlight madness" trips to this short rock structure during a full moon phase.

Sport fishers gear up for the standard surface bite in the spring through fall and then switch to rock cod in the winter. The party boats operating from this landing routinely rack up numbers of rockfish.

Tips and Tricks: Take out some freshwater spinning tackle and cast #CD-11 Magnum Rapalas in blue or silver, along with floating Rebels, off the jetty in the early morning. Bonito and pencil barries are potential biters.

Stay with soft plastics tipped with squid when pounding the Marina del Rey breakwall. The same plastics popular on the Long Beach Federal breakwall will produce on the Marina Del Rey structure. Live crawdads or mudsuckers will also work, but expect to get a share of "short" bass. Fish the outside of the wall primarily for calicos. Move to calm inside waters for sand bass.

Santa Monica Bay and Malibu

This scenic stretch of coastline runs from the Santa Monica Pier up to Bass Rock below Oxnard. The Santa Monica Pier itself intermittently kicks out bonito, halibut, a stray calico or sand bass, the prolific mackerel species, sharks, and rays. Interestingly, this public pier actually has rod racks built into the railing for the fisherman's convenience. Parking is limited and the pier is popular so get there early on the weekends. There is also a bait and snack shop on this pier.

The Malibu Pier is about on parity with Santa Monica for species variation and overall fishing. The beaches that are accessible from this point northward offer some other intriguing possibilities. Calico bass—and big bulls at that —halibut, cabezon, leopard sharks, barred perch, sargo, yellowfin croaker, and shallow rockfish are within a cast from the beach. Kelp beds and submerged reefs dot the public access beaches from Malibu to Oxnard.

Places to Fish: There is good surf fishing up to the Malibu Curve from the north of Santa Monica Pier. Look for barred perch action at small rocky outcroppings.

The larger rocks inside the bay near the Santa Monica Pier can be outstanding for nighttime bassin'. These must be reached by carefully maneuvering a small boat near these rocks. Be careful here! These rocks are not as prominently visible in the dark as they are in daylight.

Private boats and sport fishers explore the Bay for all kinds of surface-feeding game fish. Anglers in small skiffs along with party boaters sometimes get into hot bluefin tuna action in Santa Monica Bay. This Bay, and the nearby offshore waters offer some of the best halibut fishing in the Southland. Look for predominantly sandy bottoms and set up drift patterns.

Coral Beach, north of Malibu is an excellent spot for surf casting offshore kelp beds. The surfer's reef to the right of the Malibu Pier has also been a legendary haunt for big calicos. Anglers must work this reef with heavy-duty tackle and at night.

Continuing north along the Coast Highway, the next area to try is Latigo Canyon. Shoreline access is limited. Local experts prefer to launch small inflatables through the surf to work calicos in the deep potholes off the beach. Paradise Cove lies further north. This is a private facility with fees for parking and pier fishing. No surf fishing is permitted at Paradise. But you can still reach the kelp beds with a long cast from the pier.

Zuma Beach is the most desolate and windy strand along this stretch. There is a lot of "sameness" to the sandy beach. Surf casters with a keen ability to read the water can tie into some good barred perch and corbina action.

Above Zuma, the small isolated beaches, El Pescador, El Matador, and La Piedra, were previously private access but are now publicly operated by the state. You can walk down the bluffs from small parking areas to surfcast into the nearby kelp.

Pushing further north, Leo Carillo Beach offers camping nearby across the Coast Highway. Barred perch, halibut, kelp fish, cabezon, and both sand and calico bass are routinely caught by Carillo's surf busters.

Bass Rock is actually a series of rough rocky outcroppings. There are no jetties here, but the kelp is thick and often loaded with fish. Bring lots of hooks and sinkers, as much terminal gear can be lost in the sharp rocks.

North of Bass Rock heading into Point Magu, try La Jolla Beach—a flat windy stretch—for barred perch and corbina or the small breakwall at Hollywood Beach.

Best Times: As with most Southland surf fishing, there are distinct winter and summer seasons. The cabezon, shallow rockfish, and larger spawning barred perch are primarily a winter bite. Barred perch, halibut, corbina, and croakers became more active in the summer. Fish the big bull calicos in the evening. The pier and party boat activity likewise intensifies in the warmer months for the three B's, occasional yellowtail, or bluefin tuna. The halibut flurries in Santa Monica Bay are intensified in late spring with the spawning runs.

Tips and Tricks: The calico bass is the prime game fish along this span of coastline. As noted, the bull bass feed at night. Toss whole frozen squid, grunion, smelt, or anchovies on an Eagle Claw #181 #2/0 to #4/0 long-shank baitholder. You will need long rods, 11 to 14 footers, baitcasting reels with 25 to 30 pound string, and 4 to 6 ounce torpedo sinkers to drag these calicos out of the shallow reefs. Cabezon and other rockfish especially will nail the squid.

In a few areas where the kelp is much closer to the bank, try soft plastic lures on the calicos. Darker patterns such as root beer flake, purple, green, mackerel, and smoke/flake are good choices. The Salty Magic, Mojo, Power Scamper, and Lunker Thumper are perfect for this kind of calico action. If you "pothole" fish with either a small boat, inflatable, or float tube, stay with the soft plastics, or a Bomber Gumpy Jig and whole squid trailer.

The usual fare of live 'chovies or trolled plugs and spoons will take surface-feeding species along the kelp beds from Santa Monica to Point Magu.

Combination colored feathers (i.e. green/white and red/white) have traditionally produced off the Malibu Pier with Casta-Bubble bonito splashers. This tactic can even catch barries off this pier in the winter during a warm water year. Also, snag live smelt and use these for bait on trolley or sliding rigs on the Malibu Pier. Lunker halibut have been known to inhale the live smelt off this quiet wooden structure.

Ventura and Oxnard

These two cities are the gateway to the Channel Islands. Party boats operate out of Cisco's Sportfishing in Oxnard and Port Hueneme. Both 3/4 and full-day trips are available. Cisco's fleet can have you fishing Anacapa Island within an hour and a half after leaving the dock.

Ventura Sportfishing similarly offers 3/4 and full-day outings and also features specialized private charters. The party boats from this landing can also sample Anacapa, Santa Cruz, and Santa Rosa Islands. Ventura Sportfishing has a special fishing dock. Anglers can pay a nominal fee to fish the dock all day with unlimited live bait provided.

Channel Islands Harbor has complete marina facilities, including launch ramps and guest slips for private craft.

Places to Fish: Besides the Channel Islands, (which will be discussed separately) there is a wealth of kelp beds lining this portion of the coast. Ventura Harbor has decent numbers of smelt, perch, and tomcod, with a smattering of halibut and sand bass. Channel Islands Harbor is somewhat more abundant with warm water species including sandies, some spotted bay bass, and a few calicos on the outside rock walls. Halibut are fished extensively inside this harbor. Not too many boats fish the inner waters of Channel Islands Harbor. Most angling occurs from the bank.

The public fishing pier in the Oxnard-Port Hueneme area has jacksmelt, perch, halibut, tomcod, and yellowfin croaker on the menu. If we have a particularly warm water year, bonito and barracuda are a remote possibility. There are no facilities at this pier.

Halibut and barred perch are frequently caught along the beach here. This terrain is stark and very windy. Work below the naval base south of the pier at the end of Arnold Street and to the north of 5th Street. Both are barred perch and sometimes corbina hot spots. You may have to use 3 to 5 ounce pyramid sinkers to reach the perch in rough swells.

South of Oxnard in the Sycamore and Solromar region, the offshore kelp beds are loaded with grass, kelp, and olive rockfish. Calicos, sand bass, barries, halibut, and even white sea bass are found in this kelp.

Southeast of Point Mugu and west of Ventura, boaters may also encounter some hit or miss salmon activity in late winter or early spring.

Best Times: The summer period is best as warmer currents push northward. The increase in air temperature also makes fishing more tolerable along this portion of the coast.

Tips and Tricks: Use freshwater gear and fish the smelt, perch, and small sand bass in Channel Islands Harbor. The Blakemore Roadrunner, a freshwater crappie jig, is often used to fool sandies. Similarly, tiny tubular Mini Jigs fished below a bobber nail small perch and jack smelt. A Lucky Joe snag rig tipped with squid is yet another trick for the small harbor residents.

Live bait is at a premium the further north you go. As an alternative, anglers in this region will drift a frozen anchovy underneath a float while fishing for bonito off the piers. Frozen 'chovies, diced in small squares, also are highly effective on barred perch in the Oxnard-Ventura area.

Channel Islands

The remote islands that lie in the Santa Barbara Channel offer tremendous variety for sportsmen venturing out of Oxnard, Ventura, or Santa Barbara ports. Sea Landing in Santa Barbara, Cisco's in Oxnard, and Ventura Sportfishing make full-day runs to these islands. Private boats can launch from Santa Barbara and hit Santa Cruz Island 22 miles away, or from Channel Islands Harbor to the south and travel only 11 miles to Anacapa.

Santa Cruz is the big island, measuring about 20 miles in length and 5 miles in width. Surface fishing in the warmer months can be sensational here on calico bass, bonito, barracuda, yellowtail, white sea bass, and sometimes a migrating school of albacore. When the fish don't bite on top, then drop gangions to the bottom. Santa Cruz and its smaller companions, Anacapa, Santa Rosa, and San Miguel offer excellent rock codding. San Nicholas is known for its yellowtail, barracuda, and rockfish tallies. Tiny Santa Barbara Island can be a real sleeper for calicos.

Places to Fish: Work the far eastern and windward sector of Santa Cruz for surface action. San Pedro Point and Smugglers Cove are prime barracuda and bonito haunts. The western bank facing the wind along with the eastern lee side are other potential stretches for hot calico action. Barries also move into the Chinese Harbor section of the lee side of Santa Cruz. Rockfish are harvested off both the lee and windward sides of the west end. Deep-water specialists probe the east end of Anacapa, while fly-liners look for surface fish on the western tip. Rockfish and lingcod are predominantly sought on the southwest and northwest side of Santa Rosa. Slow-troll or drift the sandy bottom at Beechers Bay and around Skunk Point on Santa Rosa. The western windward lip of San Miguel Island is best for deep-water species, especially lingcod. Cuyler Harbor is another prime spot for halibut and surface feeders at San Miguel. Work the northwest and southeast kelp at San Nicholas for yellows and scooters. You can practically fish around all of Santa Barbara Island for calicos and rockfish.

Best Times: Fish Anacapa in the warmer months for some surprisingly hot yellowtail action. Bonies and scooters will also be in the area from spring through late summer. Santa Cruz has year 'round sport on calico bass and rockfish varieties. Santa Rosa sustains the rock cod bite twelve months a year. The halibut will respond best in late spring and summer. Proceed with caution fishing the waters around San Miguel. The winds and currents can be treacherous. Consult your charts for the Osborne Bank below Santa Barbara Island. This underwater pinnacle is "hot" for winter rock codding. But bluefin tuna and albacore also visit this high spot in late summer and fall.

Tips and Tricks: You can't go wrong with soft plastic lures for the calicos in the Channel Islands. Keep it simple: root beer flake, smoke flake, chartreuse flake and 'chovy colors in the Salty Magic, Pacific Eel, Mojo, Power Scampers and Caba Caba Tubes. Bottom bounce with heavier Salas, Tady, or Ironman or Jerry Jigs. Orange-red-yellow scrambled egg "rock cod" colors, solid white, and chrome work. A basic Diamond Jig is also hard to beat.

Pelagic species will strike trolled Rebels and CD-11, CD-14 and CD-18 Magnum Rapalas along the outside kelp lines. Bonito feathers will also be effective at times.

Santa Barbara Area

This quiet coastal city has a lot to offer the saltwater enthusiast. Sport fishers and party boats can fish the Channel Islands or the key One Mile and Naples Reefs to the north. Surf casters can sample some fairly decent perch and corbina action along the sandy stretches from Santa Barbara to Point Conception. Stearn's Wharf and the breakwater rocks should also be tested by pier anglers and jetty jockeys.

Boats can be launched at Gaviota, Goleta, Santa Barbara, Ventura, and Channel Islands Harbor. Party boats fish the area from Cisco's and Sea Landings. There are full bait, tackle, and marine facilities, restaurants, and hotels in the area.

Places to Fish: Apart from the Channel Islands, there are still a wealth of other locations to explore in the Santa Barbara region. The two major reefs, Naples and One Mile, are prime calico havens, but don't overlook Cambie's Reef outside the harbor. Stearn's Wharf is a local favorite for halibut. Bass, smelt, cabezon, sharks, bonito, perch, and a wayward steelhead are frequently tallied off this wharf.

The kelp south of Santa Barbara to Carpinteria is a regional hot bed for pelagic species. Bass, 'cuda, white sea bass, and assorted rockfish are local residents. Both private boats and sport fishers can sample these kelp beds.

Ledbetter Beach, Thousand Steps, Goleta, Shoreline Park, Refugio, El Capitan, and the Rincon Stretch are strong candidates for steady surf casting. Perch, halibut, corbina, sharks, bass, and cabezon can be caught from the beach. The harbor itself and the breakwater are good places to look for perch, sand bass, and halibut. The water off the Goleta pier is a primary area to try for both calicos and halibut on the drift.

Best Times: Because of this northward location, expect to experience some of the better fishing in the warmer summer months. From late spring through summer, the Santa Barbara area "blooms" with assorted angling options. Bottom fishing is the staple for the cold water period.

Tips and Tricks: Barred perch jump on miniature Scrounger lures. Frozen anchovies are the best all-around natural bait for the surf perch. Cabezon prefer frozen squid. Use this same bait for calicos and sand bass around Thousand Steps. Whole squid is also at the top of the list for serious leopard sharkin'.

Continue to probe the kelp beds off the Goleta Pier, potholing and casting with soft plastics. Salty Magics, Mojos, Lunker Thumpers, and Scampis fished on a 3/4 to 1 1/2 ounce lead head are the ticket.

I should also add that big "bull" calicos in this northern most range will strike fairly large surface jigs. Some of the best "iron" to use in the kelp beds is the Salas 6X and 7X light Tady 45 and light Jerry Jigs. Solid white, green/yellow, scrambled egg, blue/white and sardine are excellent calico killer colors.

San Luis Obispo and Morro Bay Northward

It is estimated that only about ten percent of the beach front areas above Santa Barbara ever get fished. Beach access is diminished above Point Conception due to the military installation at Vandenburg Air Force Base. Still consider fishing rock cod or a late season run of hawg-sized albacore out of Avila Bay.

Similarly, Morro Bay is a major rockfish port, along with lingcod, salmon, and albacore flurries. Further up the coastline, small relatively isolated beaches provide the surfcaster with some pretty steady perch action. The rocky outcroppings are prime poke-poling territory.

San Simeon has a state campground. Motels and excellent seafood restaurants are found in greatest numbers in the Morro Bay and Pismo Beach regions.

Places to Fish: Contact Avila Sportfishing for information on full-day rock cod trips or seasonal jaunts for salmon or albies. Virg's Landing operates sportfishers out of Morro Bay.

You can fish inside Morro Bay primarily for smelt, halibut, mackerel, and a wayward sand bass. The waters outside Morro team with blue, gopher, and copper rockfish, lingcod, and cabezon. Adjacent north to Morro Rock is a beach with excellent barred perch potential. There is also a natural "blow hole" effect that shoots water through a crevice next to Morro Rock. Fork-tail and barred perch often become trapped on this narrow passage, along with monkeyface eels, cabezon, and starry flounder.

Cayucos Beach can exhibit "hot" perch bites at times on shiners and barred varieties. Moonstone, Sandstone, and San Simeon Beach are sandy and rocky stretches with frequently great perch action. The San Simeon Pier has opportunities for barred, walleye, rubberlip and piling perch, halibut and jack smelt. There can be outstanding perch fishing 100 yards north of this pier.

From Cayucos to Point Piedras Blancas, shallow water rockfishing can be sensational for small boaters. Lings, cabezon, halibut, flounder, and petrale sole are also routinely caught here. Salmon are another possibility.

To the south, Pismo Pier is a long shot for pelagic species. In warm water periods, barracuda, halibut, corbina, and mackerel often find their way up here. Barred, fork-tail, and walleye perch are local residents of this pier. The Avila Pier and the San Luis Pier are basically tomcod, shiner perch, and magnum-sized jack smelt fisheries. The offshore waters can sustain a good run on both king and silver salmon during the prime season.

Best Times: Due to the inclement weather that plagues this shoreline, summer is the recommended time to fish it. Rock codding for the hardy is there for the taking twelve months a year. Albacore are hit and miss, usually starting in late summer.

Tip and Tricks: Fish basic five-hook gangions on the rock cod. Solid chrome, or copper-colored heavy jigs are also used on lings, cowcod and salmon grouper. Jack's Jigs, Jackpot Jigs, heavy Jerry Jigs, and the Salas PL68 are perfect models for the deep-water bite.

Sugar-cured mackerel, ghost shrimp, and sandcrabs are favored baits of the long polers tossing into the windy surf. Ghost shrimp can be pumped at Morro State Park. Pier anglers can't miss with tiny Lucky Joe or Izorline Lucky Lura mini shrimp flies for smelt and small perch. Both rock and bay mussels and frozen 'chovies are other regional offerings. You will need to cast at least two ounces of lead to hold on the surf up here.

The standard menu of squid, octopus, 'chovies, clams, and abalone trimmings are poke poler favorites. Also try soft plastics with this method.

Monterey and Carmel Bays

Party boats and smaller skiffs launching out of Monterey Bay can encounter some of the most stellar bottom fishing to be found in Northern California. Surfperch, cabezon, greenling, halibut, lings, and sanddabs are caught in the nearby waters. Seasonal runs of albacore and salmon are also typical for this famous cannery town.

There are numerous motels, seafood restaurants, and full marine facilities in Monterey proper. There are also public piers and shoreline access for non-boaters.

Places to Fish: Starting just south of Carmel heading into Monterey, the rocky shore is difficult to reach in places, but it is abundant with inshore rockfish. Greenling, olive, grass and blue rockfish, cabezon, lingcod, and surfperch are within casting range.

Surf fishermen can cast their baits along the 17 Mile Drive once they hit Fanshell Beach. Asilomar State Beach is another good local surf fishing spot.

Smelt, perch, and shallow water rockfish can be had for the taking off the pier at the eastern end of the harbor. Occasionally stripers may also show up in the catches.

Skiff operators can tackle assorted rockfish, lingcod, and sanddabs inside both Carmel and Monterey Bays. In warm water periods, bonito and barracuda can be an unexpected treat inside these sheltered harbors. Salmon can also be trolled from smaller craft in Carmel Bay, though a lot of chinook action occurs more frequently to the north above the Salinas River.

Party boats can drag these same areas for salmon or pound the deeper reefs for lingcod and rockfish. Numerous reefs from Point Sur south of Monterey to Point Pinos in the North hold major volumes of rockfish.

Best Times: Salmon can be caught from inside the bays in early spring through fall. Halibut and sanddabs are caught along the sandy bottoms in the summer and fall. The rockfish will cooperate almost anytime, while the larger spawner perch are prime in the winter. Albacore are mainly a late summer gamble with schools ranging as close to 10 miles offshore.

Tips and Tricks: Use your electronics to locate schools of suspended rockfish over shallow water reefs. Smaller spoons yo-yoed off the bottom with freshwater casting gear can be terrific sport. Try 2 to 4 ounce Diamond Jigs, the Hopkins #075, and the Haddock Jig'n Spoon, the Luhr Jensen Deep Stinger, Mr. Champ, and Crippled Herring.

Next, blitz the "rockies" with soft plastics. You name it—single or double curl-tails, straight tail or swimming-tail grubs—they will all work. Again, for maximum sport, use the freshwater outfits. The hollow-bodied tube baits have also been the rage up north here in past years. Fish the Caba Cabas in milky glow and root beer flake as solid winners!

As a final note, always watch for changes in the weather in the Monterey-Carmel stretch. There can be many rainy days in the winter, fog in the summer, and ripping, northwesterly winds in the spring. Small boaters who venture out of Monterey Bay south towards Carmel should be prepared for an extremely difficult return trip. Proceed with caution!

Moss Landing and Santa Cruz

Heading to the northern end of Monterey Bay, saltwater anglers can find additional opportunities at Moss Landing and the Santa Cruz Harbor complex. Sport fishers and private craft as well as rental skiffs can explore the offshore reefs in this area.

The menu of game fish, which is fairly identical to that of Monterey, awaits fishermen here. Rockfish, perch, greenling, cabezon, lingcod, halibut, sanddabs, smelt, salmon, and occasional stripers round out the smorgasbord out of Moss Landing and Santa Cruz Harbor.

Places to Fish: The beaches slightly south of Moss Landing are super surfperch territory. The jetty at the entrance to Moss Landing is similarly a good spot to try for perch. Starry flounder, halibut, and sometimes a wayward striper or two can also be tallied off this jetty.

The Elkhorn Slough, inland from Moss Landing, is famous for its shark and bat ray fishing. Sole and starry flounder can also make a showing in this shallow inlet.

The beaches north of Aptos range from sandy to rocky. Various surf species are candidates for the long rodder's sack. The Capitola Pier is productive for cabezon, jack smelt, perch, and shallow rockfish. The Santa Cruz Pier offers a similar array but also has lingcod, bocaccio, sculpin, sole and starry flounder.

There are numerous shallow reefs outside of the Santa Cruz Small Craft Harbor. These host some sensational lingcod and rockfish populations, accessible with smaller boats. Other popular reefs lie off of Soquel Point and Capitola south of this harbor.

Best Times: Count on catching both shallow and deep-water rockfish practically anytime off of these prolific reefs. May and June are excellent bets for king salmon in waters off Santa Cruz. June and July are prime months for chinooks along the inside stretches. Try to fish as much as possible in the morning to avoid potentially hazardous afternoon winds.

Tips and Tricks: Anglers working the shallow reefs can't go wrong with shrimp fly gangions tipped with squid. The lings will attack small, live rockfish fished on a slider or three-way swivel rig. Also try assorted soft plastics, 8 to 16 ounce jigs—and believe it or not—even surface plugs when the rockfish are stacked up above the shallow reefs.

Salmon draggers in this area prefer trolling 'chovies, herring, Krocadile, Hot Rail and Crippled Herring spoons, or hoochie jigs with 1 to 3 pound sinker release systems. Mooching can also be very productive.

Surf casters using pileworms or bloodworms will take their share of perch. A whole anchovy pitched from the beach may result in a surprise summer halibut from the surf.

Pillar Point and Half Moon Bay

Pillar Point Harbor on the inside of Half Moon Bay is one of the most diverse fisheries in Northern California. The harbor lies 15 miles south of San Francisco in the town of Princeton. Party boats and private skiffs can fish the nearby reefs for copper, olive, yellowtail, black, canary, olive, and blue rockfish, cabezon, and lingcod. Salmon, striped bass, flounder, sanddabs, sculpin, perch, and jack smelt are additional species sought around this harbor complex.

Shore anglers can try their luck off the breakwall or the pier for rockfish, perch, and maybe even a salmon, ling or striper. Poke polers can work the adjacent rocky areas for rockfish, cabezon, and eels.

Places to Fish: The reefs outside the harbor are teeming with rockfish and lingcod. The stretch from Pillar Point northward to Moss Beach is a good area to prospect for bottom fish. Pier fisherman can fish inside Pillar Point Harbor for perch, smelt, rockfish, sanddabs, and sculpin. Additional opportunities exist for the shore anglers, working the east and west jetties. Surfperch, greenling, rockfish, cabezon, and a stray lingcod or two can be targeted from the west wall. The east rocks are primarily good for flounder, sanddabs, and perch.

Best Times: October through May are the primary times to look for big lingcod in this region. The multitude of other rockfish are taken on a year around basis. Mid-February through late November is the best time frame for mooching and trolling for salmon in the Pillar Point area.

As a long shot, boats will make a run out of this harbor searching for albacore on the outer banks if the migrating schools come in.

Tips and Tricks: Bottom fishermen really tear 'em up with both iron and soft plastics. Nothing real fancy is needed. Scampis, Tora Tubes, Power Pogeys, Salty Magics, Mojos, Lunker Thumpers, and similar curl-tail lures work fine in a wide range of colors. Basic bottom-bouncing jigs such as 8 ounce to one pound Hot Diamond or Ironman Diamond Jig, Hex Bar, Salas PL68 or 7X Heavy, Tady 45 Heavy, or Di Clad models produce on lingcod. Area locals prefer to add a strip of squid to the iron for extra effect.

Pacifica Surfline

Many surf fishermen hail Pacifica as the striper capital of the West Coast. Small craft owners, party boaters, and long rodders can all sample the action on linesides in the surf (see the chapter on striped bass).

But other angling opportunities exist in the Pacifica area. The local pier lets fishermen take a shot at not only stripers but king salmon as well. Perch and smelt are more common catches. Party boats run out of Emeryville, San Rafael, Richmond, Berkeley, and San Francisco, tapping into this rich striper fishery.

Places to Fish: Stripers migrate up and down this span of coastline ranging from Pacifica to the Golden Gate Bridge. Investigate Mussel Rock, Sharp Park, Rockaway Beach, Linda Mar, Fleischacker Beach, Thornton Beach, Montara Beach and directly under the Golden Gate Bridge. Poke polers can also work the rocks at Montara, Rockaway, and Linda Mar for inshore species.

Best Times: Late June through early September have historically been the best months for striper fishing on the 7 to 12 miles of Pacific Ocean surfline below the Golden Gate Bridge. Salmon in the vicinity of the breakers can be surprisingly good in the summer, especially from the piers.

Tips and Tricks: Boaters can drift for both stripers and salmon. Live anchovies are obviously the primo bait. Salmon trollers should drag the 'chovies behind flashers from the surface down to 70 feet. Both stripers and salmon can also be taken by using drift bobbers with frozen anchovies off the piers.

A variety of regional lures will rack up the limits while making long casts from the surf. These include 3 to 4 ounce Mickey Mouse, Kastmaster, Tony Acetta Pet, Hopkins and Krocadile Spoons. Top water chuckers should consider the Cordell Pencil Popper for the surface bite. Soft plastics such as the Tora Tube, Mojo, Salty Magic, Power Pogey, Lunker Thumper and Pacific Eel can also be slow-drifted outside the surf lines.

San Francisco Bay Halibut

Bay Area party boat skippers routinely set up trips so that they may sample a variety of possibilities in determining which species is currently in a feeding mood. So-called "potluck" outings look for salmon, stripers, and halibut. The principle technique is to drift slowly to cover as much choice terrain as possible on a given day. Extensive coverage has been given to the two more glamourous species—the king salmon and striped bass. But party boaters and small craft owners can also find an additional bounty with fine-eating halibut on potluck excursions.

Places to Fish: There are some key areas to drift for halibut in San Francisco Bay. The box-like perimeter that connects the South Hampton Shoals to the Raccoon Straits, to Treasure Island, and back to the Berkeley Flats is regarded as perfect bottom bouncing terrain for these flatfish. Crissy Field outside the Marina Green on the San Francisco side of the middle bay is another halibut haunt. The Deep Hole area below and between Angel and Alcatraz Islands is a good deep-water spot. Also, fish around the major islands themselves. The northwestern portion of Treasure Island, the west side of Alcatraz, and the southwest sector of Angel Island are the areas to look for halibut. Candlestick Point is sometimes excellent for flatfishers working the southwest bay.

Best Times: Late April and early May signal the first major migration of halibut into San Francisco Bay. June through August are considered the height of the run though halibut may be found all the way through early November.

Tips and Tricks: Numerous rigging techniques perform well for halibut (see the chapter on fishing for halibut). Veteran flattie fishermen in the Bay favor live anchovies when they are available. Smelt, sardines, herring, and sometimes squid or ghost shrimp will also get bit by the 'buts. An important feature is to find hard bottoms of sand and broken shells using your electronics. This type of bottom attracts these flatfish in this large bay.

San Francisco Bay Striper

After the striped bass have thoroughly gorged themselves on schools of surfline anchovies, they begin to make their legendary migration into the waters of San Francisco Bay. Sport fishing boats from a variety of Bay Area landings stage seasonal striper hunts. Sausalito, Berkeley, Emeryville, Richmond, and San Francisco have striper fleets on call. Smaller, private vessels can be launched at Berkeley, Sausalito, Loch Lomond, San Rafael, Richmond, Oyster Point, and South San Francisco.

Places to Fish: There are a wealth of regionally renowned hot spots for Bay Area striper action. Many can be reached with a cast from shore as well as from a boat. It always helps to monitor the local outdoor press, charter boat, and sport fishing reports, and information disseminated at area tackle shops for the latest tips as to where the stripers are feeding.

Some of the historically good spots include Coyote, Oyster and Hunter's Points, Candlestick Park, Mission Rock, and Baker's Beach on the west side of the Bay. The Berkeley Flat, the Alameda Rocks, midchannel at the San Mateo Bridge, the Oakland Estuary and as far south as Dumbarton Point are striper areas in the east and south Bay area.

To the north, the Raccoon Straits, Alcatraz, Treasure and Angel Islands sustain major striper attacks. Striped bass can also be found further north at San Pedro and San Pablo Points. Fish will move into the Carquinez Straits between Crockett and Martinez up past the Mothball Fleet entering into Suisan Bay.

Best Times: Small "schoolies" start their bayward migration in summer. Bigger stripers typically move into San Francisco Bay in the latter part of August or September. They will stay in the shallow water until mid-December.

Tips and Tricks: Whenever possible, try to take a shot, at the linesides with artificial lures. Spoons like the Tony Acetta Pet, Krocadile, Mr. Champ, Crippled Herring and Kastmaster should be thrown. Popular patterns include chrome, chrome/blue, and chrome/red. Jigs such as the solid white or black Hair Raiser or Banjo Eye are time-proven winners. Other jig combinations are red head/white skirt, red head/orange skirt, and solid yellow. The Brawley Bass Bug is another popular jig for the light line enthusiast. Swimming plastics such as the Scrounger in silver or metal flake, Salty Magic or Pacific Eel are also productive. A popular combo is to drift with a Pet Spoon and a hair jig on a spreader rig.

Plugs like Rebels, Bomber Long A's, Rapalas, and Cordell Spots will work under the surface; top-water baits including the Heddon Zara Spook and Lucky 13, Storm Chug Bug, Arbogast Dasher, and Cordell Pencil Popper are perfect for a surface frenzy.

Bait fishermen can select from mudsuckers, bullheads, shiner perch, anchovies, herring, smelt, or sardines. The trick is to keep the bait moving by either drifting it, or "pumping" or "walking" it along the bottom and offshore ledges.

San Francisco Bay Sharks

As was mentioned earlier, San Francisco Bay can be an outstanding place to experience some serious monster fishing. Sport fishing boats, charter vessels, and private craft sample this kind of big game fishing from a variety of Bay Area ports.

Places to Fish: The deeper channels around Marin, west of Angels Island, the Bay Bridge, and Hunter's Point have been long-time favorite spots for northern shark hunters. Anglers also like to probe the waters off the greenhouse south of Sausalito and the main channel between the Dumbarton and San Mateo Bridges in South San Francisco Bay for these prehistoric fish.

Best Times: Leopards, soupfin, smooth hound, dogfish and 6 and 7 gill sharks can be taken at almost anytime, but look for 7 gill in spring and fall and soupfin in spring and summer. It usually helps to fish these sharks at the top or bottom of a moving tide.

Tips and Tricks: A variety of bait tactics were outlined in the chapter on sharks. When possible, try to secure some midshipmen (mudsucker-like fish) that can be gathered by hand when they spawn from June through July. They are 10 to 15 inches long and slimy. Look for them under big flat rocks at exceptionally low or minus tides. You can freeze the midshipmen in a plastic bag for future usage. Take care not to overly handle these prize bait fish. That mucous slime layer is a major treat to leopard sharks.

Other "trick" baits for the "big boys"—6 and 7 gill sharks—include the belly portions from stripers or salmon. A tail section from a small dogfish shark or a rockfish fillet will also be effective. Consider using a trap-hook bait rig to insure an extra solid hook set.

San Francisco Bay Potluck

Private boaters and shore fishermen especially take advantage of light-lining a variety of other species within the confines of San Francisco Bay. Perch, smelt, flounder, shallow water rockfish, and kingfish are frequently caught in these waters.

Places to Fish: Smelt and perch are predominant in the catch totals on the Berkeley Pier. Jacksmelt also can be red hot along the Burlingame shoreline. The wharfs and piers on the San Francisco waterfront also yield starry flounder, smelt, and perch. An excellent perch bite often materializes in a stretch of shoreline from Coyote Point to the San Francisco airport. Other strong perch possibilities include the Alameda Estuary and East Fort Baker under the Golden Gate on the Marin side.

Best Times: Spring is recognized as the prime time for focusing on the Bay's perch population. Late winter often ushers in some outstanding action on jack smelt. Starry flounder seem most prevalent in the catches in the winter and spring.

Tips and Tricks: Chunks of pileworm fished underneath a styrofoam drift bobber is the inside tip for hammering the jack smelt. Use about a #6 to #10 baitholder hook. Perch species (shiner, walleye, white, rubberlip, black, pile, striped and rainbow) can also be taken on pileworms, but split-shot live grass shrimp for the larger specimens. Small freshwater-sized spoons and Scroungers will also get bit on the larger perch. Always look for dock pilings, chunks of broken concrete, and rocky outcroppings for jumbo perch. Then take a pile of mussels and stomp on the shells, crushing the mollusks and kicking them into the water you plan to fish. This produces a super chum line for the diverse perch species.

Farallon Islands Area

Anglers making that 35 mile run from the Golden Gate Bridge to the Farallon Islands are heading into some of the finest bottom fish country found in the West. Sport fishing and charter boats from San Francisco Fisherman's Wharf, Berkeley, Sausalito, Pillar Point, and Emeryville probe the deep canyons of this rockfish mecca.

King salmon and lingcod are additional quarry for fishermen working the Farallons. The weather and sea conditions can be miserable at times in this part of the Pacific. Small boat owners should proceed with caution.

Places to Fish: A wide range of bottom fish species are taken around the islands themselves, in the nearby Fanny Shoals, or in the Gulf of the Farallons. These include salmon grouper, copper, blue, yellowtail, chilis, golden eyes, vermillion and blue rockfish. Cowcod and lings round out the catch.

Salmon are taken in the Gulf between the islands and the mainland. Troll, drift, and mooch between Duxbury Reef and the Farallons in spring. Move to the San Francisco light buoy to Duxbury Reef in the late summer through fall.

Best Times: Limit-level rockfishing is possible all through the year, particularly in the winter. Look for larger spawning lings from July to December. The king salmon with some silvers stage their flurries from mid-February through mid-November.

Trick and Tips: Standard gangions and heavy-duty gear are in order for the rockfish at 300 to 400 feet. Hexbar, Di

Clad, and Bridgeport and Luhr Jensen Hot Diamond Jigs are good alternatives for "iron strokers." Use solid chrome models ranging in size from 6 to 16 ounces. Shrimp fly rigs tipped with bait equally produce. Whole squid and dead mackerel an a three-way swivel rig are ideal for lings. Don't overlook using a small rockfish on a trap-rig for big lingcod either. I have also conducted on-the-water seminars at the Farallons emphasizing soft plastic lures. The Salty Magic, Pacific Eel, Mojo and Lunker Thumper are sensational here on the rockfish. The lingcod—and big specimens at that—clobber the Caba Caba Tubes at the Farallons.

Bodega and Tomales Bays

North of San Francisco both sport fishers and private boaters can experience great bottom fishing in Bodega and Tomales Bays. Small boat owners can launch at West Side Park and the Coast Guard station. The Tides Sportfishing Landing ruins various open party boats to the rock cod grounds and they will also chase salmon when the schools of kings migrate near the bay.

Surf fishermen and jetty jockeys can also get into the action, with numerous access points in this area. There are full service facilities at The Tides and camping is permitted through Sonoma Coast, state beaches, Doran County Park, and West Side Park.

Places to Fish: Boaters tap the lingcod and rockfish bite at the Cordell Banks. The Whistle Buoy off the mouth of Bodega Bay is a prime spot for cruising chinook salmon. You may also fish the local wharf in Bodega Bay for smelt and perch.

Rock hoppers and jetty jockeys should try the Doran Park breakwall and the outer jetty for shallow water greenling, cabezon, and assorted rockfish. Carmel and Dillar Beaches are perfect for poke polers. Wright's, Goat, Salmon Creek, and Portuguese Beaches are key places to try for smelt and surfperch.

Lawson Landing at the mouth of Tomales Bay is the center of activity in this backwater. Stripers are a possibility here as are leopard sharks and halibut. Hog Island is a hot perch hangout.

Best Times: Bottom fishing in this northern latitude can be great all year long. Surf fishing, poke poling, and rock hopping are similarly viable options twelve months a year. Salmon are sought May through July. Lingcod are prime targets in the July through November period.

Tips and Tricks: Limited striper action can be found trolling Luhr Jensen Acetta Pet Spoons tipped with pork

rind on spreader rigs. Heddon Zara Spooks are a local favorite for top-water lineside action. Blue and silver Rebels, bullheads, and shrimp round out the striper menu.

Shark hunters prefer a small whole jacksmelt, squid, or razor clams probing Tomales and Bodega Bays. Perch are suckers for pile and bloodworms fished under a bobber inside the harbors. Try silver spoons and spinners in the surfline for more perch action. Rock codders can use primarily red and yellow shrimp fly gangions or a 1 to 2 pound chrome Diamond Jig.

Ft. Ross and Timber Cove Area

This northern outpost offers some of the finest bottom fishing along the California Coast. It is a stellar spot for big lingcod as well. You can rent a boat or launch your own at Timber Cove Boat Landing. Most of the bottom plunkin' is done near the shore. Rock hoppers and poke polers can also encounter some good action along this stretch of ocean.

Places to Fish: Look for the major reefs in this area. Salt Point, Ocean Cove, Seal Rocks, Stillwater Cove, and Timber Cove itself are key bottom fishing regions. Three miles north or south of Timber Cove will put you into some of the most popular water fished.

Best Times: Late November through January are recognized as the primary time period to look for the bigger female lingcod in the shallows. Salmon trollers can sometimes hit some amazingly good runs on both silvers and kings from late April through the summer.

Tips and Tricks: The assorted bottom fish species including black snapper, yellowtail and olive rockfish, cabezon, and Chinas will readily jump on baited shrimp fly gangions. Hot Diamond, Ironman Diamond jigs and Hex Bar jigs with a squid trailer are staples with the rockfishing clan. Stripped or live bluefish make excellent fare for the giant lings laced on a shrimp fly gangion. Most salmon are taken by dragging on anchovies or herring combined with a standard dodger.

Ft. Bragg and Shelter Cove Area

For those of you motoring north toward the Oregon border, consider exploring the angling possibilities between Fort Bragg and Eureka. Shelter Cove is a rockfish mecca with a heavy emphasis on lingcod. Occasional salmon action is another possibility. The reefs off Ft. Bragg itself are excellent haunts for rockfish and are also major salmon trolling grounds.

Small rental skiffs are available at Shelter Cove, Noyo Harbor, Ft. Bragg, and Arena Cove. Anglers in private craft won't have to venture too far off the shore. Lingcod and other rockfish will be prime targets within two miles from launching.

To the south, out of Point Arena, there is pier and skiff fishing available at Arena Cove. Salmon can be trolled in this area while pier anglers plunk for greenling, rockfish, cabezon, perch, and lingcod. As is the case with most North Coast environments, be prepared for inclement weather and rough seas at all times.

Places to Fish: Local veterans are pretty much in agreement, you have to take a shot at the Bell Buoy and Whistle Buoy slightly south of Shelter Cove. Moving further south, the Tolo Banks are another hot lingcod spot. As noted, don't overlook the pocket of prime water found offshore from Arena Cove to Ft. Bragg.

Best Times: Rockfish will bite all year long in this North Coast bay. The colder winter months can be exceptionally good for big lings. Trollers will nail chinook salmon in the waters south of Pt. Delgado from May through October.

Tips and Tricks: The jumbo class lingcod are typically nailed in less than 100 feet of water. Strip bait and frozen squid are principle offerings. Also, try small sanddabs as the secret ticket for enticing the larger lings.

Standard bottom-bouncing jigs in the 8 ounce to 1 pound range will work on the gamut of rockfish including lingcod. Stay with chrome, white, blue and chrome, and orange patterns. Don't forget to drop some soft plastics over the side for these bottom dwellers. But, fish most artificial lures on 25 to 30 pound string as a minimum for prying the lings up from the rocky terrain.

Eureka and Humboldt Bay

Four mile long Humboldt Bay is recognized as one of the premier clam beds on the West Coast. But besides these delectable mollusks, ample angling opportunity also exists in this area. Surf fishermen can rack up decent tallies on walleye and redtail perch. Jetty jockeys can sample shallow water lings, black snapper, and greenling. Salmon stalkers can also encounter some decent action on kings in this northern region.

Private boats can be launched both in Humboldt Bay and near the mouth of the Eel River. There are numerous facilities available nearby on the North and South jetties of Humboldt Bay.

Places to Fish: Redtail perch action is heightened at the mouths of the Eel River and Redwood Creek. Shallow water rockfishing is the name of the game along the South Jetty in Humboldt Bay. Blue and black rockfish, greenling, lings, cabezon, smelt, perch, and even salmon are taken from this structure. Work Buhne Point on the east side of the bay from the bank for perch. The railroad bridge that rides over Eureka Slough is another key area for perch fishing. Anglers can also fish the docks at Field's Landing on the east side of Humboldt Bay.

Best Times: Like most northern environments, the shallow water rockfish bite from the shore along with offshore activity is a consistent yearlong program.

Tips and Tricks: The usual fare of cut and frozen baits works on the rockfish—squid, 'chovies, sardines, and shellfish. The redtail perch have a fondness for sandcrabs and tubeworms. Both are available at area boat stores. Salmon will jump on a frozen anchovy worked off the jetty underneath a drift bobber.

Crescent City Area

This quiet stretch of shoreline may be one of the real "sleepers" of California coastal fishery. There is a public pier and launch facility in the harbor itself. Charter boat operations are available for salmon and bottom fishing. Camping is possible at Jedediah Smith Redwoods State Park on the Smith River or Del Norte Coast Redwoods State Park south of Crescent City.

Places to Fish: Rockfish specialists have to try either St. George or South Reefs outside the harbor. Also explore the five fathom curve from Three Sister Rocks to the harbor entrance for the bottom fish. There are black, blue, vermillion, China, and bocaccio "rockies" for the taking. Pier anglers can sample flounder, perch, smelt and greenling off the Citizen's Dock.

Best Times: Bottom-hugging species like lingcod, rockfish, and cabezon are year around favorites in this colder water. Smaller silver salmon can be nailed in June, while August is the major month for kings. Poke polers can explore the rocky outcroppings all season long for monkeyface eels, rockfish, perch, and greenling. Surf casting is also a perennial option, regardless of the time of year.

Tips and Tricks: Salmon fishermen score consistently trolling for silvers and kings. Locals prefer diving planes, teamed with herring dodgers. Rockfish are scored in good numbers with soft plastics. Lunker Thumpers, Salty Magics, Mojos, Pacific Eels, Berkley Power Pogeys and Tora Tubes and Scampis are recommended. Use silver or gold flake models for rockfish and red or orange curl-tails for lingcod. Other newer popular patterns include root beer flake, milky glow, black/glitter, and bubble gum pink. Tubeworms and soft-shell crabs are the staple for surf casters looking for redtail.

Pacific Ocean Fishing Maps

A map highlighting the main features of the California Coast is on page 8 of this book. On the following pages, each of 15 sections of California's coast is detailed. All of the most productive fishing grounds and shore locales for numerous species are included. These maps are very informative, but they are not to be used for navigational purposes. The maps are adapted from *Angler's Guide to the United States Pacific Coast* (U.S. Dept. of Commerce).

San Diego Area 168
Solano Beach to Dana Point 169
Los Angeles Area 170
Santa Monica Area 171
Ventura Area 172
Santa Barbara Area 173
SoCal Islands (Map I) 174
SoCal Islands (Map II) 175
Central Coast 176
Monterey Bay Area 177
San Francisco Area 178
San Francisco Bay 179
Pt. Reyes to Ft. Ross 180
Ft. Ross to Cape Mendocino 181
Eel River to Oregon Border 182

California Saltwater Information Directory

Region	Prime Contact	Phone Number
San Diego Area	San Diego Visitor's Bureau	(619) 232-3181
San Clemente/Oceanside	Oceanside Chamber of Commerce	(760) 722-1534
Dana Port Area	Dana Port Chamber of Commerce	(714) 496-1555
Newport Area	Newport Beach Visitor's Bureau	(714) 722-1611
Catalina Island	Catalina Visitor's Bureau	(310) 510-7645
Huntington Beach/Seal Beach	Huntington Beach Visitor's Bureau	(714) 536-5511
Long Beach Area	Long Beach Visitor's Bureau	(562) 436-3645
Kings Harbor/Redondo Beach	Redondo Sport Fishing	(310) 372-2111
Santa Monica Area	Santa Monica Chamber of Commerce	(310) 393-9825
Ventura	Ventura Visitor's Center	(805) 648-2075
Channel Islands	Port Hueneme Sport Fishing	(805) 488-4715
Santa Barbara Area	Santa Barbara Visitor's Center	(805) 968-3051
Morro Bay Area	Morro Bay Chamber of Commerce	(805) 772-4467
Monterey Area	Monterey Peninsula Chamber of Commerce	(800) 649-1770
Santa Cruz Area	Santa Cruz Visitor's Council	(831) 425-1234
Pacific Area	Pacific Pier	(650) 355-0690
Bodega Bay Area	Bodega Bay Chamber of Commerce	(707) 875-3422
Ft. Bragg Area	Ft. Bragg Chamber of Commerce	(707) 961-6300
Eureka Area	Eureka Chamber of Commerce	(707) 442-3738
Crescent City Area	Del Norte Chamber of Commerce	(707) 464-3174

117° 30'

117° 30'

117°30'

32° 30'

32° 30'

San Diego Area

⛰ Shorefishing Areas

1-8 Fishing Facilities

🚤 Sportboat Operation

〰 Kelp

—20— Depth in Fathoms

TORREY PINES NORTH ALONG COAST IN ISOLATED KELP BEDS FOR:
KELP BASS
OPALEYE
HALIBUT
SHEEPHEAD
YELLOWTAIL
ROCKFISH

WHITE CROAKER
SAND BASS
BONITO
BARRACUDA
WHITE SEABASS

ESPECIALLY GOOD FOR BARRACUDA, KELP BASS, BONITO, AND YELLOWTAIL

HALIBUT
ROCKFISH

YELLOWTAIL
BONITO

LA JOLLA KELP:
BARRACUDA, BONITO, KELP BASS, YELLOW-TAIL, SHEEPHEAD, WHITE CROAKER, GIANT SEA BASS, WHITE SEABASS, LINGCOD, HALF-MOON, ROCKFISH, SOMETIMES BLUEFIN TUNA

CAL. HALIBUT
WHITE CROAKER
BONITO

STRIPED MARLIN AND SWORDFISH AT RADAR BUOY ABOUT 12 MILES OFF LA JOLLA

SPORTFISHING TRIPS TO SAN CLEMENTE FOR YELLOWTAIL, KELP BASS, ALSO TO 43 FATHOM BANK OR 35 MILE BANK FOR ROCKFISH AND ALBACORE

ROCKFISH TRIPS TO 184 FATHOM SPOT, 15 NAUTICAL MILES WEST

INTERNATIONAL MARITIME BOUNDARY

STRIPED MARLIN CAUGHT WEST OF THIS LINE, JULY TO NOVEMBER (AUG-SEPT BEST). CENTER CATCH DISTRIBUTION FROM SAN DIEGO ABOUT 15 MILES OFFSHORE

P A C I F I C   O C E A N

LINGCOD
ROCKFISH

POINT LOMA KELP:
BONITO, YELLOWTAIL, BARRACUDA, KELP BASS, SHEEPHEAD, SCULPIN, LINGCOD, HALFMOON, GIANT SEA BASS, WHITE CROAKER, WHITE SEABASS, AND ROCKFISH

CALIFORNIA
HALIBUT

BARRACUDA
ROCKFISH

CAL. HALIBUT
WHITE CROAKER
RUBBERLIP PERCH
WHITE SEABASS

Del Mar

TORREY PINES ST. RESERVE

La Jolla Canyon

Pt. La Jolla

La Jolla

Bird Rock

Pacific Beach

Pacific Beach Pier

8

Mission Bay

Ocean Beach Pier

6

Ocean Beach

Sunset Cliffs

5

Shelter I. Pier

Coronado

4

Pt. Loma

MISSION BAY:
CROAKERS
HALIBUT
BONITO
SARGO
SURFPERCH
BARRACUDA
SAND BASS
TOPSMELT
JACKSMELT

SAN DIEGO BAY:
JACKSMELT, TOPSMELT, SAND BASS, HALIBUT, SPOTFIN CROAKER, OPALEYE, KELP BASS, BONITO, SURFPERCH, SHARKS & RAYS

SAN DIEGO

National City

3

Chula Vista

2

SAN DIEGO BAY

SILVER STRAND ST. BEACH

Imperial Beach

Imperial Beach Pier

SAND BASS

HALIBUT

KELP BASS
BONITO
BARRACUDA
WHITE SEABASS
YELLOWTAIL
SHEEPHEAD

UNITED STATES (CALIFORNIA)
MEXICO

Coronado Canyon

MIDDLEGROUND:
YELLOWTAIL
BONITO
BARRACUDA
WHITE SEABASS

YELLOWTAIL

ROCKFISH

CAL. HALIBUT
WHITE SEABASS

Islas Los Coronados

YELLOWTAIL

SOUTH KELP:
SAND BASS
GIANT SEA BASS
YELLOWTAIL

Statute Miles
0 1 2 3 4 5

Nautical Miles
0 1 2 3 4 5

NOT TO BE USED FOR NAVIGATION
See NOS Nautical Charts

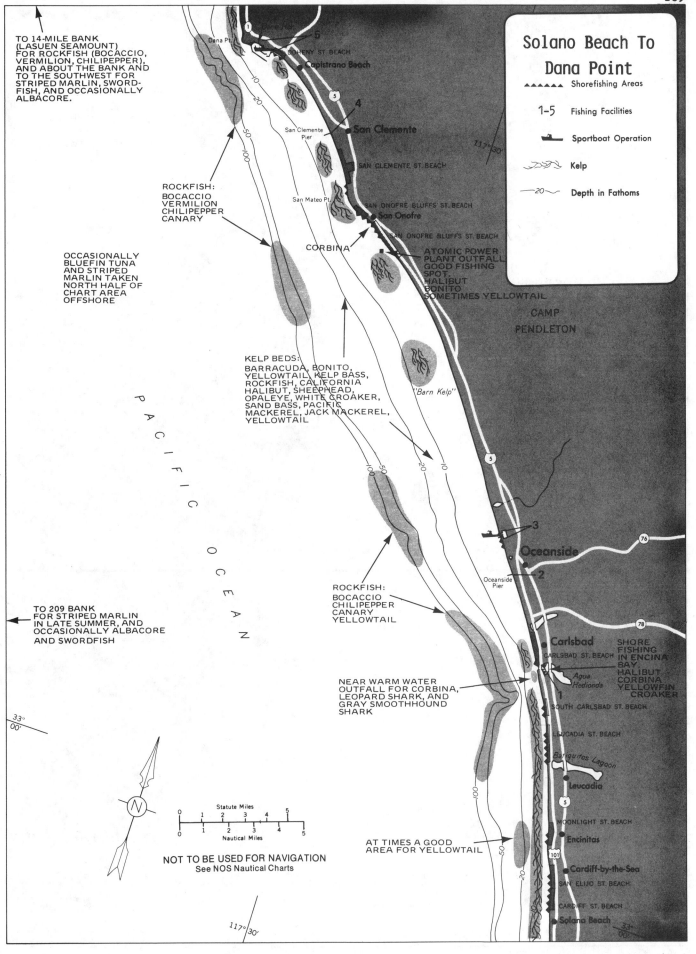

TO 14-MILE BANK
(LASUEN SEAMOUNT)
FOR ROCKFISH (BOCACCIO,
VERMILION, CHILIPEPPER),
AND ABOUT THE BANK AND
TO THE SOUTHWEST FOR
STRIPED MARLIN, SWORD-
FISH, AND OCCASIONALLY
ALBACORE.

ROCKFISH:
BOCACCIO
VERMILION
CHILIPEPPER
CANARY

OCCASIONALLY
BLUEFIN TUNA
AND STRIPED
MARLIN TAKEN
NORTH HALF OF
CHART AREA
OFFSHORE

CORBINA

KELP BEDS:
BARRACUDA, BONITO,
YELLOWTAIL, KELP BASS,
ROCKFISH, CALIFORNIA
HALIBUT, SHEEPHEAD,
OPALEYE, WHITE CROAKER,
SAND BASS, PACIFIC
MACKEREL, JACK MACKEREL,
YELLOWTAIL

P A C I F I C   O C E A N

TO 209 BANK
FOR STRIPED MARLIN
IN LATE SUMMER, AND
OCCASIONALLY ALBACORE
AND SWORDFISH

ROCKFISH:
BOCACCIO
CHILIPEPPER
CANARY
YELLOWTAIL

NEAR WARM WATER
OUTFALL FOR CORBINA,
LEOPARD SHARK, AND
GRAY SMOOTHHOUND
SHARK

AT TIMES A GOOD
AREA FOR YELLOWTAIL

33°
00'

Statute Miles
0   1   2   3   4   5
0   1   2   3   4   5
Nautical Miles

NOT TO BE USED FOR NAVIGATION
See NOS Nautical Charts

Dana Pt.

DOHENY ST. BEACH
Capistrano Beach

San Clemente
Pier
San Clemente

SAN CLEMENTE ST. BEACH

San Mateo Pt.
SAN ONOFRE BLUFFS ST. BEACH
San Onofre

SAN ONOFRE BLUFFS ST. BEACH

ATOMIC POWER
PLANT OUTFALL
GOOD FISHING
SPOT,
HALIBUT
BONITO
SOMETIMES YELLOWTAIL

CAMP
PENDLETON

"Barn Kelp"

Oceanside

Oceanside
Pier

Carlsbad

SHORE
FISHING
IN ENCINA
BAY
HALIBUT
CORBINA
YELLOWFIN
CROAKER

CARLSBAD ST. BEACH
Agua
Hedionda

SOUTH CARLSBAD ST. BEACH

LEUCADIA ST. BEACH

Batiquitos Lagoon

Leucadia

MOONLIGHT ST. BEACH

Encinitas

Cardiff-by-the-Sea

SAN ELIJO ST. BEACH

CARDIFF ST. BEACH

Solana Beach

117° 30'

117° 30'

33°
00'

Solano Beach To Dana Point

▲▲▲▲▲▲▲ Shorefishing Areas

1-5 Fishing Facilities

🛥 Sportboat Operation

〜〜〜 Kelp

—20— Depth in Fathoms

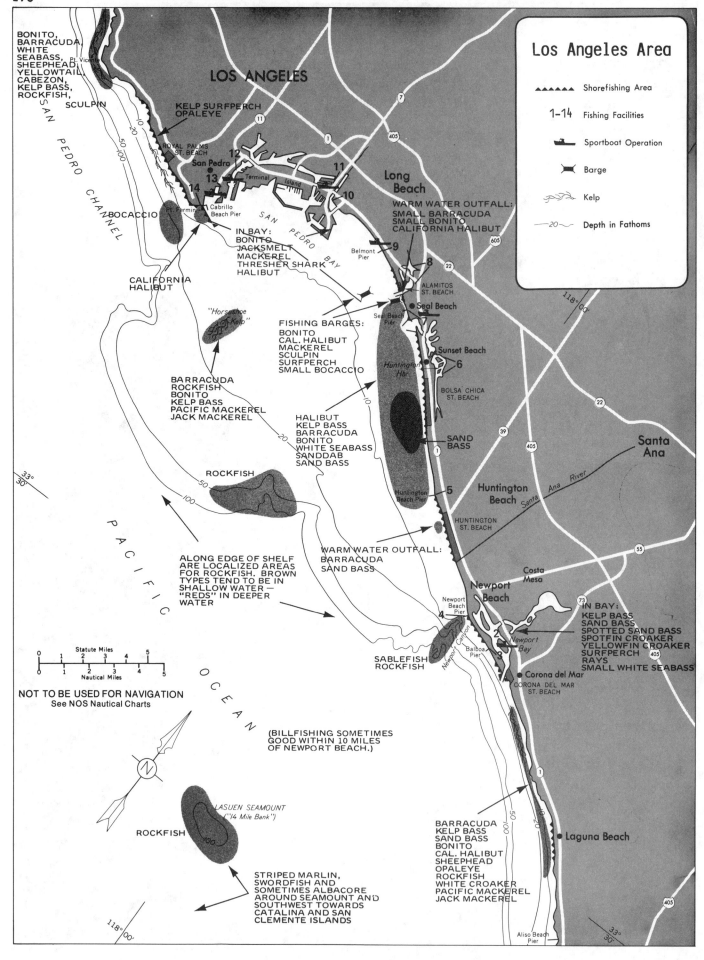

BONITO,
BARRACUDA,
WHITE
SEABASS,
SHEEPHEAD,
YELLOWTAIL,
CABEZON,
KELP BASS,
ROCKFISH,
SCULPIN

Pt. Vicente

LOS ANGELES

KELP SURFPERCH
OPALEYE

ROYAL PALMS
ST. BEACH

San Pedro

12

13

14

Terminal Island

BOCACCIO

Pt. Fermin

Cabrillo
Beach Pier

CALIFORNIA
HALIBUT

SAN PEDRO CHANNEL

SAN PEDRO BAY

IN BAY:
BONITO
JACKSMELT
MACKEREL
THRESHER SHARK
HALIBUT

11

10

Long
Beach

WARM WATER OUTFALL:
SMALL BARRACUDA
SMALL BONITO
CALIFORNIA HALIBUT

Belmont
Pier

9

8

ALAMITOS
ST. BEACH

Seal Beach

Seal Beach
Pier

"Horseshoe
Of Kelp"

FISHING BARGES:
BONITO
CAL. HALIBUT
MACKEREL
SCULPIN
SURFPERCH
SMALL BOCACCIO

BARRACUDA
ROCKFISH
BONITO
KELP BASS
PACIFIC MACKEREL
JACK MACKEREL

Sunset Beach

6

BOLSA CHICA
ST. BEACH

Huntington
Hbr.

HALIBUT
KELP BASS
BARRACUDA
BONITO
WHITE SEABASS
SANDDAB
SAND BASS

SAND
BASS

Santa
Ana

ROCKFISH

33°
30'

Huntington
Beach Pier

5

Huntington
Beach

HUNTINGTON
ST. BEACH

Santa Ana River

PACIFIC

ALONG EDGE OF SHELF
ARE LOCALIZED AREAS
FOR ROCKFISH. BROWN
TYPES TEND TO BE IN
SHALLOW WATER —
"REDS" IN DEEPER
WATER

WARM WATER OUTFALL:
BARRACUDA
SAND BASS

Costa
Mesa

Newport
Beach

Newport
Beach
Pier

4

Newport Canyon

Balboa
Pier

2

3

Newport
Bay

73

IN BAY:
KELP BASS
SAND BASS
SPOTTED SAND BASS
SPOTFIN CROAKER
YELLOWFIN CROAKER
SURFPERCH
RAYS
SMALL WHITE SEABASS

SABLEFISH
ROCKFISH

Corona del Mar

CORONA DEL MAR
ST. BEACH

OCEAN

Statute Miles
0 1 2 3 4 5

Nautical Miles
0 1 2 3 4 5

NOT TO BE USED FOR NAVIGATION
See NOS Nautical Charts

N

(BILLFISHING SOMETIMES
GOOD WITHIN 10 MILES
OF NEWPORT BEACH.)

BARRACUDA
KELP BASS
SAND BASS
BONITO
CAL. HALIBUT
SHEEPHEAD
OPALEYE
ROCKFISH
WHITE CROAKER
PACIFIC MACKEREL
JACK MACKEREL

Laguna Beach

LASUEN SEAMOUNT
("14 Mile Bank")

ROCKFISH

STRIPED MARLIN,
SWORDFISH AND
SOMETIMES ALBACORE
AROUND SEAMOUNT AND
SOUTHWEST TOWARDS
CATALINA AND SAN
CLEMENTE ISLANDS

Aliso Beach
Pier

33°
30'

118°
00'

Los Angeles Area

▲▲▲▲▲ Shorefishing Area

1-14 Fishing Facilities

🚢 Sportboat Operation

🐟 Barge

🌿 Kelp

——20—— Depth in Fathoms

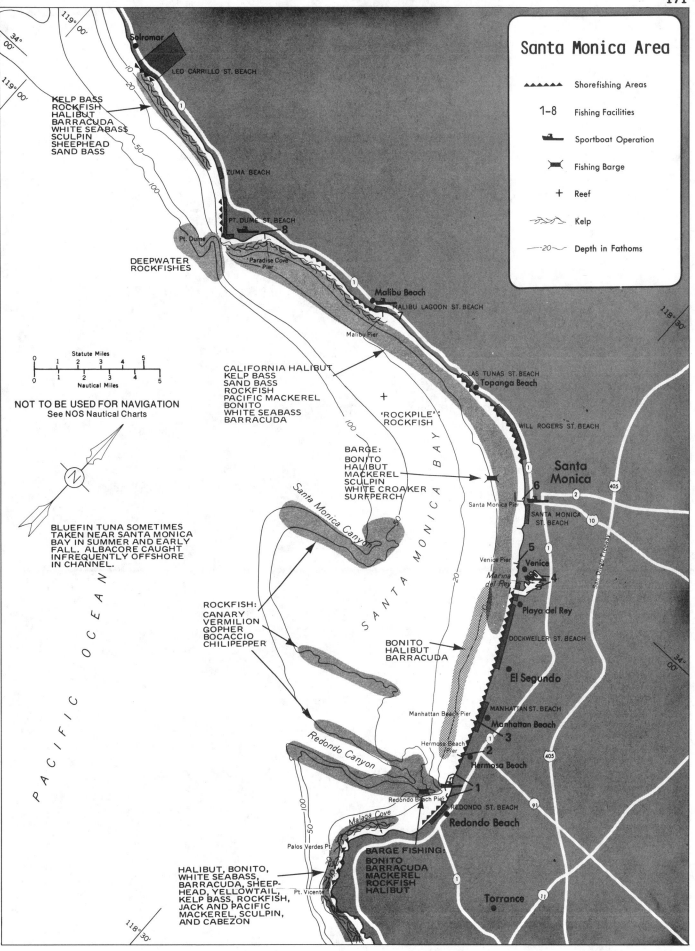

Santa Monica Area

▲▲▲▲▲▲ Shorefishing Areas

1-8 Fishing Facilities

Sportboat Operation

Fishing Barge

+ Reef

Kelp

20 Depth in Fathoms

Solromar

LEO CARRILLO ST. BEACH

KELP BASS
ROCKFISH
HALIBUT
BARRACUDA
WHITE SEABASS
SCULPIN
SHEEPHEAD
SAND BASS

ZUMA BEACH

PT. DUME ST. BEACH

8

Pt. Dume

DEEPWATER
ROCKFISHES

'Paradise Cove'
Pier

Malibu Beach

MALIBU LAGOON ST. BEACH

Malibu Pier

Statute Miles

Nautical Miles

NOT TO BE USED FOR NAVIGATION
See NOS Nautical Charts

CALIFORNIA HALIBUT
KELP BASS
SAND BASS
ROCKFISH
PACIFIC MACKEREL
BONITO
WHITE SEABASS
BARRACUDA

LAS TUNAS ST. BEACH
Topanga Beach

'ROCKPILE':
ROCKFISH

WILL ROGERS ST. BEACH

BARGE:
BONITO
HALIBUT
MACKEREL
SCULPIN
WHITE CROAKER
SURFPERCH

Santa
Monica

6

Santa Monica Pier

SANTA MONICA
ST. BEACH

N

BLUEFIN TUNA SOMETIMES
TAKEN NEAR SANTA MONICA
BAY IN SUMMER AND EARLY
FALL. ALBACORE CAUGHT
INFREQUENTLY OFFSHORE
IN CHANNEL.

5

Venice Pier
Venice

Marina
del Rey

4

ROCKFISH:
CANARY
VERMILION
GOPHER
BOCACCIO
CHILIPEPPER

Santa Monica Canyon

SANTA MONICA BAY

Playa del Rey

DOCKWEILER ST. BEACH

BONITO
HALIBUT
BARRACUDA

El Segundo

Manhattan Beach Pier

MANHATTAN ST. BEACH
Manhattan Beach

Redondo Canyon

Hermosa Beach
Pier

3

2

Hermosa Beach

1

Redondo Beach Pier

REDONDO ST. BEACH

Malaga Cove

Redondo Beach

Palos Verdes Pt.

BARGE FISHING:
BONITO
BARRACUDA
MACKEREL
ROCKFISH
HALIBUT

HALIBUT, BONITO,
WHITE SEABASS,
BARRACUDA, SHEEP-
HEAD, YELLOWTAIL,
KELP BASS, ROCKFISH,
JACK AND PACIFIC
MACKEREL, SCULPIN,
AND CABEZON

Pt. Vicente

Torrance

PACIFIC OCEAN

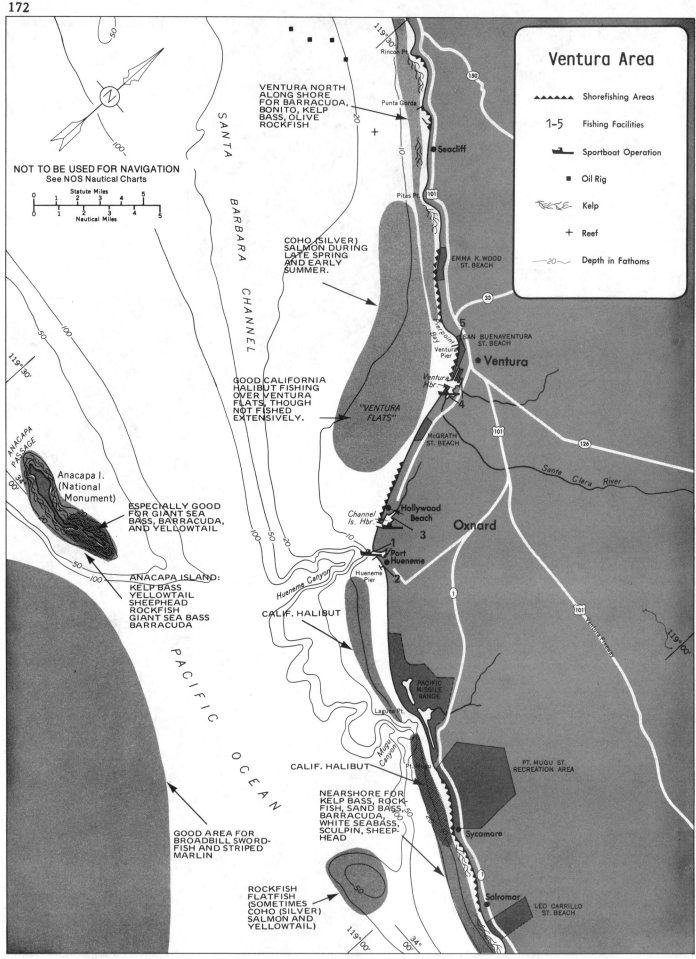

NOT TO BE USED FOR NAVIGATION
See NOS Nautical Charts

Statute Miles
0 1 2 3 4 5
0 1 2 3 4 5
Nautical Miles

Ventura Area

▲▲▲▲ Shorefishing Areas

1-5 Fishing Facilities

⛴ Sportboat Operation

■ Oil Rig

〜〜 Kelp

+ Reef

〜20〜 Depth in Fathoms

SANTA BARBARA CHANNEL

VENTURA NORTH ALONG SHORE FOR BARRACUDA, BONITO, KELP BASS, OLIVE ROCKFISH

Rincon Pt.

Punta Gorda

Seacliff

150

COHO (SILVER) SALMON DURING LATE SPRING AND EARLY SUMMER.

Pitas Pt.

101

EMMA K. WOOD ST. BEACH

33

GOOD CALIFORNIA HALIBUT FISHING OVER VENTURA FLATS, THOUGH NOT FISHED EXTENSIVELY.

Pierpoint Bay

Ventura Pier

5

SAN BUENAVENTURA ST. BEACH

• Ventura

"VENTURA FLATS"

Ventura Hbr.

4

McGRATH ST. BEACH

101

126

Santa Clara River

Channel Is. Hbr.

• Hollywood Beach

3

Oxnard

ANACAPA PASSAGE

Anacapa I. (National Monument)

34° 00'

119° 30'

ESPECIALLY GOOD FOR GIANT SEA BASS, BARRACUDA, AND YELLOWTAIL

ANACAPA ISLAND:
KELP BASS
YELLOWTAIL
SHEEPHEAD
ROCKFISH
GIANT SEA BASS
BARRACUDA

1
Port Hueneme

• Port Hueneme

Hueneme Pier

2

Hueneme Canyon

CALIF. HALIBUT

1

PACIFIC MISSILE RANGE

PACIFIC OCEAN

Laguna Pt.

Mugu Canyon

CALIF. HALIBUT

Pt. Mugu

PT. MUGU ST. RECREATION AREA

NEARSHORE FOR KELP BASS, ROCKFISH, SAND BASS, BARRACUDA, WHITE SEABASS, SCULPIN, SHEEPHEAD

• Sycamore

1

GOOD AREA FOR BROADBILL SWORDFISH AND STRIPED MARLIN

ROCKFISH FLATFISH (SOMETIMES COHO (SILVER) SALMON AND YELLOWTAIL)

50

• Solromar

LEO CARRILLO ST. BEACH

119° 00'

34° 00'

Ventura Freeway

119° 00'

119° 30'

119° 00'

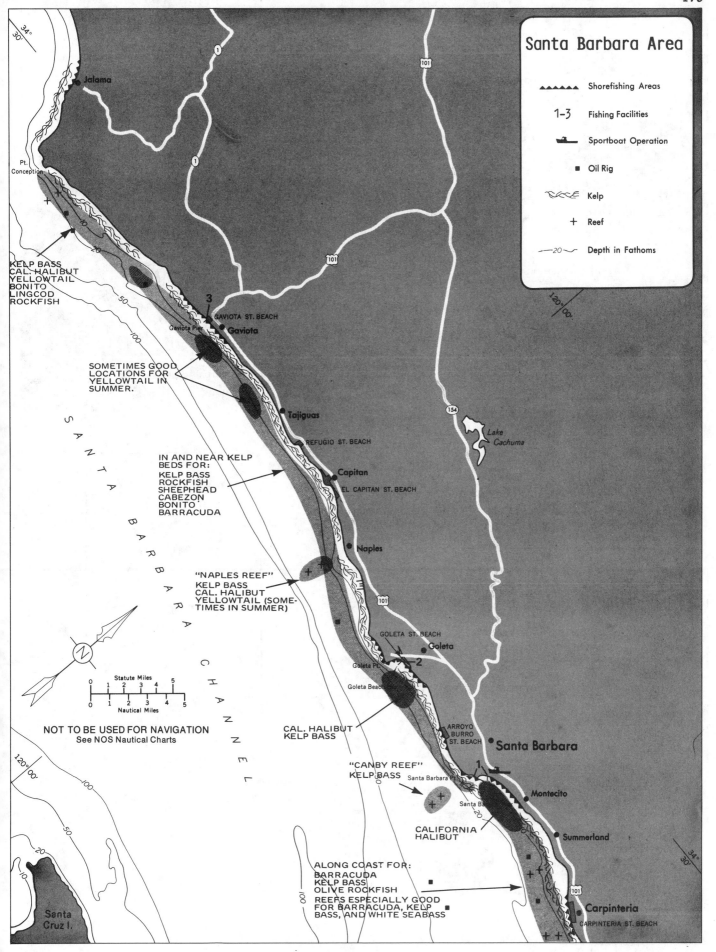

Santa Barbara Area

▲▲▲▲▲ Shorefishing Areas

1-3 Fishing Facilities

Sportboat Operation

■ Oil Rig

Kelp

+ Reef

⌇20⌇ Depth in Fathoms

Jalama

Pt. Conception

KELP BASS
CAL. HALIBUT
YELLOWTAIL
BONITO
LINGCOD
ROCKFISH

3

GAVIOTA ST. BEACH

Gaviota Pier

Gaviota

SOMETIMES GOOD
LOCATIONS FOR
YELLOWTAIL IN
SUMMER.

Tajiguas

REFUGIO ST. BEACH

IN AND NEAR KELP
BEDS FOR:
KELP BASS
ROCKFISH
SHEEPHEAD
CABEZON
BONITO
BARRACUDA

Capitan

EL CAPITAN ST. BEACH

Lake
Cachuma

Naples

"NAPLES REEF"
KELP BASS
CAL. HALIBUT
YELLOWTAIL (SOME-
TIMES IN SUMMER)

GOLETA ST. BEACH

Goleta

Goleta Pt.

2

Goleta Beach

CAL. HALIBUT
KELP BASS

ARROYO
BURRO
ST. BEACH

Santa Barbara

"CANBY REEF"
KELP BASS

Santa Barbara Pt.

1

Santa B.

Montecito

CALIFORNIA
HALIBUT

Summerland

ALONG COAST FOR:
BARRACUDA
KELP BASS
OLIVE ROCKFISH
REEFS ESPECIALLY GOOD
FOR BARRACUDA, KELP
BASS, AND WHITE SEABASS

Carpinteria

CARPINTERIA ST. BEACH

SANTA BARBARA CHANNEL

N

Statute Miles
0 1 2 3 4 5

0 1 2 3 4 5
Nautical Miles

NOT TO BE USED FOR NAVIGATION
See NOS Nautical Charts

Santa
Cruz I.

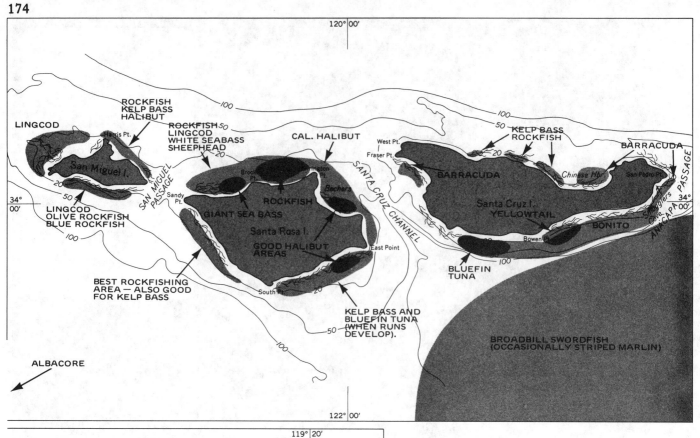

120° 00'

ROCKFISH
KELP BASS
HALIBUT

LINGCOD

ROCKFISH
LINGCOD
WHITE SEABASS
SHEEPHEAD

CAL. HALIBUT

Harris Pt.

San Miguel I.

50

20

Brock.
Pt.

ington
t.

Bechers

West Pt.

Fraser Pt.

KELP BASS
ROCKFISH

100

50

20

BARRACUDA

Chinese Hbr.

San Pedro Pt.

ANACAPA PASSAGE

34°
00'

SAN MIGUEL PASSAGE

Sandy
Pt.

ROCKFISH

GIANT SEA BASS

Santa Rosa I.

GOOD HALIBUT
AREAS

East Point

SANTA CRUZ CHANNEL

BARRACUDA

Santa Cruz I.
YELLOWTAIL

Bowen

Smugglers
Cove

BONITO

34°
00'

LINGCOD
OLIVE ROCKFISH
BLUE ROCKFISH

100

50

BEST ROCKFISHING
AREA — ALSO GOOD
FOR KELP BASS

South Pt.

100

20

50

KELP BASS AND
BLUEFIN TUNA
(WHEN RUNS
DEVELOP).

100

BLUEFIN
TUNA

BROADBILL SWORDFISH
(OCCASIONALLY STRIPED MARLIN)

ALBACORE

122° 00'

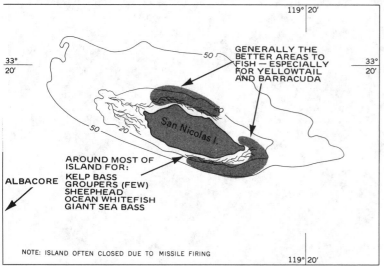

119° 20'

33°
20'

50

GENERALLY THE
BETTER AREAS TO
FISH — ESPECIALLY
FOR YELLOWTAIL
AND BARRACUDA

33°
20'

50

20

San Nicolas I.

ALBACORE

AROUND MOST OF
ISLAND FOR:
KELP BASS
GROUPERS (FEW)
SHEEPHEAD
OCEAN WHITEFISH
GIANT SEA BASS

NOTE: ISLAND OFTEN CLOSED DUE TO MISSILE FIRING

119° 20'

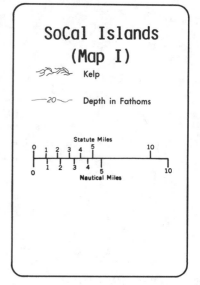

SoCal Islands
(Map I)

Kelp

─20─ Depth in Fathoms

Statute Miles

0 1 2 3 4 5   10

0 1 2 3 4 5   10

Nautical Miles

N

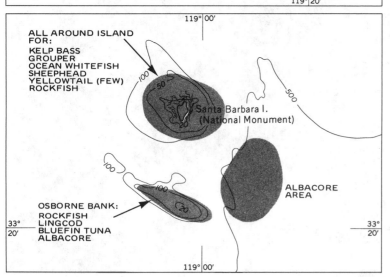

119° 00'

ALL AROUND ISLAND
FOR:
KELP BASS
GROUPER
OCEAN WHITEFISH
SHEEPHEAD
YELLOWTAIL (FEW)
ROCKFISH

100

50

20

Santa Barbara I.
(National Monument)

500

100

OSBORNE BANK:
ROCKFISH
LINGCOD
BLUEFIN TUNA
ALBACORE

100

20

ALBACORE
AREA

33°
20'

33°
20'

119° 00'

NOT TO BE USED FOR NAVIGATION
See NOS Nautical Charts

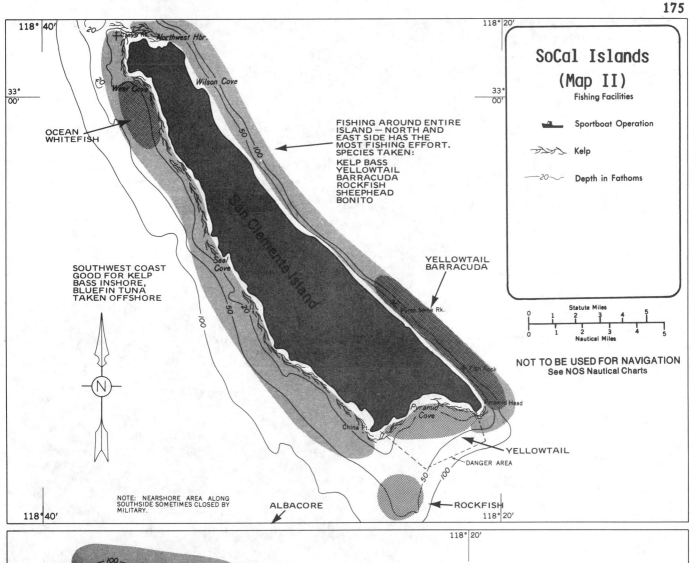

SoCal Islands (Map II)
Fishing Facilities

- Sportboat Operation
- Kelp
- Depth in Fathoms

OCEAN WHITEFISH

FISHING AROUND ENTIRE ISLAND — NORTH AND EAST SIDE HAS THE MOST FISHING EFFORT. SPECIES TAKEN:
KELP BASS
YELLOWTAIL
BARRACUDA
ROCKFISH
SHEEPHEAD
BONITO

YELLOWTAIL BARRACUDA

SOUTHWEST COAST GOOD FOR KELP BASS INSHORE, BLUEFIN TUNA TAKEN OFFSHORE

YELLOWTAIL

DANGER AREA

ALBACORE

ROCKFISH

NOTE: NEARSHORE AREA ALONG SOUTHSIDE SOMETIMES CLOSED BY MILITARY.

San Clemente Island

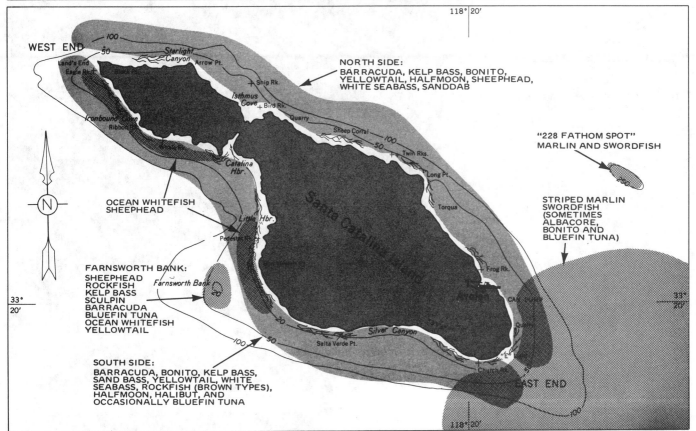

WEST END

NORTH SIDE:
BARRACUDA, KELP BASS, BONITO, YELLOWTAIL, HALFMOON, SHEEPHEAD, WHITE SEABASS, SANDDAB

"228 FATHOM SPOT" MARLIN AND SWORDFISH

STRIPED MARLIN SWORDFISH (SOMETIMES ALBACORE, BONITO AND BLUEFIN TUNA)

OCEAN WHITEFISH SHEEPHEAD

FARNSWORTH BANK:
SHEEPHEAD
ROCKFISH
KELP BASS
SCULPIN
BARRACUDA
BLUEFIN TUNA
OCEAN WHITEFISH
YELLOWTAIL

SOUTH SIDE:
BARRACUDA, BONITO, KELP BASS, SAND BASS, YELLOWTAIL, WHITE SEABASS, ROCKFISH (BROWN TYPES), HALFMOON, HALIBUT, AND OCCASIONALLY BLUEFIN TUNA

EAST END

Santa Catalina Island

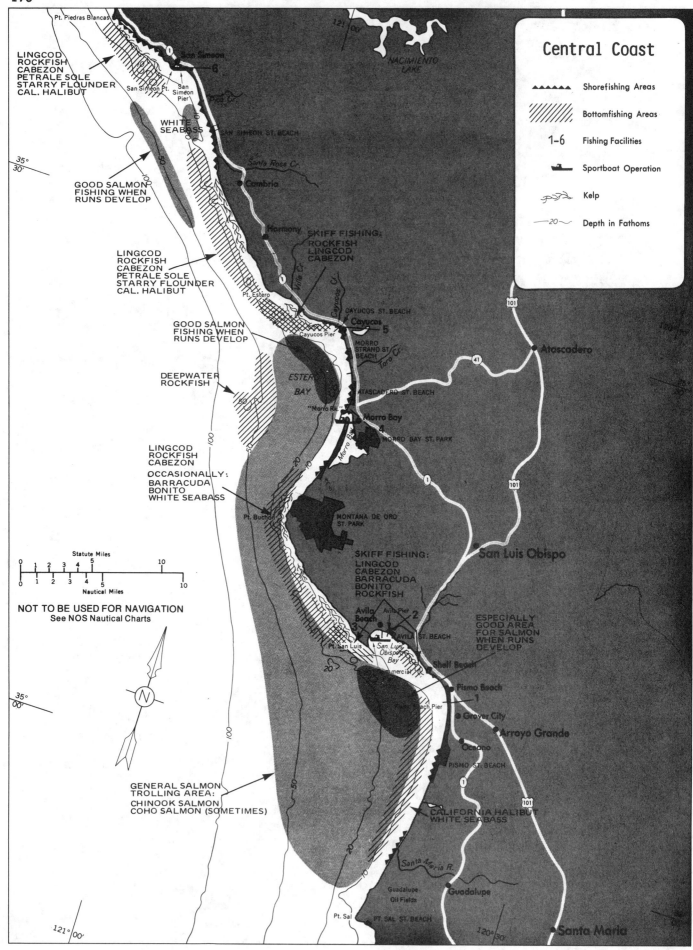

LINGCOD
ROCKFISH
CABEZON
PETRALE SOLE
STARRY FLOUNDER
CAL. HALIBUT

WHITE
SEABASS

GOOD SALMON
FISHING WHEN
RUNS DEVELOP

LINGCOD
ROCKFISH
CABEZON
PETRALE SOLE
STARRY FLOUNDER
CAL. HALIBUT

GOOD SALMON
FISHING WHEN
RUNS DEVELOP

DEEPWATER
ROCKFISH

LINGCOD
ROCKFISH
CABEZON
OCCASIONALLY:
BARRACUDA
BONITO
WHITE SEABASS

SKIFF FISHING:
ROCKFISH
LINGCOD
CABEZON

SKIFF FISHING:
LINGCOD
CABEZON
BARRACUDA
BONITO
ROCKFISH

ESPECIALLY
GOOD AREA
FOR SALMON
WHEN RUNS
DEVELOP

CALIFORNIA HALIBUT
WHITE SEABASS

GENERAL SALMON
TROLLING AREA:
CHINOOK SALMON
COHO SALMON (SOMETIMES)

Central Coast

▲▲▲▲▲ Shorefishing Areas

///// Bottomfishing Areas

1-6 Fishing Facilities

⛴ Sportboat Operation

≋ Kelp

—20— Depth in Fathoms

Statute Miles
0 1 2 3 4 5 ... 10

Nautical Miles
0 1 2 3 4 5 ... 10

NOT TO BE USED FOR NAVIGATION
See NOS Nautical Charts

N

Pt. Piedras Blancas
San Simeon
San Simeon Pt.
San Simeon Pier
San Simeon St. Beach
Santa Rosa Cr.
Cambria
Harmony
Pt. Estero
Cayucos St. Beach
Cayucos
Cayucos Pier
Morro Strand St. Beach
Estero Bay
Atascadero St. Beach
"Morro Rk"
Morro Bay
Morro Bay St. Park
Pt. Buchon
Montana de Oro St. Park
Avila Beach
Avila Pier
Avila St. Beach
Pt. San Luis
San Luis Obispo Bay
Commercial
Shell Beach
Pismo Beach
Pismo Beach Pier
Grover City
Arroyo Grande
Oceano
Pismo St. Beach
Santa Maria R.
Guadalupe Oil Fields
Guadalupe
Pt. Sal
Pt. Sal St. Beach
Santa Maria
San Luis Obispo
Atascadero
Nacimiento Lake

101
41
1

35° 30'
35° 00'
121° 00'
120° 30'
121° 00'

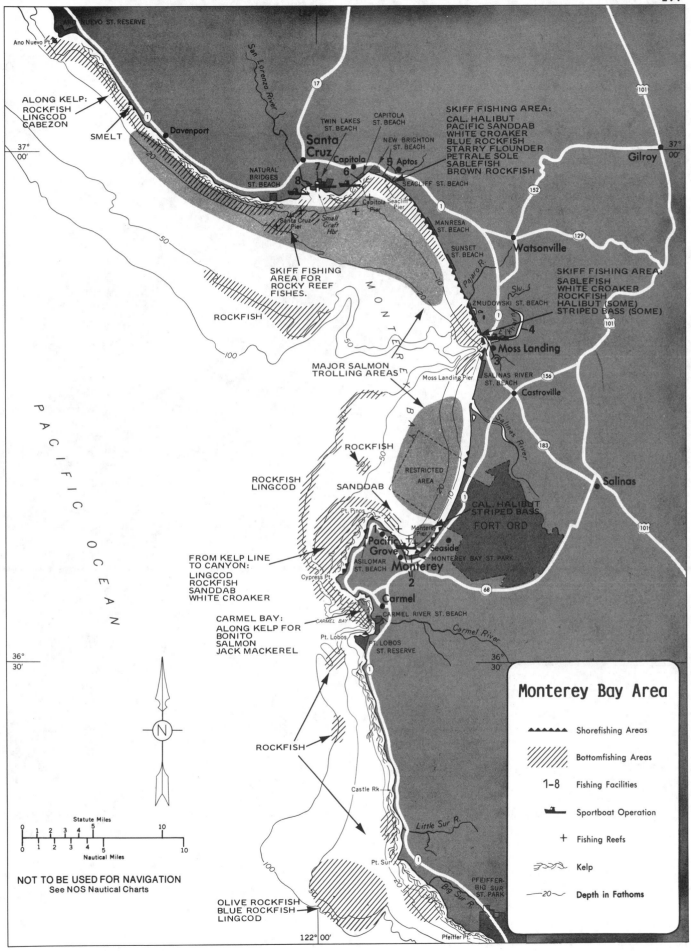

ALONG KELP:
ROCKFISH
LINGCOD
CABEZON

SMELT

37° 00'

Davenport

ANO NUEVO ST. RESERVE

Ano Nuevo Pt.

San Lorenzo River

17

101

TWIN LAKES ST. BEACH

CAPITOLA ST. BEACH

Santa Cruz

Capitola

NEW BRIGHTON ST. BEACH

Aptos

5

6

8

NATURAL BRIDGES ST. BEACH

Santa Cruz Pier

Small Craft Hbr.

Capitola Seacliff Pier

SEACLIFF ST. BEACH

SKIFF FISHING AREA:
CAL. HALIBUT
PACIFIC SANDDAB
WHITE CROAKER
BLUE ROCKFISH
STARRY FLOUNDER
PETRALE SOLE
SABLEFISH
BROWN ROCKFISH

Gilroy

37° 00'

152

1

MANRESA ST. BEACH

SUNSET ST. BEACH

Pajaro R.

Watsonville

129

SKIFF FISHING
AREA FOR
ROCKY REEF
FISHES.

MONTEREY

50

SKIFF FISHING AREA:
SABLEFISH
WHITE CROAKER
ROCKFISH
HALIBUT (SOME)
STRIPED BASS (SOME)

ROCKFISH

50

100

ZMUDOWSKI ST. BEACH

Slu.

Elk

4

101

Moss Landing

3

MAJOR SALMON
TROLLING AREAS

Moss Landing Pier

SALINAS RIVER ST. BEACH

156

Castroville

PACIFIC OCEAN

ROCKFISH

RESTRICTED
AREA

Salinas River

183

ROCKFISH
LINGCOD

50

SANDDAB

Pt. Pinos

20

CAL. HALIBUT
STRIPED BASS

Salinas

101

FORT ORD

FROM KELP LINE
TO CANYON:
LINGCOD
ROCKFISH
SANDDAB
WHITE CROAKER

Pacific
Grove

ASILOMAR
ST. BEACH

Monterey Pier

Seaside

MONTEREY BAY ST. PARK

Monterey

2

68

Cypress Pt.

Carmel

36° 30'

CARMEL BAY:
ALONG KELP FOR
BONITO
SALMON
JACK MACKEREL

CARMEL BAY

CARMEL RIVER ST. BEACH

Carmel River

36° 30'

Pt. Lobos

PT. LOBOS
ST. RESERVE

1

N

ROCKFISH

Castle Rk.

Little Sur R.

Pt. Sur

1

20

Big Sur R.

PFEIFFER-
BIG SUR
ST. PARK

Statute Miles

0 1 2 3 4 5 ... 10

0 1 2 3 4 5 ... 10

Nautical Miles

NOT TO BE USED FOR NAVIGATION
See NOS Nautical Charts

OLIVE ROCKFISH
BLUE ROCKFISH
LINGCOD

100

122° 00'

Pfeiffer Pt.

Monterey Bay Area

▲▲▲▲▲ Shorefishing Areas

///// Bottomfishing Areas

1-8 Fishing Facilities

🛥 Sportboat Operation

+ Fishing Reefs

〜〜 Kelp

—20〜 Depth in Fathoms

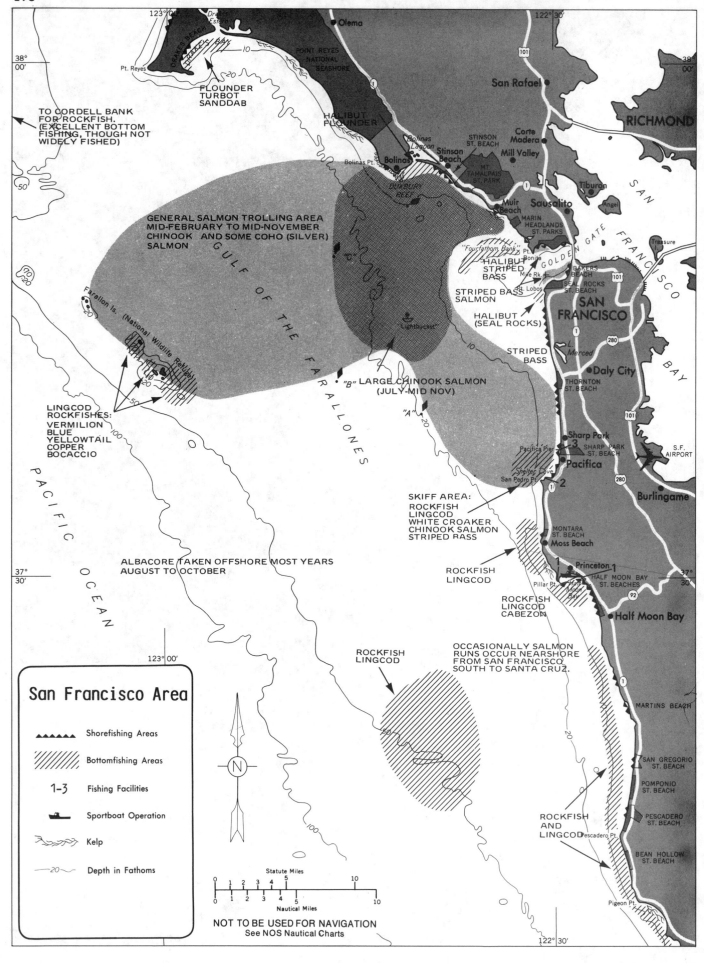

TO CORDELL BANK
FOR ROCKFISH.
(EXCELLENT BOTTOM
FISHING, THOUGH NOT
WIDELY FISHED)

FLOUNDER
TURBOT
SANDDAB

HALIBUT
FLOUNDER

GENERAL SALMON TROLLING AREA
MID-FEBRUARY TO MID-NOVEMBER
CHINOOK AND SOME COHO (SILVER)
SALMON

GULF OF THE FARALLONES

LINGCOD
ROCKFISHES:
VERMILION
BLUE
YELLOWTAIL
COPPER
BOCACCIO

Farallon Is. (National Wildlife Refuge)

"Fourfathom Bank"

HALIBUT
STRIPED
BASS

STRIPED BASS
SALMON

HALIBUT
(SEAL ROCKS)

STRIPED
BASS

"B" LARGE CHINOOK SALMON
(JULY-MID NOV)

"A"

SKIFF AREA:
ROCKFISH
LINGCOD
WHITE CROAKER
CHINOOK SALMON
STRIPED BASS

ROCKFISH
LINGCOD

ROCKFISH
LINGCOD
CABEZON

ALBACORE TAKEN OFFSHORE MOST YEARS
AUGUST TO OCTOBER

PACIFIC OCEAN

ROCKFISH
LINGCOD

OCCASIONALLY SALMON
RUNS OCCUR NEARSHORE
FROM SAN FRANCISCO
SOUTH TO SANTA CRUZ.

ROCKFISH
AND
LINGCOD

RICHMOND

San Rafael

Corte
Madera

Mill Valley

Tiburon

Angel

Sausalito

SAN
FRANCISCO

Treasure

Bakers
Beach

SEAL
ROCKS
ST. BEACH

Pt. Lobos

L.
Merced

Daly City

THORNTON
ST. BEACH

Sharp Park

Sharp Park
ST. BEACH

Pacifica

Pacifica Pier

Shelter Cove

San Pedro Pt.

S.F.
AIRPORT

Burlingame

MONTARA
ST. BEACH

Moss Beach

Princeton

HALF MOON BAY
ST. BEACHES

Pillar Pt.

Half Moon Bay

MARTINS BEACH

SAN GREGORIO
ST. BEACH

POMPONIO
ST. BEACH

PESCADERO
ST. BEACH

Pescadero Pt.

BEAN HOLLOW
ST. BEACH

Pigeon Pt.

Olema

POINT REYES
NATIONAL
SEASHORE

Drakes Estero

Pt. Reyes

Bolinas
Lagoon

Bolinas Pt.

Bolinas

STINSON
ST. BEACH

Stinson
Beach

MT. TAMALPAIS
ST. PARK

DUXBURY
REEF

Muir
Beach

MARIN
HEADLANDS
ST. PARKS

Pt.
Bonita

GOLDEN GATE

Mile Rk.

SAN FRANCISCO BAY

San Francisco Area

▲▲▲▲ Shorefishing Areas

▨▨▨ Bottomfishing Areas

1-3 Fishing Facilities

🚤 Sportboat Operation

〜〜 Kelp

—20— Depth in Fathoms

Statute Miles
0 1 2 3 4 5   10

0 1 2 3 4 5   10
Nautical Miles

NOT TO BE USED FOR NAVIGATION
See NOS Nautical Charts

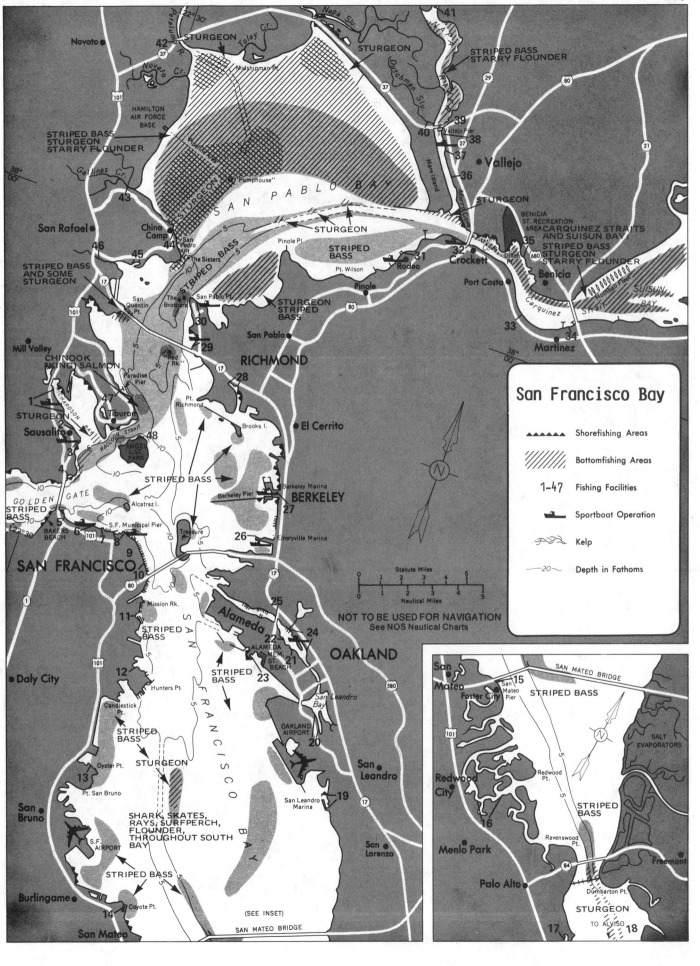

San Francisco Bay

▲▲▲▲ Shorefishing Areas

/////// Bottomfishing Areas

1-47 Fishing Facilities

⛴ Sportboat Operation

〜〜 Kelp

—20— Depth in Fathoms

NOT TO BE USED FOR NAVIGATION
See NOS Nautical Charts

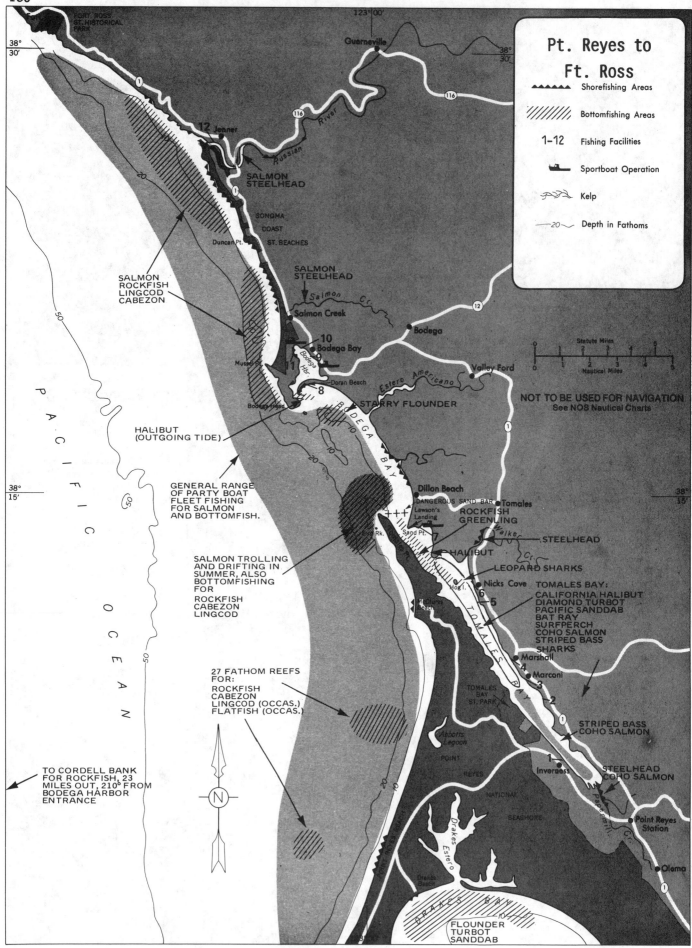

FORT ROSS
ST. HISTORICAL
PARK

38°
30'

123°00'

Guerneville

38°
30'

Pt. Reyes to
Ft. Ross

▲▲▲ Shorefishing Areas

/// Bottomfishing Areas

1-12 Fishing Facilities

Sportboat Operation

Kelp

—20— Depth in Fathoms

1

20

12 Jenner

River

Russian

116

SALMON
STEELHEAD

SONOMA
COAST
ST. BEACHES

Duncan Pt.

SALMON
STEELHEAD

Salmon Cr.

SALMON
ROCKFISH
LINGCOD
CABEZON

Salmon Creek

Bodega

12

10
Bodega Bay

Valley Ford

11 Bodega
Hbr.

Doran Beach

Estero
Americano

Mussel Pt.

8

Bodega Head

STARRY FLOUNDER

HALIBUT
(OUTGOING TIDE)

B O D E G A   B A Y

NOT TO BE USED FOR NAVIGATION
See NOS Nautical Charts

Statute Miles

Nautical Miles

50

38°
15'

38°
15'

GENERAL RANGE
OF PARTY BOAT
FLEET FISHING
FOR SALMON
AND BOTTOMFISH.

Dillon Beach

DANGEROUS SAND BAR

Tomales

Lawson's
Landing

ROCKFISH
GREENLING

Walke

STEELHEAD

Sand Pt.

HALIBUT

LEOPARD SHARKS

Nicks Cove

6

TOMALES BAY:
CALIFORNIA HALIBUT
DIAMOND TURBOT
PACIFIC SANDDAB
BAT RAY
SURFPERCH
COHO SALMON
STRIPED BASS
SHARKS

SALMON TROLLING
AND DRIFTING IN
SUMMER, ALSO
BOTTOMFISHING
FOR
ROCKFISH
CABEZON
LINGCOD

Hog I.

5

T
O
M
A
L
E
S

B
A
Y

Marshall

4

Marconi

3

P A C I F I C

O C E A N

50

TOMALES
BAY
ST. PARK

2

1

27 FATHOM REEFS
FOR:
ROCKFISH
CABEZON
LINGCOD (OCCAS.)
FLATFISH (OCCAS.)

STRIPED BASS
COHO SALMON

1
Inverness

STEELHEAD
COHO SALMON

Abbotts
Lagoon

POINT

REYES

Point Reyes
Station

N

NATIONAL

SEASHORE

Drakes
Estero

Olema

1

TO CORDELL BANK
FOR ROCKFISH, 23
MILES OUT, 210° FROM
BODEGA HARBOR
ENTRANCE

20

Drakes
Beach

D R A K E S   B A Y

FLOUNDER
TURBOT
SANDDAB

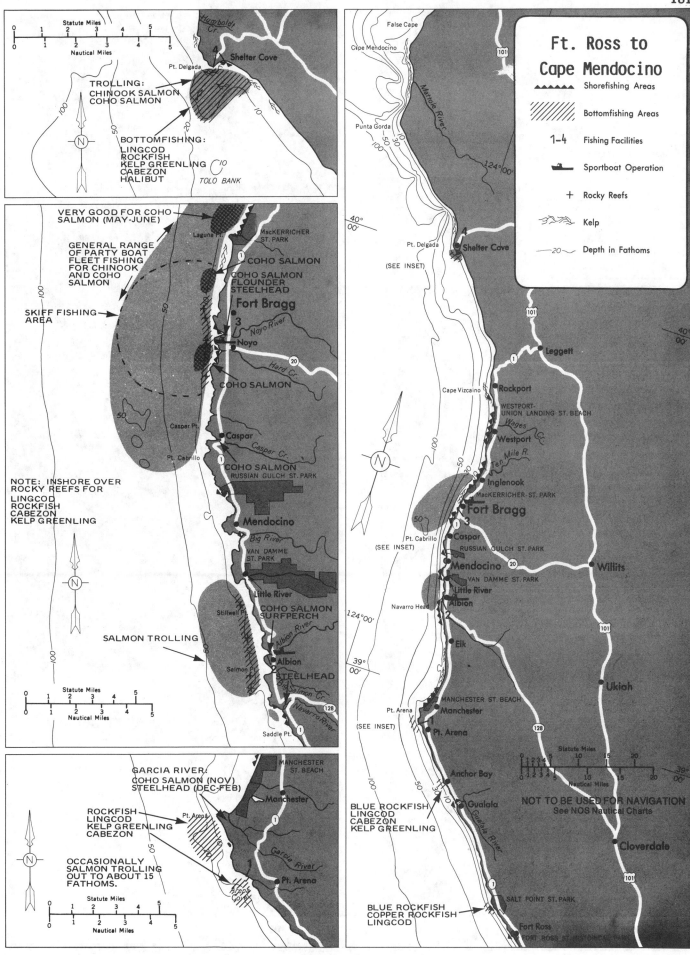

Inset (top left):

Statute Miles
0 1 2 3 4 5

Nautical Miles
0 1 2 3 4 5

Humboldt Cr.

Shelter Cove

Pt. Delgada

TROLLING:
CHINOOK SALMON
COHO SALMON

BOTTOMFISHING:
LINGCOD
ROCKFISH
KELP GREENLING
CABEZON
HALIBUT

N

TOLO BANK

Middle left inset:

VERY GOOD FOR COHO
SALMON (MAY-JUNE)

Laguna Pt.

MacKERRICHER
ST. PARK

GENERAL RANGE
OF PARTY BOAT
FLEET FISHING
FOR CHINOOK
AND COHO
SALMON

COHO SALMON

COHO SALMON
FLOUNDER
STEELHEAD

Fort Bragg

SKIFF FISHING
AREA

Noyo River

Noyo

Hare Cr.

COHO SALMON

Caspar Pt.

Caspar

Caspar Cr.

Pt. Cabrillo

COHO SALMON
RUSSIAN GULCH ST. PARK

NOTE: INSHORE OVER
ROCKY REEFS FOR
LINGCOD
ROCKFISH
CABEZON
KELP GREENLING

N

Mendocino

Big River

VAN DAMME
ST. PARK

Little River

Stillwell Pt.

COHO SALMON
SURFPERCH

SALMON TROLLING

Salmon Pt.

Albion River

Albion

STEELHEAD

Big Salmon Cr.

Navarro River

Saddle Pt.

Statute Miles
0 1 2 3 4 5

Nautical Miles
0 1 2 3 4 5

Bottom left inset:

MANCHESTER
ST. BEACH

GARCIA RIVER:
COHO SALMON (NOV)
STEELHEAD (DEC-FEB)

Manchester

ROCKFISH
LINGCOD
KELP GREENLING
CABEZON

Pt. Arena

OCCASIONALLY
SALMON TROLLING
OUT TO ABOUT 15
FATHOMS.

Garcia River

Pt. Arena

Arena Cove

N

Statute Miles
0 1 2 3 4 5

Nautical Miles
0 1 2 3 4 5

Main map (right):

Ft. Ross to
Cape Mendocino

Shorefishing Areas

Bottomfishing Areas

1-4   Fishing Facilities

Sportboat Operation

+   Rocky Reefs

Kelp

20   Depth in Fathoms

False Cape

Cape Mendocino

Mattole River

Punta Gorda

101

Pt. Delgada

Shelter Cove

(SEE INSET)

101

Leggett

Cape Vizcaino

Rockport

WESTPORT-
UNION LANDING ST. BEACH

Wages Cr.

Westport

Ten Mile R.

Inglenook

MacKERRICHER ST. PARK

Fort Bragg

Pt. Cabrillo

Caspar

(SEE INSET)

RUSSIAN GULCH ST. PARK

Mendocino

Willits

VAN DAMME ST. PARK

Navarro Head

Little River

Albion

Elk

101

Ukiah

MANCHESTER ST. BEACH

Pt. Arena

Manchester

Pt. Arena

(SEE INSET)

128

Statute Miles
0 1 2 3 4 5 10 15 20

Nautical Miles
0 1 2 3 4 5 10 15 20

Anchor Bay

BLUE ROCKFISH
LINGCOD
CABEZON
KELP GREENLING

Gualala

Gualala River

NOT TO BE USED FOR NAVIGATION
See NOS Nautical Charts

Cloverdale

101

1

SALT POINT ST. PARK

BLUE ROCKFISH
COPPER ROCKFISH
LINGCOD

Fort Ross
FORT ROSS ST. HISTORICAL PARK

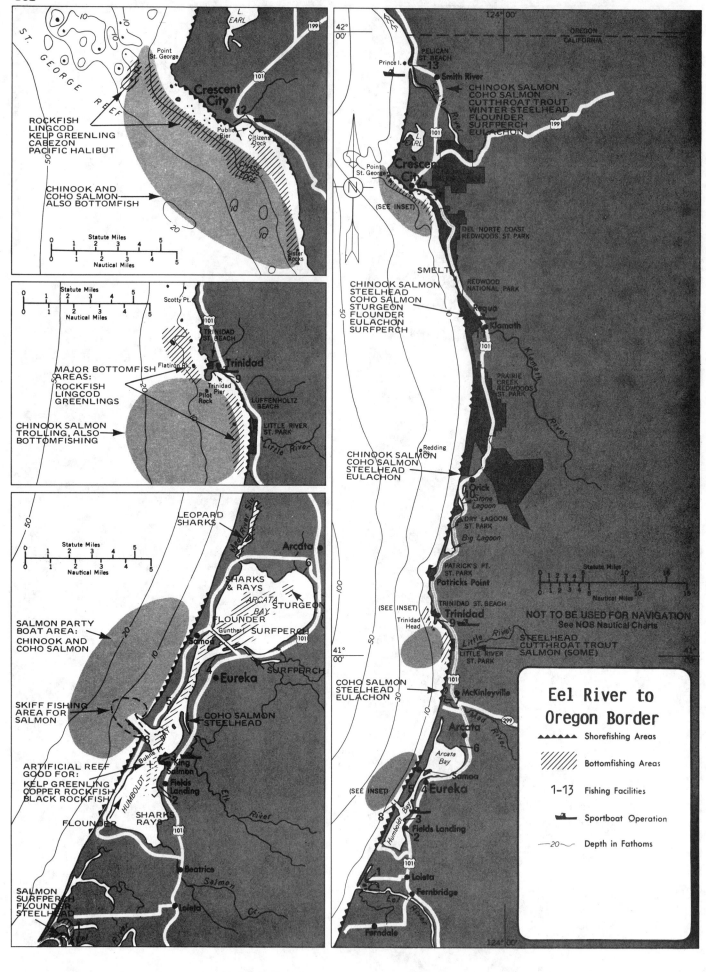

ROCKFISH
LINGCOD
KELP GREENLING
CABEZON
PACIFIC HALIBUT

CHINOOK AND
COHO SALMON
ALSO BOTTOMFISH

MAJOR BOTTOMFISH
AREAS:
ROCKFISH
LINGCOD
GREENLINGS

CHINOOK SALMON
TROLLING, ALSO
BOTTOMFISHING

LEOPARD
SHARKS

SHARKS
& RAYS
ARCATA BAY
STURGEON
FLOUNDER
SURFPERCH

SALMON PARTY
BOAT AREA:
CHINOOK AND
COHO SALMON

SURFPERCH

SKIFF FISHING
AREA FOR
SALMON

COHO SALMON
STEELHEAD

ARTIFICIAL REEF
GOOD FOR:
KELP GREENLING
COPPER ROCKFISH
BLACK ROCKFISH

SHARKS
RAYS

FLOUNDER

SALMON
SURFPERCH
FLOUNDER
STEELHEAD

Statute Miles
Nautical Miles

CHINOOK SALMON
COHO SALMON
CUTTHROAT TROUT
WINTER STEELHEAD
FLOUNDER
SURFPERCH
EULACHON

SMELT

CHINOOK SALMON
STEELHEAD
COHO SALMON
STURGEON
FLOUNDER
EULACHON
SURFPERCH

CHINOOK SALMON
COHO SALMON
STEELHEAD
EULACHON

Statute Miles
Nautical Miles

NOT TO BE USED FOR NAVIGATION
See NOS Nautical Charts

STEELHEAD
CUTTHROAT TROUT
SALMON (SOME)

COHO SALMON
STEELHEAD
EULACHON

Eel River to Oregon Border

▲▲▲▲ Shorefishing Areas

///// Bottomfishing Areas

1-13 Fishing Facilities

⛴ Sportboat Operation

—20~ Depth in Fathoms

BOOK III

More
Good
Stuff

Party Boat Lessons

The sportfishing fleets found from San Diego, California to Port Angeles, Washington comprise some of the most competitive recreational industries in the West. Boat captains must not only compete against nature, but against the rest of the fleet as well. Despite the camaraderie shared by many skippers, the bottom line is that each is vying for customers to patronize their vessels.

Pick the Right Boat

What makes one boat better than another? How does the recreational angler decide which sportfisher to select? To begin with, it is important to inspect the operation first hand if possible. Go down to the dock on a day you're not fishing. Check out the boat. Is it clean? Does it seem to be maintained properly? What about safety equipment—is it visible and accessible?

Ask the skipper or crew if you can board and look around. Does it have a galley in which you would want to eat? Does it have a posted menu of the food it serves?

Go below deck. If the boat has bunks for overnight sleeping, what are they like? Is there proper ventilation, clean sheets, pillows and adequate lighting? All of these facets of the vessel will contribute to your overall comfort and safety on a future trip. For many anglers, these amenities are ultimately more important than the number of fish caught.

On that note, there are other performance elements you can examine to evaluate the success of a given boat operation. For example, monitor fish counts. Although some sportfishers may "fudge" these dock totals from time to time, the fish count can give you some idea of just who the real "fish hunters" are. Talk to other anglers. When fishermen have a good experience with a particular boat and crew, they want to communicate that to fellow enthusiasts. Similarly, if there is a "bad rap" on a boat, other anglers will frequently relay that information. Ask pertinent questions such as "does the crew fish?"

Does the captain allow "deadheads" to hog the stern and the best baits? Is the crew ready, willing, and able when it comes to getting fish? Does the skipper seem to have solid control over his vessel and crew?

Be aware of cut rate prices and special deals that are advertised over and over for certain boats. Usually, but not always, the better operations aren't going to "give it away." They don't have to. A crew works hard to build up a reputation. Much of it is predicated on word-of-mouth testimonials among fellow anglers. Boats of this caliber will routinely carry more people because the fisherman will often return to a sportfisher that has had a successful outing.

The bottom line is that you get what you pay for—or at least you should. Be selective and careful to link up with the best operators you can. Then stay loyal to these guys, pass the word along about their boat, and tip generously!

Learn to Ask More Questions!

How can you insure that you are getting a fair shake from the captain, crew, and landing operators? The answer is simple: ask more questions. For example, inquire as to who will be running the vessel. Is the skipper the owner? Does he actually pilot the boat anymore, or does he primarily stay home to collect the checks?

Are you getting a veteran captain? What is his reputation like—surly, cantankerous, polite, laid back, aggressive? More importantly, with what type of personality do *you* feel most comfortable for a long day on the water? Understand that some of the best skippers who seem to always find fish are some of the worst when it comes to public relations. Others are great public relations people but lousy fish hunters. Try to find the best of both worlds—a good fisherman who also cares about his passengers.

As I mentioned, some boat owners have become absentee skippers. Either their business is too diverse with multiple boat ownership, or they have become lazy, or both. In either case, the vessel's reputation might be based more on past glory than how it is run today. Check it out—who is running the boat and what are his credentials? Do this *before* you charter the sportfisher or sign up for an open-party trip.

Too many skippers have taken the public for granted. Business is never "too good" in a down economy, even if the tuna or salmon show up in bountiful numbers. A shrewd party boat operator realizes that he is in the entertainment business as much as the fishing business. Customers should be treated properly to insure that they will return when the bite slows down and conditions get tough. This is when the better operations shine with loyal passengers showing up at the dock.

As a party boat passenger, voice your complaints to either the charter master, boat captain, or landing operator if you feel that something is wrong with the trip. Corrections can't be made unless the problem is addressed to the appropriate people. You wouldn't expect poor medical treatment from your doctor; a faulty job from your auto mechanic; or a lousy meal served at your favorite restaurant. There is no reason to accept poor skippering or crew work from your sport boat operator. Speak up!

Skippers on the Cutting Edge

Let's face it, there are good skippers and bad skippers, and some who fall somewhere between the two extremes. As director of the Eagle Claw Fishing Schools, I am in the business of chartering top-of-the-line sportfishing vessels. I must have those captains in the first category—the good ones—if I am to operate a prestigious on-the-water seminar program.

Did you ever wonder what separates the cream of the crop from the rest of the many people running sport boats along the West Coast? What distinguishes one skipper from being on that "cutting edge" of success while others are resigned to simply running adequate boats at best?

Here are some impressions which seem to clearly represent some of the things the best captains routinely do time after time which raises them to the top of the class.

Boat Handling

Invariably skippers must rest and let the back-up captain or first mate operate the vessel. This is an issue of crew discipline and recruitment that I'll talk about shortly. What I want to focus on, instead, is how the better captains seem to maintain an articulate control of their sportfishers.

For example, the real pro generally sets up his boat on a pinnacle or high spot after considerable monitoring of the ship's electronics. In many cases, such as shallow water rockfishing or working rock piles for calico bass, it is critical to get a pinpoint anchor set. Although the passengers often grow impatient, the shrewd skipper must frequently make many trial runs over a particular hot spot before he can position the boat properly while at anchor. Nothing short of precise accuracy will do for the captain on that cutting edge.

Similarly, when offshore tuna fishing, watch how the better skippers always seem to have a routine. They position their boats so the anglers quickly know that the drift will always start on either the starboard or port side of the vessel. There is often so much confusion when the fishermen hear the cry "JIG STRIKE," that anglers will often scramble from side to side in the stern as they jockey for position.

A captain who announces this simple routine of designating one side as the singular area to start fishing minimizes chaos and greatly improves the catch ratio. Rather than stopping and letting the passengers fish anywhere, helter-skelter, the smart skipper maintains control of the boat and establishes a sense of order for the trip.

Controlling the Crew

The best party boat operations typically involve a well-disciplined crew, carrying out the orders and representing the skipper in their on-deck behavior. I have seen many times in which a captain barely moves out from behind the shelter of the wheel house to scrutinize what his crew is doing on the deck.

Paying customers do not, for the most part, want to see deckhands fishing; nor do they want to shout for a gaff much more than that first request. The captains who pilot the better boats seem to always get personally involved with their crews when it comes to running the deck.

I have seen skippers like Buzz Brizendine of the "Prowler," Nick Cates of the "New Lo Ann," the late Steve Giffen of the "Holiday," or Ron Hart of the "Condor," routinely walk the deck. They frequently jump up on the bait tank to supervise the chumming first hand. It seems that these guys always know what their crews are doing and keep an eye out for those passengers who need help.

Better operators also seem to keep their crews together for a long time. Passengers like to feel a sense of community if not "family" between the skippers, the deckhands, and even the galley cook. Usually, when you encounter an operation that seems to regularly rotate through crew members, beware that this may reflect problems with the captain and his ability to run a tight organization.

Innovation

Those skippers on that cutting edge also seem to be some of the most innovative fishermen in the West. You will find that many boat operators are simply "me too" type captains. Their daily runs, whether for tuna or sand bass, simply amount to a "same time-same place" approach. Those on that cutting edge are willing to break from the "pack" and try to pioneer some new territory or a new plan of attack on their own.

I recall a classic example of this while fishing one day with the late Captain "Cookie" Cook out of San Pedro. For days the Huntington Flats and the Horseshoe Kelp had been pounded by every small yacht and party boat alike during the annual sand bass migration in the late spring. The bite was primarily concentrated in 90 to 120 feet of water on a hard bottom. Well, as luck would have it, we started out at this depth along with an awesome armada of over 150 other boats. By 10:00 a.m. it had become clear that something had changed and the bite was off.

Cook decided to bolt away from the fleet, heading south to the shallow waters off Huntington Beach. With decades of boat operating experience behind him, he explained how sometimes smaller schools of sand bass travel away from the mass and head into the shallow confines, not too far beyond the surf line.

Working in 30-40 foot depths, Cook found that "mother lode" of shallow biters. There were no other boats within five miles of us. By 1:00 p.m. we had all 30 anglers limited out with sand bass and a bonus round of keeper-size barracuda. Captain Cook radioed for the other boats to later join us and share in this new honey hole.

Captains like Billy Stevens, formerly of the "Cherokee Geisha," similarly demonstrate that innovative bend when it comes to locating hard-to-find offshore yellowtail and tuna. Stevens—a veteran airplane pilot—might actually fly his small plane looking for floating kelp paddies. He then radios the information to a small group of other boats. Amazingly, only a few shrewd captains are willing to share in Stevens' flying expenses, in exchange for receiving valuable coordinates for finding these floating "yellowtail motels."

Innovation also takes the form of making radical changes in tackle and lure presentation. The pioneering of San Diego's famous long-range skippers in developing an approach utilizing big surface plugs for tuna is a key example of this type of innovation. Up until recently, surface plugs were used primarily in Hawaii and for coastal striped bass fishing. Now, this obscure tactic produces some of the most spectacular tuna and dorado fishing on our local waters because the long-range operators had the vision to try these new baits deep into Mexican waters.

A Demand for Precision

The better skippers are adamant when it comes to precise presentation of lures or bait. Watch these guys carefully when they come down from the wheel house to put on a casting demonstration. Their tackle might look beat up at times, but I'll bet the rod, reel and line are precisely balanced for what they are doing. You won't see excellent anglers like these men casting a metal jig with a live bait stick, nor will you see them fooling around.

One of the most articulate captains to ever fish the Southern California scene is now-turned tackle manufacturer Russ Izor. A passenger on Captain Izor's "First String" would invariably receive a lecture on proper tackle selection from hook, line and sinker to rod and reel.

Many times Izor was confronted with horrible, weak puny anchovies while trying to fish Catalina Island in the summer months. His solution was simple: switch to an 8 foot spinning rod, lighter 12 to 15 pound test mono, and a smaller hook. Now the angler can more easily cast tiny pinhead 'chovies, with the little baits swimming better dragging against the fine diameter line. I might add that Izor's concern for precision tackle left a lasting impression with me and is a major point of emphasis on my Eagle Claw Saltwater Fishing Schools.

The Gambler Aspect

Sometimes it takes more than a concern for precision combined with innovation to find fish. Some of the best trips I recall occurred as a result of a skipper parlaying a long shot into a bonanza.

Captain Irv Grisbeck on the "Trilene Big Game" played the high-stakes game on a 3 1/2 day school I chartered during midsummer tuna season. After the first day, in rough seas out 90 miles, it was clear that the bite had fizzled and we were in store for two more days of scratch fishing at best.

Grisbeck discussed the situation candidly with my instructors and myself. One option—a calculated long shot—would be to motor south another 12 to 14 hours to the Benitos Island chain. Although we would be essentially sacrificing about one whole day of fishing time, in exchange for only about one solid day of fishing, we all agreed the risk was worth it.

As it turned out, we encountered some of the most unexpected, big 25 to 35 pound class yellowtail fishing of the season at Benitos. Our students got the trip of a lifetime, in much calmer seas, although they lost one day of fishing. Grisbeck's gamble–including absorbing the extra fuel costs—paid off in spades.

Other skippers like Captains Mark Pisano of the "Islander," Paul Strasser of the "Monte Carlo," and Fred Benko on the "Condor" are legendary in their commitment to push the time to its maximum limit. These captains depend extensively upon solid one-day yellowtail, tuna, or ling cod action during the height of the season. One-day boats also have an optimal range of about 90 to 110 miles maximum, if they are to turn around and get back to port the same day.

Often it comes down to "no guts—no glory" for the one-day fleet. The skippers must shoot craps and make the longest possible run in order to find new schools of fish. In addition to checking the fish count at the dock, consider asking when the day-boat operators usually return to the dock. The skippers who stay out the longest are usually the ones with the best scores of yellowtail and tuna.

Patience and Perseverance

The captains who are on this cutting edge of angling and fish-finding professionalism also demonstrate the highest degree of patience and perseverance. In a nutshell, they don't panic, and they don't give up.

Skippers of this caliber have been there before when it comes to piloting the boat on your particular outing. They have fished in full moon conditions, green water, cold water, and the roughest seas. They have had to work with poor bait, small bait and even no bait. Their wealth of experience combined with a gutsy approach to their profession gives them the edge over adversity compared to most private boaters and less accomplished captains.

You have to understand that these are truly "men of the sea." Without creating an excessively romantic portrait of these top sportfishing skippers, the fact remains that they are running their boats because they love what they do. Most likely they can find better paying jobs with more reasonable hours. They entered this profession because of their passion for both catching and finding fish. Unlike the less-pressured locales like Hawaii or Florida, these skippers on the West Coast really have to be with the "program" if they are to tally fish in our local waters.

Lessons to be Learned

I'm not trying to simply glorify these party boat captains. This portrait of the top skippers of this particular fleet should give the recreational angler a better idea of what to look for when selecting a first class, well-run party or charter boat anywhere along the Pacific Coast.

There are valuable lessons to be learned from the attributes of these premier skippers. The values, attitudes, and approaches they internalize are certainly worthwhile for the recreational angler to emulate. These are the individuals who routinely catch the most and largest fish year after year. Their success, like that of any angler, is more a result of hard work than pure dumb luck.

Study these captains carefully. There is room for more fishermen on that cutting edge!

More Party Boat Strategy

The San Diego fleet of sportfishers is widely recognized as one of the premier operations for this type of marine angling. Invariably, saltwater buffs from beginner to expert alike from virtually all over the West venture south to San Diego to chase yellowtail, albacore, and tuna. These are some of the most valued species caught by sportfishing boats along the Pacific Coast.

The landings that operate out of San Diego collectively offer the widest range of sportfishing boats from which to choose. These landings can accommodate you, whether you prefer a half, three-quarters, full, or multi-day trip. San Diego party boat skippers realize that their job is easier when the passengers have some basic knowledge of the inside secrets of fishing the South Coast waters. A customer who has had a successful trip is more likely to enjoy himself and therefore more likely to book additional trips.

Here then are some of the insiders' tips from six of San Diego's finest sportfishing skippers. These tips might help you to dramatically improve your catch whether you are on a party boat or your own private vessel from San Diego to Coos Bay, irrespective of the species you are attempting to catch.

Come Prepared!

Captain Billy Stephens, a veteran charter boat and open party boat captain, states that many passengers have little notion as to what to bring out on an all-day trip fishing the Pacific.

"Check the dock counts," notes Stephens, "particularly in the prime summer months. See what we are catching. The kind of fish that show up in the counts tells the angler something about the test line he should have on his reels, the lures to use, the hook size, and the type of bait to select." Stephens emphasizes that veteran party boat anglers carefully monitor the dock totals, then gear up with an array of rods and reels so they can handle almost any contingency. Scrutinize these reports from Seattle to Cabo San Lucas, utilizing local sports pages or weekly outdoor tabloids.

Develop Rapport

Veteran skipper Nick Cates of Point Loma's "New Lo Ann" firmly believes that this communication skill is vital in becoming an accomplished party boater. "Find a crew you really like," stresses Cates, "develop rapport with them, and stay with that boat. These guys will then give you the inside scoop once you develop that rapport." Captain Cates notes that the crew often reserves the better baits in the tank for customers they feel have shown a sincere interest in wanting to learn and who are willing to follow instructions.

Ralph Botticelli pilots Point Loma's half-day boat, the "Daily Double." He, too, encourages his passengers to immediately introduce themselves to his crew to set up a learning situation for the day's outing. "Also," says Botticelli, "talk to other successful anglers. Don't be afraid to ask for tips and help."

Hooking Live Baits

The party boat fisherman can also learn how to properly hook a bait from a veteran crew member. "Collar a deckhand," suggests Captain Cates, "and have him show you how to hook the baits. This is the most important thing to live bait fishing. If you learn this, you will have a better chance of catching a fish on a slow day."

Veteran skippers emphasize that the angler must closely scale the size of the hook to the test line he is casting. "An extremely small hook on 30 pound line makes no sense at all," claims Captain Irv Grisbeck of the "Trilene Big Game." "If you fish 30 to 40 pound mono, you have to use a larger hook that can withstand the pressure when you set up with the heavy line."

Captain Donny Boulette is a recognized big fish expert. "When you are chasing big fish like tuna with heavy line," notes Boulette, "don't make the mistake of using a hook that is too small. The hook size must be matched with the bait and fish. People fail to realize that a big tuna will hit a large #7/0 hook with a tiny pinhead anchovy on it."

Fish the Bow

Party boats are sometimes difficult to fish in a wide-open bite with novice anglers all bunched up in the stern. Many fishermen prefer to stay planted in the rear of the boat—often becoming so-called "stern hogs"—because this is where all the chumming occurs.

Interestingly enough, one of the most productive yet generally unfished areas of the boat is at the other end in the bow. According to Captain Grisbeck, "there comes a point where you can't get beyond the upwind corner of the stern. When this happens, consider moving to the bow. The chum from the stern gets pushed up the boat's keel and, on many boats, ends up swirling in the bow."

This explains why many shrewd party boat fishermen often relocate from the stern to the bow after that first flurry of activity, following, for example, a jig stop on tuna. There is less chance of becoming broken off by a mass of converging lines. There is also less frenzy and confusion with fewer anglers working the bow and, as Grisbeck observes, a migration of chum bait that may actually end up in the front portion of the vessel.

Understand Kelp Paddies

When the action gets really heated up in the southernmost waters, it usually coincides with the appearance of floating offshore kelp paddies. These clumps of broken kelp can become a virtual "oasis" in a wide area of otherwise "dead" water. They are sometimes affectionately referred to as "yellowtail hotels," since these fish and members of the tuna family will frequently gravitate to the schools of bait found under the floating kelp stringers. Interestingly, floating kelp paddies like these can also "hitchhike" on a warm current and travel all the way to San Francisco Bay.

One of the most critical mistakes the neophyte makes is casting too soon as the sportfisher approaches the kelp paddy. "It is important not to cast too early," observes Captain Stephens. "Give the boat a chance to stop. Wait for the skipper to give the 'okay' over the P.A. system. The fish—particularly yellowtail—will usually charge the boat once it stops." Thus, by waiting to cast, the lines will be more spread out, keeping tangles and lost fish to a minimum.

Another often overlooked dimension to working the paddies is to fish considerably deeper than is typically done on most party boats. Captain Buzz Brizendine of the "Prowler" has put on some convincing demonstrations using heavier sinkers to catch not only more but also larger 'tails and tuna by getting the bait into deeper strike zones.

"It's just Greek to most anglers," explains Brizendine. "They just don't realize how much more effective it is to use a fairly heavy sinker on kelp paddy fish. Most of the yellowtail and tuna found under paddies are at 10 to 15 fathoms, not near the surface. It's like freshwater bass fishing—if you monitor fish at 50 feet, you wouldn't throw a surface plug at them. The same goes for paddy fishing. Use a sinker—you have to get the bait to where the fish are!" (More on kelp paddies and sinker usage later.)

Another Tip—Throw Plastics!

Too many anglers are remiss in not utilizing the wealth of soft plastic lures now on the market when they fish the Pacific. Captain Buzz Brizendine of the "Prowler" observes: "Many anglers clearly overlook the seasonal versatility of soft plastic lures, particularly in colder water conditions. For example, on our trips to the Punta Mesquite reefs south of San Diego, we consistently take some of the largest shallow water rockfish, ling cod, as well as sand and calico bass on plastic baits like Tora Tubes, Scampies, Mojos, Lunker Thumpers, and Salty Magics."

Lures in this genre are available in an awesome array of colors and designs. Keep a wide selection in your tackle box to try when live bait and the "iron" fail to get bit. Brizendine suggests adding a small 1x3 inch strip of dead squid to the hook on any of these plastic baits. This will provide supplemental taste and scent for the bass and bottom fish.

Longer Rods for Live Baits

For many years, Southern Californians preferred short, powerful, 5 to 6 foot rods that allowed them to quickly "short pump" or stroke the fish quickly back to the boat. Although rods of this design are indeed strong enough to turn a big yellowtail or tuna, they are often impractical for throwing tiny anchovies with the stiffer fiberglass blanks. In contrast, anglers from San Francisco to Port Angeles, Washington have often utilized softer tip, longer rods on local trips.

Captain Ralph Botticelli of the "Daily Double" says, "It really helps to have a good bait stick, preferably 8 foot long with a good backbone and a medium light tip for throwing live baits." Botticelli notes that when the angler fishes the local kelp beds, especially for calico bass, he must be able to cast an anchovy or sardine a considerable distance. "Use the longer rod when fishing the kelp beds," says Botticelli. "Those people who can cast a live bait far away from the boat with the right rod will also have the power to pull calico bass out of the kelp. These are our most successful half-day anglers."

Remain Flexible!

One thing that all these longtime San Diego skippers recommend is for the party boat angler to remain highly flexible when fishing in this part of the south coast. The major migratory species that frequent these waters can be highly temperamental at times. One day, for instance, the yellowtails might annihilate the "iron," cast-metal jigs yo-yoed under kelp paddies. The next day the same group of fish may show no interest in artificial lures eating only a lively 'chovy on 12 to 15 pound string.

So the best advice may be to simply ask, then look and listen. Ask the skippers and crew what's happening. Look at the daily fish reports put out by these landings and watch what the successful party boat buffs are doing. Finally, listen to the deckhands and skippers when they talk about what is working for them. Each day the "program" can change. Develop a congenial rapport with the crew, learn from them, then implement the inside secrets!

The Pros' Hot Tips!

As you can see, learning to become an accomplished angler on a crowded party boat is no easy feat. Fishermen who ride these vessels frequently year after year often wonder why their success rate fails to improve. To understand this problem a little better, we must first look at the typical party boat environment. Unlike private yachts or chartered boats, a large sportfisher running an "open party" operation simply lets anyone on until they reach a full load. Passengers come from all walks of life and often range from first-time novices to longtime "regulars" who may assume more expert status.

On the better run sportfishers the captain and crew actively participate in helping their passengers both prepare for and then execute procedures during the day's outing. Unfortunately, a lot of people either fail to take advantage of a veteran crew's knowledge and assistance, or the crew itself becomes lax in assisting the passengers.

So what can you do? The single best piece of advice is to at least minimally watch what the more successful anglers do to beat the "party boat blues." Learn to adapt some of their integral "tricks of the trade" to maximize your chances on the water. Here then are some succinct tips commonly practiced by the shrewd veteran anglers. (In upcoming chapters I will elaborate more on some of these tricks as they apply to specific species.)

The Night Bite

Many three-quarter or full-day trips depart in darkness in order to reach the prime fishing grounds by daybreak. Typically, many passengers nestle into the bunks once the boat gets out of the harbor, ready to awaken at the smell of the morning bacon frying in the galley.

This is a practical approach if the vessel will still be running at dawn. Invariably with trips to the Farallons, San Clemente Island, the Los Coronados, or even the Mexican outer tuna banks, the skipper may shut the engines down in total darkness and either anchor or drift until daylight.

The smart angler will head out onto the deck when most of the remaining passengers are still down in their bunks. At the islands, this is an excellent time to target barracuda, calico, as well as sand and white sea bass in the dark! It is not uncommon for even the beginning angler to put some nice rockfish or ling cod in the sack by working in the wee, quiet hours of the morning.

These surface species usually hold at deeper depths during the night bite. This is why many anglers who take advantage of the uncrowded night bite will frequently fish live or dead bait with heavier than normal sinkers. They might also throw a soft plastic lure laced on a lead head to tap into these schools of sub-surface fish.

Many fishermen, including some die-hard veterans, firmly believe that it's not worth getting up to fish at night 70 miles out on a tuna run. Gamefish like yellowfin and bluefin tuna and albacore will definitely bite in total darkness—not just the early morning "gray" period, but even in TOTAL DARKNESS! Again, this can be a great opportunity to fish an uncrowded deck that might be in chaos later in the day.

Select Primo Baits

If you watch closely, you will note that some anglers seem to take a long time to pick a live anchovy or sardine from the bait tank. It's as if they are actually "studying" the bait. The accomplished party boater selects his baits very carefully. Put simply, not all baits are alike. This is particularly true with anchovies—the most popular live bait found on sportfishers. If you look carefully in the live

wells, you will see that some 'chovies are clearly friskier than others. Avoid selecting a large sluggish bait if a smaller more energetic specimen is available.

Next, examine the color of the anchovy's back. A majority of these baitfish will have a dark black dorsal coloration. However, a small percentage of the 'chovy population in a bait tank may have a distinctive greenish tint along the backbone instead. "Greenies" like these seem to be stronger baits than black-back 'chovies and, hence, get bit better.

Avoid picking a sardine, smelt, or anchovy that has a prominent red nose, patches of skin missing, or is wallowing from side to side on the surface of the bait well. These are usually weak baits. They won't swim well or for very long. Pass on this weak stock and look for a healthier model.

Fish Big Baits!

Although he may not catch the most fish, invariably the expert party boat angler who uses big baits will bring in the larger jackpot contenders. Let's say, for example, you are fishing calico bass primarily with anchovies. Quite frequently, a smaller population of "brown baits" consisting of tom cod, queenfish, herring, and perch is mixed in with the 'chovies.

While other passengers are culling through sub-12 inch bass trying to find a keeper fish, throw out a brown bait. The larger "bull" calicos will single out this offering while passing on the smaller anchovies that are being put in front of them. The same holds true for ling cod with voracious appetites. Other larger baits may be found mixed in with the 'chovies. Spanish and greenback mackerel, sardines, or smelt are all excellent alternatives for other species when anchovies seem to produce only smaller class fish.

Feather Your Bait!

Quite often the overwhelming majority of bait in the tanks are in a weak condition. It's tough to get gamefish to strike bait that won't swim much after they are cast. The veteran saltwater pro compensates for this situation by "feathering" the bait. Leave the reel in free spool and move the spool so slightly with your thumbs or fingertips to pull the bait back. A similar procedure can be practiced with a spinning reel. Leave the bail open and gently pull the slack line in a few inches, then manually wrap it around the spool.

This is what is meant by "feathering" the bait. The key is to pull the line in, using quick little spurts so that the bait kind of twitches and jerks on the retrieve. Frequently, inducing this erratic swimming action from an otherwise weak bait is just enough to trigger a strike from a wary surface fish.

Fish Deep!

As I mentioned with the night bite, there are times when it is better to fish deep. For example, on my Eagle Claw Fishing Schools during the summer months in southern waters my instructors work with the students to "wean" them away from the popular fly-line strategy.

Most of us learned that the best way to get bit with pelagic species is to cast an anchovy or other bait out, practically weightless, and let it peel out line near the surface. There are two problems with totally embracing the fly-line technique at the expense of a deeper approach.

1. Sometimes both the school of bait and the gamefish themselves may be significantly below the surface chum that is being thrown off the stern.

2. Some of the larger fish in the school may situate themselves below the smaller specimens and lazily pick off the weaker or crippled baitfish.

By adding a significantly larger sinker above the bait—perhaps as much as a 2 ounce ringed sinker—you may be able to tap into more and larger fish.

On our summer Eagle Claw Schools, many of the albacore in the 25 to 35 pound range were caught fishing deep bait like this. Small 8 to 12 pound yellowfin tuna provided most of the top fly-line activity.

Vary Retrieves

Too many saltwater anglers make the mistake of throwing out an artificial lure and cranking it in at the same speed, cast after cast, regardless of what species or time of year they are fishing. Some gamefish such as yellowtail or bonito prefer a cast-metal jig, for example, retrieved at a fairly high speed. The accomplished yellowtail hunter will use a reel with nothing less than a 5:1 gear ratio if the 'tails are on the surface iron or a yo-yo grind.

In contrast, barracuda typically key in on a much slower retrieve. This is true whether you are casting a candy bar style jig, a metal spoon, feather, or even a soft plastic lure for 'cuda—you have to "slow it down." Sometimes barries in particular will strike a lure on a stop-and-go retrieve. After making the cast, let the spoon or jig sink for a few seconds. Start to wind, but intermittently completely stop to let the lure sink. Invariably, the fish will attack the spoon or jig on the fall in this stop-and-go retrieve.

Other species like calico bass, stripers, or salmon will also home in on a slow-moving jig, spoon, or soft plastic bait. This is especially the case in colder water where the metabolism of the fish is slowed down and it simply won't move fast enough to attack anything.

Study the successful party boat anglers. Observe the lures they are using, as well as how they are *retrieving* them on a given day. If the bite is sporadic at best, it may pay to be experimental and mix up your retrieves until you find the pattern the fish prefer.

Checking Line and Knots

Another mistake beginners often make involves not recurrently checking line for nicks and frays. The most minuscule fracture in monofilament can result in a lost fish when you have to put pressure on the line. Veteran pros get into the habit of running their fingers over the 18 to 24 inches of mono above the hook to check for knocks and excessive kinking. If it is less than perfectly smooth—re-tie your hook and lure. Don't take a chance on a lost fish.

Equally important is to learn to tie a few good knots for saltwater trips. Not only do you need to tie the knot properly, it must be carefully cinched down or drawn tight against the lure's split ring or hook eyelet.

Too often I have seen novice anglers tie a seemingly correct knot but forget to draw it tight to prevent inadvertent slipping or even cutting which breaks the line at the knot. A handy little tip is to carefully moisten the knot with saliva before you draw the line down tight. This moisture minimizes friction and keeps the strands of monofilament from cutting into each other.

Use Your Drag

The drag mechanism on either a baitcaster or spinning reel is what you need to rely upon to tire out the fish. It is important to pre-set the drag prior to making your initial casts. My instructors and I have found that it helps to have the drag set somewhat loose for the beginning angler. Too often the novice fisher reaches for the drag knob or star wheel to tighten the drag while the fish is making a scorching run. A moderate drag setting to begin with prevents overtightening and, possibly, a broken line.

Better yet, try to keep your hands off the drag as much as possible. Ask the deckhands to pre-set it for you. They know where it should be set for the best chance of bringing in the fish.

Keep your thumb off that baitcasting spool! Sometimes there may be a tendency to use your thumb to slow the spool down when a fish is making a run. *Don't do it!* You can quickly blister your thumb from the friction generated by the line moving off the reel. Also, let your reel drag do the work. It has greater precision than your thumb. Persisting in "thumbing" the spool inevitably accounts for many lost fish by beginning anglers.

On another note, remember that saltwater live bait reels also do not have level wind mechanisms as do freshwater bass-casting models. So you should level wind the monofilament onto the spool yourself by guiding it between your thumb and index finger as you reel in.

Avoid letting the line build up on either the sides or the middle of the baitcasting reel. If a fish decides to make a fast run with the line bunched up in one spot, either the drag will fail to respond or the mono will cut into itself as gaps are formed on the spool. In either case, you will most likely lose the fish.

Follow Your Line!

On our schools, my instructors have a saying they frequently repeat on the deck: "No angles, no tangles." What this means is that it is important to keep your line in front of you at all times. This is true whether you are fly-lining on the surface, bottom-fishing, or drifting. You have optimal control over your bait or lure when you're "squared off" directly in front of the line. This also allows for a better swing and set of the fish with minimal line stretch.

This strategy also applies to playing out a fish. Once you hook up, you must *follow your fish*! This holds true for pelagic species like tuna and yellowtail, coastal predators like salmon and striped bass, as well as bottom grabbers like sharks and ling cod. All of these fish will pull you around the boat! This cannot be stressed enough for proper party boat etiquette. By following your fish, you not only keep the line in front of you at all times, but you also avoid crossing lines and tangling up with fellow passengers. If you don't move with your fish, you may lose it. When lines cross, it doesn't take much time or pressure to have the fish "sawed" off when the lines cut into each other. Move quickly and deftly to follow your fish!

Light-Lining

On our Eagle Claw Saltwater Schools we strongly encourage our passengers to use lighter tackle. Our instructors try to get party boat fishermen to move away from that 25 to 40 pound gear and scale down to 12 to 20 pound test line. This means using smaller reels, lighter action rods, and fine diameter monofilament. Anglers soon discover

that they clearly get bit more with the light tackle than other passengers using the heavier gear. Why is this so?

1. The fishery all along the West Coast tends to receive a lot of angling pressure especially on weekends. The various gamefish species are hammered with a barrage of live bait and lures. The fine diameter monofilament is simply more difficult for hook-shy gamefish to see, particularly when there is a lot of boat traffic in the area.

2. Light line makes the live bait swim more freely. A small pinhead anchovy is too tiny, for example, to be dragging out 30 pound string. This same bait on 12 pound mono becomes transformed into a highly active little dynamo palatable to even the most skittish gamefish.

Twelve to 20 pound test mono also allows smaller lures such as fathers, spoons, soft plastics, and compact cast-metal jigs to "swim" better. The light line creates less drag and resistance, with minimal impairment to the specific action of a given lure.

Multiple Outfits

On this note, the accomplished party boat pro begins to develop an arsenal of gear that can accommodate any situation encountered on a particular outing. As much as light gear has been emphasized here, there is a time and place for heavier tackle. For instance, you wouldn't want to be fishing heavy-duty freshwater bass tackle on 30 to 40 pound yellowfin tuna on a crowded party boat. In this situation, it is necessary to upscale your gear using 20 to 40 pound test mono and heavier spinning or baitcasting reels.

Similarly, even fishing for shallow water rockfish off San Simeon, for example, the angler might want to switch from standard 20 to 30 pound gear to lighter freshwater bass combos, tossing lures with 10 to 12 pound string. This can become a viable option if the rockfish are real finicky.

If you watch a longtime party boat angler, you will probably see him switching off, using light, medium and heavy outfits throughout the day. The light rig is for spooky fish, tiny baits, and small artificials. Use it with 10 to 15 pound line. The medium outfit features 20 pound string for most live bait fishing. The heavy gear relies on 25 to 40 pound line for throwing jumbo baits and larger artificial lures as well as for big fish ready to bite. As you develop more confidence in fishing party boats, carefully invest in a systematic approach with your gear, developing a tackle repertoire of light, medium, and heavy outfits.

Pros Love Lures!

I cannot emphasize enough how important it is to expand your options in becoming a better party boat angler. This translates into moving away from simply using live bait all the time and into trying an array of artificial lures.

As I noted, fishing the Pacific Coast can often be a tough proposition. The successful party boat fisherman realizes that he is in competition with the other anglers on the vessel and has live bait soaking all around him. Hence, selecting a lure to use under certain situations gives the fish something different to see besides the armada of live 'chovies commonly used on these trips.

A cast-metal jig, spoon, feather, plug, or soft plastic lure often provides the various gamefish with a different silhouette and action, which may trigger a strike in otherwise disinterested species. Sometimes more fish can also be tallied using artificials simply because the angler is able to canvass more water with more casts. This is true for salmon, striped bass, tuna, yellowtail, and the glamorous billfish species as well as bottom denizens including ling cod, flounder, halibut, and rockfish.

Similarly, artificial lures frequently account for the larger fish sacked each trip. In contrast to live bait, the expert lure fishermen will often work the artificials through deeper strike zones looking for larger specimens holding beneath the rest of the school.

The prominent profile of a jig, spoon, soft plastic, or plug offers the larger gamefish a more substantial morsel on which to focus compared to the smaller live baits used by the rest of the passengers.

Dump the Chutes!

Finally, here is a little tip worth noting to conclude these pro tips: be ready when the deckhands "dump the chutes." This is towards the end of the day when the crew calls it quits and empties the bait tanks.

This sudden commotion often creates one last feeding frenzy with the additional bait dumped off the stern. Always move to the back of the boat and try to fire off a few final casts. The sudden influx and noise of the flushing of the bait tanks can sometimes stimulate a larger fish holding far back in the outside chum line to move up to the stern for a final foray. Many jackpot winners come when the deckhands decide to "dump the chutes"!

Along this same line, don't hesitate to make a quick final cast just before the skipper moves the boat to a new spot. As he begins to pull up the anchor and move the boat forward, a lot of bait that was finding sanctuary under the hull now becomes exposed off the stern. Here again, there is a prime opportunity to nail the lone jackpot fish as the bigger specimens make a final charge at the exposed bait.

Again—Learn to Be Adaptable!

These basic tips will help you in becoming a more effective party boat angler. Above and beyond all the tricks with tackle, bait, and on-deck maneuvering, your greatest resource will be your ability to adapt quickly. Even the most accomplished saltwater buffs routinely stop to observe what is going on around them. If they are not getting bit and someone else is, they carefully analyze what the person is doing to enhance success. Novice party boaters should routinely stop and take a moment to make such observations. Then, adjust your "program," adapting to the strategies that are producing results at that time. Remember, conditions may change dramatically on a given trip from hour to hour so adaptation is an on-going process.

Do this and I guarantee you will beat the party boat blues!

How to Win Jackpots

One of the routine rituals of party boat fishing is competing in the jackpot. This is the modest cash pool anglers voluntarily contribute to prior to departure. The cost to participate usually ranges between two and five dollars per person. At the end of the trip, the deckhand will ask all anglers to bring their largest fish back to the stern, where they will be weighed on a balance bar against the other passengers' trophies.

A lot of jackpot fishing depends upon luck. Then again, it is often the shrewd veteran who knows the inside tricks and invariably takes home the "J.P." If you want to play in this low-level tournament, let me share with you some basic tips that might help produce the biggest fish of the day.

First of all, the adage "BIG BAITS CATCH BIG FISH" is definitely applicable for these party boat trips. Rather than tossing the routine menu of pinhead anchovies on a local sand bass or calico bite, be selective and look for a large "brown bait" in the tank. This collection of herring, tom cod, small shiner perch or queenfish is a favorite of big "bull" calicos, lunker-class ling cod or "barn door" halibut.

Similarly, on an offshore bite, consider fly-lining the larger sardines or mackerel instead of the standard anchovy fare. Bigger tuna, dorado and maybe even a striped marlin will home in on the larger baitfish which will stand out in a chum line of 'chovies'.

Trophy pelagic species such as bonito, salmon, stripers, barracuda, bass, yellowtail and tuna will also attack a well-presented artificial lure. Again, the cast-iron jig, soft plastic tail-swimming bait, or highly polished spoon may present a larger, more dramatic silhouette to surface-feeding gamefish on the prowl for a big morsel.

Larger gamefish will also frequently be found at deeper strike zones than the rest of the school. On our Eagle Claw Saltwater Seminars, my instructors routinely lecture the students to fish deep! While working the deck on our special charters, we will often go around from angler to angler and add larger, heavier sinkers to their setups to get them out of the strict fly-line mode. Veteran party boat skippers frequently mention, for example, that some of the largest specimens in both tuna and yellowtail tallied each season are caught in the deeper 15 fathom range. Fish deep!

Finally, steadfast perseverance may be the single most important ingredient to becoming a perennial jackpot contender. So often, the winning "J.P." fish is caught by the angler who was rigged properly and ready to cast when the captain gave the word. On the other hand, I've seen my share of jackpot fish weighed in by an angler who has confidence in what he is doing and sticking with that program until the skipper starts the engines and heads back home.

If you are fortunate to win that jackpot, also remember to share in the wealth with the crew. These past seasons have been pretty lean years financially speaking for the West Coast sportfishing industry. For you, the lucky angler, this is a form of recreation. For the crew, this is their livelihood. Give them a share of your "J.P." cash—they'll remember you the next time!

The Hidden Essentials

Many anglers who fish the Pacific Coast often overlook some of the "hidden essentials" that can make their outings even more pleasurable. Besides the basic array of reels, rods, and terminal tackle, there are several other things you might consider taking along on a sportfishing boat.

If you are packing sea sickness medication with the idea of taking it only if you start to feel ill, be aware that once you start feeling bad, it is usually too late for the medication to help. Follow directions precisely and consult your physician if necessary. Above all, if you think you may become seasick, start your medication before you leave the dock (check the box for the suggested time span).

Another preventative worth packing is sunscreen. Even on hazy, overcast days it is possible to get a nasty burn in a relatively short span of time. Dermatologists inform us that the frequency of skin cancer is on the rise, especially on the West Coast. Consider applying sunscreen before the bite heats up, since it is tough to take a break from the action.

If the bite gets red hot, plan on getting your feet wet as you move around the deck. Although boat shoes, sneakers, or sandals are more fashionable, a better long-term investment might be a pair of rubber deck boots.

On cold mornings, keep your hands warm with either mittens or gloves. You can purchase wool mittens especially designed for fishermen with the finger tips cut out to allow for a better feel. Try a pair of the new neoprene gloves like those used in scuba diving.

A hat will keep the sun from frying your head as well as keeping the anchovy scales out of your hair as the deckhands chum in the stern. Don't expect the ship's galley to have amenities like these for sale. Do your shopping before you board the boat.

Water is another overlooked essential. Some boats have water readily available in the galley, while on others it is hard to find. If you are going to need water for thirst or dehydration, consider bringing your own plastic bottle along to play it safe.

Finally, if you are taking an overnight trip, you might want to bring along some extra warm clothing to wear down in the bunks. Most sportfishers will provide you with a blanket and a pillow when you get your bunk assignment. If you have any tendency to get cold at night, bring some extra clothes for sleeping. You can strip away the layers in the morning as the weather warms. On multi-day trips where showers are available, plan on bringing your own towel.

Polarized Eyewear

One of the most overlooked pieces of equipment in the serious bass fisherman's repertoire is superior sunglasses. Over the years we have talked about the need for anglers to invest in good sunglasses as perhaps the ultimate fish-finding device. Above and beyond this, keep in mind that eyes also need the protection from ultraviolet (UV) light quality sunglasses can provide. Not all sunglasses provide these features.

So, check out the sunglasses you own now. If they are not polarized—no matter how expensive or fashionable they are—they aren't what you need for fishing. Pick a pair that will help you on the water. Polarization is the only effective method for removing dangerous and irritating glare.

Polarized sunglasses also come in a variety of lens colors which filter out varying amounts of glare and light for a variety of situations. Select the color that works best under the conditions you will be fishing.

Think about how many times you have tried to follow your cast, pick up your jig as it hits the water, or tried to "sight" fish while casting to tuna boiling on the corner? If you take this sport seriously, then consider developing a repertoire of lens colors for such critical conditions as low light, intense sun, glare, fog or haze.

Quality *polarized* sunglasses are an essential addition to your saltwater tackle collection. These glasses also help to protect your eyes under extreme climatic conditions. The investment is well worth it!

Small Craft Lessons

For many saltwater anglers, the ultimate dream is to own their own boat. In contrast to open party boats or charter vessels, smaller craft permit fishermen to come and go as they please without being tied to a specific landing's schedule. Also, to some degree, there is nothing like being your own captain, facing the challenge of making your own decisions and designing your own strategies for a given day on the water.

Basic Tactics

Smaller craft—although usually faster than large scale sportfishers—nevertheless have two key problems that may inhibit their success: 1) lack of range and 2) limited bait supply.

Still the shrewd private boater can make some specific adjustments that will diminish the potential impact of limited range and bait. Let's look at both of these issues and some of the strategies small craft owners can implement to improve their chances.

Limited Range

For the most part, few private vessels under 40 feet in length are going to have the fuel capacity to travel much more than 200 miles total distance. This puts most West Coast based boats well within the various zones for finding substantial numbers of fish.

The most obvious spots are offshore islands. Santa Catalina, San Clemente, the Farallons and the Channel Islands are all within a one-day trip range for the properly equipped private boat. Similarly, the Los Coronados Islands are only 14 miles south of San Diego Harbor again offering a potential target for even the smaller 17 to 25 foot craft.

What the novice boater often overlooks are the tremendous inshore possibilities that are so close to a variety of local landings or public launch ramps. The following are some classic examples.

The Horseshoe Kelp is a matter of a 30 to 60 minute run out of L.A. Harbor. The "Shoe" persists in providing some of the best opportunities to nail bonito, bass, barracuda, and yellowtail anywhere in the Southland. The famous Huntington Flats area, also less than an hour from L.A. Harbor, provides another haven in the late spring and summer for the small boater. Here there are a lot of sand bass and 'cuda close to shore.

Similarly, the oil rigs situated a few miles off Huntington Beach and the Barn Kelp near Oceanside are also one-day trips requiring minimal navigational skills. These spots are easy to find because invariably there are usually a few sport boats working the area. Small boat owners often pass up some of the best saltwater light tackle sport by not familiarizing themselves with our harbors and bays. Further north Morro, Avila, San Francisco, Coos, Winchester, Yaquina, and Tillamook Bays, to name only a few, are popular haunts for private boaters.

Professional saltwater guides like Mike Gardner have become legends for their prowess at working Newport and Los Alamitos Bays, using light tackle from small aluminum boats. Gardner's clients routinely tally big scores of sand and spotted bay bass along with a smattering of halibut, croaker, and corbina.

Bob Suekawa, the owner of Haddock Lures, has put on convincing demonstrations at the Long Beach Federal Breakwall tossing soft-plastic lures from freshwater bass boats in the middle of the night. Suekawa's "moonlight madness" from small boats outfitted with quiet electric trolling motors results in many big nocturnal calico bass that hunker in tight to the "wall's" rocky boulders.

On their days off, one of the most popular places to find San Diego's top deckhands is drifting San Diego or Mission Bay from small outboard skiffs. Here again, a lot of private boaters fail to realize that they might concentrate their efforts *inside* the harbor before they venture outside to test the bite.

Interestingly, party boats will seldom ever fish these harbors and bays. For one thing, skippers feel that the passengers have paid top dollar for the true "deep sea" experience. Hence, they motor outside the harbor to more scenic grounds when in reality some of the best bass and halibut fishing may be near the fuel docks, pilings, and bait receivers inside the landing basin! Further north, salmon and ling cod can be a reality in these sheltered areas, along with rockfish, greenling, turbot, and flounder. It is also often possible to find fish either in between our off islands in the prominent channel waters or at much shorter distances than the party boat fleet is targeting.

For example, it is rare to see sportfishers troll between the mainland and Catalina. Often the vessels are committed to specific offshore locales such as Catalina and San Clemente Islands. The sooner they get there, the sooner the customers get what they signed up for. For this same reason, the sportfishing fleet may be billing a trip as a serious "offshore" expedition where the anglers are pre-conditioned to look for a 70 to 100 mile boat ride—one way. Fish that are "short"—say 20 to 30 miles offshore—are often missed by the larger boats because of the way the landing is promoting longer offshore trips. Thus, the small craft owner can benefit simply by striking out on his own to explore waters—usually via trolling—that the larger vessels pass by.

Another situation that actually favors the small boat skipper is fishing the "high spots" that dot our coastal waters from the mid-Baja Peninsula to the Canadian border. Charts and books are available that clearly demarcate these rock piles, reefs, and wrecks using precise Loran readings.

For many years, my father and I fished these high spots in the Dana/Laguna area by looking for the black buoys that commercial lobster fishermen set out. These buoys invariably mark a rocky pinnacle that frequently are loaded with big "grumper" sand bass and some toad "bull" calicos along with lings and a myriad of rockfish.

Why wouldn't the larger sport vessels fish these high spots? There are easily enough fish on this structure to sustain action for 2 to 3 anglers in a small boat. There aren't enough fish to warrant a 60 to 80 foot party boat taking the time to anchor with a full load of passengers.

The issue of fuel capacity and boat range can be of paramount importance on some offshore trips—especially during tuna season. The fact remains that there is considerable water left unexplored by the large sportfishers that small craft owners can readily investigate.

Keep in mind that the faster you go, the more fuel you burn. I have fished on private boats on overnight sojourns, where the neophyte captain tries to run at nearly full throttle to get to the fishing grounds. Not only is this dangerous in the dark, but "fuel-ish." It is no coincidence that party boats average 10 to 13 knots cruising to the fishing grounds for both safety's sake and to conserve on fuel consumption. The trick is to leave earlier, run slower, and thus have more fuel left to chase down the fish.

Limited Bait

Next to fuel capacity, the issue of having a limited bait supply is crucial for the small boater to effectively strategize the outing. Without a doubt, the big 60 to 80 foot sportfishers will always have some advantage here due to giant bait tanks and massive chum power. The smart private boater can take action to offset this condition.

Don't underestimate the effectiveness of those awkward-looking canvas "diaper bags" that many boat owners hang over the stern on 17 to 40 foot craft. You can't keep many scoops of bait in these contraptions, but what you do put in usually stays fresh. Consider, however, adding a second bag to your boat. This modest addition will enhance your chumming potential dramatically. For example, you can have one diaper bag filled with smaller pinhead 'chovies which are perfect for chumming. In the other bag, you put your "hook bait" comprised of sardines, larger anchovies, live squid, or mackerel.

In harbors and bays that have a source of live baitfish, don't overlook what is in the bait receiver. Tell the attendant that you want the hot little pinheads for chum. Then ask him what else he has in the way of live squid, sardines, mackerel, or assorted "brown baits" (tom cod, herring, and shiner perch) to put in your other tank. The private boater may assume that the bait receiver only has the tiny pinhead anchovies the attendant proposes to give him when he first pulls alongside the dock.

It is also quite common for the smart private boater to "grease" the bait receiver attendant beforehand. As you pull up, tender a modest offering to insure that you get the primo baits. I've seen yacht owners offer additional cash, a fifth of liquor, a dozen donuts or even an assortment of lures to encourage the attendant to give them the best bait possible. This is no different from slipping the maitre'd at the restaurant a 20 dollar bill for a good table. Believe me—this little ploy is done all the time at the receiver by those private boaters who know how to routinely secure the best live bait.

After receiving the bait, make certain not to overcrowd it in your tank. The attendant at the bait receiver usually has a pretty good idea when you've filled the tank if you don't. The bait will often prematurely suffocate or seriously injure each other if overcrowded.

If you don't have a live bait tank on your boat, can you still compete utilizing other types of bait? The answer is emphatically *yes*! To some degree, we become spoiled out here in Southern California with fresh bait readily available and vessels equipped with aerated tanks to keep it alive. In other parts of the state and outside California, live bait becomes more problematic so alternative offerings are made.

Frozen anchovies—not salted, but instead freshly dead frozen 'chovies—often perform quite well when live ones aren't available. You can chum with the frozen baitfish either whole or cut into chunks. At times, pelagic species such as barracuda and bass will attack frozen 'chovy fly-lined or drifted among a chum line of chunked bait.

On an Eagle Claw Saltwater School to Kauai, the charter boat captain routinely relied upon fresh, dead anchovies to bring up the yellowfin tuna—both as chum and fly-line bait. Similarly, in Cabo San Lucas charter boat crews cut chunks of fresh-dead mackerel and pin them on hooks to lure dorado to the boat following a trolling jig strike. This type of chunkin' will also work for gamefish in the Southland, especially if there is no supply of live fresh chum with which to compete. Private boaters rarely try this tactic, however. (More on this later.)

Longtime party boat skipper and local expert, Captain Russ Izor, put a meat grinder on the stern of his sportfisher. Izor grinds up dead mackerel, 'chovies, squid, or sardines, and lets the "meat" drift behind the stern forming its own unique chum line. On many occasions, I have seen this trick neatly spice up the bass and barracuda action when only weak puny pinhead 'chovies were left for chumming.

When chumming, one of the best substitutes for fresh anchovies is frozen squid. Small craft operators should always carry a few one pound trays of frozen "squirts" on ice. You never know when this bait will come in handy.

You can use the squid whole, bounced off the bottom or fly-lined near the surface. I have personally caught everything from halibut to yellowtail on whole frozen squid. You can also dice it up to form a chum for perch, whitefish, sheepshead, and especially sand bass. Use a 1x3 inch strip of squid as a tippet for swimming or bottom bouncin' soft plastic lures. (I'll elaborate on these tricks with squid in future chapters.)

Although few party boat skippers ever use this tactic anymore, the private boater might consider stripping a fresh bonito or mackerel for bait. Either fly-lined or drifted along the bottom on a sliding sinker rig, the strip mackerel or bonito can be a big fish killer. Keep in mind that strip bait like this often brings in the sharks. Yellowtail, white sea bass, big calicos and sand bass frequently attack a big 8 to 10 inch long strip like this when chum is limited to small 'chovies or entirely absent.

Small Craft Trolling

As for actual boat operation, trolling and drifting allow the small bait owner the best opportunity to compete with the sportfishers in open sea. Many of the party boats won't begin to set up a trolling pattern until they are in the vicinity of their scheduled destination. Without a doubt, go ahead and try your luck at trolling if there are pelagic gamefish in your locale that are known to strike a lure presented in this fashion.

Feathers, spoons, cast-metal jigs, and especially minnow-shaped saltwater plugs make excellent trolling fare. Trolling allows the small boater to run and hunt down a quality fish here and there with almost no chum power. In contrast, the larger sportfisher has to look for a "mother lode" population of fish to accommodate greater numbers of passengers.

Soft plastic lures like the Mojo, Scampi, Lunker Thumper, and Salty Magic, however, are tough to match when it comes to lazily drifting along kelp beds, sandy bottoms, and key high spots. Keep experimenting with shapes, colors and actions of the lures until you find the pattern the fish want while drifting these baits. Keep a good supply of soft plastics in root beer/flake, lime green, and smoke glitter as the basic colors most of the major gamefish seem to prefer. Also, at 1 1/2 to 3 knots, knobtail swimbaits are terrific on the troll. Trophy yellowtail, albacore, yellowfin tuna, and dorado will nail these lures on the slow-troll.

Lots of Pluses!

Private boaters have a distinct advantage going for them over the larger sportfishing vessels. For one thing, a competent skipper can put a small boat in places where the party boats won't normally venture. You can fish the inside of the kelp beds working isolated potholes in the kelp with a smaller boat. Party boats also won't usually take time to throw at the "boiler" rocks that protrude above the surface with waves crashing over them. The white water around the "boilers" can provide sanctuary for lunker calicos and monster ling cod or trophy rockfish.

Big sportfishers won't always maneuver too close to the shore to work the surf line or next to the rocky structure of an offshore island. A skilled small craft operator can carefully explore these seldom fished areas. Finally, private boaters can fully experience the benefits of using light line and sporting tackle on major gamefish. This is usually a problem on a crowded party boat. The light gear will often get bit better, particularly in highly pressured waters.

Drift Fishing Basics

Drifting allows the small craft owner to cover more territory. Some sportfishing captains rarely use this tactic. Frequently the larger party boats will drift for rock cod, since deep water anchoring is nearly impossible at 300 foot depths. Except for rock codding, salmon mooching, and occasionally halibut or striped bass drifting, most sportfishing operators prefer to have their customers fishing from an anchored vessel. It is easier to monitor the passengers with regard to where their lines are and to make sure they are on the bottom if necessary while the party boat sits still at anchor. Long stretches of prime fish-holding water can in turn be explored by small boaters setting up drift patterns.

Drifting also permits the small boaters to work their baits closer to the beach and, again, over long spans of viable water. Along the southern coast, thick kelp beds and rocky outcroppings are primary areas to find calico and white sea bass, yellowtail, bonito, and barracuda. These are excellent places to drift. The similar terrain in the northern environment can host rockfish, ling cod, turbot, flounder, greenling and possibly salmon and stripers.

Barred sand bass typically stage their annual spawning migration over expanses of hard muddy bottom. Halibut orchestrate a similar ritual on sandy stretches. Drifting enables the angler to move through this kind of area fairly rapidly, eliminating major portions of otherwise "dead" water.

Drift Baits

The most popular lures used for drifting are soft plastic grubs and tail-swimming baits. These come in a variety of shapes and colors. This kind of lure is threaded onto a basic lead head jig and allowed to drift and bob along the bottom.

Double-tail swimming "plastics" such as the Scampi, Mojo, and Haddock's Lunker Thumper have enjoyed considerable success as a multiple-species bait among party boaters for years. When the fish want a fairly active lure, it is hard to beat one of the double-tail models. Proven colors include root beer flake, lime green, silver flake, fluorescent pink, solid white, yellow, and black.

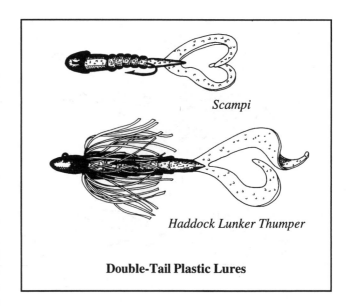

Scampi

Haddock Lunker Thumper

Double-Tail Plastic Lures

However, there are some occasions when the drift is slow with little current. In this situation, it is possible to garner more strikes from a soft plastic bait with less tail action. Lures like A.A. Worms Monarch grub are similar to the popular Scampi design, but with a flagellating single tail. Another option is to switch to a large 5 inch whip-tail grub such as those used in freshwater bass circles. The Mr. Twister model or Kalin's Salty Lunker Grub will perform quite well as a drift bait.

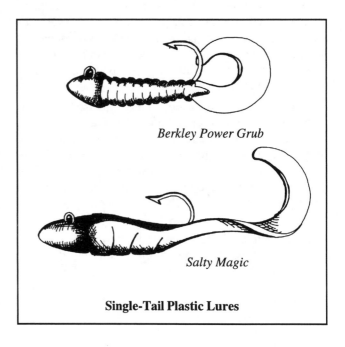

Berkley Power Grub

Salty Magic

Single-Tail Plastic Lures

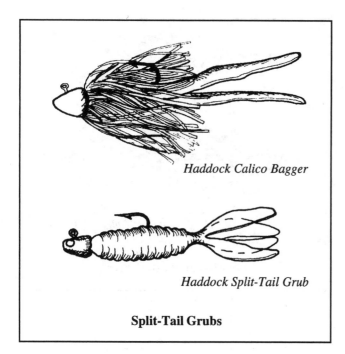

Haddock Calico Bagger

Haddock Split-Tail Grub

Split-Tail Grubs

There are times when the fish, particularly the calicos and sandies, want a maximum slow-down lure. Fat, simple paddle-tail grubs such as Haddock's Split Tail or Mann's Sting Ray can prove to be a surprising "secret weapon" when a super slow-moving bait is preferred.

Keep an adequate assortment of lead heads on board ranging from 1/2 to 1 1/4 ounces, depending upon the speed of the drift and the depth you are fishing. Some of the plastic lures such as the single-tail grubs will "swim" better with the lighter head. It is usually important to maintain good bottom contact with the bait that requires a heavier head. It is not that critical to invest time or money into painted lead heads for this type of fishing. You will lose quite a few jigs while they are bouncing through rocks and kelp.

Many veteran drift fishermen prefer to use lead heads with strong cadmium-plated hooks. These hooks won't rust and are strong enough to handle a 20 pound white sea bass. Instead I prefer jigs with bronze wire hooks. These hooks will rust and are not as strong as the cadmium versions. However, they are much sharper, offering excellent penetration especially with light mono.

The wire hooks may often bend out as pressure is applied when the jig becomes stuck. Beware if you reuse the lure by re-bending the hook—most likely the hook will be fatigued. It will probably be all right for smaller fish, but it may bend out on a big "grumper" sand bass or bull calico.

Another essential strategy to utilize in drifting soft plastic lures is to add a small strip of frozen squid as a trailer. There are some situations when the bass will only attack the baits if they are tipped with squid. Use thin 1x3 inch strips hooked on top of the plastic lure. The small strip will not impede the action of the bait as it drifts.

A variation on the soft plastics is to drift lead heads by themselves with a whole frozen squid trailer. A favorite combination has been to use a Bomber Gumpy Jig in green scale with the nylon bristles. Many anglers aren't so fancy and simply pin the squid onto a bare lead head.

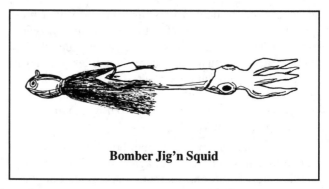

Bomber Jig'n Squid

This "squid'n jig" combo produces some of the larger calicos, sandies, a variety of rockfish, and even white sea bass. Be prepared to get a lot of "short strikes" from tom cod, lizard fish, and smaller bass. Sharks are also a possibility. When a big fish decides to eat this combination, wait until you feel solid pressure on the end of the line. You have to make certain they have eaten this lengthy offering and are not just holding onto the tail end of the squid.

Surprisingly, you can also drift with lightweight spoons. The rocking motion of the boat often imparts a sensational, erratic fluttering action from these lures as they bob up and down with the rod in the rod holder or over the gunwale. Models such as Haddock's Jig'n Spoon, the Crippled Herring, Mr. Champ, Deep Stinger and the Krocadile can account for some unexpected catches on the drift. Along with the bass species, mackerel, bonito, and barracuda will often nail one of these spoons as it lazily bobs along the bottom.

One other method is worth mentioning. It is possible to work drift patterns over hard mud or sandy bottoms with saltwater minnow imitations. These lures can also be

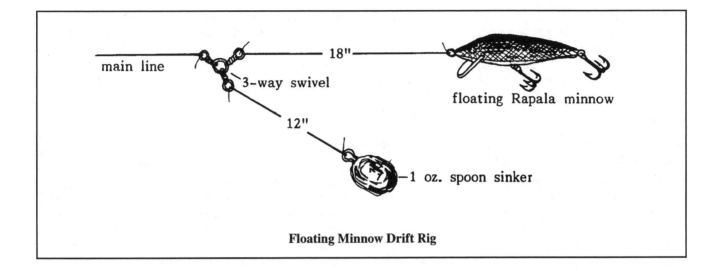

main line

18"

3-way swivel

floating Rapala minnow

12"

1 oz. spoon sinker

Floating Minnow Drift Rig

drifted over pinnacles and along kelp lines if the trebles are replaced with single Siwash hooks.

The way to use these minnows is to construct a dropper rig. Tie your mainline to a three-way swivel. Next, add a 12 inch length of leader tied to a 1 to 3 ounce flat spoon sinker. Tie a 18 to 24 inch length of 10 to 12 pound test mono with a floating Rapala minnow attached to the other remaining eyelet of the swivel.

You need to have a moderately fast drift with this tactic to generate enough action from the lures. It is best to use the floating models in the minnows, since they have more action than the sinking versions. Also a floating lure in this genre will appear to be a wayward anchovy or smelt slowly swimming above the bottom. Stay with predominately chrome patterns with blue or black backs. Halibut, stripers, rockfish, and sand bass will annihilate these baits drifted over sandy beaches or hard bottoms.

Almost any type of saltwater spinning or conventional outfit can be used for working the various soft plastic lures, spoons, or minnow plugs on the drift. However, the baits will have better action fished with lighter 10 to 15 pound test monofilament. Many "drifters" prefer a heavy-duty freshwater popping or bass rod in 6 to 7 foot lengths teamed with a level wind baitcasting reel. Premium grade mono with high abrasion resistance and minimal stretch is also a necessity.

Setting a Drift Pattern

The direction the wind is blowing is obviously critical in setting up a drift pattern. From personal experience, I have found that a wind blowing out of the west pushing the boat towards the beach is usually best. There have been days

when winds from the opposite direction have produced equally well. A mild blow coming from out of the west, however, keeps the boat near the beach where a lot of the kelp and rocky structure is located.

Try to work about two rods per passenger if space permits. You may find that for some species such as calico, rockfish, ling cod, halibut, flounder, turbot, sand and white sea bass, you may actually get bit better drifting artificials instead of live or dead baits. The trick is to mix up the menu until you hit upon the right combination that the fish seem to prefer.

For example, if three persons are fishing out of a 14 foot aluminum skiff, set up 6 outfits. One rod can have a grub; a second, a grub in a different color with a lighter lead head. The third and fourth rigs could have twin-tail swimming baits like a Scampi or Mojo. One can have a twin tail with a skirt, the other, no skirt. The final set of outfits might consist of a rod with one of the new hollow tube baits while the other might be set up with a light fluttering spoon.

The anglers let out enough line on the six different lures bouncing along at varying depths. Once the fish start keying in on one particular offering over the others, switch the baits on the remaining outfits to create a barrage of the "hot" lure at the proper depth.

Fishing multiple outfits in this manner is perfect for saltwater drifting. The anglers can work together to present the maximum array of baits at different depths in an effort to quickly determine the feeding pattern of the fish. The beauty of this is that it is possible to isolate this feeding preference without the availability of live bait for chum.

One of the most obvious places to try to drift is along the outside kelp line. Be prepared to lose some lures here. The bass species and shallow rockfish such as cabezon, sheepshead, johnny bass, and sculpin can be scattered through the thick kelp along with ling cod. As the boat is moving, invariably an open-hook lead head jig will snag a kelp stringer. It usually isn't worth the effort to start the motor to head up-swell to free the jig. Usually the speed of the drift will serve to embed the hook deep into the kelp. Break off the lure, re-tie, and continue the drift.

Always look for visible rocky outcroppings. Locals sometimes refer to these as "boilers." The swells crash over the exposed tips creating a frothy mass of white water and foam. You can spot-cast into the turbulence as you drift by. Frequently a big bull calico or ling cod will be waiting right in the foam. Definitely drift your baits along the outer edges of these boiler rocks. Quite often the rocky structure extends considerably out from what you see on the surface. Gamefish will congregate where the edge of the rocks meets the hard sandy bottom.

If you have a simple electronic depth finder on board, look for the stretches of hard bottom. Circle around in an area and determine if there are any rocky pinnacles jutting up from the bottom worth exploring. If you have a set of buoy markers, drop one over to mark a pinnacle. Sand bass gravitate to the hard bottom; calicos sometimes stack up on the rocky pinnacles. Set buoys on the rock piles that look good, motor up-swell and begin a drift that puts your lures over the pinnacle. Repeat this procedure as long as the structure continues to produce strikes.

In the wintertime, as I mentioned previously, commercial lobster fishermen can also be helpful as you look for the pinnacles. These underwater rock piles are usually too small for party boats. If you look carefully, frequently the lobster trap buoys will be directly above the pinnacle. Set your drift pattern so the boat moves along the outside edge of as many of these markers as possible. Take care not to come too close to the buoy lines. It is important not to interfere with the lobster fisherman's traps. He found the pinnacle and is basically letting you work his spot as long as the trap is left alone.

The actual "strike" that occurs while drifting can range from a gentle "tap tap" to a vicious grab that will nearly yank the rod out of the boat. Rod holders are recommended for this type of fishing. If you lay the rods over the gunwale while drifting, keep an eye on them at all times. Swing hard on the fish when you feel solid pressure on the end of the line. Avoid "short-pumping" the fish to the surface. Many species that are caught on the drift are taken between 45 and 90 foot depths. Maintain constant tension on the line following a solid hook set. This will minimize the chances of the fish throwing a hook from deep water.

Be Experimental

Drift fishing along the Pacific Coast can be an exciting and highly productive adventure. You can never really know what species will attack a lure with this presentation. It is imperative to stay alert for the strike. *Be experimental!* Without the availability of live bait and a supply of chum, it may take some innovation to fool the various gamefish into hitting the artificials.

Mix up your assortment of offerings. Keep switching baits until you discover the particular pattern the fish are keying on. Vary the depths through which the different lures are drifting. Work all types of structure from kelp and rocks to sandy and hard mud bottoms. A virtual potpourri of species await the accomplished drift fisher.

Tackle Lessons

Often the most overlooked piece of equipment in the saltwater angler's tackle box is the hook. As simple as this may sound, many fishermen working from the surf, piers, jetties, harbors, party boats or private yachts fail to put much thought into proper hook selection. Whether you are using bait or fishing with an artificial lure, the precise type of hook matched to your strategy is extremely integral to your success. Put simply, the hook is the first—and last—part of your terminal tackle with which the fish comes into contact.

Use the Right Hook

A hook that is too small can result in poor penetration, while a hook that is too large can restrict the proper swimming action of the bait. A frail hook may break on a strong gamefish, while a heavy-duty hook may alter the action of a particular lure.

Let's review some aspects of proper hook selection for saltwater angling along the West Coast.

Live Bait Hooks

The Eagle Claw #318-N short-shank live bait style hook is used extensively in the Pacific. With this type of hook, it is important to properly match hook size with live bait size rather than the size of the species sought. For example, I have seen many anglers select a size 4 live bait hook from their boxes when rigging up at the start of the trip. This size hook is popularly used with live anchovies.

The problem arises when you go to the bait tank to select a 'chovy and find that all the skipper was able to secure were tiny pinheads. If you fail to account for the small size of the anchovies and persist in using the size 4 hook, you may seriously injure the tiny baitfish. In this situation, reevaluate your hook selection and scale down to either a size 6 to 8 in this sort of hook.

Conversely, while you are using the size 4 hook with medium size 'chovies, you might spot a small tom cod in the tank. The tendency might be to continue fishing as you were, simply pinning the brown bait onto the same hook. Once again problems may arise when using a hook that is much too small for such a prominent offering. In this case, when you go to set up on the fish, use a larger hook with a fairly wide gap so it will readily tear out of the tom cod. Your best strategy here would be to either switch to another outfit with a larger hook or re-tie with your existing rig, scaling up to either an Eagle Claw #118 (bronze) or 318-N (nickel) Eagle Claw hook in #2/0 to #4/0 sizes. However, there are occasions when matching the hook to the size of the bait is totally immaterial. For instance, on a "wide open" albacore, yellowfin, or big eye tuna bite, I have seen bruiser-class fish eat pinhead 'chovies impaled on a #6/0 Eagle Claw #118MG (Magnum) live bait hook.

Thus, as a rough rule of thumb, try to match the hook to the size of the live bait. If you sense that you are in the midst of a feeding frenzy—throw out the book and select the largest hook you think you can get away with!

The actual construction of the live bait hook is another dimension to consider. Some hooks in this design are made from a thin wire construction. These are excellent on light lines, especially with a fragile bait. Although a wire hook generally provides excellent penetration, it may fatigue on a big fish. Examples include Eagle Claw's #L112, L118, L212, and L318N models.

Other hooks are made with heavy gauge wire. They are fairly strong for almost all situations. These are thicker "magnum" versions made for the toughest pelagic species such as the Eagle Claw #318-N or 118 Magnum series. Magnum class live bait hooks typically require at least 20 pound test mono to minimize line stretch. It takes somewhat more power on the set to garner adequate penetration with the magnum-style live bait hook.

Bait	Hook Size
Small, med. anchovies	4, 2
Large anchovies	1, 1/0
Sardines	1/0, 2/0
Smelt	1/0, 2/0
Mackerel	4/0
Squid	4/0
Tom cod ("brown baits")	2/0, 4/0

Eagle Claw Hooks

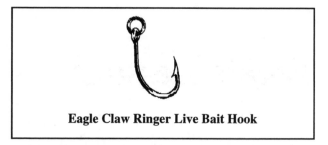

Eagle Claw Ringer Live Bait Hook

What about hook color? Well, this may be one of the truly overrated concerns among saltwater fishing buffs. Some veteran anglers, skippers, and deckhands firmly believe that a bronze live bait hook will overwhelmingly get bit better than a nickel-plated version. They theorize that the dull bronze finish is more difficult for the fish to detect and it won't reflect light unnaturally under water.

On the other hand, a majority of fishermen prefer the nickel-plated live bait hooks. These are usually more expensive than their bronze counterparts. In addition, these chrome-colored hooks won't rust as fast as the bronze models. The bottom line? Fish whichever color hook *you* have the most confidence in.

A recent innovation is to fish a unique live bait model with a larger soldered ring that slides through the eye of the hook. This is the Eagle Claw #1080G "Lazer Ringer." This hook is expensive because of increased manufacturing costs. After tying your line to the ring instead of directly to the eyelet, the hook will swivel quite freely. Some hard-core tuna fishermen adamantly feel that a bait will swim dramatically better using a ringed live bait hook. For them, the extra cost is well worth it.

Baitholder Hooks

Anglers working the surf line, break walls, and harbors commonly use a diverse menu of baits ranging from sand crabs and mussels, to cut anchovies and strips of frozen squid. The hook that is best suited for this array of offerings is a long-shank baitholder model such as the Eagle Claw #181-A series. Baitholders are usually sold in the flat bronze finish. They are characterized by one to two extra barbs found on the shaft of the hook. As you thread the bait onto the hook, it is essential to cover up not only the point but as much of the shaft as possible. The extra barbs on the shaft help to secure the upper portion of the bait so it won't slide down the hook.

It is usually more important with baitholders to match the size of the hook to the quarry you are seeking as well as to your choice of baits. When fishing at night, for example, I stalk big bull calico bass near the beach, along the surf line, and on the rocks using heavy-duty baitcasting rods and reels, 4 ounce sinkers, and 25 pound test line. My favorite offerings for calicos near the surf line or kelp bed are whole frozen squid or grunion. With bass that can easily top the 5 pound mark, I use a long-shank Eagle Claw #181-A baitholder in the #2/0 to #4/0 range.

In contrast, I switch to a light freshwater spinning outfit spooled with 6 pound mono when working from smaller yachts or uncrowded party boats. My choice of baits for smaller gamesters such as calicos, sand bass, bonito, barracuda or rockfish might be only tiny "pinhead" anchovies. In this case, I use an ultrasmall #6 or #8 live bait hook to match with the bait, the quarry, and the light spinning line. Here again, I switch back to the popular Eagle Claw #318-N model.

Wire octopus-style hooks can also be used in place of the bronze long-shank models with a similar mix of baits. These wire versions offer excellent penetration but may not be as strong for bottom scratching among the rocks and coral. An example is the Eagle Claw #L226-N Octopus hook.

I might add that a large octopus-style hook performs especially well with certain live baits such as mudsuckers or sculpin. The hook has a wide gap, pulls through tough-skinned baitfish fairly easily, and allows for good penetration. This has been a longtime staple, for example, for soaking mudsuckers while fishing for double-digit stripers in San Francisco Bay.

Lead Head Hooks

Soft plastic lures like the Mojo, Scampi, Lunker Thumper, and Tora Tube are now used extensively on the West Coast. Plastic baits of this genre are usually fished behind a lead jig head. As with baitholder style and live bait hooks, it is equally important to scrutinize the hook molded into the lead head. It is critical to use a jig head with a hook that is both long enough and has an adequate gap to match with the plastic tail section.

For example, the 3/4 to 1 ounce lead head used with a medium-size 4 inch Haddock Lunker Thumper would be too small to fish with the larger 6 inch long Thumper. The hook shaft of this lead head is too short for the longer bait. If you use it with the larger Thumper, the hook will ride too close to the head. You will miss many fish that may strike the lure more towards the mid-section. In addition, the gap—that space between the point of the hook and the shaft—will be too narrow to use the small lead head with the magnum plastic tail. You thus will need to switch to another leadhead, either the same weight or heavier, but with a bigger hook and wider gap.

Most jig heads feature a strong, heavy wire hook. These hooks are made to withstand considerable pressure. They are terrific when you are fishing a lead head lure around rocky structure as is found around jetties and break walls. Cadmium hooks also resist rusting to a great degree.

There are times, however, particularly when fishing soft plastics with light line, that it may be better to use a jig head molded around a thinner, bronze wire hook. This type of hook is somewhat weaker than the cadmium style and will rust more easily. The lead head with the thin wire hook offers superb penetration, especially when teamed with light mono. These hooks are much sharper than heavy wire and can be used right from the package.

Jig Hooks

Cast-metal jigs or "iron" usually have a specific hook affixed to the split ring. Presumably, this factory stocked hook offers the best combination of balance and "swimming" ability with the jig. Still most of these lures are sold with treble hooks and there are occasions where you may want to change them. Frequently, the manufacturer makes the mistake of using a treble hook that is too small for a particular type of "iron." If you are casting jigs for large gamefish like yellowtail or tuna, you may want to replace some of the smaller trebles with the next size up.

Similarly, the treble hooks used for jig fishing are also sold in graduated strengths, designated by an "X," Greater strength is indicated by higher numbers (i.e., 2X, 4X, 6X). When throwing the "iron" on 25 to 100 pound class fish, you might consider replacing weaker treble hooks with the stronger versions. Some manufacturers such as Tady, Ironman, and Jerry Jigs also market their jigs with

single hooks. A single hook can offer a distinct advantage over the treble.

A jig with a single hook can be fished easily through kelp stringers so it will hang up less than the "iron" with a conventional treble hook. Some pros also feel that you can get better leverage and penetration with a single hook, since twisting and torquing is more likely with a treble. Ironically, fewer fish might be lost using a jig with a single hook compared to models with the standard trebles. However, most anglers are convinced that three points are better than one and thus usually opt for the jig with the treble hook.

The single hooks on the jigs themselves can either be fixed to the lure with screws or allowed to swivel freely on a soldered ring. Manufacturers like Ironman and Tady decide which single-hooking method allows their jigs to swim best and sell them accordingly.

Spoon Hooks

Much of what was said about cast-metal jig hooks applies to spoons. Don't overestimate the propensity of these lures to nail big fish. Be aware that you may have to replace the stock treble hooks with a larger size. Some spoons like the Crippled Herring, Krocadile, and Deep Stinger are sold with a large single Siwash hook. With light monofilament, this long-shank, single Siwash with extrawide gap makes hook penetration quick, deep, and effective.

In a pinch you can use a more compact #2/0 to #6/0 short-shank live bait Eagle Claw #318-N hook in place of a Siwash style. The split rings on most spoons can be opened easily to replaced the factory treble with a live bait hook. Although this short-shank hook is not as effective as the long-shank Siwash style, it still features a fairly wide gap to enhance hook sets.

Plug Hooks

Minnow-shaped plugs are underrated lures for West Coast marine angling. Models such as the Rapala and Jensen Minnow will at times catch everything from bonito and barracuda to yellowtail and tuna. These lures require a delicate balance when it comes to hooks. The heavy-duty models usually are stocked with strong cadmium trebles. Smaller plugs like those used in freshwater will frequently feature needle-sharp bronze trebles. These are more suitable when fishing with lighter tackle.

Frequently, deckhands or skippers on party boats will request, for safety reasons, that you replace treble hooks on plugs with stainless double hooks. They feel that the double hooks are safer for their crew to handle than the 6 points on a set of trebles coming over the rail.

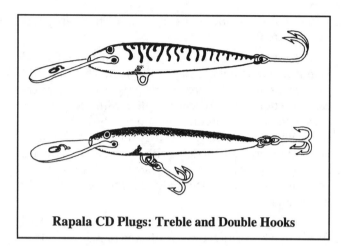

Rapala CD Plugs: Treble and Double Hooks

Be careful when replacing treble hooks on minnow-shaped plugs. Often you may inadvertently alter the balance and swimming action of the lure by switching to a set of different trebles. If possible, "tank-test" the plug after you change treble hooks by trying it in a swimming pool. Make a number of practice casts before actually using it in the field. To be sure, the treble hooks on many plugs used in saltwater, especially the bronze finish, will have to be routinely checked for excessive rusting and eventually replaced.

As a final option, you might want to replace all the treble hooks on your saltwater plugs with single Siwash models. Usually, these extra-long hooks won't significantly alter the action of the lure. Again, "tank test" the modified plug to be sure. The single hooks can be a real boon, particularly when fishing bonito or barracuda and other species with prominent teeth.

Worth the Effort!

Whether you fish with natural bait or artificial lures, avoid becoming lazy when selecting the right combination of hooks to use during your outing. Take the extra effort to properly match the hook to the baits and lures you are using as well as to the query you are seeking.

Hooks are the least expensive item in the saltwater angler's tackle box. They should be regularly sharpened and re-sharpened. Invest in a simple and widely used Luhr Jensen hook file. Keep it in your tackle box—and use it!

Rusting, rocks, kelp, and toothy gamefish can significantly reduce the strength, sharpness, and overall effectiveness of all your various hooks. Inspect them throughout the trip and, if in doubt, always replace them with new hooks. The extra effort is definitely worth it!

Circle Hooks

In the past few years, more and more California saltwater anglers are discovering Eagle Claw circle hooks. The circular design has been used by the deep-water commercial fishermen for years. Similarly, long rangers venturing to Baja's offshore islands have been fishing chunks of bait using the circle hooks to score on the big Mexican yellowfin. Well, let me tell you, the Eagle Claw circle hooks are here to stay and are a potent weapon for both surface and bottom-feeding fish.

In contrast to the J-style hook, a circle hook requires no actual hook-set. That's correct—you just throw your reel into gear and the cam-action of the circle design sets for you! Interestingly, over 95 percent of all fish hooked with the Eagle Claw circle hooks are caught on the outside of the lip. This allows for a quick release if so desired. It is also perfect for toothy species like barracuda.

Keep in mind that circle hooks are marketed in a different size nomenclature. For example, a 4/0 circle hook is equal to a 2/0 in a traditional J-bend style.

Add the following Eagle Claw circle hooks to your West Coast arsenal: #2004, #200S, and #197. Be aware, circle hooks are only for soaking baits. The built-in cam-action will not work if you use the circle design with faster moving lures.

Hooking Strategies

An angler may own the finest tackle in the world yet not have productive days on the Pacific because he does not know proper hooking methods for presenting his baits. Let's then review the assorted baits used for fishing the Pacific Coast and the ways the pros hook these different offerings.

Anchovies

These small baitfish remain the staple option for most small craft and party boat fishing along the coast. There are basically three ways to hook a 'chovy. For fly-lining the bait totally weightless without a sinker, it is best to gently run a short-shank live bait hook under the skin directly behind the gill cover. It is important not to actually penetrate the hard gill cover itself. This might quickly drown the anchovy if the gills fail to operate. This technique is termed "gill-hooking" even though the gills of the tiny baitfish remain unimpaired. You can continue to use this gill-hooking tactic as you add no more than 1/4 ounce of weight. This allows the 'chovy to suspend slightly below the surface.

As you begin to use a heavier sinker, you will have to take measures to keep the anchovy from prematurely drowning or having its swimming ability severely impaired. A gill-hook strategy might not be the best option in this situation. Instead, carefully run the short-shank Eagle Claw #318-N hook through first the lower and then the upper lip of the bait. This serves to keep the mouth of the anchovy pinned shut so that an inordinate amount of water is not pushed through its gills.

This lip-hooking technique is suitable for fishing an anchovy directly on the bottom, while drifting for halibut, for example. It can be used in deep open water when you want to "plunk" a bait 50 to 150 feet deep on an offshore kelp paddy for albacore, yellowtail, or tuna.

A final, though seldom-used option is to carefully run your hook across the narrow body section of the 'chovy directly ahead or behind its anal pore. This kind of "butt hooking" is highly suitable for fly-lining. In this situation, you may want to get the bait to swim down below the surface but you don't want to add any unnatural resistance with even the smallest sinker.

Anal-hooking an anchovy with a fly-line presentation can be quite effective in getting the bait below pesky small school fish such as mackerel in order to reach bigger prey like yellowtail or calico bass.

One final point is worth mentioning when it comes to hooking anchovies. We instruct our students in our Eagle Claw Saltwater Schools to routinely check their hands, rod butts, and reel seats for loose scales. This is usually the telltale sign that the novice is grasping the anchovy too firmly which may quickly injure the small baitfish. Be "kinder and gentler" with these little baits when handling them in the hooking process. "Cradle" the 'chovy in your hand as you walk from the bait well to your rod at the rail. Apply minimum pressure in grasping the bait as you proceed to hook it.

Sardines

The proliferation of this larger baitfish has been an absolute boon to the West Coast party boat fleets these past years, after a prolonged period of near extinction in our waters. Much of what I discussed about properly hooking anchovies will apply to sardines.

If the 'dine is only 3 or 4 inches long, gill-hook the bait for fly-lining as you would a small 'chovy. You can also use butt hooking to make the sardine swim deeper without the addition of extraneous weight.

Employ a lip-hooking strategy on the smaller 'dines. If you want to fish these baits down deep, try "plunking" with a heavier sinker. However, this technique has to be modified in the case of casting magnum-size sardines between 7 and 10 inches in length. In this situation, it is more effective to run the short-shank live bait hook through the nostril pores on the bridge of the 'dines snout.

This is called nose-hooking. Care must be taken not to break through the thin gristle that forms a bridge between the nostril pores. The sardine must be gently lob-cast with this method to insure that the hook does not pull through the gristle. 'Dines are stellar baits for everything from ling cod and halibut to salmon and striped bass to yellowtail and tuna. Handle them with care, keeping your hands wet when you bait your hooks.

Mackerel

Both Spanish (brown) and the greenback mackerel can be cast with the nose-hooking technique mentioned above for large sardines. Of course, with bigger baitfish in this genre, you will have to dramatically scale up in hook size. Many anglers make the mistake of not using a large enough hook with the "mack." When a big calico, yellowtail, or tuna decides to eat the mackerel, it will typically attack the baitfish at the head with some viciousness. When they decide to eat this kind of bait, they eat it hard! Hook size is not as restrictive as it is with more delicate baits like pinhead anchovies.

In recent years, deckhands and party boat skippers have been encouraging their passengers to fish small nickel or cadmium-plated treble hooks for mackerel. Use the treble in place of a short-shank baitholder. However, be certain to insert only one of the three points into the nostril-pores when nose-hooking a mackerel with a treble hook. At first glance it may appear rather strange to have two remaining totally exposed points left outside the "mack's" nose portion. When yellowtail are "on" mackerel, the treble hooks won't deter the strike and may actually increase catch-to-strike ratios.

Occasionally, both types of mackerel may also be hooked behind the anal fin. Sometimes when fishing thick kelp stringers for bull calicos, it helps to hook the "macks" in this manner to force them to dive deeper into the kelp beds where the big bass live.

Brown Baits

This collection of small baitfish includes tom cod, herring, queenfish, 7-11 perch, and baby pompanos. The brown coloration comes from the hues surrounding many of the dorsal, caudal, and anal fins of this array of baits. Brown baits hooked across the snout through the nostrils can be fished quite effectively weightless. You can also cross-hook them above or behind the anal fin if more depth is desired on the fly-line.

Frequently, however, the best bite with these fairly large baits occurs at 60 to 120 foot depths, particularly when probing for big calicos over submerged rock piles, reefs, and underwater wrecks. You can fish the brown baits, lip-hooked, on a "plunker" rig ahead of a large split-shot or a rubber-core sinker. There are some other hooking possibilities worth exploring.

First, run your line through a 1/2 to 2 ounce sliding egg sinker so it rests directly above your hook. Now, hook the brown bait through the lower and upper lips and let the sinker take the baitfish deep, possibly to the bottom. Instead of using a sliding egg sinker, try a variation on this theme. Take a 1 to 3 ounce lead head—painted or unpainted (whichever you have confidence in)—and lip-hook the brown bait with the jig. This is another example of a rather strange hooking procedure, but it really works when fishing deep structure!

The calicos do not seem to be bothered by the exposed lead head or the large hook. The long-shank cadmium hooks commonly molded into the lead head also provide the angler with an extraordinarily strong hook with a large gap to generate maximum penetration at depths over 60 feet. (More on this when I talk about "bull" bass fishing in upcoming chapters.)

This "jig-and-brownie" combo has personally produced some stellar catches for this author in both sand bass and big bull calicos while fishing the high spots in the Horseshoe Kelp region.

Squid

Live, fresh-dead, and frozen squid can be hooked in identical fashion. The simplest and most widely used procedure is to run an Eagle Claw #118, #118MG, or #318-N hook in sizes #2/0 to #4/0 short-shank live bait hook once through the tail portion of the squid. The bait can be fly-lined with this hooking. Either a big split-shot or rubber-core sinker may also be added 12 to 18 inches above the hook for greater depth.

The little ploy mentioned utilizing a sliding-egg sinker resting against the hook also works super for fishing a live or frozen squid deep. The fish typically eat the squid head first. As they pull and tug on the bait, the squid moves freely through the sliding egg sinker with the yellowtail, sea bass, halibut, or rockfish feeling minimal resistance.

Squid can also be bounced on the bottom pinned behind a jig head. Here again, the lead head can be bare, painted, with or without feathers or a vinyl skirt. This setup is known as the "jig-and-squid." It has been highly effective on the various bass species, especially when you need to get the squid to penetrate through a mat of thick kelp.

Give the fish some time to eat this jig-and-squid combo before setting up on the initial strike. The overall rig is fairly long and the bass may not always strike near the tail portion where the lead head and the hook are situated.

Strip Baits

Saltwater buffs in Southern California may often be remiss in not trying more strip baits. Their north Pacific counterparts recognize the merit of strip baits well. There are situations when gamefish simply want a more prominent offering and/or live bait is not available. Here is where the shrewd angler might consider cutting a small filet of mackerel or bonito as a strip bait. I like to actually cut the filet into somewhat of a triangular, wedge-like shape, wide at the top, tapering nearly to a point at the bottom.

Then simply run a fairly large Eagle Claw #118, #118MG, or #318-N 2/0 to 5/0 short-shank live bait hook, a longer Eagle Claw O'Shaughnessy model #254-N hook, or a lead head once and through the wider portion of the filet strip. The strip can be fished on the surface as it drifts back into the current. It can also be allowed to sink by adding either the lead head or a sinker and then S-L-O-W-L-Y "pumped" back to the boat following the cast. As you lift-and-drop the rod tip "pumping" the strip back in, it will undulate in the water as if it is alive.

In warm water years, you can also strip giant squid into foot long pieces. These should be cut from the main body of the squid and would not include the tentacles. This bait can be terrific fly-lined or "plunked" below the surface for yellowtail at a time when smaller squid would normally not be available. The hooking of the giant squid strip would be similar to that of mackerel or bonito filets— once through the head portion of the lengthy squid strip.

'Dads

Finally, some coastal fishermen have found that freshwater crawdads are excellent for shallow water rockfish, sheepshead, and even calicos along the break walls or on outside reefs and pinnacles. When fishing 'dads, I recommend a thinner, long-shank baitholder hook such as the Eagle Claw #181-A. Surprisingly, the best place to hook these little crustaceans are not through the tail but rather between the eyes through the gristle bridge that forms a point. Hooked like this, the crayfish will be able to propel itself more freely than if its movement was restricted with a tail-hooking ploy.

Match the Hook!

It is imperative to routinely check the hook you are using to match up with the available size bait. For example, you may need to fish tiny pinhead anchovies on a #6 live bait

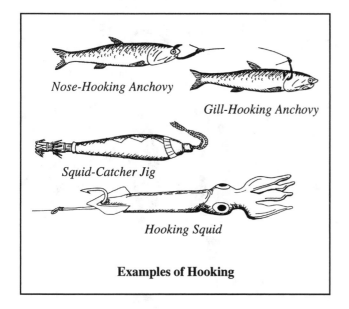

Nose-Hooking Anchovy

Gill-Hooking Anchovy

Squid-Catcher Jig

Hooking Squid

Examples of Hooking

hook. When you grab a small Spanish mackerel out of the bottom of the same tank, you will have to switch to a larger Eagle Claw #118 or #318-N (regular or magnum) 2/0 to 4/0 hook. Also, be prepared to switch from finer wire hooks with small baits and/or light line, to heavier gauge "magnum" hooks for big baits and 25 to 50 pound mono.

Too often I have watched novice anglers make the same mistake over and over of thinking that one size hook will be suitable for all the different baits available for the day's fishing. Study the diverse menu that is on deck that day—'chovies, 'dines, "macks," squid, brown baits. How about the more exotic offerings such as frozen squid, strip filets, or even freshwater crawdads?

Whatever your selection, make sure to match your hook to the particular bait so that you are able to present your offerings in the most lifelike manner.

Use Good Line!

I am always amazed at how otherwise dedicated anglers seem to treat monofilament line as a secondary piece of equipment and feel my advice applies to everything but line. Even with a new high-speed baitcasting reel and custom-wrapped rod, the most important link between you and the fish is your line. After spending upwards of over 200 dollars on a first class outfit, the last thing you want to do is scrimp on your monofilament.

Premium grade line has a number of distinct advantages over the "cheaper spread" usually sold at discount on large bulk spools. A quality monofilament made by a name-brand manufacturer will usually demonstrate three significant qualities: 1) uniformity, 2) abrasion-resistance, and 3) knot strength.

Although the big bulk spool of discount mono may seem on the surface to be a good deal, in reality you are probably purchasing line of varying diameters and breaking strengths. The test strength marked on the spool is the average for the entire run. This number varies little with quality line, but inexpensive mono may demonstrate wide variations with weak spots or differences in diameter between the beginning and end of the spool.

Second, a premium grade monofilament exemplifies a relatively uniform diameter and breaking strength, while maintaining a measure of abrasion resistance. If you cast where the fish live, then invariably your monofilament will be subject to the nicks and fractures caused by making contact with rocks, kelp, and the toothy critters themselves. A premium grade mono can withstand considerable abrasion before it weakens; the cheaper grades will not.

Finally, whenever you tie a knot in the monofilament, it will weaken to some degree. This occurs as the mono cuts into itself as the knot is drawn. As with abrasion resistance, a better grade line suffers minimal reduction in knot strength when it is pulled against itself and the metal of the hook eyelet or lure split ring.

What about line color? I personally believe that this is one of the most overrated concerns confronting the saltwater buff. Speaking from personal experience on both coasts, I think line color is more a matter of personal preference and confidence than "scientific fact." Fish clear, blue, green, or even pink—as long as you feel confident with your choice.

I will say, however, that when it comes to "serious fishin'" for pelagic species such as yellowtail, tuna, salmon, and marlin, I prefer not to use any monofilament with a fluorescent hue. There have been too many times when anglers using a mono that "glows" have been thoroughly stymied on yellowtail, while those fishermen who got bit used the flat-colored lines. On the other hand, don't overlook the fluorescent mono for surf-fishing, trolling, and bottom bouncin'.

Light-Line Fever

"Light-liners" are usually into a world of their own. They won't always gravitate to the stern of a crowded party boat, especially with everyone else fishing 30 to 40 pound string. They can't afford to get "sawed off." They aren't the back-breakin', stand-up strokers either who like to tackle tuna "mano-a-mano" with locked down drags and 50 to 80 pound gear.

Light-liners represent more of the "finesse" dimension of the sport. We like to use smaller reels, longer, softer, more parabolic rods, scaled-down lures and, of course, fine-diameter monofilament. Granted, light-liners lose their share of fish, but they may also get bit more often and frequently land jackpot winners.

There are a number of reasons why light-liners get bit so well these days. To begin with, the live bait situation in many locales up and down the coast is a "hit or miss" proposition. One day you find "race horse" size anchovies at the bait receiver; the very next day the live wells are loaded with tiny pinheads.

Smaller and, for that matter, weaker bait swims with less drag and resistance when hooked on lighter 10 to 15 pound test monofilament. Pinhead 'chovies and even larger specimens cast more easily using lighter line, especially when you need to fly-line the bait without the use of a sinker.

Lighter monofilament also permits certain saltwater lures to "swim" better than if you were throwing them on heavier string. Spoons, minnow-shaped plugs, bonito and 'cuda feathers, as well as a parade of soft plastic baits move through the water better if they are retrieved with lighter line and, thus, with less resistance.

There is also the simple fact that it is more difficult for the fish to see finer diameter monofilament. A good example of this is when it comes to stalking bluefin tuna on an inshore bite. In contrast to those found on the outer banks, it can be a real test of skill to persuade fish near the coastline to eat a live bait.

Invariably you will see veteran bluefin tuna experts scaling all the way down to 10 to 12 pound mono to get these finicky tuna to bite. Some reels become spooled and some bluefin are lost on the spider web-like line. The point is by light-lining these fish you do get bit. (More on this strategy later.)

Keeping your tackle in perfect working condition is imperative for successful light-lining. Reel drags must be perfectly smooth and the same holds true for rod line guides. The slightest rough spot on a guide can nick the thin diameter mono and then you have problems. Buy only premium grade monofilament in the smaller breaking test. Re-tie knots and change line often. Light-line fever—catch it!

No Dinkers with Sinkers

For some reason, many recreational anglers fail to realize the importance of selecting the right sinker for the precise conditions encountered. In southern waters, for example,

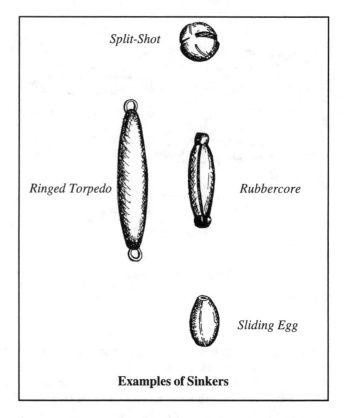

Examples of Sinkers

it seems that we are drilled from the start by deckhands, skippers and veterans alike, to "Fly Line That Bait"!

Without a doubt, there are many occasions when an anchovy, sardine, mackerel, or live squid performs best when frantically swimming on the surface unencumbered by any weight. Shrewd pros realize that this is the time to select a sinker to probe the mid-depths to the bottom for not only more but larger fish once the surface action begins to fizzle.

For example, it is common to see many novice fishermen fly-line anchovies at the beginning of the yearly sand bass migration into 30 to 120 depths in Southern California. Let the truth be known, however, that those bigger 6-8 pound "grumper" sandies are going to be laying on or near the bottom and sometimes at that 90-120 foot range. If you want these trophy sand bass, you will have to use anything from a large split-shot, rubber-core, or sliding-egg sinker, somewhere between 3/4 to 1 1/2 ounces in weight.

Similarly, it is common knowledge among longtime tuna skippers that some of the best meter marks found on offshore trips are at 15 fathoms. Most anglers cast fly-lined baits following the initial jig stop or sliding onto a kelp paddy. The smart veteran might start by "plunkin'" that 90 foot range with a heavy 1 to 2 ounce sinker for the larger yellowfin, bluefin, and even that rare albacore!

During post El Nino albacore trips, invariably many of the tuna caught on my Eagle Claw Fishing Schools have been tallied using 1-4 ounce chrome torpedo sinker "plunkin'" setups. Fishing at 90 to 250 foot depths, the chrome weight refracts light, generating the illusion of a school of anchovies or sardines. Your single-hooked bait trails behind the chrome sinker ready to receive the deep-water strike.

These same sinker strategies work for bonito, calico bass, barracuda and yellowtail. So often, the smaller, more aggressive members of the schools are found crashing on the chum near the surface. Forget these "dinkers"— be smart and work your sinkers for those better fish, lazily swimming at the greater depths. In later chapters I'll review specific rigs and the precise sinkers that should be used to complete these key terminal setups.

When Equipment Fails

Did you ever wonder how much luck truly plays in becoming a successful saltwater angler? During our schools, my instructors and I routinely hear students comment that the angler with the big fish "sure is lucky."

The truth of the matter is that luck probably has a minor roll in a successful day on the water. If you really scrutinize what the apparently "lucky" anglers are doing, you will soon find that they minimize the chances that something might go wrong. Without question, proper hook, line, sinker, and bait selection is integral for putting together your successful "program" for a day on the water. There are other factors that may contribute to a lack of success on the water. Here are some core issues that we have isolated in our schools which deal with proper equipment. We teach our students the importance of handling each one as essential to becoming an accomplished Pacific fisherman.

Spooling

As simple as this sounds, many novice anglers fail to sufficiently fill their reels with enough line. As you get further and further down into the spool, casting distance becomes more difficult to obtain. This is particularly the case with spinning reels. Many times when the fish are boiling on the far outside chum, a long cast is imperative to getting bit. If you fail to fill your reel with enough line, you may miss out on the action.

In addition, it is important to keep your thumbs off the spool when a fish starts to take line from a casting reel. Many neophyte anglers panic when they encounter the first surge of line from a big fish. They quickly put thumb pressure on the spool, thinking that if they don't, the fish will run out all the line. Let your drag do its job! The chances of becoming spooled are rare, especially if you took the time to fill your reel to capacity.

Finally, don't forget that with casting reels, you have to level wind the line yourself. Move the monofilament from side to side on the spool using your thumb and index finger. If you fail to do this rudimentary procedure, the line will invariably build up in one area of the spool. When a big fish tries to take out drag, the uneven line on the spool digs and cuts into itself rather than smoothly paying out from side to side. This may cause the monofilament to quickly break.

Extraneous Hardware

If you need to use hardware such as snaps, swivels, or snap-swivel combinations, *keep it simple*. A snap-swivel, in particular, is very tempting to use, especially when it comes to conveniently changing jigs, spoons, or plugs. However, this little device usually dramatically kills the action of the saltwater lures. Most lure manufacturers market their baits with the appropriate snaps or split rings that have been pre-tested to insure that the lure will generate the best action.

If when trolling, for instance, you need to use hardware, invest in quality goods. When it comes to swivels, split rings, or snap-swivel combos, the cheap varieties won't usually hold up on a big fish. Invest in quality terminal tackle, perhaps even ball-bearing swivels if necessary.

Wrong Lure—Wrong Time

It is a mistake to fish the same diameter monofilament over and over based on past successes. The same holds true for lure fishing. Just because a particular jig worked one week doesn't mean it will be equally effective at the same spot the next week.

Water clarity, prevalence of specific natural baits, and overhead sunlight can affect the role color plays in selecting a particular lure. A white jig might have been dynamite last week when the white sea bass were in the area feeding on squid. Next week, the best pattern might be the same jig in blue and white as the sea bass shift to feeding on 'chovies or sardines.

It pays to be equally flexible when it comes to selecting size and action of soft plastic lures, spoons, and plugs. Don't take anything for granted based on prior success. Today is a new day—give the fish what they want.

Advanced Lure Lessons

Over the years on our Eagle Claw Fishing Schools, we have discovered a wealth of new strategies. We have also refined older established methods for catching not only more but better quality fish ranging from bottom grabbers to pelagic gamesters. Here are some of the most potent technique we routinely utilize on our programs fishing exclusively with artificial lures.

Soft Plastics on Parade

It would be difficult to find a group of anglers who are as innovative as the ones who fish the Pacific Coast. Many of the major strategies for catching marine gamefish had their origins out West. This is certainly the case with the proliferation of soft plastic lures now widely used from coast to coast. Many of these unique baits were designed, tested, and perfected by Western saltwater buffs.

For years, the staple lures used for Pacific party boat fishing included a basic menu of spoons, feathers, cast metal jigs, and occasionally a handful of minnow-shaped plugs. Today, however, Western fishermen would be severely remiss if they didn't carry a complete array of "plastic," as the deckhands term these baits, on both offshore and coastal outings.

Let's briefly examine then the evolution of this family of soft plastic lures and the popular models used up and down the Pacific Coast today.

The History of Soft Plastics

Up until the mid-1970s, very few soft plastic lures were sold for saltwater angling. Most that were being manufactured at this time were targeted for sales in the Southern Gulf Coast states. The rather unspectacular-looking Bagley Salty Dog and Boone Tout were some of the first lures of this material to find their way West. These baits were nothing more than thick chunks of soft plastic with a flat tail section. They were fished on a lead head and supposedly mimicked a shrimp hopping along the bottom.

Local deckhands in Southern California's party boat fleet began using these lures, initially on sand bass. They found that a chunk of plastic bounced off the bottom would also nail calico and white sea bass, halibut, and a smorgasbord of shallow-water rockfish.

At about this same time, another hearty band of fishermen were working the breakwalls in the Long Beach-San Pedro Harbors at night. These "wallbangers" began experimenting with various soft plastic worms and jig trailers normally used for freshwater largemouth bass. They soon discovered that hungry calicos and sand bass would readily jump on these baits fished off the rocks at night.

Finally, a third group of anglers was exploring the possible effectiveness of soft plastics in coastal harbors and bays. The advent of the curl-tail worm extensively promoted by Mr. Twister ushered in still another application of soft plastic lures in saltwater. Spotted bay bass, sandies, halibut, croaker, and even perch, sargo, and corbina, were found to like these strange new worms in places like Newport and San Diego Harbors.

Nowadays, the saltwater buff can visit any tackle store and have an awesome array of soft plastics from which to choose. Let's review some of the options available and how and where these different lures are best used.

Fork-Tails

This bait basically evolved from the body design of the early Bagley Salty Dog. The Scampi was one of the first to expand upon this lure shape, by adding a double-tail section to the bait. The thick thorax portion of the Salty Dog remained intact with the Scampi design. Other manufacturers followed Scampi with a variety of other fork-tail models. These included the Mojo, Haddock's Lunker Thumper, and Shabby Shrimp.

You will find some of these models to be mass-produced through the injection-molding process. Other fork-tail lures are made from a more labor intensive, hand-poured procedure. The latter type of bait is usually characterized by more elaborate, multi-layered color schemes and a distinctively softer body. Hand-poured plastic lures in this genre are frequently more potent than the standard fare represented by the harder, more bland-looking injection-molded baits. Expect to pay more for the soft plastic models and to lose them more frequently because they become torn up more easily by toothy critters.

Soft plastic baits made from either of these processes excel for calico and sand bass fishing along with rockfish and ling cod. They can be casted, yo-yoed, or drifted along the bottom. Deep-water rock codders have also found that the jumbo-size fork-tails fished on a 10 to 16 ounce lead head can be dynamite on big ling cod, salmon grouper, and "cow" cod.

One little tip is worth mentioning again here when using these lures. Cut a strip of frozen squid about 2/3 the length of the plastic and pin it onto the jig head hook. The squid trailer will ride above the plastic tails, but it will not affect the action of the bait. This serves as a "tantalizer" of sorts, when the bass seem finicky and won't eat the straight plastic offerings. Do this with both injection-mold and hand-poured models.

Another ploy to use with these lures is to add a plastic or vinyl skirt behind the jig head. This skirt should be reversed to make the strands of vinyl or plastic flair out when the bait sits on the bottom. The addition of the skirt will also make these lures fall more slowly through the water. This is an excellent option to try when the fish are hitting the offering on the "sink."

Skirts will also add a nice contrast to these baits, especially the less-spectacular, injection-molded models. You can purchase the skirts from most coastal tackle stores. They are the same type used with freshwater bass spinners. Be creative here, mixing and matching colors of the skirts and the plastic fork-tails. Quite frequently you may come up with a super "hot" customized combination that no one else will have on the boat that day!

Freshwater bassers should also consider bringing out the light gear and some of their miniature counterparts in fork-tail jigs when fishing off the rocks, breakwalls, bays, or jetties that dot the coast. Lures such as Garland's Spider Jig, Canyon Lures' Cap'N Gown, and Haddock's Kreepy Krawler are excellent calico and sand bass baits when fished on 1/4 to 5/8 ounce lead heads and 8 to 20 pound test. They are also perfect for light tackle rock fishing in northern kelp beds and reefs using freshwater bass gear.

In the Southland, hard-core breakwall fishermen have been tallying some hefty limits on mixed catches of calicos and sandies tossing these three freshwater lures along the rocks at night on the various breakwalls. Here too, as was recommended to do with saltwater fork-tails, it helps to add a 1x3 inch piece of cut squid as a trailer to these smaller baits.

As a bonus, you will most likely find an awesome array of colors available in the freshwater fork-tails since they are in considerable demand among tournament bass fishermen.

Tube Baits

Hollow-bodied tube baits clearly evolved from freshwater bassin' circles. Lures like Bobby Garland's Fat Gitzit have become legendary bass killers on Western impoundments. These and other versions of the "tubes" often produce sensational results in the marine environment as well. More and more saltwater tackle stores are adding both freshwater and larger size "tubes" to their floor stock.

You can start out by using the basic freshwater 2 to 3 inch models with an 1/8 ounce jig head inserted inside the hollow body. This size tube bait is perfect for pitchin' around the docks, pilings, and boat moorings found in harbors up and down the coast. All sorts of perch, croakers, halibut, as well as bay and sand bass will bushwhack these tubes as they sashay down along a piling.

Larger 4 to 6 inch tube baits produce on deeper outside waters. These soft plastic lures replicate a slow-moving squid when they are either drifted or casted. Models like the Tora Tube and Crappie John's Turbo Jig are perfect for salmon, stripers, calicos, sand bass, bonito, barracuda, halibut, ling cod, a wide variety of rockfish and, believe it or not, deep-water yellowtail!

These big tube baits have been generating spectacular catches from the Farallon Islands to below Ensenada, Mexico on ling cod and other rockfish. On an outing to the Farallons, for example, all the jackpot contenders were caught on the giant tubes. Similar results have occurred when rockfishing in more southern waters. This tube bait is an absolute "hawg hunter"!

You can also run your line through the head of the giant Tora Tube and then through a series of egg sinkers shoved into the hollow body. Tie the line onto a larger single Siwash hook and you have an intriguing new trolling lure. This is an interesting alternative to trolling with feathers for larger offshore species. Tuna, albacore, yellowtail, and wahoo will strike this magnum-size tube bait on a relatively fast troll.

Saltwater tube baits can be even more potent if the hollow cavity is filled with liquid fish attractant. Stuff a small cotton wad up into the tube and soak it with some Berkley Saltwater Attractant. As the tube glides through the water, the bait will emit a "chum slick" of the scent. This may again generate strikes when the fish seem especially hook-shy.

One other rather unusual application for saltwater tube baits is to use them to construct the "soft spoon." This is simple to make. Take a slender narrow-bodied spoon like the Crippled Herring, Deep Stinger, or Haddock Jig'n Spoon and carefully slide a medium-length tube bait over the lure. Push the line eyelet at the head of the spoon up through the nose of the tube bait. What you now have is a metal spoon encased in a soft plastic tube.

As the spoon is either casted and retrieved below the surface or yo-yoed off the bottom, the tiny tentacles in the tail section of the tube bait seductively flair in and out. The weight of the metal lure will help it sink faster or cast further than a tube bait on a lead head, yet still resemble a squid on the retrieve. Furthermore, when the fish strike the soft plastic outer cover, it will feel more lifelike compared to a hard metallic surface.

Tube Driftin'

Tubes are excellent as a drift bait. Both party boat anglers and private craft fishermen can cover a lot of terrain by slow-drifting tubes. The secret is to make solid bottom contact. As the lead head bounces along, the lure will sort of rise and fall with the tentacles flaring similar to a live squid. A typical drift for halibut, sand or calico bass, salmon, stripers, or even white sea bass requires using a 1 to 3 ounce lead head with the tube bait bottom bouncin' in 60 to 120 feet.

Start with the lighter head. If the current picks up, switch to the heavier jig heads. The motion of the waves and the current is usually enough to impart the necessary action to this kind of lure. However, to enhance the effectiveness of the tube, squirt some liquid fish attractant up into the hollow cavity. As you drift with the lure, the scent is slowly emitted, creating a chum slick of sorts to call in the fish.

Tube baits are terrific on a cast-and-retrieve strategy. Occasionally, a more aggressive fish may nail the lure on a straight wind such as a bonito or tuna. Invariably the more potent method is to carefully "pump" the tube back to the boat.

To do this, let the lure sink to the desired depth. Then lift the rod tip from the 3 o'clock position. Drop the tip back down parallel to the water, allowing the tube bait to slowly fall. "Pumping" the tube in this manner has the effect of making the lure kind of dart up and down while the tentacles seductively pulsate on this type of stroking retrieve.

Bottom dwellers such as ling cod, halibut, and shallow-water rockfish frequently chase down the tube "pumped" like this off the bottom and viciously attack the lure. More surface-feeding species such as calico bass, bonito, barracuda, and even yellowtail and tuna will strike a tube slow-pumped through 15 to 60 foot depths.

The S-L-O-W Yo-Yo

Tube baits also excel with the vertical yo-yo technique. Here too bottom contact is essential. After the lure reaches the bottom, throw the reel into gear and lift the rod tip up anywhere from 1 to 8 feet. Let the tube slowly sink, hit the bottom, then start the lift-and-drop sequence all over again.

There are times when the more exaggerated yo-yoing works best with the tube bait jumping 6 to 8 feet off the bottom. Invariably, most of the strikes will occur on the fall. Look for any sudden dramatic slack in the line. This usually signals that a fish has inhaled the tube on the sink. Swing and set!

Often in colder deeper water a very subtle short rod lift, perhaps not more than 1 to 2 feet, is most effective. The fish may not want to move too far or too fast in the colder environment. Thus, the S-L-O-W vertical yo-yo makes the tube an easy target to attack. This yo-yo tactic with tube baits has proven effective not only on shallow-water rockfish but on prize gamefish as well. Both yellowtail and white sea bass will sometimes annihilate one of these squid-like soft plastics when they are feeding in deep water on schools of "squirts."

Larger 8 to 10 ounce Tora Tubes can be yo-yoed in much deeper 30 to 50 fathom water for larger rock cod. Better yet, attach a dropper loop about 18 inches above the jumbo Tora Tube and hitch on a smaller 1 ounce Berkley Power Tube as a trailer. This can be a dynamite one-two punch for red rockfish, salmon grouper, and ling cod. Often a smaller fish might hit the little Tube only to have a larger predator strike the big Tora Tube on the way up. Catching two deep-water rockfish on one drop is quite common with this double tube bait setup.

You can also thread small to medium-size brightly colored Berkley Saltwater Power Tubes onto the multiple hooks of a rock cod gangion. Definitely add either live or cut bait to the hook along with the colorful tubes. If the deep-water species steal the bait, the soft plastic tubes will act as a backup offering. You can thus keep the gangion rigs down for longer periods without having to reel up from these greater depths.

Swimbaits

These fish-shaped lures probably had their origins back with the French-made Vivif or the Weber Hoochy Toad. These were fairly hard plastic replicas of mackerel with big double hooks and a whippy knob-tail. They were super big fish killers for "bull" calicos and yellowtail. Neither of these baits are made today.

Instead, soft plastic manufacturers have a series of knob-tail models that have greater utility for a spectrum of gamefish. These lures are fished on a lead head jig similar to fork-tails. They are basically designed as cast-and-wind baits with the knob-tail pulsating and shaking on the retrieve.

Smaller 3 inch models such as the A.A. Worms' swimbait have been the rage among bay fishermen in Southern California. These are effective on practically all species of gamefish found in these harbors. They are best worked on a slow retrieve with a 1/8 ounce, darter-head jig teamed with 6 to 8 pound monofilament.

Larger size knob-tails like the A.A. Worms' swimbait or the unique Optimum lure are made to look like small tom cod, herring, or queenfish. These "brown bait" look-alikes can be highly productive on calicos and sand bass when the fish seem to be keying in on a larger offering. I want to emphasize, however, that the knob-tails clearly are most effective with a relatively S-L-O-W retrieve, with barely enough speed to keep the tail throbbing.

Whip-Tail Grubs

These soft plastic lures have also garnered a reputation among freshwater bassers. Most of the models used on our Western bass lakes will work in saltwater, primarily in the harbors and back bays, and off the rocks or piers.

Grubs also fish best with light line and tiny 1/8 to 1/4 ounce jig heads. Models such as Kalin's Lunker Grub, the Mr. Twister Grub, and the new Berkley Power Grub are excellent baits to fish in moving water such as the eddies found in Newport Harbor all the way to Coos Bay.

Grubs featuring these prominent tails can also be rigged with freshwater plastic worm hooks combined with sliding bullet sinkers. The hook is re-embedded back into the thick body of the grub, making this plastic bait particularly weedless.

Both shallow-water rockfish enthusiasts and dedicated deep-water rock codders would be wise to carry some of these little grubs in their offshore tackle boxes. A whip-tail grub added onto either a gangion or dropper loop hook will add considerably more action to a piece of strip bait as it dangles from the same hook.

Sickle-Tails

A lesser known class of soft plastic lures are distinguished by long, narrow sickle-shaped tails. These are usually single-tail variations of the fork-tail baits utilizing the same basic head and thorax design. Only the shape of the tail differs.

A.A. Worms' Monarch grub exemplifies this genre of soft saltwater plastics. After many years of experimenting with these lures, I can state with accuracy that there are definitely times when the diverse species key in on the sickle-tail and won't make the slightest pass at the more popular fork-tail models.

Sickle-tail lures have caught sand bass, calicos, halibut, lings, and rockfish drifted or retrieved along the bottom. Interestingly, these soft plastics also perform quite well at time with other pelagic species.

Barracuda will eat them on a slow "pump." Bonito will nail them on a fast grind. Yellowtail, albacore, skipjack, dorado, and yellowfin tuna have all been taken on sickle-tail lures like these primarily on the "slide" as the boat came to a stop following a jig stop on a trolling feather. However, there were also occasions, when shrewd anglers casting from the bow with light tackle, caught these exotics dragging a sickle-tail lure near a floating kelp paddy.

Split-Tail Grubs

Even less common than the sickle-tail design are those saltwater plastic lures which feature tails that are split in half or sometimes even into quarters. Haddock's Split-Tail Grub and Calico Bagger illustrate this type of subtle tail configuration.

These lures are used off the breakwalls for nighttime calico and sand bass safaris. However, I have personally found the split-tail grubs to be highly effective as bottom-bouncing baits, working drift patterns in 45 to 100 feet of water. Practically anything that is near or on the bottom will eat these lures, especially if they are tipped with a piece of cut squid. This is an excellent shallow-water rockfish offering!

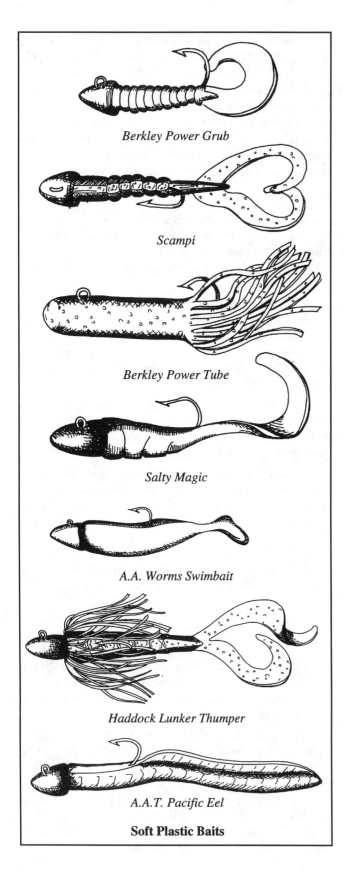

Berkley Power Grub

Scampi

Berkley Power Tube

Salty Magic

A.A. Worms Swimbait

Haddock Lunker Thumper

A.A.T. Pacific Eel

Soft Plastic Baits

Split-tail grubs have minimal action compared to other soft plastics. During the winter, the pelagic bass species will typically be in a slow-down mode and so won't always attack a lure with more vigorous erratic tail action. Try the split-tail grubs under these conditions, with or without a single skirt. Some of the largest "bull" calicos and "grumper" sand bass I have ever caught came on these split-tails while slow drifting in the dead of winter!

Versatile Lures!

So there you have it—a full parade of soft plastics widely used by the Pacific fishermen. As you can see, these soft plastic baits are extremely versatile lures for marine conditions. Try to work these lures with as light as line as you can possibly use. The tail action of these baits is greatly enhanced with the fine diameter monofilament.

More on Lead Heads

I love lead heads. As a longtime freshwater bass fisherman, I learned to fish everything from the pig'n jig to the Spyder and the Kreepy Krawler. Anyone who chases largemouth bass the West quickly comes to realize that there is nothing better than plowing a lead head jig across the bottom for locating fish holding on deep structure.

Well guess what? These simple lures have even greater utility in saltwater. Armed with a coffee can full of lead heads in 1 to 3 ounce weights, the Pacific angler is ready to tackle anything from sand bass, rockfish and even yellowtail and ling cod.

Lead heads are cheap to buy and even less expensive if you cast your own. The trailers that you lace behind them vary from soft plastic grubs and fork-tails to frozen squid and live herring. The various lures you can assemble from the basic lead head jig are practically endless and extremely simple to put together. Here are some of my favorite combos:

Squid'n Jig. This is one of my longtime favorites. In the "old days" we used to use Bomber Gumpy Jigs with the nylon tail bristles and a whole frozen squid pinned on tail first. The Bomber or any other colorful lead head with feathers or plastic skirt will still work with this squid'n jig combo. As simple as this sounds, you can produce good catches of bass and rockfish by using a cheap, unpainted lead head with the whole squid.

Brown Bait Plunker. Take a lead head and lace the hook through the upper and lower lip of a live small to medium-size tom cod, herring, or shiner perch. This rig doesn't look too attractive but it gets the "brown bait" down deep where the big "bull" calicos, halibut, and ling cod live.

These are just two of my favorite tricks using lead heads above and beyond combining them with soft plastic trailers. Keep plenty of these jigs on hand. When you bounce the bottom, you are going to lose some. They are fairly inexpensive and it won't take a huge investment to assemble an awesome lead head arsenal. Keep it simple— fish lead heads!

Also, be certain to pre-sharpen all the hooks used with lead heads. Many lead jig heads are poured with cadmium hooks. These are not as sharp as bronze hooks but they won't rust as quickly either. Many times our local species will gently "mouth" the soft plastic, so solid hook penetration is necessary.

On this note, consider using a graphite rod to increase your hook-to-strike ratio with lead head combos. Because the "strike" is not often so pronounced, the graphite blank is more sensitive and responsive to nail those delicate feeders. Many anglers are now stepping onto sportfishing boats additionally armed with 7 or 7 1/2 freshwater graphite bass trigger-grip rods, and light level wind baitcasting reels spooled with 10 to 15 pound string strictly for fishing soft plastics and lead heads.

Pumpin' the Eel

I am fortunate to be both an outdoor writer and the director of the Eagle Claw Fishing Schools program. Frequently, I have the chance to preview, test, and help refine a variety of new products over the seasons. In past years, students in our on-the-water seminars have had the opportunity to be among the first to try the now popular Tora Tubes. Next came the soon-to-be marketed Salty Magic curl-tail baits, the Rapala jumbo Shad Raps, Berkley Power Grubs, Tubes and Scampers and, most recently, the hot new Jerry Jigs surface irons. We have tried them all, and they have all performed quite well in our schools.

At one of our land-based Penn Fishing University symposiums, one of my guest speakers, Mike Gardner, a renown light-tackle saltwater guide, handed me some of the most bizarre-looking lures I had ever seen. These were 10 inch long, hand-poured, soft plastic eels. Now I've used eels before in freshwater bass lakes, but they were smaller 6 inch specimens. I might add that I was first introduced to these baits back in the mid 1960s and I rarely ever see eels sold in the West anymore—until now.

Gardner's monster versions were made by Tony Paino of A.A. Worms. They were obviously created to resemble rainbow trout, a natural prey for big largemouth bass at Lake Castaic outside Los Angeles. So, to be polite, I took the sample baits and stashed them in my saltwater box.

A few weeks later, I was leading one of my schools down to San Martin Island about 155 miles south of San Diego. We had been picking at log size 'cuda, a smattering of yellowtail, and some calico bass all day. In the late afternoon, we anchored on a high spot in about 180 feet of water. This was a recognized pinnacle for big red rockfish and sometimes ling cod. The bite was especially slow. Scrounging through my tackle box, I found one of the AA eels—in rainbow trout color no less—and laced it on a 3 ounce lead head. I fished the eel on 12 pound string, matched with a graphite 7 foot freshwater poppin' rod. On the first drop, I was hammered. I slowly wound up a nice 7 pound red rockfish. The next drop I was nailed again by a red of equal size. Initially, both my instructors and deckhands alike snickered at my weird eel. After the second big red hit the deck, and coughed up a 6 to 8 inch "real" baby eel, my skeptics soon asked if I had any more of these new baits.

This story has been repeated many times as I take my eels to sea. Big chuckleheads, lings, "grumper" sand bass, and toad "bull" calicos will also eat them. As I discovered, bass like most bottom grabbers, such as reds, lings, whitefish, and halibut, feed on small eels in their natural habitat. It's not so strange then that the soft plastic imitation works so well.

The soft plastic eels are big fish baits. Don't worry about short strikes—the keeper fish bite the eel at the head. Don't fool around with tricky stinger hooks in the tail. As for colors—I've used about every pattern sold and all work fine. It's the size, silhouette, action, and uniqueness of these new eels that makes them so effective!

Saltwater Scents

Saltwater angling, like other sports, has evolved into a hi-tech industry. We now have everything from big game reels with lightning-fast gear ratios and sophisticated lever drag mechanisms to lines made out of Kevlar. There are electronic fish finders that scan from side to side as well as supplying a vertical picture of the bottom. Hooks are now manufactured with laser technology and lures are marketed with incredible natural fish-like finishes. Everything is going hi-tech.

A somewhat less glamorous member of this cavalcade of hi-tech tackle is the multitude of fish scents and attractants that are now on the market. You can purchase waxes, liquids, and solid compounds that are designed to encourage the fish to bite your offering. Much of this emergent scent technology, however, was spawned in the freshwater bass and trout fraternities. It has only been recently that anglers have been taking a serious look at these mixtures and how they might have application in a marine capacity.

As director of the Eagle Claw Fishing Schools, I have had the opportunity to investigate many of these compounds while conducting our various on-the-water seminars in California, Baja, Hawaii, Alaksa, and the Florida Keys. I also have a strong background using scents and attractants on freshwater lakes while running my bass and trout guide service in the Southland. My freshwater experience has been especially helpful, I might add, for generating a myriad of applications for these concoctions for my instructors to use while at sea. Here are some of the more intriguing applications we have discovered.

Home Remedies

Some of the best fish attractants for saltwater are actually products of home experimentation, passed on from one angler to another and are fairly simple to put together.

An example of this is what veteran lure manufacturer, Bob Suekawa, of Haddock Tackle, does when preparing to use soft plastic grubs and jigs fishing the Long Beach Federal Breakwater at night. Parlaying the propensity of both calico and sand bass to key in on smell during a nocturnal bite, Suekawa frequently pre-soaks his lures in squid juice during and prior to the trip.

"The stuff is simple to extract," notes Suekawa. "I just let a block of frozen squid thaw out and collect the natural juices in a bucket. I then let my Kreepy Krawlers and split-tail grubs soak for a while in the natural juice. This produces a lot of strikes when I fish the "Wall"—more so, than if I fish plastic lures without the juice."

Other natural sources also produce "juices" that are excellent when applied to soft plastic baits. One in particular is the result of crushing fresh rock mussels and collecting the juice. Small curl-tail grubs dipped in this scent will perform along the surf line, off the piers, and along the docks and pilings in secluded harbors and bays.

For years, freshwater bassers have relied upon oil of anise as a "secret sauce" of sorts. This oil not only gives the lure the distinctive licorice odor, it also "greases" the bait, giving it a slick lifelike appearance. Small tube baits like the Fat Gitzit, Berkley Power Tube, or Fatzee are excellent when pitched under docks, piers, and moored boats in the backwaters of Southland harbors. Dip these soft plastic lures as well as curl-tail grubs and knob-tail minnow-like baits in the anise oil for greater effect.

You can also create some unique, one-of-a-kind, custom smelly soft plastic lures by putting a variety of different baits into a poly bag with a spoonful of anise oil. Seal the bag and let it sit in the sunlight for a few days. A virtual rainbow of interesting patterns will develop as the different colors of soft plastic bleed into one another. The oil seems to facilitate this "bleeding" process with the by-product of having the anise scent permeate more deeply into the soft lure.

This little trick is a good way to recycle some of those old, torn-up plastic worms that may be stashed away in your freshwater bassin' box.

Liquid Blends

Far and away, the most prominent representation of fish attractants and scent is in liquid form. Some of the popular varieties include Berkley Fish Attractant, Dr. Juice, and Pro Cure.

Some of these mixtures are oil-based, creating that slick-looking effect similar to the anise-soaked baits I mentioned. Others, like Berkley Fish Attractant, are water soluble, creating a less spectacular effect as far as lure finish is concerned, but presumably emitting a particular chemical to encourage the fish to attack the bait.

The manufacturers of true liquid scents and attractants have also been careful to market all these products in different odors to be employed for a particular species. Dr. Juice, for example, comes in a saltwater, trout, salmon, panfish, or catfish blend.

Like the home remedies discussed, the liquid formulas would seem to have greatest utility in conjunction with soft plastic baits. The simplest technique is to either spray on or add a drop or two of the liquid to the saltwater lure. Most of these mixtures are relatively expensive and highly concentrated. In my experience, it doesn't take a lot of the liquid scent or attractant to dress up the lure.

One thing worth noting, however, is to be sure to apply the liquid especially to the head and mid-thorax portion of the bait. Popular soft plastic lures like the Mojo, Lunker Thumper, Scampi, or A.A. swimbait will commonly be attacked near the head section of the bait. If you add too much oil to the tail portion of these lures, expect to see a lot of little fish short-striking the bait, ripping at the tail.

These liquid formulas should also be used in conjunction with a natural bait trailer or with natural bait by itself. For instance, a common ploy is to add a small 1x3 inch strip of cut squid to the hook on a soft plastic bait as an added attraction if the lure is not drawing strikes. Better yet, add a few drops of your favorite scent for even greater potency. Again, this stuff is expensive and a few drops will go a long way.

Another intriguing tactic we pioneered on our Eagle Claw Schools was taken directly from our freshwater bass guide logs. For years, so-called "finesse" bassers have been injecting both plastic worms and grubs with liquid scent or attractants using a hypodermic syringe. A less unusual version of this little ploy is to fill the hollow cavity of popular tubular lures with these liquids.

Take a medium-size Tora Tube, Berkley Power Tube, or a Crappie John Turbo Tube and fill it with an ample amount of one of these liquid compounds. As the soft plastic tube glides down on the sink, it emits a sort of "vapor trail" of the liquid scent, calling the fish in to investigate. This strategy has produced stellar catches of sand bass, calicos, barracuda, shallow-water rockfish, ling cod, and even deep-water yellowtail. Through informal controlled tests, my instructors and I firmly conclude that the "tubes" injected with the liquid attractants or scents overwhelmingly get bit better than those that are fished "dry."

A variation along this theme is also worth noting. To conserve on the liquid along with creating perhaps a longer time-release effect, many anglers now stuff a small amount of cotton into these hollow tube baits. Then they saturate the cotton plug with the various liquid formulas. While once participating in a major billfish tournament, an enterprising angler drilled out small portion of the core of a marlin jig head. Then he inserted a cotton plug soaked in liquid attractant. On a slow-trolling program, the liquid would again be released gradually presumably creating a chum slick around the lure.

Liquid scents can also be used in conjunction with natural bait to create an even more potent chum concoction. One proven trick is to take strips of bonito, mackerel, barracuda, or pieces of squid. Put them into a milk carton and mix in a few cups of sand. Then add an ample amount of liquid fish attractant. The scent adheres to the sand while the sand adheres to the slimy natural bait. You can then throw out pieces of this combo as chum, similar to the way East Coasters "chunk," utilizing portions of cut bait to bring the fish to the boat. The attractant is slow to leave the natural bait, since it is mixed in with the sand that coats the bait. This specialized "chum pot" works great for sand bass!

Pastes and Slime

One of the problems in using liquid fish attractants is that they will not adhere properly to hard baits such as cast-metal jigs, spoons, or plastic plugs. Some time ago, the people at Berkley marketed a powdery substance called "Alive." It comes in a canister, and if you run across some on a dusty shelf, buy it! When mixed with water, Alive produces a thick syrupy slimy solution into which you can dip hard baits. It is still basically a water soluble product like Berkley's liquid attractant, but it is much more sticky.

The late Bob Bringhurst, a former world record holder and renown big fish expect, started coating his trout-colored plastic plugs with this stuff while stalking trophy rainbows and browns. He shared this little trick with me, and I soon found that Alive would also work in saltwater. For example, I took a group of students to fish giant amberjack in Key Largo on the "iron." Our 83 pound jackpot fish was nailed when I recommended the angler dip his heavy jig in a bucketful of Alive.

Two new compounds are now available that are similar to the slimy Alive. Both Smelly Jelly and Scent Wax approach a more solid state. Each of these mixtures will, to a great degree, adhere to smooth metal surfaces like those found on a saltwater spoon. Similarly, both the wax-like and gel attractants can be used to coat a jig or a plastic minnow-shaped plug.

Built-In Scents

Perhaps the most intriguing application for scent technology in the saltwater field has been the recent proliferation of soft plastic lures that feature "baked in" attractant. For years, freshwater bass fishermen have experimented with this technology by hand-pouring their own plastic worms with everything from vanilla extract to salt crystals added into the molten plastic. The theory behind this concern for built-in scents is twofold: 1) the scent will mask human odors and 2) it will also actually attract fish into striking the artificial lure.

A soft plastic bait impregnated with one of these substances also presumably has the added benefit that the fish will actually hold onto the lure longer than if it was simply plain, unadulterated plastic. Berkley led the way with the advent of their "Power" series of grubs, worms, and tube baits. Experimenting with these basic freshwater bass lures on our saltwater schools has produced remarkable results!

My instructors and I have found that everything from sand bass and calicos to ling cod and halibut will viciously strike the Power Grubs, and Power Tubes. Many jackpot fish were taken this past season when anglers fished one of these soft plastic lures which are essentially impregnated with the same materials as those found in the liquid Strike compound.

Jim Bloomfield and Reuji Suenaga are in the business of hand-pouring soft plastic bass baits. Also concerned with eliminating messy external applications of scent, Bloomfield and Suenega started adding Smelly Jelly to their Bonzai Worm products.

Another entry into this saltwater attractant market is the series of Culprit Shrimp Tidbits, Sea Ray I, and Shad Tail Grubs. These soft plastic lures also have scent and flavor enhancements built in to product harder, more pronounced strikes. These are basically shrimp-like or knobby-tail designs.

Bonzai baits have also produced spectacular results on recent Eagle Claw Fishing Schools targeting shallow-water rockfish. As with the Berkley Power series of baits, we have found the lings and other rockfish to readily attack these most recently introduced scent-laden lures.

The most effective way we have devised to utilize these soft plastics with the built-in scent is on a dropper loop rig. Tie on either a heavy cast-metal jig or spoon with a dropper loop about 12 to 18 inches above the lure. Attach a #4/0 live bait hook to the loop then thread on one of these smelly grubs, worms, tubes, or leeches. Proceed to "bounce" the jig or spoon off the bottom. Invariably if you stick only one fish, it will be on the dropper loop and the soft plastic bait. Double hook-ups are frequent with the soft plastic lure usually accounting for the larger of the two fish. These scent-laden baits are also sensational thrown on light bass-casting gear while fishing harbors and bays or coastal reefs and rock piles. Any bottom-dwelling fish might eat one of these lures laced on a lead head and retrieved or drifted slowly.

You can also take the tiniest Power Tubes and insert one over each of the points of a big treble hook on a jig or spoon. Now the lure has acquired a modicum of "smell" without jeopardizing its performance. A jig or spoon with three miniature tubes sticking off the treble hook looks rather weird—but it definitely gets bit!

Be Creative!

As you can see, there are endless applications for using fish scent in saltwater. I have touched on only a few tricks I have come across this past season. Undoubtedly, there are many more to be discovered.

I must confess that I, like most anglers, also use only the compound prescribed by the manufacturer for a single gamefish species. This obviously facilitates more multiple sales for the scent and attractant companies. I certainly encourage you to be innovative and perhaps try some freshwater compounds in the marine environment. It just might lead to some interesting results as a halibut homes in on a grub soaked in rainbow trout scent!

South Coast Trolling

Trolling is one of the most productive ways to catch the major pelagic species in Southern California and Baja California waters. This is especially true for small private boats that have limited chumming capabilities. Even sportfishing skippers will attest that there are situations when trolling allows them to cover expanses of open water efficiently in an effort to locate schools of marauding gamefish.

The five major surface species caught in the Southland—bass, bonito, barracuda, yellowtail, and tuna—will all strike an artificial lure dragged behind the boat. Here is a brief rundown of how to set up a trolling program for each of these distinct gamefish. Keep in mind that some of this material is repeated in greater detail in the individual sections on the different gamefish species. This is merely a basic "primer" on trolling.

Bass on the Troll

Many anglers are remiss in not trolling for bass when the opportunity arises. Both calicos and sand bass can be tallied with this technique. Calico bass will frequently nail the "iron" as a cast-metal jig is slowly pulled behind the boat. The emphasis here is S-L-O-W-L-Y. Jigs in this genre will have a tendency to spin if they are trolled too fast. You can throttle down to a plodding 1 to 3 knots if you want to drag the iron.

Two kinds of jigs will work on calicos with the trolling strategy. If you are cruising along the outside kelp lines, I recommend a small compact "heavy" model such as an Ironman #2 or Salas Christy 2. These jigs pull nicely on 20 to 30 pound mono and, at least initially, they should be tied directly to the line. If the jig begins to spin even with a slow trolling speed, use a ball-bearing swivel with a leader. Tie your main line to the ball bearing swivel and add a 4 to 6 foot length of leader. Then tie your jig directly to the other end of the leader line. Don't snap a swivel to the split ring on the jig. This usually kills the distinctive side-to-side swimming action of the "iron."

As for colors, these smaller jigs are made to replicate mackerel, sardines, or anchovies. Time-proven patterns are blue/white, blue/chrome, and definitely green/yellow for calicos.

There are other times when the calicos—particularly the bigger "bull" bass—are up feeding near the surface of the kelp stringers. This is an excellent opportunity to slow-troll a lighter surface jig. Larger models like the Jerry Jig Light series, Ironman Candyman, Salas 6X or 7X or Tady 45 in a "light" weight are perfect for this type of trolling. Consider switching to the less popular single hook versions in these jigs. They will swim through the kelp stringers better than conventional treble hooks models with less snagging. With these longer jigs, a blue and white pattern with a painted black underbelly is a terrific pattern used by many of the big calico experts. Another "sleeper" color is a dull, almost General Motors green jig.

A prime situation to drag one of these larger jigs is on a party boat while the deckhand is setting up a chum line. The skipper will typically circle a prime spot while chum is tossed out to bring up the fish. Troll one of these larger surface jigs through the initial chum—you just might get nailed by a big bull bass!

Both calicos and sand bass will also strike a big soft plastic tail-swimming lure on the slow-troll. Small boats can cruise near the bank keeping an eye open for so-called "boilers." These are small, rocky outcroppings that the surge will crash over at low tide. Calicos and sometimes sandies will be found in the foamy water created by the "boiler." Pull a larger fork-tail Scampi, Mojo, or Lunker Thumper near the white water. The single hook lead head used with these soft plastics makes the lure practically weedless. Soft plastics like these also slow-troll well along the kelp stringers or through a chum circle. Stay with the ever popular root beer/flake, chartreuse, or smoke/sparkle colors with the fork-tail lures.

Sand bass, more so than calicos, will often stratify or suspend. It is not uncommon to meter sandies stacked up from 20 to 40 feet above a 100 foot bottom. One seldom used method is to slow-troll a weighted plug through these deeper strike zones. Using 20 to 30 pound line, tie your main line to a ball-bearing snap-swivel. Clip the swivel to the ring on a 10 to 16 ounce torpedo sinker. Clip another snap-swivel to the other ring on the sinker. Next add a 4 to 6 foot length of lighter 12 to 15 pound line tied onto the swivel at the bottom of the sinker. Lastly, tie on a medium-size, minnow-shaped plug such as a Rapala CD-11, CD-13, or CD-14 Magnum model.

On a moderate slow-troll, the torpedo sinker will take the lightweight plug down fairly deep. The sand bass readily attack the anchovy look-alike providing the boat skipper with an excellent means to target suspended bass!

Troll for Bonito

"Bongos" are by far the easiest of the pelagics to fool with a trolling program. Like calicos, they will eagerly attack a smaller metal jig when it is slow-trolled. The heavier Ironman #1 and #2, along with the Salas Christy #1 mini Jerry Jig and Pee Wee models, are great for this slow-troll strategy. Blue and white as well as solid chrome patterns would be hard to beat.

Bonito will also annihilate smaller minnow-shaped plugs. The Jensen Minnow, Rapala CD-9, CD-11, and CD-13 Magnum lures are excellent choices when trolling for bongos, along with a 4 inch Possum Lure. Usually these artificial minnows produce best for this species tied directly to the line and pulled a few feet below the surface. These plugs are also small enough to be trolled with freshwater bass gear, producing terrific light-line sport on 10 to 12 pound spinning or baitcasting outfits.

Surprisingly, soft plastic baits can also be trolled for bonito and at a fairly fast speed—well over 6 to 7 knots. The classic fork-tails work well along with the recently introduced Tora Tubes. Pull brighter shades such as fluorescent lime, chartreuse, blue, or red while trolling soft plastics for bongos.

Metal spoons are also a viable option. More than ever, with these lures, S-L-O-W is the word if you want to troll them. The slab-shaped models like the Crippled Herring, Deep Stinger, Champ, and Haddock Jig'n Spoon will erratically dart back and forth near the surface on the slow-troll. The wobblers with their curvier wider bodies such as the Krocadile and Hot Shot series most definitely must be pulled S-L-O-W-L-Y. Avoid adding a snap-swivel to these spoons—it will kill their slow-seductive action.

All of these spoons are available in chrome or prism-scale finishes. Both patterns seem to work equally well. A lot of times the bonito will eat a slow-trolled spoon when faster-moving less subtle lures are producing.

Day in and day out, however, it is hard to beat feathers as your best overall option for trolled bonito. The old standby—a chrome, single-hook, lead head with turkey feathers—still works. It can be pulled fast or slow, rides fairly weedless, and persists in getting bit. The basic array of colors still produces with these feathers: blue/white, red/white, and green/yellow.

If you feel that you may be getting into some larger bonito, perhaps in double-digit weights, you might consider trolling a large, more conventional 15 mm tuna feather. These lures are sold rigged or unrigged, usually with a strong double hook. Particularly while running offshore near the outer banks and around the islands, a larger tuna feather like this might result in a big monster bonito or tuna! More on this strategy shortly.

Barracuda on the Troll

Rounding out the three B's, barracuda are also prone to attack a lure slowly trolled. Barries will eagerly hit soft plastics, small to medium size iron, feathers, spoons, and minnow-shaped plugs on the troll. With soft plastics, switch to Mojos and Lunker Thumpers in fluorescent lime or smoke/sparkle. A small Tora Tube in blue/flake is dynamite on the 'cuda pulled slowly behind the boat. Barracuda like a solid white jig slow-trolled. My favorite choices in this situation would be an Ironman #2, #3, or #4, or a Salas Christy 1, 2, or 6x Junior in heavier versions. Blue and white, along with blue and chrome models, can also be effective, but solid white in the "iron" remains the inside secret of the 'cuda experts.

Barries will also tear up your smaller plugs on the troll. You will get a lot of action and great sport using 10 to 12 pound string but be prepared to lose some of your lures with these toothy critters. You might be better off dragging plugs on 15 to 20 pound mono when it comes to 'cuda.

The CD-13 Magnum Rapala is a staple for barracuda on the slow-troll. However, some of the large 7 to 9 pound "stove pipes" will be scored trolling a longer and distinctively larger Rapala #SL-20 "Sliver" model. These are elongated, jointed-minnow plugs that can sometimes drive a barracuda crazy. Troll the Slivers in the more opulent fluorescent orange and chartreuse finishes while staying with the traditional blue or black models in the CD-13 Rapalas.

'Cuda will also sometimes nail a single-hook bonito feather slow-trolled especially in colder water conditions. Longtime barracuda aficionados will attest that the solid white feather with the chrome head and red glass bead eye would be the one to pull.

As for spoons, the same arsenal cited for bonito will work equally well for barracuda on the slow-troll. However, don't hesitate to experiment, scaling up considerably in size, trolling a large 2 to 4 ounce Krocadile or 2 1/8 ounce Haddock Jig'n Spoon. Again, the trick is to keep your trolling speed down but don't go so slow as to eliminate the action from the spoon. Dragging a big spoon like this may result in a "log" barrie that may home in on a bigger morsel while smaller school 'cuda are chasing 'chovies.

Drag Lures for Yellowtail

Many anglers fail to take advantage of a trolling opportunity when it comes to stalking 'tails. Trolling will often generate catches—both on shore and off—when fishing is especially slow or the yellows are scattered over a large area. The best overall strategy is to either drag tuna feathers or plugs for yellowtail. A basic 15 mm head is the appropriate size feather to troll alongside offshore kelp paddies. The 'tails will frequently race out from under the floating kelp to strike the tuna feather.

This same basic feather combo can also be pulled while cruising for breezing fish. This method works especially well inshore when you are working in the general vicinity where yellows have been sighted.

Sometimes, however, these "breezers" will be in a sub-surface mode. Tie on a 10 to 16 ounce ringed torpedo sinker about 4 to 6 feet above the feather. Rig the sinker with ball-bearing swivels at each end as previously discussed. The torpedo weight will drag the feather into slightly deeper strike zones. This subtle trick often produces bonanza catches on "breezers." Traditional tuna colors—blue/white, red/white, and green/yellow—are suitable for yellowtail trolling.

'Tails will also chase a minnow-shaped plug pulled at 3 to 6 knots. Smaller CD-13 Rapalas match well for 6 to 10 pound "peanut" class yellows. Drag the larger CD-14 and CD-18 Magnum Rapala or the giant #SL-20 Rapala Slivers if you are looking for bigger fish. The saltwater version of the Rapala Shad Rap also works for yellowtail on the troll. It has to be dragged fairly slow but it really mimics greenback and Spanish mackerel in size, color, and shape. Usually you won't be able to troll both feathers and plugs together. Drag either one class of lure or the other. Trolled together, the plugs may track too close to the feathers on their natural swimming motions and inadvertently cross lines.

Although it is rarely practiced, yellowtail will also respond to a large size candy bar style jig trolled at a fairly slow pace. A hefty size Salas 6x or 7x, a Tady 45 or an Ironman #3 or #5 may prove effective on the slow-troll. Stay with the lighter versions and definitely drag them in the stern as you set up the chum. Pull blue/white, mackerel, sardine, or scrambled egg colored jigs for yellowtail.

Tuna and Dorado on the Troll

Like yellowtail, almost all the major tuna species will home in on a trolled feather or plug. Historically, in the last decade or so the albacore as well as the yellow, bluefin, and skipjack tuna seem to overwhelmingly prefer a 15 mm head. These can be rigged with the traditional double hook or with a single Siwash model.

Popular tuna feather colors include "the basics"—blue/white, yellow/green, and red/white—along with more exotic combos such as purple/black, black/green, sold white, "Mexican flag" (yellow/red/green) or "zucchini" (yellow/orange/red). All the major manufacturers such as Braid, California Lures, Area Rule Engineering, Severstrand, and Zucker market tuna feathers in these combinations. Not all of these feathers are actually "feathers," per se. The tail portion of these trolling lures might also be plastic or vinyl.

Over the years, I have experimented by stacking two 15 mm heads on top of each other. This produces numerous, sometimes unusual, custom color combinations. For example, one of my favorites is to stack a red/white feather on top of a blue/white model. I call this hybrid the "Fourth of July." Stacking smaller feathers like this also creates a "jointed" or hinged effect with the lure. This increases the motion of the jig and gives the fish something new and different to look at.

Also keep in mind that there are different head shapes in these trolling feather lures that you can try. Braid, for example, markets a blunt-nose Wombat and a pointed cone-head shape Albie Teaser. There are also metal heads with holes drilled in to generate a stream of bubbles behind the lure. Popular models are made by Severstrand, Zuckers, and Area Rule Engineering.

Larger 25 mm class feathers are used for the big eye tuna. These 40 pound(+) fish prefer a bigger offering. However, there are times when they may want a sleeker, longer lure without the bulky 25 mm head. Here is where two stacked 15 mm feathers may be the hot ticket. I might add that I have even had striped marlin hit the slim profile double-stacked jig!

Other somewhat larger feathers or models with plastic skirts will also produce catches of big eye. The Zuckers "3.5" was designed primarily as a striped marlin jig. Big tuna and dorado will eat these large lures readily if they are in the area. The Severstrand Kona Jet and Area Rule Engineering Hoo-Nob are other mid-size trolling lures that can be deadly on the big eye tuna.

The members of the tuna family also attack trolled plugs. The large Rapala CD-14, CD-18 Magnum, and

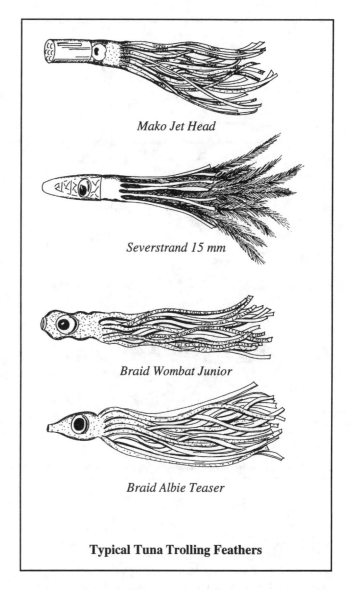

Mako Jet Head

Severstrand 15 mm

Braid Wombat Junior

Braid Albie Teaser

Typical Tuna Trolling Feathers

#SL-20 Slivers are excellent options to feathers if the fish seem to be highly finicky and reluctant to bite. The Braid Speedster and Reflecta models, both lipless plugs, are recent additions to the parade of trolling plugs and have enjoyed success with tuna on both local and long-range trips.

Even more important than the double or single Siwash hooks commonly used with trolling gear, the treble hooks on many of these big minnow-shaped plugs must be presharpened before you drag the lure. Tuna and dorado caught on the troll can apply tremendous leverage and force against the hooks combined with the boat traveling in the opposite direction. Insure solid penetration by taking the time to sharpen these big trebles.

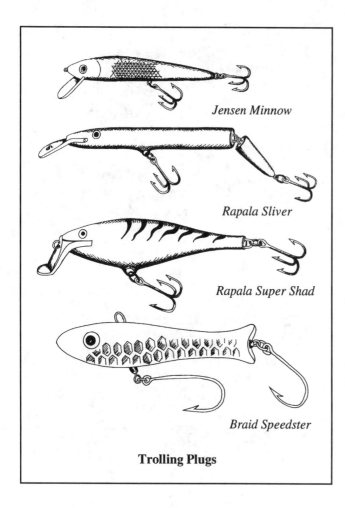

Jensen Minnow

Rapala Sliver

Rapala Super Shad

Braid Speedster

Trolling Plugs

More Trolling Tips

Irrespective of which pelagic species you are trolling for, always make sure that your rod and reel are secured to withstand the sudden impact from that initial strike. You may want to use auxiliary ropes tied to solid brass or stainless steel clips that attach to the posts of your conventional reel for extra insurance. The ropes are hitched to the railing in the stern of the boat.

On that note, you don't always have to troll with casting gear. I have had some outstanding sport dragging light jigs, plugs, spoons, plastics, and feathers on spinning tackle. If you want to troll with a spinner, be certain to use a reel with a quality drag system; otherwise many fish will be lost following that initial surge with a sticky drag that can happen with an inexpensive spinning reel. Similarly, check your baitcasting reels. These drags must also be in top-notch condition for a trolling program.

Another tip is to always monitor your boat speed and the distance from the boat where the lure is riding. After you get bit and wind the fish in be careful to duplicate the same trolling program. Let out the same amount of line and maintain the identical boat speed. Many novice trollers forget to account for these factors, which often produce only random success at best.

Finally, trolling is far from an exact science. Be experimental! Work with the entire menu of lures for a particular species. However, be careful in mixing different classes of baits at the same time. Usually spoons won't troll well next to plugs, or plugs with feathers. Always check your trolling lures to ascertain that they are "swimming" properly to generate the maximum results. Good luck!

Spoonin' the Pacific Coast

Metal spoons are one of the most versatile but underrated lures in a Pacific angler's tackle box. Spoons are an all-season lure. They will catch everything from pelagic species like bonito, barracuda, salmon, striped bass, yellowtail, and even tuna, to bottom dwellers including almost every kind of rockfish, halibut, and ling cod. Spoons are relatively simple to use once you understand their basic design and application.

Types of Saltwater Spoons

Spoons can be divided into two basic shapes: 1) wide-bodied wobblers and 2) narrow slab-shaped spoons. These are the simple yet fundamental styles we use here along the Pacific Coast from the north to the south.

Wide-Bodied Models. These spoons are larger versions of popular models often seen in Western trout circles. The spoon most widely used for marine conditions is the ever-popular Luhr Jensen Krocadile. Spoons in this design feature a fairly wide metal body that wobbles from side to side on the retrieve. This kind of spoon also has terrific fluttering action, mimicking a wounded baitfish as it slowly sinks. Other wide-bodied spoons that are highly suitable for Pacific coastal and offshore saltwater fishing include the Flutter Spoon, Diamond King and Mister "J."

Slab-Shaped Models. These spoons are characterized by their narrow bodies and sleek appearance. Models like the Hopkins, Deep Stinger, Champ, Haddock Jig'n Spoon, and Crippled Herring spoons have tremendous wind resistance and can be cast great distances. Slab-shaped spoons are designed to sink quickly and bounce off the bottom. However, these spoons may also prove to be deadly as surface lures. Let's look at some of the major gamefish species found off the Pacific Coast and how to catch these fish using simple spoons.

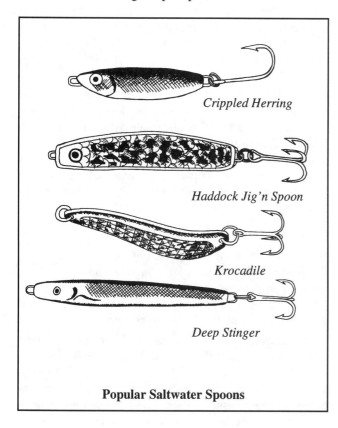

Crippled Herring

Haddock Jig'n Spoon

Krocadile

Deep Stinger

Popular Saltwater Spoons

Bass on Spoons

Calico and sand bass comprise an integral component of the yearly catch for sportfishing fleets in southern California. Both of these saltwater bass species will readily attack a shiny spoon.

In the colder months, both calicos and "sandies" will be situated near the bottom structure at 60 to 90 foot depths. One of the best ways to reach these fish is with a slab-shaped spoon vertically yo-yoed off the bottom. The trick is to make good bottom contact. Depending upon wind and current, fish either a Deep Stinger or Crippled Herring spoon in 1 to 3 ounce models. Watch for sudden slack in the line as bass suspended off the bottom may strike the spoon as it is sinking. Once on the bottom, use an exaggerated lift-and-drop sequence, raising and lowering your rod tip from the 3 to the 12 o'clock position. The object is to make the spoon literally "jump" off the bottom, then flutter down replicating a dying squid, anchovy, mackerel, or sardine.

For bass, use the Deep Stinger in pearl/blue back, pearl/green back, or nickel/neon green patterns. In the Crippled Herring series, the blue/over chrome and bluish green back/over chrome finishes are great for calico and sand bass.

As water temperatures warm, switch to a sub-surface cast-and-wind retrieve with a Krocadile spoon. Depending upon the size of the bass in the school, select from 5/8 to 2 + ounce models. Remember, however, "big spoons catch big fish." Occasionally pause in the retrieve to let the "Kroc" lazily flutter down a few feet. Always be prepared for a sudden jolt as a bigger "bull" calico or sand bass practically "inhales" the Krocadile on the sink.

Time-proven colors for this style of saltwater bassin' are chrome, chrome/blue mackerel, chrome/green mackerel, and chrome/silver prism lite. The Luhr Jensen Krocadile spoon is available in all these finishes.

Spoon 'Cuda!

Veteran saltwater buffs in Southern California have known for years that big 'cuda love a shiny spoon! Although a lot of smaller barracuda may be caught on live bait, the trophy 7 to 10 pound "logs" are frequently taken by accomplished spoon fishermen.

In the early spring, the barries can stack up on the bottom all the way down to 120 feet. These fish will be semi-lethargic, but they will eat if a lure is placed right in front of them. Here a heavier 1 1/2 to 3 ounce spoon yo-yoed off the bottom can be deadly. The Luhr Jensen Deep Stinger and Crippled Herring along with the large Haddock Jig'n Spoon are perfect for deep-water 'cuda. In addition to the patterns recommended for bass, try a Deep Stinger in solid white or pearl/pink back patterns. Barracuda are notoriously fond of white and pearl finish lures. The Haddock models in prism scale finishes all seem to work equally well. Similarly, fish a Crippled Herring in the fluorescent blue back over a pearl white body. This particular pattern should always be a staple in the serious 'cuda fisherman's arsenal.

When the barries are "up" near the surface, it is hard to find a lure better than the Krocadile. The basic patterns used for saltwater bass are also perfect for barracuda. 'Cuda will also go crazy over some other, more esoteric finishes in the Krocadile series that are worth adding to your spoon inventory. The hammered brass/fire stripe has been a longtime local favorite along with the chrome/fire stripe. You may also want to switch to a Krocadile with the optional single hook arrangement. This spoon is a lot easier to remove from a toothy customer like the barracuda, using a single hook instead of the traditional treble hook configuration.

Another well-kept secret is to throw either the Luhr Jensen Super Duper or Hot Shot Wobbler spoon on light line for these fish. The Super Duper and Hot Shot are hallmark lures for Western trouters. Skilled saltwater anglers casting these spoons in brass/fire stripe patterns know that finicky barracuda will also find a Super Duper or Hot Shot Wobbler to their liking!

Bonito Spoonin'

These powerful little members of the tuna family are readily taken on a shiny spoon. "Bonies" in deep water will jump on a Crippled Herring, Haddock Jig'n Spoon, Hopkins, or Deep Stinger spoon yo-yoed off the bottom. Any of these models in some variation of chrome finish will perform admirably. Scale down in size, however, from 3/4 to 2 ounces.

When bonito are on the surface feeding on schools on anchovies, start throwing those Krocadiles! A 5/8 to 1 1/2 ounce "Kroc" thrown on a light baitcasting or spinning outfit makes a potent combination on bonito. Here again, almost any finish in the Krocadile series will be effective on the bonies as long as it has some trace of chrome in it.

Yellowtail Spoons

These fish are one of the most prized gamefish sought along the Southern California and Baja coastlines. There are times, particularly when the "yellows" are feeding near the surface, that they will attack a spoon.

With most specimens in the 12 to 25 pound range, don't hesitate to throw a larger 3 1/4 to 5 ounce Krocadile on schools of boiling yellowtail. Be careful not to reel the "Kroc" in too fast. A steady retrieve to keep the spoon from spinning is best for yellows.

The chrome/blue mackerel, chrome/green mackerel, chrome/silver prism-lite, and blue mackerel finishes are favorites when throwing big Krocadiles on feeding yellowtail.

However, don't overlook slow-trolling these big spoons to locate schools of "breezing" yellows. Throttle down the boat speed to a few knots and slow-troll "Krocs" in yellowtail territory. The big spoons will look like errant mackerels or sardines—prime morsels for hungry yellows!

Tuna Spoons

Yes, tuna will definitely nail a spoon on the outer banks! As the boat slides to a stop following an initial strike on the trolling lines, quickly fire off a cast with either a Krocadile, Deep Stinger, Haddock Jig'n Spoon, or Crippled Herring spoon. Lure color isn't too critical in this situation when fishing "the slide." Any of these spoons in a variation of chrome finish will work fine. As the spoon sinks away from the boat, charging yellowfin, bluefin, or albacore tuna may intercept it as it is sinking. After the spoon has sunk to roughly 90 to 150 feet if you don't get bit, start a steady retrieve back to the surface.

The offshore strike can be voracious on these lures with tuna in the 15 to 35 pound range. After you catch one on the slide, continue to free-cast the spoons, fishing them fairly deep for the schooling tuna. Some of the largest specimens caught on a tuna trip are invariably taken by an accomplished angler fishing lures like these spoons on "the slide."

Spoon Bottom Grabbers

Halibut, ling cod, and the myriad of shallow-water rockfish found all the way north to Vancouver are eager biters when it comes to the shiny spoon. As was mentioned with saltwater bass fishing, bottom contact will be essential when vertical spoonin' for these bottom dwellers.

The heavier 1 1/2 to 4 ounce models in both the Deep Stinger and Crippled Herring spoons are excellent for this type of bottom-bouncin'. The vertical lift-and-drop yo-yoing technique works best. As you fish these spoons below 120 foot depths, color becomes less important to the fish. The key again is to make solid bottom contact, keeping the spoon in the deep strike zone.

I want to reiterate how important it is to occasionally pin on a strip of cut mackerel or dead squid to one of the points on the spoon's treble hook when you start to do some serious deep-water spoonin'. This adds a lot of "flavor," giving the spoon a more lifelike scent at these greater depths where the fish rely more upon smell than sight and color!

Salmon Spoons

Both chinook and coho salmon are eager to strike a trolled spoon as the boat pulls these lures with the current. This kind of lure clearly mimics crippled baitfish which comprise the bulk of the salmon's diet. Wobbling spoons such as the Krocadile are usually the best choice for salmon. You need to have that distinctive side-to-side action to trigger strikes.

Both coho and chinook salmon can be highly temperamental when it comes to spoon color choices. Be prepared to switch back and forth between certain models throughout a day of trolling. Depending upon where the salmon are stratified—and this is where good electronics come into play—different colored spoons will reflect or refract light better than others.

For example, a red spoon trolls best at the surface down to about 30 foot depths. Any deeper, and this color is filtered out. Yellow and chartreuse models in contrast, will be effective down to about 60 feet with green and blue spoons working somewhat deeper. By understanding this simple color gradation, you will be able to select the most effective colored spoon when trolling for salmon off the Pacific Coast.

Compared to other spoonin' strategies, salmon trolling can be done with a wide range of set ups: surface (flat line), keel sinker, Dipsy Diver plane, downriggers, and Dodger rigs. (These tactics are explained in greater detail in the general section on salmon fishing.) Salmon can also be caught slowly drifting spoons in open water. This method is simple to master. Free-spool the spoon to the bottom or desired level. Raise the rod tip from about 6 inches to 6 feet to start the sequence. Then drop the rod tip sharply causing slack line. This allows the lure to flutter back to the starting level. Pause a few seconds after the line tightens up and begins another lift-and-drop sequence.

Spoon Stripers!

Most of the same spoonin' tactics that work for pelagic species such as bonito, barracuda, and calico or sand bass will work equally well for striped bass. In fact, stripers often put on the most voracious surface-feeding frenzies where a well-thrown spoon gets bit instantly. Both wobblers and slab-style models are effective with this northern gamefish.

Like salmon, striped bass can also be spooned on the drift or slow-trolled from the surface to mid-depths utilizing everything from diving plans to downriggers to keep the spoon at specific strata. Proven striped bass colors in metal spoons for medium to deep spoonin' are blue or green in combination with nickel (either hammered or smooth surface). For spoonin' striped bass near the surface use chartreuse green or red in prism scale or pointed finishes as well as standard metallic gold or chrome finishes. Refer to the more detailed section on stripers for additional information.

All-Season Lures!

As you can see, saltwater spoons are truly multi-species all-season lures. Carry an array of these various models in a variety of sizes, shapes and colors with you when fishing the vast Pacific coastal waters.

When other anglers are struggling with live bait, try these spoons! More fish and larger "jackpot" contenders are always a possibility when you start using simple yet effective spoons along the West Coast!

Packing Iron

As the director of the Eagle Claw Saltwater Fishing Schools, I travel around the country to look for new locales to serve as sights for future programs. In my travels to the Florida Keys, Kauai, Kona, and Cabo San Lucas, I have realized that the cast-metal jig or the "iron" as it is termed, is basically a Southern California phenomenon. For example, on a trip to the Keys to sample the giant amberjack suspended in 300 to 400 feet of water, I was amazed to see 45 to 75 pound "ambers" practically inhale a big an Ironman #6 or Salas 6 or 7x size jig every drop.

Deep-water yo-yoing in this manner is still foreign to most charter boat operations in Florida. When you talk about "jigs," many skippers quickly point to a painted lead head with bucktail feathers. A search through the various tackle stores in the Keys also proved futile—they just don't stock this style of lure.

On a trip to Cabo San Lucas, our students experienced one of those rare days when the marlin simply refused to strike either live bait or a trolled lure. As we were jigging for mackerel (a prime marlin bait), in mid-afternoon, one of the anglers in our party decided to drop a heavy blue and white metal jig down about 200 to 250 feet to see if there were fish below the bait.

Sure enough, almost instantly, he got bit on the yo-yo by huge 10 to 13 pound class skipjack tuna. Soon, we were all yo-yoing the iron for these second-class tuna as a means of salvaging an otherwise long, unproductive day of marlin fishing. Needless to say, we had some great sport fighting these monster "skippies" on light tackle teamed with the heavy jigs. A similar scenario was repeated for yellowfin tuna and dorado while tossing the iron following a Cabo jig strike on the troll.

These are clear examples of why it pays to "pack iron" with you wherever you venture Pacific. You can't go wrong by always having a few of the heavier sinking versions handy. These jigs will allow you to fish the optimal strike zones quickly. They are relatively easy to use, either yo-yoing up-and-down, or simply winding in on a steady retrieve. Salmon, striped bass, ling cod, and rockfish are also prime candidates for the serious jig fisherman working the colder northern waters.

As for color schemes, there seems to be a basic selection of patterns in this sort of lure that are effective on the Pacific coast. Keep a few jigs in chrome, blue and white, green and yellow, and solid white in your tackle box at all times. These are popular colors for most pelagic species. As an added trick, throw a few marking pens into your tackle box. Using permanent black, blue, red, or green ink, you can custom-color almost any one of the basic jig patterns while in the field to adjust for particular species preferences.

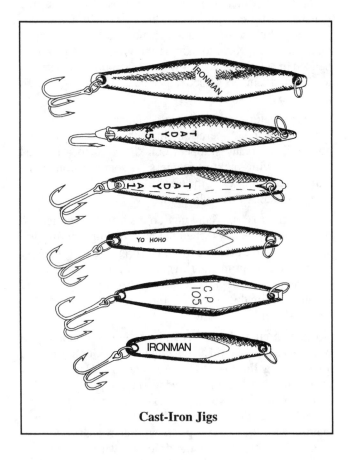

Cast-Iron Jigs

Bottom dwellers also chomp on solid chrome, blue/white, scrambled egg, green or blue/chrome, mottled purple, orange or red, and solid white. As for the "light" versions, or surface jigs, the color menu includes solid white or chrome, scrambled egg, blue/white, and green/yellow. Here is a succinct listing of the most popular models, weights, and colors of cast-metal jigs we routinely use on the Eagle Claw Fishing Schools with great success.

Species	Recommended Jig Models	Preferred Colors
Calico bass	Ironman #2 Salas Christy 2 (H) Tady 45 (L) Jerry Jig Light	blue/white, green/yellow, General Motors green
Sand bass	Ironman #2 Salas Christy 2 (H) Jerry Jig Light	blue/white, blue/chrome, solid white, solid chrome
Striped bass	Ironman #2, #3, #5	solid white, solid chrome
Bonito	Ironman #1, #2	blue/white, blue/chrome, green/chrome
Barracuda	Ironman #2, #4 Tady A1 (H) Salas 6xJR (H) Jerry Jig Light Ironman Candyman	solid white, blue/white, blue/chrome, scrambled egg
Yellowtail	Ironman #3, #5 Tady A1(H) and 45(L) Salas CP105 Jerry Jig Light Ironman Candyman	scrambled egg, blue/white, solid chrome, dorado
Yellowfin tuna	Ironman #3, #5 Tady A-1(H) Salas CP105 Jerry Jig Heavy	scrambled egg, blue/white, blue/chrome, dorado
Bluefin tuna	Ironman #5, #6 Tady A1 (H) Salas CP105 Jerry Jig Heavy	blue/white, blue/chrome
Albacore	Ironman #3, #5 Tady A1 (H) Salas CP105 Yo Yo #4 Jerry Jig Heavy	blue/white, blue/chrome, scrambled egg, red/white
Dorado	Ironman #3 Tady A1 (H) Jerry Jig Light	dorado, blue/white, scrambled egg, blue/chrome
White sea bass	Ironman #5 and Salas 6x and 7x (H and L) Jerry Jig Light	solid white, blue/white, solid chrome glow-white
Ling cod	Ironman #5, #6 Salas 6x, 7x (H) Jerry Jig Heavy	solid white, blue/white, blue/chrome, solid chrome
Rockfish	Ironman #2, #5, #6 Salas 6xJR Jerry Jig Heavy	solid white, solid chrome, blue/white, scrambled egg, blue/chrome, green/chrome

The Inner Game of Fishing

By now you have hopefully garnered some core insights into the technical aspects of fishing a variety of species found along the Pacific Coast. The lessons from the Eagle Claw Fishing Schools concentrate on the real "nitty gritty"—the specific how, when, and where—of how to catch everything from bottom grabbers to major league billfish. The preceding chapters have focused on the specific technical elements of challenging these West Coast species.

To conclude this series of lessons, I want to focus on an aspect of fishing that is equally important—the mental aspect or "inner game" of angling. The accomplished saltwater fisherman realizes that his mental outlook has a strong effect on his fishing success. It may be more important than all the technical information.

Creative Fishing

All fishermen—fresh and saltwater alike—seem to become stuck in a rut at times. We are hung up on tossing the same anchovies, the same jigs, or the same plastic lure trip after trip. Often it simply pays to try something "off the wall," giving the fish a lure or bait that is more bizarre to look at. Let me give you some firsthand examples of this out-of-the-ordinary approach.

On one of our Eagle Claw Fishing Schools we were scratchin' out a few legal size calicos south of Tijuana on the Salsipuedes kelp. One of the students, in the dead of winter, started throwing an old "General Motors" green surface jig on the outside kelp stringers. Wouldn't you know it? A 6 pound bull bass skyrocketed up from one of the kelp pockets to inhale the iron despite the cold water. There was no sign of surface activity. The angler simply wanted to take a shot at throwing something different. A jackpot resulted!

Similarly, on our Eagle Claw Fishing School in Key Largo, Florida, we teach our students to fish giant Atlantic amberjack Pacific Coast stand-up style, yo-yoing the

iron. On the third day of fishing, one angler with limits of 65 pound "ambers" decided to pin on an 18 inch long length of strip bonito to the treble hook on his yo-yo iron. The next drop, he nailed an 85 pound amberjack—and you guessed it—the big fish jackpot for the trip.

On one school where we were targeting shallow-water rockfish, I received some miniature Power Tubes from Berkley. These are similar to the tiny tube baits used for freshwater panfish, only laden with Berkley's fish scent. I had all the students lace one of the little Power Tubes onto their live bait hooks or onto the trebles on their jigs and spoons. The rockfish and ling cod annihilated them!

I have been on other trips where shrewd anglers brought out their own private stock of fresh shrimp or even octopus. I watched one fisherman nail one sheepshead after another on the fresh shrimp when nothing else would interest these finicky "goats."

On still another outing, I observed my instructors replacing the trebles on saltwater spoons with single hooks. Then they threaded on a soft plastic curl-tail grub. As bizarre as this spoon-and-grub combo looks, I have seen it catch a lot of bass and rockfish when no other hardware was working.

These are all firsthand examples of how it pays to be experimental, trying unusual lures and baits that might rarely be used otherwise. Let your imagination run wild at times while rummaging through your tackle boxes. Don't worry about what skippers, deckhands, or friends might think—go for it—try something new. A jackpot just might be out there waiting for the guy who takes a chance at fishing the bizarre!

Catching vs. Fishing

On the Eagle Claw Fishing Schools I have encountered an interesting question: Can I guarantee fish? As director of these schools, I charter the best vessels with accomplished captains and veteran crews for these trips. We cannot make the fish appear or more so require them to take the bait if conditions are not favorable. As much as we are in the business of "*fishing*," we of course want to practice as much "*catching*" as possible. Unfortunately, there are no guarantees in this sport.

There is a myriad of unpredictable variables that can affect a potential bite. Let's itemize a few of the more critical ones.

Water Temperature

Our local waters can be unpredictable and water temperatures can suddenly turn colder when it seems they should by warming up instead. For instance, in the middle of March, we found 61 degree water at San Martin Island, 150 miles south of San Diego. When conditions are right, this is prime yellowtail territory. That day, 160 'tails succumbed to cast-iron jigs in an area that receives relatively little angling pressure.

Three weeks later, with considerable "press" and hoopla, we took another group to this same area with the intention of repeating our previous feat. There was not a yellowtail to be had. An up-welling of cold water hit the island and surface temperatures plummeted to a chilly 55 degrees.

Water Color

Similarly water color can change rapidly and have an equally devastating effect on the bite. One day you may be "catching" tuna in classic dark blue water The next day you are "*fishing*" in a band of dirty green water and the tuna have disappeared. Mother Nature can be highly unpredictable.

Current

Shifts in current can be subtle but even so they can be a killer for inshore fishing. At Catalina Island, for example, you might have all the live squid you can stuff in a bait tank, again with high expectations of a bonanza day ahead. Even this primo bait can be worthless if subsurface water current is not moving—and in the right direction, I might add—to take the squid to the fish. Here again, you end up "*fishing*" instead of "*catching*."

Bait

Finally, the bait situation can be critical. One week the bait receivers are plum full of frisky hook-size anchovies. The barracuda, bass, and yellowtail go crazy for this hearty bait. The next day, the bait boat fails to score on the anchovies and instead fills the receivers with racehorse-

size sardines. Back at the same location, the skipper finds the fish won't give the big hefty 'dines even a glance; so once again it's back to "*fishing*."

So always try to be understanding of the skippers and charter masters who put these trips together. The best operators always try to maximize their chances but the fickleness of nature is obviously something that even these experts cannot control. Unfortunately, this sport does not come with a guarantee.

So plan to enjoy yourself with or without the fish. Remember there is a difference between "*fishing*" and "*catching*" You'll enjoy every trip if you aim to have a great day "*fishing*" and remember that "*catching*" is always a special bonus.

Everyone Welcome

Why are women distinctively absent from most passenger lists on party or charter boat trips? Well, probably because "deep sea fishin'" has been glamorized in the lore and tradition of the past, as one of the last major frontiers for man to battle nature one-on-one. The sea is where men can push their personal strength and stamina to its maximum while combating both the elements and the prey at the other end of the line.

Female athletes on the other hand have penetrated the barriers of most major sports such as golf, tennis, bowling, archery, softball, basketball, volleyball, auto and horse racing and even trap and skeet shooting. But female anglers remain distinctively absent on the "Big Pond."

Well guys, let me share with you some major insights I've gleaned from watching a modest number of ladies fishing on my Eagle Slaw Saltwater School charters. To begin with, the women seem to demonstrate a tremendous amount of inner peace and patience. This is probably due to the fact that the females on these trips don't construct a "man vs. nature" scenario out on the water. Relying upon that kinder, gentler, softer side of human personality, the ladies do not seem to internalize any pressure to prove anything while maintaining respect for nature and the marine environment.

The female angler to be sure is every bit as tough as the male. What she may lack in sheer brute strength, she makes up for in perseverance, stamina, and level-headedness. In all my 40(+) years of saltwater fishing, I have never seen a single woman "lose it" at the rail during a wide-open bite, cursing, yelling, screaming and pouting, like some men do when they lose a fish.

Instead, the ladies I've watched at the rail under heavy "combat" conditions, simply shrug off a lost fish, return to re-tie, bait up again, and get right back into the thick of the action with a smile on their face. Most ladies simply don't consider fighting a fish a life or death proposition, or a "rite of passage" into greater womanhood, as do many of their male counterparts.

Female anglers also seem to have a great sense of touch. They tend to be excellent light-liners, good live bait enthusiasts, with a high level of patience during the slack periods. It is not just luck or mere coincidence why many woman end up winning the jackpot, while males who put a lot of pressure on themselves are often stymied.

Men—we can learn from the so-called "weaker sex" when it comes to saltwater fishing. Study their patience, gentleness, and overall attitude in treating the trip as an occasion to have some fun. The female angler can usually hold her own on a party boat. As novices some may appreciate help or guidance. But this holds true for male or female beginners. One thing the lady fisherman doesn't need is patronizing or being treated like she is a "little girl."

The sportfishing industry depends on bringing more and more "new blood" into the sport. Let's give the women a chance guys—we may learn something from them. Share this idea with someone you love, and bring 'em out on a trip!

"Positive Fish Attitude"

When I was growing up, I devoured every piece of written material about fishing that I could get my hands on. From the campfire lore of Ted Trueblood to simplified fly fishing by Lefty Kreh, I tried to read all the great outdoor authors of that time. Of all the features I collected back in those days, one really stuck with me down through the years.

Unfortunately, I can't remember who wrote the article for I would certainly like to both credit and thank him for the piece. Nevertheless, he talked about what is perhaps the most important ingredient necessary to become a successful angler. The writer termed this component, P.F.A.—Positive Fish Attitude.

What is P.F.A.? Well, basically it is belief that the fish will bite. No matter how bad the weather, how rough the water, or how negative the reports are, P.F.A. means you approach your quarry with victory in mind.

Positive Fish Attitude was coined way before notions such as "visualization" or the "inner game" hit the popular press. But P.F.A. is definitely akin to this type of "affirmative mind set."

I have fished and worked with some of the great fishermen of this past decade. Party boat skippers Ron Hart, Mark Pisano, Paul Strasser, Fred Benko, Buzz Brizendine, and Russ Izor certainly are at the top of their sport. World-class trophy hunters like the late Bob Bringhurst and Don McAdams were the best at their specialties. Similarly, western guides like Mike Gardner know how to sustain when the pressure is on.

All of these super fishermen have one thing in common—P.F.A. Even before they set out, they conceptualize a successful game plan for the fishing day. Once on the water, even when things turn sour, they "gut it out." They maintain the strong belief that they not only deserve to catch fish, but that they *will* catch fish. Most importantly, they internalize this positive fish attitude from start to finish—no matter what the prevailing conditions are.

This is not some kind of psychological "mumbo-jumbo" I'm espousing here. By assuming this positive posture, the accomplished saltwater angler is able to assess the situation clearly and draw upon a repertoire of tactics that will work. The motivation level remains high all day long with fishermen of this caliber.

I've seen veteran deckhands, skippers, and "dead heads," for example, continue to fire off casts with as much intensity at the end of the day as when they started. I've watched them go into a "two minute drill" with seconds before the boat pulled up the anchor, meticulously and positively continuing to dissect the water. So many times these saltwater pros will tell you that they "pulled it out" in the last cast. You know why? P.F.A.!

Practice Catch and Release

To conclude this book, I leave you with a simple request. Keep only the fish you are planning to eat—release the rest. The Pacific Coast fishery is not an endless warehouse of the myriad of species I have talked about in this book. Take a look sometime at pictures of the quantities and size of halibut, bass, etc. that were caught earlier in this century and you'll see how greatly this fishery has changed.

More and more it is evident that this is a fragile ecosystem impacted by everything from commercial fishing and pollution to increased recreational traffic. It can take many years for this body of water to replenish diminished stocks of a given species. So don't take this fishery for granted—practice catch and release.

Good Luck!

Saltwater Sportfish Identification Guide

The main purpose of this guide is to help identify the species of fish caught off California. Recently, the State of California's Department of Fish and Game (DF & G), in conjunction with several other agencies, published *Marine Sportfish Identification—California*. This publication was instrumental in preparing the information on the following pages, including the "Fishing Information" sections. This fishing info, in most cases, should be considered an adjunct to the detailed material that is the heart of **Saltwater Fishing in California**.

Copies of *Marine Sportfish Identification—California* are available from DF & G offices for approximately $4.00. This version is tackle-box size and includes color reproductions of all 78 species. Speaking of species, there are over 500 species of fish found in California's coastal waters. The most common 78 are described on the following pages.

Spiny Dogfish	233	Sea Bass, Giant	243
Shark, Common Thresher	233	Bass, Kelp	243
Shark, Bonito	233	Bass, Barred Sand	244
Shark, Gray Smoothhound	233	Bass, Spotted Sand	244
Shark, Brown Smoothhound	234	Mackerel, Jack	244
Shark, Leopard	234	Yellowtail	245
Shark, Blue	234	Sargo	245
Shovelnose Guitarfish	234	Queenfish	245
Bat Ray	235	White Sea Bass	245
Round Stingray	235	Yellowfin Croaker	246
Sturgeon, Green	235	California Corbina	246
Sturgeon, White	235	Croaker, White	246
Salmon, Chinook (King)	236	Croaker, Spotfin	246
Salmon, Coho (Silver)	236	Opaleye	247
California Lizardfish	236	Halfmoon	247
Pacific Hake (Whiting)	236	Surfperch, Silver	247
Pacific Tomcod	237	Surfperch, Walleye	248
California Grunion	237	Surfperch, Shiner	248
Jacksmelt	237	Surfperch, Redtail	248
Sculpin	238	Surfperch, Rubberlip	249
Rockfish, Black	238	Surfperch, Barred	249
Rockfish, Blue	238	Sheephead, California	249
Bocaccio	238	Barracuda, California	249
Chilipepper	239	Giant Kelpfish	250
Cowcod	239	Mackerel, Pacific	250
Rockfish, Olive	239	Skipjack	250
Rockfish, Yellowtail	240	Bonito, Pacific	250
Rockfish, Canary	240	Albacore	251
Rockfish, Vermillion	240	Tuna, Bigeye	251
Rockfish, Copper	240	Tuna, Bluefin	252
Rockfish, Widow	241	Tuna, Yellowfin	252
Rockfish, Greenspotted	241	Swordfish	252
Rockfish, Starry	241	Marlin, Striped	253
Sablefish	241	Halibut, California	253
Lingcod	242	Sanddab, Pacific	253
Kelp Greenling	242	Sanddab, Longfin	253
Pacific Staghorn Sculpin	242	Halibut, Pacific	254
Cabezon	242	Founder, Starry	254
Bass, Striped	243	Sole, Petrale	254

Spiny Dogfish

a spine at the origin of each dorsal fin

Family: Squalidae (Dogfish sharks)
Genus and Species: *Squalus acanthias*
Description: The body of the spiny dog-fish is elongate and slen-der. The head is pointed. The color is slate gray to brownish on top, sometimes with white spots, becoming white below.

This species and the horn shark are the only sharks along the California coast with spines at the beginning of both dorsal fins. These spines may be mildly poisonous and provide a defense for the spiny dogfish.
Range: Spiny dogfish occur in temperate and subtropical waters in the Atlantic and Pacific Oceans. In the eastern Pacific Ocean they are found off Chile, and from central Baja California to Alaska and to Japan.
This species is common in nearshore waters along most of the coast. It is generally found in waters up to 1,200 feet deep though spiny dogfish have been taken to depths of 2,400 feet.
Natural History: The spiny dogfish feeds upon practically all smaller fishes such as herring, sardines, anchovies, smelts and even small spiny dogfish as well as crabs.

The females are larger than the males, and produce from 3 to 14 young at a time and in alternate years. Most adults are 2 to 4 feet long.
Spiny dogfish are long lived and non-migratory; as a result, heavy fishing pressure in a given area will lower the population level of this slow growing, low reproductive species quite rapidly.
Fishing Information: You are most likely to catch a spiny dogfish with anchovies or invertebrates on a rock cod jig, They are commonly taken in commercial bottom trawl nets.
Other Common Names: dog shark, grayfish, Pacific grayfish, spinarola, California dogfish.
Largest Recorded: 5.25 feet; no weight recorded; however, a large fat female about 4 feet long will weigh 15 pounds.
Habitat: Shallow Sandy Environment

Common Thresher Shark

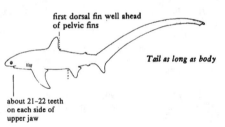

first dorsal fin well ahead of pelvic fins

Tail as long as body

about 21-22 teeth on each side of upper jaw

Family: Alopiidae (Thresher sharks)
Genus and Species: *Alopias vulpinus*
Description: The body of the common thresher shark is moderately elongate. The snout is rather short, and the mouth crescent shaped. The first dorsal fin is large, and located midway between the pectoral and ventral fins. The second dorsal and anal fins are very small. The tail is distinctive since it is very long, almost as long as the rest of the body. The coloration may vary from brownish gray, bluish or blackish above to silvery, bluish or golden below. The dorsal, pectoral and ventral fins are blackish and sometimes the pectoral and ventral fins have a white dot in the lip.

The bigeye thresher also occurs off the California coast. It can be distinguished by its large eye; however, if you can count the teeth in the upper jaw, the common thresher has 21-22 on each side while the bigeye thresher has 10-11 on each side.
Range: The common thresher shark occurs worldwide in warmer seas. In the eastern North Pacific, it is found from central Baja California, to the Strait of Juan de Fuca, British Columbia. The common thresher is an inhabitant of the upper layers of deep offshore waters and is most abundant in areas of steep bottom contour along the edges of the continental shelf. During the spring and summer months smaller thresh-ers may occur near shore where they are often seen leaping completely out of the water.
Natural History: The food habits of the thresher are not well known, but on the California coast they feed mostly upon small fish such as sardines, anchovies, mackerel, and squid. They are said to use their long tail as a flail to frighten or stun their prey.

The common thresher shark bears live young and appears to become sexually mature in 6 or 7 years. Four pups are produced annually. A 18 foot female contained four young that weighed 13.5 pounds each and were 4 to 4.5 feet long.
Fishing Information: Most thresher sharks caught off California have been taken on live sardines, anchovies, or mackerel. Best localities

have been the San Francisco Bay area, the inshore coastal water between Point Conception and Port Hueneme, and Santa Monica Bay, especially around Malibu and Paradise Cove.

They are most abundant during the summer months. Considered a fine game species on light or medium tackle, they often put on an aerial demonstration. At other times the battle is entirely beneath the surface and consists of brute strength and shift-towing tactics.

An angler would do well to bait a live mackerel on a 9/0 hook attached to 10 or so feet of heavy wire leader.
Other Common Names: thresher, blue thresher, green thresher, longtail shark, swiveltail, fox shark, sea fox.
Largest Recorded: 20 feet; 1,000 pounds. Largest taken off California by a recreational angler: 527 pounds.
Habitat: Pelagic Environment

Bonito Shark

insertion of pectorals well ahead of origin of 1st dorsal fin

Family: Lamnidae (Mack-erel shark)
Genus and Species: *Isurus oxyrinchus*
Description: The body of the bonito shark is elongate but rather stout. The snout is long and pointed. The first dorsal and the pectoral fins are large, but the second dorsal and anal fins are very small. This species is a deep blue or dark gray above and white below. There is a black spot at the base of the pectorals.
Range: This shark is found worldwide in warm and temperate seas; in the eastern Pacific from Chile to the Columbia River, Washington, including the Gulf of California, but not in the tropics.
Natural History: The diet of the bonito shark includes fishes and squid, often large ones. Whenever possible, the bonito shark takes its food in one gulp. With its tremendous speed, it is unquestionably a dangerous shark. Bonito sharks bear live young.
Fishing Information: The bonito shark is one of the larger sharks to inhabit California waters. By all accounts, it is as dangerous as any shark, and it probably swims faster than most.

The best way to hook a bonito shark is by trolling with a whole tuna, squid or mackerel. You can also use lures, and chumming does help. Watch out, when you catch one, because this is a dangerous fish that will not hesitate to attack you or your boat.
Other Common Names: mako, mackerel shark, spriglio, paloma, shortfin mako.
Largest Recorded: 13 feet; 1,000 pounds. 11.5 feet; 1,030 pounds (California). Largest taken by a recreational angler off California; 299 pounds.
Habitat: Pelagic Environment

Gray Smoothhound

midpoint of base of 1st dorsal fin closer to origin of pelvic fins than to insertion of pectoral fins

Family: Carcharhinidae (Requiem sharks)
Genus and Species: *Mustelus californicus*
Description: The body of the gray smoothhound is elongate, slender, tapering from behind the dorsal fin to a long slender tail. The snout is comparatively long and flattened. The color is brown to dark gray above and whitish below.

The gray smoothhound can be distinguished from other smoothhounds by scales present on the posterior one-fifth of the dorsal fin and the teeth having sharp points.
Range: This species occurs from Mazatlan, Mexico, to Cape Mendocino, California; and is found in shallow waters to depths of 150 feet.
Natural History: The diet of the gray smoothhound includes crabs, shrimp and small fishes. The female bears the young alive.
Fishing Information: Although the gray smoothhound is of relatively minor importance to sport anglers, it is commonly taken in the surf. It is edible, but not as tasty as the brown smoothhound.

If you're fishing in southern California, you are most likely to catch a gray, and in central California, you are most likely to catch a brown smoothhound.
Other Common Names: shark, dogfish, paloma, sand shark, gray shark.
Largest Recorded: 5 feet 4.25 inches; no weight recorded.
Habitat: Shallow Sandy Environment

Brown Smoothhound

Family: Carcharhinidae (Requiem sharks)
Genus and Species: *Mustelus henlei*
Description: The body of the brown smoothhound is elongate, slender, tapering from behind the dorsal fin to the long slender tail. The snout is comparatively long and flattened. The color is brown or bronze above and silvery below.

The back one-fifth of the dorsal fin is without scales. The teeth are blunt, without sharp points. The brown and other smoothhounds can be distinguished from the soupfin shark since their second dorsal fins originate well in advance of the beginning of the anal fin; while in the soupfin, the second dorsal begins behind the origin of the anal fin.
Range: The brown smoothhound occurs from the Gulf of California to Humboldt Bay, California. It is found at depths from shallow water to 360 feet.
Natural History: The diet of the brown smoothhound includes crabs, shrimp, and small fishes.

Females bear their young live, as do most other sharks.
Fishing Information: The brown smoothhound is a relatively small shark, and is one of the most abundant sharks in the central California sport fishery.

This is a good sport species on light tackle, and can be taken in bays from San Francisco to Point Conception. Good baits to use include crabs, shrimp and small fishes. The brown smoothhound is considered a very good table fish.
Other Common Names: mud shark, dogfish, paloma, sand shark, Henle's shark.
Largest Recorded: 3. feet 1 inch; no weight recorded.
Habitat: Shallow Sandy Environment

Leopard Shark

Family: Carcharinidae (Requiem sharks)
Genus and Species: *Triakis semifasciata*
Description: The body of the leopard shark is elongate, and the snout is short and bluntly rounded. This shark is easily identified by the gray coloration over most of its body, and the black spots and crossbars on the back and side. It is white underneath.
Range: Mazatlan, Mexico, to Oregon. This well decorated species is abundant in bays and along sandy beaches of southern and central California in shallow water. During the fall, large numbers may be found in San Francisco and Monterey Bays.
Natural History: The leopard shark eats a variety of fishes and invertebrates like anchovies, squid or crab, all of which make good bait.

Females, which bear their young live, usually produce 4 to 29 pups in a lifter.
Fishing Information: It is considered a relatively harmless shark and is timid around divers; nevertheless, handle a live leopard shark with care.

The leopard shark is very good eating, and has been compared favorably to salmon.
Other Common Names: cat shark.
Largest Recorded: 7 feet; 70 pounds.
Habitat: Bay Environment

Blue Shark

Family: Carcharhinidae (Requiem sharks)
Genus and Species: *Prionace glauca*
Description: The body of the blue shark is elongate and slender. Its head is slender and the snout is long and pointed. The color is blue or light bluish gray above and white below.

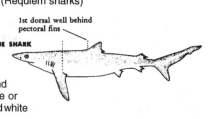

This species has up to three rows of functional teeth in each jaw and there are 14 or 15 serrated teeth in each side of each jaw. The pectoral fins are long and sickle shaped.
Range: The blue shark occurs worldwide. In the eastern Pacific, blue sharks are found from Chile to the Gulf of Alaska, but not in the tropics. It is common off southern California most of the year, but during warm water periods occurs much further north.
Natural History: Blue sharks do not mature until they attain a length of 7 or 8 feet. Of several thousand blue sharks taken on longline gear, the smallest female was 7 feet long.

A female weighing 95 pounds and 7 feet 7 inches long, contained 26 apparently fully developed young ranging in length from 15.5 to 17.75 inches, As many as 54 young have been counted in a single adult female captured in the Mediterranean Sea.
Fishing Information: Most are taken incidentally by albacore or rockfish anglers. Should you wish to specifically fish for blue sharks, they are easily taken once located. Either casting a bait at a previously located fish or chumming in an area known to be inhabited by blue sharks will usually produce results.

Dead fish or squid make excellent bait, and ground up anchovies make good chum. Blue sharks tend to "roll up" on the line, so it is necessary to use a long wire leader to avoid cutting the line on the shark's skin.

The blue shark is not considered a man-eater, but is probably responsible for many attacks upon injured swimmers, after boating, airplane, and other accidents at sea. It should be considered dangerous because of its numerical abundance and attraction for blood, if for no other reasons.

The fish may be eaten, but it is necessary to bleed it while it is still alive. After it is dead it should be cleaned, skinned and soaked as soon as possible to avoid the taste of urea in the meat.
Other Common Names: blue whaler, great blue shark.
Largest Recorded: No length recorded; 231 pounds (California); however, a 5 foot 9 inch male weighed just 49 pounds. A 12 foot 4 inch blue taken off southern California was not weighed.
Habitat: Pelagic Environment

Shovelnose Guitarfish

Family: Rhinobatidae (Guitarfishes)
Genus and Species: *Rhinobatos productus*
Description: The body of the shovelnose guitarfish is depressed and gradually tapers into the tail; the disk is longer than wide. The snout is rather long and rounded at the tip. The color is gray above becoming lighter below.

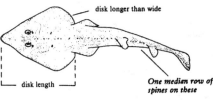

This species is distinguished from the banded guitarfish by the absence of dark crossbars on the back. It can be separated from most others of this flattened and plated group by the presence of a tail fin and two dorsal fins. Its sharp pointed nose distinguishes it from the other guitarfishes.
Range: Gulf of California to San Francisco, California. The shovelnose can be found, sometimes in large numbers, over sand or mud sand bottoms in colder, shallow coastal waters.
Natural History: The guitarfish diet consists of a variety of crustaceans, worms and clams. They have been observed feeding on sand crabs in water less than 3 inches deep. At times they are left stranded on the beach by receding waves and must wiggle their way back into the water much like grunion.

Shovelnose guitarfish bear live young, with as many as 28 from a single female. Mating takes place during the summer months and the young, apparently born during the following spring and summer, are 6 inch miniatures of the adults.
Fishing Information: Shovelnose guitarfish are caught in the surf, in bays and from piers. They take live or dead bait including clams, mussels, sand crabs and almost any other bait or lure. The flesh, especially the tail and back straps, is considered quite good.
Other Common Names: shovelnose shark, pointed nosed guitarfish, guitarfish.
Largest Recorded: 5 feet 1.5 inches; 40.5 pounds.
Habitat: Shallow Sandy Environment

Bat Ray

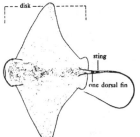

Description: The bat ray has a distinct head that is elevated above the disk. The tail is whip-like and as long or longer than the width of the disk with the sting located just behind the body. The color is dark brown to dark olive or almost black above and white below.

This species can be distinguished from manta rays or mobulas (that rarely occur off California) by the absence of the armlike projections manta rays and mobulas have on their heads.

Range: Bat rays are found from the Gulf of California to Oregon, from surface waters to depths of 150 feet.

Natural History: Bat rays feed chiefly upon mollusks and crustaceans. In bays and sloughs they feed heavily upon clams, oysters, shrimp and crabs. On the open coast they eat abalones and various other snails. When feeding, they swim along the bottom until they encounter currents of water expelled from the siphons of clams. They dig clams by suction created by flapping their wings. The shell of the ingested clam is crushed by their millstone like jaw teeth.

Mating takes place during the summer months and the young are born alive, apparently the following summer, when they are 12 to 14 inches in width and weigh about 2 pounds. The young are always born tail-first with their wings rolled up over the body. They come equipped with a stinger and can cause severe painful wounds.

Females apparently weigh at least 50 pounds and males 10 pounds before they are mature. Females of 50 to 60 pounds usually have two to four young; whereas, females of 130 to 140 pounds may have 10 or 12 young.

Fishing Information: Most sportfishing for bat rays takes place in protected bays and estuaries. Although bat rays may be taken in the open ocean, anglers prefer to catch them in sheltered waters. Heavy tackle is recommended since anglers often encounter large rays. Favorite baits include shrimp, clams, crabs or even cut mackerel.

Other Common Names: sting ray, eagle ray, batfish, stingaree, bat sting ray.

Largest Recorded: Width 4 feet, 9 inches; 181 pounds.

Habitat: Shallow Sandy Environment

Round Stingray

Family: Dasyatididae (Stingrays)

Genus and Species: *Urolophus halleri*

Description: The disk of the round stingray is nearly circular. The back of this species is brown, often mottled or spotted, and the underside is white to orange.

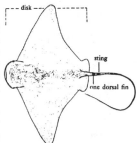

The round stingray is one of six rays found in California waters which have a stinger on the tail. It can be distinguished from the others since it is the only one with a true tail fin. The others have either a whip-like tail or very short tail with no fin membrane.

Range: This species occurs from Panama to Humboldt Bay, California, including the Gulf of California. Round stingrays are most abundant off southern California and northern Baja California at depths up to 70 feet.

Natural History: Round stingrays obtain much of their food by burrowing in the substrate. Their diet includes worms, crabs, snails, clams and small fishes.

It takes 3 months for the round stingray young to develop and they are approximately 3 inches wide at birth. Sexual maturity is reached in 2.6 to 3 years, and mating occurs from May to June and in December. There are one to six pups, depending upon the size of the female.

Fishing Information: Most round stingrays are taken incidentally by anglers fishing for other species. However, should one wish to go after them specifically, marine worms or pieces of clam are good bait. Sandy or muddy bottoms along a beach or in a bay should provide good fishing.

Round stingrays are potentially dangerous because of the wounds they can inflict. If an angler is stung, the wound should be cleaned thoroughly and bathed in water. One should see a doctor if pain persists or infection occurs.

Other Common Names: ray, stingray, stinger, stingaree.

Largest Recorded: 22 inches; no weight recorded; however, a male 20 inches long weighed 1.5 pounds.

Habitat: Shallow Sandy Environment

Green Sturgeon

Family: Acipenseridae (Sturgeons)

Genus and Species: *Acipenser medirostris*

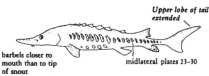

Description: The body of the green sturgeon is long, roughly cylindrical and has five rows of bony plates on its back. The snout is narrow, long, and cone-shaped, and more or less depressed below the level of the forehead. The mouth is toothless, protruding, and sucker-like. Four fleshy projections, or barbers, extend from the underside of the snout. The color is olive green above, whitish below, with olive stripes on the sides.

The green sturgeon can be distinguished by its olive green color, the number of bony plates along the side of the body (mid lateral plates; 23 to 30), a very pointed snout, and the barbels are closer to the mouth than to the tip of the snout.

Range: Ensenada, Baja California, to the Bering Sea and Japan. The green sturgeon is commonly found in brackish water (part saltwater, part freshwater).

Natural History: The green sturgeon sifts muds and silts for food and feeds upon small invertebrates and fishes. Since it has no teeth, it must swallow its food whole. The green sturgeon is anadromous, spending its adult life in the ocean but ascending coastal streams in the winter where it remains to spawn the following summer.

This species appears to reach sexual maturity in 10 or 15 years and may live to be over 100 years old.

Fishing Information: In California, the green sturgeon is regularly caught in San Francisco and San Pablo Bays, but is not considered to be a good food fish.

Other Common Names: none.

Largest Recorded: 7 feet; 350 pounds.

Habitat: Bay Environment

White Sturgeon

Family: Acipenseridae (Sturgeons)

Genus and Species: *Acipenser transmontanus*

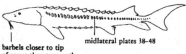

Description: The body of the white sturgeon is long, roughly cylindrical, and has five rows of bony plates on its back. The snout is bluntly rounded and more or less depressed below the level of the forehead. The mouth is toothless, protruding, and sucker-like. Four fleshy projections, or barbels, extend from the underside of the snout. The fish is overall gray in color.

The white sturgeon can be distinguished f rom the green sturgeon by its overall grey color, 38 to 48 bony plates along the side, a round snout, and the barbels are closer to the tip of the snout than to the mouth.

Range: This species occurs from Ensenada, Baja California, to the Gulf of Alaska.

The white sturgeon is the largest fish found in North American freshwaters. The white sturgeon is anadromous, and spends more of its time in the brackish (part salt, part freshwater) waters of bays than in the open ocean. Most anadromous fish spend their adult life in the ocean or brackish water, and spawn up freshwater streams.

Natural History: White sturgeon are bottom feeders and their diet consists predominantly of clams, grass shrimp, crabs and herring roe. All can be used as good baits to catch fish that are most commonly under 300 pounds. Rocks, twigs and other odd things have been found in their stomachs and a white sturgeon caught in the Snake River had eaten half a bushel of onions that it had found floating in the river.

This species is long lived and may live to be over 100 years old.

Fishing Information: A good food fish, the white sturgeon in California has been taken commercially in the past for its eggs (caviar).

Other Common Names: Sacramento sturgeon, Oregon sturgeon.

Largest Recorded: 12 feet; 1,285 pounds. Largest recreational caught in California: 468 pounds.

Habitat: Bay Environment

Chinook (King) Salmon

Family: Salmonidae (Salmons)
Genus and Species: *Oncorhynchus tshawytscha*
Description: The body of
the chinook salmon is elongate and somewhat com-
pressed. The head is conical. The color is bluish to
dark gray above, becoming
silvery on the sides and
belly. There are black spots
on the back and on both lobes of the tail.

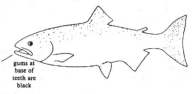

gums at
base of
teeth are
black

While five species of salmon occur along the Pacific Coast, over 99% of all salmon caught in the ocean off California are either chinook or cohos. Chinook and coho salmon can be distinguished by the color of the lining of the gums at the base of the teeth. In chinook salmon, this lining is blackish, while in cohos it is white.

Range: Chinook salmon occur from San Diego, California, to the Bering Sea and Japan. Generally, the fishery begins off San Luis Obispo County, California, and continues north.

Natural History: Chinooks and all salmon are anadromous—that is, they spend part of their life in the ocean and then enter fresh water to spawn. The adults spawn principally in large river systems, primarily from the Sacramento River system north. At spawning time, male chinooks turn very dark and usually have blotchy, dull red splotches on the sides and develops a hooked nose.

Most all chinook spawn when either 3 or 4 years of age but some, predominately males, will spawn at age 2. These precocious males are called jacks, chubs or grilse. Some rivers have large chinooks that do not spawn until 5 or 6 years old.

Sacramento River female chinook salmon produce an average of 6,000 eggs each. This, however, is an unusually high number since female chinook salmon from other river systems normally average only 3,500 to 4,500 eggs each.

Fishing Information: In the ocean, chinook salmon are fished princi-pally by trolling dead bait or artificial lures. Occasionally, live bait will be used while still-fishing or drift-fishing. Chinook salmon normally stay well beneath the surface of the ocean, usually 40 to 250 feet or more and a heavy weight or downrigger is necessary to keep trolled bait at the desired depth.

Other Common Names: king salmon, Sacramento River salmon, spring salmon, black mouth, Columbia River salmon, tyee.
Largest Recorded: 4 feet 10 inches; 126.5 pounds.
Habitat: Pelagic Environment

Coho (Silver) Salmon

Family: Salmonidae (Salmons)
Genus and Species: *Oncorhynchus kisutch*
Description: The body of the
coho salmon is elongate and
somewhat compressed. The
head is conical. This species
is dark metallic blue or blue
green above, becoming silvery
on the sides and belly. There
are spots on the back.

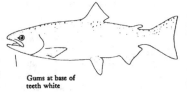

Gums at base of
teeth white

The main distinguishing fea-ture between the coho and chinook salmon is the color of the gums at the base of the teeth. Chinook salmon have a blackish lining while coho has a white lining. Cohos also have black spots only on the upper part of the tail fin, whereas chinook tail fins are completely covered with black spots.

Range: Coho salmon occur from Chamalu Bay, Baja California, to the Bering Sea and Japan.

Natural History: Cohos, as all salmon, are anadromous and spawn in fresh water. At spawning time the males turn dusky green above and on their head, bright red on their sides and blackish below. The females turn a pinkish red on their side after they enter fresh water.

Coho salmon enter streams, move upstream, and spawn from Sep-tember through March. The bulk of spawning takes place from Novem-ber through January. Adult males enter streams when they are either 2 or 3 years old, but adult females do not return to spawn until 3 years old. Almost all female coho salmon will spawn at age 3. All coho salmon, whether male or female, spend their first year in the stream or river in which they hatch. All adults die after spawning.

Generally speaking, the larger the female the greater the number of eggs produced; however, numerous counts have been made that

indicate most females will spawn from 1,500 to 3,500 eggs. The average number produced per female appears to be about 2,500.

Fishing Information: In the ocean, coho salmon are fished primarily by trolling with dead bait (anchovy, herring, etc.) or any of several types of lures. Occasionally, live bait is used while drift fishing. The fish are usually caught within 30 feet of the surface and a heavy weight is normally used to keep a trolled lure at the desired depth. Several devices are used by recreational anglers to detach this weight when a fish strikes or is hooked. Best trolling speed appears to be about 2 knots per hour.

Some coho salmon are taken off southern California; however, the ocean angler is most successful from Monterey Bay north. The bulk of the sport catch contains 6 to 10 pound fish, about 24 inches in length.
Other Common Names: silver salmon, silver sides, hookbill.
Largest Recorded: 38.5 inches; 31 pounds.
Habitat: Pelagic Environment

California Lizardfish

Family: Synodontidae (Liz-ardfishes)
Genus and Species:
Synodus lucioceps
Description: The California
lizardfish has an elongate cy-
lindrical body with a head

gill membranes and pelvic
fins yellow

and mouth which are lizard-like in appearance. The body is a uniform brown on the back and sides shading to tan or white on the belly.

Because of its elongated body and mouth full of sharp teeth, California lizardfish are occasionally mistaken for the California barracuda. The barracuda, however, is silvery rather than brown and has two dorsal fins of approximately equal size with a wide space between them. The lizardfish has only a single dorsal fin with a tiny fleshy fin behind it.

Range: The California lizardfish occurs from Guaymus, Mexico, to San Francisco, California, but is not common north of Point Conception, California. This species generally occurs over sandy bottoms in shallow water ranging from 5 to 150 feet, but has been taken at depths up to 750 feet.

Natural History: The California lizardfish spend most of their time sitting on the bottom with the body at a slight angle, propped up in the front end by the ventral fins. This inactivity ends rapidly when small fishes or squid swim into the area and the fish dart upward to grab one, usually swallowing the prey in one gulp.

This species is believed to spawn during the summer months when adult fish have been observed to congregate on sandy patches. Young lizardfish, less than 3 inches long, are nearly transparent, elongate, scaleless, with a row of large black spots under the skin of the belly.

Fishing Information: The California lizardfish, while not sought by most anglers, is taken incidentally in fairly large numbers by anglers fishing for other shallow water bottomfishes like halibut.

California lizardfish can be caught on a wide variety of cut baits fished on the bottom.
Other Common Names: candlefish, lizardfish.
Largest Recorded: 25.17 inches; no weight recorded; however, it is reported to reach 4 pounds.
Habitat: Shallow Sandy Environment
a Pacific halibut that large. The fish are typically caught on crab, shrimp, squid, and other invertebrates.
Other Common Names: alabato, northern halibut, right halibut, genu-ine halibut, real halibut.
Largest Recorded: 8.75 feet; 507 pounds.
Habitat: Deep Sandy Environment

Pacific Hake (Pacific Whiting)

Family: Merlucciidae* (Hakes)
Genus and Species: *Merluccius productus*
* *Gadidae (American Fisher-
ies Society)*
Description: The body of the
Pacific hake is elongate, slender, and moderately com-
pressed. The head is elongate and the mouth large.

deep notches in 2nd dorsal
and anal fins

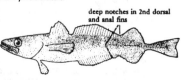

The color is gray to dusky brown, with brassy overtones and black speckles on the back. The elongated shape, notched second dorsal and anal fin, and the coloration separate Pacific hake from other fish in this group.

Range: The Pacific hake occurs in the Gulf of California (isolated population) and from Magdalena Bay, Baja California, to Alaska and along the Asiatic coast. It is found to depths exceeding 2,900 feet.

Natural History: The diet of this species includes small fishes, shrimp and squid.

Pacific hake spawn in the winter, beginning at 3-4 years of age, off southern California and Baja California, Mexico. After spawning the adults migrate northward to Oregon, Washington and Canada and return to their spawning areas in the fall.

Fishing Information: Pacific hake are most commonly caught incidentally by anglers seeking salmon or bottomfish.

Pacific hake support one of the larger commercial fisheries off the Pacific Coast. Considered a nuisance by many anglers, they are generally discarded if caught. If kept chilled immediately after capture, Pacific hake have good food qualities. However, the fish becomes soft and undesirable if not cared for properly. Pacific hake may be caught with salmon or groundfish baits such as squid, herring or anchovy.

Other Common Names: Pacific whiting, whitefish, haddock, butterfish, California hake, popeye, silver hake, ocean whitefish.

Largest Recorded: 3 feet; no weight recorded.

Habitat: Deep Sandy Environment

Pacific Tomcod

Family: Gadidae (Codfishes)

Genus and Species: *Microgadus proximus*

Description:.The body of the Pacific tomcod is elongated, slender and moderately compressed. The head is elongate and there is a small fleshy projection, a barbel, on the lower jaw. The color is olive green above, creamy white below, and the fins have dusky tips.

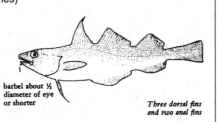

barbel about ½ diameter of eye or shorter

Three dorsal fins and two anal fins

Three spineless dorsal fins and the small chin barbel separate the Pacific tomcod from any similar appearing fish, except its cousin, the Pacific cod. The Pacific cod has a barbel as long as the diameter of the eye while the Pacific tomcod has a barbel that is less than one half the diameter of the eye.

The Pacific tomcod is a member of the true cod family. It is one of the smaller members of the group and is often confused with the white croaker. Again, the three spineless dorsal fins will distinguish this species from the others.

Range: The Pacific tomcod occurs from Point Sal, California, to Unalaska Island, Alaska, in near surface waters to depths of 720 feet.

Natural History: The diet of the Pacific tomcod includes anchovies, shrimp, and worms.

A 10.3 inch female Pacific tomcod contained an estimated 1,200 eggs.

Fishing Information: Pacific tomcod are occasionally taken by recreational anglers in central and northern California. This is usually incidental to fishing for other species of fish. Since these are rather small fish, light line and small baited hooks are the proper gear. Small pieces of cut fish make good bait.

Other Common Names: tomcod, piciata, California tomcod.

Largest Recorded: 12 inches; no weight recorded.

Habitat: Shallow Sandy Environment

California Grunion

Family: Atherinidae (Silversides)

Genus and Species: *Leuresthes tenuis*

Description: The California grunion has an elongate body and head that are more or less compressed. The mouth is small. The scales are small, smooth and firm.

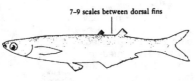

7–9 scales between dorsal fins

This species is bluish green above, silvery below, and a bright silvery band tinged with blue and bordered above with violet extends the length of the body.

Range: The California grunion occurs from Magdalena Bay, Baja California, to San Francisco, California; however, the principal range is between Point Abreojos, Baja California, and Point Conception, California.

Natural History: The food habits are not well known; however, they do eat small crustaceans and fish eggs.

The life span of California grunion is usually 3 years, with some individuals surviving 4 years. The most rapid growth takes place during the first year, at the end of which they are 5 inches long and capable of spawning.

The spawning behavior of grunion is one of the more unusual of all marine fishes. They are the only California fish known to strand themselves on the beach to deposit their reproductive products in the moist sand.

Females, accompanied by one to eight males, swim onto the beach, dig themselves into the sand up to their pectoral fins and lay their eggs. The males wrap themselves around the female and fertilize the eggs. With the next wave the fish return to the sea. During spawning activities, grunion may make a faint squeaking noise.

Spawning takes place from early March through September, and then only for 3 or 4 nights following the full moon during the 1 to 4 hours immediately after high tide.

Most females spawn from four to eight times a year producing up to 3,000 eggs every 2 weeks.

California grunion are non-migratory, and are most often found in schools a short distance from shore in water 15 to 40 feet deep.

Fishing Information: California grunion may only be taken by hand. No appliances of any kind may be used, and no holes may be dug in the beach. The season is closed April and May.

While the California grunion may not be taken during April or May, these are good months to observe spawning activities.

Other Common Names: smelt, little smelt, grunion, lease smelt.

Largest Recorded: 7.5 inches; no weight record; however, a 7 inch female full of eggs weighed less than 2 ounces.

Habitat: Surf Environment

Jacksmelt

Family: Atherinidae (Silversides)

Genus and Species: *Atherinopsis californiensis*

Description: The body of the jacksmelt is elongate and somewhat compressed. The head is oblong and compressed, and the eyes and mouth are small. The color is greenish blue above, silver below, with a metallic stripe bordered with blue extending the length of the body.

10–12 scales between dorsal fins

insertion of dorsal fin well in advance of beginning of anal fin

Jacksmelt, topsmelt, and California grunion are members of the silversides family and are not considered true smelt.

These three species look very similar except for the location of the first dorsal fin. In the jacksmelt, the first dorsal fin is forward of a line drawn perpendicular to the vent (anus); in the topsmelt, it is just about over the vent and in the grunion, it is behind the vent.

Range: Jacksmelt occur from Santa Maria Bay, Baja California, to Yaquina, Oregon.

Jacksmelt are found in California bays and ocean waters throughout the year. They are schooling fish which prefer shallow water less than 100 feet and are most common in 5 to 50 foot depths.

Natural History: Jacksmelt feed on small crustaceans.

Jacksmelt that are 13 to 15 inches long are 8 or 9 years old. A 16 inch, 1 pound male was 11 years old.

They will spawn first when 2 years old and about 6 inches long. The spawning season extends from October to March. Large masses of eggs, about the size of small BB's, are attached to shallow water seaweeds by means of long filaments.

Fishing Information: Jacksmelt are one of the most common fishes taken by pier anglers, but are also caught in the surf.

Sometimes a number of coiled up worms are found in the flesh. These are intermediate stages of spine headed worms, the adult of which are harmful to sharks, pelicans and other fish predators. The worms are harmless to humans when the fish is thoroughly cooked.

Other Common Names: silverside, horse smelt, blue smelt, California smelt.

Largest Recorded: 17.5 inches; no weight recorded; however, a jacksmelt 16 inches long weighed 1 pound.

Habitat: Bay Environment

Sculpin

Family: Scorpaenidae (Scorpionfishes)
Genus and Species: *Scorpaena guttata*
Description: The body of the sculpin is stocky and slightly compressed. The head and mouth are large, as are the pectoral fins. The

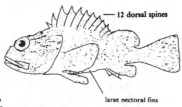

— 12 dorsal spines

large pectoral fins

color is red to brown, with dark blotches and spotting over the body and fins.

Range: The sculpin occurs between Uncle Sam Bank, Baja California, and Santa Cruz, California, with an isolated population in the Gulf of California. They are caught over hard, rocky bottoms at depths ranging from just below the surface to 600 feet. Some may occasionally be taken over sand or mud bottoms.

Natural History: The diet of the sculpin includes crab, squid, octopus, fishes and shrimp.

Sculpin first spawn when they are 3 or 4 years, and they may live 15 years or longer. Spawning takes place from April through August, and probably occurs at night. The eggs are embedded in the gelatinous walls of hollow, pear shaped egg-balloons. The paired egg-balloons, each 5 to 10 inches long are joined at their small ends. The walls of these "balloons" are about 0.1 inch thick, transparent or greenish in color, and contain a single layer of eggs. Each egg is about 0.05 inch in diameter. The "balloons" are released at the bottom of the sea and rise rapidly to the surface. The eggs hatch within 5 days.

Fishing Information: Sculpins readily take a hook that has been baited with a piece of squid or fish and lowered to the bottom in a rocky area where they are known to inhabit. A lot of rebaiting time can be saved by utilizing a "difficult to steal" bait. At times, a considerable amount of chumming with ground fish will attract sculpins to the surface. Hooked sculpins are not noted for their fighting qualities.

The sculpin is the most venomous member of the scorpionfish family in California. Its dorsal, pelvic and anal fin spines are associated with venom glands and are capable of causing an extremely painful wound. Penetration of the skin by any of these spines is followed almost immediately by intense and excruciating pain in the area of the wound.

Many treatments have been used for sculpin stings, but immersion of the affected part in very hot water seems to be the most effective. Multiple punctures can be quite serious, producing shock, respiratory distress or abnormal heart action and may require hospitalization of the victim.

Other Common Names: spotted scorpionfish, scorpion, rattlesnake, bullhead, scorpene, California scorpionfish.
Largest Recorded: 17 inches; no weight recorded; however, a 15.25 inch female weighed 3.5 pounds.
Habitat: Shallow Rocky Environment

Black Rockfish

Family: Scorpaenidae (Scorpionfishes)
Genus and Species: *Sebastes melanops*
Description: The body of the black rockfish is oval or egg-shaped and compressed. The head has a steep upper pro-

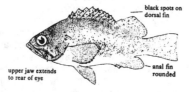

black spots on dorsal fin

upper jaw extends to rear of eye

anal fin rounded

file which is almost straight; the mouth is large and the lower jaw projects slightly. The color is brown to black on the back, paler on the sides, and dirty white below. There are black spots on the dorsal fin.

This species is easily confused with the blue rockfish; however, the anal fin of the black rockfish is rounded while the anal fin of the blue rockfish is slanted or straight. The black rockfish has spots on the dorsal fin, the blue rockfish does not.

Range: Black rockfish occur from Paradise Cove, California, to Amchitka Island, Alaska. They are wide-ranging fish that can live on the surface or on the bottom to 1,200 feet near rocky reefs or in open water over deep banks or drop-offs.

Natural History: The diet of the black rockfish includes squid, crab eggs, and fishes.

Black rockfish are ovoviviparous, like all members of this family—fertilization and development of the embryo take place in the body of the mother. When embryonic development is complete, the female releases the eggs and the exposure to sea water activates the embryo and it escapes from the egg case.

Fishing Information: These fish are commonly caught from commercial passenger fishing vessels and when trolling for salmon. Use similar fishing techniques as for blue rockfish.
Other Common Names: black snapper, black bass, gray rockfish, red snapper.
Largest Recorded: 23.75 inches; 10.5 pounds.
Habitat: Shallow Rocky Environment

Blue Rockfish

Family: Scorpaenidae (Scorpionfishes)
Genus and Species: *Sebastes mystinus*
Description: The body of the blue rockfish is oval or egg-shaped and compressed with similar dorsal and ventral profiles. The head is relatively short and bluntly pointed. The mouth

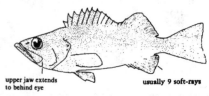

anal fin slanted or straight

is relatively small with the lower jaw slightly projecting. The color is dark blue or olive brown to grayish black on the back becoming lighter below; blotched with lighter shades on back and sides.

The presence of five spines on the preopercle (gill cover), easily distinguish this species as a rockfish rather than a perch, a bass or a halfmoon which is of similar color.

The black rockfish can be confused with this species; however, the black rockfish has spots on the dorsal fin while the blue rockfish does not. The anal fin of the black rockfish is rounded while that of the blue rockfish is slanted or straight.

Range: The blue rockfish occurs from Punta Baja, Baja California, to the Bering Sea. It is a schooling species that is often caught in large numbers over rocky bottoms and around kelp beds. It is most commonly caught from the surface to 100 feet, although it has been taken from depths as great as 300 feet.

Natural History: Blue rockfish principally eat small fishes, shrimps, other crustaceans and small pieces of algae or seaweed. Algae may be accidentally ingested while picking up small shrimp and other tidbits.

As with other rockfishes, fertilization is internal and live young are born which are quite small and helpless. A 16 inch female contained just over 500,000 eggs. The main spawning season runs from about November to March. Blue rockfish may attain an age of at least 15 years.

Fishing Information: Blue rockfish can be caught in quantity near rocky shores and around breakwaters, sunken ships, piles of rubble and similar localities along the entire California coastline, especially north of Point Conception. They are caught just beneath the surface in and around kelp beds, but where there is no kelp they live mostly near the bottom. Two or more hooks can be used with good success and almost any kind of cut fish will prove productive bait. Mussel, clam, crab, shrimp and squid strips work almost equally as well, as do some kinds of wet flies and other artificial lures. Blue rockfish are noted for putting up an excellent battle when hooked.

Other Common Names: blue bass, blue fish, reef perch.
Largest Recorded: 21 inches; no weight recorded; however, a 15 inch female weighed 1.75 pounds.
Habitat: Shallow Rocky Environment

Bocaccio

Family: Scorpaenidae (Scorpionfishes)
Genus and Species: *Sebastes paucispinus*
Description: The body of the bocaccio is elongate and compressed. The head is pointed, the mouth large, and the lower jaw greatly protruding. The color varies from

upper jaw extends to behind eye

usually 9 soft-rays

shades of brown to reddish and extends down over the belly.

Young fish are generally light bronze with speckling over the sides and back. As they mature, their color generally becomes darker and the speckling gradually disappears.

Range: Bocaccio occur from Punta Blanca, Baja California, to Kruzof Island and Kodiak Island, Alaska. Young bocaccio 1 or 2 years old travel in loose schools and move into shallow water where they may be captured in quantity. With increasing age they seek deeper water and move from near the surface to near the bottom. Adults are commonly found in waters of 250 to 750 feet over a somewhat irregular, hard or rubble bottom. They have been found at depths as great as 1,050 feet.

Natural History: The diet of bocaccio includes mainly fishes such as surfperch, jack mackerel, sablefish, anchovies, sardines, Pacific mackerel, deepsea lanternfish, other rockfishes and sanddabs. Squid, octopus, and crab also are eaten.

Females start maturing when they are 17 inches long. As with all rockfish, fertilization is internal and development of the embryos takes place within the ovaries of the female until they are ready to hatch. A 28 inch female was estimated to contain nearly 1.5 million eggs. The main hatching period runs from December through April. The newly hatched young, about 0.25 inch long, does not completely absorb the yolk from the egg stage for a period of 8 to 12 days.

Fishing Information: Almost any rocky or rubble bottom at depths of 250 to 750 feet will yield good catches of bocaccio. The usual rig is made up of three to six hooks above a sinker that is heavy enough to take the line to the bottom on a fairly straight course. Because of the depths fished, it takes a considerable amount of time to let down and haul up this rig; consequently the bait should be sufficiently tough to remain firmly on the hook while being nibbled and chewed upon by the quarry. Pieces of squid are ideal.

Other Common Names: salmon grouper, grouper, mini-grouper (juveniles), red snapper, Pacific red snapper.

Largest Recorded: 3 feet; 21 pounds.

Habitat: Deep Rocky Environment

Chilipepper

Family: Scorpaenidae (Scorpionfishes)
Genus and Species: *Sebastes goodei*
Description: The body of the chilipepper is slender and rather elongate. The head is elongate, pointed and

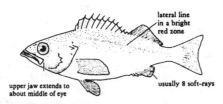

lateral line in a bright red zone

upper jaw extends to about middle of eye

usually 8 soft-rays

with no spines; the lower jaw is projecting.

The chilipepper is generally pinkish becoming whitish below. The middle of the chilipepper's side, the lateral line, stands out clearly, as a lighter, bright red zone.

In comparison to the bocaccio, it has a smaller mouth with an upper jaw that extends only to about the center of the eye, not past it.

Range: This species occurs from Magdalena Bay, Baja California, to Vancouver Island, British Columbia.

Chilipeppers are not taken as frequently as other rockfishes because they are rarely caught in depths less than 360 feet along the coast of California. They generally occur over rocky bottoms and have been taken as deep as 1,080 feet.

Natural History: Adult chilipepper feed on small crustaceans, small squids, or on such fishes as anchovies, young hake, small sardines, and lanternfishes.

Approximately 50 percent out the males mature when 8.75 inches long and 2 years old; while 50 percent out the females are mature when they are 12 inches long and 4 years old. Chilipeppers may live to be at least 16 years old.

As with other rockfishes, fertilization is internal and live young are born. The number of developing eggs increases from 29,000 in a 12 inch female to 538,000 in a 22 inch female.

Fishing Information: The usual rig for chilipepper is made up of three to six hooks above a sinker that is heavy enough to take the line to the bottom on a fairly straight course. Chilipepper are often fished in midwater as well on the bottom. Because of the depths, it may take a considerable amount of time to lower and raise this fishing rig; therefore, the bait should be tough enough to remain on the hook while being chewed upon. Pieces of squid, dried salted anchovies or strip bait, or cut bait as it is commonly known, consists of small strips of flesh with the skin still on from freshly caught rockfish, mackerel or other fishes are ideal.

Other Common Names: chili, red snapper.

Largest Recorded: 22 inches; 5.25 pounds.

Habitat: Deep Rocky Environment

Cowcod

Family: Scorpaenidae (Scorpionfishes)
Genus and Species: *Sebastes levis*
Description: The body and head of the cowcod are

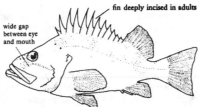

fin deeply incised in adults

wide gap between eye and mouth

somewhat compressed. The head is very large. The mouth is large with a projecting lower jaw.

Adults are uniform pale pink to orange in color. Young fish have four dark vertical bands on their sides which gradually fade into dusky blotches as they increase in size.

Their heads are large and spined, the dorsal fins are deeply notched, and there is an unusually wide space between the eye and the upper jaw. These three characteristics help to distinguish cowcod from other reddish colored rockfish.

Range: Cowcod occur from Ranger Bank and Guadalupe Island, Baja California, to Usal, California. This is a deeper water species occurring at depths from 60 feet (young) to 1,200 feet.

Cowcod are found over rocky bottoms, particularly where there are sharp, steep drop-offs.

Natural History: The diet of the cowcod includes mainly fishes, octopus, and squid. Juvenile cowcod eat small shrimp and crabs.

Like all members of the genus Sebastes, the cowcod gives birth to live young. These are less than 0.5 inches in length and are produced in great numbers. The young are free floating and may be found in shallower water; however, as they grow larger they move to deeper water.

Fishing Information: Because of its large size, the cowcod is one of the most sought after rockfishes in southern California.

Live squid and oversized metal, lead and rubber jigs are often effective baits for this species. Live or salted anchovies or frozen squid are also considered good baits for the cowcod.

Sometimes cowcod are caught while attacking smaller rockfish which have already been hooked and are being brought to the surface.

Other Common Names: cow, cow rockfish, cowfish, red snapper.

Largest Recorded: 37 inches; 28.5 pounds.

Habitat: Deep Rocky Environment

Olive Rockfish

Family: Scorpaenidae (Scorpionfishes)
Genus and Species: *Sebastes serranoides*
Description: The body of the olive rockfish is elongate and compressed. The upper profile of the head is almost

no reddish-brown speckling on scales

usually 9 soft-rays

straight, and the snout is long and pointed. The lower jaw is projecting.

The olive rockfish is dark olive brown on the back, often with some light areas under the dorsal fin. The sides are a lighter olive green, and the fins are yellow.

This species is very similar in appearance to the yellowtail rockfish. The olive rockfish always has nine soft rays in the anal fin; the yellowtail rockfish usually has eight.

Range: This species occurs from the San Benito Islands, Baja California, to Redding Rock, California.

Olive rockfish are generally caught in nearshore waters. They are found primarily around reefs and kelp beds in water less than 150 feet deep, but have been caught as deep as 480 feet.

Natural History: The diet of olive rockfish consists primarily of fishes; however, crab, shrimp, and squid also are consumed in smaller quantities.

Olive rockfish mature and spawn for the first time when they are 3 or 4 years old. As is true among the other rockfish, fertilization is internal and live young are born. The main spawning season is from December through March and a large female may spawn as many as 500,000 young during the season.

Fishing Information: Olive rockfish may be found in almost every kelp bed along the mainland shore south of Monterey Bay, California.

The best rig employs a single hook on monofilament nylon and calls for a lively anchovy. The bait should be cast directly into the floating fronds of kelp and no sinker should be used. It there are any olive rockfish around they will hit the bait right at the surface, usually so hard that they set the hook themselves. The ensuing battle is excellent in every respect and the larger the fish the better the fight. Olive rockfish will also strike a streamer fly or a properly worked metal lure or small wooden plug.

Other Common Names: johnny bass, johnathans.

Largest Recorded: 24 inches; no weight recorded.

Habitat: Shallow Rocky Environment

Yellowtail Rockfish

Family: Scorpaenidae
(Scorpionfishes)
Genus and Species:
Sebastes flavidus
Description: The body of
the yellowtail rockfish is
elongate and com-
pressed. The head is
rather long and the upper

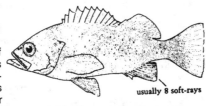

usually 8 soft-rays

profile is steep and slightly curved. The lower jaw projects, but not beyond the upper profile of the head.

The color is grayish brown above which shades to white below. The sides are finely spotted with yellow. The tail is yellow, while the other fins are dusky yellow. When the fish is fresh, reddish brown speckling is visible on some of the scales.

As with many of the rockfish, identification can be somewhat difficult. Some of the distinguishing characteristics of the yellowtail rockfish include a convex (surface curves outward) space between the eyes, the absence of spines on top of the head, a projecting lower jaw, an anal fin with eight (rarely seven) soft rays and the lining of the belly is white.
Range: The yellowtail rockfish occurs from San Diego, California, to Kodiak Island, Alaska; however, it is most often caught by recreational anglers off of central and northern California. It is regularly found over deep reefs from the surface to depths of 1,800 feet.
Natural History: Adult yellowtail rockfish feed on small hake, ancho-vies, lanternfishes, and other small fishes, as well as on small squid, and other shrimp-like organisms. These are all good baits to use for the yellowtail rockfish.

A few yellowtail rockfish mature when 11 inches long or 3 years old. Fifty percent are mature when 13 inches long or 5 years old. They may live to be 24 years old.

As with other rockfishes, fertilization is internal and live young are born. The number of developing eggs increases from 50,000 in a fish 12 inches long to about 633,000 in a fish 19 to 21 inches long.
Fishing Information: When fishing for yellowtail rockfish in deeper waters, the typical rockfish rig and bait is appropriate (see bocaccio). Since this species occurs quite often at or near the surface, standard surface fishing techniques and baits such as anchovies or squid fished on a small hook are effective. Small silvery lures or small lead and rubber jigs also work well.
Other Common Names: red snapper, yellowtail.
Largest Recorded: 26 inches; no weight recorded; however, a yellow-tail rockfish 24 inches long will weigh about 7.5 pounds.
Habitat: Shallow Rocky Environment

Canary Rockfish

Family: Scorpaenidae
(Scorpionfish)
Genus and Species:
Sebastes pinniger
Description: The body of
the canary rockfish is
elongate, moderately
deep and com-
pressed. The head is
large with an upper
profile that is some-
what curved. The

black blotch in fin in fish measuring up to about 14 inches

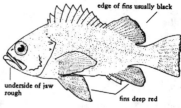

underside of jaw smooth

color is yellow orange with gray mottling on the back and paler, near white, below. The fins are also yellow orange. The middle of the sides are in a clear, gray zone. There is often a black spot near the back of the first dorsal fin in fish shorter than 14 inches.

Although the canary rockfish resembles the vermilion rockfish super-ficially, the two are easily separated. The underside of the lower jaw of the canary rockfish has no scales and feels smooth to the touch when rubbed from back to front. The vermilion rockfish has scales on the underside of its lower jaw so that it feels rough when rubbed forward.
Range: Canary rockfish occur from Cape Colnett, Baja California, to Cape San Bartolome, Alaska.

Canary rockfish are usually caught at depths of 50 to 300 feet, although juveniles have been taken at the surface and adults have been taken from depths as great as 900 feet. They are found around reefs and over soft bottoms.
Natural History: Adult canary rockfish feed on small crustaceans as well as anchovies, sanddabs, and other small fishes.

The canary rockfish, like all members of the genus *Sebastes*, pro-duces live young. Fertilization and embryo development take place within the body of the mother. The number of eggs increases from 260,000 in a 19 inch female to about 1,900,000 in a female 26 inches long. About 50 percent of canary rockfish are mature at a length of 14 inches, or when they are 5 to 6 years old. They may live to be at least 22 years old.
Fishing Information: The typical rockfish rig and bait may be used for canary rockfish (see bocaccio). This species contributes to the recre-ational marine anglers mixed rockfish bag.
Other Common Names: red snapper, fantail, canary, orange rockfish.
Largest Recorded: 30 inches; no weight recorded; however, a 24 inch canary rockfish weighs about 7 pounds.
Habitat: Deep Rocky Environment

Vermilion Rockfish

Family: Scorpaenidae (Scorpionfishes)
Genus and Species:
Sebastes miniatus
Description: The body of the
vermilion rockfish is moderately deep and compressed.
The upper profile of the head
is somewhat curved; the
mouth is large, with the lower

edge of fins usually black

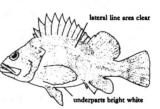

underside of jaw rough

fins deep red

jaw slightly projecting. The color is bright red on the body and fins; many with black and gray mottling on back and sides. On fish shorter than 12 inches, the mottling is much more apparent and the fins are often edged with black.

The yelloweye and canary rockfishes are similar in appearance to the vermilion, but the bottom of the yelloweye and canary's lower jaws are scaleless and feels smooth to the touch. The vermilion rockfish has scales on the bottom of the lower jaw which make it rough to the touch.
Range: Vermilion rockfish occur from San Benito Islands, Baja Califor-nia, to Vancouver Island, Canada. They are generally caught over rocky bottoms at depths of 1 00 to 500 feet, although they have been taken from depths as great as 900 feet.
Natural History: The tree swimming young of the vermilion rockfish feed primarily upon shrimp-like organisms, while the larger, bottom-living adults feed almost exclusively upon fishes, squid and octopus. Most fishes that are eaten are other smaller kinds of rockfish.

Vermilion rockfish appear to mature and spawn for the first time when they are 3 or 4 years old. As with all other rockfish, fertilization is internal and they give birth to living young. A vermilion rockfish that was 20 inches long was estimated to contain 282,000 eggs. By this measure a 30 incher might contain as many as 500,000 eggs. The principal reproductive period lasts from December through March.
Fishing Information: Because a good rockfish "hole" often will yield a dozen or more kinds of rockfishes on any given day, it has been said that rockfish fishing is colorful, interesting, productive, and mysterious. Vermilion rockfish usually are found in the bag of "red" rockfish taken from one of these "holes."

The same rig, bait, and technique used for bocaccio works for vermilion rockfish. Again a lot of rebaiting time can be saved by using a tough, difficult to steal bait such as a piece of squid or salted mackerel.
Other Common Names: red snapper, red rock cod.
Largest Recorded: 30 inches; no weight recorded; however, they attain a weight of at least 15 pounds.
Habitat: Deep Rocky Environment

Copper Rockfish

Family: Scorpaenidae (Scorpionfishes)
Genus and Species: *Sebastes
caurinus*
Description: The body of the copper rockfish is moderately deep
and compressed. The head is large

lateral line area clear

underparts bright white

with a slightly curved upper profile; the mouth is large and the lower jaw projects slightly. The color is copper brown to orange tinged with pink. The back two-thirds of the sides are a clear, light pink area; the belly is white.
Range: The copper rockfish occurs from San Benitos Islands, Baja California, to the Kenai Peninsula, Alaska. It is found in shallow rocky and sandy areas, and is generally caught at depths of less than 180 feet; however, some have been taken as deep as 600 feet.

Natural History: The diet of copper rockfish includes snails, worms, squid, octopus, crabs, shrimps, and fishes.

Copper rockfish, like all species in the genus *Sebastes*, give birth to fully developed embryos. Fertilization and development of the embryo take place in the body of the mother. Upon being expelled from the female, the fully developed embryo is released from the egg.

Fishing Information: The copper rockfish is often the last species to die in a bag of rockfish. Some individuals continue to twitch long after members of other species have died.

Other Common Names: never die, whitebelly, chucklehead.

Largest Recorded: 22.5 inches; no weight recorded.

Habitat: Shallow Rocky Environment

Widow Rockfish

Family: Scorpaenidae (Scorpionfishes)

Genus and Species: *Sebastes entomelas*

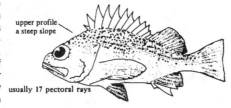
upper profile slightly curved

anal fin slanting, membranes black

Description: The body of the widow rockfish is elongate and compressed. The head is relatively short, and the upper profile is slightly curved. The mouth is relatively small, the lower jaw projects slightly.

The color is brassy brown over most of the body with the belly generally lighter in color, often with a reddish cast. The fin membranes, particularly in the anal and pectoral fins, are black.

Specimens smaller than 10 inches are lighter in color and are tinged with vague streaks of orange.

Range: Widow rockfish occur from Todos Santos Bay, Baja California, to Kodiak Island, Alaska.

Natural History: Adult widow rockfish feed extensively on small free floating crab-like animals. Occasionally salps, small squids and anchovies are eaten.

A few mature when 12 inches long and 3 years old. Fifty percent are mature when 12.75 inches long or 4 years old. Widow rockfish may live to be 16 years old.

As with other rockfish fertilization is internal and the young are born live. The number of developing eggs increases from 55,000 in fish 12.75 inches long, to about 900,000 in a fish 20 inches long.

Fishing Information: Widow rockfish are generally caught by sport anglers fishing on or just above the bottom in deep water up to 1,200 feet, although young fish may be taken at or near the surface. On occasion, widow rockfish form huge schools in midwater where they feed on small plants. At such times, they are vulnerable to recreational anglers as well as commercial trawling gear and are often taken in great quantities.

Other Common Names: widow, widowfish, red snapper.

Largest Recorded: 21 inches; no weight recorded; however, a 20 inch widow rockfish will weigh about 4 pounds.

Habitat: Deep Rocky Environment

Greenspotted Rockfish

Family: Scorpaenidae (Scorpionfishes)

Genus and Species: *Sebastes chlorostictus*

Description: The body of the green spotted rockfish is elongate and moderately compressed. The upper profile of the head is rather steep with a nearly straight slope. The jaws are even when

upper profile a steep slope

usually 17 pectoral rays

closed. The color is yellow pink with distinct green spots over the back and top of the head. There are three to five white blotches with green borders along the upper back, and the pectoral fins carry 17 rays. The underside of the lower jaw has no scales and is smooth to the touch.

Two other species, the green blotched rockfish and pink rockfish, are nearly identical to the greenspotted rockfish. Nevertheless, they can be distinguished from the greenspotted rockfish by the small patches of scales on the underside of their lower jaws. These two look-alike species attain a larger size than the greenspotted rockfish, but are not encountered as frequently since they usually inhabitat deeper water.

Range: The greenspotted rockfish occurs from Cedros Island, Baja California, to Copalis Head, Washington.

Greenspotted rockfish are caught around offshore, rocky reefs at depths ranging from 160 to 660 feet.

Natural History: As with other rockfishes, fertilization is internal and live young are born. The young are born during the period of April through July.

Fishing Information: The greenspotted rockfish is a common species in the deep-water rockfish catch. It is not considered very desirable, however, because of its small size.

Other Common Names: chucklehead, red rock cod, bolina.

Largest Recorded: 19.75 inches; no weight recorded.

Habitat: Deep Rocky Environment

Starry Rockfish

Family: Scorpaenidae (Scorpionfishes)

Genus and Species: *Sebastes constellatus*

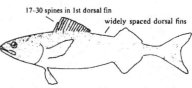
underside of jaw usually without scales

Description: The body of the starry rockfish is elongate, robust, heavy forward tapering to the tail. The head is rather pointed in profile and the mouth is large with the lower jaw projecting only slightly beyond the upper jaw when the mouth is closed.

The body is red orange and profusely covered with small white spots. There are four or five large whitish blotches along the back. It is a very distinctive fish that is not easily confused with any other rockfish.

Range: The starry rockfish occurs from Thetis Bank, Baja California, to San Francisco, California, and is found around rocky offshore reefs at depths of 80 to 900 feet.

Natural History: As with other kinds of rockfish, fertilization is internal and live young are born. The young are usually born during March through May.

Fishing Information: Starry rockfish contribute to the recreational anglers offshore reef catch. The typical rockfish rig and baits are appropriate gear (see bocaccio).

Other Common Names: spotted corsair, spotted rockfish, chinafish, red rock cod.

Largest Recorded: 18 inches; no weight recorded.

Habitat: Deep Rocky Environment

Sablefish

Family: Anoplopomatidae (Sablefishes)

Genus and Species: *Anoplopoma fimbria*

17-30 spines in 1st dorsal fin

widely spaced dorsal fins

Description: The body of the sablefish is quite elongate, slightly compressed and tapering to the tail. The head is rather large and elongate. The sablefish is blackish gray on the back and sides, and gray to white below. Two well separated dorsal fins, very small teeth and the uniform coloration distinguishes this species.

Range: The sablefish occurs from Cedros Island, Baja California, to the Bering Sea and Japan; at depths ranging from the surface (juveniles) to 6,000 feet. They are usually taken in 80 to 600 feet of water; however, schools of small individuals occasionally enter shallow areas.

Natural History: The diet of sablefish include marine worms, crustaceans and small fishes.

About 50 percent of the male sablefish are mature by the time they are 24 inches long and 5 years old, whereas 50 percent of the females first mature at 7 years, when they are 28 inches long.

A 28 inch female weighing 6.5 pounds and 7 years old is capable of spawning about 100,000 eggs; while a 40 inch female that is 20 years old will contain approximately 1,000,000 eggs.

Fishing Information: During some years, young sablefish abound in inshore waters and can be caught in large numbers close to the surf zone. Most of the time, however, they live on the bottom in deeper water. There is a tendency for sablefish to move deeper during the winter spawning season; thus, the heaviest catches, which are made during summer months, are made in shallower water.

Considering the depths at which one must fish, a lot of reeling in to rebait can be avoided by using more than one hook and by using bait that is difficult for the fish to steal. Chunks of salted mackerel or fresh squid are both excellent baits. Sablefish are feeble fighters at best, but large fish have a weight advantage that makes hauling them from the depths a back breaking ordeal.

The flesh is pure white and oily with a very mild flavor.

Other Common Names: butterfish, blackcod, coalfish, candlefish, skilfish, coal cod, bluecod, bluefish, deep sea trout, black candlefish, skill.

Largest Recorded: 3 feet, 4 inches; no weight recorded; however, a sablefish 3 feet long weighed 40 pounds.

Habitat: Deep Sandy Environment

Lingcod

Family: Hexagrammidae (Greenlings)

Genus and Species: *Ophiodon elongatus*

Description: The body of the lingcod is elongate, tapering and only slightly compressed. The head is elongate and conical, the mouth is large with numerous large teeth.

blotches on upper body

large mouth, large teeth

adult

juvenile form

Lingcod are generally dark brown with lots of spots and blotches on the upper part of the body, but come in a variety of colors ranging from blue green to red brown.

Range: Lingcod occur between Point San Carlos, Baja California, and Kodiak Island, Alaska. They are not abundant south of Point Conception except in a few localities. They live at or near the bottom, generally in close association with rocky areas and kelp beds, especially where there is a strong tidal movement. They occur most abundantly at depths ranging to about 350 feet, but will often go into deeper water and have been caught as deep as 2,700 feet off southern California.

Natural History: Young lingcod feed primarily upon shrimp and other crustaceans until they are big enough to eat fish. Once started on fishes, it seems that any kind coming within reach is fair game.

Male and female lingcod first mature when they are 3 years of age and about 23 inches in total length. Nearly all are mature at age 4 when they are nearly 26 inches long. Spawning usually takes place from December through March. The eggs are large (0.17 inch in diameter) and adhesive, sticking in large masses to rocky crevasses, generally on subtidal reefs. The male lingcod guards the eggs after fertilization until they hatch. A female 30 inches long may lay approximately 60,000 eggs; whereas, a 45 inch female may lay more than 500,000 in a single season.

Fishing Information: Lingcod are easily caught on standard rockfish rigs using anchovies or squid pieces. Larger baits such as live squid, mackerel or even small rockfishes often produce catches of very large lingcods. Large chrome-plated metal jigs, large lead-head and rubber jigs, and lead-filled pipe jigs are also favorites of avid lingcod anglers. When sportfishing, live bait is more effective than dead bait, and dead bait usually more than metal jigs. Whatever the bait, it seems more effective if jigged or bounced up and down along the bottom.

Care should be taken when unhooking one of these toothy beasts. The lingcods teeth, as well as the gillrakers, are extremely sharp and can cause serious injury to the fingers of careless anglers. Unless you are wearing heavy gloves, NEVER put your fingers into the mouth or gill chamber of a lingcod. The safest way to pick up a lingcod is to place the thumb and first finger of one hand in the eye sockets and grab the tail with the other hand.

Other Common Names: ling, greenlinger, slinky linky, buffalo cod, cultus cod.

Largest Recorded: 52 inches; 54 pounds (California).

Habitat: Deep Rocky Environment

Kelp Greenling

Family: Hexagrammidae (Greenlings)

Genus and Species: *Hexagrammos decagrammus*

Description: The body of the kelp greenling is elongate and somewhat compressed. The head is conical, blunt in profile, and the mouth is rather small.

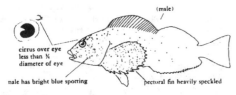

(male)

cirrus over eye less than ¼ diameter of eye

male has bright blue spotting

pectoral fin heavily speckled

Male and female kelp greenling can be readily distinguished by their coloration. The forepart of the body of the male has numerous sky blue spots, each surrounded by a ring of rusty spots. The female is rather

uniformly covered with round reddish brown spots. Certainly, the kelp greenling is one of the most boldly colored fishes found along our coast.

The kelp greenling has small, unfringed flaps of skin (cirri) over the eyes and the mouth is yellowish inside; whereas, the rock greenling has a pair of large, fringed flaps of skin over the eyes and the inside of the mouth is bluish.

Range: Kelp greenling occur from La Jolla, California, to the Aleutian Islands, Alaska, but are quite rare south of Point Conception. They live in relatively shallow water along rocky coasts, around jetties and in kelp beds.

Natural History: Included in the kelp greenling's diet are various seaworms, crustaceans, and small fishes.

In British Columbia, spawning occurs in October and November. Pale blue eggs are laid in large masses on rocks. In California, eggs and young have been collected in March suggesting that spawning takes place during the winter months throughout the total range.

Fishing Information: Kelp greenling is one of the major species in the rocky shore angler's bag in central and northern California. The jetties at Eureka comprise the number one greenling "hole" in the state. They can be caught with hooks baited with cut pieces of fish, clams, mussels, shrimp, squid, worms and crab backs. Once hooked, the kelp greenling is difficult to land because of its habit of entangling the angler's line about rocks, crevices or kelp. Kelp greenling are excellent bait for lingcod anglers.

Other Common Names: greenling sea trout, rock trout, spotted rock trout, kelp trout, kelp cod.

Largest Recorded: 21 inches, no weight recorded; however, a male 12 inches long weighed 1 pound.

Habitat: Shallow Rocky Environment

Pacific Staghorn Sculpin

Family: Cottidae (Sculpins)

Genus and Species: *Leptocoffus armatus*

Description: The body of the Pacific staghorn sculpin is elongate and scaleless. The head is long and depressed, and the mouth is large. The body coloration often blends

spines in dorsal fin

antlerlike projections or spines just forward of the gill slit on the gillcover

with its environment and shows such varieties as greenish brown or gray above, and white to yellow below. The spinous dorsal fin has an obvious black spot and the pectoral fins are yellowish with dark cross bars. The most striking characteristic of this species is an antler-like spine located just forward of the gill cover.

Range: The Pacific staghorn sculpin occurs from San Quintin Bay, Baja California, to Chignik, Alaska. They frequent California's bays, estuaries, lagoons, and shallow coastal waters, and are wide ranging from the intertidal zone to a depth of 510 feet.

Natural History: The diet of the Pacific staghorn sculpin includes crabs, shrimp, worms, mollusks, and many kinds of juvenile and adult fishes.

These fish become sexually mature when 1 year old. Spawning takes place between October and April. The average sized female produces about 5,000 eggs in a season.

Fishing Information: The Pacific staghorn sculpin is attracted to a variety of baits, preferably small invertebrates. It is not highly prized as a food or sport fish. On the other hand, it is a popular bait fish for the San Francisco Bay Delta striped bass sport fishery. Caution is recommended when handling this species because the spines located on the gill cover can leave nasty cuts if the fish thrashes around in your hands.

Other Common Names: bullhead, staghorn sculpin, smooth cabezon, buffalo sculpin, smooth sculpin.

Largest Recorded: 12 inches (California), 18 inches (Canada); no weight recorded; however, a 10 inch fish weighed 0.5 pounds.

Habitat: Bay Environment

Cabezon

Family: Cottidae (Sculpins)

Genus and Species: *Scorpaenichthys marmoratus*

Description: The body of the cabezon is elongate and stout. The head is large,

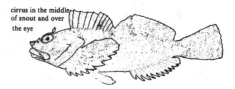

cirrus in the middle of snout and over the eye

broad and the snout is bluntly rounded. The mouth is large. The color is usually dark brown, but a variety of colors ranging from blue green to reddish brown occur and there is much mottling. It looks somewhat like the lingcod, and sometimes has blue colored flesh.

It is a member of the true sculpin family and it can best be distinguished from the similar looking lingcod by: the absence of scales on its body; and by the presence of a small flap of skin, a cirrus, over each eye and in the middle of the snout. The lining of its mouth is a pale to dark blue and it also lacks the large teeth of the lingcod.

Range: Cabezon occur from Point Abreojos, Baja California, to Sitka, Alaska. Cabezon are usually found on the bottom around rocky reefs and kelp beds in water less than 100 feet deep, although they are known to occur as deep as 250 feet.

Natural History: The cabezon's diet is made up of about 50 percent crabs and 50 percent mollusks and fishes. Small abalones are swallowed whole and the shells are regurgitated after some digestion takes place. These shells are sometimes beautifully polished by the action of the acids.

Male cabezon first mature when about 2 years old and 13.5 inches long, females when 3 years old and 17.5 inches long. Females grow faster and attain larger sizes than do males.

Spawning takes place from November through March, peaking in January. The adults tend to congregate at nesting sites. The eggs are laid in large masses on cleared rocks. The individual nest is guarded by the male who will drive away any intruder. A 3 pound female will lay an average of 48,700 eggs and a 10 pounder, 97,600.

The eggs and young are free floating, some having been taken more than 200 miles from shore. The young enter the tide pools and inshore areas during the spring when they are about 1.5 inches long. They then lose their silvery color and take on the pattern characteristic of adults.

Fishing Information: Cabezon are caught by rocky shore anglers in every suitable area from border to border. Larger numbers are caught in the central and northern part of the state. They are one of the most sought-after rocky shore inhabitants.

Suitable baits include abalone trimmings, mussels, clams, squid, shrimp, worms, cut or strip bait, and live bait when available. Here again is a bottom rock dweller that can be most difficult to land if allowed to retreat to the shelter of rocks or seaweeds after being hooked.

Cabezon eggs are poisonous, so do not eat the roe. Consumption of cabezon roe has produced near fatal results in humans.

Other Common Names: bullhead, cab, cabby, bull cod, giant sculpin, scorpion, marble sculpin.

Largest Recorded: 39 inches; 25 pounds.

Habitat: Shallow Rocky Environment

Striped Bass

Family: Serranidae (Sea Basses) or Percichthyidae
Genus and Species: *Roccus saxatilis**
* Also known as Morone saxatilis

6-9 blackish stripes along the sides

Description: The body of the striped bass is elongate and slightly compressed. The head is a narrow, cone-shape, and the mouth is large. The color is greenish above, silvery on the sides, and white below. There are six to nine horizontal blackish stripes on the side. In southern California, the much smaller salema occasionally is mistaken for young striped bass; the salema, however, has orange-brown stripes and larger eyes than those of striped bass.

Range: Striped bass were brought to California from New Jersey in 1879. They now are found from northern Baja California to Barkley Sound, British Columbia. In California, they most commonly are found in the Sacramento-San Joaquin Delta, San Francisco Bay and adjacent ocean areas.

Natural History: Examination of stomach contents show that shrimp and anchovies are most important during the summer and fall while a variety of small fishes are eaten during the winter.

Females usually mature at 5 years of age when about 24 inches long and many males mature at age 2 when about 11 inches long. A 5 pound fish may spawn as many as 25,000 eggs in one season; while a 12 pounder will spawn 1,250,000 eggs. A 75 pound striper produces as many as 10,000,000 eggs.

Striped bass are believed to spawn only in fresh water in which there is an appreciable current. In California, they spawn from March to July with a peak in April and May.

Fishing Information: By far the largest part of the striped bass catch is made in San Francisco Bay and the Delta. Good fishing occurs during late summer, but is best in the fall. Stripers occur along the coast only during late spring and summer at which time surf fishermen get a chance at them.

A variety of artificial lures and chunks or strips of standard bait fish will attract stripers. The beaches immediately adjacent to the Golden Gate are generally the best coastal spots, but occasional good runs are encountered as far south as Monterey and as far north as Bodega Bay. In San Francisco Bay, trolling with live bait is popular, with common catches under 10 pounds.

Juvenile striped bass have been planted in San Diego, Mission, Newport and Anaheim Bays since 1974 to provide sportfishing.

Other Common Names: striper, streaked bass, squidhound, rock bass.

Largest Recorded: 4 feet; 90 pounds (California); however, in the Atlantic Ocean to 6 feet and 125 pounds.

Habitat: Bay Environment

Giant Sea Bass

Family: Serranidae (Sea Basses) or Percichthyidae
Genus and Species: *Stereolepis gigas*

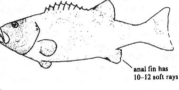
anal fin has 10-12 soft rays

Description: The body of the adult giant sea bass is elongate with dorsal spines that fit into a groove on the back. The head is robust, and mouth is large with teeth in the back, Giant sea bass are usually reddish brown to dark brown in color on all but their stomachs and, at times, many have dark spots on their sides.

Perch-like in appearance, juvenile giant sea bass differ radically from adults and are often mistaken for a different fish. Coloring on juveniles is distinct with the body being sandy red with white and dark patches spread along the sides.

Range: Giant sea bass occur throughout the Gulf of California and from Cabo San Lucas, Baja California, to Humboldt Bay, California. In California, the appearance of this species north of Point Conception has been sporadic.

Natural History: Giant sea bass feed upon a wide variety of items. Small fish taken of this species off our coast contained mostly anchovies and white croakers. Pacific mackerel, jack mackerel, sheephead, ocean whitefish, sand bass, cancer crabs, and red crabs have all been found in the stomachs of large giant sea bass. By their very bulk they appear to be slow and cumbersome, yet they are capable of outswimming and catching a bonito in a short chase.

Giant sea bass apparently do not mature until they are 11 to 13 years old. A fish of this age will weigh between 50 and 60 pounds. The ovaries of a 320 pound female weighed 47 pounds and contained an estimated 60 million eggs. This fish was ready to spawn and the larger eggs were about 0.04 inch in diameter. The main spawning season for giant sea bass occurs during July, August, and September.

Fishing Information: There has been a moratorium, which will probably last many years, on landing giant sea bass in California. All fish must be returned alive to the water. Occasionally, fish taken by anglers will "float" to the surface as their gas bladders expand. They may be returned by carefully inserting a hypodermic needle through the side of the fish into the gas bladder and allowing the air to escape.

Please be aware that it is illegal to take or possess giant sea bass.

Other Common Names: black sea bass, jewfish, giant bass.

Largest Recorded: over 7 feet; 563 pounds (Anacapa Island, 1968).

Habitat: Deep Rocky Environment

Kelp Bass

Family: Serranidae (Sea Basses)
Genus and Species: *Paralabrax clathratus*

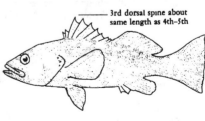
3rd dorsal spine about same length as 4th-5th

Description: The body of the kelp bass is elongate and compressed. The head is relatively elongate, compressed and has a pointed snout. The mouth is large. The color is brown to olive green, with light blotches, becoming lighter below.

Kelp bass can be easily distinguished from sand bass by the fact that the third, fourth and fifth dorsal spines of kelp bass are about the same length; while in sand bass, the third dorsal spine is much longer than the fourth and fifth spines.

Range: Kelp bass occur from Magdalena Bay, Baja California, to the Columbia River, Washington. They are taken regularly from Point Conception south to central Baja California in depths down to 150 feet.

Natural History: Small shrimp-like crustaceans are very important in the diet of kelp bass of all ages. However, with increase in size there is a corresponding increase in the amount of fish eaten. Anchovies, small surfperch, and other small fishes are part of the diet.

By the time kelp bass are 10.5 inches long and 5 years of age, nearly all are capable of spawning. The spawning season usually extends from May through September with a peak during July. As with most members of the bass family, growth is slow and a 9 year old fish is only about 16.5 inches long.

Fishing Information: Kelp bass are caught primarily with live anchovies fished at or near the surface in and around kelp beds. They may be taken throughout the water column by trolling near kelp beds with live or dead bait. Numerous anglers also catch them on cast plugs, spoons, lures, and jigs. These anglers obtain their best catches with a yellowish, bronze, or white colored jig. In localities where kelp bass are not spoiled by offerings of live bait, they willingly accept hooks baited with strips or chunks of anchovy, mackerel or squid. Kelp bass are noted for their fighting qualities regardless of the type of bait or lure used.

Other Common Names: calico bass, bull bass, kelp salmon, cabrilla.

Largest Recorded: 28.5 inches; 14.5 pounds.

Habitat: Shallow Rocky Environment

Barred Sand Bass

Family: Serranidae (Sea Basses)
Genus and Species: *Paralabrax nebulifer*
Description: The body of the barred sand bass is rather elongate and compressed. The mouth is large and the lower jaw protrudes slightly. The color is gray white on the back, white

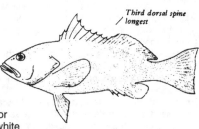

Third dorsal spine longest

on the belly and there are dark vertical bars on the sides. Barred sand bass can be easily distinguished from kelp bass by the height of the third dorsal spine. In barred sand bass, this spine is the longest of the dorsal spines, while in the kelp bass, the third, fourth and fifth dorsal spines are of about equal length. Barred sand bass can be distinguished from spotted sand bass by the lack of spots on the body.

Range: Barred sand bass occur from Magdalena Bay, Baja California, to Santa Cruz, California. This species occurs from shallow water to depths of 600 feet; however, most fish are taken in 60 to 90 feet of water.

Natural History: The barred sand bass diet includes crabs, octopus, squid, and small fishes.

The adults aggregate and spawn during warmer months, The eggs are free floating. The striped young appear in southern California nearshore areas and eelgrass beds during fall and winter.

Fishing Information: Most barred sand bass landed in California are taken between May and October. They are fished in three main areas: Horseshoe Kelp to Newport Beach, Dana Point to Oceanside and the Silver Strand off San Diego.

The best method for catching barred sand bass is to search a sandy area with an echosounder until a school is located. The boat then can be anchored and fishing commenced with live anchovies. Barred sand bass will usually "build" or gather under the boat when chummed so it pays to wait for awhile before moving.

Other Common Names: sand bass, sandy, ground bass, sugar bass, kelp bass, California sandbass, rock bass.

Largest Recorded: 26 inches; 11.1 pounds.

Habitat: Shallow Sandy Environment

Spotted Sand Bass

Family: Serranidae (Sea Basses)
Genus and Species: *Paralabrax maculatofasciatus*
Description: The body of the spotted sand bass is moderately elongate and compressed. The mouth

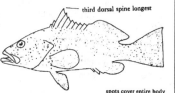

third dorsal spine longest

spots cover entire body

is large and the jaw protruding only slightly. The color is olive brown with round black spots on the body, head and fins.

Spotted sand bass can be easily distinguished from kelp bass by the height of the third dorsal spine. In spotted sand bass and barred sand bass it is the longest of the dorsal spines, while in the kelp bass the third, fourth and fifth spines are of about equal length. Spotted sand bass differ from barred sand bass by the presence of spots that cover the entire body.

Range: Spotted sand bass occur from Mazatlan, Mexico, to Monterey, California.

Spotted sand bass are confined to large bays in southern California. Because of this, they are taken less frequently than kelp or barred sand bass. They may be taken in the open ocean but this generally occurs only when drifting through the kelp.

Natural History: Spotted sand bass eat primarily crustaceans, and a Pacific halibut that large. The fish are typically caught on crab, shrimp, squid, and other invertebrates.

Other Common Names: alabato, northern halibut, right halibut, genuine halibut, real halibut.

Largest Recorded: 8.75 feet; 507 pounds.

Habitat: Deep Sandy Environment

Jack Mackerel

Family: Carangidae (Jacks)
Genus and Species: *Trachurus symmetricus*
Description: The body of the jack mackerel is rather elongate, somewhat compressed. The body tapers to a tail, which is as broad as it is deep. The color is metallic blue to olive green above becoming silvery below.

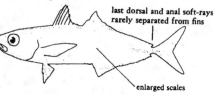

last dorsal and anal soft-rays rarely separated from fins

enlarged scales

The jack mackerel, which is not a true mackerel, is quite similar to the Mexican scad, but can be distinguished by the enlarged scales along the side and by the last rays of the dorsal and anal fins being attached to the body. These rays are isolated finlets on the Mexican scad.

Range: Jack mackerel occur from Magdalena Bay, Baja California, to southeast Alaska, and from the surface to depths of 150 feet. Adults may be found over 500 miles offshore.

Natural History: Jack mackerel are known to feed heavily upon anchovies, lantern fish, or juvenile squid. Food studies indicated that more than 90 percent of the identifiable items found in the stomachs of jack mackerel are crustaceans and small, free swimming mollusks.

Half of the 2 year old females are sexually mature and will spawn. All are spawning when they are 3 years old. Spawning takes place from March through June, and occurs over an extensive area from 80 to over 240 miles offshore.

Jack mackerel regularly live 20-30 years and weigh 4 to 5 pounds. For fish with such a long lifespan, they become sexually mature at a very young age. They are quite common near the islands and banks off southern California up to 3 or 4 years of age, and then presumably move offshore or northward.

Fishing Information: Younger jack mackerel do not feed extensively on anchovies, do not readily bite on baited hook or lure, and thus are a much less common addition to the catch of a sport angler. They can be jigged, however, on small feathered hooks and frequently are used as a bait for larger game fish by the experienced ocean angler. These younger fish are taken by the southern California commercial purse seine fishery since they occur in large schools.

Jack mackerel are most frequently taken as 15+ year-olds by commercial albacore trollers and bottomfish trawlers, generally in northern California waters and further offshore. These larger, older fish have been found in offshore waters from Baja California to the Aleutian Islands.

Other Common Names: horse mackerel, Spanish mackerel, mackerel-jack, jackfish, Pacific jack mackerel.

Largest Recorded: 32 inches; a fraction of an ounce more than 5 pounds; a 28.5 inch jack mackerel weighed 5.25 pounds.

Habitat: Pelagic Environment

Yellowtail

Family: Carangidae (Jacks)
Genus and Species:
Seriola lalandi*
* Also known as S. dorsalis.

dark horizontal line along the side

Description: The body of the yellowtail is elongate, somewhat compressed, tapering to the sharp snout and the slender tail. The head is more or less conical. The color is olive brown to brown above, with a dark streak along the side of the body. The fins are yellowish. Yellowtail are easily distinguished from other fishes by the darker horizontal stripe along the side of the body, as well as a deeply forked yellow tail.
Range: Yellowtail occur from Chile to southern Washington including the Gulf of California, and from the ocean's surface to depths of 228 feet. Most fish landed in California are taken between Point Conception and the Coronado Islands, Baja California.
Natural History: Yellowtail feed primarily during the day and are opportunistic feeders, eating anything that is abundant in the area. Red crabs, anchovies, squid, and most small fishes are food items.

Spawning occurs from June through October. Many yellowtail are sexually mature in 2 years; all will spawn when 3 years old. A 3 year old female will weigh about 10 pounds and spawn approximately 450,000 eggs; however, a 25 pound female will produce more than 1 million eggs.
Fishing Information: Prime yellowtail areas are found around the Coronado Islands, La Jolla Kelp, the area between Oceanside and Dana Point, Horseshoe Kelp, Palos Verdes Peninsula, Santa Catalina Island and San Clemente Island. Most yellowtail taken by California anglers are landed on boats which anchor at spots where yellowtail are known to aggregate and then chum the fish to the boat with live anchovies. As the fish mill about the boat, anglers then use anchovies, mackerel or squid to catch them. Small boaters may take yellowtail by trolling jigs or feathers in areas where these fish occur.
Other Common Names: California yellowtail, forktail, mossback, amberjack, white salmon.
Largest Recorded: 5 feet; 80 pounds (California).
Habitat: Pelagic Environment

Sargo

Family: Pristipomatidae (Sargos)
Genus and Species:
Anisotremus davidsonii
Description: The body of the adult sargo is a compressed oval shape with the back elevated. The head has a steep, straightish upper profile and a small mouth.

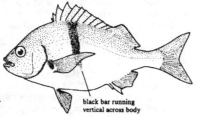

black bar running vertical across body

The color is metallic silvery, with a grayish tinge on the back and silvery below; with a distinguishing dark vertical bar running across the body. Occasionally, sargo are entirely bright yellow, orange or pure white.

Young sargo, up to 4 inches, have several dark horizontal stripes. The vertical bar begins to appear when they are 2 or 3 inches long.
Range: The sargo occurs from Magdalena Bay, Baja California, to Santa Cruz, California, and is found inshore and in bays. Sargo occur from the surface to depths of 130 feet, but are most common in water about 25 feet deep. They are usually found in areas with rock or combination rock-sand bottoms, around pilings or similar submerged structures.
Natural History: Examination of stomach contents indicate sargo are bottom feeders, eating different small shrimps, crabs, clams, and sea snails.

Sargo spawn when they are about 7 inches long and 2 years old.

Spawning occurs in late spring and early summer. The 1 inch young appear in late summer and fall in shallow water, schooling loosely with young salema and black croaker. At a length of 5 inches, when they are about 1 year old, they join adult sargo schools. All through their life they are capable of displaying the striped pattern characteristic of juveniles.
Fishing Information: Sargo are commonly caught incidentally to other fishing, primarily during the summer months. Anglers fishing from the rocks catch a few as part of their mixed fare and good runs are occasionally encountered in southern California bays. Sargo make a piglike grunting sound when pulled from the water.

Almost any type of animal bait, such as clams, mussel, shrimp or pieces of fish, does well. Because of their habit of swimming a few feet off the bottom in loose schools and in shallow water, they are a prime target when spear fishing. Probably more are taken in this manner than by hook and line.
Other Common Names: China croaker, blue bass, black croaker, grunt.
Largest Recorded: 17.4 inches; 3.7 pounds.
Habitat: Shallow Rocky Environment

Queenfish

Family: Sciaenidae (Croakers)
Genus and Species:
Seriphus politus
Description: The body of the queenfish is elongate and moderately compressed. The head is com-

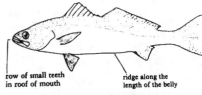

depression of upper profile

base of dorsal and anal fins about same length

pressed with the upper profile depressed over the eyes. The mouth is large. The color is bluish above becoming silvery below and the fins are yellowish.

Queenfish can be distinguished from other croakers by their large mouth, the base of the second dorsal and anal fins being about equal, and the wide space between the two dorsal fins.
Range: Queenfish occur from Uncle Sam Bank, Baja California, to Yaquina Bay, Oregon. They are common during summer in shallow water around pier pilings on sandy bottoms. They are found at depths up to 180 feet; however, occur more often from 4 to 27 feet.

Queenfish are common in southern California, but are rare north of Monterey, California.
Natural History: Queenfish feed on small, free swimming crustaceans, small crabs, and fishes.

Adult queenfish spawn in the summer. The eggs are free floating. Tiny young queenfish, less than 1 inch long, appear in late summer and fall; first at depths of 20 to 30 feet, gradually moving shoreward until they enter the surf zone when 1 to 3 inches long.
Fishing Information: Queenfish may be caught using live anchovies as bait. They are quite often the most commonly caught fish by anglers from piers.
Other Common Names: herring, kingfish, herring croaker, shiner.
Largest Recorded: 12 inches; no weight recorded.
Habitat: Shallow Sandy Environment

White Sea Bass

Family: Sciaenidae (Croakers)
Genus and Species:
Cynoscion nobilis*
* Also known as Atractoscion, nobilis.
Description: The body of the white sea bass is elongate, and somewhat compressed. The head is pointed and slightly

row of small teeth in roof of mouth

ridge along the length of the belly

compressed. The mouth is large, with a row of small teeth in the roof; the lower jaw slightly projects. The color is bluish to gray above, with dark speckling, becoming silver below. The young have several dark vertical bars.

The white sea bass is closely related to the California corbina, but is the only California member of the croaker family to exceed 20 pounds in weight. They are most easily separated from other croakers by the presence of a ridge running the length of the belly.
Range: White sea bass occur from Magdalena Bay, Baja California, to Juneau, Alaska. They usually travel in schools over rocky bottoms and in and out of kelp beds.
Natural History: The diet of white sea bass includes fishes, especially anchovies and sardines, and squid. At times, large fish are found which have eaten only Pacific mackerel.

At the minimum legal length of 28 inches, the average white sea bass is about 5 years of age, weighs about 7.5 pounds and has been sexually mature for at least one spawning season.
Fishing Information: White sea bass are fished primarily with live bait in relatively shallow water, but they will also take a fast-trolled spoon, artificial squid or bone jig. Live squid appear to be the best bait for a white sea bass, but large anchovies and medium-size sardines are also good.

At times, large white sea bass will bite only on fairly large, live Pacific mackerel.

The young of this species are exceptionally vulnerable to sport anglers for two reasons. The first is that as juveniles they inhabit shallow nearshore areas, bays, and estuaries, and the second is that they are not easily recognized as white sea bass by the average angler. Commonly, these young fish are mistakenly called "sea trout" because of their sleek profile and vertical bars or "parr marks." To add to the confusion, these bars fade as the fish grows.

There is a 28 inch size limit and current fishing regulations should be checked concerning bag limits.

Other Common Names: sea trout (juvenile), weakfish, king croaker.
Largest Recorded: 5 feet; 83 pounds.
Habitat: Deep Rocky Environment

Yellowfin Croaker

Family: Sciaenidae (Croaker)
Genus and Species: *Umbrina roncador*
Description: The body of the yellowfin croaker is elliptical-elongate with the back somewhat arched. The head is coni-

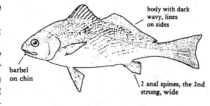

body with dark wavy, lines on sides

barbel on chin

2 anal spines, the 2nd strong, wide

cal and blunt. The color is iridescent blue to gray with brassy reflections on the back diffusing to silvery white below. The sides and back have many diagonal dark wavy lines. The fins are yellowish except for the dark dorsal fins.

The yellowfin croaker differs from other California croakers in having a single fleshy projection, a barbel, on the lower jaw and two heavy spines at the front of the anal fin.
Range: Yellowfin croakers occur from the Gulf to California, Mexico, to Point Conception, California. They frequent bays, channels, harbors and other nearshore waters over sandy bottoms. These croakers are more abundant along beaches during the summer months and may move to deeper water in winter.
Natural History: The diet of the yellowfin croaker consists mainly of small fishes and fish fry; however, invertebrates such as small crustaceans, worms and mollusks are also eaten in large numbers.

Spawning takes place during the summer months when this species is most common along the sandy beaches. Maturity is apparently not reached until the fish are slightly over 9 inches long.
Fishing Information: Yellowfin croaker are most often taken by surf anglers using softshelled sand crabs, worms, mussels, clams or cut fish as bait.
Other Common Names: Catalina croaker, yellowtailed croaker, golden croaker.
Largest Recorded: 20.13 inches; no weight reported. However, an 18 inch yellowfin croaker weighed 4.5 pounds.
Habitat: Shallow Sandy Environment

California Corbina

Family: Sciaenidae (Croakers)
Genus and Species: *Menticirrhus undulatus*
Description: The body of the California corbina is elongate and slightly compressed. The head is long and the mouth is small, the upper jaw scarcely reaching a point

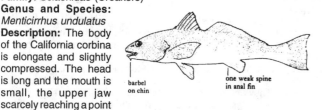

barbel on chin

one weak spine in anal fin

below the front of the eye. The color is uniform grey with incandescent reflections, and with wavy diagonal lines on the sides.

This croaker and the yellowfin croaker are the only two of the eight coastal croakers present in California waters to have a single fleshy projection, a barbel, on the lower jaw. The California corbina usually has only one weak spine at the front of the anal fin, while the yellowfin croaker has two strong spines.
Range: California corbina occur from the Gulf of California, Mexico to Point Conception, California, and is a bottom fish found along sandy beaches and in shallow bays. This species travels in small groups along the surf zone in a few inches of water to depths of 45 feet.
Natural History: Adults have been seen feeding in the surf, at times in water so shallow that their backs were exposed. They scoop up

mouthfuls of sand and separate the food by sending the sand through the gills. They are very particular feeders, apparently spitting out bits of clam shells and other foreign matter. About 90 percent of the food they eat is sand crabs. Other crustaceans and clams are of lesser importance.

Males mature when 2 years old at a length of about 10 inches and females at age 3 when about 13 inches long. Spawning extends f rom June to September, but is heaviest during July and August. Spawning apparently takes place offshore as running ripe fish are not often found in the surf zone. The eggs are free floating. Young corbina, 1 inch long, have been observed outside the surf in 4 to 8 feet of water in August.
Fishing Information: California corbina are caught throughout the year along southern California's sandy beaches, although fishing is at its best from July through September. They are very wary and difficult to hook as many an avid surf fisherman can affirm. Perhaps one reason is that they tend to mouth and chew their food and don't strike solidly very often. Sand crabs (usually softshells) are the preferred bait, though some anglers swear by blood worms, mussels, clams, pileworms, and ghost shrimp.
Other Common Names: California whiting, surf fish, sucker. California corbina should not be confused with corvina which are taken in the Salton Sea.
Largest Recorded: 28 inches; 8.5 pounds.
Habitat: Surf Environment

White Croaker

Family: Sciaenidae (Croakers)
Genus and Species: *Genyonemus lineatus*
Description: The body of the white croaker is elongate and somewhat compressed. The head is oblong and bluntly rounded, with a mouth that is somewhat underneath the head.

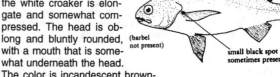

(barbel not present)

small black spot sometimes present

The color is incandescent brownish to yellowish on the back becoming silvery below. The tins are yellow to white.

The white croaker is one of five California croakers that have mouths located under their heads (subterminal). They can be distinguished from the California corbina and yellowfin croaker by the absence of a single fleshy projection, or barbel, at the tip of the lower jaw. The 12 to 15 spines in the first dorsal fin serve to distinguish white croakers from all the other croakers with subterminal mouths, since none of these has more than 11 spines in this fin.
Range: White croakers have been taken from Magdalena Bay, Baja California, to Vancouver Island, British Columbia, but are not abundant north of San Francisco. White croakers swim in loose schools at or near the bottom of sandy areas. Sometimes they aggregate in the surf zone or in shallow bays and lagoons. Most of the time they are found in offshore areas at depths of 10 to 100 feet. On rare occasions they are fairly abundant at depths as great as 600 feet.
Natural History: White croakers eat a variety of fishes, squid, shrimp, octopus, worms, small crabs, clams and other items, either living or dead.

While the ages of white croakers have not been determined conclusively, it is thought that some live as long as 15 or more years. Some spawn for the first time when they are between 2 and 3 years old. At this age they are only 5 to 6 inches long and weigh less than 0.10 pounds.
Fishing Information: These fish can be caught on almost any kind of animal bait that is fished from piers or jetties in sandy or sandy mud areas. In fact, they are so easily hooked that most anglers consider them a nuisance of the worst sort. If a person desires to fish specifically for white croakers a tough, difficult-to-steal bait, such as squid, is recommended. When hooked, they put up little or no fight. Fishing and catching is good throughout the year.
Other Common Names: kingfish, shiner, Pasadena trout, tommy croaker, little bass.
Largest Recorded: 16.3 inches; no weight recorded; however, a 14.5 inch white croaker weighted 1.41 pounds.
Habitat: Shallow Sandy Environment

Spotfin Croaker

Family: Sciaenidae (Croakers)
Genus and Species: *Roncador stearnsii*

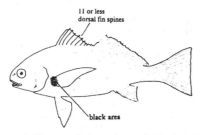

11 or less dorsal fin spines

black area

Description: The body of the spotfin croaker is elongate, but heavy forward. The upper profile of the head is steep and slightly curved, and abruptly rounded at the very blunt snout. The mouth is underneath the head (subterminal). The color is silvery gray with bluish luster above and white below. There are dark wavy lines on the side, and a large black spot at the base of the pectoral fin.

The subterminal mouth, absence of a fleshy barbel and the large black spot at the base of the pectoral fin distinguish spotfin croakers from all other California croakers. Small "spotties" are sometimes confused with small white croakers, but a count of the dorsal fin spines will quickly separate them; the spotfin croaker has 11 or fewer (usually 10), while the white croaker as 12 to 15. So-called "golden croakers" are nothing more than large male spotfin croakers in breeding colors.

Range: Spotfin croakers occur from Mazatlan, Mexico, to Point Conception, California, including the Gulf of California. In California, they are most commonly found south of Los Angeles Harbor. They live along beaches and in bays over bottoms varying from coarse sand to heavy mud and at depths varying from 4 to 50 feet or more. They prefer depressions and holes near shore.

Natural History: Spotfin croakers eat a wide variety of food items. Apparently they prefer clams and worms. Small crustaceans are also eaten extensively. They use the large pavement-like pharyngeal (throat) teeth to crush their food.

Male spotfin croakers first mature and spawn when 2 years old and about 9 inches long. Most females mature when 3 years old and 12.5 inches long. All are mature by the time they are 4 years old and have reached a size of 14.5 inches. The spawning season runs from June to September and apparently takes place offshore, since no ripe fish have been caught in the surf zone. One inch juveniles do appear in the surf in the fall.

Spotfin croaker travel considerably but with no definite pattern. They move extensively from bay to bay. For example, fish tagged in the Los Angeles Harbor were later taken as far south as Oceanside. Spotfin tagged in Newport Bay moved to Alamitos Bay and vice versa.

Fishing Information: Although some are caught throughout the year, late summer is best for spotfin croaker fishing. Good fishing seems to depend on runs. When a "croaker hole" is found and a run is on, good fishing can be had by all present whether in a bay, from a pier or in the surf. Most spotfin croaker caught are small to medium sized fish.

Other Common Names: spotties, spot, golden croaker.
Largest Recorded: 27 inches; 10.5 pounds.
Habitat: Shallow Sandy Environment

Opaleye

Family: Girellidae (Nibblers)
Genus and Species: *Girella nigricans*

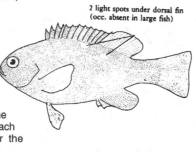

2 light spots under dorsal fin (occ. absent in large fish)

Description: The body of the opaleye is oval and compressed. The snout is thick with an evenly rounded profile. The mouth is small. The color is dark olive green, and most have one or two white spots on each side of the back under the middle of the dorsal fin.

The opaleye is California's only representative of the nibbler family. Bright blue eyes and the heavy, olive green, perch-like body quickly distinguish it from any other species.

Range: Opaleye occur from Cape San Lucas, Baja California, to San Francisco, California.

Opaleyes are residents of rocky shorelines and kelp beds. Young ones, 1 or more inches long, live in tide pools, but they seek deeper water as they grow larger. The largest concentrations of opaleye are in 65 feet of water.

Natural History: Opaleye primarily eat marine algae with or without encrustations of organisms. Food items include feather boa kelp, giant kelp, sea lettuce, coralline algae, small tube dwelling worms, and red crabs.

Ripe adults have been taken in April, May and June. They form dense schools in shallower water where spawning takes place. The eggs and larvae are free floating and at times are found a number of miles from shore. The juveniles form schools of up to two dozen individuals. When about 1 inch long they enter tide pools. As they grow they seek deeper and deeper water. They mature and spawn when about 8 or 9 inches long at an age of about 2 or 3 years.

Fishing Information: Few fish are harder to hook than the opaleye and few fish will put up more fight pound-for-pound. Long considered one of the better sport fish, they take mussels, sand crabs, pieces of fish or invertebrates on a hook. Since opaleye are primarily vegetarians, some anglers find it easier to catch them using various "mosses" for bait.

Other Common Names: green perch, black perch, blue-eyed perch, bluefish, Jack Benny, button-back.
Largest Recorded: 25.5 inches; 13.5 pounds.
Habitat: Shallow Rocky Environment

Halfmoon

Family: Scorpididae* (Halfmoons)
Genus and Species: *Medialuna californiensis*
*** Kyphosidae (American Fisheries Society)**
Description: The body of the halfmoon is oval and compressed. The head is blunt and rounded and the mouth is small. The color is dark blue above, shading to blue gray on the sides and becoming white below. The tail is halfmoon shaped. The soft rays of the dorsal and anal fins are nearly hidden by a thick sheath of scales. The halfmoon most closely resembles the blue rockfish, but lacks the 5 spines on the front section of the gill cover, which are common to all rockfishes.

Range: Halfmoon occur from the Gulf of California, Mexico, to the Klamath River, California. They are most common in southern California, particularly around the Channel Islands. Halfmoon occur over shallow rocky areas and in kelp beds. They have been observed as deep as 130 feet, but are most commonly taken by anglers from waters from 8 to 65 feet deep.

Natural History: Halfmoon feed on a variety of plant and animal matter such as red, green and brown algae, and sponges. In the turbulent areas of the rocky coasts they have been seen catching bits of upsurging seaweed.

Spawning takes place during the summer months. Ripe adults are taken from July through October. The eggs and young are free floating and the young, like opaleye, are found some distance from shore. One inch halfmoon, are found at the outer edges of kelp beds. Only adults are commonly found in the inshore area. They reach maturity when about 7.5 inches long.

Fishing Information: Halfmoon are abundant throughout the year. They are scrappy and are good eating. Anglers, fishing from the rocks, have good success using mussels and shrimp; opaleye anglers occasionally catch them on moss bait. Anglers, fishing offshore, are most successful using fresh cut bait such as anchovy, sardine or squid.

Other Common Names: Catalina blue perch, blue bass, black perch.
Largest Recorded: 19 inches; 4.75 pounds.
Habitat: Shallow Rocky Environment

Silver Surfperch

Family: Embiotocidae (Surfperches)
Genus and Species: *Hyperprosopon ellipticum*
Description: The body of the silver surfperch is oval and strongly compressed. The head is small and the mouth is moderately large. The body is silvery with dusky (brownish to gray) coloration on the back and dusky bars on the sides. The tail is usually pink with an occasional orange spot on the anal fin.

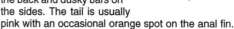

tail usually pinkish

The specific name ellipticum refers to its elliptical body outline. It looks similar to the walleye surfperch but lacks the black coloration on its pelvic fins.
Range: Silver surfperch occur from Rio San Vicente, Baja California, to Schooner Cove, near Tofino, Vancouver Island, British Columbia.

These small surfperch primarily frequent the sandy surf zone although they are also caught among shallow rocks from piers, and in bays.

Natural History: The diet of silver surfperch includes shrimp, crustaceans, amphipods and algae.

As with all surfperch, the young are born alive and are relatively large. Mating occurs during the fall and early winter months. The male approaches the female from below; both swim with vents close for 2 or 3 seconds, then separate and repeat the process. Three to 16 young are born the following spring and summer.

Fishing Information: Silver surfperch rank among the top ten in numbers caught by recreational anglers in central and northern California, even though the average weight is 0.1 pound.

They are plentiful, easy to catch and occur in large numbers in surf, shore and pier catches.

Other Common Names: silver perch, shiner.
Largest Recorded: 10.5 inches; no weight recorded.
Habitat: Shallow Sandy Environment

Walleye Surfperch

Family: Embiotocidae (Surfperches)
Genus and Species: *Hyperprosopon argenteum*
Description: The body of the walleye surfperch is oval and strongly compressed. The head is small and the eyes are large. The mouth is small and slanted downward. The color is silver with faint dusky shading on the back. The tips of the ventral fins are black as are the borders of the anal fin and tail.

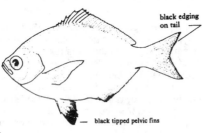

black edging on tail

black tipped pelvic fins

The walleye surfperch can be distinguished from other surfperch by the distinctive black tips on the ventral fins and black borders on the tail and anal fins.

Range: Walleye surfperch occur from Point San Rosarito, Baja California, to Vancouver Island, British Columbia. This species is found in dense schools along sandy beaches, near rocks and around piers. They appear to move into embayments such as Humboldt Bay during summer.

Natural History: Walleye surfperch feed primarily on small crustaceans.

Mating takes place in October, November and December when the usual dense schools break up and the males and females pair off. The encroachment of another male is immediately countered by a quick charge from the courting male toward the intruder's snout. Between 5 and 12 young, depending on the size of the mother, are born the following spring. They average a little over 1.5 inches in length at birth. They reach maturity the following fall and winter; in fact, the largest proportion of the breeding population appears to be young of the year.

Walleyes are probably short-lived as are most other surfperches. A 10.5 inch walleye was only 6 years old.

Fishing Information: Walleyes can be caught in the surf, from rocks, and from piers anywhere along the open coast. They usually are the most abundant surfperch caught from piers. A small hook baited with mussels, pieces of fish, worms, squid or shrimp will catch walleyes any season of the year. Often occurring in dense schools 6 to 8 feet thick, comprised of several hundred fish, the walleye can provide very rewarding fishing.

Other Common Names: walleye surf fish, walleye seaperch, china pompano, white perch.

Largest Recorded: Reported to reach 12 inches; however, largest recorded is a 10.75 inch female; no weight recorded.

Habitat: Bay Environment

Shiner Surfperch

Family: Embiotocidae (Surfperches)
Genus and Species: *Cymatogaster aggregata*
Description: The body of the shiner surfperch is elongate oval and compressed. The head is small and the mouth is small. The

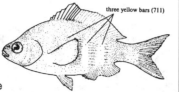

three yellow bars (711)

body is gray to greenish above with vertical lemon yellow cross bars in the shape of a "71 1" and eight horizontal sooty lines along the sides. During courtship and breeding the males are dark gray, almost black, in color and have a black spot on each side of the snout.

The island surfperch is a close relative found around the channel islands off southern California. This species is much more slender than the shiner surfperch.

Range: Shiner surfperch occur from San Quintin Bay, Baja California, to Port Wrangell, Alaska.

They prefer calm water and are most abundant in bays around eelgrass beds and the pilings of wharfs and piers. They have been captured in trawl nets fishing in 350 to 480 feet of water and have been observed by divers at depths as great as 120 feet, but are more numerous in shallow inshore waters.

Natural History: The diet of shiner surfperch consists mostly of small crustaceans and other invertebrates. They are frequently observed around pier pilings nipping off the appendages of barnacles.

Mating takes place during the summer months in most localities, and the young are born the following spring and summer. During courtship, the male closely follows the female, their movements remarkably well synchronized. He will leave her side frequently to chase off other fish, many of which are not the least bit attracted to his mate.

They are apparently short-lived as a 6 inch female (large for shiner surfperch) was only 3 years old.

Fishing Information: Shiner surfperch are caught from shore, docks, piers, rocks, and almost any other fishing area. They are probably the number one fish caught by youngsters along the California coast. They can be taken on almost any type of bait and any type of fishing equipment from handline to spinning gear so long as the hook on the end of the line is small enough for the fish to get in their mouths.

Other Common Names: shiner perch, shiner, shiner seaperch, yellow shiner, bay perch, seven-eleven perch.

Largest Recorded: 7 inches, reported to 8 inches; no weight recorded; however, a pregnant female 6.75 inches long weighed just under 3 ounces.

Habitat: Bay Environment

Redtail Surfperch

Family: Embiotocidae (Surfperches)
Genus and Species: *Amphistichus rhodoterus*
Description: The body of the redtail surfperch is oval and compressed. The upper profile of the head is nearly straight from the snout to the dorsal fin except for a slight depression above the eye. The body color is silver with olive green mottling and bars on the side. The tail is pink to deep purple.

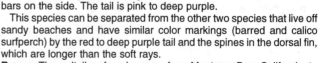

dorsal spines much longer than dorsal soft-rays

tail fin purplish-red

This species can be separated from the other two species that live off sandy beaches and have similar color markings (barred and calico surfperch) by the red to deep purple tail and the spines in the dorsal fin, which are longer than the soft rays.

Range: The redtail surfperch occurs from Monterey Bay, California, to Vancouver Island, British Columbia, and is the most often encountered surfperch from Bodega Bay northward.

Redtail surfperch are predominantly surf dwellers off sandy beaches, but have been taken in rocky areas adjacent to beaches. They are common in estuaries and protected embayments during the spawning season.

Natural History: Small crustaceans are the major food items preferred by this species; however, small crabs, shrimp, mussels or marine worms are also attractive, to redtail surfperch.

Like all surfperch, the redtail gives birth to live young. The young are carried inside the mother until birth when they emerge as miniature replicas of the adults. Males mature at age 2 and females at age 4. They breed in fall and give birth in spring and summer, primarily from June to August. Females contain up to 51 young with the average of 27.

Fishing Information: Redtail surfperch concentrate just before spawning in sheltered inshore waters during the spring and early summer. They are frequently caught in large numbers at this time. The average size of redtail surfperch that an angler usually catches is 1.8 pounds, although 3 pound fish are not uncommon.

Light tackle with No. 406 hooks and crab backs for bait is the preferred method of take in Humboldt Bay. For surf fishing, 20 pound test line and 6 to 80 ounce sinkers are usually used with sand crabs, tube worms or clams for bait.

Other Common Names: rosy surf fish, redtail seaperch, porgie, Oregon porgie.
Largest Recorded: 16 inches; no weight recorded.
Habitat: Surf Environment

Rubberlip Surfperch

Family: Embiotocidae (Surfperches)
Genus and Species: *Rhacochilus toxotes*
Description: The body of the rubberlip surfperch is oval and compressed. The mouth is comparatively large and the lips are extremely thick. The lower jaw is slightly shorter than the upper.

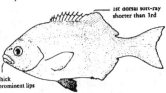

The color is variable but it is generally whitish with brown to brassy overtones on the back fading to tan below. The lips are whitish or pink. Juveniles have one or two vertical dusky bars on the body, although these usually are not found on adults. Its large size and thick prominent lips distinguish it from all other surfperches.
Range: Rubberlip surfperch occur from Thurloe Head, Baja California, to Russian Gulch State Beach, California. They frequent rocky areas, tidepools and kelp beds on the outer coast as well as bays and harbors.
Natural History: Adults feed upon crabs, shrimps and octopus. Juveniles feed on typical surfperch food such as worms, small crabs, mussels, and tiny snails.

Like all surfperch, the rubberlip surfperch bears its young live. A 16.5 inch female, that was 8 years old and weighed slightly less than 3 pounds contained 21 young that averaged a little over 3.5 inches in length.
Fishing Information: While modest numbers of rubberlip surfperch are taken by recreational anglers, it is the leading species of the commercial surfperch catch in the Monterey Bay area.

Recreational anglers catch rubberlip surfperch from skiffs, piers and the shore. The greatest number have been taken from piers in the Monterey Bay area, with the average size caught by sport anglers being 2 pounds. Most hook-and-line catches are made using mussels, clams, sand worms, cut shrimp or similar bait.
Other Common Names: pile perch, rubberlip seaperch, porgee, sprat, liverlip, buttermouth.
Largest Recorded: 18 inches; no weight recorded; however, a 16.5 inch rubberlip surf perch weighed nearly 3 pounds.
Habitat: Shallow Sandy Environment

Barred Surfperch

Family: Embiotocidae (Surfperches)
Genus and Species: *Amphistichus argenteus*
Description: The body of the barred surfperch is oval and compressed. The head is blunt and the mouth is comparatively large. The color is

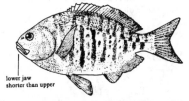

olive green to yellow green on the back becoming silver below; with bronze, brassy or yellow vertical bars and spots on the side.

This surfperch is one of three living off sandy beaches with similar color markings; however, it can be distinguished from the other two (calico and redtail) by its lower jaw being slightly shorter than the upper, and by the absence of red or reddish color on its fins.
Range: The barred surfperch occurs from Plaza Maria Bay, Baja California, to Bodega Bay, California. It is more abundant than the calico and redtail south of Cayucos, California. Barred surfperch are found in the surf zone along sandy beaches where they seem to congregate in depressions on the bottom. They have been taken from water as deep as 240 feet.
Natural History: The major portion of the barred surf perch diet is sand crabs, with other crustaceans, bean clams and small crabs comprising the remainder.

Barred surfperch give birth to living young from March to July. As few as four and as many as 113 have been counted, but the average is 33 per female. They are about 2.5 inches long at birth, and mature when about 6.5 inches long and 1 or 2 years old.

This species is relatively short lived with the oldest males being about 6 years old and 12 inches long. The oldest females are about 9 years old and up to 17 inches long.

Tagging studies indicate barred surfperch move very little, usually less than 2 miles, although movements up to 31 miles have been recorded.
Fishing Information: The most popular bait for barred surfperch is soft shelled sand crabs, but blood worms, mussels, cut fish, and small artificial lures also work. Fishing is usually best on an incoming tide when the perch are feeding inside the breaker zone.
Other Common Names: barred perch, silver perch, surf perch, sand perch, silver surf fish.
Largest Recorded: 17 inches; 4.5 pounds.
Habitat: Surf Environment

California Sheephead

Family: Labridae (Wrasses)
Genus and Species: *Semicossyphus pulcher* (male)
Description: The body of the California sheephead is elongate, robust, and compressed. This species is a "protogynous hermaphrodite"; meaning that it begins life as a

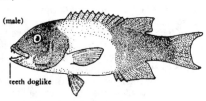

female, but then becomes a male later in life. Females mature at about 8 inches in length when they reach 4 to 5 years of age. Most females transform to males at a length of about 12 inches at 7 to 8 years of age.

This sex change is accompanied by a marked change in appearance. Younger fish (females) are a uniform pinkish red with a white lower jaw. As they age and become males, the head and rear third of the body turns black, the midsection of the body remains red and the lower jaw remains white. In all stages of their development, sheephead have unusually large dog-like teeth.
Range: California sheephead occur from Cabo San Lucas, Baja California, to Monterey Bay, California, with an isolated population in the Gulf of California. They are uncommon north of Point Conception. California sheephead are generally taken in rocky kelp areas near shore, in water from 20 to 100 feet deep, although they do occur as deep as 180 feet.
Natural History: Crabs, mussels, various sized snails, squid, sea urchins, sand dollars, and sea cucumbers are typical food items. The large canine-like teeth are used to pry food from rocks. A special plate in the throat crushes shells into small pieces for easy digestion. Occasionally, large adults have been observed out of the water in the intertidal hanging onto mussels after a wave has receded.

Spawning takes place in early spring and summer. Young about 0.5 inch long occur in late May through late December and do not resemble the adults. They are brilliant red orange with two black spots on the dorsal fin and a black spot at base of tail fin. Pelvic and anal fins are black, trimmed in white. Occasional lemon yellow young are seen.

The young live close to rocks at depths from 10 to well below 100 feet, particularly around beds of gorgonian corals (sea fans). When disturbed, they seek shelter in sea fans or among red seaweed.

The following summer, juveniles are 3 to 4 inches long and have faded to dull pink. At 2 years they are 6 to 8 inches long, have lost all spots, and have a typical female color pattern.
Fishing Information: Sheephead will take a variety of live and cut baits, such as anchovy or squid, fished on the bottom. Those interested in trophy-sized sheephead may try a whole, live mackerel fished on the bottom. The angler who hooks a California sheephead is usually in for a strong, tugging battle. A battle that commonly ends in disaster when the "catch" runs through or around a kelp plant, or under the nearest rocky ledge.
Other Common Names: sheepie, goat, billygoats (large), red fish, humpy, fathead.
Largest Recorded: 36 inches; 36.25 pounds.
Habitat: Shallow Rocky Environment

California Barracuda

Family: Sphyraenidae (Barracudas)
Genus and Species: *Sphyraena argentea*
Description: The body of the California barracuda is very elongate and slender, and almost round. The mouth is large with canine-like teeth. It has a sharply pointed snout with a projecting lower jaw. The color is grayish black with a bluish tinge on the back becoming silvery or

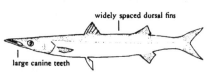

white on the sides and belly. The tail is yellowish and the dorsal fins are widely spaced.

Range: California barracuda occur from Cape San Lucas, Baja California, to Kodiak Island, Alaska. This species is found from the surface to depths of 60 feet, but is rare north of Point Conception, California.

Natural History: The California barracuda's main forage is anchovies and other small fishes. The spawning season in southern California may extend from April through September, but most spawning takes place in May, June and July. An individual probably spawns more than once each season.

About 75 percent of the California barracuda will spawn when they are 2 years old. The ovaries of a 3-inch female weighed 0.75 pounds and were estimated to contain 484,000 mature eggs. Young barracuda up to 6 inches in length are usually found in shallow water close to shore.

Fishing Information: Most California barracuda are taken with live bait fished at or near the surface; however, they will take an assortment of trolled artificial lures. If you see a very large barracuda, in the 10 pound range, chances are it's a female. Positive identification can be made because the female has a charcoal black edge on the pelvic and anal fins, whereas the male fins are edged in yellow or olive.

Three pound barracuda are common, but generally they are large enough to put up a good fight. Caution should be taken when you land a barracuda to avoid their needle sharp teeth.

Other Common Names: barracuda, scoot, scooter, snake, barry, Pacific barracuda.

Largest Recorded: Reported to 5 feet, but recorded to 4 feet; 18.1 pounds.

Habitat: Pelagic Environment

Giant Kelpfish

Family: Clinidae (Clinids)
Genus and Species: *Herterostichus rostratus*
Description: The body of the giant kelpfish is very elongate and compressed. The head is slender, compressed and pointed. The color may vary from light brown to green and purple with lighter areas of mottling.

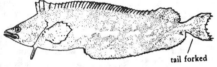
tail forked

Giant kelp fish are easily separated from other family members because they are the only ones with forked tails; other members have rounded tails.

Range: Giant kelpfish range from Cabo San Lucas, Baja California, to British Columbia, and from surface waters down to 130 feet. Rocks covered with seaweed and kelp beds surrounding them provide the forage and habitat giant kelpfish desire.

Natural History: The diet of the giant kelp fish is predominantly small crustaceans, mollusks, and small fishes.

Spawning occurs during March through July. During spawning, which occurs in a territory established by the male, the female releases her eggs on seaweed while she quivers with the male next to her, sometimes head to tail. Pink to greenish eggs are attached to the seaweed by entangling threads that extend from egg coverings. The male remains to guard the eggs. Transparent post larvae appear from April through August, usually in shallow water f rom 5 to 30 feet. Giant kelpfish school until approximately 2.5 inches long when they begin to assume adult colors and become solitary, living close among seaweeds.

Fishing Information: Anglers pursuing giant kelpfish should drift through giant kelp beds since the fish are closely associated with the plants. When fishing for this species, small hooks are recommended since the fish have small mouths. Small shrimp, juvenile clams and other small invertebrates are used as bait. Squid can also be used if cut into small pieces.

Other Common Names: kelpfish, eel, iodine fish, butterfish, kelp blenny.

Largest Recorded: 24 inches; no weight recorded; however, a 16.2 inch giant kelpfish weighed 1.2 pounds.

Habitat: Shallow Rocky Environment

Pacific Mackerel

Family: Scombridae (Mackerels and Tunas)
Genus and Species: *Scomber japonicus*
Description: The body of the Pacific mackerel tapers at both ends, is rather elongate, and

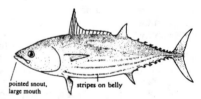
wavy lines extend onto head
4–6 finlets

somewhat compressed. The head is pointed and the mouth is large. The head is dark blue, the back is dark blue with about 30 dark wavy lines, and the undersides are silver green.

The widely separated first and second dorsal fins serve to distinguish Pacific mackerel from all of the other tuna-like fishes that inhabit our waters, except for the frigate and bullet mackerel. Pacific mackerel and bullet mackerel can be differentiated by counting the dorsal finlets. Pacific mackerel typically have four to six, while bullet and frigate mackerel have seven to eight finlets.

Range: Worldwide in temperate seas; in the eastern Pacific from Chile to the Gulf of Alaska.

Natural History: Larval, juvenile or small fishes appear to be the most important natural food of Pacific mackerel, but there are times when they rely heavily on small crustaceans. They feed upon squid to a lesser extent, and eat whatever other bite-sized organisms they may encounter.

Off southern California, spawning normally reaches a peak during the early spring months, especially March, April and May. Pacific mackerel eggs are about 0.045 inch in diameter and float free in the upper layers of the ocean, usually within 300 feet of the surface. At average water temperatures they will hatch 4 or 5 days after being spawned.

Fishing Information: Pacific mackerel have long been cast in the role of an intruder or nuisance fish by most anglers, especially those seeking larger sportfish like yellowtail or barracuda. Nevertheless, they have been the most frequently caught species on hook and line in California waters in recent years.

Known as a voracious, indiscriminant feeder, Pacific mackerel will devour a live anchovy, engulf dead cut bait, strike readily on lures and often on flies. When in a feeding frenzy it has been known to hit a piece of rag soaked in fish gurg. While it is relatively small in size (3 pounds or 18 inches would be trophy size), it scores high for power (ounce for ounce) and beauty. Pacific mackerel put up an excellent fight against light tackle.

Other Common Names: American mackerel, blue mackerel, greenback jack, chub mackerel.

Largest Recorded: 25 inches; 6.3 pounds.

Habitat: Pelagic Environment

Skipjack

Family: Scombridae (Mackerels and Tunas)
Genus and Species: *Euthynnus pelamis*
Description: The body of the skipjack is cigar-shaped (tapers at both ends). The snout is sharply pointed and the mouth is relatively large. The color is dark blue to purple on the back become silvery or white below, with four to six dark horizontal stripes on the belly.

pointed snout, large mouth
stripes on belly

Range: Skipjack occur worldwide in warm seas. They are found in the eastern Pacific from Peru to Vancouver Island, British Columbia. Skipjack usually visit California waters in the fall when water is relatively warm (about 68°F) and the currents are from either the south or southwest.

Natural History: The diet of the skipjack tuna includes fishes such as anchovies and sardines as well as squid; however, shrimp eggs and similar organisms are a major component of the diet.

Skipjack tuna do not spawn in waters off California, but further south in the eastern Pacific spawning takes place during the summer months. A skipjack tuna that is 18.5 inches long and weighs 5.5 pounds lays an estimated 113,000 eggs, while one that is 22.1 inches long and weighs 13.1 pounds produces 600,000 eggs. The young fish grow rapidly and when 1 year old are 18 inches long. They rarely live beyond 7 years.

Fishing Information: Most skipjack are taken incidentally to other fishing activities, especially albacore or tuna fishing. They bite a feather eagerly and will readily come to the boat when live anchovies are used as chum.

Most anglers do not actively seek skipjack because of their small size and the undesirability of the meat when fresh. However, skipjack is good if processed and most is consumed after it is canned. Most fish taken off California weigh 2 to 12 pounds, with the vast majority in the 4 to 6 pound range.

Other Common Names: skippies, oceanic bonito, striped tuna, arctic bonito, watermelon, victor fish.

Largest Recorded: No length recorded; 26 pounds (California).

Habitat: Pelagic Environment

Pacific Bonito

Family: Scombridae (Mackerel and Tunas)
Genus and Species: *Sarda chiliensis*

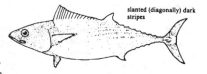
slanted (diagonally) dark stripes

Description: The body of the Pacific bonito is cigar-shaped and somewhat compressed. The head is pointed and conical, and the mouth is large. The color is dark blue above, dusky on the sides becoming silvery below. There is a number of slanted darkish stripes along the back.

Pacific bonito are the only tuna-like fishes on the California coast that have the slanted dark stripes on their backs.

Range: Pacific bonito occur discontinuously from Chile to the Gulf of Alaska, with the greatest area of abundance in the northern hemisphere occurring in warm waters between Magdalena Bay, Baja California, and Point Conception, California.

Natural History: The preferred food of bonito appears to be small fishes, such as anchovies and sardines. Occasionally, they rely heavily upon squid in their daily diet.

Bonito may not spawn successfully every year in California, but successful spawning does take place further south each year. The bulk of southern California spawning appears to take place from late January through May. The free floating eggs require about 3 days to hatch at average spring water temperatures.

Young fish resulting from local successful spawnings are usually first observed by the various live bait haulers when they are 6 to 10 inches long in the early summer months. These fish will often weigh 3 pounds or more by the fall of the year and by May of the following year many will weigh 6 or 7 pounds.

Fishing Information: Pacific bonito are excellent fighters and have hearty appetites. Once a school is aroused they will take almost any bait or lure that is tossed their way. Most Pacific bonito are taken by a combination of trolling and live baitfishing. The schools are located by trolling feathers and live anchovies or squid pieces are used to bait the fish once located. Fishing for bonito generally takes place offshore in 300 to 600 feet of water, but may occur next to kelp beds when the fish are near shore.

Pacific bonito may arrive off of California as the ocean warms in the spring, but may never show up if oceanic conditions dictate colder than normal water temperatures.

Bonito anglers generally catch 1 to 4 year old fish, weighing between 3 and 12 pounds. Pacific bonito fishing tapers off in the fall as the water cools, but persistent anglers still find good bonito fishing around warm water outfalls associated with power plants.

Other Common Names: bonehead, Laguna tuna, magneto, striped tuna, California bonito, ocean bonito.

Largest Recorded: 40 inches; 25 pounds.

Habitat: Pelagic Environment

Albacore

Family: Scombridae (Mackerels and Tunas)
Genus and Species: *Thunnus alalunga*

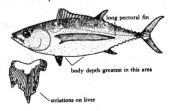
long pectoral fin
body depth greatest in this area
striations on liver

Description: The body of the albacore tapers at both ends (cigar-shaped). The head is long and the mouth fairly large. The color is dark gray to metallic blue on the back becoming white to gray below.

Albacore are easily distinguished from the other tunas occurring off California, with exception of the bigeye, by the extreme length of their pectoral fins (they extend well past the anal fin). Albacore and bigeye can best be distinguished by the characteristics of their livers. The albacore has a heavily striated (covered with blood vessels) liver while the liver of the bigeye is only lightly striated along the edges.

Range: Albacore occur worldwide in temperate seas; in the eastern Pacific they range from south of Guadalupe Island, Baja California, to southeast Alaska.

Natural History: The food of the albacore varies, depending upon where they are feeding in the water column and what items are available at the time and place the albacore are feeding. A majority of the food consists of small fishes, but at times squid, octopus, shrimp-like and crab-like organisms are extremely important.

There are indications that albacore spawning takes place in the mid-Pacific, probably north and west of the Hawaiian Islands. Large specimens caught in that area during late summer on long line gear have had nearly ripe eggs in their ovaries.

The albacore is one of the world's fastest migrant fish. Annual trans-Pacific migrations have been documented by tagging. Fish tagged off California were captured off Japan, nearly 5,000 miles away, 294 days later. Traveling "as the crow flies", this is equivalent to more than 17 miles a day.

Fishing Information: Albacore are the most sought after of the tunas by California anglers. Most fishing for albacore takes place 20-100 miles offshore in central and southern California. They are rarely taken near shore. Albacore have a preference for deep blue oceanic water and mild temperatures. Studies indicate that 57 of every 100 albacore caught are hooked in water ranging in temperature between 60 and 64 F

Albacore travel in loosely knit schools which are located by trolling or observing surface signs (feeding birds, etc.). Once located, they are fished with hook and line using live anchovies for bait. They may also be caught on a trolled feathered jig.

Other Common Names: longfin, albie, pigfish, Pacific albacore, German.

Largest Recorded: 5 feet; 79 pounds (California).

Habitat: Pelagic Environment

Bigeye Tuna

Family: Scombridae (Mackerels and Tunas)
Genus and Species: *Thunnus obesus*

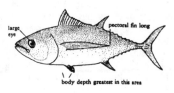
large eye
pectoral fin long
body depth greatest in this area

Description: The body of the bigeye tuna is cigar-shaped (tapered at both ends). The head is pointed and the eye is relatively large. The color is dark metallic brownish blue to dark yellow on the back becoming gray or whitish below. There often is a bluish stripe on the side.

In most individuals, the length of the pectoral fins should enable one to identify the species properly. Both bigeye and yellowfin tuna look similar, but bigeye tuna have pectoral fins which extend well past their anal fin, while yellowfin tuna have much shorter pectoral fins. Tuna which cannot be distinguished by external characteristics can be positively identified by liver characteristics. Bigeye tuna livers are striated (covered with blood vessels) along the trailing edges, while yellowfin tuna livers are smooth.

Small bigeye tuna also may be distinguished from albacore by the characteristics of the liver. The liver is heavily striated in the albacore while the bigeye tuna liver is only striated along the trailing edges.

Range: Bigeye tuna occur worldwide in warmer seas. In the eastern Pacific these tuna range from Peru to Iron Springs, Washington. They are occasional visitors to California, entering our fishing grounds in June and remaining until November. These fish prefer temperate water in excess of 70°F, but significant catches have occurred in water as cool as 65°F.

Natural History: The diet of bigeye tuna includes fishes, squid, and crustaceans. Like most other tunas, they feed on what is most abundant in the area.

Bigeye tuna do not spawn in waters off California, but spawn further south in the Pacific. Bigeye tuna are approximately 3 years old at first spawning. In the equatorial regions of the Pacific, the peak spawning is between April and September.

A bigeye tuna weighing 159 pounds will produce an estimated 3.3 million eggs per year. The young are fast growing and weigh about 45 pounds when they first mature. They live 7 or 8 years.

Fishing Information: Bigeye tuna generally are not accessible to recreational anglers because they travel far below the surface during the day. Only rarely are they seen on the surface, and then, only momentarily while feeding. This makes the fish hard to locate since they leave no telltale surface signs nor can they be easily located by trolling. Most bigeye tuna are taken incidental to albacore or marlin fishing.

The best way to fish for them is to troll marlin lures in an area where the fish are known to occur. Most bigeye tuna taken in southern California weigh 50 to 100 pounds, with an occasional 150 to 200 pounder landed.

Other Common Names: gorilla, tuna, patudo
Largest Recorded: 80 inches; 435 pounds; 215 pounds (California).
Habitat: Pelagic Environment

Bluefin Tuna

Family: Scombridae (Mackerels and Tunas)
Genus and Species: *Thunnus obesus*
Description: The body of the bluefin tuna is cigar-shaped and robust. The head is conical and the mouth rather large. The color is dark blue above and gray below.

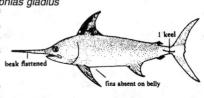
pectoral fin not reaching the beginning of the 2nd dorsal fin

Bluefin tuna can easily be distinguished from other members of the tuna family by the relatively short length of their pectoral fins. Their livers have a unique and definitive characteristic in that they are covered with blood vessels (striated). In other tunas with short pectoral fins, such vessels are either not present or present in small numbers along the edges.

Range: Worldwide in all but the coldest seas. Bluefin tuna range throughout the eastern North Pacific Ocean with fish being taken from Magdalena Bay, Baja California, to Shelikof Strait, Alaska.

Most bluefin tuna landed by California anglers are 1 or 2 year olds and weigh between 15 and 30 pounds.

Natural History: Examination of a number of stomachs indicates that while in California waters anchovies make up the bulk of the diet. Sanddabs, surfperches, and white croakers are also consumed.

Fishing Information: Bluefin tuna are seasonal visitors to California waters. They usually appear in May and depart by October. Since they are temperate tunas, their availability to anglers depends on water temperatures in the 62° to 68°F degree range. They can be located by either trolling feathers or anchoring at a spot known to be frequented by bluefin tuna, and chumming with live anchovies. Once the fish are attracted, anglers must use light line (12# test or less), small hooks (#4's or smaller), and the "hottest" bait available that season (usually live anchovies or pieces of squid).

Other Common Names: leaping tuna, tuna, footballs, tunny, shortfin tuna, ahi, great albacore.
Largest Recorded: No length recorded; 363.5 pounds (California). Weight to 495 pounds in the Pacific Ocean, and 1,500 pounds in the Atlantic Ocean.
Habitat: Pelagic Environment

Yellowfin Tuna

Family: Scombridae (Mackerel and Tunas)
Genus and Species: *Thunnus albacores*

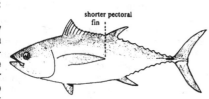
shorter pectoral fin

Description: The body of the yellowfin tuna tapers at both ends (cigar-shaped), and the head is conical. The color is dark brownish blue to dark yellow on the back becoming gray or whitish below.

Identifying tunas can be difficult, especially when yellowfin and bigeye tuna are involved.

In most cases, the length of the pectoral fins can distinguish each species. The yellowfin has pectoral fins which do not extend past the anal fin; while in bigeye, the pectoral fins extend well past the anal fin.

Tuna which cannot be distinguished by external characteristics can be positively identified by liver characteristics. The surface of a yellowfin's is smooth while the liver of the bigeye is striated, containing many small blood vessels along the trailing edge.

Range: Widely distributed in the Pacific Ocean. In the eastern Pacific, yellowfin tuna occur from Chile to Point Buchon, California. They occasionally enter California waters when ocean temperatures are warm. They usually are not taken in waters less than 70°F with best catches occurring in waters above 74°F.

Natural History: The diet of the yellowfin tuna includes juvenile fishes, crustaceans, and squid. They are opportunistic feeders taking whatever is most available in the area.

Yellowfin tuna do not spawn off the coast of California; however, they do spawn further south in the eastern Pacific.

Some spawning takes place during every month of the year, but off Central America it peaks during January and February.

Young fish grow very rapidly and by the time they are 1.5 years old they weigh around 7.5 pounds. At t years old they weigh approximately 150 pounds. The largest yellowfin tuna taken are 10 or more years old. These larger fish sometimes have an elongated second dorsal fin.

Fishing Information: Yellowfin tuna are fished in much the same manner as albacore; jigs are used to locate the schools, and live anchovies are chummed to keep the fish around the boat.

Most yellowfin tuna taken in California weigh 30 to 50 pounds, fish over 200 pounds are occasionally landed. The smaller fish are 1 to 2 years old while the larger ones may be over 10 years of age.

Other Common Names: Allison tuna, ahi, Pacific yellowfin.
Largest Recorded: No length recorded; 239 pounds (California); weight to 450 pounds.
Habitat: Pelagic Environment

Swordfish

Family: Xiphiidae (Swordfishes)
Genus and Species: *Xiphias gladius*
Description: The body of the swordfish is elongate and somewhat compressed. The upper jaw is very much extended, forming a long, flat sword. The color is dark gray to black above becoming gray to yellowish below.

beak flattened
1 keel
fins absent on belly

Swordfish are readily distinguished from other billfish by their flattened bills, lack of fins on the belly, and the presence of only one keel (small projection) on the base of the tail adjoining the fish.

Range: Swordfish occur worldwide in temperate and tropical seas. Off southern California, they are most commonly encountered between the mainland and the Channel Islands.

Natural History: The diet of swordfish includes fishes such as anchovies, hake, jack mackerel, rockfishes, lanternfishes, pencil smelt, as well as squid.

Swordfish do not spawn off the coast of California, but in 1958 a ripe female was harpooned off Santa Catalina Island. It contained an estimated 50 million eggs.

In areas like the Mediterranean, where spawning has been studied, some females lay eggs during every month of the year, but the spawning peak is in June and July. The eggs take 2.5 days to hatch. While there is little information available on swordfish age and growth, they probably grow quite rapidly and do not live for a great number of years.

Fishing Information: Swordfish are taken from May through November, and occasionally landed in December. The average California recreational fishery take is between 10 and 20 fish per year, but more than 125 fish were landed in 1978, the best year on record.

Most recreational fishing for swordfish involves visually searching for a fish that is finning (presenting itself at the surface) and then maneuvering a baited hook in front of it. Live Pacific mackerel or dead squid are the preferred baits, although some anglers use live California barracuda.

Once hooked, swordfish are strong and stubborn fighters with average encounters lasting more than 4 hours. Some fish are landed in short time (10 to 15 minutes) because the fish may swim within gaffing distance of the boat early in the battle.

Most fish taken off southern California weigh between 100 to 300 pounds. Occasionally, a fish weighing more than 400 pounds is landed.

Other Common Names: broadbill, broadbill swordfish.
Largest Recorded: 15 feet; 503 pounds (California).
Habitat: Pelagic Environment

Striped Marlin

Family: Istiophoridae (Billfishes)
Genus and Species: *Tetrapturus audax*
Description: The body of the striped marlin is elongate and compressed. The upper jaw is much extended, forming a rounded spear. The color is dark blue above becoming silver below, with light blue bars or vertical spots on the sides.

— dorsal height about equal to or longer than body depth

rounded spear

Of the billfishes that occur in California waters, the striped marlin is difficult to confuse with the others. Marlin have scales, fins on the belly, and a rounded spear which set them apart from swordfish which have no scales or ventral fins and have bills that are flat. Sailfish have an extremely high dorsal fin not found among the marlins, and shortnose spearfish do not have the long spear on the upper jaw nor the body weight of the marlin. The striped marlin normally develops conspicuous stripes along the sides of its body after death. This feature is unique to striped marlin.
Range: Striped marlin occur in tropical and warm temperature waters of the Indian and Pacific Oceans. On the west coast of the United States they range as far north as Oregon, but are most common south of Point Conception, California. They usually appear off California in July and remain until late October.
Natural History: The food of striped marlin is predominately fishes, squid, crabs and shrimp. The latter three make up lesser portions of the diet than do fish.

The spear of the marlin is sometimes used both as a weapon for defense and as an aid in capturing food. Wooden boats frequently have been rammed by billfish, and in one instance the spear penetrated 18.5 inches of hardwood-14.5 inches of which was oak. When it uses its bill in capturing food, the striped marlin sometimes stuns its prey by slashing sideways with the spear rather than impaling its victim, as some believe.
Fishing Information: Most striped marlin are taken by trolling artificial lures in are as they are known to inhabit. Blind strikes are generally the rule, but one can occasionally tempt a "finner" or "sleeper" (marlin swimming along the surface) to strike if lures are trolled past the fish. Live bait also works well but requires more effort since the fish must usually be first spotted visually. Once a striped marlin is located, the angler should cast a bait in front of and past the fish so it can be reeled back towards the animal. Strikes usually result from properly presented live bait.

Most striped marlin anglers prefer Pacific mackerel as bait. The best California fishing locality is in a belt of water which extends from the east end of Santa Catalina Island offshore to San Clemente Island and southward in the direction of the Los Coronados Islands.
Other Common Names: striper, marlin, Pacific marlin, spikefish, spearfish.
Largest Recorded: 13.5 feet; 339 pounds (California).
Habitat: Pelagic Environment

California Halibut

Family: Bothidae (Left-eyed flounders)
Genus and Species: *Paralichthys californicus*
Description: The body of the California halibut is oblong and compressed. The head is small and the mouth large. Although a member of the

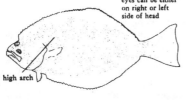

eyes can be either on right or left side of head

high arch

left-eyed flounder family, about 40 percent of California halibut have their eyes on the right side. The color is dark brown to black on the eyed side and white on the blind side.

Their numerous teeth, very large mouth and a high arch in the middle of the "top" side above the pectoral fin make them easily distinguishable from other flatfish.
Range: California halibut occur from Magdalena Bay, Baja California, to the Quillayute River, British Columbia. A separate population occurs in the upper Gulf of California.
Natural History: California halibut feed almost exclusively upon anchovies and similar small fishes. At times they are observed jumping clear of the water as they make passes at anchovy schools near the surface.

Males first mature when 2 or 3 years of age, but females do not mature until 4 or 5. A 5 year old fish may be anywhere from 11 to 17 inches long. Spawning takes place in relatively shallow water during the months of April through July.
Fishing Information: California halibut are pursued by anglers throughout the year, but the best landings usually occur in the spring. In central and northern California fishing is best in summer and early fall. At that time California halibut move into shallow water to spawn.

Drifting for halibut is the most successful fishing method with anglers using live anchovies, queenfish, white croakers, shiner perch or Pacific mackerel as bait. Artificial lures work well at times although they are not always effective.

California halibut are found over sandy bottoms.
Other Common Names: flatty, fly swatter (small), barn door (large), alabato, Monterey halibut, chicken halibut, southern halibut.
Largest Recorded: 5 feet; 72 pounds.
Habitat: Shallow Sandy Environment

Pacific Sanddab

Family: Bothidae (Left-eyed flounders)
Genus and Species: *Citharichthys sordidus*
Description: The body of the Pacific sanddab is oblong and compressed. The head is deep; the eyes are on the left-side and are large. The color is light

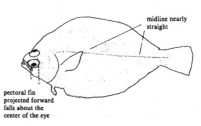

midline nearly straight

pectoral fin projected forward falls about the center of the eye

brown mottled with yellow and orange on the eyed side and white on the blind side.

Although three kinds of sanddabs live in the waters off California, only two are commonly used for food—the Pacific and longfin sanddabs. The third, the speckled sanddab, is so small (only about 5 inches) that it is only important to the diet of other fishes.

The Pacific sanddab can best be distinguished from the longfin sanddab by the length of the pectoral fin on the eyed side. It is always shorter than the head of the Pacific sanddab and longer than the head of the longfin. Sanddabs are always left "handed" (eyes on the left) and can be distinguished from all other left "handed" flatfish by having a midline that is nearly straight for its entire length.
Range: Pacific sanddabs occur from Cape San Lucas, Baja California, to the Bering Sea. They seldom inhabit water that is shallower than 30 feet or deeper than 1,800 feet. They are most abundant at depths of 120 to 300 feet.
Natural History: Pacific sanddabs eat a wide variety of food. In addition to such items as small fishes, squid, octopus, they eat an assortment of eggs, luminescent sea squirts, shrimp, crabs, and marine worms.

During the peak of the spawning season, which is July, August and September, the females spawn numerous eggs. These fish probably spawn more than once during a season.
Fishing Information: If the depth is correct and the bottom suitable, it is extremely difficult to keep sanddabs off the hook. Sportfishing entails the use of small hooks, usually more than one on each line. A variation from the typical rig involves use of an iron ring or hoop around which are dangled several dozen baited hooks of small size. This contraption is lowered on a stout line to a position just off the bottom and allowed to remain a sufficient period to fill all the hooks. Normally this does not require as much time as is needed to rebait the rig after removing the catch. Small pieces of squid or octopus are good baits because they are tough and stay on the hook, but pieces of fish work equally well.
Other Common Names: sanddab, soft flounder, sole, mottled sanddab, megrim.
Largest Recorded: 16 inches; no weight recorded; however, an 11.5 inch female weighed just over 0.5 pound.
Habitat: Deep Sandy Environment

Longfin Sanddab

Family: Bothidae (Left-eyed flounders)
Genus and Species: *Citharichthys xanthostigma*
Description: The body of the longfin sanddab is oblong and compressed. The

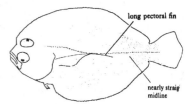

long pectoral fin

nearly straig midline

head is deep; the eyes are large and on the left side. The mouth is large. The color is uniform dark brown with rust orange or white speckles, and the pectoral f in is black on the eyed side; the blind side is white.

The longfin sanddab can best be distinguished from the Pacific sanddab by the length of the pectoral fin on the eyed side. It is always shorter than the head on the Pacific sanddab and longer than the head on the longfin. Sanddabs are always left "handed" and can be distinguished from all other left "handed" flatfish by having a mid-line that is nearly straight for its entire length.

Range: Longfin sanddabs occur from Costa Rica to Monterey, California. These flatfish are usually on sandy, muddy type sea bottoms from 8 to 660 feet.

Natural History: Longfin sanddabs eat a wide variety of food. In addition to such items as small fishes, squid, and octopus, they eat an assortment of eggs, luminescent sea squirts, shrimp, crabs, and marine worms.

Females are larger than males and normally mature when 3 years old and about 7.5 inches long. They produce numerous eggs and each fish probably spawns more than once a season. The peak of the spawning season is July, August and September.

Fishing Information: If the depth is correct and the bottom type is right, it is extremely difficult to keep sanddabs off the hook. Sportfishing entails the use of small hooks, usually more than one on each line. A variation from the typical rig involves use of an iron ring or hoop around which are dangled several dozen baited hooks of small size. This contraption is lowered on a stout line to a position just off the bottom and allowed to remain a sufficient period to fill all the hooks. Normally this does not require as much time as is needed to rebait the rig after removing the catch. Small pieces of squid or octopus are best because they are tough and stay on the hook best, but fish works equally well as a bait.

Other Common Names: sanddab, soft flounder, Catalina sanddab.
Largest Recorded: 15.75 inches; no weight recorded.
Habitat: Deep Sandy Environment

Pacific Halibut

Family: Pleuronectidae (Right-eyed flounders)
Genus and Species: *Hippoglossus stenolepis*
Description: The body of the Pacific halibut is elongate, rather slender, diamond shaped and compressed. The head is elongate and the mouth is large. Both eyes are on the right side of the body. The color of the body is dark brown to black with fine mottling on the eyed side and white on blind side.

corner of mouth forward of eye

eyes always on right side of head

The Pacific halibut can be distinguished from the California halibut by looking at the end of the jaw. In the Pacific halibut, it extends to the front edge of the eye, while in the California halibut it extends beyond the eye.
Range: Pacific halibut occur from Santa Rosa Island, California, to the bering Sea and the Sea of Japan, at depths from 20 to 3,600 feet. In California, however, most are in nearshore areas from Fort Bragg northward, with the largest numbers being taken by anglers offshore north of California.
Natural History: The diet of the Pacific halibut includes fishes, crabs, clams, squid and other invertebrates. Females become mature at 8 to 16 years of age (average 12); however, males mature earlier.

Spawning takes place from November to January. A large female of 140 pounds may produce as many as 2,700,000 eggs. The eggs and young drift casually with the currents gradually rising toward the surface as development proceeds. When first hatched, the young swim upright; however, they soon start to turn to their left side and the left eye migrates to the right side.

By early spring, the transformation is complete and the young settle to the bottom in shallow waters.
Fishing Information: Recreational anglers have caught Pacific halibut up to 346 pounds, but California anglers would be hard pressed to find a Pacific halibut that large. The fish are typically caught on crab, shrimp, ~uid, and other invertebrates.
~er Common Names: alabato, northern halibut, right halibut, genu- ~libut, real halibut.
~t Recorded: 8.75 feet; 507 pounds.
~ Deep Sandy Environment

Starry Flounder

Family: Pleuronectidae (Right-eyed flounders)
Genus and Species: *Platichthys stellatus*
Description: The body of the starry flounder is broad, relatively short, somewhat diamond shaped and compressed. The head is relatively short and the eyes and mouth are small, the lower jaw slightly projecting. While a member of the right-eyed flounder family; the majority of starry flounders are left-eyed. The color is dark brown on the eyed side with alternating white to orange and black bars on the dorsal and anal fins; white on the blind side.

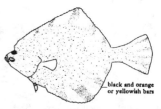

black and orange or yellowish bars

Its name comes from the rough, star-like scales on the eyed-side.
Range: Starry flounders occur from Santa Barbara, California, to Arctic Alaska and the Sea of Japan.

They occur over sand, mud and gravel bottoms in coastal ocean waters, bays, sloughs and even fresh water. Starry flounders are found from depths of a few inches to more than 900 feet.
Natural History: Small starry flounders eat mostly worms and small crustaceans. As they grow they eat progressively more crabs, clams, sand dollars and brittle stars. Large individuals also eat some fishes, among them sardines, sanddabs and surfperch.

Females grow faster and attain larger sizes than do males. Males spawn at the end of their second year when they are about 14.5 inches long, and females in their third year at approximately 16.25 inches. The spawning season extends from November through February with greatest activity in December and January.

Studies in California indicate that spawning occurs in water shallower than 25 fathoms.

Like other flatfishes, the young are born with an eye on each side of the head. By the time they reach about 0.5 inches in length, both eyes are on the same side and they resemble their parents in all respects.
Fishing Information: Starry flounders are one of the most numerous fishes of central and northern California backwaters, particularly San Francisco Bay. Starry flounders can be taken throughout the year but are caught more frequently between December and March. They accept a variety of baits, including chunks of sardine, clams, shrimp, squid, and worms.
Other Common Names: rough jacket, great flounders, grindstone, California flounder, emery flounder, sand paper flounder.
Largest Recorded: 3 feet; 20 pounds.
Habitat: Shallow Sandy Environment

Petrale Sole

Family: Pleuronectidae (Right-eyed flounders)
Genus and Species: *Eopsetta jordani*
Description: The body of the petrale sole is elongate, moderately slender and compressed. The head is deep, and the mouth is large. The eyes are large and on the right side, The color is uniform dark to light brown with dusky blotches on the dorsal and anal fins on the eyed side and white on the blind side.

no high arch

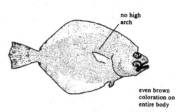

even brown coloration on entire body

Petrale sole are often confused with California halibut because of their similar color and large mouths. However, petrale sole have an even, brown coloration and do not have a high arch in the lateral line.
Range: Petrale sole occur from Cedros Island, Baja California, to the northern part of the Gulf of Alaska. They are found at depths of 60 to 1,500 feet.
Natural History: The diet of the petrale sole includes crabs, shrimp, and fishes such as anchovies, hake, small rockfish and other flatfish.
Fishing Information: Although this flatfish is not often sought by recreational anglers, its large size and excellent eating qualities make it a good sportfish. Probably the entire sport catch for this species is taken incidentally by anglers on rockfish trips aboard commercial passenger fishing vessels. These anglers fishing in waters from 100 to 300 feet deep catch petrale sole on the sand surrounding rocky reefs.
Other Common Names: sole, round-nosed sole, Jordan's founder, California sole, brill.
Largest Recorded: 27.5 inches; no weight.
Habitat: Deep Sandy Environment

Extra:
The "Non-Mono" Controversy

Since 1985 I have been in the business to educate western anglers. Between all my writings, fishing schools, seminars, and radio and television programs, I don't think I have ever seen a more controversial subject than the advent of modern day non-monofilament lines.

Let me start out by saying, I am clearly not a technically knowledgeable authority on these lines. I am writing from the perspective of the recreational angler who typically reaches some sort of crossroads as to: "Do I use it, or do I not?"

Since 1989 I have "graduated" over 11,000 students from our Eagle Claw Fishing Schools. In recent years, I have observed both a number of positive and negative features among weekend anglers who use such non-mono as Spectra, Spiderwire, Fireline, or Whiplash.

First, and most obvious, is their great application for shallow-to-deep water bottom fishing. I have witnessed stellar catches made of ling cod, red snapper, oceanic whitefish, and salmon grouper, by anglers fishing the "non-monos" in 180-300 foot depths. These lines have practically no significant stretch with incredibly fine diameters compared to monofilament with similar breaking strength. This latter feature permits the light tackle enthusiast to actually use gossamer diameter line but with high breaking test on lighter rods and reels.

Offshore trollers like Captain Allyn Watson of the charter boat "Dreamer," are also proponents of "non-mono" technology. The fact that these lines exhibit minimal stretch will translate into excellent hook-sets on big tuna, striped and blue marlin.

Long-range specialists such as Pete Haynes from Izorline International also embrace the "non-mono" program. One of the problems that world-class tuna fishermen face is how to fight 200-300 pound yellowfin comfortably, while standing up, harnessed into larger, more awkward reels.

With the ultrathin diameter "non-monos," long-rangers can now spool a lot of line onto smaller more comfortable reels. A twist in this strategy is to run, say, 200 yards of standard monofilament spliced to and backed with over 500 yards of some kind of "non-mono." This allows the angler to fish a large bait with traditional monofilament, yet have an incredible amount of "non-mono" as excellent backing. Again, with this combination, smaller less cumbersome reels may also be employed.

As a former freshwater bass guide, I too have personally experimented with these new lines. There were days last spring in which I caught over 50 largemouths in a single outing using super thin 6 pound test Berkley Fireline. This line was so effective, I eventually tied my lures directly to the Fireline without using a monofilament leader. It didn't seem to make any difference. Fishing bass at depths over 15 feet, I really appreciated the non-stretch feature of this new technology.

So, what's the "beef" with these new "non-mono" lines? My impression is that objections come primarily from the saltwater skippers and deck hands. Many of these guys are still highly traditional and somewhat hesitant to try anything new and radical. Crew members especially find much of the "non-mono" products to be more difficult to work with when trying to untangle lines. Also, they complain that the "non-monos" with such extremely thin diameters are more dangerous to pull on when attempting to dislodge a jig from the bottom, or when removing a hook quickly. Thus, some boat operators emphatically do not want to see the "non-mono" lines on wide-open, surface action.

It is probably safe to say that these new lines will not replace today's monofilament completely. They are also more expensive than a comparable yardage of monofilament. Still, they are here to stay, with new niche applications emerging each season. If you haven't tried this stuff yet, you're in for a surprise. When a two pound starry rockfish snaps your jig off the bottom using this "non-mono," it will feel like a fish five times that size wants to yank the rod out of your hand. It's tough to miss even the slightest bite with this new technology!

Ronnie Kovach